THEN ATHENA SAID

Unilateral Transfers and the Transformation of Objectivist Ethics

Kathleen Touchstone

University Press of America,® Inc.
Lanham · Boulder · New York · Toronto · Oxford

4501 Forbes Boulevard
Suite 200
Lanham, Maryland 20706
UPA Acquisitions Department (301) 459-3366

PO Box 317
Oxford
OX2 9RU, UK

Printed in the United States of America
British Library Cataloging in Publication Information Available

Library of Congress Control Number: 2006924498
ISBN-13: 978-0-7618-3519-6 (paperback : alk. paper)
ISBN-10: 0-7618-3519-9 (paperback : alk. paper)

™ The paper used in this publication meets the minimum requirements of American National Standard for Information Sciences—Permanence of Paper for Printed Library Materials, ANSI Z39.48—1984

Dedicated to D. S. Lliteras

Table of Contents

Preface

The impetus for this book was a statement by David Kelley in his interview with John Stossel on a television special called "Greed" in which he stated that Michael Milken had done more for humanity than Mother Teresa had. Kelley indicated that to go into slums and suffer, as he said Mother Teresa had done, was not a value. What is important is what people produce ("And to Think" 1998, 4). His point was that producers such as Milken create wealth whereas Mother Teresa did nothing more than distribute wealth created by producers ("A Slogan" 1998, 4).

David Kelley is an Objectivist philosopher. Objectivism is a philosophy founded by Ayn Rand. The purpose of this book is to explore charity and other unilateral transfers within the framework of Objectivist ethics (OE). OE is an individualistic ethics. It is egoistic and biocentric. Rand closed the is/ought gap with the proposition that what man is determines what he should do. According to OE, a man's life is his ultimate value. OE's cardinal values are reason, productive purpose, and self-esteem; the corresponding cardinal virtues are rationality, productive work, and pride (Rand 1964a, 25). All of Rand's cardinal virtues and values are achievable by man alone on a desert island; other people are not a fundamental part of reality (Peikoff 1991, 252–53).

In chapter 1, I ask, how are the cardinal values and virtues in OE derived? Rand viewed ethical principles as being those actions that if consistently followed will yield success—man's survival *qua* man. One possible approach to their derivation is on the basis of long-run probabilities. I examine two ways in which probabilities may be applied to principles.

In chapter 2, I challenge the idea that others are not a fundamental part of reality by making a (weak) case for including reproduction as a primary value and nurturance as a primary virtue. Rand's main social principle is the trader principle—the exchange of value for value between independent equals (Rand 1964a, 31). The interaction between parent and child is primarily unilateral, from parent to child. Reproduction can be regarded as productive in OE, but it is not (nor can it be) life-sustaining. In OE, it is morally optional (1968, 3). I argue that "reproductivity" is sufficiently dissimilar from productivity to warrant a separate category. My case for reproductivity is based on the Objectivist position that concepts are required for man's existence, that concepts require two or more existents (1979, 15), and on the concept "man."

In chapter 3, I ask, why must principles be general? Why can't a principle have an escape clause that permits force or fraud (of any stripe, to include trespass, default, assault, theft, rape, murder, etc.) if it can lead to gain? I refer to these infringements as forced unilateral transfers since an individual's person or property is used by another without the victim's consent and without compensation. Bilateral interaction employing game theory's Prisoner's Dilemma (Axelrod 1984, 8–9) is used to analyze this question. Human nature offers insights. A practical reason for not defaulting is the threat of retaliation. Rand's trader principle, justice, is rooted in voluntary interaction. This is broadened to include the principle of reciprocity. To uphold this principle, not only would retaliation be required in response to default in an original state of nature, I argue that it would be the moral response (with qualifications).

In chapter 4, I examine economic decision-making for a man alone on a desert island under very restrictive assumptions. Productivity, which includes saving, is the central virtue in OE. Consumption is a value, but no virtue. The decision facing the castaway is basically a consumption decision which involves the trade-off between the pressure to consume in order to live today (time preference) and postponing consumption in order to produce more of one's life in the future (return). Although simplistic, the model supports Rand's contention that decision-making is long-term in nature (Rand 1964a, 24; Peikoff 1991, 300). It is also noted that bequests are not relevant to a man alone.

In chapter 5, I consider decision-making between two individuals in an original state of nature. Rand recognized only two appropriate states for man—alone on a desert island or living among other men under a proper government (1964g, 107). She did not analytically fill the gap between these two states. Game theory is used to show how conventions can emerge in a state of anarchy (Sugden 1986). Rand (1964c) claimed that conflicts of interests would not exist among rational men. However, if property rights are not recognized, conflicts (zero-sum in nature) cannot be ruled out. When ownership is in place but enforcement is lacking, the Prisoner's Dilemma can be utilized to uncover strategies for the emergence of cooperation. Robert Axelrod found that on repeated trials, a strategy of reciprocity was successful (1984, 55). It is noted that for cooperation to take hold, retaliation in response to default is necessary.

In chapter 6, I challenge the Objectivist position that interaction with others is optional (Rand 1961a, 133; 1964g, 107), at least for some fundamental relationships. According to OE, interaction, when it occurs, is between independent equals. Although Rand did not use the Crusoe device analytically, it would be a logical starting point for modeling behavior for a man alone, and to analyze interpersonal interaction between individuals when a second person is added. However, there is one relationship that is not optional and that is the one between mother (parent) and child. I call this the Primary Social Unit (PSU). It is primary (in the sense of being the first relationship a person has), universal (applicable to everyone), and essential in that one person is inherently dependent on the other for his survival. It is not the dependency per se that renders it required. Rights are involved. I argue that the positive right to care (by the parent for the child) is a basic right.

Chapter 7 discusses negative and positive rights. According to Objectivists and Libertarians (Rand 1964h, 94; Machan 1998a, 119–20; Den Uyl and Rasmussen 1991, 107), negative rights are basic. Positive rights are derivative and secondary (Den Uyl and Rasmussen 1991, 107). The latter may be based on consent or contract. Positive rights may also result if one person (either intentionally or unintentionally, if the latter was foreseeable and avoidable) infringes on the rights of another. Rothbard (1998, 100), an anarcho-capitalist, had a more restrictive position on what positive rights entail than did Rand. He claimed that children do not have a positive right to care from their parents. Bissell (1981, 30) used a liability argument for parental care for their children. This argument is valid, but it puts childbirth in the category of being an infringement of the child's rights. Unlike other positive rights, I do not regard the right to child care from parents as being reciprocity-based (in the "implied contract" sense). In this chapter, I make two arguments for positive rights other than those generally recognized by Objectivists and Libertarians. Both are related to children and those with diminished capacity.

Chapter 8 is on property rights, concentrating primarily on the acquisition of original ownership. Once all space is owned, the right to property has implications for ethics; in particular, others become a fundamental part of reality, since it is through voluntary exchange with others that a propertyless person has access to space within which to act. Also considered in this chapter is the establishment of ownership for resources that move. It is noted that efficiency and inefficiency can have ethical implications.

Intellectual property is discussed in chapter 9. Rand (1967i) made a case for property rights for copyrights and patents, but argued that they should be of limited duration. She was opposed to property rights for the discoverers of new knowledge. She regarded inventors and discoverers as permanent benefactors of mankind. I point out that it is because these individuals are not fully compensated for their contributions that they bestow unilateral benefits upon others.

Chapter 10 utilizes the social contract as an analytical device in discussing the establishment of government. The definition of the social contract that I employ is the exchange of protection of rights by government for the relinquishing of the right to retaliate (except if one's life is in imminent danger). I offer two cases for the existence of government. One is based on the violation of the equal rights protection principle in a state of anarchy—specifically, the systematic exclusion of children and those with diminished capacity (as a condition of their existence) who are abused by their guardians. The other case involves the conflict of rights that exists between the accused and the victim of a crime. The decision can be cast as one in which a person, who faces being potentially accused of a crime, compares the risks of being treated justly if reliance is on private retaliation versus the risks if justice is turned over to an impartial third party under the condition that everyone else also agrees to do so.

Chapter 11 compares Rand's theory of value (Peikoff 1991, 207–213; Rand 1964a) with that of economic theory. Chapter 12 does the same for productivity (Rand 1964a; Sciabarra 1995, 246–48; Peikoff 1991, 292–303). These chapters are relevant since, according to Objectivists, humanitarians do not produce anything of value; they merely redistribute income created by others.

Chapter 13 is on replacement capital and presents my second, stronger argument for including reproduction as a cardinal value. It follows from Nathaniel Branden's statement that to be worthy of inheritance, a person should use it productively (1963, 22–23). I take this to mean that the inheritor should keep its value intact. This is also a principle of economics with respect to the value of the capital of a business. To keep the value of the capital intact, a sinking fund can be set aside. Economist Gary Becker (1995f, 358–59) implied that a parent has the option of endowing his child with physical capital or with human capital investment. I note that to keep one's human capital intact, one could set aside a sinking fund. However, I also point out that a person's child is his sinking fund. Maintenance of endowments (whether physical or human capital) can be viewed as intergenerational reciprocity.

Chapter 14 returns to the discussion that was begun in chapter 4 on the consumption-production decision, currently and over time. In the short run, there is a trade-off between consumption and production, but if the long view is taken—which is consistent with Rand—both more consumption and more production are not incompatible objectives. Time preference and risk aversion tend to be positively related to the amount consumed out of an additional dollar of wealth (marginal propensity to consume, MPC) in the current time period. The interest rate and a bequest motive are negatively related to the MPC out of current wealth. A decrease in the probability of survival tends to increase the MPC. Once life's uncertainty is introduced and a bequest motive is accounted for, then an increase in the probability of dying on the MPC is ambiguous. If there is a strong bequest motive, an increase in the probability of dying has a negative effect on the MPC; if the bequest motive is weak, the opposite is true (Fischer 1973). Increases in risk aversion, the rate of time preference, and the probability of dying tend to decrease the growth rate of consumption over time. An increase in the interest rate and a bequest motive tend to increase the rate of consumption (and therefore production) over time (Yaari 1965). One conclusion is that if productivity is valued, as it is in OE, then, if a person cares not only about his own life, but also beyond his life, production will be greater. Chapter 14 can be omitted without loss of continuity for those unacquainted with the economic theory in this chapter.

Chapter 15 is concerned with ethical decision-making. I argue that both a rule-based approach and the maximization principle are consistent with decision-making in OE, depending upon context. Based on my interpretation of Rand's Benevolent Universe Premise (BUP) (Peikoff 1976; quoted in Binswanger 1986, 50–51; see also Paterson 1968, 250–51), I regard the expected loss to the ethical action as irrelevant when deciding between an ethical and an unethical action. The expected loss of the unethical action should not be ignored, however. When deciding among ethical alternatives only, the expected loss associated with each alternative can be ignored so long as the expected losses are the same across all alternatives. If, among the ethical actions, the expected losses are unequal, then the expected loss is not irrelevant to the decision. This does not mean, however, that the action with the lowest expected loss will be chosen. Even if the risk of death is high for a given action, a person may still rationally choose it; at least, I argue that it would not be unethical to do so, even though life is one's ultimate value. This conclusion is consistent with Rand. The reason I offer is that both humans and principles are mortal, but for humans death is inevitable; for ethical principles, it is merely possible. To be kept alive, principles must be acted upon. There may be those instances in which the only way to keep a principle alive is by risking one's life. In doing so, one keeps alive the best that is within oneself—principles embodied as virtues.

In chapter 16, I discuss charity from a number of perspectives. According to Rand (1961c, 80) and Kelley ("A Slogan" 1998, 4), humanitarians are not productive, and no one should devote full-time to a profession that is supported primarily by almsgiving rather than by trade (Berliner 1995, 83, 544–45). I argue that humanitarians can be productive. Theirs is not the only profession that relies on contributions. Charity has public goods characteristics. Public goods and near public goods are supported entirely or in part by contributions because they are not subject to the price mechanism typical of market goods. There is no price to provide information or incentives to act on information. The self-regulating tendency of the market is absent. Rand maintained that charity was acceptable as long as it was marginal. It is a minor virtue at best (1964d, 49). If charity were pursued on a major scale, occupying all of a person's time and income, it would be suicidal to both the giver and the recipient. It is not self-sustaining. Viewed in this way, even a marginal contribution could be regarded as mildly self-sacrificial. This latter perspective might have some merit if individuals had never been net beneficiaries of the actions of uncompensated others. However, I argue that many people have received benefits from others for which they have not paid. The benefactors to whom I refer are inventors, discoverers of new knowledge, the founders and protectors of liberty. None of these were fully compensated for the endowments they bestowed on others. Like the inheritance of physical capital, it is my view that these endowments should be kept intact. Invoking the trader principle, I argue that giving to (worthy) others would not be self-sacrificial. Since charitable giving has public goods characteristics and is outside the market mechanism, the question of how much to give is addressed. Based on the BUP, success is the to-be-expected. I see the expected loss of an action as irrelevant to a decision-maker, since it is incidental—the not-to-be-expected. If one is successful, then the expected loss is a bonus and can be used for charitable giving. As a rule of thumb, I suggest that the expected loss may be approximated by the probability of dying multiplied by yearly income. The probability of dying would not be specific to oneself. It would be an average. In chapter14, I derive and analyze several "permanent" probabilities of dying, using as a starting point an equation for a net level premium for life insurance. These are merely suggestive. The analysis provides insights into the importance of both death's uncertainty and its inevitability in the charitable-giving decision.

In chapter 17, I look at other unilateral transfers; specifically, gifts and forgiveness. Gifts may appear to be unilateral, but there is often implied reciprocity involved. Forgiveness is unlike other gifts in that it is not given to the "innocent." I do not regard forgiveness as an unqualified virtue. If forgiveness is unwarranted, it is an act of cowardice. I also discuss Rand's view on the confluence of a person's emotions with his thoughts. Unlike Rand (1969a, 29), I believe that it may not be unusual for an ethical person's emotions and thoughts to be out of sync. This is because of the dynamic nature as life and learning. Rand (1964a, 15, 21; 1964d, 44) saw the decision process as one of choosing between a value and a non-value (or something with little value). I think many decisions involve choosing between two or more values, both or all of which rank high in one's value system. This makes decision-making more difficult. It is complicated by the introduction of a second value that ranks on par with productivity in one's value system—childrearing.

Acknowledgments

My thanks to Professor Tibor Machan for suggesting that I submit my manuscript to the Rowman & Littlefield Publishing Group, and to Troy University for awarding a research grant that allowed me to complete this book. My appreciation to Hampton Roads Publishing Company for their copyediting and typesetting assistance; to my in-laws, Mecca and Frank (deceased), for the interest they have taken in my work; and to my parents, Jack and Wanda, from whom I continue to learn.

Finally, this book could not have been completed without the continued devotion of my husband, Danny Lliteras, to whom it is dedicated.

CHAPTER ONE

The Basis for Objectivist Ethics

The purpose of this book is to examine unilateral transfers, focusing primarily on Objectivist ethics (OE), the philosophy founded by Ayn Rand. OE are individualistic, egoistic, and based on human nature (biocentric). This chapter introduces Objectivism's cardinal values—reason, productive purpose, and self-esteem; and the cardinal virtues—rationality, productivity, and pride (Rand 1964a, 25). It discusses two methods that have been attributed to Rand in deriving her ethical principles: the general species approach and the long-run probability approach.

The General Species Interpretation

Rand's ethics are rooted in human nature. It is by examining what man is that one determines what he ought to do (1964a, 17). Man has no automatic means of survival. He must rely on his mind. He must choose to do so. Man's fundamental decision is to think or not. He must create his means of survival. He must be productive. Values are those things he acts to gain or keep. Virtues are the actions by which he gains or keeps that which he values (Rand 1961a, 121). Life is man's ultimate value. Reason, productive purpose, and self-esteem are man's cardinal values. Rationality, productivity, and pride are his cardinal virtues. Rationality forms the basis for all other virtues. Productivity is man's central purpose (Rand 1964a, 25).

Rand claimed that her virtues apply to every man. Eric Mack took issue with this, arguing that every man's survival does not depend upon his rationality and his productivity. A single man may survive, and live a long life, by being a parasite (1986, 136). Mack interpreted Rand as having used a generic species approach to form her ethics. His argument hinged on her use of the phrase "man as such." He saw Rand as deriving an abstract principle based on what promotes the survival of the species. Another interpretation envisions any particular man as an instance for the concrete application of a general principle (1986, 140–41). Although Rand used the phrase "man *qua* man," she did not believe that, metaphysically, there is man as such, only individual men. She distinguished between "man," the abstraction that applies to every man, and "mankind," a collective noun that applies to man in general (Berliner 1995, 561–62). The universality of her principles follows from man's common human nature.

Rand saw man as the relevant unit of analysis. To understand what man is, one must first understand what is meant by an entity. An entity cannot be subdivided nor aggregated beyond what it is. One can speak of an entity's attributes for purposes of analysis, but they are not separate existents. Parts, however, can be materially separated from an entity. Still, in neither instance is the entity a sum of its attributes or its parts. It is an integrate; it is not an aggregate. Similarly, an entity cannot be subsumed within some larger collective, and then the collective be regarded as the relevant unit insofar as ethical issues are concerned (Sciabarra 1995, 147). To Rand, it is the individual that is relevant, and, insofar as questions of ethics are concerned, man is the relevant entity. This does not mean that Rand subscribed to an atomistic individualism. She saw man in context—in relation to other men (1967a, 15).

Man is an entity that has a particular identity. What distinguishes him from other beings is his rationality—his conceptual faculty. Man thinks in terms of concepts. A concept is the mental integration of two or more existents that share common features. They are abstractions. They do not exist in reality (1969a, 23). They are epistemological devices. But they are based on existents in reality. A concept, like all knowledge, is contextual (1979, 55). It has limited application. Concepts have the advantage of permitting unit economy. A man need not know every concrete in existence in order to understand a thing. By using concepts, he can think in numerical terms that are multiples of what he could retain if limited to the perceptual level of his consciousness (1979, 83–85).

Principles express a relationship between or among concepts. They, too, are abstract. They lay claim to universality. Their universality is derived from man's common human nature. A moral code saves man from the paralysis of analyzing every situation he encounters "from scratch." Like concepts, principles permit a kind of unit economy. Consistent application of a principle can save a person from the cost of gathering information to analyze every event on a case-by-case basis. Consistency can be cost-effective. Is there anything in human nature that would lead one to think or act consistently? There is some evidence that humans, as well as some other animals, detect patterns in the environment even though they may not be able to explicate these patterns in terms of rules. Many of the advances in knowledge are in fact efforts to uncover, make explicit, and gain an understanding of these patterns. The implicit learning of these patterns may not be veridical. But, like the informal learning of language, the "unconscious" use of grammatical rules may be sufficiently accurate to facilitate understanding among individuals (Reber 1993, 118–19). In experimentation, individuals have also been found to be able to implicitly detect relative frequencies underlying events on repeated trials. At times, humans have been found to event match (decide on the basis of the underlying relative frequencies), which is sub-optimal (at least for the conditions underlying the experiment). They have also been found, at times, to submit to the gambler's fallacy (1993, 32). Still not quite understood is how repeated exposure to consistent patterns wires cell assemblies in the brain. It is believed that neurons that "fire together wire together" (Begley 1996, 61).

In addition, our nervous system seems to predispose us to some acquired habits. Some addictions, notably opiates, are thought to result, in part, from the drug occupying natural opiate receptors within the body. Morphine receptors are located in the limbic system, an area associated with emotion, and the medial thalamus, an area associated with pain impulses. Endorphins are natural opiates produced by the pituitary. It is thought that endorphins may be involved in some way in the acquisition of some habits (Restak 1979, 335–48). These examples are hardly exhaustive but are mentioned simply to show that there is some basis for consistency in thought and action in human nature. Consistency in thought and behavior is part of what defines a person's identity.

Although there is some basis in human nature for consistency, this does not substantiate it as a good thing. Habits or patterns of behavior or thought can be good for a person or bad. Some things may be beneficial under some circumstances but have potentially harmful side effects. Post-surgery use of morphine as a painkiller can be helpful, but there is nothing positive about morphine dependency.

Principles and Probability

Rand pointed out that moral principles are readily grasped; what is not so easy is to apply them (1964e, 72). This requires rationality. Morality is not a mindless knee-jerk application of abstract principles to the events of everyday life. Application of principles depends on context. Like concepts, principles do not have unlimited application. As Chris Sciabarra pointed out in his book *Ayn Rand: The Russian Radical*, a person would not necessarily be truthful with someone who had kidnapped his child (1995, 245).

Thus, to Rand, adhering to principles does not mean mindless adherence to rules regardless of context. This is not the same thing as having principles that allow for exceptions. Gregory Johnson (1999, 145) asked, in effect, why not have a principle (such as being honest) that allows a person to violate that principle (for instance, lie) when it would be to his advantage to do so? Since it is to a person's advantage to appear to be honest, presumably this exception would only apply when the chance of being caught being dishonest was extremely unlikely. So, one would, presumably, only lie if the risk of detection is low. Thus, if one is deciding whether or not to lie, he must also calculate the probability of detection. This involves another cost, that of acquiring the information necessary to make this estimation. The calculation of the probability of detection would seem to be inherent in Johnson's "rule." Johnson added that if one gets caught, admit it (1999, 145). He took issue with Peikoff's stand that there is a tendency for individuals to persist in a lie once told. Would there be any rationale for a person to do this? I believe there is, and that it has its basis in risk categories. Again, probabilities are a factor.

Probabilities also figure into Ronald Merrill's interpretation of OE. Like Mack, Merrill acknowledged that a man may be immoral—he may be a parasite—but if he pursues this course and remains successful, it is due to luck. Merrill stated that Rand recognized the stochastic in life. But luck, good or bad, should not form the basis for ethics. To do so would be to commit the fallacy of converse accident. Merrill claimed that Rand based her ethics on those actions that if persistently undertaken would yield long-term success. One may still be unlucky and fail, but that formula is the best way to bet (Merrill 1991, 115–17). Probability, it would seem, is inherent in an inconsistent rule that allows lying (stealing, cheating, killing—force or fraud of any stripe) if the chance of detection is low. Probabilities also figure into Merrill's approach to principles (which he attributed to Rand), which is to base them on the long-run probability of success. How do the two approaches to the use of probabilities in ethical decisions differ?

There are at least two approaches to defining probabilities. One is the frequency approach, the other the classical approach. The frequency approach requires, according to some interpretations, that events be random, independent, uniform, and repeated under identical circumstances. Probability is defined as the long-run relative frequency of an event. The classical approach calculates the percentage of times a given event is possible out of the total number of possible events. The classical approach, it is thought, requires the assumption of equiprobability. So, if there are two possible alternative outcomes, the probability of each would be 1/2. This is sometimes called the outcome based on chance. The relative frequency approach calculates the percentage of the occurrence of an event based on repeated trials (see, for instance, Beals [1972 10–24]). If, upon repeated trials, the outcome is found to be different from chance, one asks why. One does not, however, discard the theory of probability. One looks for reasons why the outcome is different from chance. For instance, the probability of heads for a fair coin is 1/2. If a coin were tossed on repeated trials, and the relative frequency for heads were found to be 2/3 instead of 1/2, it could be because the coin is unbalanced. If that were the case, there would exist an element of determinism to the outcome. Still a stochastic element would remain. One cannot know the outcome until the coin is tossed.

In a coin-toss experiment, the same coin is tossed over and over. It is not based on the results of a number of coins, some of which are loaded and others which are fair. Does this mean that one cannot apply the theory of probability to a population of unlike elements or individuals? Not necessarily. In fact, differences between groups can lead to further inquiry about causal factors. If one is interested in long-run success, that is, in identifying those things that will increase the odds of success in the long term, it is in discovering the determinants of success that one is ultimately interested. There is still the recognition that even when one has identified the determinants of success for one's life and is living in accordance with them, a stochastic element will remain.

Mortality tables are based on relative frequencies of death for the population in general. But, in general, the longevity for males is different from that for females. This has an effect on mortality rates, and thus on life insurance premiums. If one examines longevity for both males and females grouped together, variability from the mean will exist in part because the longevity for females is different from that for males. The reason for the difference between the two is not entirely known. But it is known that longevity is dependent on gender or something related to gender. If data for the two sexes are separated into two categories, this will eliminate the effect of gender on the respective means. If such an effect exists, each group will become more homogeneous. Each mean would be more representative of the actual for each group. There would tend to be less dispersion around their respective means than there would be for the combined mean. But even within each group are found differences.The probability of dying is not the same for each person within a given gender group. Mortality tends to increase with age, in general. Age is related to (if not correlated with) mortality. As age increases, so does the mortality rate, generally speaking. Age changes the odds; as does cigarette smoking. In preparing mortality tables for insurance companies, actuaries separate smokers from non-smokers. It is not entirely known why gender, age, and smoking are related to death; only that, like weighting the side of a coin or loading a die, they change the odds.

Examining the determinants of long-term success using probabilities as a guide (usually as aids to further inquiry) is not the same as estimating the probabilities of detection. Rules that permit inconsistent behavior are applied on a case-by-case basis. The relevant probabilities in such decisions are not, generally speaking, long-term in nature, but are for unique events. Probability theory informs us that calculation of probabilities for unique events may be more difficult, even impossible, to estimate. This is, I believe, a strike against the use of inconsistent rules. But it does not stop there. If a person lies (steals, etc.) again and again, this may increase the probability that he will be caught. This sounds like the gambler's fallacy, but is it? The gambler's fallacy assumes independent events. But would the events in such a circumstance be independent? The same person is involved, over and over, and he has an identity, which, in part, means that there is a pattern to his behavior. The events are, therefore, correlated or related in some way. They are not independent. So the probability of detection may increase upon repetition of a given type of behavior by the same person.

I believe that probability categories and their link to reputation may also lend a clue to why a person may perpetuate a lie once told. So long as a doubt remains about one's dishonesty, a person is not in a "high risk" category, so to speak. If he admits to a lie, doubt is removed. Once in a different probability category, doubt concerning a person's previous and subsequent veracity may be in question. Thus, it may be expedient for a person to continue a lie once told. So long as he denies the lie, a doubt remains.

The cost savings of consistent behavior, the tendency for humans to "look for" consistency and to behave consistently, the relative difficulty of calculating probabilities on a case-by-case basis, the increased likelihood of detection if a behavior is perpetuated because of one's identity (consistency in behavior), the tendency to perpetuate a lie in order to remain in a "truthful" probability category, all weigh in favor of Merrill's approach to principles relative to those rules that permit inconsistent behavior.

But one must also use caution in accepting Merrill's approach to principles (which he attributed to Rand). Probabilities are not proof. When Rand, who smoked more than two packs of cigarettes a day for forty years, was advised against the habit, she said, according to biographer Barbara Branden, ". . . don't tell me about statistics; I've explained why statistics aren't proof. You have to give me a *rational* explanation" (1986, 380). Yet, when she was told she had lung cancer, Branden said that Rand "knew that the odds were not in her favor" because of the degree to which the malignancy had advanced (1986, 381). Are these two statements inconsistent?

Not necessarily. Statistics are not proof. Correlation is not causation. There is a strong correlation between cigarette smoking and lung cancer, but evidence is not limited to statistics. Cigarette smoking is inadvisable. Statistical statements are part of the information required, but some statistical evidence is better substantiated than others. Once someone has been diagnosed with a condition, however, a different decision is in order. Once diagnosed, a person faces odds of a different sort. One is in another risk (probability) category. One faces different odds for a different kind of decision.

If one used probabilities as a guide to longevity, women would be advised to neither marry nor have children. Most women would be perceived as living in opposition to their best interests, which is irrational. So a knee-jerk response to probabilities is not recommended. If the word "probably" is to be assigned to any aspect of Rand's ethics, it is probably within the confines of its definition as "that which can be supported by good argument."

When ten-year-old Jane Eyre is told that wicked girls go to hell after they die and was asked what she must do to avoid going to hell, she answered, "I must keep in good health, and not die" (Brönte 1981,18). Her answer is endearing because it is so logical, yet so naïve. For a toss of a balanced coin, the probability of heads is 1/2. The probability of two consecutive heads is 1/4; three out of three is 1/8. There is a probability, however minute, that one could always toss heads. But there is no probability, no matter how remote, that one will never die. At any point in time one may live or die. There are two possible outcomes, but the odds are not, as with a balanced coin, fifty/fifty. Each day one does not face the same odds as he did the day before. And there is no probability, no matter how infinitesimal, that one will always live. Death is inevitable. I will later argue that this inevitability weighs heavily in the way in which we regard virtues.

CHAPTER TWO

Reproductivity

All of Objectivism's cardinal values are achievable by a man alone. Other people are not a fundamental part of reality (Peikoff 1991, 252–53). It follows that procreation, although productive, is morally optional (Rand 1968, 3). Rand's most important social principle, justice, is the Trader Principle, the exchange of value for value between independent equals (Rand 1964a, 31). Much of the interaction that takes place between parent and child is unilateral in nature, from parent to child. In this chapter, I argue that reproduction is sufficiently dissimilar from production to warrant a separate category. I note that because "reproductivity" is outside the market (and should be), because it is nonremunerative, and because there is no price mechanism, children may be "under-produced." I make a weak case for including reproduction as a primary value and nurturance as a primary virtue. The case is based on the Objectivist contention that concepts are required for man's existence (Peikoff 1991, 120), that concepts require two or more existents (Rand 1979, 15), and on the concept "man."

Desert Island Ethics

According to one interpretation, Rand could be said to have used a long-run probability approach in deriving her ethics. Ronald Merrill, in effect, said this. Another interpretation, one of two put forth by Eric Mack, viewed Rand as using a collective species approach (Mack 1986, 140). Merrill used jaywalking to illustrate that if longevity were the ultimate value, then jaywalking would be inadvisable. The odds would be against it as a general practice. One might survive a given instance of it, but if one did, it would be because of luck (Merrill 1991,

114–17). A collective species approach, on the other hand, might conclude that if everyone were to jaywalk it would be detrimental to the species, so no one should do so.

Chris Sciabarra saw Rand's approach to ontology and epistemology as analytically breaking down reality into understandable "relational units" and tracing the interconnections; then reuniting them into "an organic whole" (Sciabarra 1995, 128). I believe that this is the approach that Rand used to determine the centricity of purpose that work serves in man's life as well as her other cardinal values and virtues. Some of her remarks, and particularly some of the statements of Objectivist Leonard Peikoff, indicate that Rand may have first analytically isolated man from other men, and then asked what would be required of a man alone to sustain his life. Once these were established, she integrated this representative man into a society of other men.

Den Uyl and Rasmussen pointed out that, according to Rand, it does not matter whether a person is on a desert island or in society, he needs a moral code. It is necessary in either circumstance because morality "is dependent on human nature and not on the number of human beings" (Den Uyl and Rasmussen 1986a, 79n23). In Galt's speech in *Atlas Shrugged*, Rand said, to those who believe that morality is a social construct, it is when man is alone on a desert island that morality is most needed (1961a, 127). Peikoff echoed this sentiment, stating that, alone on a desert island, dependency would be impossible. A man would have to use his mind and produce or face the consequences. "He would have to focus on reality or perish" (1991, 252).

This is reinforced by Rand's view of reality—that it does not fundamentally include other people. Merrill stated that, to Rand, morality is not fundamentally concerned with dealing with other people. It is a guide for dealing with nature (Merrill 1997, 70). David Kelley said that the cardinal virtues are how a man primarily deals with reality; which means that relationships "cannot be assigned the same degree of fundamentality" (1996, 24). Nature or reality, in the contexts in which Peikoff, Merrill, and Kelley used these terms, does not include people, other than oneself. Kelley clarified that that he was referring to adults (1996, 63n24).

Children and other so-called "marginal cases" (Register 1997, 9) have not been fully integrated into OE in a systematic way. As Kelley noted, an ethical code that is biocentric must start with the adult stage. Then only can the special needs of those who are wholly or partly dependent (children and the elderly) be identified ("Roundtable" 1996, 9). In *The Fountainhead*, Rand's character Howard Roark said: "A man thinks and works alone" (Rand 1961a, 82). One man cannot live for another. It is impossible for him to share his body or his consciousness (1961a, 80). Man not only works to live, i.e., to sustain his life; he lives to work, i.e., to fulfill a psychological need. Roark said: "The creator lives for his work" (1961a, 79). He does not need others; others are not his primary objective. Those for whom others are primary are parasites (1961a, 79). Here we have moved from the desert island, so to speak, to society, but the values and virtues required remain the same as those for a man in isolation. Rand pointed out that once a man lives among others rather than on a desert island, he is not relieved of the responsibility "of supporting his own life" (1964c, 52).

Once off the desert island, Rand stressed the importance of trade and an institution of government (1964c, 52; 1964g, 107–108). Rand's conception of man was not narrow or one-dimensional. Like Rand, Kelley pointed to the vast improvements in knowledge and wealth that can be achieved from living in the society of others (1996, 24–25). Peikoff, as did Rand, underscored the relevance of friendship (1991, 236–37). Yet what Peikoff emphasized was that the same principles are at work in society as on a desert island. A man's nature does not change, nor do "the requirements of his life" (1991, 252).

Based on a "desert island" perspective, each man must be rational. He must learn those things necessary for his survival. He must engage in productive work. Other virtues are also required. Reality is the ultimate arbiter. Alone he cannot fake reality; he must be honest. He must have integrity; alone he can cheat no one but himself. Reality is the testing ground. If he were to lie to himself or try to trick himself—either would result in failure. Alone, each man must be rational and productive. His survival depends upon it. He must be honest and have integrity. Rand saw man as efficacious. He is capable of discovering what he needs to know and do to survive. As Merrill (1991, 115) pointed out, there are no guarantees he will succeed. But if he does nothing, he is certain to fail. His life is his ultimate value, so he must do these things if he wants to survive. This is not a collective species approach to ethics. It is instead a process of isolating and analyzing. Rand, of course, integrated man back into society. Although she never stated explicitly that she used a "desert island" approach, it is clear from the quotes above that she indeed used this as a proverbial springboard on more than one occasion.

Reproduction

Rand used the "desert island" approach as a metaphorical abstraction. It could be argued that, based on her comments, Rand, in fact, believed that in reality man could survive alone; that is, living among others was entirely optional. At least, this is the way in which Larry Sechrest (1999, 89) interpreted Rand. He drew this conclusion from her statement that living in a society can be very beneficial to man "*—but only on certain conditions*" (Rand 1967d, 329).

There are many things man cannot do alone. The one that is essential to the survival of the species is reproduction. If there is an argument that Rand did not use a collective species approach in deriving her ethics, as Mack proposed, it is this. If she had, reproduction would have been the centerpiece of her ethics, since the survival of the species depends upon it. One man need not reproduce, but if all chose not to do so, the species would become extinct. Of course, one man by himself cannot reproduce. Rand asked, what must a man do to survive? Not every man needs to reproduce. Not any man needs to reproduce. Any man can live a lifetime without reproducing. Reproduction is, according to Rand, not only optional, it is morally optional. She said, "The capacity to procreate is merely a potential which man is not obligated to actualize" (Rand 1968, 3). Reproduction is not a cardinal value. Cardinal values are concerned with how man primarily deals with reality; thus, those virtues relating to other individuals "cannot be assigned the same degree of fundamentality" (Kelley 1996, 24). Reality does not (fundamentally) encompass other people. Rand examined man in isolation and said it is man alone who must be the most moral (1961a, 127), for alone he cannot depend on others for his own survival. He must use his mind, he must be rational, he must produce, he must have pride. Reproduction is not required for man's survival. In fact, for a man alone it is not possible.

Rand claimed that "independence is the only gauge of human virtue and value" (1961c, 82). A man can share neither his body nor his consciousness with another (1961c, 80). But to reproduce one does depend on another. One cannot do this alone. For a while, during gestation and nursing, one does share one's body with another. These are not exceptional cases in the existence of man. They are required for the existence of everyone who has been born. They may not be required of one's life in that one must procreate in order to survive, but they are required in order that one may be alive.

Peikoff described Rand's Razor as: "Do not begin to philosophize in midstream" (1991, 139). Peikoff stated that, because all of "reality is interconnected," no one entity is an isolated existent that neither affects nor is affected by others. Ultimately, no aspect can exist separately from the total (1991, 23). According to Kelley, a biocentric code of ethics must start its analysis with the adult stage ("Roundtable 1996," 9). Rand asked what is required in order that an adult survive. Reproduction is not required. By starting her analysis in the middle of man's life, did she overlook something else essential to man's nature? I am confident that she did not think so. Sciabarra described Rand's method as "breaking down the whole into graspable elements" (1995, 128), which requires identifying essentials and abstracting these from the whole, analyzing them, then reintegrating them. I believe Rand did this, if not analytically at least metaphorically, by first asking what would be required of a man alone. But she did not leave man isolated from society. She did reintegrate him into it, asking what would be necessary for his existence among men; what preconditions would be required. Her trio of cardinal values and corresponding virtues remained unchanged—what is required of man alone is required of man in society. Productive work remains his central purpose.

Both Peikoff (1991, 123) and Sciabarra (1995, 144) stated that, according to OE, reality is an interconnected whole that consists of interacting entities (1991, 123). Yet, again and again, it is emphasized that reality does not (fundamentally) include other people. Kelley reiterated that the cardinal virtues are how man deals with reality; therefore, others "cannot be assigned the same degree of fundamentality" (1996, 24). Rand stated that relationships cannot rank first in a man's life (1964b, 7). Peikoff made it clear that that which comes first in man's consciousness is reality, not other individuals. Fundamentally, a person acts among others as he would alone. "In principle, he is as alone in society as on a desert island" (1991, 252–53).

Rand's ethics are biocentric. As Merrill (1997, 88) has pointed out, Rand's description of life, which forms the foundation of her ethics, is: "a process of self-sustaining and self-generated action" (Rand 1964a, 15). He also noted that the description (which was not intended to be a formal definition) makes no mention of reproduction. He offered two scientifically accepted definitions, both of which include reproduction as an essential feature of life. Merrill asked, if man has no instinct for reproduction "why go to the trouble and expense of having children at all?" (1991, 121)

In Rand's philosophy, instincts carry no weight in any event, since man has none. There are inherent biological needs, such as food, but a man can survive without procreating. I am not suggesting that biological inclinations are not present and important to the issue of procreation, but, in Rand's philosophy, instincts play no role. If instinct is not a reason for reproduction, others do exist. In response to Merrill, Coates asked:

> Does [Merrill] merely mean that Objectivism would be better off if someone wrote a careful essay explaining the selfish joy of having children, how it can be a major form of creativity and productivity and visibility for many, many psychologically healthy human beings, and why, for them, this is well worth giving up certain lower values? Or does he mean that having children is a duty for all, and one is immoral or acting against one's own interest if one chooses not to have them? (Coates 1998, 223)

Merrill clarified that he was not suggesting that everyone should have children. It was not his intent to imply a "moral criticism of persons choosing to remain childless" (Merrill 1998, 228).

What of Coates's question as to whether having children "is a duty for all, and one is immoral or acting against one's own interest if one chooses not to have them?" (Coates 1998, 223) Rand attached a specific meaning to duty. Whereas some might think of duty as synonymous with obligation or responsibility—such as in "I have a responsibility or an obligation or a duty to pay my bills"—she did not use these terms interchangeably. To Rand, it meant the moral imperative to behave in a given way based solely on "obedience to some higher authority" (1982a, 96), with no consideration for a person's happiness or interest. OE's guiding principle is causality, not duty (1982a, 99). Duty cannot be a reason in Rand's ethics for procreating.

Marsha Enright countered Merrill's claim that Rand's description of life does not include reproduction as an essential feature. She asked, "What is reproduction, but a means by which a life form sustains and generates its particular process of action beyond the existence of an individual life?" (Enright 1998, 231) This statement is true; however, if reproduction were essential, it would be regarded as a cardinal value. She, like Coates, also emphasized the joy children can bring to one's life (Enright 1998, 232).

Since both Coates and Enright mentioned joy as a reason for having children, consider how this fits into Rand's philosophy. To Rand, an emotion is not a reason to do a thing. Emotions are important. They are the means by which men enjoy their lives. But they are not guides. They are not a means of cognition. (See Enright 2002.) The guide is one's mind; emotions are the effect or result, not the cause, of one's actions. These cannot occur in reverse order (1964b, 6). If one is looking for reasons to reproduce, joy cannot be a reason. It may be a result, but not a guide for that decision. If one is interested in reasons, one must look elsewhere.

According to Rand, man's own happiness is his "*highest moral purpose*" (1964a, 27). Happiness is not the standard of ethics, however. Life is the standard. Rand's ethics are not hedonistic, but egoistic. Happiness is the consequence of achieving one's values (Shelton 1995, 23). Although Rand insisted that "virtue is not its own reward" (1961a, 131)—happiness is life's reward (ibid.)—she connected happiness to virtue. Rand explained that happiness and the maintenance of one's life are not separate achievements, but two aspects of the same thing. "Existentially, the activity of pursuing rational goals is the activity of maintaining one's life; psychologically, its result, reward and concomitant is an emotional state of happiness" (1964a, 29).

This passage links happiness more closely to life's maintenance, or productive work. Rather than being the consequence of the achievement of values, happiness is their achievement from a psychological perspective. Ray Shelton noted that since both productivity and happiness are the purpose of life, at some level, Rand equated the two (1995, 43n73). Rand did not regard work as drudgery or a duty. Valérie Loiret-Prunet (1999, 101) quoted Andrei, a character in Rand's novel *We the Living*, who said: "There is no such thing as duty. If you know that a thing is right, you want to do it" (Rand 1959, 79). Psychologically, there should be no conflict between man's mind and his emotions (Rand 1964b, 6). One's reason and feelings should be in harmony if one's personality is fully integrated (1969a, 29). As Kelley pointed out, if one continually felt no interest in his job, then this would indicate that one's premises were at odds with his emotions. If a man accepts a moral principle, he will inevitably feel the emotions that correspond to it (1996, 35).

Peikoff contended that it is not simply material needs one satisfies by working, but that work is also a profound psychological need (Peikoff 1991, 301). In Rand's view, without a central purpose—that of productive work—as the standard, one cannot determine the relative importance of other values; one cannot prioritize them nor integrate them into one's life (Peikoff 1991, 299; Rand 1964b, 6). Peikoff stated that even if a person is financially independent, whether due to his own efforts or good fortune, he still must have a career (1991, 301–302).

But it seems to me that claiming that an activity satisfies a psychological need is straying somewhat from the biocentricity originally claimed for Rand's ethics and for productive purpose. Thus, values in Rand's ethics may be psychological phenomena. This is true for productivity, the central purpose of life in Rand's philosophy. I regard a psychological basis for an argument as something somewhat different from a biological rationale. This is not to say there cannot be more than one justification for a thing and that each does not fit into a larger piece that could be called "survival *qua* man." (However there are some occupations that may satisfy a psychological need, but in later years may be physically life threatening as one's skills deteriorate. So, in some instances, the psychological need to work and one's own survival may be at odds.)

As for whether reproduction is a duty or not, I would think that, if it is essential, the same statements would apply to reproduction as were said of productive work: It is necessary for one's life both from a biological and a psychological perspective ("Roundtable" 1996, 9; Peikoff 1991, 301). If something is right, it is not a duty. And one should want to do it (Loiret-Prunet 1999, 101). Doing it will bring one joy (Rand 1964a, 29). There should be no conflict between reason and one's emotions (1969c, 29).

Must everyone reproduce? That would depend on whether it is in some sense essential. Enright implied that it is. According to Rand, productive work is essential. It is necessary for one's survival. On a desert island, one must work to survive. There is no option. In society, the same principle applies. It is possible, once one lives among others, to live off of others. One could take from others by force—through theft or fraud. Or one could live off of others voluntarily—through charity or trust fund stipends or lottery winnings or inheritance. One may even survive by not living off others but by living off physical capital one has accumulated by virtue of one's own prior efforts. But none of these are consistent with moral behavior in Rand's ethics, because work satisfies not only one's material needs, but a psychological need as well. So even though it may be possible through predation or gifts or one's own prior effort to forgo work once one lives among other men, work is still an ethical requirement. If reproduction were essential, the same logic would hold.

But as has been noted, one cannot reproduce alone on a desert island. This does not present a problem because, about this, Rand was clear. Reproduction is not fundamental to survival. It is morally optional (Rand 1968, 3). It is not a cardinal value and there are no cardinal virtues that specifically relate to reproduction, since cardinal virtues are those that deal with reality and reality does not (fundamentally) include other people. So even if reproduction is implicit in Rand's description of life, as Enright suggested (1998, 231), it is not an essential feature of survival. If it were essential, it would be accorded the same degree of fundamentality as productive work, in which case the desert island metaphor would be an inadequate starting point to relate the cardinal values and cardinal virtues in Rand's ethics. At least one other person would have to be considered part of "reality." Virtues dealing with relationships with others (at least some others) would have to be assigned the same degree of fundamentality as those that deal with (other aspects of) reality.

But assigning reproduction to a category separate from production may be unnecessary. According to Coates, having children may "be a major form of creativity and productivity and visibility" (1998, 223). So reproduction is production; it is simply one of the many kinds of productive activity that cannot be undertaken on a desert island. Even though it is not obligatory, Peikoff regarded motherhood as a career, if it were pursued as such and so long as the mother has a productive purpose once her children leave home (1991, 302). This is essentially the same view Rand expressed in her *Playboy* interview. The interviewer, Alvin Toffler, asked: Given that work is the highest goal within her philosophy, would she consider immoral someone who placed family and friends above work. She answered in the affirmative. Friends and family cannot come first in man's hierarchy of values. Would a woman be immoral, Toffler asked Rand, if instead of a career, she chose to dedicate her life to her home and to her family? Rand answered that, rather than immoral, she would find this impractical, since this would not constitute full-time employment except during the time the children were young. She added that motherhood was important, so long as it was approached scientifically, not merely to indulge one's emotions (Rand 1964b, 7).

Parenthood may be a career, but what is not mentioned by Peikoff or Rand is the obvious, i.e., it is not remunerative. Not only does it not pay, it should not pay;

i.e., children do not "owe" parents. Nathaniel Branden pointed out that the support a parent gives his children is owed them by right. Once he is grown, if his parents need financial help, "it is not his *duty* to help them regardless of the cost to himself. There can be no *unchosen* obligation of this kind" (N. Branden 1962, 55). So one does not and cannot undertake this career because of expected financial return.

A Unilateral Transfer

When one has a career of parent, Rand's trader principle is violated; or more accurately, it does not apply. Rand stated that a trader treats others as independent equals whereby, based on their respective judgments, they engage in voluntary interaction in which there are mutual benefits (1964a, 31). However, a child is not an independent equal to a parent. Both parties, parent and child, may benefit, but exchange is not between equals based on their own independent judgments. A child does not voluntarily enter the "birth" contract, and throughout his rearing there very well may be an element of coercion from parent to child in many of their "exchanges." A child is not entirely capable of rational choice and independent action. The trader principle applies strictly to adults who have these capabilities. Such is not the case between parent and child. The trader principle refers to bilateral exchange. The interaction between parent and child is predominantly unilateral from parent to child.

Objectivists have recognized that there are nonmonetary rewards to productive effort. For instance, Kelley pointed this out within the context of his discussion of benevolence in his monograph *Unrugged Individualism.* He said that the money received is the "social recognition" of the value created; however, the value a person places on that which he creates carries more weight in a person's value system than monetary return (1996, 49). Roger Donway countered:

> Certainly, a person ought to earn money by creating that which he judges to be objectively valuable to humans. But the money a person receives for creating such values is not only a social recognition of his having created the values . . . it is the vehicle by which his creation of those values is turned into support for his life. Thus, there would be no point in his creating the values if he did not expect people to pay him for them. ("Roundtable" 1996, 6)

In response, Kelley agreed that Donway had made a significant point, but that there was a psychological need to create value, even if a person were independently wealthy ("Roundtable" 1996, 9). Kelley regarded what one does for one's children as something other than benevolence. Still, if parenthood is a career, the question arises—as Donway expressed it—why would someone undertake the creation of value if he did not expect a monetary return? Although Kelley was speaking in general terms, not specifically of parenthood, his answer was that a psychological need exists even if one is wealthy enough not to need to work for pay. This is essentially the point Peikoff was making about the central purpose of work in one's hierarchy of values; that is, there is a psychological need as well as a monetary reward to productive work (1991, 301). But most workers, including parents, have not been financially independent. Most parents work at jobs for pay as well as have the responsibility of taking care of their children.

Rand said that motherhood is only a full-time job while one's children are young (1964b, 7). Even if this is true, if a person has more than one child, one is still considering an expanse of twelve to eighteen years of full-time (or at the very least, significant part-time) work. And as Peikoff noted, if one does devote full-time effort to rearing one's children, one must also prepare to have a productive career once the children are independent (1991, 302). Considering the nonremunerative time and effort that are required for parenting, a legitimate question is, why wouldn't the psychological need to create value be sufficiently satisfied by one job—the one for pay? Why also undertake a second career, one that not only does not and cannot pay, but one for which a person must incur, as Merrill pointed out, a (considerable) cost? (And if a person must support himself as well as his child or children, would he not have more than a single purpose in life? And if a person is to have a single purpose, as Rand seems to have suggested in the *Playboy* interview, it would seem to follow that, within the confines of OE, that purpose would more logically be one for which pay is received.)

The Productivity of Parenthood—An Economic Perspective

To be productive is to produce a good or a service. Goods produce services, so to be productive is to ultimately produce a service. One may produce a good that is used to produce other goods or produce a good that is consumed (either immediately or over time) or one may provide a service directly to the consumer (who may be oneself). Thus, if parenting is productive, the parent is producing something—that is, a good that will be used in the production of other goods (parents are investing their time, effort, and other goods in the creation of human capital), and/or a consumer good (a durable consumer good that provides services over time).

In his *Principles*, Alfred Marshall recognized that, regardless of class, women were assigned the task of investing their time without receipt of any direct income in the improvement of males' human capital (Pujol 1992, 122–23). Investment in human capital, according to Marshall, depends upon the willingness of parents to sacrifice for the future of their children (1992, 125). It is a *duty* of parents to educate their children. Women, in particular, are asked "to sacrifice themselves for the sake of their children" (1992, 126). Primarily, what women are expected to sacrifice is their own (paid) employment (along with the development of their own human capital).

From an economic perspective, parenting results in the development of human capital. However, the primary beneficiary of that investment in human capital is the child himself, or at least should be, according to OE. From the parents' perspective, economist Gary Becker regarded the production of one's own children as creating consumer durables (1995a, 259–60). Becker envisioned the household as a firm or factory in which the objective is to maximize utility (Febrero and Schwartz 1995b, xxii; Becker 1995b, 186; Becker 1995f, 360; Becker 1995c, 651–53). His emphasis was on consumption rather than, as in the theory of the firm, production. In a firm, it is assumed that the objective is to maximize profits, but since the end of production is consumption (as first put forth by Adam Smith), consumption was Becker's focus. His position was that basic goods are produced by consumers, oftentimes at home. The inputs to this production process are goods purchased in the marketplace as well as one's own (as well as other family members') time. The relevant prices are shadow prices since basic goods do not go through the market and thus do not have explicit prices (Febrero and Schwartz 1995b, xxi; Becker 1995e, 93–98, 186).

One of the things produced at home is one's own children (Becker 1995a, 246), since children cannot be bought in the marketplace. Children may provide income, but they are primarily a source of utility—psychic income (1995a, 242–43). Thus, children provide a flow of services—psychic and, perhaps, monetary—over time. They also necessitate the incurrence of costs (both explicit and implicit) as income goes up. For the mother, the largest cost as income goes up is her opportunity cost. Although Becker mentioned the "imputed value of the parents' services" (1995a, 244) as a cost of children, he did not mention specifically the opportunity cost of the mother's time. If the mother forgoes income, either by not working or not working fully outside the home, or if she works outside the home full-time but sacrifices career advancement in some way, this is a cost. (There is also a sense in which investment in a child's human capital can compete with investment of the mother in her human capital.) Because of the expected benefits and costs over time, the decision to have children is an investment decision, whereby the quantity of children is weighed against that of other consumer durables, nondurables, and services (Febrero and Schwartz 1995b, xxviii; Becker 1995a, 242–43, 256).

Becker believed children to be normal goods, which means as income goes up, so should expenditures on children (Febrero and Schwartz 1995b, xxviii; Becker 1995a, 243). However, higher-income parents tend to have smaller families (Febrero and Schwartz 1995a, xxxviii). Becker identified two effects at work as income rises. One is the quality effect. Wealthier families buy, not necessarily more durable goods, but higher quality durable goods. Similarly, Becker believed that as income rises, parents spend more on children and in doing so produce children of greater quality (1995a, 245). The increased demand for children as income increases translates into an increase in child quality rather than in quantity (Febrero and Schwartz 1995b, xxix). Another effect is that expenditures on children increase with income—there is a price effect. The higher expenditure decreases the quantity of children demanded.

As income rises, one of the costs that increases is the opportunity cost of the mother. This cost increase has no effect on quality; it is a pure price effect. Becker did not give this cost any particular weight in his discussion. The result of the increase in opportunity cost is to decrease the quantity demanded of children. However, if the mother chooses to work outside the home, the resulting increase in family income will increase the demand for all normal goods, including the demand for children. There are other factors that, according to Becker, probably have a negative effect on the demand for children, such as prohibitions on child labor and compulsory education. In addition, technology in the home has not kept pace with that outside the home, which has resulted in the higher relative cost of children. Becker maintained that even though children may be "purchased" with a lower down payment than other consumer durables, which may encourage earlier "acquisition," their lack of liquidity (there is no resale market) encourages their postponement (1995a, 257).

Harvey Leibenstein argued that as income per capita has increased, it has become less necessary to depend on children as sources of income. He reasoned that since higher incomes are in part due to more education, as income increases parents are more inclined to spend more on their children's education and training, and children are more likely to require more education and training in order to attain a given (or improved) standard of living. Consequently, there is less time available for children to spend contributing to family income (Becker 1995a, 269n9). Becker contended that as income increases, parents choose to have children of higher quality, which in turn requires greater expenditures on education as well as other goods and services.

Commenting on Becker, Bernard Okun said that Becker assumed that the wealthy choose children of higher quality, but he asked whether they have a choice (1995a, 265). James Duesenberry indicated that the choice may be limited. Expenditures may have to increase mechanically (in "fixed proportions") as income rises. He stated that Becker equated quality with expenditures (1995a, 262), and Okun further noted that Becker equated quality with utility (1995a, 264). Becker claimed that the quantity elasticity of demand for children may be small, but the quality elasticity is high (1995a, 244).

Okun did not agree. He pointed out that the decline in the birthrate is calculated by dividing the number of children by some aspect of the population; for example, women of child-bearing age. Each child is weighted the same. No distinction is made for quality. In terms of explicit expenditures, it is irrelevant whether they are for child "quality" or for other costs. Okun believed the "quantity income elasticity of demand for children may well be negative, or if positive, be very low" (1995a, 266). To Okun, the relevant variable was spending per child. This has been going up considerably (1995a, 265). Real per capita income tripled in the United States between 1860 and 1960. Over the same period of time, children went from being a net producer good ("providing rather than using income" [1995a, 245]) to a consumer durable. In 1980, the annual cost per child (exclusive of college expenditures) was estimated between $3,400 and $3,800 (Ogden 1986, 214). In the late 1990s, a figure of $150,000 to bring up a child was mentioned in a news article on the subject (Matera 1999, 15). (These are, of course, out-of-pocket expenditures.)

For women, the decision to marry and have children has historically been an economic one, whether recognized as such or not. Writing in the nineteenth century, John Stuart Mill branded the choice of matrimony for women as Hobson's choice, "that or none" ([1869] 1970, 156). A woman's fate was decided by her father, her husband, and nature: "Until a late period in European history, the father had the power to dispose of his daughter in marriage at his own will and pleasure, without any regard to hers" ([1869] 1970, 157–58). A "yes" at the wedding ceremony was merely a formality, not an expression of consent. "By the old laws of England, the husband was called the *lord* of the wife; he was literally regarded as her sovereign, inasmuch that the murder of a man by his wife was called treason" ([1869] 1970, 158).

Legally and technologically there have been momentous changes since Mill's time (in market-oriented democracies). Women have become enfranchised. Labor-saving technologies in the home have relieved or lessened the burden of many household chores. Technology outside the home has made many jobs less physically demanding than they were formerly and opened up a substantial white-collar service industry—consisting of occupations more suited to women.

While technology has increased opportunities outside the home for women, other technology has increased the opportunity for women to have more control over how many children they have as well as their timing. Birth control has become more reliable and dependable. Biology is no longer destiny for women. Freedom implies choice and, prior to the pill, choice was constrained. Of course, Okun noted that the fertility rate was declining in the 1800s, "by more than 50 percent from 1800 to 1870" (Becker 1995a, 267)—even before the dissemination of birth control.

There have also been cultural shifts that have increased the burden of responsibility on some women with children. The likelihood of divorce has increased to over 50 percent. So, for a woman, it is more probable that she will be primarily responsible for the care of the child—not only in the traditional ways a mother has been responsible but also monetarily. Even though courts award child support, as Annegret Ogden pointed out, this may be insufficient:

> The court may order the husband to pay anywhere from 10 to 25 percent of his income for child support. The amount decreases for higher incomes. . . . Recent data have shown that less than half of all the divorced mothers who were entitled to child support collected any money at all after two years, that only 20 percent receive regular support, and that only 8 percent receive alimony. (1986, 213)

Women, then, must rely on their own incomes. Yet, as Ogden noted: "In 1977, the average income of American women—from employment, investment, alimony, and child support—was less than $6,000. For those who worked full-time, year-round, the annual income rose to $8,620 compared with men in that category who earned $14,630. . . . [M]ore than a third of the nation's women still had no personal income at all" (1986, 216). In 1995, estimates still put women's earnings at 74 percent of men's for the same work (D. Smith 2000, 17). These cultural changes may encourage women to have fewer children.

According to Okun, the quantity elasticity of demand for children may be low or negative. As per capita income increases, the expenditures on children must increase; thus the demand for children falls (Becker 1995a, 266–67). (Here it sounds as if Okun confused the increase in cost—a price effect that results in a decrease in the quantity demanded (a movement along a curve)—with the income effect, which could result in an increase or a decrease in demand (a shift in the curve) depending upon whether the "good" is normal or inferior.) The income elasticity does not have to be negative for the number of children to be fewer than replacement. If the cost (both implicit and explicit) of children increases (the supply curve shifts leftward) so that a lower quantity is demanded, yet demand increases as a result of higher income (since children are "normal goods"), however, because the income elasticity is positive but low, the (rightward) shift in demand does not offset the decline in "quantity demanded," then the number of children "demanded" will fall. The birth rate is currently less than replacement in most industrial countries.

Extinction—A Possibility?

If incomes continue to grow along with the cost per child (both explicit and implicit) and *if* the quantity income elasticity is negative, is there a threat of population decline and possible extinction? Ownership is the cornerstone of a free market system. Without clearly defined property rights, the price mechanism cannot perform its rationing function. Prices signal certain things—they provide information. They also provide the incentive to act on that information. Supplying information is oftentimes not enough. For instance, people can be told a resource (say, the whale) is becoming extinct, but still overutilize it or overharvest it to the point of exhaustion or extinction. Prices provide information and incentives not only about animal populations, but also with respect to other resources used as inputs in the production process.

What does this have to do with children? Becker has called children consumer durables (1995a, 259) and has said that the decision to have children is an economic one, in which parents compare costs with the expected benefits (utility or psychic income) over time. Children are not purchased in the open market but are produced at home. There may be a cost to having them and rearing them, but there is no explicit price. Nor is there a resale market. For most durables, resale is possible. No such market exists for children. Parents have children. But are children owned by their parents? Do property rights exist for children per se, and, if so, are they clearly defined? What are the implications of the lack of a pricing mechanism and a market for offspring?

Ownership is the right to acquire, use, and dispose of an object. Anything less than that does not qualify as full property rights. Children cannot be acquired or disposed of (bought or sold), and, although they may be enjoyed, they cannot be (ethically or legally) used in the sense of being enslaved or abused by parents. So, in no sense of the word are children owned. The purpose of property, Sciabarra said, based on his reading of Rand, "is the material means of sustaining life, it is crucial to the actualization of the human potential" (1995, 277). Rand defined property as "the product of a person's labors. It refers to all the material assets [a person has] created, earned, exchanged, and legitimately appropriated for survival as a rational being" (ibid.). Although parents do perform a creative function in having and rearing their children—and children may be, in part, a product of their efforts—they cannot be appropriated by their parents. Children are unique in that sense.

Yet Rand believed all property "apart from some tangential public property linked to narrowly defined governmental functions, . . . should be privatized" (1995, 278). Forests, oceans, airwaves—all should be privately owned; however, rights do not apply to the unborn or nonhumans (ibid.). Adults, of course, own themselves. What of children? Following Rand's assertion that everything should be owned, children should be owned by someone as well. Do children own themselves? What are their rights? Bryan Register wrote:

> In fact and in logic, Objectivism advocates a rights-respecting approach to all persons and notes that individuals have rights in virtue of their potential rationality,

> not in virtue of what actual use they make of it. Other, more marginal cases (those of children and the retarded, for instance) have not yet come under Objectivist analysis; this is a gap in the Objectivist political perspective. (1997, 9)

William Thomas, who has written on the legal status of children, stated:

> The "right to life" of an infant . . . amounts to little more than an entitlement not to be harmed or killed by force. Such a "right" does not prevent the infant from being manhandled, vaccinated, diapered, restrained, washed, and otherwise cared for without the slightest rational consent. (1999a, 18)

I conclude from the discussion thus far that everything, except for minimal government property, should be owned, and that one should own the fruits of one's labor. Ownership amounts to having certain rights—the rights to acquire, use, and dispose of an object. Children are, in part, the product of the creative efforts of parents. But they cannot be bought or sold, used, or disposed of. They are not owned. An adult owns himself. He owns himself by virtue of his potential rationality. He has certain rights that follow from that ownership. But a child does not own himself. He is not capable of the rationality and autonomy required for full ownership in himself. He has a right to life but only in a very limited sense, which may be considered more of a "protection" than a right. (Children's rights are discussed in a chapter 7.) A child is, therefore, unowned.

The fact that children are unowned does have implications insofar as the working of the price mechanism is concerned. There is no explicit price for children, but there is a cost. Becker assumed that greater expenditures on children (higher costs) reflect greater utility (1995a, 243–44). It is true that higher costs tend to shift supply curves to the left. The supply curve will intersect the demand curve at a higher price (or shadow price if there is no explicit market), which reflects (if one accepts marginal utility theory) a higher marginal utility. In a free market, increased scarcity of a thing will be reflected by a higher price.

An increase in demand may result in higher prices relative to costs. This would signal current producers of a thing to produce more. This may also encourage potential producers to enter the market. Higher prices signal and encourage producers of substitute products to produce more. If no or few substitutes exist they may encourage innovation—the creation of new products to compete with existing products. The realization of some or all of these possibilities tends to have a moderating effect on the price of the thing in question. The price mechanism, and more specifically profit, performs this function. For the price mechanism and profits to perform this function, property rights must be clearly defined. There must be a market, or the existence of a market must be possible (for new "goods" as well as a resale market); otherwise, profits cannot encourage more production.

Profit, the difference between revenue and costs, is not earned when something is produced at home for one's own consumption or use. When something is produced at home there is no explicit price, but there is a value to the person producing and consuming the product (a shadow price exists). There is also a cost to producing the good. The decision-maker compares these costs with expected benefits in his decision to produce the good himself. Examples abound—homegrown tomatoes, homemade clothes, etc. Children share these features with other products produced at home. But, unlike tomatoes that can be bought and sold in a market, children cannot. A price does not and cannot exist for children. Higher costs (without an explicit market) can provide information and incentives. They encourage the curtailment of production on the part of producers and conservation on the part of consumers (in this case the same people). They also encourage the substitution of similar goods to the extent that they exist. Returning to Becker, the substitutes for children are durable consumer goods.

Becker assumed that demand for children (due to increases in income) keeps pace with rising costs (1995a, 259–60). In general, higher costs, *ceteris paribus*, will cause the supply curve to shift to the left. With a free market and ownership, higher prices may encourage more production if prices rise relative to costs; i.e., profits exist. But when price increases because of higher costs, profits will not be realized except for those who already own the good. Those individuals can receive capital gains by reselling in "secondhand" markets. For those who already own the product, the price will have increased relative to historical costs so that on resale they will experience a capital gain. But they will experience the capital gain only if they can sell what they already own. If they cannot, then they will not experience the capital gain. If costs have gone up, this will not encourage production within this market, because it is the higher costs that have shifted the supply curve and that have caused prices to go up. It may encourage, in the longer run, the production of substitutes, however, and this may have a moderating effect on the price of the scarcer good because of a movement away from the scarcer good. That is, the demand curve falls for the scarcer good.

For price to rise relative to cost, the demand for a good must increase (or costs decrease). Becker believed that children are normal goods, so that as income increases, the demand curve for children will shift outward. So higher incomes make costs go up—but demand also goes up, he would counter. Specifically, the demand goes up for children of higher quality. This has not translated into a significant increase in the quantity. But, insofar as the population is concerned, it is the quantity that counts. To sustain a population, a certain number is needed. If the quantity income elasticity of demand is negative, as Okun suggested, then increases in income will shift the demand curve for children downward (1995a, 265). With the supply curve shifting to the left, and the demand curve shifting downward, it is at least theoretically possible that at some point there could be no demand for children at the prevailing cost.

Demand and supply curve analysis is static partial equilibrium analysis. It does not tell the whole story. Restricting assumptions to a few can have implications that are not consistent with reality. Malthus came to the conclusions he did about population because he assumed, among other things, fixed resources and a population that was increasing geometrically (and agricultural production increasing arithmetically). This is not sufficient to reach his conclusions, however (Barnett and Morse 1963, 51–58).

The purpose here is not to present a "theory of population," nor to be an alarmist about threats to population growth, but simply to indicate that the free market operates to ameliorate conditions of scarcity by providing incentives through the price mechanism. But its cornerstone is private ownership. If property rights are not clearly defined or do not exist, then there can be problems. (The population of England was about 250 and that of France approximately 10,000 during the early Paleolithic era [Pipes 1999, 81], yet man managed to survive. This is an analysis of tendencies, only.)

Clarification

Economists regard human beings as inputs in the production process. To some extent, they are substitutable for equipment or land or raw materials (and vice versa). But human beings are not like equipment, etc. They have minds. They create. They create the equipment, not the other way around. But if the fact that capital equipment can be substituted for labor in some circumstances were ignored, then some very poor business decisions would be made. Labor-saving capital has been a major source of productivity. Tractors replaced horsepower and manpower as well. Vending machines have been substituted for vendors. Electronic computers have taken over many of the tasks done by human computers.

In part, expenditures on education result in the creation of human capital. When costs and income as well as other long-term benefits are involved, a decision is in part an investment decision, whether the investment is in physical capital, human capital, or a consumer durable. This is true not only of education, but also in the decision to have children. Are children durable goods? No. But do people consider costs over time relative to benefits when they consider having them? To some extent, yes. For some, perhaps, to a very great extent. In general, as costs of having children have risen, the number of children (per adult female of childbearing age) has declined in many countries. Are costs relative to benefits the only reason? People have children for a number of reasons, many which have not been addressed here. Also, procreation is not always based on a reasoned choice. Some have children by "accident," for example.

It is no coincidence that as job opportunities have increased for women, the number of children per adult female has decreased. Greater job opportunities for women increase the opportunity cost of having children because the mother's time has a greater monetary value. From one perspective, the job of homemaking and childrearing has been an occupation for women; historically, one of the few, and it was largely a full-time job. Now there are more occupations, many of which pay better since childrearing pays (explicitly) nothing at all. Some interpret economic theory as indicating that individuals will rationally choose more income to less. This is not accurate. It is assumed that for two jobs that are identical in all other respects, a rational person will choose the job that pays more. Of course, childrearing and other jobs are not identical. So even if the former pays nothing explicitly, there are still benefits that weigh in its favor, what is called psychic income. Even though from the perspective of the economy as a whole (and from the perspective of the children themselves), parents may be seen as investing in human capital by rearing and educating their children, from the parent's perspective, children are consumer, not producer, durables.

Historically, this has not always been the case. But now, from the perspective of parents, children are no longer regarded as income-earning assets. They do not provide a positive source of net income to the family. They do not pay for their own keep, in money or in kind. They no longer provide a form of old-age security for their parents nor do they provide physical security. They are not apprenticed in work their parents do. They must receive most of the training they need for a livelihood formally, outside the home, and at considerable expense. They are consumer goods, very time-intensive, expensive, consumer durables—consumer goods that can only be produced at home, that command no explicit price, that cannot be sold or resold.

The fact that children neither are owned nor command an explicit market price is not to argue in favor of a "market" for children. The concept of property rights does not apply in the case of children. Children do have certain protections, and parents have certain responsibilities toward them (both positive and negative—that is, they have some responsibilities for them as well as some limitations on what they can do to them). But because ownership does not apply, the market mechanism is not fully operational in their "production." This is important to keep in mind since the decision to have children is to an extent an economic decision. Costs are incurred over time when one has children. Parents derive benefits from having children. As income increases, both implicit and explicit costs increase. This has the effect in most markets, other things equal, of reducing supply. In other markets, those people who (already) own goods that have increased in price because of scarcity can sell their goods and receive a capital gain. The capital gains and higher prices may encourage the production of similar or substitute products. Capital gains cannot be realized with children because there is no resale market.

An increase in income has the effect of increasing the demand for a good if it is a normal good. Even if the good becomes scarcer (the supply curve shifts to the left), this will encourage production so long as demand keeps pace with higher costs. This is what Becker assumed. The higher implicit cost, i.e., the opportunity cost of the mother, is a pure price effect in that it is not related to quality (of children)—something Becker did not acknowledge. Apparently, the income elasticity is low or negative. If a good is inferior, as the income elasticity for children would suggest (1995a, 265), then the demand for the good falls with increases in income, further discouraging production. At least *theoretically* these dynamics could result in a dried-up demand for children. But should this be a *primary* concern for an ethics based on egoistic individualism?

Man Alone—Again

In constructing an ethics one must start with concepts. Concepts are the building blocks of knowledge. Principles are expressed as relationships among concepts that reflect a universality or generality. One of man's distinguishing characteristics is that he thinks conceptually. Peikoff stated that even on a desert island man needs concepts: "Just as man would need concepts (including language) on a desert island, so he would need logic there, too. Otherwise, by the nature of human consciousness, he would be directionless and cognitively helpless" (1991, 120). By definition: "*A concept is a mental integration of two or more units possessing the same distinguishing characteristic(s), with their particular measurements omitted*" (Rand 1979, 15). As Sciabarra pointed out, a concept (e.g., man) includes every man "that has ever lived and will live" (1995, 172).

A concept requires two or more existents that have the same essential characteristics. Man thinks in terms of concepts. Principles express relationships among concepts. As Peikoff noted, concepts are needed on a desert island; otherwise a man would be cognitively adrift. One concept that is fundamental to a man is the concept "man." Two or more existents are required for the existence of the concept "man." The question I pose is, if a man is alone on a desert island, how does he know that other men exist? There must be at least one other man in existence for the concept "man" to have meaning. If he is alone we cannot assume that he knows that other men exist. (In fact, when he employed the Crusoe device, Murray Rothbard assumed that the castaway had amnesia [1998, 29].) One could rebut that this is an abstraction, and with abstractions we can make assumptions, and we can just assume that he knows other men exist. Can we have it both ways?

Can it be assumed that man knows that others exist and then assume that he does not? Then conclude that other men are not part of reality. Then state that fundamental virtues are concerned with how man deals with reality but others are not (fundamentally) part of reality.

One could claim that I am making a categorical error here, that I am confusing the meaning of man (epistemologically the meaning or definition of a concept) with the meaning of man (metaphysically, the meaning or purpose of man). The argument does not hinge on the meaning of meaning. Either man is on a desert island, as Peikoff suggested, or he is not. Either concepts are necessary on a desert island or they are not. Either concepts mean two or more existents of a particular kind or they do not. Either reality (fundamentally) includes other people or it does not. This is important because it is from observing man in isolation that cardinal values and virtues are derived, values and virtues that are primary. (At least, this is what Peikoff was metaphorically suggesting.)

It may seem as if I am switching from epistemology to ethics and back (see Peikoff on Heisenberg's Uncertainty Principle [1991, 16–17].) However, to claim that the concept man is needed for a man on a desert island and that in order to have that concept you do in fact have to have two or more existents, etc. is not sleight of hand, because reason in Rand's epistemology is concept-formation (1964a, 20). Metaphysically there is no hierarchal distinction between one and one million. However, from an epistemological perspective, the number "two" is critical, since, in order for a concept to exist, there must be at least two existents in reality so that their common features can be observed and generalized (1990, 198).

Theory or lack of it does not change the facts of reality. Paraphrasing Stephen Jay Gould, Newton's apple did not remain suspended midair awaiting his discovery of the law of gravity (1981, 35). So a man's survival on a desert island would not await his discovery of the concept "man," which would be impossible so long as he remained alone. The fact that the concept "man" would not exist would not negate the actuality of a single man's existence. Yet, Rand said, man cannot long survive at the perceptual level of existence. He depends on his conceptual faculty. Reason is man's means of existence. It is the cornerstone of epistemology. "The faculty that works by means of concepts is: *reason*" (Rand 1964a, 20). Metaphysics—"the study of existence as such or, in Aristotle's words, of 'being qua being'" (1982d, 3)—tells us about man and his relationship to the universe. Man is by nature a rational animal (1961a, 122). In ethics, reason is man's cardinal value, because it is man's tool of survival (1971b, 227). Rationality is the primary virtue; the source of all others (1964a, 25).

Concept-formation is the faculty of reason. Reason is man's means of knowledge, according to Objectivist epistemology. However, reason is also man's primary value, and rationality is his primary virtue. It is this that links the concept "man" to ethics. Rand said: "This—the supremacy of reason—was, is and will be the primary concern of my work, and the essence of Objectivism" (1971d, 1). If reason were not linked from epistemology to metaphysics to ethics, then the concept "man" would not need to have any referents in reality. It could be a concept of method, such as infinity in mathematics, that has no metaphysical content (Rand 1990, 148). If reason were not required for man's existence—even on a desert island—then concepts (specifically the concept man) would not be needed.

Suppose that the man on the desert island does not know whether there is another man in existence. There either is or is not another man in existence. Suppose that he assumes that there is no other man in existence; what are the implications of that? If he is the only man in existence he cannot form the concept "man." He, therefore, cannot derive principles since they are expressed as relationships among concepts, one of those concepts necessarily being man. He will be cognitively adrift. Now suppose he assumes there is one other man in existence. With this knowledge he can now form the concept "man." He can derive principles. However, he now faces the mortal's dilemma. If the other person dies first, he is alone; the concept, man, "dies" as well. If he dies first, the concept is "alive" as long as he is. In order for the concept to remain in existence as long as he, he must die first. If life is the ultimate value to a person, this is not a desirable outcome, and it has an inherent contradiction. If he wants greater assurance (to increase the odds, since there are no guarantees) that the concept "man" will outlive him, he can reproduce with the other person in existence (assuming the other person is of the opposite sex and consents). In this way there will be at least three persons in existence. This means that if any one of them dies, the concept "man" will still have meaning. (Also since his offspring is younger than he and since the chance of death increases with age, it is more likely that the concept, man, will outlive him, since it is likely that his offspring will outlive him.)

This solves the problem for the man alone—although he is no longer strictly alone. Now once a man moves off the desert island, he will become aware that other men exist. He will notice that others are procreating, so he may conclude that the concept "man" is not threatened since the extinction of man is not likely—especially in his lifetime, which is, after all, his ultimate concern. But by "letting others" keep the concept of man alive by procreating, is he shirking? One could answer—if there is no possibility of extinction of man, how could any one individual be responsible for its perpetuation? But is there no threat? If one looks at Western industrialized countries where an element of freedom has existed for some time, population is just at or less than replacement for most countries. (In 1995, it stood at replacement for the United States and Sweden, and at less than replacement for Norway, Ireland, Australia, Canada, France, the United Kingdom, Belgium, Denmark, Switzerland, Austria, Germany, Greece, Portugal, Spain, and Italy. This was based on an SPSS® data file. The data was compiled for 109 countries using 1995 almanacs. Some of the data was inconsistent across sources [SPSS 1999].)

One could say that we could be hit by an enormous meteor and become extinct. What's the point? The point is a meteor is exogenous to the philosophical system (ethics). However, there are forces within the philosophical system described above that make extinction a theoretical possibility (however slim). As mentioned, for children—although a source of creativity and productivity—property rights do not apply. Costs exist, but there is no explicit price; therefore, the price mechanism is not fully functional. Those who do procreate may be doing so for their own selfish reasons, but there are spillover effects—benefits to third parties. The benefit to third parties is not that others perpetuate the species, per se, since perpetuation of the species is not a direct, *primary* concern of any particular individual. Third parties benefit because of the reasoning expressed above. That is, since man thinks in terms of concepts, concepts are required on a desert island; otherwise man is directionless and cognitively helpless. Concepts are the building blocks of knowledge, and principles express relationships between concepts. Two or more men are needed for the concept of man to exist. Thus a particular man selfishly needs the existence of at least one other man, and to avoid the mortal's dilemma, at least one more who can potentially outlive himself. If he does not procreate, he benefits directly (not indirectly) by the reproduction of others.

Spillover Effects

When a third party benefits from the availability of a good supplied by others, economists say that there are spillover effects and the good provided has public good characteristics. Public goods have nothing to do with the way in which the goods are financed, but have to do with the benefits they provide (Gwartney 1976, 519). Public and quasi-public goods tend to be jointly consumed. Now, obviously everyone does not "consume" or enjoy other people's children in the same way as the parents of those children do. But goods—all goods—have more than one aspect and can be consumed in more than one way. Recall that an entity is its attributes. Attributes are embodied in the entity. They cannot be isolated from the entity as separate existents. The point is that at least one aspect of others having children may be the benefit mentioned above. Since nonpayers cannot be excluded from enjoying this particular aspect, it qualifies as having public good characteristics (even if children are not public goods, per se).

If others benefit without having to pay, they are free riders (1976, 519–22). When someone receives a benefit without paying for it, he is receiving the unearned. According to Rand, a rational man "never seeks or desires the *unearned*" (1964c, 52). Rand said: "One must never seek or grant the unearned or the undeserved, neither in matter nor in spirit (which is the virtue of Justice)" (1964a, 26). James Gwartney stated:

> [W]hen external benefits are present, decision-makers lack the incentive to carry the activity far enough. Potential gains are present, but they may go unrealized because the pricing mechanism does not make it possible for a decision-maker to appropriate or capture the gains that he bestows on others. (1976, 517–18)

This is an example of market failure. It can exist in a free market system and may be exacerbated if property rights are not clearly defined and the price mechanism consequently fails to fully perform its function.

As has been discussed, having children shares only some of the characteristics of private market transactions. Although having children is a creative endeavor, children are not owned; ownership does not apply. There is no explicit price for children, although there is a cost. There is no market for selling children or for reselling them. There is no profit. The price-profit mechanism cannot provide the signal-incentive mechanism to encourage production as the "good" becomes scarcer. I have argued that it is conceivable that in developed (freer) countries, children may be "underproduced" because of the possible negative quantity income elasticity of demand and rising explicit and implicit costs with rising incomes. There are many goods that are no longer produced because demand has declined over time as costs increased.

Children are unique in that they cannot be owned, do not own themselves, yet have certain protections (ethical and legal). As a consequence, they cannot be subject to the "overuse" characteristic of other unowned "goods." Still, because clearly defined property rights and a fully operational price mechanism (and the resultant remuneration) cannot exist for children, they may be underproduced. Something may be underproduced because of the lack of ownership and a pricing mechanism in the sense that some potential benefits exist that are not being met. The benefits may go unrealized not only by primary beneficiaries but also by third parties. Primary beneficiaries may underproduce because they cannot realize gains that would exist through the market (both new and resale markets) since there is no market. Specifically, in the case of children, as the opportunities in other markets (occupations) have increased (particularly for women), the (non-remunerative) career of parenting has become less attractive.

For third parties, who receive potential spillover benefits (discussed above), the "good" may be underproduced as well. If a "good" has public good characteristics, third parties, external to the transaction, benefit. To the extent that these characteristics exist, there is market failure. Potential benefits go unrealized because the price mechanism does not permit producers to capture the gains that are received by third parties. If there is a threat of a decline in population, it is not external, but internal to the (economic) system. It could potentially result from any or each of these and their interaction.

In human capital theory, it is recognized that since people cannot sell themselves, their human capital is an inadequate source of collateral in obtaining funds to invest in one's own productivity (Febrero and Schwartz 1995b, xxvi). Employers are unlikely to invest in general training for their workers, unless workers pay the full cost (including the opportunity cost), since general training is transferable to other employment. The improved productivity is embodied in the worker and the worker takes the training with him when he changes jobs (Becker 1995d, 36–90). Individuals who invest in themselves may have a problem obtaining loans for general education or training (since repossession is not possible). Although there may be some "indenture-like" agreements (e.g., schoolteachers who promise to work in inner cities in return for scholarships), these are generally not available because of the difficulty in making the agreements binding in free societies. Therefore, there may be an under-investment in human capital because it cannot be used as collateral.

The forgoing is introduced only to acknowledge that economists are aware that problems can exist for decisions related to human capital. Procreation involves the creation of human capital. Marshall believed that women should sacrifice (other employment) in order to create a better workforce (Pujol 1992, 122–23). His reasoning was based on the benefit to the economy as a whole. This is not the argument here. Third parties may benefit from the procreation of others, but it is not from the perspective of the economy or from the perspective of the species that the benefit is of relevance, insofar as an individualist ethics is concerned. It is, in the first instance, from the perspective of an individual alone on a desert island and (as Peikoff noted) his need for concepts for his survival, in particular the concept "man." If there is a tendency for children to be underproduced on this account—i.e., because of market failure—then the answer to the question: is someone shirking his responsibility by not procreating, would be yes.

One could counter that, even though the population in this country (and other relatively free countries) is at, or less than, replacement, many countries have large or growing populations. It is hard to make the case that the world is going to be threatened by human extinction any time in the near future. But one could say much the same thing about a man's productivity once he lives among men (more specifically, men who are free). As Mack (1986, 139) implied, a man living among men may not have to work to survive. A man may pursue a parasitical course. However, to Rand, the same principles apply when one lives among other men as would apply on a desert island (Peikoff 1991, 252). Parasitical avenues would not be open to a man in society because man has a psychological need to be productive. How is reproduction different? One could argue that the population may not be threatened if one person does not reproduce, but perhaps—like production—reproduction satisfies not only a material need but a psychological need. How is it different from production in that regard? If man should not live off of the productivity of others, if he is not entitled to the unearned in the productive sphere, why should he be entitled to an unearned benefit by virtue of the reproductivity of others?

Reproduction—A Separate Category

Perhaps reproduction is not different from production. Perhaps it is just one aspect of production (considered in chapter 13) or one type of production (discussed here). If reproduction is simply one type of production among many, then by producing—whether having children or engaging in some other creative way—one satisfies whatever psychological need there is. One could observe that empirically many people both work and have children. If work for pay satisfies the psychological need Rand was speaking of, why do vast numbers also have children? Do children satisfy another need? One answer may be no. This is why as women's opportunities outside the home increase they feel less inclined to procreate. Procreation has been a job, the only or the main job open to many women. Now that other paying jobs are available for women, the psychological need to be creative is being filled by alternative (paid) employment. The other answer is yes, procreation is different, and people do have a psychological need to reproduce. They may also reason, as I have above, that they may be in some sense shirking their responsibilities if they do not reproduce, so they do—not out of duty but out of reasoned choice (that if man is alone, there is no concept of man, etc.). There may also be some who reason this way, but because of market failure, they leave the child-bearing to others. They shirk.

So reproduction may be just another type of production or it may fill a niche that cannot be satisfied by any other kind of production. In some ways reproduction is like other production. It is a creative process and it is an economic decision in that it involves long-term benefits and the incurrence of costs over time. It requires tradeoffs with other purchases and investment of one's time and money and other resources. But unlike other production, there is the lack of ownership of the fruits of one's labor, the lack of a price-profit mechanism, the absence of remuneration, and the breakdown of the trader principle (it does not apply) between parent and child. It is also different from production (for the purposes of survival) in that production can be done alone and reproduction cannot. Reproduction requires at least one other (adult) person—at least for the time necessary to conceive—and it involves the care of another person (child). Because it requires another person, it also requires principles related to how one relates to another person. Because of these differences, reproduction may be sufficiently different from production to be considered as a separate category. So in answer to the question of whether one is shirking by not having children, I offer a tentative and very qualified "yes" (to be revisited later).

Reproduction—A Cardinal Value?

Now, if reproduction is a separate category and if it is a value, can it be said to be a cardinal value? It certainly cannot be performed by a man on a desert island. To reproduce, one is not independent in the limited sense that one needs another (adult) person—at least for the span of time it takes to conceive. Unlike other work, it is something one cannot perform alone. And when one reproduces, one does share one's body with another (one's offspring). Nor does the trader principle apply between parent and child. But if man needs concepts on a desert island and the concept "man" requires two or more existents, then two or more men are needed. And to avoid the mortal's dilemma, more than two are needed, one of whom has a life expectancy that extends beyond one's own. To avoid the inconsistency of a man alone not having the concept "man" on which to build the principles he needs for survival, then a man needs at least one other man to comprise his "reality," and to avoid the mortal's dilemma, one more (younger) person. Reproduction is conceivably a primary value and, for the reasons listed above, a category separate from production.

Concerning production, Rand said: "Men have been taught that the highest virtue is not to achieve, but to give. Yet one cannot give that which has not been created. Creation comes before distribution—or there will be nothing to distribute" (1961c, 80). Production is the precondition of consumption. It must come first. But it seems to me, one could equally say: "Rand has said, that which one values is not procreation but one's life. Yet one cannot live unless procreation has taken place. Procreation comes before life—or there would be no life to live." The counterclaim is that reproduction may be necessary so that one may come into existence, but it is not necessary for a person's continued survival. However, if, as Peikoff claimed, work is a psychological need even if one is wealthy enough not to work, why wouldn't reproduction also be a psychological need? Reproduction, it would seem, is more fundamental (basic or primary) than production. Even though reproduction is not necessary to sustain a person's life, neither would be productive effort if one were independently wealthy. Reproduction is a value. As a value, it must be validated to remain viable. It must be sustained by action. Action keeps values alive.

However, every value need not be acted upon by everyone. Art, according to Rand, is necessary for man's survival (1969a, 17). Yet, every man need not be an artist. But art is a productive activity. Reproduction is a category separate from production. Reproduction is a precondition for life and, therefore, for production. Work is a psychological need in order to anchor and prioritize one's values. But reproduction is more basic to survival than production (in the sense of being a precondition for it). If production is a precondition for consumption, reproduction is a precondition for production. If the psychological need that is satisfied by work serves to anchor and prioritize values, it would seem that a value that is more basic than work would also be a psychological need.

Discussion: Virtues for Reproduction?

Virtues are those actions that are necessary to attain or preserve values. If reproduction is a value, a related question is: Are there virtues required for reproduction that are different from those needed for production? For production, one must be honest and have integrity. Although not cardinal virtues, these were found to be important to a man on a desert island, and, likewise, when living among other men. Certainly these are important for reproduction as well. Reproduction, however, unlike production, requires by its nature another (adult) person (at least in the short term). In addition to the primary virtues listed thus far, Rand also included justice as a virtue that is required when dealing with others. Kelley added benevolence (1996, 32–33). These, justice and benevolence, are not primary in OE since they deal with others. But if others (at least one other) are fundamental to reality, then these virtues would be important as well. But justice applies to independent equals. The main justification for benevolence, according to Kelley, is the possibility of future traders. Traders are also independent equals.

David Axel pointed out that Kelley's discussion on benevolence does not "pay adequate attention to childhood" ("Roundtable" 1996, 7). He mentioned that during that part of our lives we depend on others for our survival. Kelley acknowledged this, but that was beyond the scope of his monograph. He said that "the reasons why parents care for their children are more specific—and more powerful—than benevolence" (1996, 9). I agree. Children are dependent. Neither the trader principle—which is the basis for justice—nor benevolence applies to one's children. Children are not independent, entirely rational, agents making choices on their own informed judgments. And parents are not trading value for value in transactions with children. Values may, indeed, be traded. But the other requirements for the trader principle do not apply. If a virtue (or virtues) is required for having and rearing children, it (or they) probably relates to nurturance or some aspect of nurturance. It is an area of ethics that demands adequate explication, but suffice it to say, at this point, that nurturance would appear to be related to the virtue involved.

What about arguments such as everyone cannot afford to have children or that everyone does not have the requisite virtues or temperament for children? To both of these I would direct the answer back to what Rand has said about productivity. Rand said, in effect, that to be moral one must be productive (1964b, 6–7). She did not say one must be productive unless one does not have the requisite skills; that one should work, unless one cannot afford to get the knowledge necessary to do the job. Acquiring knowledge is part of the requirement. One must acquire whatever skills are needed. Rand said that one must support one's own life—sustain one's own existence. And she thought humans were efficacious enough to do so.

What of the corresponding virtues? She did not say, be honest unless it does not work for you. Or have integrity unless you cannot get a job except by sacrificing your integrity. You must have these virtues. Why should reproduction be any different from production? If reproduction is required, then one should be able to afford it. Since man is efficacious, he should be able to sustain his life and—if necessary—that of his offspring. If certain virtues are required, he should have them. One does not say: Have integrity unless it is not in your temperament to have it. Why should one be excepted from having a nurturing nature if that is what is required for the job, for the creation of the associated value? If something is a value that is necessary, and one's virtues are the means by which one achieves or maintains that value, then one must have that virtue. We do not have the option of picking and choosing our virtues from a cafeteria plan—if they are required, if they are primary, if they are the way in which man deals with reality—then a man must acquire them. If other people (even a select few) are part of "reality," one should acquire the necessary virtues to deal with that reality.

Reproduction is different from production in that it cannot be done alone. Dependency (of a particular kind) is involved. Another person is needed (in a specific way). One shares one's body with another—one's offspring (for a limited period of time). It is also different in that another virtue or other virtues are required, a virtue related to nurturance, perhaps. In addition, it differs in another fundamental way; consent is required. One can produce alone. If one trades, consent is required. But one can potentially survive without trading. One can potentially produce all of what one needs to survive alone. One cannot reproduce alone and consent is essential. One must have qualities that are attractive to another person.

Since some aspect of a nurturing nature is needed to rear a child, one aspect of one's character that may need to be exhibited is that of a nurturing nature. The reason it may need to be exhibited is that one cannot be nurturing with one's own child unless one has a child. So this is a Catch-22 situation. It is similar to the problem of needing job experience to get a job when one has never had a job. How does one exhibit the qualities needed to show a potential employer he is or will be productive? One (although not the only) way to exhibit productivity is to complete some training to show that one has learned some skills, that one has initiative, that one has the tenacity to complete a task, and so on. One may exhibit a nurturing nature a number of ways as well. One may do so by showing in some way that one is cognizant of others in dependency situations and by indicating by one's actions one is sensitive to others in those circumstances.

Peikoff (1991, 292) said that there cannot be too much productivity. What about too much reproductivity? Rand does not address this. Reproduction may be a source of creativity. She left it at that. She said it was morally optional, but did not set limits on how much one should reproduce or if there should be some reasonable limit. Like everything else, she left this to the individual. As with other decisions, one should approach this rationally. Personal responsibility is paramount. One should not have more children than one can reasonably afford, of course, since it is the parents' responsibility and obligation to rear them. I will return to this topic in chapter 13.

CHAPTER THREE

Forced Unilateral Transfers and Retaliation in a State of Nature

This chapter addresses what I call forced unilateral transfers, which would include such things as defaulting on trade, stealing from others, assaulting, raping, and killing others. Bilateral exchange is voluntary and forms the basis for Rand's principle of justice—the trader principle (Rand 1964a, 31). There are mutual gains to trade; however, there are incentives to cheat (default, for instance). This incentive structure can be modeled in a Prisoner's Dilemma (Axelrod 1984, 8). This model is used to analyze the question, why must principles be general—why shouldn't principles have an escape clause that allows for cheating (a forced unilateral transfer) if it can lead to gain? One reason that I examine is the threat of retaliation. Rand's trader principle is broadened to include reciprocity. I argue that in an original state of nature, retaliation would not only be necessary, it would also be moral (with certain qualifications). Also noted is the tendency to rely on tribal justice when government is absent.

State of Nature and Human Nature

Rand claimed that all cardinal values and virtues can be practiced by a man in isolation; a Robinson Crusoe existence in a state of nature, so to speak. Although Rand did not use the "Crusoe" technique to derive her cardinal values and virtues, the process of abstracting man from other men in order to examine essentials specific to a given question is not unusual. Murray Rothbard used it in *Man, Economy, and State* and again in *The Ethics of Liberty*. About it, Rothbard said that the abstraction process of isolating a few individuals and analyzing their interactions on a "desert island" facilitates a clear understanding of the fundamental truths underlying interpersonal behavior, which would remain hidden if the world were examined "only whole and of a piece" (1998, 29).

State-of-nature analysis has received some criticism in the literature. With reference to Hobbes's use of it, Douglas Den Uyl and Douglas Rasmussen maintained that "state of nature analysis is usually parasitical upon civilization. No one could disseminate Hobbes's rules for peace (as found in Chapter XV of *Leviathan*) who was unfamiliar with civilized life" (Den Uyl and Rasmussen 1997, 9~38). In its defense, Tibor Machan said that it is a "meaningful analytic device to understand the development of ideas about human conduct" (1975, 20). This chapter will continue to assume an original "state of nature." However, now more than one individual may be relevant to the analysis.

Why Be Moral?

In chapter 1, it was asked, "why pursue consistency at all costs?" (Johnson 1999, 145) A somewhat similar question was asked by Robert Nozick in "On the Randian Argument." Nozick asked why must each person "follow the *same* principles"? (Nozick 1971, 292); that is, why couldn't a rational person have an exclusionary clause recommending "parasitism under certain conditions"? (ibid.) In response to Nozick, Den Uyl and Rasmussen made the following points: First, a salient feature of human nature is that "generality is inherent in our very being" (1978, 193). Second, every human has the same nature. Third, a consequence is that each human must abide by the same principles. Fourth, if exclusionary clauses are permitted, then one is not "talking about principles" (ibid.). And finally, if there is an argument to be made for parasitism, it should be made in the form of a general principle.

The points that Den Uyl and Rasmussen made with regard to principles and human nature were discussed to some extent in chapter 1. To Rand, principles are related to man's survival. It is in man's self-interest to be moral. Virtues, such as honesty, are selfish. According to her: "Truth is the recognition of reality" (1982i, 14). In *Atlas Shrugged*, she said: "Honesty is not a social duty, . . . but the most profoundly selfish virtue man can practice" (1961a, 129). From observing man in isolation, one can see that truth is necessary for man's existence. Isolated in nature, one must accept the facts of reality in order to survive.

The same principles apply when among others as when alone. Although Rand said that honesty is not a social duty, this does not mean that it is not a social virtue, and that there are not instances in which one *rightfully* deserves the truth from another. If a person offers you something to eat and he knows that the food is poisonous, you would be justified in being told the truth (before you eat it). If you have paid for the delivery of a piano to be received in one week and the person has no intention of delivering it, you are justified in knowing that before you pay the person.

According to Den Uyl and Rasmussen, if establishing principles is the objective, then there would have to be a general principle recommending dishonesty. Some individuals lie all the time, such as those who suffer from Korsakov's disease (or, to be more accurate, what they say is not consistent with reality) (Restak 1979, 272–74). When individuals lie all the time, they are fairly easily found out and usually undergo medical and other examinations to uncover the cause. One reason that people do not lie all the time is that the ultimate arbiter of truth is reality, and many of the facts of reality are patently demonstrable. So one may want to appear truthful so as not to be labeled a fool or worse.

But why should one care if someone else lies or not? When the truth is ostensive, one may not care. But much of what we know is not obvious. Truth has value. We depend on it for our survival since truth can be regarded as reality revealed, i.e., discovered. Much of what we know is not discovered by each of us "from scratch." We rely on the communication of knowledge from others to ourselves. It is important that others impart truthful information. Many of us depend on trade for our livelihood. Trade is largely based on trust. If I give someone money with the understanding that he will deliver something later, I depend upon his honesty. If I want someone to give me money for something I promise to produce and deliver, my hope is that he will perceive me as honest. Honesty has value for interpersonal relationships. If someone offers to feed your cat while you are on vacation, you hope he is being truthful with you. One benefits from being honest with oneself. If one deludes oneself into thinking he can fly unaided, he will suffer the consequences.

In "On the Randian Argument," Nozick presented an example of a child who, on the arrangement of his father, has had an implant inserted in his head that allows the child to forget misdeeds. The child could then, throughout his life, murder and steal, yet forget, and thus live a blissful life. In response, Den Uyl and Rasmussen replied that since the person forgets his transgressions, his actions have no moral relevance (1978, 201). However, the question insofar as principles are concerned, for those who are morally culpable, is why not have a principle that permits dishonesty, if one can benefit from it?

One could equally ask—why not kill someone if one could get away with it if he can "gain" by doing so? One argument relies on the benefits that can be gained through cooperative interaction. Rand was aware of the advantages to cooperative behavior. But those advantages are not primary reasons for not killing others. Still, I think they may be regarded as reasons, even if they are not primary. As in the case for truth, communication is a valued form of cooperative interaction. One can learn more through communication with others than if one had to rely solely on oneself. There have been a few documented instances in which a child managed to survive virtually alone, because the child was either abandoned or kept isolated. The familiar case of Genie is particularly extreme because not only was she isolated for her first 13½ years but she was punished when she made any noise (Springer and Deutsch 1989, 242–43). Tragic instances such as this allow the contrast of knowledge so acquired with that acquired living among others. Although one must rely upon his own mind, much of what is in one's mind is attained through communication with others.

Gain from trade is another example of the benefits from cooperative behavior. Although the advantages of trade would seem to be intuitively clear—why would individuals voluntarily engage in trade if there were no benefit to it?—Adam Smith was the first to identify the underlying principle involved. He realized that unfettered trade leads to "more." Through unrestrained voluntary trade, a greater quantity of goods and services can be produced. Although his argument was based on absolute advantage (Spiegel 1971, 255), David Ricardo followed with an explication of the principle of comparative advantage (1971, 328–29). In a simple world of two people, it can be shown that if each specializes in that which he does relatively better, more can be produced. This is true even if one of the two individuals is better in an absolute sense in both endeavors. The law of comparative advantage demonstrates that trade is not a zero sum game, for two individuals or any number. Unlike predation where one person benefits only at the expense of another, in trade more is created. There are mutual gains to trade.

Of course, more is produced in a quantitative sense only after each party has specialized. But even if two individuals were limited to their initial endowments—so that there is no more between the two of them in a quantitative sense—so long as each is endowed differently from the other, there can be gains to trade because of the different ways in which each person values the other's goods relative to his own. The differences in relative valuation will result in mutual gains if trade takes place, even though the total quantity of goods available is unchanged. The same principle applies regardless of the number of participants.

In addition to communication and trade, individuals are also enriched by friendship with others. And, even though Rand did not address it, there are benefits to reproduction—the obvious benefit being the perpetuation of the species. None of these benefits to cooperative behavior will be apparent from examining man in isolation, however. It would be fallacious to assume that a man in isolation would be cognizant of these benefits if he were to encounter someone for the first time. These advantages are not self-evident even to those who have had the advantage of living among and observing men in society. It took several hundred years for someone—Smith and later Ricardo—to identify the laws of mutual advantage underlying voluntary trade (Spiegel 1971, 255, 328–29). A man in isolation would have to be prescient to know of these advantages in advance of ever having observed them. This would be akin to envisioning the flame from the head of a match before having heard of such a thing or seen one struck.

Similar comments apply to reproduction. It took some time for man to understand paternity and its relationship to sex and reproduction. If one had never encountered the opposite sex, one would hardly be aware of the benefits derived from perpetuation of the species as a motive for cooperative behavior. Gains from trade or from perpetuation of the species cannot be known by a person in isolation, a priori. Knowledge of these is dependent upon subsequent interaction.

Golden Opportunities: Forced Unilateral Transfers

The Crusoe metaphor is relevant since in isolation predation is impossible. One must be self-reliant if he is to survive alone. He cannot evade reality. If one is not honest with oneself, he risks sacrificing his existence. And if he is honest with himself, he cannot be dishonest with others since he cannot become someone else around others and himself when he is alone. However, what of those "golden opportunities" in which detection of cheating is virtually nonexistent? Why not adopt a rule to lie/murder/etc. in these instances? Some of the mutual benefits to voluntary bilateral interaction (exchange) have been mentioned. However, if one could default on his side of the bargain without detection, then he could retain what he agreed to give up, as well as have that which the other person agreed to hand over. This would be, in effect, an involuntary unilateral transfer—what I call "truncated trade." This kind of interaction is not limited to default on trade in which there was an initial agreement to the transaction by the victim, but could apply to any forced unilateral transfer in which one person benefits at the expense of another person (without the latter's consent)—which could include the victim's property or person.

A payoff matrix reflecting the decisions for both parties to this interaction can be constructed. In game theory, the underlying incentive structure of this model is known as a Prisoner's Dilemma. In the Prisoner's Dilemma, there are assumed to be two players facing a set of payoffs. The following matrix can be used to explain a generalized Prisoner's Dilemma:

	Column Player	
Row Player	m,m	s,t
	t,s	d,d

(m,m) are the payoffs for mutual cooperation, (d,d) are the payoffs for mutual defection, t is the temptation (default or theft) payoff, and s is the sucker's payoff (Axelrod 1984, 8–9). The payoffs are assumed to be small, but m does not have to equal m, and the same for t, s, and d, so long as $t>m>d>s$ for each player.

Outcomes to the decisions of the two players include three possibilities: (1) no interaction (d,d); (2) one of the players defects, (s,t) or (t,s); (3) exchange takes place (m,m). The dilemma is that, even though there are mutual benefits to bilateral exchange (m,m), each party has an incentive to cheat (to follow the unilateral alternative, since t exceeds m for both players). However, if both parties defect (d,d), then each ends up with less than if each had followed through with the exchange.

In my view, Rand would say that each person would want to follow through—choose (m,m)—because it would be in his long-run interest. This conclusion could be drawn from the fact that predation would be impossible to a person alone; therefore, it would not be in his interest otherwise. Or it could be based on a long-run probabilities approach, as per Merrill. In either case, the mutual benefits argument would be secondary to Rand. Also, according to Rand, since a person's emotions follow from his thoughts, one would want to do the right thing.

Robert Frank (1988), in his book *Passions within Reason*, acknowledged that an individual may want to do what is right (not defect); however, there may be impulses to cheat. There are, or may be, competing emotions involved. Frank addressed this question. His interest was in solving what he called the commitment problem—the commitment to virtuous behavior. When there is a low chance of detection, why not give into the impulse to cheat? Frank's answer was that people give clues to their intent—both passive and active. Passive clues are those over which a person has no voluntary control. They are expressions or mannerisms that have evolved incidental to the emotion in question that cue others to one's underlying emotion or intent, and they are difficult to fake (Frank 1988, 114–45). Active clues are those over which a person has a measure of control—such as his reputation. But why would reputation be a giveaway? After all, reputation is based on observed behavior, for the most part. Why would not a person simply be honest when observed and dishonest otherwise?

The reason is what Frank called the impulse control problem. Frank argued that consistent behavior is necessary in order to sustain the emotions required to solve the "the commitment problem." A person must be committed to honest behavior in those instances when it pays to appear honest—that is, when one's behavior is being observed. Certain emotions tend to sustain that behavior. However, if a person acts dishonestly when there is a "golden opportunity," he will have difficulty sustaining emotions required for honest behavior when detection of cheating is not low. Furthermore, the gains to cheating are now, the costs later. There is a tendency to discount the costs and, thus, to undertake dishonest behavior, even when the risk of detection is not zero or even low. If a person fails to control his impulses when confronted with a "sure thing," he will have difficulty doing so when the risks are higher. So, if someone has a good reputation, it is likely that he is more than simply a clever pragmatist (1988, 75–95). I would also add the point made in chapter 1 that probabilities of detection are difficult, if not impossible, to calculate for isolated events.

From Ethics to Rights

In "On the Randian Argument," Nozick offered what he regarded as a more promising approach to an argument against parasitism, that is, to concentrate on rights. "Each person has a right to his own life" (1971, 293), he stated. Den Uyl and Rasmussen rebutted that "for Rand it makes no sense to jump into rights-talk from out of nowhere (as Nozick does here) because the notion of rights is for Rand, a moral concept. Thus one's ethical and thereby value theory must be intact before one can legitimately move to rights-talk" (1978, 196). An abbreviated version of this transition from ethics to rights would be: that man values his life, that life is his ultimate value, that to sustain that life he must work, that to do so he must be free to use his mind and to act on his own judgment. This follows from man's nature—that he is a rational animal; that rationality is not automatic; that man must be free to decide and to act on his decisions. For another to interfere with that would be to jeopardize his life. Therefore, it is wrong for others to keep him from using his mind and undertaking those actions to sustain his life. He has a right to his life.

One might ask, just because a man has reasoned that he has a right to his life, in what way does this keep him from taking the life of another? Rand's opposition to predation was based on her nonsacrificial principle, according to which "each person is an end in himself" (Mack 1986, 157). Sacrifice—whether oneself to others or others to oneself—is not in one's rational self-interest. Although Rand never resorted to game theoretics to distinguish between narrow self-interest and rational self-interest, it is clear that what she meant by rational self-interest was not the short-term or narrow interest associated with the default option in the Prisoner's Dilemma. Both "players" have incentives to cheat (that is, to pursue the zero-sum alternative), but if both do so then the outcome is worse for both players than if they had cooperated (pursued the positive sum alternative). Individuals are best served by following their long-term interest, which is associated with the positive sum choice (m,m). This latter view of interests is consistent with Rand.

Eric Mack envisioned "a dual role for the principle that each person is an end in himself" (1986, 157). According to Mack, Rand endorsed both the doctrine of egoism (rational self-interest) and the doctrine of rights by way of what he called "the rational incumbency thesis." This says "that the adoption of egoism makes it rationally incumbent upon one to adopt rights as well" (1998, 3). Mack's point was that Rand's argument for rights implies that a person (A) would not interfere with another's (B's) rights insofar as it would harm A, but that does not explain why B has the right not to be infringed upon. Rand made, in Mack's estimation, the bold claim that "persons' rational interests never clash" (1986, 158). If the interests of rational men do not conflict, then A would never pose a threat to B. But one may envision circumstances in which a person's (A's) interests might clash with another's (B's). Mack said that in such a circumstance, an egoistic ethics would claim that A could (and should) violate B's rights if it is in A's interest.

If interests never clash, then this would not be an issue. But this depends on what is meant by interests. Rand took the long-range view of interests. It may be true that if one looks at a situation from a short-sighted perspective (the default or zero-sum option in the Prisoner's Dilemma), individuals apparent (i.e., short-sighted) interests may be regarded as clashing. But this would not be in the interests of both parties if both took the broader view. It is by respecting rights that both parties achieve mutual gains—which exceed that which would be received if each party pursued his narrow interest and defaulted. (That is, if both default, they end up at [d,d].)

This analysis has to do with respecting rights that have already been established. Later on, I point out that a zero-sum outcome is also possible if property rights have not been established in the first place. Trade is predicated on ownership. A person must own something before he can exchange it. If a resource is not owned by either party, then there is the potential for conflict. A zero-sum outcome is possible—that is, there may be a winner and a loser in the dispute over an unowned resource. However, this results because of a lack of ownership rights, not because, as in the Prisoner's Dilemma, one of the parties defaults on an exchange. It would seem then that the establishment of rights is necessary before rights can be respected and the gains from trade can be realized. It could also be argued that the establishment of property rights, the respect for rights, and the gains from trade are simultaneously determined. In theory this may be true, but in practice, a resource, if it is sufficiently abundant, may be used for some time before property rights need to be established. If a resource is not scarce, it need not be owned. Many individuals may use a resource before establishment of property rights is necessary. It may not be apparent who the owner of the resource should be once it becomes scarce. A conflict may emerge once scarcity of the resource sets in.

And Another Motive for Not Initiating Force Is . . .

In Nozick's hypothetical example of the child with the brain implant, the child could murder and steal, yet forget, thus live a happy existence (Den Uyl and Rasmussen 1978, 201). One could take the question Nozick raised a step further.

Why surgically implant a device for forgetting? Why not simply teach the child that it is perfectly all right to steal and murder? In that way he could be prosperous (for the sake of argument, although this is not a forgone conclusion), retain his memory, and still be happy. Why not adopt a principle that recommends killing? Is this not what one might conclude from Hobbes's state of nature? Machan implied this:

> Hobbes believed that outside civil society, with no legal system prevailing, it is right for each person to do whatever he will do. In a sense each person has a natural right to do anything, to act however or possess whatever he can, with no limits. (1975, 19)

Hobbes saw man as concerned with his self-preservation. A general principle recommending killing might seem to follow—that is, kill or be killed. Although Rand claimed that it is not in man's self-interest to initiate force, Hobbes's view of man's nature differed from Rand's in that he regarded man as a being driven by his passions. The initiation of force is prevalent in Hobbes's state of nature, and the initiation of force is right, or, at least, within one's rights, in such a state—or so one might interpret.

There may be another, practical, reason for not sacrificing others to oneself even if a person had no moral compunction to do otherwise, and that is that the rights violator would face legal consequences for his actions against others. Suppose, however, that the question is limited to a state of nature—one in which it is assumed there is no established law enforcement agency, so that one is in no threat of repercussions from authority if one initiates force against another. In such a setting, why would it not be advisable for a parent to teach his child to murder, steal, prosper, and enjoy it? Some reasons were discussed in the previous section; however, one that was not mentioned is that if one initiates force against another, the other may strike back. One might suspect this would be the case, particularly in a state of nature, since in such a state there would be no government to enforce justice. Risk of retaliation by the victim may not be the most important reason from a moral perspective for not initiating force against another, but it is of practical relevance. This reason does not appear to have been appreciated by either Nozick or Den Uyl and Rasmussen. According to Mozes (based on an example used by Peikoff in a course on Objectivism), in a state of nature in which force is used by one person against another, nothing more can be said (1992, 92, 93n7).

According to Herbert Spencer, ethics is concerned with the "perfect" man ([1892] 1954, 51). He said that pure ethics cannot acknowledge evil or the conditions generated by evil. "It entirely ignores wrong, injustice, or crime, and gives no information as to what must be done when they have been committed" ([1892] 1954, 52). When a principle has been violated, ethics can only inform you that it has been violated. If one person assaults another, all that can be said is that the law has been violated. Ethics cannot supply an answer. Such a violation "is a disturbance of social equilibrium" (ibid.). The moral philosopher can only treat the *straight* man. "A problem in which a *crooked* man forms one of the elements is insoluble by him" ([1892] 1954, 53).

Does this mean that ethics cannot consider questions of retaliation? One definition of retaliate is "to return like for like, especially to return evil for evil; to pay back (an injury) in kind" (*American Heritage* 1969). Spencer's perspective appears to be in agreement with the spirit of this definition. "All violence," he said, "involves criminality" ([1892] 1954, 186). And by violence he meant not only the initiation of force by the aggressor but defensive force as well, whether the latter is on behalf of the individual or on behalf of a nation. "Ethical law is as certainly broken by the deeds of judicial authorities as by those of a defensive army," ([1892] 1954, 241) was Spencer's view. Yet he viewed passivity as an absolute wrong ([1892] 1954, 243). He was not unaware that if all force is declared wrong, this creates a dilemma.

Rand recognized the individual's right to self-defense. She also acknowledged that retaliation is a moral imperative. Although she regarded it as an individual right, it is *that* right that the individual entrusts to government and government alone. Like Spencer, she acknowledged that nonresistance is wrong. She recognized that a "pacifist" society would be at the mercy of any thug who chose to act immorally. Instead of eradicating evil, pacifism "would encourage and reward it" (1964g, 108). But the right of retaliation is delegated "to government, for the purpose of an orderly, legally defined enforcement" (1967e, 46). Although she was an advocate of individualism, and even though retaliatory force is an individual right, it "cannot be left at the discretion of individual citizens," according to Rand (1964g, 108). Thus, the individual has a right to retaliation, but it is not a right he should exercise—that is, it is a right to which one does not have a right, a curiosity among rights.

Like Hobbes, Rand believed "if a society provided no organized protection against force" (i.e., government), then it would degenerate into gang rule (ibid.). Thus, her insistence on the delegation of retaliation to government is because it cannot be entrusted to individuals. Rand stated that man does not have to live alone. Yet he should live among others *"only on certain conditions"* (1964g, 107). She regarded government as the only means to rights protection. But if one chooses to live alone, there is the possibility that one will be confronted by an aggressor, and if one has the right to one's life, in my view, he must have the right to defend himself.

Retaliation on a Desert Island

Consider a case in which there is an immediate threat to one's life. Two broad categories of immediate reaction are to fight or to flee. Since Rand's ethics are biocentric, it may be pertinent to consider the physiological responses to threat. Frank explained that because an individual's energy is scarce, the body's arousal mechanism responds in proportion to the degree of threat. If the threat is significant, this elicits intense fear, which triggers the autonomic nervous system. This is referred to as the "flight or fight" response. If a person's survival is at risk, he "has no reason to hold anything back" (Frank 1988, 118). If one does not fight or flee but stays stationary, this fear will be expressed via pathways over which the individual has the least conscious control, outwardly manifested by trembling, for example. Nature's responses then are to fight, flee, or to remain stationary and exhibit outward signs of fear. How a person actually responds to a threat on his life will to some extent be determined by preexisting ethical principles he has learned and accepted and acted upon, training or experiences he has undergone, as well as the time and ability to consciously analyze the situation and make a decision.

In an original state of nature, a person who is attacked by another may not be able to immediately defend himself. If so, the alternative would have to be to respond later. Still, why would one choose to retaliate at all (by this I mean delayed retaliation)? The obvious answer is to restore what has been taken. However, some things may be destroyed or the victim may be injured. These cannot be recouped, per se. Retaliation does not literally mean an eye for an eye. It may be something equivalent to an eye. That which is sought is retribution, defined as "something given or demanded in repayment; especially, punishment." The payment in the case of retaliation should be in some measure equivalent to that taken. Restitution is "1. The act of restoring to the rightful owner something that has been taken away, lost, or surrendered; 2. The act of making good or compensating for loss, damage, or injury; indemnification; reparation; 3. A return to or restoration of a previous state or position" (*American Heritage* 1969).

One could say, what is past is past. What is done is done. One cannot change the past. Retaliation will not bring back what is lost. David Ross has said that Objectivists should not be concerned with the past. "'As rational egoists, all we care about, fundamentally, is the future . . .'" ("What Is Justice For" 2000, 23). Does this mean we should simply forget transgressions? Ridley noted that this would be a sensible way to react, and that many animals do not seek revenge (1996, 13–36). They respond when immediately threatened much the same as humans do—they fight or flee—but many animals (although not all) do not retaliate against transgressors after the fact (Ridley 1996, 71). For those who do not retaliate, it may not be a matter of "forgetting" transgressions but of not remembering them in the first place.

To reciprocate, one must be able to recognize and remember specific others. Frank pointed out: "Man, of course, has the greatest capacity of any animal to recognize and remember the past behavior of other members of his species" (1988, 28). He noted that there is a particular region of the human brain associated with face recognition. Ridley has suggested that the human brain is an exchange organ that "looks for ways to check those who might cheat" (Ridley 1996, 130). So, there is at least some evidence that delayed retaliation is part of human nature. Although one could say, "Forget the past, it cannot be changed," one would still have to address the question of why we would have to forget. That is, why do we remember in the first place? If we have a capacity to remember such things, then perhaps this capacity is related to our survival.

Frank argued that revenge is irrational. Revenge is not undertaken because it pays, since it does not, according to Frank. Individuals retaliate out of anger. However, revenge is productive if potential predators anticipate that their victims will respond by exacting revenge. A victim's commitment to seek retaliation if wronged will deter predators. Frank put great stock in emotion to solve the commitment problem and thereby achieve that which is in one's long-term interest. A person's anger commits him to a course of revenge if wronged. Others, being aware of this, are less prone to initiate force against him. Thus, he achieves what is in his long-term interest, that is, not to be aggressed against. Frank contended that if one had to rely solely upon short-run cost-benefit calculations, one would choose to forgo retaliatory actions (1988, 51–56). Whether one agrees or disagrees with Frank's thesis that emotions help solve the commitment problem, it still may be true that the anticipation of retaliation for wrongdoing may be a deterrent to those considering such actions.

Thus, it appears that, unlike many animals, humans are equipped with capacities that facilitate retaliation in the event one is wronged. At least two factors, memory and recognition, contribute to this tendency. Recognition and memory would be unimportant insofar as retaliation is concerned if individuals did not have identities; if their behavior could not be predicted based on that identity. The aggressor has an identity and the victim recognizes him as an aggressor. Part of what makes up identity is consistency in thought and behavior. Individuals can change, but the probabilities favor consistency. If one has been an aggressor in the past, the likelihood is that he will be one in the future. The aggressor also has a memory of the victim. The victim has an identity. He has been identified by the aggressor as a victim. If the victim fails to retaliate, he will be identified as a victim who does not fight back.

Even though the threat of retaliation may help to solve the commitment problem, there are oftentimes moral sanctions against it. These moral codes are usually found in conjunction with legal restrictions prohibiting it on the part of private individuals when retaliatory measures have been assumed by government. In Frank's words:

> Most cultures not only do not encourage the pursuit of vengeance, they take positive steps to curtail it. Contrary to impressions, the biblical reference, "an eye for an eye, a tooth for a tooth," is not an exhortation to *seek* vengeance, but a plea to *restrain* it to the scale of the original provocation. (1988, 39)

The appeal in the quote above is for retaliation, a form of revenge in which there is proportionality. According to one definition, revenge is "to inflict punishment in return for (injury or insult)" (*American Heritage* 1969). Some definitions of revenge include presumed accompanying emotions. Bidinotto, citing one source, said that revenge is "the carrying out of a bitter desire to injure another for a wrong done to oneself or to those who seem a part of oneself" (2000, 9). Revenge does not necessarily carry with it bitter desires. One may be reluctant to carry it out. One may be afraid of being harmed in the process or not want to expend the energy or time or other resources that may be involved. There are many emotions that may or may not accompany revenge. Insofar as the definition is concerned, the emphasis here is on the action, not on the emotion.

The principle of proportional retribution has been ostensibly adopted by the criminal justice system in this country; that is, the punishment should fit the crime. Personal retaliation, however, is by and large prohibited by law. As noted by Frank, there exist moral tenets against revenge as well. Christian dogma has been popularized to encourage forgiveness, which some have interpreted to mean that one should not seek retaliation. Originally the appeal to forgiveness was within the context of Jews forgiving one another so as not to further weaken themselves against their oppressors. Personal retaliation is now regarded negatively in most cultures and prohibited by law. Still, where the power of the law is weak, (private) retaliation is quite common (Frank 1988, 2).

By definition in a state of nature, there is no government. Yet there may be "law," according to anarcho-libertarians such as Murray Rothbard. Rothbard argued that where there is no government, an individual would justifiably have the right to "take the law into his own hands" (1998, 90). Frank's argument for retaliation is that it solves the "commitment problem." This is retaliation viewed as a deterrent. Rothbard regarded deterrence as a utilitarian principle and dismissed it as a principle of justice. Rothbard favored retributive justice (by individuals or their agents). He reasoned that the victim is entitled to the value of the damages imposed by the aggressor plus compensation for the fear and uncertainty (1998, 88–89), a principle that has been described as "two eyes for an eye" (Hoppe 1998, xxxviii). He argued that if deterrence were the relevant principle, then since there is more petty theft than murder, the punishment for the former should be greater than the latter (Rothbard 1998, 92–93). This would violate the principle of the punishment fitting the crime. Rothbard is correct in that if deterrence were the sole criterion for justice, then other principles, such as the right to life, might be violated as well.

Rothbard also dismissed the "humanitarian" criterion of rehabilitation of the criminal as a justification for punishment. A petty thief may require years to rehabilitate; a murderer a few weeks (1998, 94). The punishment would not fit the crime in either case. As sole principles, both the deterrence and the rehabilitation criteria were found lacking by Rothbard.

Reciprocity and Justice: Another View

Objectivists have debated the rationale underlying retribution. David Ross said that rational egoists should not look to the past but to the future; that punishment of criminals was necessary to prevent future crimes. Robert Bidinotto countered Ross by saying that although deterrence is a value and a utilitarian justification for advocating punishment, it is not a principle on which to base retributive justice ("What Is Justice For" 2000, 23). Like Rand (1982d, 10–11; 1964g, 108), both Ross and Bidinotto were referring to justice meted out by government.

Bidinotto defined justice as "*a punitive response to a criminal that penalizes him in direct proportion to the harm he has done to actual individuals*" (2000, 9). Retribution, he has said, is reflective. "The fundamental strategy of moral retribution, then, is to reflect those negative consequences of harm and injury back onto the criminal who caused them" (ibid.). Ross, on the other hand, failed to see how retribution could be the principle for justice since "justice is a virtue, and virtues aim at future values. Retribution looks to the past" ("What Is Justice For" 2000, 23).

Both Bidinotto and Ross were attempting to uncover the Objectivist roots of justice. Rand focused on cooperative, voluntary behavior and the social virtue related to that behavior, i.e., justice—her trader principle. Exchange in this context is quite broad. It includes not only exchange in the economic sphere but also communication as well as friendship and romantic love; that is, both the material and the spiritual (Rand 1964a, 31). Irfan Khawaja, who claimed to be making an Aristotelian-Thomas-Objectivist argument (1997, 96–97), based his account of justice on reciprocity. He defined reciprocity as "the disposition to use another person ('s traits) for mutual advantage, where the traits in question are mutually recognized to enhance each actor's ability to achieve his good" (1997, 120). It has been assumed, according to Khawaja, that morality is concerned with the "adjudication of conflicts of interests" (1997, 122). Reciprocity can result in "a concord of interests between rational agents" (1997, 120). As a mode of interaction it is in our interest because it best promotes man's survival *qua* man (1997, 121).

I agree that reciprocity can lead to cooperation and mutual benefits to parties to an exchange. However, reciprocity encompasses more than voluntary exchange. It recommends the restoration of (moral) equilibrium if there is an involuntary unilateral transfer. Trade is the voluntary exchange of value for value. It is not the exchange of identical things, but of things that have the same value in the estimation of the traders. In the economic sphere, the trade often involves a delay in time on the part of one of the parties to the transaction. If the reciprocating party whose action is delayed defaults, he has received a value for which he has not paid (in cash or kind, depending on the nature of the transaction). He has, in effect, stolen something from the other party. It may not have been his intent at the time of the agreement, but it is the effect. The person who has been cheated out of payment deserves compensation. It is his by right. The person who has defaulted on the trade owes the other party to the transaction. The trader principle has been violated. The principle of reciprocity need not be.

As I see it, the root of *in*justice here is that someone has received something for which he has not paid and that which he received belonged to someone else. The point is that one person reneged on payment and what is owed is that payment or some proportional compensation to the injured party. To restore balance (reciprocity), payment should be made to the injured party, and the reason it should be made is that the injured party has given up something involuntarily and unilaterally that he owned. It is by the nature of the transaction that justice is backward-looking—the thing that was taken belonged (past tense) to someone else. It is forward-looking because the person remains uncompensated for that which has been taken, and the person who owes it still must pay (in the future). One does not say of a voluntary transaction in which there is contracted delay in payment that the debtor does not have to pay because "virtues aim at future values" ("What Is Justice For" 2000, 23). Nor does one say that the past is the past—why should the debtor pay now? A consumer does not say to the power company, for instance, that the electricity has already been used; that he cannot bring it back; that paying now will not change what has been done in the past. It is understood that the nature of trade is such that value is exchanged for value, whether that which was received was received in the past or whether that which is owed is to be paid in the future.

Default on payment may be done with forethought, or it may result because of circumstances subsequent to the trade agreement. The former would, generally speaking, carry more weight as a moral breach, even though both violate the trader principle. Theft oftentimes violates the trader principle in two respects. Not only is payment not made in return for a value received, but there is not even the pretense of agreement in the first place. The thing of value is taken by force in the first instance. Based on the trader principle, which subsumes voluntary agreement, what is owed is the value of that which one surrenders. Since that which was taken was taken without any agreement whatsoever in the case of theft, one could argue, as did Rothbard (1998, 88–89), more is required in compensation. According to him, what is owed, in addition to that which has been taken, is an equivalent amount to that which has been stolen plus compensation for fear and uncertainty. This is not to imply that all that should be remitted in the case of default is simply the value of that which was taken (plus interest). If an element of fraud was involved, more than that value would be owed the injured party.

When something has been taken (through default or some other type of force), this is, in effect, truncated trade. It is a unilateral transfer of a value; an "exchange" in which the aggressor pays a zero price. Trade is a form of reciprocity. It is the exchange of value for value, but trade is voluntary. All reciprocity is not necessarily based on voluntary exchange. Retaliation is also rooted in reciprocity. When a value has been taken by force without compensation, the principle of reciprocity demands value for value, that is, retribution. Justice is based on reciprocity, but the basis for that reciprocity is that in the first instance something is owned. If there were no rights—rights to life and other property—there would be no justification for reciprocity.

As sole principles, both the deterrence criterion and the rehabilitation criterion were found wanting. However, proportional retribution may have a discouraging effect on crime and may encourage criminals to change. If an action that yields rewards has no cost, if it is "free," it is encouraged. Those for whom ethics are not the basis of their behavior will be more likely to undertake activities that yield positive returns if those actions can be undertaken at an explicit price of zero. In this sense, crime is no different from any other good or service. If it is free, more of it will be "consumed" (by those with no moral compunction to behave otherwise).

Rehabilitation is complex. As mentioned, one's identity is defined in part by consistency in thought and deed. Individuals can change and do, but exactly how and why a particular individual changes is still not entirely known. What is known is that if an activity has a cost, it may discourage even habitual practitioners. It is also known that on a very basic level, all living organisms tend to avoid pain. When there are no (apparent) negative consequences to a behavior, it is not discouraged. If there is some punishment, it may encourage change.

A generally accepted principle of reciprocity as a mode of interaction may lead to cooperation. Certainly, trade is cooperative. But reciprocity also subsumes retaliation, which results when one party to an exchange has defaulted. Since government has assumed the role of retaliator in most cultures, many have come to think of justice and punishment as a function of what is owed to society and what is good for society—what promotes peace, concord, cooperation, and safety in society. What has been overlooked has been that the primary reason for retaliation is that someone (his person or other property) has been injured. It is the injured party who has surrendered something of value involuntarily and is owed something in return by right. What he is owed is compensation by the perpetrator for that which the victim has given up. Retaliation may lead to a more cooperative society because it discourages uncooperative behavior (with respect to rights violations) from those who are inclined to be uncooperative. Deterrence may be an effect of retaliation but not the sole justification. The justification is reciprocity founded on ownership.

Virtues to Retaliation

My question is, should the victim take action if his rights have been violated? When someone initiates an aggressive action, a principle has been violated. If one believes in a principle, then one should uphold that principle. If one does not uphold the principle, then it is weakened. Like life-forms, principles, too, can be mortal. Whether they survive depends on whether they are affirmed. One's life is the realization of one's philosophy. It is an enactment of belief in one's values. Actions are the concretization of the principles one holds. Ideals must be defended to remain viable. Not to do so would be to default on one's principles. For those who have previously established and defended and maintained principles, this would be to default on their efforts as well. If, among a society of men, there is cooperation, it may in large measure be due to the efforts of the current members but also the efforts of those who have come before.

Maintaining principles requires vigilance. Affirming a principle does not simply mean tacitly agreeing with it, it means living in accordance with it and taking action (effort) to uphold the principle when violated, especially if you are the victim. If it is not upheld, there is a "little death" to the principle. Thus, one must have good reasons not to uphold and defend a principle when it is violated. (This is why another may step in to uphold a principle when the victim is incapable of upholding it, because of the value with which he holds the principle, regardless of how he feels about the particular victim.)

It is the value of the principle that one is upholding when one makes a decision to retaliate. It is this that is being upheld when the government takes action against an aggressor. In a state of nature, the principle is no less important. The difference is that it is the individual who must uphold and defend it. If he does not, he has defaulted on his responsibility. If the society continues to be peaceful despite his lack of effort, it will be due to the efforts of others. In this sense, he will have accepted the unearned. Recall Rand's admonition that one should not give or receive the unearned; one should neither sacrifice himself to others nor others to himself (1964a, 27). If one fails to retaliate when wronged, yet continues to benefit from cooperative exchange, it is as a result of the vigilance of others. He is receiving an unearned benefit. In an indirect sense, he has also allowed another—the aggressor—to receive the unearned. Since the victim has chosen not to retaliate, the aggressor has received an unearned benefit. Retaliation is a moral course. It takes certain virtues—prudence, temperance, moral and physical courage—to carry it out. Physical courage is vital to all cultures, particularly those that are lawless.

A number of assumptions are implicit in the forgoing. One is that the aggressor is known. If the aggressor is not known, there are other costs, such as the cost of determining who the aggressor is; that is, of investigation. The victim is at an obvious disadvantage since the costs are many. He must investigate, weigh the evidence, be as impartial as possible, and carry out retaliation without physically harming innocent people. He must be detective, prosecutor, jury, judge, and "executioner" (i.e., he must execute justice). These all require special talents, time, and energy, and there are forgone opportunities related to these. There are also the risks of being wrong and of future retaliation as well as physical risks. The expectation is that the threat of future aggression is lessened if one takes action. Of course, there is always the possibility that an unethical person will take action regardless of whether one retaliates or not (unless he is eliminated).

There are costs associated with not retaliating that can be seen as benefits if one does retaliate. A significant cost is the risk of being a victim again, not only of this aggressor but of others as well. Again this goes to human nature, memory, and the strategic nature of interpersonal relationships. If one does not retaliate, one may get the reputation of being a moral and/or physical coward, whether true or not. To maintain a reputation of one who is not a victim (a pragmatic consideration) and/or one who stands by his principles (a moral consideration), one needs to retaliate.

Is it wrong not to fight an injustice? The cost may be very high. This is where context may enter the picture. "Should" implies "can." If one is incapacitated, it may be impossible to follow through on what one considers one's obligation. Even if one is not incapacitated, one cannot pay all debts at once. There are those debts one enters voluntarily (to pay for one's subsistence) and even those are often paid on "time," i.e., on the "installment plan." No one blames someone, nor can one blame oneself, for not being able to pay a cost that is not within his means that was not a result of his own choice. This is a debt imposed on one by circumstances beyond one's control. It was not "chosen." However, it could be argued that one does not choose to be hungry, to have shelter, to get well from a disease, either. These are realities of life and must be taken care of, as must justice. This debt need not be paid at once, but there may be costs if it is not.

If one chooses to retaliate but postpones it, there are costs associated with that. There are strategic reasons having to do with human nature for not postponing retaliation if the aggressor is known with certainty, or for searching for the aggressor if he is not known. To contrast human nature with nature in general, compare an injury suffered because of the actions of an aggressor to that of an illness. If one is ill, one tries to get well by finding out if there is a cure based on known medical treatments. But one is not obligated to investigate the cause of the disease, if it is not known, or to discover a cure or treatment if one is not available or if what exists is inadequate. What is the difference between this kind of injury and one caused by the willful act of another person? The difference goes to the issues of character (identity), memory, and the nature of strategic interaction because of these factors. How one "re-acts" depends on what action is expected in the future. Another cold virus might overtake you, but it is not a conscious act. If it does, it is not because it has been knowingly successful in the past. Similarly, acts of nature do not "reason" in this way. But humans can and do.

There is also a principle involved in the case of human action. There is the risk the principle may eventually not be observed if it is allowed to be violated without reaction. Only individual action can uphold principles and keep them alive. Since forgiveness is a big part of our culture, the question of whether forgiveness is a viable option should be addressed. This goes to the question of motive and character of the aggressor. Again, complex issues are involved here. It is difficult to mine the human psyche. One would not want to rule out the possibility that the person is insane (in which case some other action besides retaliation may be warranted). Character is difficult to discern. That is why reputation would carry weight in a lawless society. Character is identity and identity has an element of consistency. Reputation is not character but what others think of a person based on experience over time. If an aggressor is known to have been a person of good character but has fallen on hard times, then if he asks to be forgiven and is willing to make amends of some kind in the future, it may be acceptable to forgive him and not seek further retaliation. However, if the person has been merely expedient in the past or has been lucky and now has gotten caught and says he is remorseful, it is likely he is not—except for having gotten caught. If he is willing to pay restitution, then it may be worthwhile to forgive him and take the wait-and-see approach. A person with a reputation for aggression cannot be forgiven, since he feels no remorse. It is a very high-risk gesture to forgive a person with a known reputation for aggression.

As before, one could ask if a person can change and what kind of action is likely to encourage change. Will simply forgiving a person, especially if little or no restitution is in order, encourage change? Incentives matter. If there is a cost to an activity, it is less likely to be undertaken. One cannot count on (expressions of) remorse alone to bring about a change in behavior.

There is also the matter of the principle being attacked; that is, the principle that one should not initiate force. To uphold a principle it must be affirmed. You may choose to forgive the transgressor. But if you do, you must also forgive yourself for not fighting for your principles.

Retaliation When You're Dead

Now, I ask, what if the unprovoked act of violence results in your death? One cannot retaliate on one's own behalf if one is dead. How then is justice to be achieved? This is a case in which one must rely on others. Should a person feel obligated to avenge the death of another? Rand would not agree that avenging another's murder would qualify as a legitimate activity. But if one were to apply the principle of reciprocity to avenging the death of another, then, based on Randian ethics, a person would do so only if it were in his own interest. That is, one should not accept an unearned debt or obligation (N. Branden 1962, 55).

How then would one arrange (in an enlarged state of nature) justice in the event of one's death? One could enter a contractual arrangement; that is, arrange that if one is murdered a named party will be paid (say, out of one's inheritance if it exists) to take action (Rothbard 1998, 86). Or one could enter a pact with another—if I am murdered, you will avenge my death and vice versa. (Contracts and the difference between contracts and other promises will be discussed later.) Of course, if you go first, you must trust the other to fulfill his promise, and you must rely on his integrity. The other person may not feel obligated, since he no longer has someone to avenge his murder if something were to happen to him. As to who might be trusted, blood-ties seem like the obvious choice, in part, simply because we are accustomed to hearing about relatives avenging the murders of loved ones. However, this does not mean that the relative is under obligation to avenge such a murder simply by virtue of being kin. It would depend on whether there was such an agreement (and the degree to which it was explicit). If there were no such agreement, a relative might feel some sense of obligation because of his feelings for the victim or because he feared future action or because of how he felt about the principle that had been violated. He would have to determine the benefits and costs of his action. The costs are often high. The benefits are justice for the relative, upholding the principle of justice in general, and the avoidance of the cost associated with not retaliating—the probability that he might be a target of the aggressor in the future. All of this assumes that retaliation is justified. One may have to incur the cost of investigation before reaching this conclusion.

What of the idea considered earlier that the past is past? Retaliation does not bring back the victim (the life, lost limb, work of art, or other object of ownership). This is akin to saying the past does not exist. Or it is the same as saying cause, which necessarily precedes effect, is not tied to effect. The past, per se, does not exist. But it has existed. It is etched on our memories. It exists in us. It is part of what we have been and part of what we are. The future, which does not exist nor has, exists in us as potential. Most animals have no memory for actions of the kind discussed here. They do not engage in retaliation. Ingersoll said: "In nature there are neither rewards nor punishments; there are only consequences" (Peter 1977, 356). Man makes his consequences where other men are concerned to a considerable degree. The nature of man is such that the past is past but it affects the future. Trade, largely, links past to future. Violation of the trader principle calls for restoration of balance. Identity also links past to future. To a large extent people are what they are—which means they are what they will be. They will particularly remain who they are if there is no intervening action that might change how they act or react in the future. If there is no cost to aggression, there is no deterrent to aggression.

Gangs, Etc.

It is easy to see how a dispute between two people in a state of nature can escalate into disputes that are tribal in nature. Once retaliation evolves to the "pack" or "gang" level it can quickly degenerate from the pursuit of justice to nonspecific retaliation or revenge. That is, the reaction taken is not necessarily against the aggressor of an action but against anyone related to or associated with the aggressor. Guilt or innocence of the punished individual becomes irrelevant. Action is against the group, not the individual.

Must the state of nature necessarily result in packs, gangs, or leaders with trained warriors or henchmen? There is safety in numbers and there may be economies to combining, especially if they have a common goal or enemy. Game theory—the Prisoner's Dilemma—indicates there may be cooperation in the state of nature. It also reveals that there can be cooperation within groups coupled with confrontation among or between groups (Axelrod 1984, 146–50).

Dam Butlab Dam

Revenge is no longer an accepted practice in most cultures. Frank related the familiar tale of the Hatfields and McCoys of nineteenth-century Appalachia, a time and place in which "few citizens had faith in the power of law to resolve their disputes" (1988, 2). Presently, in the Near and Middle East, cycles of revenge persist. This phenomenon is not unusual "where the force of law is weak" (ibid.). *Lex talionis*, the law of retaliation, is a near-Eastern tradition that has been in effect since long prior to Muhammad. It was common to Mediterranean culture, but among Arabs, it continues to be valued as an important principle (Patai 1983, 209). It has survived nomadic, village, and now urban life. Its practice rivals the police and judiciary, complicating their work. According to Tribal Law: *Dam butlab dam*, "blood demands blood" (1983, 80). Honor among the victim's *khamsa* (male relatives removed by up to five male links) is restored only if a member of the *khamsa* retaliates or *sulha*, i.e., reconciliation, is arranged with compensation (ibid.).

The practice of revenge among early nomadic peoples is understandable to a large extent, in my view. With law enforcement virtually nonexistent, self-defense and delayed retaliation would have to be undertaken by the members of the tribes themselves. In early nomadic culture, property in land did not exist, per se. Land may not have been considered scarce except possibly under certain conditions, for example, times of the year. Ownership was confined to one's self and some transportable items. A single individual living and traveling alone would be particularly vulnerable to unscrupulous aggressors. In such a situation, there might be strength in numbers. A logical extension of oneself is one's family. But if the scope is limited to one's immediate family, one is more vulnerable still, since it may consist of two or fewer adults and one's children, the latter of whom are defenseless. There is little security in numbers if others look solely to oneself for protection. One is responsible then for defending not only one's own life but one's dependents as well. The company of other adults would seem to be in order.

An extended family would be one answer. Why family? There is a natural protective spirit that exists among family members, particularly parents for their children. It is one of the primary duties of caregiving. Other protective attitudes may spring from that. As children mature, they may in turn feel protective toward their parents. Older children may feel somewhat protective of younger siblings. This is particularly true if they have had occasion to be put in charge of caregiving. If siblings remain within the family unit once they become adults, shared domestic responsibilities may generate feelings of protectiveness toward the children of other family members. Since one of the benefits of an enlarged family unit is that there are advantages to specialization, economies of scale, and safety that sheer numbers provide, protection when needed will be provided by several adults acting jointly. Consequently, one would be protecting not only oneself but others as well. When a good or service is jointly produced, it is difficult, if not impossible, to separate the marginal products of each individual involved. Thus, one person in conjunction with others provides an umbrella of protection for oneself and others as well, the dimensions of which may not be attributable to each of the individuals providing protection. This may work to reinforce the general spirit of protection among family members.

Historians and anthropologists inform us that in reality, family, particularly as traced along bloodlines, was an emphatic value to early societies. First, before paternity was understood, family bloodlines were naturally traced matrilineally. Then once the concept of fatherhood was discovered, at first bloodlines may have continued to have been traced matrilineally by many cultures, but the whole concept of family was transformed. Eventually, blood was traced along male lines.

Although it may be logical for an individual who is nomadic to be a member of an extended family for purposes of protection, the self may seem to slip in relative importance. The shift in emphasis may be not only apparent but real. The individual may be doing what is in his own interest given the limits within which he can operate. The range of choice with respect to work may be severely restricted from the vantage point of current Western life, but anything other than nomadic life for those involved may not be viable.

Alone on a desert island, one's opportunities would be likewise constrained. In a nomadic culture, one may have few more options than on a desert island. Perhaps fewer, since when one is alone one faces no threat of aggression from other humans. One deals with one's survival within the constraints set by nature (*sans* man) only. In a nomadic culture, one lives with the threat of possible aggression from other humans. One must provide for one's sustenance, shelter, and so on, as one would on a desert island; however, part of one's survival effort must now be devoted to protection. By protection, I mean the readiness to defend oneself if attacked and/or to retaliate later, if necessary.

When there is more than one individual, specialization can lead to improved productivity. Responsibility for threats outside the group may be assumed for the most part by the male members. Males, by nature, tend to be relatively stronger and more aggressive, particularly during their youth. If threats are ever-present, these traits will be valued. That which is valued tends to be reinforced. In addition to strength and aggression, an individual must be willing to defend or retaliate on one's own behalf and that of others within the group.

When one is alone on an island and then is confronted by another, one only has oneself on which to rely for protection. Within a group, there is the possibility that one may shirk, or be perceived as shirking. If the group remains viably intact despite one's shirking, the shirker will have received an unearned benefit. For this reason, the other members of the group may impose a social cost on the shirker in the form of a loss in status or loss in honor. His reputation will be in some measure diminished among the group. If bravery is valued and cowardice is not, then the coward may have to pay a (nonpecuniary) price for his inaction. (Protection is a public good for which there are incentives to be a free rider. Solving the Prisoner's Dilemma associated with public goods may be more easily achieved for small groups since shirkers are more readily identified. Also if virtues or social mores emerge that are related to protection, these may be used as coercive measures to encourage compliance and thereby solve the dilemma.)

Specialization may extend to older males who are no longer strong and who lack the aggressive impulse. Their wisdom and experience may be valued and put to use in other ways (see Patai 1983, 80). Their knowledge and reputation may be suited to peacemaking both within and between groups. It is readily seen that when one's interest is so intimately tied to the group, it may become subordinate to the group. In such a culture, protection is vital to one's survival. It could become one's primary occupation. The primary virtue required for this work is bravery (physical courage), although other virtues such as integrity and prudence would also be important. It may seem as though if one's primary occupation were providing protection, one would have to be willing to sacrifice oneself for others. In a real sense, this is part of the job, but the risk of injury or death would exist regardless and is, in theory, reduced by the presence of others.

Within the social unit there may evolve a kind of governing through custom. Not everyone in the social unit is involved in protection. Females are less inclined. Young men who are physically incapable may be exempt, as would younger children and the elders. So in a sense the responsibility for protection would be delegated from some individuals to others. Even so, a large proportion of the group may be responsible for protection. All others in the group who were not suited for this work would not be seen as shirking. Through the division of labor and custom, they would be performing other necessary activities. In a sense, these would be dictated by supply and demand. There are real differences in the extent to which one can compare free market supply and demand to situations in which occupation may be largely dictated by custom, however. In the latter case, one's fate may be entirely or almost entirely dictated by others.

As for those providing protection, since each member of the group must stand ready to retaliate against an aggressor (or else suffer the consequences to one's reputation within his group), anyone within the group is a target to someone outside the group. And since protection is for the group, not just the self, retaliation may tend to become nonspecific. The self would then tend to slip in importance since one's actions and the consequences of one's actions would no longer be directly tied in this regard. Action and reaction would not be specific to the individual. An individual in a group may suffer the consequences of the misdeeds of another member and vice versa. One is less accountable for one's own actions in this sense. According to Raphael Patai: "A characteristic expression of kinship cohesion surfaces in connection with disputes. . . . [T]he obligation to support one's kinsman in a quarrel with an outsider exists all over the Arab world, irrespective of the question of right or wrong" (1983, 231). When matters of kinship override consideration of right and wrong, a system of personal ethics breaks down. One may still be operating within a socially forged code of behavior, but without a personal code of ethics.

Rand realized that tribal communities benefited from the safety of numbers and that the tribe may have been necessary for the survival of the individual. However, what could spring from tribalism is an ethic of self-sacrifice—the individual for the group. Rand claimed that: "the morality of *altruism* is a tribal phenomenon"

(1982e, 50). Modern-day factionalism is rooted in this mentality, but it is a psychological phenomenon, not one based on physical threat as it had been for tribal communities predating formal government (ibid.).

The retaliatory principle can persist even after government has taken over the function of protection. This could be because individuals continue to see protection of oneself and one's loved ones as a personal responsibility. If they fail to take action, they may see themselves as shirkers. This is after all what they may have come to regard as their work. They may have acquired traits ("virtues") that accompany this kind of occupation. They may have skills that are pertinent to this type of work, skills that they are adept at performing and for which they see themselves as suited. By way of analogy, one might ask, if the government took over the function of charity, would one feel obligated to quit giving? If a principle has been held in esteem, if the corresponding virtues have been prized, if one regards action related to this principle as one's responsibility, it is unlikely one will be anxious to abandon it. This is not peculiar to Arab tradition. Spencer, writing in the nineteenth century, related that it is a misconception to believe that once man proclaimed: "'Let there be law'" ([1892] 1954, 236), it automatically took hold. The old system of settling differences privately was replaced by state provision gradually. It took time for the state to be acknowledged as the protector of rights. The feudal lord would have been disgraced had he turned to government for protection of his rights. "It is only after public morality has gained a certain ascendancy that the civil power gets strong enough to perform its simplest functions" (ibid.). Those who abandon the principle of retaliation might argue that they are not becoming more moral but exchanging a principle for something else; that is, state provision of protection services.

The Oresteia

The transition from the rule by men (blood revenge) to the rule of law (trial by jury) was depicted in the first trial drama, *The Oresteia* by Aeschylus (Casson 1966, x). The Furies, old goddesses of the soil and family, protectors of bloodlines and Matriarchal Law, stood for strict justice—blood for blood (Barrett 1962, 277; Casson 1966, x). They argued that Orestes, who had slain his mother, should be found guilty since he committed the one unpardonable sin, matricide; that is, killing the closest blood relative. Athena, who was born not from woman but who emerged full-grown from the head of Zeus, cast the deciding vote in Orestes's favor, saying that all of her heart praised the male (Goodrich 1989, 148). Thus commenced "a rational means for dispensing justice" (Casson 1966, xi).

Apollo said that the mother is simply the nurse. The father, who can procreate without the mother, is the parent, pointing to Athena as proof (Fagles and Stanford 1979, 80). Apollo is regarded as the pro-masculine god of enlightenment;

the Furies are the chthonian goddesses of the earth. The play reflects the battle between nature and civilization, matriarchy and patriarchy, darkness and light, the unconscious and consciousness, emotion and intellect, the irrational and the rational, revenge and justice (Barrett 1962, 277–78; Paglia 1991, 101–102).

Then Athena said to the Furies that they were not defeated or dishonored. The Furies knew better. Athena convinces them to take their abode beneath the earth where they will be revered as "Kindly Ones," guardians of Athens and protectors of children (Paglia 1991, 101–102; Aeschylus 1982, 89). Athena promises to endow jurors with a deity's sense of reason and fairness. From this time forth, justice would be dispensed by men, unmoved by blood lust (Casson 1966, xi). The Furies had been defeated.

CHAPTER FOUR

Decision-Making on a Desert Island

Chapter 4 examines economic decision-making for a man alone on a desert island under very restrictive assumptions. In Rand's ethics, the fundamental alternative is life or death (Rand 1964a, 15; Peikoff 1991, 209). Productive work is the central virtue since it is the means by which a person sustains his life—his ultimate value. In this simple illustration (a variation on an example of Irving Fisher [1930, 186–92] in *The Theory of Interest*), it is assumed that a castaway has a single resource, a limited quantity of hardtack, which will just sustain his life if he consumes it judiciously. There is no production in this example, except insofar as the castaway is kept alive. The decision is that of consumption over time.

The competing incentives for the castaway are to consume as much as he can today, since tomorrow he may die, or to postpone consumption so as to have more of himself (his life) in the future. The former is a basis for time preference and the latter is related to the rate of return. These two are determinants of the interest rate. The relevant probabilities are for surviving and for dying. These are used to calculate the individual's expected lifetime consumption value ("human capital"). Depreciation is the change of value from year to year; a sinking fund would not be relevant. The discount rate in this case would be derived from the ratio of the probabilities of survival between two adjacent periods. The "return" would be the extension of the castaway's life beyond that expected. Although simplistic, the analysis reveals how the fundamental alternative is related to decision-making as well as the importance of thinking long-term. It is useful in that it lays the foundation for other, less simplistic analyses. It is noted that alone on an island, bequests are of no relevance to a person.

Assumption of Scarcity

In OE, a man's life is his ultimate value. He sustains his life by productive effort. Productive purpose is the central value. Productive work is the central virtue (Rand 1964a, 25). Consumption is a value, but not a virtue. Saving, when used for investment, is productive (1982f, 130–32). There is some tension, at least in the short run, between consuming and saving. The pressure to consume must be weighed against the productivity of saving.

Let us return to the man on the desert island and ask, what kind of decisions must he make for his survival? Although this analysis is highly abstract, there are some basic decisions that have general relevance. The man alone faces the fundamental alternative of life or death. Since life is his ultimate value, he faces the pressure to live today. However, man thinks long-term. He will make decisions that affect today, as well as the future. If resources were infinitely abundant, this would pose no problem, but resources are scarce. Scarcity is a fact of reality and is fundamental to life. It forms the basis for economic theory. It is also fundamental to ethics, since ethics deals with how man relates to reality. The Crusoe device can be a relevant starting point since, in OE, others are not fundamental to reality.

It is typically assumed in a state-of-nature scenario that scarcity sets in immediately. Of course, a person's time is always limited, but it is assumed that other resources are limited as well. Some resources may be finite; others may be limited in the short run, but renewable. Renewable resources are not necessarily in danger of being fully exhausted with use. There are many instances in nature in which, if some present consumption is sacrificed, future consumption may exceed the consumption that is currently forgone. Receiving a return in the future may require no more than waiting. A forest may yield more board feet of lumber if allowed to mature. That would mean cutting during the current time period would be forgone.

Böhm-Bawerk recognized that this phenomenon of receiving a return in the future by virtue of forgoing present consumption was one of the factors that caused the interest rate to tend to be positive (Green 1978, 203–208). His emphasis in this regard was on net productivity, particularly with respect to techniques of production that require time. Present consumption may be forgone in order to produce capital goods that will be used to produce more goods in the future than can be produced at present. For instance, in order to produce more crops in the future, a farmer may have to forgo current consumption so as to invest in equipment—a plow, for example.

Time Preference

A person cannot forgo all consumption. Life is a value that must be sustained in the present. That is the nature of living things. This pressure to consume today is related to another determinant of the interest rate, time preference. Simply put, time preference is the tendency for individuals, other things equal, to attach a premium to a unit of a good today relative to a unit of the same good to be received in the future (Fisher 1930, 62). Irving Fisher saw time preference as a rate of impatience reflecting the desire for a unit of real income now relative to a unit deferred (1930, 65).

According to Fisher, the rate of time preference is, under most circumstances, a determinant (along with the rate of return) of the interest rate. There are a number of reasons for the existence of time preference. Mortality is one reason, along with the uncertainty related to when one will die. But the timing of one's death is not the only uncertainty in life; there are others as well. Fisher also included, as determinants of impatience, the size of one's expected future income stream, its composition in terms of goods and services consumed, its distribution over time, and the probability of its receipt (1930, 71).

Net Productivity—The Rate of Return

The rate of return over cost is not the rate of interest, but it is one of its determinants. Fisher used the now familiar example of determining when to cut a forest. In this case the income accrues all at once when the forest is cut. The decision rule is to equate the rate of growth of the forest with the rate of interest. This would seem to support the idea that the interest rate and growth rate are one. But the decision depends on the interest rate; thus it cannot be the growth rate (1930, 164–65).

Irving Fisher regarded the interaction of two rates—the rate of return and the rate of time preference—as determinates of the interest rate. However, in some instances one or the other of these rates may dominate, according to Fisher. As an illustration of how return rather than time preference may drive the interest rate, Fisher considered three cases of castaways stranded on a desert island barren of any other goods, save one. He used these cases to illustrate how the (marginal) rate of return (over cost) can under extreme circumstances have a dominant effect on determining the rate of interest (1930, 182). In one hypothetical case, 100 sheep are assumed to be able to produce for current consumption 100 units (of mutton and wool) or, alternatively, 10 percent a year for the next and all subsequent years if consumption is sacrificed. In such a case, the rate of return will drive the interest rate and the rate of time preference, according to Fisher. Here, they will equal 10 percent (1930, 193).

Standard Income Defined

The two extremes in the sheep example are either to consume 100 sheep in the current time period or to consume none today and in all future periods. The latter would result in an accumulation of capital, that is, sheep. Neither would be life-sustaining in the long run. If one were to start with a stock of 100 sheep, and the return were 10 percent per year, then that 10 percent could be consumed leaving the stock unchanged. (Replacement would equal the amount consumed leaving the stock unchanged—i.e., there would be no net accumulation). The present value today of 110 sheep to be received one year hence would be 100. The rate of return would be 10 percent. For the economy as a whole, Alchian and Allen defined standard income as wealth (which they limited to the physical stock of goods) multiplied by the interest rate. If, for instance, a given stock of wealth could grow by 10 percent, then the society could consume that increase while keeping the original stock intact (Alchian and Allen 1977, 160).

Fisher, like Alchian and Allen, also defined standard income. However, instead of defining standard income as that which society as a whole could receive while keeping the original capital stock intact, Fisher defined standard income as the income an individual "*would* receive if he chose to keep his capital unimpaired and unincreased" ([1906] 1965, 110). For a single asset, such as a house that is rented, the standard income, or earnings on capital, would be undepreciated rent (actual—or what Fisher also called realized—income) net of other costs and amortization ([1906] 1965, 110; 246). Generally speaking, standard income (which Fisher also referred to as earnings or ideal income) is not equal to actual income ([1906] 1965, 333).

Fisher regarded only consumption (income detached from capital) as (actual) income. He regarded saving as an addition to capital ([1906] 1965, 254–55). Standardized income would be uniform and perpetual if the interest rate did not change and if future income were known with certainty. A change in the rate of interest may affect capital values. Fisher presented two competing concepts of standard income ([1906] 1965, 396–98). One assumes constant capital value and variable income (as the interest rate changes, the capital value remains unchanged). The other assumes a variable capital value and constant income (as the interest rate changes, capital value changes).

For an asset that depreciates, "it is possible to obtain its capital-value by the discounting process; its value-return, by division of [actual] income by capital; its depreciation, by comparing its capital values at successive dates; and its earnings [standard income], by deducting depreciation from realized [actual] income" ([1906] 1965, 235). Value-return is the actual return. Standardized income is the interest on capital for a given capital value. Fisher stated that, given an asset that has a present value based on discounted income, if actual income and standard income (i.e., interest) are equal, the value of the asset will remain unchanged. If actual income is greater than standard income, the value of the asset will fall by the difference. If actual income falls short of standard income, capital value will rise by the difference ([1906] 1965, 237–38). Thus, actual and standard income "differ by the appreciation or depreciation of capital" ([1906] 1965, 238). Similarly, the rate of value return exceeds the rate of interest by the rate of depreciation, or is less than the rate of interest by the rate of appreciation. These decreases and increases in the value of capital are anticipated over time. Houses will be expected to depreciate over time as they age, and forests appreciate as trees grow to maturity.

Unanticipated changes in capital value may occur for a number of reasons. For example, obsolescence may result in a capital loss—a decline in capital value that is unanticipated. A sudden shift in tastes in a favorable direction to the asset in question may lead to a capital gain. These, like anticipated changes in capital value, will affect value return. Alchian and Allen demonstrated that for a particular asset, capital gains may affect standard income. If the market value of an asset were to increase in value by more than standard income, the net gain would be profit (Alchian and Allen 1977, 161). For example:

> If your wealth today is $100, . . . and market value [jumps] to, say, $120 . . . [y]our unpredicted (by the market) $20 increase in wealth value is a capital gain, or *profit*. Thus, at a 10 percent interest rate, you now foresee that you can get $2 more standard income per year every year thereafter—$12 per year instead of $10. That profit can be *expressed* either as a wealth gain of $20 or an increase in the standard income flow of $2 per year. (ibid.)

The rate of interest is associated with the net productivity of investment, defined as "the net rate of increase in wealth from a dollar more investment" (1977, 435). It is similarly associated with the rate of time preference, the individual's valuation of future income that is equivalent to a dollar's worth of current consumption. In a money economy, individuals do not trade present goods for future goods, but money now for money in the future. Thus, the interest rate is the price of credit. It is the rate of return on loans or on bonds. There is also the rate of interest that equates the present value of future yields to the price of capital goods. These rates are brought into equality by adjustments in various financial and goods markets. When they are all equal their common value is the rate of interest (1977, 435–36).

Fisher's Two Other Cases

Fisher had two additional examples for which the interest rate may be driven by productivity, and time preference adjusts to it. In a second example in which the hypothetical castaways are stranded, Fisher assumed the stock under consideration is perishable to the extent that it deteriorates at a rate of 50 percent per year. If the stock were figs, the "fig rate of interest" would be negative 50 percent, as would the rate of time preference (Fisher 1930, 191–92). (Here the rate of return is negative; deterioration is figured in.)

Fisher's objective was to show how technical conditions could drive the rate of interest. In the sheep example, the interest rate is determined by sheep reproduction given that consumption is forgone. In the fig example, a good that perishes at given rate per time period yields a negative rate of return and therefore a negative rate of interest and of time preference. In Fisher's third case, the hypothetical castaways have nothing more at their disposal than a given quantity of hardtack. The castaways can consume it all in one year or spread it over two or more. One unit of present consumption can only be achieved at the cost of one unit a year from now, so the "hardtack rate of interest" would be zero. This would also equal the rate of time preference, according to Fisher. With no interest, everything consumed per time period would have to be classified as depreciation. (The latter is my conclusion based on Fisher's definitions.)

In these abstract cases, investment productivity dominates, and the rates of interest and impatience adjust. The opposite case could also be hypothesized. That is, if, as a group, society rigidly adhered to a particular rate of time preference, the marginal rate of return over cost would respond (1930, 183). Fisher claimed that when the income stream is fixed or inflexible and no alternative exists, there is no opportunity cost and thus no rate of return over cost. However, a rate of time preference is not as easily dispensed with so long as there is any exchange between present and future (1930, 184).

In the hardtack case, the rate of return is technically limited to zero. The rate of impatience must adjust, according to Fisher, because an individual is limited to trading a unit of hardtack today for a unit of hardtack in the future. If hardtack is squandered today, this will reduce the future stock, which will result in the present price adjusting relative to the future price such that their ratio will ultimately equal unity (1930, 189). There is something unsettling about this conclusion because if the rate of time preference is zero, one could interpret this to mean that it does not matter to the individual whether he consumes a unit of hardtack today or a unit tomorrow. He is equally indifferent between consuming a unit today or a year from now or one hundred years from now. The trade-off is the same.

A Return to Hardtack?

It could be said that what hardtack produces is a human life. If so, the return to hardtack, like other inputs, should be stated in relation to that which it produces. The decision is a production decision in this context. The rate of return on hardtack would be expressed in terms of that which is produced, a human life—or in production terms, human capital. Like other inputs that are used in the production of goods, the value of hardtack would be considered a derived value. It is derived from the value of that which it sustains. If so, it might be argued that the rate of return is positive. So long as the person remains alive, the return on hardtack would be positive.

On an island barren of all but hardtack, with no other chance to produce or consume; the value of a person's life in an earning (human capital) sense would be low. (That is, there would be no employment and therefore no alternative uses of one's time.) This conclusion could in part be based on Rand's contention that one's primary purpose in life is to produce. If that is not possible, one's life loses much of its meaning. From a purely economic perspective, one's human capital has no value if there is no prospect of earning income. One might say that the abstraction process is so unrelated to reality in the hardtack case that it is devoid of implications. But I think there are insights that can be gained. One is that even if there appears to be no alternative use for a resource (hardtack), it still has value if it is put to a valuable use—in this case keeping someone alive.

Typically we measure goods such as hardtack in dollars (or some unit of currency or account) and a human life—for human capital purposes only—in dollars. The dollar value of a human life is the discounted value of expected future income. But since there is only hardtack, it would have to be the unit of account. Let's assume there is only a single castaway, there are 10,000 units of hardtack, and that is enough to sustain a person for 10 years. How then is a human life measured? Even if the human has no way of earning income, he may still value his life and, presumably, be able to impute a value to his life. If he were to consume 1,000 units a year, he could nevertheless value his life at more than 1,000. If he did so, then wouldn't hardtack's value be derived from a year of the person's life measured in units of hardtack and thus be worth more than 1,000? How could 1,000 units of hardtack be valued at more than 1,000? It could be said that this occurs through the process of transformation. The objective of the production process is to create something the value of which is greater than the value of the inputs used to produce it—the total becoming greater than the sum of the parts. Since hardtack is the unit of account, it does not matter if the value is 1,000 or 1,200. With no other goods to compare these with in the current time period, either value would suffice. So the value of a year of a human life could be set equal to 1,000. A person is what he eats, so to speak.

Of course, this is not literally true. Even if a quantity of hardtack and a unit of a human life were said to have the same value, the stock of hardtack would not be equivalent to a human life. An obvious difference in the two is that one is not living and one is. From a purely economic perspective, there are important implications that follow from this. A stock (asset) such as hardtack derives its value from that which it produces. The stock exists. It has an expected productive life.

The stock may not change significantly in a physical sense over time. It will change in a physical sense (assuming no physical deterioration) only to the extent it is used up. It has value to the extent that it contributes to a human life. If that which it produces is no longer produced nor can be (i.e., if the person is no longer alive), and there are no other alternatives, then the stock may exist, but it would have no value. A human may be alive now, but he "grows," or his life is extended, by a process of nourishment. The nature of a human being is that he is a living being and cannot, as is the case for some pieces of equipment or many natural resources, sit idle, neglected, and untended for an extended period of time. A day may be skipped, but not a year or ten years or even several days.

For purposes of illustration, it is assumed that it is possible for a person to measure the value of a year of his life in terms of hardtack and that it is equal to 1,000 units. Suppose further that he values each year the same. (This is a simplifying assumption.) If the interest rate is assumed to be zero, it might be concluded that the value of the person's life is 1,000 units per year multiplied by the number of years more he expects to live, which is assumed to be 10. The value of the entire life from an economic perspective would be the value of a consumption stream (or income stream, using Fisher's definition) over one's lifetime, or 10,000 units.

Is the concept of depreciation relevant here? Does a human life depreciate? In human capital terms, something that is equivalent to depreciation can be calculated. If depreciation is defined as the difference in the value of capital from one time period to another (Fisher [1906] 1965, 235), then it would exist in the case of human capital. Human capital is the discounted value of an expected income (consumption) stream. If the discount rate is zero (and, for the moment, it is assumed that consumption per time period is *not* adjusted by the probability of being alive), then the value of human capital would simply be, as figured above, 10,000 units. The value return would increase each year. The first year the rate of value return would be 1,000/10,000. Depreciation would be the difference between the value the first year and the value the second. Since 1,000 are used up the first year, then 9,000 would be available and with a zero interest rate, that would be the value in year two. The depreciation would be the difference between the values for the two years, or 1,000 units. All return would be depreciation. The depreciation rate would be the same as the rate of value return. The net return ("interest") would be zero.

However, to determine the value of the consumption stream, one should take into account that the mortality rate tends to increase as one ages (not just due to aging alone, but if that probability were separable from other factors that account for death over time, then one might limit the probabilities of dying to those that result from aging only). So, consumption would have to be factored by the probability of being alive to consume it. This could be regarded as equivalent to expected lifetime consumption (or income, in the Fisherian sense), since if one is not alive, then one consumes nothing ($\pi d_t C_t = 0$, where πd_t is the probability of dying at time t, C_t is consumption at time t). This assumes that bequests are irrelevant to the castaway. Thus, the value of human capital would be the sum of hardtack consumption per year (say 1,000 units) weighted by the probability of being alive each year for ten years, or the sum of expected consumption per time period over time. In human capital terms, the value return would increase each year, since the 1,000 units would be divided by a number that shrinks over time. The "net return" ("interest") would be the value return adjusted for "depreciation."

If the probability of dying (force of mortality) is assumed to be constant and equal to 10 percent per year, then the value today of the consumption stream that extends over the expected life would be 6,144.44. (Although I use the term "value" here, it is expected value to which I refer, not present value. See appendix 1.2.) The value after one year's time would fall to 5,758.89. "Depreciation" between the two periods would equal 385.55 units. The other part of the "income" of 1,000 per year can be thought of as "interest." For the first year, the rate of "value return" would be 1,000/6,144.44, "depreciation" as a percentage of the value of capital would be 385.55/6,144.44, and the "rate of return" would be (1,000-385.55)/6,144.44, or 10 percent. (These values assume that the force of mortality is a constant percentage, which may not be realistic. It is also assumed that the probability of being alive in the first period is less than 100 percent. If the period of time is short enough, a 100 percent probability may not be unrealistic.)

The "return" of 10 percent is equal to the force of mortality of 10 percent, which it must. I have said that the probabilities are based on age. If they are the result of unforeseen "accidents," then to the extent that the person lives and receives the "return," it is due to luck. If, on the other hand, the individual has some control over the probabilities, then that percentage return could be seen as a result of his own effort. For instance, if a person smokes, his expected life span is shortened and the probabilities of dying increase over the course of his life. If a smoker quits smoking and thereby reduces the probabilities of dying attributable to smoking, then that difference (between the probabilities of dying with and without smoking) can be thought of as a return to his decision, not the result of luck. At this point, I do not make this kind of distinction. I simply introduce the probabilities of dying in rather generic terms. The distinction becomes important in chapter 16 in the discussion of decision-making for charitable giving.

Hardtack and the Fundamental Alternative

Fisher (1930, 189) claimed the hardtack rate of return is zero and that this rate would dominate the rate of time preference. The interest rate would thus be zero. The only exception to a zero rate of time preference that he addressed is if one's survival were in imminent peril. The rate of time preference would then be positive. If the rate of time preference is zero, it makes no difference to the person whether he consumes a portion of the hardtack today or ten years from now. It may appear that, rather than consuming any of it today, one could wait ten years to consume some or all of it, and consequently never consume any. This interpretation would not be quite accurate because the rate is determined at the margin. Still even at the margin one might question whether a zero rate of time preference makes intuitive sense.

As mentioned, the nature of a human being is that he is a living being and cannot, as with nonhuman capital, remain unattended for an extended period of time. At some level, the alternative in a real sense is between consuming a unit of hardtack and remaining alive and not doing so and risking death. This is a factor that will drive the rate of time preference, which is more likely to be positive rather than zero. In other words, Fisher's "exception" about the rate of time preference being positive when death is imminent is the "rule." Death is always immanent in the sense that there is always a positive probability of dying associated with the next instant.

The Hardtack Decision

The value of hardtack is derived from that which it produces—additional units of a human life. In production, to be profitable, the value of what is produced exceeds the inputs for production. But in this case, what is produced is human capital in the service of one's own life only. Since the castaway is, by abstraction, limited only to hardtack, nothing else can be produced except himself. The decision, then, at some level is between consuming a unit of hardtack today relative to a unit in the future. It is a consumption decision. If one has a very limited supply, consuming another unit today may translate into a shorter life span. Once the point has been reached at which one can sustain oneself at present (in terms of calories, for instance), additional consumption will have a psychic benefit but will not extend one's life. At that point, the psychic value of additional units must be traded off against the sacrifice of units of one's life (which can also be expressed in psychic units, i.e., utility).

One might think that as soon as subsistence is attained, the additional psychic value of consuming a unit today would be overwhelmed by the loss of value of losing units (of one's life) in the future. Life is such that it requires nourishment to sustain it, but no amount of nourishment can sustain it indefinitely. There is a limit to how long one may live. It is also true that no one is guaranteed that he will live T years and then die. The cumulative probability of survival declines over time (the mortality rate increases) as a person ages. Intuitively one may see himself after a certain point as trading off the psychic value of an additional unit today with the value of an additional unit of one's life at the end of one's expected life. The value today of an additional unit of one's life toward the end of one's life is unlikely to be as great as the value of an additional unit of one's life is at the present moment. This is because the value today of an additional unit of one's life toward the end of life would be weighted by the probability of being alive at that time. The value today of an additional unit of one's life at the expected end of one's life may be outweighed by the additional psychic value a unit adds today when those values are multiplied by their respective probabilities of survival.

Although it is true that there may be pressure to consume more today than in the future, that does not mean that the individual will do so. As shown in appendix 1.1, when limited to two adjacent periods, the optimality condition for consumption for both periods will be given by equating the ratio of the marginal values (utilities) for two consecutive periods under consideration, multiplied by the ratio of their respective probabilities of survival, to the ratio of the respective relative probabilities of survival. There is pressure to consume today (time preference). However, there is a competing incentive not to consume so as to have a return (in this case, more of one's life) next period. Because the ratios of the respective probabilities of survival appear on both sides of the equation, consumption will be equal across both periods.

Implications

The assumptions underlying the hardtack decision can be modeled as a consumption decision over one's lifetime (as I have shown in appendix 1.1). Although simplistic, this view of the decision-making process is not inconsistent with Rand, who saw man as choosing fundamentally between life and death (1964a, 15), but she saw this decision as long-range, not range of the moment. That is, the decision is not only for the moment but encompasses the future life expectancy. Implicit in the modeling of this decision is that life has value to the decision-maker. The tension between consumption and saving is relevant, as is the importance of planning over time. Since in Objectivism, consumption is a value and saving is a virtue, there are ethical implications to the decision. The fundamental alternative of life or death is represented by probabilities of survival and figures prominently in the decision. The discount rate in this case would be derived from the ratio of the probabilities of survival between two adjacent periods. Analogues to depreciation and interest can be calculated from expected lifetime "income" (consumption). The "return" is based on the survival of the individual and is equal to the force of mortality in this particular case. Bequests would be irrelevant to a person on a desert island (as would "replacement capital"). The analysis is important because it lays the foundation for less simplistic analyses to be considered later.

CHAPTER FIVE

Decision-Making with Two Players

Rand recognized only two proper states for man—alone on a desert island, or among other men under a proper government. To Rand (1964a), virtues are selfish. A man alone would not rely on force or fraud, since it would be impossible for him (if he wants to exist). Among others, the same values apply. There are mutual gains to voluntary cooperation among men. But to Rand, this reason is secondary (1967a, 20). One should not engage in force or fraud, because in so doing, a person cheats himself. Eric Mack (1986, 158) added that in order for a doctrine of egoism to translate into a doctrine of rights, Rand (1964c) added the caveat that there is no conflict of interests among rational men. However, as noted in this chapter, if property rights are not defined, conflict can arise.

Rand did not examine the transition from an original state of nature to government. The focus of this chapter is on decision-making in an original state of nature with two individuals. The maximin criterion for decision-making under uncertainty and the Bayes criterion under risk are considered (Baumol 1977, 460–66). Game theory is used to address problems of coordination and of conflict in which property rights do not exist. Conventions of ownership are modeled as games of conflict. Using the Prisoner's Dilemma, strategies that lead to cooperation in a state of nature in which there is ownership but no enforcement are discussed. In repeated plays of the game, Axelrod (1984) found that a strategy of reciprocity won based on long-run success. In order for cooperation to emerge, retaliation is needed in response to default.

Decision-Making under Uncertainty with Two Players

Other people are not a fundamental part of reality in OE. The man on the desert island has been used as a starting point in analyzing decision-making. He was considered in discussing the values and virtues in OE. His life would be his ultimate value, and his fundamental alternative would be whether to live or not. Following a hypothetical case similar to one first explored by Irving Fisher (1930, 186–92), I, by abstraction, assumed the only resource available to the castaway was hardtack, a limited and depletable stock; one of which the castaway could not produce more. The decision facing the castaway was a simple one. It involved weighing the consumption of an additional unit today relative to the future. The preference for the present had to be weighed against the return in the future—more of his life. The relevant probabilities that were assumed to affect the decision were those related to living and dying.

A decision necessarily involves more than one alternative. When there is "certainty," it means that for each alternative there is a known outcome. When there is uncertainty or risk, there is more than one outcome for each alternative; thus if one chooses to take a given action, he cannot be certain what the outcome will be. The outcome will be dependent on the "state of nature." (The states of nature associated with a given decision are to be distinguished from a state of nature in which man lives without government.) Economists distinguish between uncertainty and risk. Uncertainty is when the probabilities for the states of nature are unknown or not estimable. Risk exists when probabilities are known or estimable. (However, I often use the word "uncertainty" when referring to either possibility, except in examples in which I am making a distinction between the two.)

In order to make a decision, there must be some basis on which to determine whether one alternative is better than another. Under certainty, it is assumed that each alternative has a payoff. Depending on the decision, the payoff may be expressed in terms of money, units of output (or some other physical unit), or utility (a psychological measure of satisfaction or value). When there is more than one outcome for a set of alternatives, a payoff matrix can be constructed. A good deal of information may be necessary to create a payoff matrix. To make a decision, even without probabilities, a person must have some idea of what the possible outcomes could be to various courses of action. There must be some way of measuring or weighing these alternatives in order to compare one with the other.

Given the payoff matrix, different criteria may be used to choose among the alternatives. For instance, the maximin criterion is defined as choosing the best alternative among the worst possible outcomes that the decision-maker faces. The maximin criterion assumes that the decision-maker is risk averse, but is otherwise a would-be maximizer (Hillier and Lieberman 1967, 81–82). The maximin criterion assumes that nature is an opponent and is malevolent (Baumol 1977, 460).

This assumption is at odds with Rand's Benevolent Universe Premise (BUP) (Rand 1964d, 48; Peikoff 1976; Paterson 1968 250–51). If a person is alone and is simply facing "nature," rather than a thinking opponent, then the assumption that nature is "out to get you" is unnecessarily pessimistic. Nature is neither malevolent nor benevolent; it simply is. However, Rand's BUP was based on her belief that man is efficacious; that is, if man acts rationally, he can, accidents excepted, expect success. The maximin criterion applied to a set of alternatives when man is alone in a state of nature would be unduly risk averse.

Another criterion, the Bayes or Laplace criterion, like the maximin, assumes that the probabilities are unknown. However, the Bayes criterion simply assigns equi-probabilities (chance) to each state of nature (at least, initially [Chou 1969, 682]), thereby permitting the calculation of an expected value for each alternative. The alternative that has the highest expected value is chosen. Two problems with the Bayes approach are that the (initial) assumption of equal probabilities may be unrealistic and that if the number of categories (states of nature) changes, this changes the probabilities (Baumol 1977, 463). (Both the maximin and Bayes criteria for decision-making are revisited in chapter 15.)

When an individual is alone, as on a desert island, space is not an issue. Scarcity is more a time-induced than a space-induced phenomenon. This is particularly true in the naïve case in which there is a castaway with a given quantity of hardtack. The castaway is prohibited by the restrictive assumptions of the case from so much as manipulating his environment to create more of a good. Once a second person is introduced into the analysis and the number of resources is expanded (although still assumed scarce), space becomes relevant. Again the maximin criterion may be employed, but now it is a decision criterion used against a real "opponent," not nature, in a zero-sum game.

Rand did not believe that nature limited men to a single resource over which they were forced to battle (Berliner 1995, 354). She did not believe that there were conflicts of interests among rational men (Rand 1964c). Interaction, it could be concluded, is not zero-sum so long as men are rational. If an interaction is zero-sum, it is not due to the nature of the "game," but because one (or both) of the parties to the interaction forces it to be zero-sum. That is, Rand believed that mutual gain (a positive sum outcome) was the rule, not the exception, to voluntary interaction between men. If one of the "players" forced the other to relinquish something he owned (an involuntary unilateral transfer of one's person or property to another), then the outcome would be zero-sum (there would be a winner and a loser). However, the "game" itself is potentially positive sum. It is the use of force on the part of one of the parties to the interaction that would lead to a zero-sum outcome. (That is, as the Prisoner's Dilemma illustrates, exchange leads to the positive sum (m,m) outcome. If one of the players defaults, (s,t) or (t,s), the game becomes zero-sum.)

There are two implications here. One is that a person in an interaction cannot lose what he does not have. For instance, if two applicants vie for the same job, the "loser" is not in fact a loser because he never had the job in the first place. "Interests" here is synonymous with "rights." If a person does not own a thing, he has no right to it; that is, he has no interest in it. The underlying assumption is that property rights have been defined, assigned, and should be respected. The presumption seems to be that if men are rational, they recognize that property rights should exist, know how they should be assigned in a given case, assign them, and respect them. (For a given resource that was once abundant and becomes scarce, it is not always obvious that property rights are necessary, or to whom the rights should be assigned.)

Another implication to the idea that the interests of rational men do not conflict is that interaction tends to be positive-sum (once property rights have been defined). Adam Smith ([1776] 1937, 423) is credited with being the first to recognize this in the economic sphere. But these gains are predicated on the existence of property rights. If property rights are acknowledged and assigned, then a positive-sum interaction can be transformed into a zero-sum interaction if one of the participants violates the rights of the other.

The maximin criterion could apply to a dispute over an unowned resource. If it is assumed that there is a single payoff matrix (which would apply if one player's gain is automatically the other player's loss) and that the game is zero-sum, then the player could employ the maximin criterion. If he did so, then the best response strategy for the opponent would be to play the minimax criterion (choose the lowest of the largest possible costs) (Baumol 1977, 438–42). Both players are assumed to be risk averse, but this is not unrealistic when a person faces an opponent, not nature. Each player may follow a pure strategy, or a mixed strategy may result. An example of a mixed strategy is when a player X chooses a strategy Y, Z percent of the time (Chiang 1974, 754). A mixed strategy could apply, for instance, to the shared use of a resource by two players when ownership is not established.

According to my interpretation of Rand, if property rights have been assigned, then zero-sum games would be rare, except in the case in which one person is trying to forcefully infringe on another's rights. There are exceptions to this. Most voluntary games or competitions are zero-sum, as are political elections. Market share among competitors, expressed in percentage terms, is necessarily zero-sum; even though, when expressed in absolute terms, one competitor's gain is not necessarily at a rival's expense.

Conventions in a State of Nature

When a strategy is played routinely by players in a given circumstance, then that strategy may be regarded as a convention. Two individuals credited with examining the emergence of conventions using game theory analysis are David Lewis (1969) and Robert Sugden (1986). Lewis saw conventions as emerging from coordination problems (Lewis 1969, 14). Sugden believed conventions could also emerge from so-called games of conflict (Sugden 1986, 33). Both acknowledged that conventions could not arise from a one-time encounter (game) (Sugden 1986, 16; Lewis 1969, 42). And both defined a convention as a rule of behavior that could develop out of two or more possible rules (Lewis 1969, 70; Sugden 1986, 32). Unlike social contracts—which may be unique—conventions are not (Lewis 1969, 95). Conventions emerge spontaneously and are not encoded as laws. (A convention may become encoded in positive law, but then it is a law, not a convention.) Sudgen's objective was to examine how conventions could take hold in a Hobbesian state of nature. The games were assumed to involve two participants selected at random playing for small stakes in repeated games (Sugden 1986, 1–16).

Many of the conventions that Sugden examined involved disputes over space. Coordination problems tend to involve use of a resource by two or more parties that may lead to both (all) parties arriving at the same space at the same time. The resource need not be owned by either party. Conventions such as "yield right of way" or "drive on the right side of the road" are examples of those arising from coordination problems. A dispute may develop between two parties over the permanent dispensation of a resource. This is more appropriately modeled as a game of conflict. Several possibilities could result. Both parties could divide the resource. One person could be assigned the exclusive right to the resource; i.e., a settled rule of property could result. In some cases, the resource may be dissipated during the conflict so that nothing is left.

Sudgen introduced three games to explain how property rights to an unowned resource could be established by a convention. Each game assumed something about human nature. In the Hawk-Dove game, individuals were assumed to be either aggressive or submissive. In the War of Attrition, it was assumed the players would weigh the persistence time of fighting against its cost. In the Division game, it was assumed that each player would claim some percentage of the resource. All three games—the Hawk-Dove, the War of Attrition, and the Division game—either can result in conflict or can be resolved peacefully. In a game, either an asymmetry can be recognized or not. An asymmetry is some salient feature of the game that is observed by the players, which cues them to follow a particular strategy. If no asymmetry is observed (that is, if the game is symmetrical), then the emergence of a convention (following a consistent strategy when a particular feature is present) is far less likely. When the games are symmetrical, they can be resolved peacefully if: in the Hawk-Dove game, doves meet doves; in the War of Attrition, the players' persistence times are zero; and in the Division game, the claims of the two players do not sum to more than 100 percent. The first two equilibria are unstable. If one player is a dove, it pays to "play hawk." If one player has a persistence time of zero, then it pays to persist. In the third game, if the sum of the claims exceeds 100 percent, fighting ensues. All three games can lead to force or the threat of force (Sugden 1986, 70–8).

Once an asymmetry is recognized, a convention will more readily be established. Conventions can allow for the peaceful settlement of disputes. One asymmetry that Sugden discussed was possession. Possession of a resource may be a "natural" basis for property rights, according to Sugden, and if so, then conventions of property would be natural laws. Sugden invoked Hume's claim that humans detect relationships among objects to back up his argument. He also cited Locke's basis for property rights, that of the expenditure of effort. Biological evidence was also offered. Territoriality is innate in many animals; it may be natural to humans as well (Sugden 1986, 93–103).

To be a bona fide convention, however, there must be an alternative to the convention favoring possessors. Conventions favoring challengers (where it is assumed, as in all games, players are chosen at random) would have to be observed to have taken hold in reality. However, Sugden offered no evidence of that. It would seem to me that a convention favoring challengers, if one were to arise, would tend to be inherently unstable. If possessors voluntarily relinquished their resources to challengers simply because they were challengers, then they would become dispossessed and therefore become the new challengers. They would thus have a right to reclaim the resource by virtue of being challengers. Then the newly dispossessed would again become the challengers, and so on. If a convention favoring challengers is unrealistic, then a convention favoring possessors might be unique. If so, then it would not qualify as a convention, according to Sugden's definition of the term. This does not mean that generally accepted rules of social conduct could not emerge that would be consistent with natural law, i.e., property rights (and that they might be based on possession). What it would mean is that these generally accepted rules, i.e., property rights, would not be conventions.

This does not mean, however, that all laws that actually encode generally accepted rules of behavior *vis à vis* property are consistent with property rights (i.e., property rights as applicable to all men—natural rights, not property rights as special rights or privileges of some men). Property rules (as well as positive property laws) may be confined to those individuals who meet certain criteria such as age, gender, race, and/or ethnicity. They may be related to certain capacities such as sanity or I. Q. or literacy. The theory of conventions discussed by Sugden (1986, 22) assumes that "players" are chosen at random. When "games" are played repeatedly over a large number of individuals, random selection has the effect of eliminating extraneous differences on the outcome over repeated plays; that is, players would tend to be evenly matched. If individuals are not evenly matched, then those who are less equal (in a game theoretic sense of being less evenly matched) may be at a disadvantage. That is, in reality the salient feature that results in the asymmetry could be that some players are less "powerful" than others. There may be other reasons (ostensible or real) for property laws that favor some individuals relative to others (separate from possession). Laws prohibiting the ownership of property by some may be based on "protecting" those who are "less equal."

When man lives among others, Rand (1964g) believed that man should live under a proper government. This means that property rights would not be established by convention or custom, but be encoded in positive law and protected, not by individual retaliation, but by government. A constitution ("social contract") would not emerge spontaneously, but require the rational application of thought and effort. This does not exclude the possibility, it would seem to me, of rational social customs or conventions arising over time that would be consistent with property rights. If rational social customs or conventions emerge that are consistent with natural rights, I do not think that this would be inconsistent with Rand's concept of rationality since she did not regard rationality as cut off from reality. One way of arriving at knowledge (here, knowledge of property rights) might be a combination of rational thought and trial and error, since rational men can learn from experience to the extent that they correct former errors in judgment. Logic is not limited to deduction from a set of self-evident or a priori propositions. Propositions are derived from observation of reality.

Cooperation in a State of Nature

Like Sugden (1986), Robert Axelrod (1984) was interested in investigating the emergence of cooperation in a state of nature (more specifically, one in which there was no central authority (Axelrod 1984, viii)). Unlike Sudgen, Axelrod did not examine how property rights might be established in a state of nature. Axelrod was primarily interested in cooperative economic interaction. However, for economic exchange to occur, the parties to the transaction must own that which is exchanged. Ownership must already have been established in some way. Axelrod did not explicitly address the establishment of ownership. Perhaps one might think of the situation he presented as one in which there is possession, and customs have emerged that cover trading that which a person possesses. The lacking ingredient to exchange under such a circumstance would be enforcement. That is, there would be no governmental enforcement agency. So, if an exchange were agreed upon and one of the parties defaulted, there would be no authority to whom the aggrieved party might turn for justice.

If the incentive structure were such that both parties had an incentive to cheat and both gave in to these incentives, then there would really be no problem of enforcement. There would be no basis for a dispute. Neither party would have a grievance. Trade simply would not take place. Each person would be an island, so to speak. There would be no interaction. However, there is a payoff to exchange. Mutual gains to trade are possible. Each person can potentially end up with more after an exchange than if each remained self-sufficient. The incentive structure thus described can be modeled as a Prisoner's Dilemma. Axelrod (1984) used the Prisoner's Dilemma to explain how cooperation could take hold in a state of nature. Sugden (1986) similarly examined cooperation—or more generally, a convention of reciprocity—in a state of nature.

The one-shot Prisoner's Dilemma (one-time interaction) is typical of the incentive structure underlying the "golden opportunity" discussed in chapter 3. If there is no possibility of future interaction (and if the game is anonymous), the incentive would be to cheat—to default on the trade. According to Axelrod (1984, 9–17), defection is the dominant strategy even when future interaction is possible so long as the number of interactions is finite and the number is known. The defection strategy has been called a "nasty" strategy (Sugden 1986, 109). However, if in anticipation of defection, no trade takes place because neither party enters an agreement in the first place, then this strategy would have no particular moral content. Even though survival is the ultimate value and trade results in more productivity, there is nothing morally objectionable in Objectivism about a man being solitary.

There is an ethical dimension to mutual defection. But mutual defection has an inherent punishment for the defectors since the payoff is less for both than would exist if both had followed through on the agreement. There is a broken contract (or perhaps a broken promise) on both sides. More damaging than mutual defection is when one person defects and the other does not. Here a defection is actually a default on payment. In Rand's view, this is equivalent to theft (Rand 1964g, 111). With unilateral defection, one person gets something (which results in an involuntary unilateral transfer) for which he does not give anything in return.

If only one person defects, the other receives nothing. The sucker's payoff is zero. (It is actually less than zero since he is giving up something for which he receives nothing.) This is a zero-sum outcome. This hypothetical case assumes that there is no further possibility of interaction for these two individuals. But if this had not been an assumption, the behavior on the part of the defector would virtually assure it, at least so long as the other player wants to avoid being put in the position of being suckered once again. The defector has not only eliminated the possibility of future exchange, but has also quelled the potential for the exchange of information, goodwill, and friendship with the other.

In a strictly one-shot scenario, these losses would not be recognized as such. But if future interaction were even a possibility, these potential gains would be included in a payoff matrix of a rational decision-maker. If a person has never interacted with another, he may not fully understand the implications of what is lost through default—knowledge that remains unshared through lack of communication and other experiences. In isolation, it is impossible to conceive of that which has never been—the potential benefits from trade, which are derived from specialization, capital formation, and innovation.

One way of "solving" the Prisoner's Dilemma is for there to be an understanding on the parts of both players that these potentialities exist and that they are being sacrificed if one party to the transaction defects. Nozick presented the evidential argument to solving the dilemma. That is, if each party believes the other is sufficiently like he is, and he does not want to defect, then both may avoid defection and trade may take place (Nozick 1993, 50–59). The question then is, how does one surmise that the other is sufficiently like oneself? One way is to rely on reputation. Reputation would not appear to be relevant to a participant in a one-shot exchange. This would seem to be particularly true if the partners were never to interact again (in any other way).

However, Frank pointed out why reputation can be a factor in a one-shot game. He believed that those emotions which commit a person to being honest are sustained by consistent behavior (1988, 16–19). There are strong societal pressures to conform to a social rule once it has become an accepted norm (Touchstone 1995, 93–100). People may conform because of what Nozick (1993, 26–35) called the "symbolic utility" associated with an action. Certain actions may cue others to the possession of certain character traits. Reputation can matter. It can matter because one's livelihood may depend on it, for instance. If a person is regarded as trustworthy and honest, he is more likely to be viewed as a potential trading partner. And it is through exchange that we earn a return on our labor services and acquire homes, consumer goods, financial instruments, businesses, education, and so on.

Game theoreticians point out that rules such as those in mathematics are not conditional. Two plus two equals four (Ridley 1996, 57). Rules of conduct are conditional. Of course, when one is alone, one's behavior is conditional as well. It is unwise to go sailing when a hurricane is expected. But interpersonal interaction is more complex than that of an individual alone trying to make a decision. A person may consider weather conditions in making his decision, but the weather does not take into account the human's decision. An individual (A) may enter an exchange with another (B) because A expects B not to cheat him, but whether the trade in fact takes place will also depend on whether B expects A to be honest as well.

There is another reason that a person would be encouraged to be cooperative in a one-shot exchange, and that is the possibility that there might be retaliation if he defaults. Reputation encompasses more than being known for honesty; it can also include knowledge of how a person reacts if someone else is dishonest in trade—whether he will retaliate or not. The threat of retaliation would require at least the possibility of future interaction for that purpose.

Axelrod stated that it is because players could encounter each other again that the emergence of cooperation is possible. Axelrod noted that the future carries less weight than the present, giving two reasons why this would be true for individuals who interact. "The first is that players tend to value payoffs less as the time of their obtainment recedes into the future. The second is that there is always some chance that the players will not meet again. An ongoing relationship may end when one or the other player moves away, changes jobs, dies, or goes bankrupt" (1984, 12). Thus, the next move will count less than the current move. Future payoffs are discounted. The less important the future is in one's decision, the higher the discount rate. But now the discount rate depends not only upon one's own mortality and its uncertainty, as considered in chapter 4, but also on the mortality of another as well as his disappearance, financial condition, and commitment.

Axelrod illustrated that once the time horizon is lengthened (future interaction is possible), cooperation is more likely by examining extended Prisoner's Dilemma games in a computer tournament in which various strategies were pitted against each other. Axelrod found that the Tit-for-Tat strategy yielded the greatest overall rewards (1984, 50–55) and was collectively stable in repeated games (that is, another strategy could not successfully invade it) (1984, 56). In Tit-for-Tat, an individual initially cooperates, then subsequently cooperates or retaliates depending upon whether one's opponent cooperated or defaulted in the previous play. Tit-for-Tat is a strategy of reciprocity. Always defect (All D) was also a collectively stable strategy. However, "not nice" strategies over the long haul would tend to "destroy the very environment [they need] for [their] own success" (1984, 117).

Still, Axelrod found reciprocity unsavory because of "its insistence on an eye for an eye" (1984, 137). He did not regard retaliation as virtuous. (Similar sentiments were expressed by Ridley (1996, 140) and Frank (1988, 34–35).) Rand did not regard personal retaliation as a virtue. She believed government should be solely responsible for this type of justice (Rand 1964g, 109). Axelrod acknowledged that retaliation may be necessary in a state of nature, since there would be no governmental body or agency to perform this function. He said: "When there is no central authority to do the enforcement, the players must rely on themselves to give each other the necessary incentives to elicit cooperation rather than defection" (1984, 138). A community, using a principle of reciprocity, can police itself. It is because the uncooperative are punished that the "deviant strategy" is rendered unprofitable. "Therefore the deviant will not thrive, and will not provide an attractive model for others to imitate" (ibid.).

In Tit-for-Tat, one retaliates by refusing to interact with someone who had defected in the past. This means a person may "get away with" a single defection. In chapter 3, I tied retaliation to restitution. In game theory, it is assumed that games are played for small stakes, so it might be justifiable for a person to forgo the attempt to get restitution for a single defection. Refusal to interact further with the defector may be a sufficient response. Even so, one can build into games reparation for past defections, so that if someone defects he pays by having it cost him to reenter future games. He may get away with a single defection but if he wants to play again, he must pay to play. Sugden stated that reparations can be made "sufficiently burdensome to deter deliberate defections" (1986, 115).

Comparisons with Rand

Parallels with Rand's ethics are notable (1964a). Rand's ethics are based on strategies for long-term success. The exchange of value for value is the basis of Rand's trader principle—the principle of justice, her primary social principle. Rand was not interested in a strategy that might work on a one-time basis or one based on "chance" or luck. Axelrod (1984) found Tit-for-Tat, a strategy of reciprocity, to result in the greatest long-term rewards and to be stable. He discovered parasitic strategies to be impractical as general or long-run modes of behavior; a finding consistent with Rand's nonsacrificial principle. However, unlike Axelrod, Rand was not interested in cooperation, per se. She was interested in the individual and what he should do to have a successful life. Voluntary trade is cooperative behavior and a symbol of respect among men. It has the advantage of delivering mutual gains to participants. But the mutual gains are not the (sole or primary) reason that individuals should respect others' rights or cooperate with others (Berliner 1995, 259).

Axelrod concluded that it pays for individuals to be "nice," by which he meant that one should cooperate so long as one's partner cooperates and not be the first to defect (1984, 113). This is consistent with Rand's idea that one should grant a stranger "generalized respect and good will . . . until and unless he forfeits it" (1964d, 46). The Golden Rule or unconditional cooperation, as expressed by Axelrod, is similar to the way in which Rand viewed altruism. She did not regard altruism—the idea that one should put others above oneself—as a virtue. Yet Axelrod (1984, 136), Ridley (1996, 145), and Frank (1988, 57) commented favorably upon altruism. The definitions they employed varied. At one point, Frank referred to altruism as a refusal to sacrifice others to oneself (1988, 57) rather than the willingness to sacrifice oneself to others. Only the latter would be consistent with Rand's definition of altruism. Although Axelrod regarded the Golden Rule as a morally superior standard, he acknowledged its inherent flaw:

> The problem with this view is that turning the other cheek provides an incentive for the other player to exploit you. Unconditional cooperation can not only hurt you, but it can hurt other innocent bystanders with whom the successful exploiters will interact later. Unconditional cooperation tends to spoil the other player; it leaves a burden on the rest of the community to reform the spoiled player, suggesting that reciprocity is a better foundation for morality than is unconditional cooperation. (1984, 136)

Axelrod recognized that cooperation was more likely if individuals did not regard exchange as a zero-sum game, and if individuals did not yield to envy. In trade, one person's gain is not at another's expense as it is in zero-sum interactions. If a person regards trade as zero-sum, in which he may be the "loser" in an exchange, he may be reluctant to trade with others or to trade honestly. He may be tempted to default. He may also be envious of the success of another if he regards another's success as being at the expense of other people (himself included). Invidious comparisons with another person, when the other person's success has been achieved through his own efforts and through honest exchange, are self-destructive. Axelrod found that the long-run success of others "is virtually a prerequisite of your doing well for yourself" (1984, 112).

Like Axelrod, Rand also wrote of the destructive nature of certain manifestations of envy. If envy leads to appeals for everyone to be equally bad off, it is destructive. It can lead not only to a win-or-lose outcome (i.e., to one that is zero-sum), but to a lose/lose outcome (one that is negative sum). Rand gave as an example a doctor who, instead of treating a man with a broken leg, crippled other men in order to make his patient feel better and to "equalize the 'unfairness' of nature" (1971c, 170). Voluntary exchange is positive sum. One person's success is not at the expense of another or others.

Neither Frank (1988, 21–23), Ridley (1996, 44–46), nor Axelrod (1984, 6–7) regarded self-interest as a virtue, which is, of course, the basis for Rand's ethics. However, each recognized the tendency for an individual to be concerned with his own interest. Rationality also was not an assumption of their explorations (Axelrod 1984, 18; Ridley 1996, 6; Frank 1988, 2). So even though the conclusions reached by Frank, Ridley, and Axelrod may share some important commonalities with Rand's philosophy, their undertakings were not designed with that intent. Their discoveries can be seen as providing independent theoretical support for some aspects of Rand's philosophy.

Chapter Six

The Primary Social Unit (PSU)

In this chapter, I challenge the idea in OE that interaction with others is optional (Rand 1964g, 107; 1968, 3; 1961c, 79; Peikoff 1991, 252)—at least for some basic relationships. A proper society, if one opts to interact with others, is comprised of independent equals voluntarily exchanging value for value. Although Rand did not employ the Crusoe abstraction as an analytical device, it would seem to be an obvious starting point for an ethics that does not consider other people to be a fundamental part of reality. A second person can then be added in order to derive interpersonal ethics, conventions, and/or rights. Adding a second adult would seem to be a logical extension of the analysis if society is viewed as consisting of independent equals—a position held by Rand. However, Rand's ethics are considered biocentric. There is one social unit that by its nature is necessary, and that is the relationship between mother and child. I refer to this as the Primary Social Unit (PSU). It is a social unit because it has two individuals and is long-term in nature. It is primary because it is the first relationship a person has, and it is universal in that it is required for each human being. It is essential because one of the individuals is inherently dependent on the other for his survival. Although it is biologically necessary, that is not what makes it a socially necessary unit. An issue of rights is involved—positive rights from parent to child. I analytically expand society to include more than the PSU. The steps by which this abstraction process continues depend on whether the concept of paternity is understood or not. Although paternity has been understood for some time, analytically examining what is "primary" or "natural" is an abstract process in which assumptions are initially simplistic and then become increasingly more complex.

Society

In Rand's philosophy, men are independent and may choose to interact so long as they can do so voluntarily as traders, exchanging value for value. The social virtue in her moral code is justice, which is the trader principle. Men may choose to live alone, but if they choose to interact, the interaction need not be long-term in nature, since men are independent. To Rand, interacting with others is optional (1964g, 107). A man alone may produce those things necessary for his survival. There are many things that are only produced with others, such as a football game or an orchestral concert, but it is possible for a man to survive alone—to acquire those values necessary for survival, i.e., to reason, to produce, to have self-esteem. Rand's primary values can be achieved alone. There is one thing that is basic to the survival of man, the species, that cannot be done alone, however, and that is reproduction. If one wants to reproduce, then one must interact with another.

I regard reproduction as necessary to the individual for two reasons (at this point). One is the argument presented in chapter 2. That is, the concept man is parasitic on the existence of other men. Other men must exist—and continue to exist—in order for the concept to be viable. The second is that, as Peikoff noted, "every organism *owes* its existence" to reproduction (1991, 231; italics added). Since one's life is one's ultimate value, it would seem to follow that reproduction would be an essential value since it is required in order that one may exist. The nature of reproduction is that an inherently dependent person is created. The survival of the offspring is dependent on another person. The relationship between offspring and parent itself is also primary or fundamental rather than secondary or marginal because it is the first relationship an individual has, and it is universal because it is required for every human being. Every human being is born dependent, so one other person is required for his survival until he is independent. It is not need that renders it required, however. The child has a right to care from the adult (because of the prior actions of the adult—both the laws of causality and identity apply).

With the introduction of reproduction comes the necessity of a long-term relationship between two individuals—mother and child, which I label the Primary Social Unit (PSU). I define a social unit as one that has two or more individuals and is long-term in nature. The PSU is primary because it is fundamental to humans, universal, and essential. It is a social unit because it has two members, the minimum number for a social unit, and because it is inherently long-term. The reason for the latter qualifier or ingredient for the existence of a society is that, as both Sugden (1986, 16) and Lewis (1969, 58) noted, conventions of social behavior require for their establishment more than one interaction. As Axelrod (1984, 16) discovered, cooperative strategies were more likely to emerge with a lengthened time horizon. For "society" to exist, more than a single interaction (a one-shot game—in game theory parlance) is required. (This does not mean that when there is only a one-time encounter between individuals rights have no meaning. Rights exist for a one-time interaction. But a one-time interaction does not qualify as a society of people.)

The state-of-nature device can be used to examine man alone. Rothbard called Crusoe ethics the "most elementary human situation and problem" (Hoppe 1998, xxii). A second man is added to explore interactive decision-making, conventions, and rights. This is not the basic social unit, however—the most elementary societal situation. In this chapter, I analyze that unit—the PSU. The approach I use is similarly abstract. It is not based on historical or anthropological data. Historical and anthropological data are only referenced to clarify specific points. In this analysis, I isolate one or two features of social interaction that I regard as essential and build on that.

Initially, the focus is on the PSU. It is a relationship that is necessarily of long-term duration; it is not optional. Other long-term relationships may arise for many reasons and they may be beneficial to the parties involved, but they are not inherently necessary. The interaction here is necessary because it is essential for the survival of one of the individuals—the child. It is inherently dependent (the survival of one of the individuals depends on the other), but that is not what makes it required. It is the issue of rights that renders it a required relationship. The child has a positive right to care. The right that is relevant here (at least while the child is an infant) is the positive right to care of the child. The negative right to life of the child is redundant since it is subsumed in the positive right to care. The negative right of the mother does not apply since the child (at least initially) would not be culpable even if the child could harm the mother. (Early on, the mother would, in effect, be in the same position as if alone on an island where rights do not apply.) The primary right then, in the sense of being first, is the positive right to care. Since Rand put survival or life at the center of her ethics, I believe it follows that if a social unit is primary it should be tied to survival—at least to the survival of one of the parties. As for the independent individual—the adult—Rand was correct that one person's survival does not depend on others so long as this statement is limited to an adult's survival among other adults. (The basis for rights will be discussed in chapter 7.)

A relevant question is, what is the nature of the interaction within the PSU? Sugden (1986), Axelrod (1984), and Ridley (1996) were all interested in showing how cooperation could arise in a state of nature. Cooperative interaction to their way of thinking is the basis for society. Axelrod found that cooperation could best be achieved through reciprocity. Although cooperation could be achieved in a single-shot case, it is more likely to flourish if there is the possibility of future interaction. When there is a relationship that has the possibility of duration, Axelrod indicated that reciprocity can emerge (Axelrod 1984, 129). Is the PSU a candidate for reciprocity? Ridley noted the main condition necessary for Tit-for-Tat to take hold is a relationship that is stable and repetitive. The greater the likelihood for the encounter between two players to be casual and opportunistic, the less probable Tit-for-Tat will be successful at fostering cooperation (1996, 63). This would seem to apply to the PSU, but Tit-for-Tat is a rule that favors cooperation between individuals who are not kin. Ridley pointed out: "Babies take their mother's beneficence for granted and do not have to buy it with acts of kindness" (ibid.).

In an exchange situation, it is assumed in OE that the participants are evenly matched (independent equals). The mother/child relationship is unequal. What is being traded? As discussed in chapter 2, the mother is productive. There is the creation of wealth—human capital—and property, in the broad sense that the child will one day own himself. There is no transfer of property. The producer does not own the product of his effort. The mother cannot buy or sell rights to ownership. The mother is investing in a long-term investment, but the return is primarily to the child. The child is under no obligation to reciprocate; that is, the parent has no right to reciprocity. What are the rights involved? At least initially, the right of the child to care. As Nathaniel Branden wrote: "A child is the responsibility of his parents, because (a) they brought him into existence, and (b) a child, by nature, cannot survive independently" (1962, 55).

What of the possibility of defection? The child does not have to reciprocate and therefore there is no basis for defection. The mother could defect, but it would be wrong to do so. How does retaliation fit in? There may be a basis for retaliation. Since only the child (infant) has positive rights here (that is, the right to receive care), if the mother in some way violated the child's rights, then the child may at some point retaliate. Of course, the idea of rights for a child is different from that for adults. A child would have a right to care, but the relationship is one of dependence of the child on the parent. It is inherently unequal since the child has a less than fully developed rational faculty. There may be an element of coercion on the part of the parent. Parents may restrict the movements of a child to a particular place—a play area, for instance. A parent may reprimand a child. The trader principle does not apply to parent and child, nor is there a Prisoner's Dilemma in the usual sense.

Is there a basis for reciprocity? There may be a basis for reciprocity during the child's adult years at which time both parent and child are independent (assuming the parent is still alive and is not dependent). Once an adult, the child may choose not to defect on exchanges with the parent. Whether there is cooperative interaction may depend, in part, upon whether the parent has been able to instill in the child values such as trust and the respect for rights. (See Morse (2001, 38–44).) If the child embodies these virtues, then this may form the basis for cooperative interaction with the parent and form the basis for a mature social unit.

So, as I see it, the mother/child relationship is the fundamental social unit; it is the only relationship that inherently requires (by "requires" I mean for the survival of one of the parties) interaction on a long-term basis (until the child is mature), and the relationship is required for each human. All other relationships of a long-term nature are optional. It is inherently dependent, long-term, essential, universal, fundamental, and has a basis in rights.

Specialization and the Division of Labor

There are several bases for cohesiveness among individuals that result in, or bolster, society. A natural foundation for society, in the sense of being grounded in human nature, is family. Shared responsibility is another basis for society. This can take the form of specialization that results in the division of labor. Pooling of risk is another form of shared responsibility.

Ridley noted that the sole division of labor notably present in every society is that between males and females; particularly, between married people (1996, 49). Ridley did not believe that nepotism was the basis for how society got off the ground in the first place. I agree with Ridley that the division of labor between men and women may not get society off the ground—particularly if the concept of paternity is not understood. Axelrod made a similar point in his discussion of promiscuity and the ill-defined nature of paternity and the bearing relatedness has on cooperativeness. He indicated that a cue to relatedness is cooperative reciprocity (Axelrod 1984, 97).

Ridley pointed out that specialization by gender may not have taken place until possibly 100,000 years ago. Both males and females engaged in foraging. Each was self-sufficient since there was apparently little opportunity to take advantage of gains from trade from the division of labor (1996, 94). It is not known when the switch happened, but it is likely to have occurred with the institution of marriage (1996, 94). The implication of the television program *The Neanderthals* (2000) was that early man did not specialize. Although small groups of individuals banded together, each person tended to fend for himself. Women were portrayed on the program as relying (at times, apparently) on scavenging to support themselves. This makes sense, particularly if women were also responsible for their offspring. Scavenging, however, is high-risk (in the sense that the game is not fresh).

In his discussion of specialization, Ridley's focus was largely on the division of labor among men. He commented that: "It is hard to imagine any group of grown men working together as a team for a fairly long period of time (as ancestral hunters would have done) without some similar sort of specialization emerging" (1996, 48). Rand noted that a man can survive alone. The question is, what would bring men together initially? Earlier I mentioned the pooling of risk. Two categories of risk pooling that are particularly relevant for early man are pooling for protection and for hunting.

One of the distinguishing characteristics of man is that he is a walking animal. His body was "built" for walking. It has been noted that: "[T]he human locomotor apparatus is definitely not designed for speed, it is well adapted to long-distance locomotion with minimum energy expenditure" (*Anthropology Today* 1971, 180). One of the methods of large-game hunting of early man was to track an animal for several days until the creature dropped from exhaustion (ibid.). Early man "moved away over prodigious distances" (Bronowski 1973, 45). This led to a species that, even though small in number, was widely dispersed over the planet. Males as a gender are particularly mobile because they are not biologically tied to their offspring during gestation or nursing as are females. Mobility can increase a person's opportunities. But one man traveling alone is extremely vulnerable. There is safety in numbers. One man has an incentive to pair up with another man or team up with several other men for protective purposes. There is strength in numbers, a pooling of risk. Protection is one reason for cooperation among men. It is particularly important when venturing into unknown territory.

Ridley offered hunting as the first great opportunity for cooperation (1996, 89). Although it may not be the first, it is important. Ridley stated: "According to one calculation, six hunters who pool their game will reduce the variability in their food supply by a massive eighty per cent compared with six hunters who do not pool their game. This is known as the risk-reduction hypothesis for food sharing" (1996, 102; Winterhalder 1986). Seasonal changes affect vegetation and animal migratory patterns. Mobility is attractive because it opens up hunting opportunities. Mobility also offers the attractions of adventure, discovery, and, unfortunately, marauding. One does not have to look far to find examples of men that engage in cooperative interaction over extended periods of time.

Many of the skills required for protection overlap those needed for hunting. Hunting and protection are also similar in that both may have public good characteristics. That hunting, particularly of big game, has public good features was noted by Ridley (1996, 108). The reason for the latter is twofold. Hunting is partly luck. If a group goes out instead of a single hunter, the probability of returning with a kill may increase. Hunting together reduces the risk (1996, 116). Second, as Ridley noted, it was not possible to prevent meat sharing; "a dead mammoth was essentially public property" (1996, 108).

With public goods, exclusion of nonpayers is difficult (or impossible). There is an incentive for individuals to be free riders. In the case of hunting, shirkers would be the "nonpayers." However, when the group is small and consists of able-bodied men, shirkers are more easily identified and are unlikely to be tolerated.

This does not mean that every man will necessarily engage in hunting, or even protection since, through division of labor, some may take on other tasks. However, each person is more likely to be seen as pulling his own weight, or he risks facing expulsion from the group. Exclusion of shirkers is not only possible, but likely.

It is more difficult to cull from a group those who do not pull their own weight when they cannot do so. Children, particularly young children, cannot. If paternity is not understood, there is less of an incentive for a man to team with women with children in work that requires mobility over long distances for extended periods of time. Since there is the potential for having children among childless women, teaming with other males would tend to be preferred, other things equal. Protection is more of a "public good" when children are present. Children, generally speaking, cannot pull their own weight. If children are present, it is also possible that it may even be more difficult to identify and cull from the group adults who are shirkers.

Others, who are not protectors or hunters (of larger game), may perform work that is more individualized in nature. Their work may not have "public good characteristics." Ridley made this point about the work of gatherers (1996, 101–102). If, within a group, there are individuals (such as children) who cannot contribute on the scale of an adult, or shirkers, who do not do their part, protectors may see themselves as contributing more to (some) others than they receive in return. They may feel a sense of "sacrifice" in providing protection. This is one reason that, *ceteris paribus,* there may be a tendency among travelers to prefer adults. Second, there is more speed without children in tow. With children, the group is more vulnerable since, instead of providing protection, children must be protected. Third, adult males tend to be stronger than children and women. And, fourth, with children, a surplus must be produced to provide for their sustenance. This is particularly apparent when each person is (just) self-sufficient. Even if children are only dependent for a few years, it can still pose a considerable strain on a marginal society. The increased caloric intake needed for a pregnant woman, coupled with her inability to produce enough to sustain herself, was depicted as creating a drain on the small social units that were typical of Neanderthals (*The Neanderthals* 2000).

For these reasons, other things equal, a group who traveled and worked for an extended time period would tend to be comprised of independent equals. Although the society itself may be interdependent, those who did not pull their own weight would tend to be winnowed from the group. The PSU is comprised of an independent and a dependent person. It is vulnerable. Frank stated: "One person acting in isolation will never get far trying to raise a family" (1988, 66). Of course, the concept of marriage arose with the understanding of paternity. Without that understanding, there is less of an incentive from the male's perspective for long-term domestic specialization between him and a woman with a child. However, because of the vulnerability of the PSU, a female may prefer this kind of domestic specialization. One woman could share domestic chores with another female or females as well, but it is likely that there would also be responsibility for additional children with other females. Still, specialization with other females would be preferable to tending to oneself and one's children alone, since a division of labor among women could, through economies of scale, lead to the creation of a surplus—enough perhaps to provide for those children who could not be productive.

Unlike men, women, particularly women with children, tend to be less mobile. Since women tend to be encumbered with children, why then would a man remain (stationary) long-term in a community that included women if the concept of paternity is not understood? We are accustomed to thinking that love is a reason that a man may remain in a long-term domestic relationship with a woman or may want to remain in a community near a woman (as opposed to being mobile—primarily working with other men). (This dichotomy between being mobile and remaining stationary is an abstraction. The choice need not be either/or. However, by making it either/or, certain motivations or incentives can be isolated.) Before paternity was understood, there is some evidence that promiscuity (short-term interaction) was not uncommon. The idea of romantic love has evolved over time. When there was no understanding of paternity, the notion may have been less common if it existed at all. However, without an understanding of paternity, there is one male/female relationship that has duration, and that is between mother and son.

One reason men may remain long-term in a community that includes women might follow in part from the relationship that a son develops with his mother. This is the basic social unit (mother and child). If certain values are learned by the child—such as trust and respect for others—then there may be an incentive on the part of the child to engage in cooperative behavior with the mother as an adult. There most likely would be an emotional attachment to the mother as well. Emotional attachments need not be limited to the mother but may extend to siblings and others with whom a man may have formed cooperative bonds while growing up. In Rand's philosophy, love is an outgrowth of shared values. One objective of parenting is to instill values in one's offspring. If successful, one's offspring becomes the embodiment of one's own values. (I do not mean this narrowly, as will be clear later.) So the incentive for a man to remain in a cooperative environment with women may in the first instance be formed by the bond of values and affection he may share with the mother.

This is not an unreasonable conjecture since primitive societies are often matrilineal. Without the understanding of paternity, family can be defined along the mother's bloodline. The objective of the parent is, as Nathaniel Branden noted "to equip the child for independent survival as an adult" (1962, 55). This would be true in this setting as in a setting more socially advanced. This does not necessarily mean leaving family ties behind and going out on one's own. Family bonds can be strong. Shared values and customs (culture) can be cohesive.

Now the choice is not necessarily one of staying in one place (as women may be somewhat more inclined) or of being as mobile as one would like if one had no dependents or potential dependents. The choice may be to travel as a group. If seasons affect the migratory patterns of animals and the availability of vegetation, the whole group may be nomadic in response. Travel would be at a much slower pace with children in tow than if it were confined to a community of men, but the group would be more mobile, most likely, than if it consisted solely of women. Here I have examined some reasons why there may be cooperative ties within a group. This does not mean, however, that cooperation between groups will follow.

Group versus Group

The positive side of cooperative interaction includes the mutual benefits of trade, knowledge, friendship, and reproduction. Reciprocity can result in intragroup cohesiveness. Shared values may both encourage and bolster cooperation. Ridley acknowledged that there may also be a downside to group cohesion. If, as a group, cooperators separate themselves from others, another force evolves—"one that pits groups against each other, rather than individuals" (1996, 147).

Within the groups themselves, there will tend to be a division of labor. One of the primary divisions of labor appears to be that which is often seen between the sexes, (pre-agriculturally) hunting being the purview of males and gathering that of females. Ridley noted that this division has left its imprint on their relative skills (1996, 95). There is an overlap in the skills that are suitable for hunting and those that are required for protection. Men have largely assumed both roles. Protection of the group enables cohesion within the group. If men have reasons for remaining with women in groups, then the burden on protectors is greater, since those who cannot protect themselves—children—live with the group. It is in the self-interest of individuals to combine to form a stronger protective force than would exist if one were left to one's own devices. This would be true for both men and women. But if there are dependents—those who cannot pull their weight—the services provided by the protectors have "public good" characteristics.

Without an awareness of paternity, if a male assumes the role of protector, there may be an element of self-sacrifice on his part. He may perform the service anyway for a number of reasons. There may be a sense of gratitude he feels toward his mother, a desire to protect her as well as his younger siblings, even extending perhaps to his sister's children. This may not be purely "altruistic."

Growing up around others may have afforded the opportunity to perform reciprocal services, favors, and acts of kindness. These may continue into adulthood. So, although he may see himself as protecting unrelated others—dependents—he may also be protecting those for whom he has received, and may still be receiving, services. That is, it may spring from an overall sense of general reciprocity, or even reciprocity that is more specific in nature.

Now a rather naïve question is, why would a group of people need protection? As Ridley related, once groups are formed, the Hobbesian war continues, but between groups rather than between individuals. At least there is the potential for battles between factions once cooperation exists within groups. Axelrod, using the Tit-for-Tat strategy, showed how labeling can reinforce stereotyping. Once groups are identified by labels, and the strategy is for one to cooperate with one's kind but defect with all others, the labels become reinforcing. If one individual tries to deviate, he will be rebuffed and return to the stereotype expected. Axelrod noted an obvious indication that players are all worse off than they could be is that "mutual cooperation between the groups could have raised everyone's score" (1984, 148).

Ridley related that tribal societies tend to have a "them versus us" mentality. This tendency is particularly acute for what is termed a "fraternal-interest group," which is made up of related males and their wives and children. "[T]he more men stay in their native bands while women migrate, the more antagonism there is between groups. Matrilineal and matrilocal societies are a little less prone to feuding and warfare" (1996, 165). Ridley's conclusion was that men are more aggressive than women. So once paternity is understood and the shift is toward families being defined along patrilineal rather than matrilineal lines, the resulting groups will be more aggressive, since they are comprised of related, rather than unrelated, males. I think Ridley has a point. But I think an important factor may be the extent to which the group in question is nomadic, because I believe nomadic groups have a tendency to be more combative.

Patrilineal groups may permit this kind of mobility even more since, once paternity is recognized, a man would be more likely to form bonds with his family and therefore the group. Men are more mobile without families, so a group with men would tend to be more mobile than if it were limited to one of women (and children) only. Also, mobility requires protection, and men may feel more protective of the group once they recognize children as their own rather than as unrelated dependents of the group.

But why would a nomadic group need protection more than a group that is settled? Wouldn't a settled group be a "sitting duck," so to speak? Certainly a settled group could be. But if two groups are otherwise evenly matched, the settled group may have less reason to be challenged by other groups than one that is nomadic. I believe there may be a number of reasons for this. In nomadic cultures, ownership of land is less likely. Without ownership, disputes are more likely. Also, if groups are nomadic, onetime encounters with nongroup members are more likely. In onetime encounters, default is more likely. If default is expected of another, then it is more likely that one will be suspicious of another. This reinforces the tendency to default.

This tendency to defect in a Prisoner's Dilemma when one player is unlikely to encounter the other again was noted by Axelrod. According to him, anthropologists have found that Gypsies approach non-Gypsies suspiciously and vice versa (1984, 115). But if the temptation to cheat is greater for nomads, there may also be a greater chance that the slighted party may make the effort to seek out the defector and exact revenge. Nomadic cultures may be less likely to have a central enforcing authority to whom to turn in case of disputes. Disputes would then have to be resolved by the groups themselves. If each group must protect itself, rather than turning to specialists, more people may be involved in protection.

A point with respect to settled property was made by Sugden (1986, 96). Even if property rights have not been formalized in positive law, those who are settled on a piece of property (i.e., possess it) may feel justifiably emboldened to fight harder and/or longer to keep it if challenged. If this is generally recognized, then challengers may be less inclined to confront possessors. However, even after groups are no longer nomadic, if they have had a history of nomadic culture, ethics and traits favorable to retaliation may have been established. The effect of a perpetual conflict is that an enemy threat strengthens group identity and solidarity. Ridley stated group cohesion is advanced by having an external threat (1996, 174). Customs that emerge will tend to be perpetuated. One group may become more unlike the other.

Sacrifice

Ridley stated that humans have a tendency to form groups that are hostile with each other, and that groups successful at instilling cultural conformity perform better than ones that do not. Repetitive thoughts and actions are, it seems, "wired into our brains," so to speak. They also are reinforced, or can be, by our central nervous system. They are buoyed by emotion. Ritual is a way of establishing and reinforcing custom. Ridley credited anthropologist Lyle Steadman with the argument that ritual is not only about accepting tradition, but also encourages cooperation and sacrifice (Ridley 1996, 189). Customs that appear capricious, arbitrary, and even dangerous can arise, yet people follow them. Ridley recounted pressures that may generate cultural conformity. His five include: there is punishment for not following convention (which he calls fashion, and is not exactly the same thing as convention); there are rewards to following what others do; people are irrational sheep; everyone draws the same conclusion independently; and, some people (the "first" people) tell other people what to think. He dismissed all of these in one way or another and chose the safety of the herd. He also pointed out that it is less costly to do as others do, and, after all, others may be right (1996, 184–86). There may be truth in most of these. It is costly to go against the herd. The fear of alienation or worse is an effective stick.

There is also the carrot of approval, the feeling of belonging that accompanies following convention. Humans also realize that the truth is necessary for existence and that loved ones care for one's future and try to the best of their ability to pass on the truth. Each individual accepts a good deal of what they learn from others as truth partly because of this reason. It would be very costly to validate every piece of information one receives. There is also a stigma of going against the norm because sometimes those who do so are evil or insane. Not all deviations from the norm fall in this category, but humans have a tendency to categorize and sometimes fail to do so correctly. They may see a deviation from the norm as deviant. Those who may be considering a different path may be fearful that they are insane or abnormal or fear that others think they are. And, in order to go against convention, there must be some viable alternative. One must recognize that an alternative exists and also believe it to be possible as well as have the courage to follow through with it. If there were no negative repercussions from deviating from the norm, courage would not be a factor (Touchstone 1995, 93–102). Although conventions may or may not be useful or rational, it is easier in some sense to understand why people follow them than to understand how they arise in the first place.

Ridley noted that there is a tendency among people to become emotionally attached to groups, even those that seem to be arbitrary. However, even though we are extremely groupish, we are not "group-selected" in an evolutionary sense. Group selection means that individuals put the group's interest above their own. This is not our nature, according to Ridley. His view was that we are constructed "to exploit the group for ourselves" (1996, 188). If Ridley is right, that is, if we do enter cooperative relationships for our own interest, why then the association of tribal society with sacrifice?

Within the hierarchy of the group, the more powerful may be the protectors since their function is essential to the survival of the group if conflict is commonplace. They may be more influential in setting rules and customs. Thus, conventions (or, more accurately, customs) may not simply emerge but may be dictated. Axelrod showed, using the Prisoner's Dilemma, that hierarchies can be established and perpetuated (1984, 149). Why others go along with this is understandable for many reasons. Ridley dismissed fear as a reason (1996, 184–86), but it is a factor—particularly for the less powerful. Power, after all, is the ability to have others do as one would have them.

The idea behind ritualized sacrifice is to reinforce the necessity of sacrifice. Rand regarded the morality of sacrifice to be a tribal phenomenon (1982e, 50). Sacrifice implies a unilateral transfer, which in itself is not evil. It is the sacrifice of a greater value (the greatest being one's life) for a lesser (the group) that is evil. Why in a tribal society would sacrifice be seen as necessary? One could say sacrifice is necessary because one must sacrifice for the group through custom in order to get approval and stay in the good graces of the group, but that begs the question: Where did the idea of sacrifice arise in the first place? I think there may be two sources (although these need not be the only sources) in which there are unilateral transfers that are vital to the family/tribe and that may also have the added potential of being life-threatening.

One is related to "reproductivity" and the necessity of parents providing care for dependent children. Childbearing is potentially life-threatening, and childrearing requires the provision of unilateral transfer of benefits for a significant period of time. Another source for the idea of sacrifice is the protective service itself. Protection has the qualities of a public good and it is high risk. As Rand pointed out, the fundamental decision is between life and death, and all values can be traced to that decision. Protection involves risking one's life in a more immediate sense than some other types of productivity. One must be willing to do this and to do it on an ongoing basis. So the idea that one is risking one's life for others may seem more directly related to the idea of sacrifice for the group. Since protectors have a larger role in tribal culture, the idea of sacrifice may assume significance as a value. Self-sacrifice may gain importance as a trait or virtue. Since protectors may have influenced rules and customs, sacrifice may be prized and encouraged among others who have no particular need to regard themselves as otherwise sacrificing.

Not only may a protector perceive himself as being willing to risk his life for others, there is also the possibility that others may shirk. With the presence of dependents in the group, shirkers may be more difficult to identify and the group may even be less willing to banish them. This may strengthen the notion among protectors that they are sacrificing for the group. This could be a reason that the idea of the sacrifice on the part of others (who are not protectors) may gain strength in the minds of the protectors. If protectors are influential in making rules, the idea of the sacrifice of others may be formalized into custom, or ritualized. Ritualized sacrifice may not be thought of as entirely unilateral, but, in some sense, a way of "paying back." (Although it would be a stretch to call this a "social contract," this has elements of the basis for a "social contract.")

Property

Ridley (1996, 169) made the point that matrilineal or matrilocal groups tend to be less prone to intergroup friction. The implication is women are less warlike.

There are just as many men in matrilineal or matrilocal groups. The difference is that the men are less related by blood in the latter, so there is, presumably, less cohesiveness among them. This may be true; however, I think it may be the case that there could be less conflict among groups (that are evenly matched) if the groups are not nomadic. If they are not nomadic, then, whether patrilineal or matrilineal, there may be less need for protection. If there is less need for protection, then the protectors may have less power within the group. If they have less power within the group, they may have less influence on rules and customs. If they perceive themselves as sacrificing for the group, then this notion may not have as much weight in the value system. (Since protection is not the only form of sacrifice, there may be other sources for sacrifice to still be considered a value.) Other values, such as physical courage, will not be as extensively prized.

Although I believe that women as a gender may be inclined to be less mobile, I do not believe it is necessarily true that the reason people settle is because of women (the nesting hypothesis). Some accept the theory that "women were responsible for the development of agriculture, as an extension of their food-gathering activities" (Stone 1976, 3). According to Joseph Campbell in *Primitive Mythology*:

> Here it was the women who showed themselves supreme; they were not only bearers of children but also the chief producers of food. By realizing that it was possible to cultivate, as well as to gather, they had made the earth valuable and they became, consequently, its possessors. (Stone 1976, 19)

There are many reasons people may settle rather than be nomadic. Settling in one place allows for many things that mobility does not. The obvious benefits are the possibilities of sturdier dwellings and the cultivation of land. The reason I think it permits more cooperation among individuals, and perhaps groups of individuals, is that permanent proximity permits the possibility of future interaction, and the possibility of future interaction—as has been shown by Axelrod (1984, 161)—increases the possibility of cooperation. Another reason that cooperation may be fostered once societies are settled is that there are more likely to be settled rules of property in land. If so, there may be less or no conflict over the resource itself. Once the resource itself is no longer a source of conflict, then a firmer foundation for trade is established. The mutual benefits to trade can overcome other disinclinations to interact in noneconomic ways that may stem from cultural differences. There are other kinds of interaction. Marriage is one. Marriage tends to take place between individuals of similar background.

Groups define themselves in many ways. Individuals belong to many groups—a family, a religion/culture, a country. Tribal groups tend to define themselves by family lineage. Group coherence is furthered by common values and customs. That which connects the individual to the group may shift from the tribe to the culture. Once groups become settled in a specific geographic region, alliances with kin may gradually give way to alliances on the basis of territory. Richard Pipes noted that some primitive cultures that were bloodline-based also acknowledged geographical bonds. In England, during the seventh century, bonds of kinship were recognized, yet people who lived next to each other thought of themselves as related, whether they were or not. "The transition, therefore, may be marked not so much by the replacement of one system by another as by the emergence of the territorial principle from a subordinate to a dominant position (Pipes, 1999, 96). Ridley pointed out that Craig Palmer has argued that in large measure the notion of human groups is a myth. Although people think in terms of groups, they do not live separately in isolated groups. Ridley noted that groups tend to co-mingle. Even in patrilineal societies, some of the mother's culture is absorbed. "Human groups are fluid and impermanent" (Ridley 1996, 187).

Once a group is settled, there may still be the tendency to think in terms of group identity, and there may still be challengers to the "group" for one reason or another. But for two equally matched groups, the possessor of property may have an edge over a challenger on his own turf in battle. Simple familiarity of the region may be one reason. Another, as Sugden pointed out, is that a possessor may fight harder than a challenger because of his attachment to it (1986, 93). A challenger, on the other hand, may not fight as hard if he does not believe he has the moral edge. This knowledge—that the possessors have a psychological edge and that this may give them an edge in battle—may have a deterrent effect—at least on an equally matched opponent.

With intermarriage come potential changes in customs, values, and ideas. But once land is settled, marriage also has another effect. It results in a combining of property outside bloodlines. This forms bonds that may not otherwise exist and may form the basis for reciprocity—cooperation in the form of trade. Customs that are arbitrary, capricious, and even harmful may be broken down somewhat by marriage, communication, and trade. Bonds formed when property in land is involved may form a firmer foundation for trade. Trade and marriage may offer opportunities for individuals to become aware of alternative ideas and customs. One reason some ideas are accepted as true is because of lack of awareness of alternatives. Even with awareness, the alternatives may not seem viable. Encounters with other cultures allow for observation of alternatives. This does not mean that capricious or dangerous customs of a culture will be abandoned, but there may be an erosive effect on them over time.

Of course, once land becomes cultivated (along with domestication of animals and animal husbandry), the need for hunting eventually is lessened, and the skills that it requires are also lessened. These skills overlap those necessary for protection. If the need for protection and the skills it subsumes are lessened, then the protection function may be specialized even further so that all or nearly all young men are no longer expected to contribute. (The transfer of the protection function to government is one view of the "social contract" to be considered in chapter 10.) This has a freeing effect upon those who were formerly pigeonholed into this function, permitting them now to pursue other types of work. It also may shift the power base within the culture from protectors to those engaged in cultivation and perhaps to those engaged in trade. This too can have an effect on the customs abandoned, adopted, and perpetuated. (It is also true that mobility, not "nomadity," can have an effect of eroding customs as evidenced once the nailed horseshoe was introduced (see Spiegel 1971, 51).) Values related to self-sufficiency and independence may gain in esteem and those pertaining to physical courage and sacrifice may be regarded as important but may take different forms or be less extensively practiced.

Implications for Decision-Making

One implication of this analysis, as I see it, is that the female thinks of life beyond her own life. Part of this tie is physical (biological) because of the very nature of procreation. Another is that when she raises the child and instructs him in her values, he becomes the embodiment of her values. Her values have a potential existence beyond her own life. So there is an incentive to think in terms of consumption and production beyond one's own life. This would have implications beyond those found for the hardtack example discussed earlier for a single castaway. More generally, production and consumption decisions would not be limited to one's life, but may also include bequests.

Once groups of individuals are settled, and the land they settle becomes part of the decision process, it too may lengthen the time horizon for the individual. Land has a permanence that other resources (including human beings) do not. So if an individual starts to regard a piece of land as his own, he may extend his decision-making time horizon beyond that of his own life simply because land extends beyond his life. The question becomes one of what happens to the land beyond one's life. To whom does it belong?

CHAPTER SEVEN

Rights: Positive and Negative

According to Objectivists and classical liberals, negative rights—the right to noninterference—are basic natural rights (Rand 1964h, 94). Positive rights—claim rights—involve others and are secondary, derivative rights that do not apply to everyone (Den Uyl and Rasmussen 1991, 107). They may be the result of bilateral (or multilateral) consent or contract. Murray Rothbard's position on positive rights was more restrictive than Rand's. To him, because a person cannot alienate his will, children have no positive right to care (1998, 100). Whatever a parent would do on a child's behalf would thus be classified as a gift or charity. Parents can neglect their children if they wish. He dismissed the causality argument for the positive right to childcare, one to which Objectivists subscribe (N. Branden, 1962, 55). Besides consent and contract, there are other bases for positive rights. Whenever there is a forced unilateral transfer involving a person's property or person, whether intentional or due to avoidable neglect, the victim has a positive right to redress—either proportional retribution or compensation. Roger Bissell's (1981, 30) case for childcare by parents is a liability argument. This is a valid argument; however, it puts childbirth in the category of being an act of aggression against the child. The liability argument is that the helplessness of one person was created by the actions of another, because the former's rights were violated by the latter. I argue that the positive right to childcare is a basic right. It is unilateral in nature, not reciprocity-based, as would be a positive right based on trade or on the prior infringement of a negative right.

To Rand, the basis for rights is man's rational faculty. Reason is man's means of survival. He must be free to use his mind (Rand 1967a, 17). In this chapter, I attempt to define what life is—that is, whether it is a biological event or a metaphysical phenomenon. I weigh in on the former. I make two additional cases for positive rights. Both relate to children and those with diminished capacity. Objectivists and classical liberals would say that, when these individuals' rights are violated by their caregivers, others may take over guardianship as long as it is voluntary (Machan 1975, 178). My (stronger) case for positive rights is based on the argument that if an individual in this circumstance cannot care for himself, and no one else agrees to, then the person would be in a position of trespass, but would not be culpable because of lack of a fully functioning rational capacity. Rand (Berliner 1995, 560) has said that the legal system applies to rationally capable adults—if someone can be "proved" to be insane, then he can be put in an asylum. I broaden this to include those with less than a fully functioning rational capacity, and I include other nonpunitive care facilities in addition to asylums.

The weak case for positive rights assumes that all individuals (who do not violate others' rights) have full negative rights regardless of their rational capacity. Since coercion is a violation of a person's negative rights, then if any of a person's rights were withheld (due to a less than fully functional rational capacity), this would be unjustifiably punitive. It would follow that the person would be entitled to a positive right to redress—compensation commensurate with that which is denied.

What a Right Is—Negative Rights

To Rand, a right is a right to action. It is "the moral sanction of a *positive*" (1964h, 94): to act on one's own uncoerced, independent judgment. The obligation that rights impose is *negative*: not to infringe on the rights of others (1964h, 94). Rothbard echoed this "negative" aspect of rights, stating that no man can compel another to perform a positive act (1998, 100). Machan and Den Uyl and Rasmussen agreed that rights to life, liberty, and property are negative (Machan 1998a, 121–22; Den Uyl and Rasmussen 1991, 107). Positive rights impose duties on a person *vis-à-vis* a rights-holder. Positive rights are not basic (Machan 1998a, 122). Basic rights are those that are "not derivable from other rights" (Den Uyl and Rasmussen 1991, 82).

Equal Rights

To Rand, each and every man has the same rights at all times (n.d., 6). This view is shared by classical liberals. Machan stated that, within the context of human nature, all men are "equal in moral capacities" (1975, 247). Natural law and natural rights provide the basis, according to Machan, for justice, which includes as its tenet that all men are equal under the law (1975, 165). Herbert Spencer examined the question of the alternative to equal (negative) rights. If rights were unequal, how would the relative assignments be gauged? What is the basis for assigning less than equal rights for one person relative to another? What is the unit by which this is to be measured? (Spencer [1892] 1954, 100) In similar fashion, Rothbard's argument for 100 percent self-ownership shares commonalities with the case Spencer made for his law of equal freedom. If one is not entitled to full ownership of oneself, Rothbard asked, what are the alternatives? The alternatives are that either an equal portion of ownership of each person is vested in all other persons (universal and equal other-ownership), or there is partial ownership of one group by another. The second alternative cannot serve as a universal principle of natural law. The first alternative, although theoretically universal, would in practice reduce to the second because of the unwieldiness of its implementation (Rothbard 1998, 45–46).

Source of Rights

To Rand, the source of rights is the law of identity. Rights provide the conditions for man's survival (Rand 1961a, 182). Rights, to Rand, are primarily a requirement of man's mind—his rational faculty—because his survival depends on reason (1967a, 17). In a similar vein, Rothbard claimed that man's rights follow from his nature—his capacity to reason and make conscious decisions (1998, 155). In contrast, to Den Uyl and Rasmussen, rights "seek to protect the self-directedness or autonomy of every individual in the political community" (1991, 82).

Natural Rights/Negative Rights

Although rights pertain to action (and only to action) (Rand 1964h, 93), they are not conduct. They are, according to Rand, "conditions of existence" (1961a, 182). Rights have been described as boundary setting. To Den Uyl and Rasmussen, they are conditions that define a "sphere of moral territory" (1991, 104). Similar to Nozick, Machan viewed rights as providing a "sphere of moral jurisdiction" (1998a, 122).

Den Uyl and Rasmussen stated that by "natural rights" they mean those that exist "prior to any convention or agreement, regardless of whether someone is a member of a particular society or community" (1991, 83). Although natural rights exist separate from custom or convention, there is a connection between natural rights and law. To Rand: "*Individual rights are the means of subordinating society to moral law*" (1964h, 92). Den Uyl and Rasmussen's position differed from Rand's in that she regarded rights as moral principles, that is, as providing behavioral guidance (1991, 111). Den Uyl and Rasmussen saw rights as meta-normative principles. They said that rights provide the normative foundation for positive law. They give guidance and justification for the development of a constitution (1991, 112).

Den Uyl and Rasmussen believed "rights are negative because they stem, in the first instance, from an obligation to self" (1991, 107). Since morality is expressed through the perfection of self, according to Den Uyl and Rasmussen, rights are needed "to provide the individual with a context for eudaimonic achievement" (1991, 108). Machan saw rights as negative because their function is to provide a sphere of moral space, since individuals "have moral tasks in life that they ought to fulfill" (1998a, 122). Rand did not see rights as being *for* a purpose (Berliner 1995, 365). The link between rights, rationality, and life is much more tenuous in Den Uyl and Rasmussen's approach to rights than in Rand's. For Den Uyl and Rasmussen the link between rights and virtue is more direct. Their emphasis is on virtue. Rand's emphasis was on man's survival (*qua* man) (1961a, 182). One can lose the thread of her argument if the focus becomes self-perfection (eudaimonia). The link between purpose and survival can be lost in Den Uyl and Rasmussen's conception of man's ultimate end.

Positive Rights

To Rand, the sole obligation rights impose is to respect others' rights (1967h, 227). Den Uyl and Rasmussen claimed that a right is not a moral claim or entitlement (1991, 107). Rights must have "universal and uniform application" (1991, 84). Positive rights are special rights. Den Uyl and Rasmussen stated that positive rights are reflective of obligations. They are other-oriented (1991, 107). They do not apply to everyone. Rights are concerned only with the universal (1991, 113), according to Den Uyl and Rasmussen. Positive rights are particular and contingent. Rights, therefore, must be negative (1991, 83).

Positive rights are derived through consent, according to Den Uyl and Rasmussen, although they were hesitant "to claim that *all* positive norms will be a function of consent. The special relationships (such as parent to child) one may have with others may imply certain obligations that are not easily reducible to consent alone" (1991, 107). Objectivists acknowledge that children are entitled to receive childcare from their parents by right (N. Branden 1962, 55).

Right to Do What Is Right

Mack (1986, 153) stated that Rand could be interpreted as believing that man has rights so that he may do what is right. She said: "'[I]t is *right* for [man] to use his mind, it is *right* to act on his own free judgment, it is *right* to work for his values and to keep the product of his work'" (1961a, 182). This sounds as if man has the right to do only that which is right. This is not what Rand meant, however. She made it clear that man is not infallible. He must be free so that he may decide—but he may be right or wrong. Freedom protects this right to be wrong so long as it does not infringe on the rights of another.

Rand specified that rights are conditions of existence. They are not the conduct within those conditions. Rights are rights to action, but they are not the actions themselves. They are rights to action within prescribed limits. Thus when Rand said that rights are right for individuals, she was not referring to right actions on the part of those individuals. What is meant is that rights are conditions that are right for man. They are right in that they are the conditions necessary (although not sufficient) for his survival.

In my view, by recognizing rights as conditions instead of actions, one avoids the problems posed by Den Uyl and Rasmussen. Although rights are conditions, not ethics, per se, this does not mean that one cannot reason that one should not kill (or steal from) another person in the same way that one might reason that one should not lie. The ethic that one should not kill another person may follow along the logic that Rand used against parasitism as a course of action. Parasitism in any form is not, in the long run, life-enhancing. One line of reasoning that would lead to this conclusion could be to look at what leads to long-term success. Another approach would be to use a process of abstraction and ask what would be required of a person alone on a desert island, then conclude that once man lives among other men, those requirements do not change. A third approach (one that is not attributable to Rand as an argument) would be to look at the long-term benefits of cooperating with other people. Retaliation could be reasoned as well. Not killing others and retaliating if one has been attacked (or one's property damaged) by another are ethics that can be reasoned. Ethics are expressed in terms of action. Rights are expressed in terms of conditions, although they limit and sanction action (Rand 1964h, 93–94). (Even though rights are not virtues, having rights and having them observed are values, and violating a right is an ethical breach.)

Primacy of Will? Discussion

Gregory Johnson and David Rasmussen stated: "The conceptual sleight of hand by which Rand reduces man's life to freedom reveals a contradiction in her account of the relationship of reason and the will" (Johnson and Rasmussen 2000, 256). One problem with Rand's ethics, as Johnson and Rasmussen saw it, is that one is said to choose to be rational. The question is how does one choose to be rational without using reason? This is where ethics meets epistemology.

Philosophers have turned to the cognitive sciences for insights into this question. I will not review those here. All I will address is one small aspect of that discussion—that is, that humans are not born with fully developed cognitive skills. It is very likely that actions initially are not entirely self-directed. Actions could be entirely random or simply responsive to stimuli. If they are random (or even if they are not), there may be some error-reduction learning process involved, based on feedback from the environment (reality). That is, some learning may be "trial and error." However, by their nature, humans have the capacity for choice. This means they can make the wrong choice (Boydstun 1996, 202; Boydstun 1994,

127). They can choose to ignore the feedback from their environment. One could say that the choice not to ignore feedback from one's environment (that is, not to ignore reality) is rational. This is one way of learning. The fact that humans do not automatically respond to their environment can work to their advantage, however. That is, the fact that humans may persist in behavior that results in negative consequences may be a way of learning—at least within certain parameters. Mark Twain's adage about the cat is revealing in this respect; that is, if a cat sits on a hot stove, he will never again sit on a hot stove, but he will never sit on a cold one either. Cats could be said to "overgeneralize." In this respect, humans are not as quick to "learn" as cats.

Does this mean that humans continue to learn by trial and error as they mature? No. What they may eventually learn from these experiences is that if they learn (gather information) before they act, instead of acting first, they may be better off. However, learning up front takes effort. In the long run, it may take more effort to learn (assuming one does) by relying solely on one's mistakes than if one were to put in the effort to gather information before taking action, but this is a lesson a person may refuse to learn. Thus the decision becomes, whether one puts forth the effort to gather information to make a decision. This is the decision before the decision. (Reason does not necessarily involve gathering more information. It may involve choosing not to ignore the information one already has. The effort involved would be that needed to face the facts of reality one already is aware of—but evades—and using one's rational faculty to make a choice based on that.)

The other issue Johnson and Rasmussen addressed is that, since choice precedes reason, will must be primary. Their argument seems to be that because will is primary (precedes reason), the basis for rights is the individual's will, not reason. Den Uyl and Rasmussen regarded volition and reason as, "not two separate faculties but distinct aspects of the same conscious act" (1991, 93). Den Uyl and Rasmussen saw rights as being based on the "rightness" of volition (1991, 92–96), and in that respect, they would have been in agreement with Johnson and Rasmussen. To Rand, man's volition (free will) "is an attribute of his consciousness (of his rational faculty)" (1982d, 25). Like Den Uyl and Rasmussen, she regarded volition (free will) as an aspect of rationality.

Unlike Rand (at least, my interpretation of her), Den Uyl and Rasmussen regarded volition as a virtue, however. Den Uyl and Rasmussen said that self-directedness or autonomy is "*the* virtue which makes all other virtues possible" (1991, 113). Volition is choice; it is not chosen (1991, 74). Virtue involves making the right choice. Thus, I do not think volition is a virtue, as did Den Uyl and Rasmussen. They linked volition to virtue since it is inherent in every virtuous act (1991, 94); however, it is also present in every evil act. In that respect, it is like sensation. One does not choose to have sensations. They, too, are an aspect of cognition. Freedom is the right to exercise one's free will. But the basis for rights is man's rational capacity, not his free will alone, because his free will is not his means of survival.

Rand as Reductionist: Discussion

Johnson and Rasmussen's criticism of Rand was that her approach was reductionist; specifically, she reduced both creativity and freedom to reason, and replaced reason with will in her theory of rights (2000, 254–55). Freedom is the condition necessary to exercise one's free will. Freedom is a social concept. It relates to the degree to which others in society can interfere with the exercise of a person's will. A man has volition when he is alone. He cannot be said to have freedom alone. Volition is a part of man's cognition. It is not social in nature. Nature (exclusive of man) limits one's free will. A person must accept reality—he cannot change physical laws by an act of will. Freedom's boundaries are dictated by human nature. Freedom protects free will, the freedom to act on one's will, but only within limits set by the rights of others.

Reason is not a choice among alternatives; it is the best choice among alternatives that one is capable of making. Man is capable of error. One's rights are not confined to doing only what is right. One has the right to do something wrong so long as it does not infringe on another's rights. Still, even if another person is not adversely affected by one's actions, if one does something that is wrong, there are consequences. The consequence is that one's self is affected. That is what is meant by a wrong action. It has adverse consequences. If an action were neutral in its effects, it would have no moral content. Behavior that is wrong ultimately affects one's survival. So one has an incentive to try to determine what is right and to do it. One has that incentive because right behavior is life affirming. Freedom is important in that with it one must accept the consequences of his actions; he cannot shift them to someone else.

Reason is the means by which we learn about reality and deal with it. It governs our good (i.e., realistic) choices. In Rand's view, man's creativity is at the root of all progress. But she did not say that freedom is needed to protect man's creativity—although it is. Creativity is an outgrowth and an aspect of man's reasoning ability. He must understand the material elements of the world, their laws and properties, to innovate or to create. He must be able to choose and to act on his choices. Productive purpose is the central value in Rand's ethics. The virtue—productivity—requires rationality, but it cannot be reduced to reason. Reason is required for every virtue. It is the primary value. But Rand's epistemology makes it clear that reason is a mental process. It is the means of knowledge. Rand defined production as "the application of reason to the problem of survival" (1967a, 17). Productive work requires mental effort, but productive work must be embodied. Creation is defined as "the power to bring into existence an arrangement (or combination or integration) of natural elements that had not existed before" (1982b, 25). To be realized, material elements are required.

Mature Manifestation

Rand limited rationality to its mature manifestation, that of the adult. Den Uyl and Rasmussen made the related comment that to understand living organisms, it is necessary to understand their *mature* state of being (1991, 44). Machan claimed that negative rights "provide *adult* persons with a sphere of moral jurisdiction" (1998a, 122). Rothbard asserted that the self-ownership right of each individual "has been established for *adults*"(1998, 97). [Italics added in above quotes.] Spencer, unlike the others quoted above, regarded *all* individuals as having equal rights under the law.

Spencer maintained that a rule, such as equal freedom, permits no exceptions. Referring to British law at that time, he said that the basis for the unequal treatment of women was that women were considered mentally inferior. He challenged this in two ways: first, arguing that women are not mentally inferior; then stating that if rights between the two sexes are to be assigned on the basis of relative intelligence, then the same criterion should be applied among males ([1892] 1954, 140–41). The true basis for unequal treatment of women, Spencer maintained, is not their intelligence or lack of it, but a belief that "women have no souls" ([1892] 1954, 143).

The law of equal freedom also applies to children, said Spencer. Rights are derived from faculties. The fact that a child's faculties may not be as developed as the adult's is immaterial. The rights of children and adults are equal, whether or not their faculties are. The child has a right to exercise what faculties he possesses ([1892] 1954, 156–57). If children are not accorded the same rights as adults, then there remains the problem of trying to determine at what point a child becomes an adult. Spencer found it impossible to definitively draw a line between childhood and adulthood. There is also the problem that if children do not have rights, then infanticide, child slavery, etc. are permissible ([1892] 1954, 154). Since rights are negative, it would follow that, like an adult, a child would have a zone within which no one can interfere—whether that zone is limited to one's own person or to his person as well as his property. Any coercion is wrong in that it violates the child's rights ([1892] 1954, 158). This includes coercive education and any form of coercive punishment ([1892] 1954, 168), according to Spencer.

Rothbard's position on the negative rights of children would appear to be the same as Spencer if one were to confine his remarks to those in which he said that, once born, each infant, by virtue of being a separate existent and potential adult, has the negative right not to be aggressed against by his parents—that is, not "mutilating, torturing him, etc." (1998, 100). Spencer permitted no exceptions—children cannot be coerced, period. Rothbard seems to have left wiggle room for what might be regarded as coercion in that he said, since parents own their home, they "have the right to set down rules" (1998, 103) for their children and others who live there.

A further reading of Rothbard makes clear that he did not believe children own themselves in the full sense. He said the parent(s), in particular the mother, since only she is the certain parent, is the owner of the baby by virtue of being his creator. An infant is not a self-owner in any sense of the term (1998, 99). He is instead a "*potential* self-owner" (1998, 97). What does this ownership by the mother entail? Ownership is the right to acquire, use, and dispose of an object. It is the right to action with respect to an object. How then does the mother (parents) acquire a child? In the same way that original property is acquired in Rothbard's theory, and that is by homesteading. The mother is the "natural or 'homesteading' owner" (1998, 99). But parents do not have 100 percent ownership of the child. For the child, self-ownership is exclusively limited to the right not to be aggressed against his person and the "absolute right to run away or to leave home at any time" (1998, 104). Children, then, have negative rights.

Rothbard meant two things insofar as ownership by parents is concerned. One is that others may not seize the child by force. Thus, seizing a child by force is not a violation of the child's right not to be aggressed against, but a violation of the parents' right to the child (1998, 99). If the right to ownership were truly limited to negative rights of the child, then the parental right in this regard would appear to be an extra layer of rights that is redundant. The second respect in which parents own their children, according to Rothbard, relates to the ownership right of disposal. Recall that disposal through exchange requires the voluntary consent of the parties to the exchange. Here is where it must be acknowledged that children are in some way different from adults. Parents, according to Rothbard, have the right to sell their children. The children are not regarded as parties to the exchange. They are that which is exchanged. The selling of adults is a violation of their rights. But children, without their consent, may be exchanged. Rothbard noted that such exchanges already take place but at a zero price, i.e., adoption (1998, 103–104). Rothbard's position is, in effect if not intent, that "any state interference in the autonomy of families should be anathema" (Hoppe 1998, xli). It would appear that it is the family, not the individual, who has rights.

However, the right of ownership of children by parents is limited. It is limited in *kind*, Rothbard said. The idea that a libertarian who held the principle of self-ownership would support the parent's right to kill or torture his child "would be grotesque" (1998, 100). In addition to being limited in kind, it is also limited in *time*. Otherwise, a middle-aged adult would be under the exclusive legal control of his aged parent, a situation Rothbard found bizarre (ibid.).

Even though Rand, Machan (Rand n.d., 6; Machan 1975, 165), and Spencer ([1892] 1954, 25) stated that all men were equal under the law, and Rothbard argued that individuals had 100 percent self-ownership, Rothbard claimed that children have less than 100 percent self-ownership. This contradicts his statement that there is no viable alternative to full ownership (1998, 45–46). However, if rights are limited to the right not to be aggressed against, then children cannot be said to have 100 percent ownership of themselves, depending on what is meant by aggression. If aggression is an action upon a person to which he has not consented, and if transfer of care from one guardian to another without the consent of the person being transferred qualifies, then a child cannot be said to have full negative rights. There is a second circumstance under which force may be used against a child, depending upon one's definition of force. That is, he may be forcibly evicted from the home in which he lives. Rothbard said that the child must abide by the parents' rules so long as he stays in the home. Just as Rothbard did not set an age when a child becomes an adult or when he can leave home, he set no age concerning when a child can (or cannot) be forcibly evicted from his parents' home. Thus, there is nothing (from the perspective of rights) to prevent the parent from forcibly evicting a child regardless of age and from doing whatever is necessary to prevent the child from returning home.

Rothbard said that a child has full ownership rights in himself once they are demonstrated in nature; that is, when he leaves home (1998, 103). This can occur at any age and the parent cannot compel the child to return. If there is no virgin space on which the child may homestead (which is the presumed situation [1998, 55, 244–45]), then the child would have to live on property owned by others. This requires the consent of the property owner. If a child leaves home because he has found a place to live (say, he is five and the next-door neighbor entices him with a puppy), what is to prevent the parents from regarding this as a seizure of the child? Recall that the parents have exclusive trustee ownership unless they voluntarily transfer it to someone else. Yet, Rothbard said that regardless of age the child has a right to leave home. It is the child's absolute right. But is it?

Rothbard pointed out that when an exchange is made, what is being exchanged is rights to ownership (1998, 36). In a free market there is a voluntary exchange of ownership titles (1998, 36, 41, 133). To be consistent, for trustee ownership, there should be a contract to specify the exchange of ownership (1998, 103). A parent does not have to have a title of ownership to acquire a child since that ownership is based on "homesteading." However, if a child is exchanged, it would seem to follow that a title of ownership would be required. As long as the parent holds the title, then it would seem that if the child—voluntarily or involuntarily—transferred to another household without the parents' (owners') transfer of title to either the child or the person on whose property the child will live, the transfer can be viewed as seizure of the parents' property. (I do not agree with this, since I do not think children are the property of their parents.)

Alienability, Restitution, and Indentured Servitude

Rothbard claimed that a transfer of title of ownership, that is, a contract, is only valid and binding for property that is *alienable* by man (Rothbard 1993, 134; Evers 1978, 7–8). All tangible property qualifies as alienable (Rothbard 1998, 134). The concept of inalienability, according to Den Uyl and Rasmussen, means that one cannot surrender that which is inherently essential to human nature—that is, human reason and volition (1991, 84). Rothbard said that this means that a person cannot sell himself into voluntary slavery since he would be surrendering his will in advance (1998, 40–41).

An anarcho-capitalist, Rothbard opposed any form of government, even the "minimalist" state accepted by some libertarians as necessary. Thus, contracts are enforced by individuals themselves. If a contract is broken, or if someone attempts to take property by force instead of through voluntary contract, the damaged party would have recourse through a private court and police system or he could "take the law into his own hands" (Rothbard 1998, 90–91). The victim's right to restitution or retribution follows from his right to self-defense. The debt that is owed is to the victim, not to "society." For nonassault grievances, restitution is appropriate. If the criminal cannot pay, he should be forced to work until restitution to the victim has been satisfied. With regard to the latter case, Rothbard stated that ideally, the criminal is placed into a position of enslavement to the victim—that is, "just slavery"—until redress has been made (1998, 86).

Machan regarded punishment as "like the payment of a debt or the delivery on a promise: it is the logical, moral consequence of a freely chosen act" (1975, 248). If restitution is paid to the victim rather than the criminal paying "society," then the loss of freedom is not *like* the payment of a debt, it *is* in fact the payment of a debt. Rothbard's state-of-nature analysis makes this clear.

Children—No Positive Rights

Rothbard claimed that the only legal right a person has in a free society is not to be aggressed against and he is only legally obligated to respect the negative rights of another. Thus, a parent has no legal right to aggress against his child; however he has no "*legal obligation*" to care for his children since this would require positive acts. "[T]he parent should have the legal right *not* to feed the child, i.e., to allow it to die" (1998, 100). Rothbard responded to two arguments for why children should have a legal right to be kept alive by their parents (1998, 101).

They are (1) the argument from helplessness and (2) the argument from creation. Both of these reasons were given by Branden for parents having an obligation to support their children (1962, 55).

The argument from need alone does not hold up insofar as rights are concerned since rights are negative—noninterference (Rothbard 1998, 101). Rothbard dismissed the argument from creation since parents can sell or give away their children and the guardians then would not have created the child. Thus guardians would not be legally required to take care of their children if they had not created them. Also, Rothbard asked, if creation were an accepted rationale, when would the obligation stop? The obvious response is, when the child becomes an adult. But Rothbard asked, why stop then? (1998, 102)

To address these issues, I return to Rothbard's own previous statements. If there is a right to care for a child by a parent (or any guardian), then that right would be transferred with guardianship. This would be no different than for any other property. If a person homesteads a piece of land, then all of the rights and obligations are transferred with new ownership. This is why one checks to see if there is a lien against a piece of property before one purchases it. The question of why obligation would stop with adulthood of the child is no different or more complex than why 100 percent self-ownership is acquired in adulthood, adulthood being defined by Rothbard as when a child leaves home. These responses both assume that the parent is responsible for the child; they do not justify that responsibility.

The next argument in favor of positive rights for children that Rothbard addressed was the "contract" argument. The rationale for this argument is that the consensual act of the parents in having a child creates a (implied) contract that obligates parents to support the child. Rothbard (1998, 103) dismissed this argument for many of the same reasons that he dismissed the arguments against abortion. His arguments are consistent with those of Evers (1978, 7–8). Rothbard's contention was that such a "contract" would have to be with the fetus (1998, 103). The mother, even though she may have consented to the conception of the child, has not entered a contract. At best this would be in the nature of a promise and Rothbard did not regard promises as enforceable. Secondly, there could be no contract per se "since the fetus (fertilized ovum?) can hardly be considered a voluntary and consciously contracting entity" (1998, 98).

Even if it were granted that there was a contract, one's will is inalienable, according to Rothbard. Within libertarian theory, slave contracts are impermissible (ibid.). Since the will is inalienable, it follows that anyone has the right, regardless of promise or contract, to quit his job at any time. This would mean that the Armed Forces draft, as well as enlistments, would be illegal in a libertarian society. A soldier could, legally and without fear of punishment, desert or go AWOL at any time. "[E]very man has the right to change his mind at any time over the disposition of his body and will" (1998, 136–37). When an exchange takes place, there is an exchange of titles of ownership—a contract. But one can transfer only that which is alienable. One's labor is alienable, but one's will is not.

This creates a big problem for an exchange economy since what is often being exchanged is labor services. Contracts are necessary because there is oftentimes a delay between payment and receipt of services. However, if what is being traded are titles to ownership, then what title is attached to labor services? Taken literally, it would seem that there could be no transfer of labor services at all since there is no transfer of title of ownership of labor. Although Rothbard (1998, 138) did not address this inconsistency directly, he did offer a way to deal with this dilemma, and that is by way of a penal (or performance) bond. This is a promise that a worker will pay a certain amount of money if he does not follow through on a contract. One's will is not alienable, but money is. This discourages the worker from bailing out on a contract without requiring him to alienate his will.

Libertarians Rothbard and Evers apparently recognized some situations in which a person may not simply quit a job whenever he feels like it. One example would be the case of an airplane pilot who "bails out on a whim, leaving the passengers to crash" (Evers 1978, 3). The pilot's agreement to fly others creates a legal duty founded on the creation of peril. However, even in these cases, Evers noted, "the supposed duty to aid the imperiled does not have the property of universality, a property which legitimate legal duties (such as the duty *not* to assault) possess because they are generalizations based on the nature of man and reality" (ibid.).

Whether acknowledged by Rothbard and Evers or not, duties may arise without the consent of the person who is responsible for an obligation. In the case of liability for another's injuries (loss of pay and other compensation) in which a car accident is caused by an intoxicated driver, the driver does not have to agree to be responsible. Intent is not an issue either. Concerning reproduction, Evers stated that he doubted "whether it is proper to call sexual activity a consciously purposive act intending procreation" (1978, 7). But in the case of a car accident that causes bodily injury to another innocent driver or pedestrian, one's intent is immaterial for the most part. Bissell pointed out that: "The right to child support . . . springs from the same basic source as the right to compensation for disablement when caused by someone else" (1981, 30).

In the case of the injured party to a car accident caused by a drunk driver, the drunk driver by his actions has violated another's rights. He has injured the victim's person (right to life) and if the victim was also a motorist, his vehicle (right to property). So one can become responsible for another's care without entering into a contract in the same way one is responsible if he robs another's home or assaults him. One could argue that, unlike the liability argument involving the drunk driver and a victim, in the case of reproduction, a parent has not violated the child's rights. If a drunk motorist hits a pedestrian, it is an act of aggression (whether intentional or not). Where is the violation in the case of childbirth? When a person is forced to act without his consent, his negative rights are violated (Rand n.d., 6). If positive rights are restricted to those specified by Rothbard, then since a child does not give his consent when born, the only alternative is that his negative rights are violated. Birth, by this reasoning, is an act of aggression against a child, since the child is forced to be born without his voluntary agreement.

An alternative to birth being an act of aggression against a child is that there is implied consent. If one accepts the contract idea and thinks of procreation as an implied contract with the child, then there is an implied exchange. The nature of the exchange is the child belongs to the parent (in a custodial sense), and the parent cares for the child until the child acquires self-ownership. The child then would have an implied claim on the parent until reaching maturity. If the implied contract theory applies, then Rothbard's second objection to the idea that a child has a claim for parental care is that such a contract would not be valid anyway because one's will is inalienable. With other contracts for labor, one could deal with this problem by a performance (or penal) bond. If the worker reneged, the contracting party would not have the labor services, but its equivalent—its dollar value. In the case of the care of a child that might translate into a trust fund, a fund to be used in the event that the parents cannot or will not take care of their child.

For now, I'll avoid the problem that one cannot explicitly contract with an infant because such an agreement would be impossible to negotiate. Consider any labor contract for which one puts up a performance or penal bond to be paid in the event one reneges. Suppose one reneges on the bond, what recourse does the claimant have? Like any other default or theft, the claimant has a right to recompense. In Rothbard's view, if payment cannot be in the form of cash (restitution), then it should be in the form of labor. One becomes the "just slave" of the creditor until the debt is repaid (1998, 86). Thus, although voluntary slavery contracts may not be explicitly recognized, they can be achieved in effect through a circuitous route. A person may not be able to alienate his will contractually, but he is still responsible for his actions if he defaults on a debt, and can thereby become an involuntary servant to another until the debt is repaid.

If one accepts the implied contract argument for parental care of one's child, then what recourse is there if the parent defaults on the contract and does not feed his infant? In Rothbard's theory, if someone has defaulted on a contract (or otherwise violates a person's rights), it is up to the victim to seek recourse. The victim may take the law into his own hands, or he may rely on a private agency. According to implied contract argument, the parent is responsible for the care of the child; this would include seeking justice on the child's behalf. But if the parent is the one who has defaulted, he would have no incentive to do so. Thus, in effect, Rothbard would be correct. The child would not have a positive right to care.

Children: No Negative Rights Either

If someone harms or abuses or kills a child, it is the child's rights that have been violated, but it is also the parent's rights—the right to ownership of the child (according to Rothbard). The child has the right to seek justice, but, because he is helpless, he cannot. The parent has the right to seek justice if someone harms the child. In Rothbard's thinking, this would be a positive act and therefore not required of the parent (1998, 100). It is even doubtful that another person could do this on a child's behalf, if, as mentioned, "any state interference in the autonomy of families should be anathema" (Hoppe 1998, xli). If the parents are the abusers, there is no requirement that the parent seek redress on behalf of the child, nor would there be an incentive for the parents to do so. Not only does the child have no positive rights to care; in effect, the child has no negative rights to noninterference if it is the parents who are the rights violators.

Even if it is argued that the child has a positive right to care from the parents (based on either the liability argument or the implied contract argument), if the parents are the abusers, the child has a positive right for the parents to seek justice on his behalf, but the parents have no incentive to do so. If the parent is the abuser, not only does the child, in effect, have no positive right to care, he has no negative right to noninterference.

Positive Rights—Basic Human Rights

The concept of rights, according to Rand (1964h, 93–94), Rothbard (1998, 100), Spencer ([1892] 1954, 95), Den Uyl and Rasmussen (1991, 82), and Machan (1998, 121–22), is negative. That is, basic rights are rights to noninterference. No person has the right to compel another to perform a positive action (Rothbard 1998, 100). Positive rights are derivative. They impose obligations to act with respect to another person or persons. They are "fundamentally other-oriented" (Den Uyl and Rasmussen 1991, 107), and, according to Den Uyl and Rasmussen, they do not have the universal application that negative rights have (1991, 113). Where these authors differ is on what may legitimately form the basis for positive rights. Of these authors, Rothbard appears to have been the most limiting in his assessment of what constitutes a positive right. Positive rights in his estimation would be based solely on explicit consent (contract), in which a person could not alienate his will. If one accepts Rothbard's constraint on the categories of rights, childbirth would be regarded as an act of aggression against the child (according to my interpretation). The liability argument would be a valid case for positive rights to childcare from parents.

It is generally agreed that positive rights result from a voluntary contract. If person A purchases a product from person B, then person A must pay B. Purchase confers a positive right for B to receive payment from A. If A defaults, then B has a claim on A. B is within his (positive) rights to demand restitution in some equivalent form from A (plus damages, perhaps). Contracts are not required for a positive right to exist. If A takes something from B by force, B's negative rights have been violated; B therefore has a claim on A (based on a positive right). Rand said, "Whenever a man is made to act without his own, free, individual, *voluntary* consent—his right has been violated" (n.d., 6). B is within his rights to exact retribution (personally and/or through the criminal justice system depending on the "state" in which he lives). Person A may be liable if he has caused harm to B, whether due to intent or avoidable negligence. By his actions, A has infringed on the person and/or property of B. The injured party, B, has a (positive) right to receive compensation. If B is rendered helpless, A is responsible for B's care.

The latter argument was the analogue to the case for the positive right to parental responsibility for children. If positive rights are based solely on consent, then it would follow that a child's rights have been violated by virtue of his being born. It would follow also that if a person (B) were the object of any action of another (A) in which B's consent was not given, B would have a claim against A regardless of what form that action took. For instance, if a person (A) gave CPR to a person (B) who was having a heart attack and unconscious, or otherwise incapable of giving consent, this would be regarded as an act of aggression. (See a related point by Johnson [1999, 146].) Person B would have a claim (based on a positive right) against A. (Whether or not A was successful in his efforts would be immaterial.)

Rand recognized that accidents were a part of life and believed individuals should help others in emergency situations (so long as their own lives were not in danger) (1964d, 45–47). Coming to the assistance of another in such a circumstance is usually regarded as a virtue, not an infringement on the rights of the person receiving assistance. To deal with these possibilities in life, people support fire and rescue units and buy health insurance. These are tacit signals that if they cannot give explicit consent, they nevertheless have agreed before the fact to receive help. There are times in which laypersons or off-duty professionals may come to the aid of a person in such a circumstance. Those who do so are taking a risk. There have been cases in which rescuers in these situations have been subsequently sued by those for whom assistance was given. It is not a forgone conclusion that a person who comes to the assistance of another (without the person's consent) will not be construed as infringing on the latter's rights in some cases. Helping others is not risk-free, even if it does not involve risking one's life. By and large, however, if one comes to the assistance of another and the intent is not to harm him but to save his life, this is not regarded as an infringement. The person who is rescued (B) would not have a claim on the rescuer (A). Every act by one person (A) that impacts another (B) for which the latter has not given consent cannot automatically be characterized as an infringement on B's rights, and does not automatically confer a positive right for B to have a claim against A. The issue insofar as positive rights are concerned is whether A intentionally (or through avoidable neglect) caused the helpless or injured state of B.

To arrive at (negative) rights, Rothbard (1998, 29) began his analysis with a Crusoe state of nature. With the introduction of Friday, rights become relevant. Rand considered only two states in which man could live (*qua* man), either alone on a desert island or among other men within a proper government. To Rand, living among other men was optional (1964g, 107). It may be true that man may live alone "on an island" if he so chooses, but no man is born alone. Peikoff recognized this, saying "every organism owes its existence" to reproduction (1991, 231). A man may opt to live alone, but there is one relationship that by its nature is not optional for each person who is born, and that relationship is between mother (a parent) and child, which I have labeled the PSU.

Since rights follow from the nature of the beings under consideration, the question is, what is the nature of the persons within this social unit? The basis for rights in Rand's ethics is that man has no automatic means of survival; he must rely on reason, and reason takes effort. Therefore another person should not interfere with the exercise of one's rational faculty. The nature of the child is that he has no automatic means of survival. He has a rational faculty and it will take effort to exercise it. In fact it will take *years* to develop it, and it cannot be developed in isolation. The relevant right insofar as the child is concerned is his positive right to childcare (which is needed by every human being to develop his rational faculty).

According to Evers, negative rights "have the property of universality . . . because they are generalizations based on the nature of man and reality" (1978, 3). The positive right to care by a child from his parent(s) is universal, since it applies to every human being and is based on a human being's nature and reality. The source of rights is man's rational faculty—his survival depends on it. A human being's nature is that he is born with less than a fully developed rational faculty. The right to care is needed because reason is required for man's existence and it is not automatic—it takes years to develop, and it cannot be developed by a person alone. The right to care is necessary for the development of the requisite capacity needed for a person's survival.

It could be argued that the child has a negative right not to be killed. But if, by definition, childcare means the actions taken by the parent to sustain a child, then this right—the negative right not to be killed—would be an unnecessary extra layer of rights. The nature of the PSU is that there are two individuals, an adult and a child. So long as the child is totally helpless (an infant), the adult is in no threat of physical aggression against his life or property from the child (and even if he were, an infant would not be culpable). A parent with an infant is in the same position as a man alone on a desert island—rights are irrelevant. The only relevant right for the PSU, at least during the child's infancy, is that of the child—his positive right to childcare. The positive right to childcare from the parent is the basic natural right. It is required first in every person's life before any other right becomes relevant. Without this right one would not survive to maturity and no other rights would ever become relevant.

As the child matures and develops, he could pose a threat to his parent's life and/or property and be culpable for it. Therefore, negative rights become relevant, for the adult as well as the child. And, of course, once the child has matured to adulthood, positive rights to childcare are no longer relevant. When there is more than one adult in a social unit (Crusoe and Friday), negative rights are relevant, but living in a social unit for an adult is entirely optional and is not required by his nature. All human beings are children first, and by their nature the first rights that are relevant are positive rights of childcare from their parents. Without these rights, future rights would be immaterial since humans would not survive (nor develop the rational capacity on which those rights are based) to benefit from them. The fact that a person does not have that positive right all of his life is not relevant. Negative rights are not relevant over the course of the entire life of either the adult or the child if the analysis is confined to the PSU.

Whether or not two adults, Crusoe and Friday, combine to form a social unit is optional because of the nature of adulthood. The smallest social unit required by nature is mother and child because this is, in essence, how every human being begins his life. This society, although primary, is no more realistic, however, than the hypothetical man on the desert island. In actuality, men do live among other men.

Personhood

Gregory Johnson and David Rasmussen argued that to be consistent with Rand's theory, rights should apply to humans and life should be fundamental to the definition of rights. They claimed that she equated "being human as such with being a healthy adult human" (Johnson and Rasmussen 2001, 473). Johnson and Rasmussen maintained that Rand, as well as those who have interpreted her (Machan 2001 and Tabarrok 2001), made a distinction between humans and persons, even though they did not use this terminology. The distinguishing characteristic of being human is the capacity for rational thought. But since this characteristic does not apply to all humans, Johnson and Rasmussen believed this is more accurately a description of personhood (2001, 469–476).

The idea of personhood has a long theoretical and legal history (Wise 2000, 95–118). Rationality and the ability to exercise it have been a key feature in this discussion. More recently the concept of personhood has been taken up by bioethicists. Bioethicist Robert M. Veatch is quoted as saying: "'The essence of human existence is the presence of integrated mind and body. . . . For the human to exist in any legal, moral, or socially significant sense, these two features must be present'" (Fletcher 1974, 13–14; quoted in W. Smith 2000, 174). In his book *Animal Liberation*, bioethicist Peter Singer expressed the view, according to Wesley Smith, "that the moral worth of lives . . . is roughly equal to their cognitive abilities" (2000, 192).

Tied to reasoning and cognitive ability is "moral agency." Rationality is the primary virtue in Rand's ethics because it is on man's rational faculty that he depends for his survival. It is because man has the capacity to choose the wrong action, as well as the ability to know the difference between that and the right action, that his rational faculty requires freedom from the interference of others (Rand 1967a, 17). The idea of moral agency is consistent with Rand's perspective on rights, even though she never used that term or the term "personhood."

John Harris, professor of bioethics, tied morality to personhood by claiming that the standard for personhood should be based on identifying those individuals "'who have the "highest" moral value or importance'" (W. Smith 2000, 211). He asserted that "a person is 'a being that can value existence'" (2000, 212). Philosophy professor R. G. Frey further asserted that the "'value of life is a function of its quality'" (Beauchamp and Childress 1994, 25; quoted in W. Smith 2000, 212). These statements have some parallels with Rand's ethics. She regarded life as a man's ultimate value. This is directly tied to rights. Her position was that if man's survival is taken to be axiomatic, then man's rights must be acknowledged (Berliner 1995, 307–308). Secondly, rights are required for man's proper survival, *qua* man (Rand 1961a, 182). Since life is fundamental to the concept of rights, the next two sections will address its end—death—as well as its beginning.

Death Defined

To the layperson, death would seem to be a straightforward biological event, but it has been subject to redefinition over time. One accepted medical definition of death is brain death. The American Academy of Neurology has described this as "'the irreversible loss of the clinical function of the brain'" (Fletcher 1979, 85; quoted in W. Smith 2000, 171). This means that the brain and its components are neither separately nor as a unit functioning, nor is there any significant neural electrical activity. Also absent are respiratory drive and brain stem function (W. Smith 2000, 171). There may be a few people who think this definition a bit too liberal since bodies that are declared brain dead may still be kept functioning artificially.

On the other hand, the advantage of this definition of death is that it "is a measurable, medically determinable, objective biological event" (2000, 172). At issue primarily is accuracy of diagnosis, not the validity of the concept as such.

What is more controversial than the definition of brain death has been the attempt to extend the definition of death to include those who are still alive, specifically those who are permanently unconscious. Wesley J. Smith, author of *Culture of Death*, stated: "To these advocates, human life per se is not morally meaningful; what matters is rationality" (2000, 173). Medically, the diagnosis of permanent unconsciousness is unreliable. As an example, Smith referred to a case of a woman who had been unconscious for sixteen years, who went from being fed by a tube on one day to being able to dress herself, write a letter, and walk unassisted the next (2000, 175).

This definition of death (permanently unconscious) "transforms death from a biological, objectively determinable event into a subjective, metaphysical concept based on one's view of 'what it means to be human'" (2000, 174–75). Advocates for this redefinition of death are bioethicists, whose objective, according to Smith, is to increase the supply of organs for transplant (2000, 173). Smith said: "Transforming death from a biological event into a value judgment would effectively obliterate the dead donor rule—which may be the point of the whole redefinition-of-death enterprise" (2000, 176). The definition of personhood is relevant here. Organs have already been harvested from anencephalics, infants who are terminal because they have been born without much of their brain. They are regarded as less than full persons (2000, 177), or as nonpersons. According to one bioethicist, nonpersons cannot be said to have been deprived of life because they are incapable of valuing their lives (2000, 212). Because of the lack of a rational faculty, they do not qualify for rights.

Abortion

Rand stated that the unborn are not human beings (Johnson and Rasmussen 2001, 469). A fetus is "a piece of protoplasm," and "a piece of protoplasm has no rights," according to Rand (1975, 383). Johnson and Rasmussen noted that Rand hedged on this position for the latter stages of pregnancy (2000, 259n3). Johnson and Rasmussen claimed to have relied on biology to define the concept of human being; accordingly, human life originates at conception. Rand's argument that the unborn is a nonhuman is strictly a biological question, according to Johnson and Rasmussen. They argued that, although a fetus is a piece of protoplasm, it is not undifferentiated. It is a distinct organism with a unique genetic identity. Legal rights start, not at birth, but at conception (2000, 248–52).

Alexander Tabarrok's reply to Johnson and Rasmussen was that whether the unborn is human or not is irrelevant. At issue is whether a fetus is a rights-bearer

(Johnson and Rasmussen 2001, 474). Since a fetus cannot will, set goals, or act to attain them, it is not a rights-bearer (Tabarrok 2001, 459). Bissell examined the abortion issue, basing his inquiry on Rand's claim that a rational faculty was the distinguishing feature of humans. The question is, according to Bissell, when in a fetus's development "a *human being* may be truly said to have made its appearance" (1981, 28). Based on Rand's definition of reason as "'the faculty of perceiving, identifying, and integrating the evidence of the senses'" (ibid.), Bissell reasoned that the defining feature of a reasoning capacity in humans is the ability to perceive.

The issue becomes one of trying to determine at what point in fetal development the brain becomes sufficiently capable of distinguishing objects of perception as opposed to detecting undifferentiated sensations. Bissell turned to neurophysiology for an answer. Based on observations by neurophysiologist Steven Rose, Bissell noted that at the twenty-eighth week, EEG patterns corresponding to those found in adults begin to appear. Prior to the twenty-eighth week, the patterns are markedly different. Bissell coupled this with neuroscientist Dominick P. Purpura's definition of brain life as "'the capacity of the cerebral cortex, or the thinking portion of the brain, to begin to develop consciousness, self-awareness and other generally recognized cerebral functions as a consequence of the formation of nerve cell circuits'" (1981, 29), to pinpoint personhood at the twenty-eighth week after conception. At this point a fetus has "rights to life, liberty, and property—and support" (ibid.).

Bissell pointed out that this definition of personhood avoids the problems of categorizing as nonpersons, and therefore subject to threat of being killed, those who may be regarded as inferior, misfits, or in some other way undesirable. Candidates for consideration as nonpersons would be limited to fetuses prior to the twenty-eighth week as well as "babies born without a cerebral cortex or who would otherwise never be able to function conceptually; and individuals who, because of severe brain damage, will never again be able to function conceptually—the Karen Quinlan types" (1981, 30). I think this definition may still lead to an abuse of the definition of person. For instance, "babies . . . who would otherwise never be able to function conceptually" is open to broad interpretation. In contrast to Bissell, some might argue that any activity in the cerebral cortex would qualify as "brain life." I would think it preferable to advance the more restrictive definition of brain life, whether applying the concept to abortion or to the definition of legal death.

The criterion for brain death, according to an article by Virginia Postrel, is "when human brain activity, measured by an EEG, ceases" (1989, 12). If one used the same standard for fetal life as a yardstick, this would equate to between the fourth and sixth week of pregnancy since some EEG activity can be detected around that time (ibid.). Tabarrok stated that brain waves become evident around the eighth week. This is when the fetal stage of pregnancy begins (Tabarrok 2001, 465n3). One problem with this criterion, according to Postrel, is that this is before many women discover that they are pregnant. A second issue is that the patterns at that time are different from adult readings. Postrel stated:

> A more politically feasible standard, which is also philosophically attractive, is to declare that life begins at 20 weeks of pregnancy. That state represents the earliest operation of the human brain system critical to cognition and awareness—the cerebral-reticular complex. After this stage, the fetus begins to demonstrate both behavior and EEG patterns we generally recognize as human. (1989, 12)

If the criterion for brain death were applied to when a "human life" appears, then that standard would be the lack of significantly measurable brain activity. That criterion would apply to termination of pregnancy. The fact that many women may not be aware that they are pregnant as early as four to eight weeks would be a nonissue insofar as the criterion is concerned.

Animal Rights

Rand did not regard rights to be extendable to fetuses or to nonhumans (Sciabarra 1995, 278). Rothbard stated: "There is, in fact, rough justice in the common quip that 'we will recognize the rights of animals whenever they petition for them'" (1998, 156–57). It is because this capacity is not of their nature that they do not have rights, according to Rothbard. To the claim that infants cannot petition, he responded that, unlike animals, babies are potential adults (1998, 156–57).

Machan recognized that the question of whether animals have rights cannot be answered with certainty. He explained:

> Proving a negative is, of course, impossible. That animals do not qualify as rational beings and, therefore, basic rightsholders is something we know not from a syllogistic proof but from reflecting on the evidence and putting forth an explanation that makes better sense than any other. (1998a, 115)

Having said that, he did argue that the concept of rights does not apply to animals. The concepts of life, liberty, and property are applicable to humans because humans are capable of moral and immoral acts. Humans are therefore in need of moral space. Animals cannot be blamed for their actions. They should not be tried for crimes committed against others (1998a, 106–107).

One reason Machan gave for humans having rights and other animals not having them is that "we are more important or valuable than other animals and some of our projects may require the use, even killing, of animals so as to succeed" (1998a, 109). A second reason, as mentioned in the quote above, is that unlike humans, other animals are not rational beings (1998a, 115). Unlike humans, who depend on thinking for their survival, animals do not seem to have a "central, crucial need of thinking" (1998a, 116). They depend instead upon their instincts. Although some minimal abstract thought has been discovered to exist among some animals, Machan saw this as being induced by scientists in experimental settings.

Johnson and Rasmussen and Tabarrok appear to have agreed that rights increase in scope "to the extent that our nature requires them and is capable of exercising them" (Johnson and Rasmussen 2001, 475). This is the idea of proportionality as it applies to a human being over the course of his life as well as to particular humans who may have less than normal capacities. The principle of proportionality is not a new one. It was discussed by Aristotle. The idea is that rights are attributable "in proportion to the possession of qualities to less-than-normal degrees" (Wise 2000, 86). Rights, then, would be based on some characteristic—rationality being one that is consistent with Rand's ethics. Normal adults would have full-fledged rights by virtue of possessing that characteristic. Others may be "eligible for some part of that right" (ibid.). Carl Wellman has identified three dimensions on which rights might vary. One dimension is a quantity measure. Some may have fewer rights than others. Another is a limit on the degree to which one has a particular right. A third dimension is that one may have only some elements of a complex right (Wise 2000, 86–87).

If rationality is the yardstick, rights could be apportioned along a spectrum that reflects the degree of cognitive ability. Peter Singer has used the moral worth approach to argue for rights for animals. This approach broke with the welfare model that was prevalent prior to the mid-1970s (W. Smith 2000, 190). Using a continuum of rationality or cognitive ability approach to rights across species, disabled infants might have less moral worth than some animals. Moral worth as a gauge of rights might, through the proportionality principle, assign fewer rights to the infant than to an animal. Commenting on Singer, Wesley Smith said: "The advocacy tactic of using disabled infants as examples of humans with lower capabilities than animals is one to which Singer resorts repeatedly, whether he is promoting animal 'liberation' or his other hobby horse, creating a moral and legal license for infanticide" (2000, 191–92).

Recall that Harris used as a standard of personhood, "'a being that can value existence'" (W. Smith 2000, 212). This principle, according to Harris, could be applied across species or even to machines. Disqualified as persons would be the unborn, newborns, and "people with significant cognitive disability or dementia" (ibid.). Nonpersons, in Harris's thinking, have no rights to life. They can be deprived of existence without moral consequence because in so doing they are not being deprived of something they value.

The idea that there is a spectrum of cognitive ability across species is highly suspect. In certain areas of "cognitive" ability, it could be argued that some animals far exceed that of humans. Bats innately have superior radar detection capabilities, and birds have better implicit navigational abilities (Gallistel 1990, 48–49, 492). The idea of using cognitive ability as a ruler on which to base degree of moral worth and apportioning rights on that basis is untenable if for no other reason than cognitive ability is not some unidimensional quantity.

There have been significant advances in the understanding of the cognition of other species, however, and to ignore that would be an act of evasion. If human rights are justified on the basis of man's rational faculty, then, to the extent that rights apply to other animals, they may be based on cognitive ability as well. A very good case for rights for certain primates has been made by Steve Wise (2000) in his book, *Rattling the Cage*. I will not re-create his argument here, but it is based on both legal and scientific grounds. The evidence he presented on the relatively high cognitive ability of some primates is persuasive (2000, 217–30). Wise's case is that these primates are deserving of some rights, which, at a minimum, would include the right to life. This right would apply primarily to killing or taking such animals from the wild, particularly for invasive and life-threatening experimentation. Wise presented evidence that even experimentation that one might regard as nonthreatening has not always been carried out in ways that would qualify as humane (2000, 173).

Although the percentage of primates used for experimentation is low in relative terms—less than one-third of one percent (W. Smith 2000, 199)—it is still too high if they have rights to the contrary. If they are brought into captivity for whatever reason, they may be entitled to positive rights in addition to the negative right to life. I mention this because some chimps that have been used to test language-learning capability have been subsequently sent back to the wild or used in life-threatening experimentation. For instance, language-trained chimps have been later used in pesticide testing and AIDS research. One argument for not recognizing the rights of some animals is that they are incapable of propositional expression. An animal will be given freedom when he asks for it, to rephrase Rothbard (1998, 156). But if that is the only criterion, then the request has already been made. One language-using chimp named Booee was subsequently transferred to a hepatitis testing facility and infected. After he had been there for six years, a student from the Chimpanzee and Human Communication Institute was dispatched there to visit Booee in his cell. When the student signed to the chimp, the chimp responded "*Key out*" (Wise 2000, 240). Booee remained in the cell for seven more years.

The right to life could be based on cognitive ability and could be made on a case-by-case (species-by-species) basis to the extent that it would apply. The character of the rights for nonhumans, assuming they exist, would be different from those of humans. Those who advocate rights or protections for animals vary considerably in the form those rights and/or protections should take. The right to life would apply to primates (particularly, higher primates). What that right would entail might differ among primates, but for, say, chimpanzees, it would involve physical integrity.

This does not eliminate arguments for protecting animals based on other criteria. The motive for such protections may not lie in the characteristics of other creatures but in ourselves. For instance, the humanitarian concerns related to the avoidance of pain and suffering could be based on the way in which their suffering makes us feel rather than the pain of the animals as such. A nonrights argument would not be supported by Objectivists or libertarians, however.

Rights of Prisoners

In the civilized world, there is the concept of cruel and unusual punishment. There is also the idea that the punishment must fit the crime. These two notions can be at odds with one another. Rothbard never mentioned cruel or unusual punishment. According to Rothbard, even if a person has not been convicted of a crime, he may suffer from cruelty. For instance, he stated that one may torture a suspect so long as one is willing to suffer the same in the event the tortured person is found not guilty (1998, 82). (However, he later contradicted himself, in principle, in his discussion of Nozick [Rothbard 1998, 241].) Rothbard was a strict adherent to proportional justice—i.e., the punishment fitting the crime (1998, 88). For crimes of property, he recommended monetary compensation. If monetary compensation is not possible, he recommended "just" slavery. For assault, he recommended the same assault, but more so. If someone breaks your leg, you can break both of his. The problem is that a mass murderer of innocent lives has only one life to lose—one of lesser moral quality than those he has taken. Justice can never be proportional in cases such as this.

Den Uyl and Rasmussen said that one does not lose his rights when he violates the rights of others. What is being respected is the lack of the right to act in a non-rights-respecting way (1991, 85). But what does this mean? One may be incarcerated and his actions limited to a given space. He may be forced to perform actions that he otherwise would not. But how far can the incarcerators go? Is there a limit to what may be done to prisoners? Proportionality may be a guide. Still, there is a long-standing belief that torture, medical experimentation, sexual abuse, and using remains for food are wrong. But are these simply morally wrong, or do prisoners retain certain minimal rights that cannot be breached, regardless of what they have done to others? If prisoners have some basic rights, what is the basis for those rights?

I think an argument could be made that individuals have minimal rights related to the infliction of bodily pain. Cruel and unusual punishment in respect to physical pain may not be inflicted upon another. Even if a person is sentenced to death, there may be prohibitions on how that sentence can be carried out so as to minimize unnecessary physical suffering. The basis for this argument would be that a man has the *right to life*. Since the right to life is based on human nature—what a human being is—then there may be some aspects of being human that should be protected regardless of whatever other rights one may forfeit through one's actions, so long as the person is alive. One aspect of human survival is the ability to experience pain and pleasure (physical sensations). These provide cues to one's environment that a sentient creature uses to help him survive (see Rand 1964a, 18–19). Man cannot rely on them exclusively, but they are input to the reasoning process. So the basis for the argument is not feelings (sympathy for those who feel pain) but the capacity for (physical) pain that humans have that aids them in their survival. A person may forfeit the right to life, but not all rights related to that right. No new or additional basis for rights for humans would be needed. By virtue of being alive, there would simply be some minimum rights that a person was entitled to regardless of what crime he had committed.

The other possibility, insofar as rights are concerned, is that the right not to suffer cruel and unusual punishment is based on something other than a characteristic that is uniquely human. Since sentient creatures can feel pain to one extent or another, the capacity for pain may form the basis for some rights for prisoners. At issue here is not that a human being is capable of feeling pain but rather the capacity to feel pain per se. And if ability to feel pain is a basis for rights, then it is possible that other creatures besides man may have some minimal rights. They may have a right not to be the subject of cruel and unusual treatment. This does not mean that all animals would have a right to life. It would simply mean that animals should not be subjected to unnecessary pain, so long as they are alive. If one uses the capacity for pain as the basis for the argument for other animals, one does not have to begin with the right to life for those animals. This would open up a new basis for rights, or possibly protections.

One could make a case against cruel and unusual punishment separate from a rights argument. It could be based on how meting out such punishment makes us feel rather than how it makes the criminal feel. This was also said with respect to "protections" for animals. As a legal justification, such arguments are weak, or more accurately unacceptable, in Objectivist thought. Laws should be rights-based, not based on morality or emotions.

Consent and Personhood

If not incarcerated and otherwise free, humans are free to experience pain and take other risks (so long as they do not involve unwilling others). This may even include the right to commit suicide. It would seem to follow that if one owns one's life, he has the right to end it. This is not as straightforward as it sounds, however. There is the question of consent. If one commits suicide, there is no doubt that the person consented. But there may be at least two problems with this from a rights perspective if the issue is assisted suicide. One is that the person may not be capable of making a rational decision. (Whether the decision itself is rational or not is another issue.) The other is that if there is a delay between the decision and the act, there may be a change in one's attitude. This is the issue of euthanasia. Euthanasia is also used to describe nonconsensual termination of life. In the latter case, the person cannot give consent (because he is unconscious or not fully capable of rational choice).

If one is rational and either commits suicide or is assisted in doing so, a case could be made that this is one's right based on the right to life. If there is a delay between the decision and the action, how binding the agreement should be is a function of a number of factors (for example, if the person is terminally ill, the length of the delay, to name two). (For a discussion of assisted suicide from an Objectivist perspective see Goldberg [1998, 7–9].) The more difficult cases are when the person either has diminished capacity and consents, or cannot consent because he is unconscious. These two cases are only marginally different. If one gives consent but is severely mentally disabled, there is consent, but it is in name only. In both cases, there is the issue of personhood. Much of the discussion related to abortion applies, in principle, to euthanasia. In both cases, the issue of personhood is central to the discussion (see Richard Epstein's review of Ronald Dworkin's book on abortion and euthanasia [1993, 58–61]).

There are basically two arguments here. The first is, if a person is incapable of rationality (he is permanently unconscious or mentally incapacitated), he does not qualify for personhood and therefore has no rights. His life can be taken because he cannot lose something he is incapable of valuing. The second argument is, if a person is not rational, he cannot give consent; therefore, he cannot agree to assisted suicide, and thus, his life cannot be taken because his consent is impossible to attain. Any action that is taken without his consent infringes on his right to life. This blanket statement would include medical care given to him when he is unconscious. If any action one takes *on behalf of* another without his consent is deemed a violation of his rights, then receiving life-saving medical care when unconscious would qualify as an infringement. This latter argument was considered earlier and dismissed.

David Norton said, with respect to individuals "who appear to be incapable of any degree of actualization, we have a choice. Either we deem them nonpersons, e.g., 'vegetables,' or the like, and treat them accordingly, or else we regard them as children who in all likelihood will remain such" (1976, 333n*). He regarded the second choice to be "dictated not by charity alone, but likewise by prudence and reason" (ibid.). Unfortunately, Norton did not give his reasons for not treating the "lesser number" to which he referred as vegetables. It would seem to me that if a person cannot give his consent, then an action to end his life would be an infringement upon his rights. Now why he cannot give his consent may be an issue in considering what his rights include or exclude, but at a minimum, it would seem to me that he would have a right to life. Insofar as death is concerned, brain death would seem to be a good definition, i.e., no significant neural activity.

Although new definitions may follow from new scientific information and measurement, what is not appropriate is to redefine death to suit some other agenda—such as to increase the number of organs for transplant. Expanding the definition to include those individuals with measurable brain activity as nonpersons, and therefore eligible to be donors, does not rely on new scientific information relevant to death per se.

Positive Rights Revisited

Unlike Rand, Rothbard believed human life begins at conception. His argument for abortion was that if and when a mother decided she did not want to carry the fetus any longer, she could abort it because once she made that decision, the fetus—although a human being—was violating her person and she could evict it, so to speak. The fact that the child may have been voluntarily conceived is irrelevant to the argument, according to Rothbard (1998, 98–99).

The trespassing argument is inconsistent with Rothbard's other statements as well as with reality. A fetus cannot be considered a trespasser if he was "invited" by virtue of the person's voluntary actions. Secondly, in Rothbard's claim that the mother is the natural owner of a child, his basis for this claim was that the mother was the homesteader of the child. A person cannot be a homesteader of an infant and at the same time regard a fetus as a trespasser. The argument has the same weaknesses as the one Rothbard made with respect to a parent's right to let his child starve. Bissell's response to that was as follows:

> Clearly, the problem here is not just whether abortion is ever justifiable. The broader question is whether any child has a right to be supported by its parents—rather than killed, abandoned, or simply neglected—until it becomes an independent person capable of surviving by its own effort and initiative. (1981, 30)

Bissell argued that a child has a positive right to care from his parents just as a victim of an accident would have a right to compensation from the person who caused his incapacitation (ibid.). Consent (involving the exchange of property) is generally acknowledged to form the basis for mutual claims (positive rights). Positive rights are also conferred as a result of an infringement of a negative right. The principle of reciprocity demands compensation for the property lost through the unilateral "transaction." Default on payment, trespass, theft, vandalism, assault, and rape are all examples of involuntary unilateral transfers in which one person has been forced to relinquish his property or person to another for which the victim has not been compensated. The victim has a positive right to restitution and/or retribution. Whenever the actions of others result in a condition of helplessness of (or harm to) another, the former are responsible for the latter. There are some qualifications to the previous statement. One is that the outcome must have been to some extent foreseeable (and avoidable). Refusal to acknowledge that the outcome was probable would be an act of evasion. Now it is true that, unlike a person becoming incapacitated as a result of the actions of a drunken driver, a child's rights have not been violated by having been conceived. Although the child does not consent to being born, one's birth is still not an infringement on his rights. So I believe rights that follow from reproduction are in a different category of positive rights from those that arise through consent or through an infringement on one's negative rights.

What of a person who is helpless, say mentally incapacitated to the point that he is unable to care for himself; is anyone "responsible" for him? The Objectivist philosophy would claim that the helpless person does not have a positive right to care. Unless someone has caused the person's helplessness, either willfully or through avoidable neglect, no one is responsible for that person in the sense that the helpless person has a claim on anyone. Of course, so long as the mentally incapacitated person can pay for care, he has a positive right to care. This is a nonissue insofar as positive rights are concerned. A person has a positive right to anything he pays for, so long as it does not infringe on the rights of others.

There is a problem here, however, and that is, since the person is mentally incapacitated, who determines what is in the best interest of the person? Someone or some persons must make decisions for the benefit of the helpless person. A person who is permanently helpless is not the victim of the kind of temporary condition that arises in emergencies when consent cannot be given. The permanently helpless must rely on the decision-making of others all the time. This can lead to abuses by those in charge. There could be, for instance, needless testing that could be costly and drain the helpless person financially. Still, the question of whether a helpless person has a positive right to care is not an issue so long as he has the funds to pay for it. The issue of the right to care as such only emerges once the funds run out.

Once the ability to pay is completely exhausted, the helpless person is in the position of being a trespasser of private property, be it a hospital or nursing home or a private dwelling that has been sold to pay for bills to care providers. As a trespasser, he can be forcibly removed from the property. If the helpless person owns no property, then wherever he goes he is trespassing, unless someone voluntarily "takes him in." No one is under any obligation to do so, however, if individuals are only entitled to the observance by others of their negative rights. So, if the person has no property and no one voluntarily permits him to live on their property, he is a trespasser and is subject to ejection from property owned by others. From an Objectivist perspective, all property should be owned (i.e., private property); therefore the helpless person would necessarily be a trespasser.

Trespassers are violators of the negative rights of others and because of that are subject to punishment of some kind. However, if the person truly has diminished capacity as a condition of his existence, he cannot be responsible for his actions. He is violating the rights of others by his presence on their property, but he is innocent in the sense that it is not a willful violation of the rights of others. It is not willful because the person cannot be said to have will or the capacity to exercise it. Rand recognized that punishment for crimes should apply to those who have the capacity to know that they have committed a crime. She said the penal code was relevant for responsible adults. For a person who infringes on the rights of another or others but is not a responsible adult, Rand stated that if it can be proven that a person is not legally responsible by virtue of being insane, then he can be committed to an asylum (Berliner 1995, 560).

Punishment does not usually apply to those who have significant diminished capacity. (And by diminished capacity, I mean one that is a condition of the person's existence, not induced by abusing drugs or alcohol.) Rand mentioned insanity as an example of diminished capacity, but this may not be the only form it takes. She also recognized that the person may qualify for positive care—specifically, an insane asylum. There may be other examples of facilities or homes that provide care, but the point is that she recognized a positive right to care that is nonpunitive in nature for those who infringe on the rights of others but who did not do so with intent because they have diminished capacity as a condition of their existence.

I think a similar case for the positive right to care can be made for orphaned or abandoned children. Machan said that: "[P]arents, by creating human life, take on responsibilities which they have no right to abandon. . . . [T]hey might . . . give up their children if some others *volunteer* to take care of them" (1975, 178). Bissell expressed a similar sentiment (1981, 30). Rand would agree that no person should accept an unchosen obligation. However, if children are abandoned and no one voluntarily takes care of them, then their options depend on their degree of helplessness. If they are too young to earn a living, then they will not be capable of buying, renting, or maintaining property. If they are propertyless, then, like those who have diminished capacity (as a condition of their existence), they are trespassers. As trespassers they are infringing on the rights of others, but they are innocent insofar as being punishable for their acts of infringement. Since the penal code should not be used to impose punishment on those who are not responsible adults, the justice system may be in the same or a similar position that it would be in if an insane person violated another's rights. The justice system may have to provide nonpunitive care.

There are many questions that arise from this analysis. For instance, is it necessary for the justice system to wait until a "crime" has been committed? Rand said that if insanity could be *proved*, a person might be entitled to care (an insane asylum in her example). Another is that a person should not be "punished" if he has committed no crime. A free society does not want the justice system forcing individuals into care facilities or worse if they do not belong there. Although the care facilities are not "punishment" in the strict sense of the word, such care may very well involve a limitation on one's rights.

If a person has diminished capacity, it follows that he cannot exercise all of the rights of a responsible adult. He may be unable to make life-preserving decisions, work a job, own and maintain property. He may not be able to exercise other rights that responsible adults are entitled to exercise. He may not be able to own a firearm, for instance. A person who is helpless may not be able to exercise these rights by the nature of his helplessness. If a person is deemed helpless (without evidence to support it and before he has violated another's rights) and is assigned to a care facility, he may be deprived of these rights by virtue of the nature of care he receives and the nature of the facility.

Rand believed that a person who is not capable of rationality does not have the rights of a rational person (Berliner 1995, 560). Yet, an implicit assumption in the analysis thus far has been that all people have the same rights—i.e., negative rights of noninterference—but that some people may not be able to exercise those rights because of diminished capacity. This was essentially Spencer's stance on children. He first presented the counterargument that, given that rights are based on faculties, children cannot have the same rights as adults because they do not have the same faculties ([1892] 1954, 156). This is a nonargument, according to Spencer, because the person has "*perfect* freedom to exercise *all* his faculties" (ibid.), whatever those faculties may be. Children then should have full political rights, rights to property, and rights to noninterference. He said that "the use of coercion is wrong" and "that the relationship now commonly existing between parents and children is therefore a vicious one" ([1892] 1954, 158).

If one takes Spencer's perspective, then children and those with diminished capacity have the same rights as a "responsible adult." It would seem to follow that if the former cannot properly take care of themselves and end up abandoned, homeless, trespassing on others' property or worse, then the government can prosecute them as they would any other rights violator. Then it would be up to the defense to show that the defendant had diminished capacity or otherwise could not be held accountable for his actions and therefore not rightfully punishable (assuming that would be a defense that Spencer would accept). The justice system may then be responsible for following up on placement, etc., following the argument that I have laid out above.

If it is agreed that humans have full rights regardless of age, as Spencer asserted, then if children or those with diminished capacity are denied a right, this would qualify as an *infringement* on their rights. So if a child or a person with diminished capacity is denied the right to own a firearm or to vote or to buy alcohol, etc., this would be an infringement on their rights. Earlier it was stated that when a person infringes on the rights of another, then generally speaking, this confers a positive right on the person whose rights have been violated. For instance, if a person sells a product to a person, and the buyer defaults, the seller has a positive right to payment (and possibly damages). It could be argued that if each person—solely by virtue of being human—is entitled to full negative rights, and if he is denied rights based on his limited capacity for rationality, then that is an infringement on his basic human rights. Since his rights have been violated, this confers upon him a positive right of some kind. A positive right is a claim on others, a claim for payment or compensation or a benefit of some kind. The basis for the claim is that a person cannot have his rights infringed upon, so that if he is entitled to full rights by virtue of being human, and those rights are restricted for some reason, then he should be justly compensated. A qualification here is that the person's rights are limited because of something that is beyond his control, not because of any actions he has taken. If he had committed a criminal act, he would justifiably lose some of his rights so long as he was regarded competent. But the denial of rights on the basis of diminished capacity as a condition of a person's existence (not as a result of his actions—for example, abusing mind-altering drugs which temporarily incapacitate him) is predicated on something over which the person has no control.

This case suffers in a couple of respects. First, even though it is generally true that if one person infringes upon the rights of another, then the person whose rights are violated has a positive claim against the violator, it is not clear that every denial of a right is an infringement of one's rights. The argument is premised on the idea that each person does have full rights regardless of mental capacity. Although an argument can be made that every person has a right to life (from what I have termed "brain life" at eight weeks to "brain death"), one could also make a case that every individual is not entitled to full rights. Negative rights do assume that a person has a certain capacity to reason, make decisions, and to act on those decisions in order to create the means of survival. One needs noninterference in order to use one's mind so as to survive. Negative rights also entail the respect of others' negative rights. The ability to exercise one's negative rights assumes that one is capable of understanding the rights of others and that others' rights cannot be infringed upon.

Another way of viewing children and those with diminished capacity is that they have the negative right to life (and based on the argument presented previously, this right would extend to fetuses—that is, the unborn eight weeks old and older—as well as to certain primates as argued by Wise [2000] in his book *Rattling the Cage*). The negative rights a child and a person with diminished capacity would have would be commensurate with their capacity to exercise those rights. Johnson and Rasmussen stated that "philosophers and psychologists, most eminently Jean Piaget, have shown that the human rational faculty develops and unfolds its capacities over time. Yet, at every stage of its development, the rational faculty is still the rational faculty. Reason is reason, whether in its earliest stages of development or in its full maturity. Reason is reason, whether in a state of dormancy or in a state of activity" (Johnson and Rasmussen 2000, 251). Tabarrok stated what was needed was a theory to explain why "the number and scope of rights increases with adulthood" (Tabarrok 2001, 460).

I think it would be an infringement to limit a person's rights based on nothing more than an assumption that he is incapable of exercising his own rights or respecting the rights of others. That is why in many cases a person is assumed to have full rights until he demonstrates that he is not entitled to those rights because he has violated the rights of others. If the infringement was perpetrated by one with his faculties intact, then he would be eligible for punishment. If the person had diminished capacity, he would not be subject to punishment, but may be subject to restrictions on his freedom because he is incapable of exercising his rights and of respecting (because he is incapable of understanding) the rights of others.

Because of what is known about child development, it is understood that infants are incapable of fully understanding and appreciating the concept of negative rights. It is not necessary, therefore, to grant children full rights (as Spencer suggested), then wait until it is demonstrated that infants are incapable of exercising their own rights or of respecting the rights of others. Thus rights can be limited for children based on what we know about the nature of normal human development. Those (negative) rights may grow in number and scope with age (so long as the child develops normally). It is more difficult to argue that adults with diminished capacity should be denied rights until they have somehow properly demonstrated that they are capable of understanding, exercising, or respecting them. This does not mean that they cannot be denied certain rights if, by their actions or inaction, they are found incapable of understanding, exercising, or respecting rights.

It is better to err on the side of assuming that adults have full rights than to assume that they do not and to make them prove otherwise. The latter is akin to assuming individuals are guilty until proven innocent. The possibility emerges that a competency test for rights would be required for everyone. That is, the assumption that a person has diminished capacity until he demonstrates otherwise could lead to testing to determine what rights he is entitled to have based on how well he scores on a "rationality examination." This is counter to the idea that individuals have inalienable rights.

In some cases this dilemma is easily remedied. There can be preemptive measures that are taken without being invasive of others' rights. Nursing homes, hospitals, and other facilities that care for people who are incapacitated to the point that they cannot look after themselves usually know a great deal about the individual's capacity to care for himself, his financial status, and the extent that he can rely on family or others for care. They have this information because they are the caregivers, they diagnose these conditions, and because they require financial information as a condition of admission. Since these institutions would not be required to continue providing care once a person could no longer pay (that is, the person does not have a positive right to care if he cannot pay), then the institutions would be within their rights to evict the person. However, if the person is evicted and has no property or other means of support or care, he would become a trespasser. It could be argued that the care facility has an obligation to notify the justice system of such an eventuality.

There is precedence for this kind of notification. If a person knows that another person is going to commit a crime, then it is morally incumbent on that person to notify the authorities. It could be argued that it is legally incumbent upon the person to do so as well. If a care facility knowingly discharges a person who has no property and who will (because of diminished capacity and lack of property) be in a position of trespass once he is evicted from the facility (because of lack of funds and inability to care for himself), then the care facility would have knowledge of a criminal act before the fact. (The act itself, trespassing, is criminal, even though the person who commits it may be legally innocent because of diminished capacity.) The care facility would be under greater obligation than a private citizen who might suspect a crime will be committed, since the care facility would know with certainty of the violation and because it would be involved in it by virtue of evicting the care receiver. If care facilities are required to notify the authorities about these individuals, then it would not be necessary to wait until they break the law before the justice system intervenes to place them in another facility. This would not be the same as the authorities depriving a person of his rights by claiming that he has diminished capacity and assigning him to a facility without justification. Nor would the authorities have to wait until a person is homeless and a trespasser before they stepped in.

Although there are numerous issues I have not addressed here, the point I have made is this—that one can argue for positive rights based on some other criterion besides agreement. The argument for the positive right to care for those who have diminished capacity that is not the result of the actions of others is circuitous. I have presented two. One argues that within the narrow constraints I have identified, a person with diminished capacity may be eligible for care if he has no property and therefore is a trespasser and is innocent by virtue of his condition. This argument is in principle very similar to Rand's case for the placement in asylums of those (who have violated laws) who are proven insane. I simply do not limit those with diminished capacity to the insane and care facilities to asylums, but the principle involved is identical to Rand's.

The other argument is much less tenable. That argument assumes that everyone, by virtue of being human, has full rights, and if rights are denied a person because of diminished capacity, then that is a violation of his rights. If one's rights have been infringed upon for reasons beyond a person's control (that is, he has diminished capacity), he is deserving of positive rights. It is more reasonable to assume, however, that those with diminished capacity have fewer rights, than it is to claim that they have full rights with some of those rights denied. Theoretically, the argument of fewer (negative) rights for those with lesser capacity is tenable. There may be some problems with implementation. For instance, it would be a violation of a person's rights, generally speaking, to assume that he has diminished capacity and then require him to prove otherwise. Yet if the justice system waits until someone with diminished capacity has violated the rights of others before limiting his rights, then this could hurt others as well as the person with diminished capacity. There are ways of reducing the latter possibility before the fact, as suggested above.

There are two other important questions. They are: How much care should be given and who should pay? The question of "how much" is not only a problem with this question—that is, those with diminished capacity to care for themselves who are in the position of trespass or potential trespass. It also pertains to anyone who receives governmental services for the protection of their negative rights. Does everyone have a right to a personal bodyguard, a tank, a security system? Stating that every person has a negative right to noninterference does not provide a clue about how much is too much or how much is enough protection of one's rights. The same would be true for the kind of care considered here.

The second question is: Who pays? If a person has violated the negative rights of another and is incarcerated as a result, the citizenry pays. If a person is evicted from a care facility and is in a position of trespass, he is ostensibly violating the law, but is not legally culpable. However, he would still be entitled to care based on the above argument. I would say that those who should pay would be the same people who pay for criminal justice, since what is at issue is the infringement on property rights (through trespass), even though the innocent should not be treated as criminals. In Objectivist philosophy this should be provided voluntarily, not through taxation or other coercive means. I will revisit this discussion later. A related question is, how much is owed "by right" and how much is charity? It is not a forgone conclusion that because a person is helpless, he has a right to be taken care of by the justice system. The justice system may have some role to perform, but it may not be to house, feed, provide medical care, schooling, and so forth to everyone who is helpless. It may provide, at a minimum, a placement and oversight function, yet the bulk of the care may be provided through private charities.

CHAPTER EIGHT

Ownership

This chapter discusses property rights, particularly the ownership of original resources. According to Rand, the source of property and all other rights is the right to life (1967a, 18). She referred to the Homestead Act as an appropriate method of distributing original resources (1967g, 123). Rand's position was that ownership of land should be 100 percent. Mavrodes (1972, 249–50) saw an inconsistency in Rand's view of land ownership and her view on ownership of pure knowledge by its discoverers. Spencer ([1892] 1954, 103–122) claimed that private land ownership violates the law of equal freedom, and Kohr (1974, 52) held that property—not property rights—is necessary in order to be free, since freedom is the freedom to act. Ownership of original resources is relevant to OE because others are not fundamentally a part of reality. However, once all original resources are owned, other people must become fundamentally a part of reality for the propertyless, since the latter must acquire property from others. I conclude that ethics concerning others become of primary, not secondary, importance. Rothbard (1998, 98) argued that, since a person cannot alienate his will, a person cannot sell himself into slavery. Although I argue that one could do this by a circuitous route, if one accepts Rothbard's case, then it would seem to follow that a person could not alienate himself from the space he occupies (his property). If that argument is valid, then if one has offspring, he would have to yield some of his own space (property) to his child in order for his child to be free.

I also examine the problem of assigning property rights to resources that move. There appears to be no single efficient method of assigning private property rights (in the strict sense) to these resources. Efficiency considerations are not unrelated to ethics. For one, efficiency is related to productivity, which is required for survival. Second, the problem with nonoptimal (inefficient) property arrangements is that the individual does not take into account the costs his actions impose on others. This violates the Objectivist "nonsacrificial" tenet that one should not give or receive the unearned.

What Is the Source of Property Rights?

To Rand, the source of property rights is the source of all rights and that is the right to life (1964h, 94). Man has no automatic means of survival. He must produce to sustain himself, and he should be able to keep the product of his efforts. That is his property, and it should belong to him. Rand said: "Man has to work to produce in order to support his life. . . . Without property rights, no other rights can be practiced" (1967a, 18).

Machan, Den Uyl and Rasmussen (1991, 104), and Nozick all claimed that man needs what Nozick called "moral space," since, to be a moral agent, a person needs a realm of "personal jurisdiction" (Machan 1998a, 68) within which to act without interference from others. To varying degrees, their emphasis was on property rights permitting one to act morally—which in turn results in successful living. Rand's emphasis was on acting rationally (i.e., morally) so that one may produce and therefore live. She always tied rationality, productivity, and property to sustaining one's life.

How Is (Original) Property Acquired?

In *The Ethics of Liberty*, Rothbard used the Crusoe approach first to examine what property is in the context of being alone, and then, by introducing others, extended the analysis to rights to property. He subscribed to the homestead principle; that is, the first person who occupies or finds land and transforms it for use owns it. However, Crusoe could not, by what Rothbard called the "Columbus complex," claim the entire island (1998, 47–48). Later Crusoe could leave the property idle; the hand of the original owner would nevertheless be apparent, according to Rothbard (1998, 65).

When Friday arrives on the island, he could acquire property by applying his labor to any remaining unowned land. If none is left, he could either trade something he owns (for example, his labor) for some of Crusoe's land, assuming Crusoe is agreeable. Alternatively, Crusoe may, if he is so inclined, give a share of his property to Friday; or, Friday could attempt to take Crusoe's property by force. The latter would be a violation of Crusoe's rights, however. Having a right to property means not only the right to exclusive use, but also the right to enter voluntary contracts transferring that property to another party (1998, 133).

Rand's view of original acquisition shares features with that of Locke, who stated:

> Though the earth and all inferior creatures be common to all men, yet every man has a "property" in his own "person": this nobody has a right to but himself. The "labour" of his body, and the "work" of his hands, we may say, are properly his. Whatsoever, then, he removes out of the state that Nature hath provided and left it in, he hath mixed his labour with it, and joined to it something that is his own, and thereby makes it his property. It being by him removed from the common state Nature placed it in, it hath by his labour something annexed to it that excludes the common right of other men. For this "labour" being the unquestionable property of the labourer, no man but he can have a right to what that is once joined to, at least when there is enough, and as good left in common for others. (Locke 1984, 30)

Specifically, Rand believed that in order for a resource to be of value, it requires the "application of human knowledge and effort" (1967g, 122). It is the function of government to provide for the orderly dispensation of unowned resources. She offered as an example the Homestead Act of 1862 (1967g, 123). (This begs the question of how a government becomes established without formerly existing in geographic space in the first place.)

Den Uyl and Rasmussen believed that Locke was wrong about nature providing man with a stock of resources from which he could devise a set of rules for just dispensation. Like Rand, they believed that the best nature supplies is "the potential for transformation" (1991, 117). To them, as to Rothbard and Rand, property is "produced through an act of transformation" (1991, 120). Similarly, they claimed that preexisting wealth was a misnomer (ibid.). To Den Uyl and Rasmussen, all wealth is the result of thought and effort (1991, 118). This is reminiscent of Rand, who said "the base of all property rights [is] a man's right to the product of his mind" (1967i, 130), and Rothbard, who noted that underlying each good that is produced "is an *idea* . . . a manifestation of man's spirit" (1998, 31). Sciabarra attributed to Rand a labor theory of value in that an idea "is the creative force behind the production of material values" (1995, 291).

Rather than adopting a variation on Locke's view of "mixing one's labor" with nature in the acquisition of property, Machan advocated Sadowsky's idea that the property owner "performs an entrepreneurial function" (1998a, 68). A property owner may take "unimproved" land and do nothing to it if he thinks that will result in the greatest increase in value over time (Sadowsky 1974, 89). This does not address the question of original acquisition, however, unless it is done by "claiming." (The idea that transforming a resource will raise its value is fallacious, according to

Sadowsky [ibid.]. His view of value is at odds with a labor theory of value. Although the two are sometimes confused, a labor theory of value is not synonymous with nor a necessary consequence of a labor theory of original acquisition.)

Other Views on Land Ownership

Although Den Uyl and Rasmussen envisioned property as being produced by a process of transformation, they were unconcerned with original acquisition as such. Their position was: "[R]ules of original acquisition are less a matter of morality than they are a matter of getting co-operative society off the ground" (1991, 123–24). Kelley dismissed original acquisition as well, claiming that what is important is being able to keep the results of one's labor (1992, 59).

The utilitarian position is to accept all existing property rights arrangements, regardless of how property rights were originally established (Rothbard 1998, 52). Rothbard took exception to this, arguing that the current possessor could claim legitimate title to a piece of property if it could not be proven that he or his ancestors criminally attained the property (1998, 57). A proviso was that, even if the ancestors criminally attained it, if the original owners (their ancestors) could not be identified, the current possessor could legally claim it.

Neither Kelley nor Den Uyl and Rasmussen embraced the utilitarian position, but since they did not regard original acquisition of particular significance, it could be argued that they accepted it by default. However, if, as Kelley believed, property rights and justice are linked after property rights are established, then it would seem to follow that the way in which property rights are originally established should be just. Another reason that original acquisition is important is that when new (unowned) resources are discovered, they must be distributed in some way. Rand's (1967g) article on the airwaves illustrates this. There are endangered species and there is the question of whether property rights should be assigned to them in order to protect them from extinction and if so, how. There are water pollution and air pollution and questions related to assignment of property rights to air and water. If there are just ways of assigning property rights, then they should be explored.

Another point relates to ethics. To Rand, the same cardinal values apply whether man is alone or among others under a proper government. But, if in the latter situation, all property is owned, what are the implications for the concept of reality? This is relevant in OE because its view is that other men are not fundamentally a part of reality. Its cardinal values and virtues can be practiced by man alone. However, man alone on a desert island has direct access to original resources. This is not true of a propertyless person born into a world where all property is owned.

Spencer stated that once all of the earth is owned, then the propertyless "can exist on the earth by sufferance only. They are all trespassers. Save by the permission of the lords of the soil, they can have no room for the soles of their feet" ([1892] 1954, 104). They can act "only by the consent of the landowners" (ibid.). Spencer believed that original land belonged equally to all men in common ([1892] 1954, 103), and that property in land violates the law of equal freedom. His solution was to shift from the present landlords to a system of land tenure based on a joint stock company, i.e., government ([1892] 1954, 112, 116, 118) (an idea he later abandoned [{1850} 1946, 49, 72]).

It was because of the difficulties in pinning down just rules of original acquisition of nature-given resources that George Mavrodes questioned whether a moral justification could be given for the ownership of original resources. His argument for limiting the duration of land ownership is similar to that made by Rand for limiting rights to patents and copyrights. Rand's case was that intellectual property, unlike material objects, is not used up when consumed. The same is true for land, Mavrodes noted (1972, 260). At one point, Mavrodes questioned the notion of land ownership altogether. His justification was based on Rand's contention that laws of nature cannot be owned, since the discoverers do not create them (Rand 1967i, 130). The same is true for nature-given resources, according to Mavrodes. Finding nature-given resources, like discovering laws of nature, may take considerable effort, but that effort does not justify ownership, since the resources, like laws of nature, are not produced (Mavrodes 1972, 250).

Mavrodes's recommendation included a system of land taxation, the proceeds of which could be used for "opportunity grants," so that each generation may have the equivalent of original resources. Another suggestion was the assignment of fragmented rights, limiting the duration of ownership to the life of the resident (1972, 261). Writing in response to Mavrodes, John Hospers asked: Why is the government entitled to the property? The government has a dynamic of its own. If evicted, the propertyless person has nowhere to go if the government owns the land (Hospers 1972, 269, 271). If a private landowner evicts a tenant or raises the rent, a propertyless person may have a number of other dwellings from which to choose.

Hospers, like Rand, preferred government distribution of original property. His justification for private ownership was utilitarian, although he stated that the same facts he presented for his utilitarian argument would support a natural-rights doctrine. Hospers looked at the empirical facts: Man's survival depends on the production of goods; nature supplies raw materials but man must apply his labor and ingenuity to convert these into products to sustain him. If he owns that which he produces, he will be encouraged to be more productive and efficient. He will be encouraged to specialize, to sell the surplus he produces, to purchase those things that are produced relatively more efficiently by others. As a result, more *in toto* will be produced; the standard of living will improve. Hospers also endorsed

Locke's position that man is the steward of the land and as such he may hold the title to it during his lifetime and may forfeit his right to it if he neglects or abuses it (1972, 271–72).

The Propertyless

Man's life is experienced over time, and he lives in space. Property has duration. It also has a spatial dimension. It is the spatial dimension that Rand focused on when she remarked that "only a ghost can exist without material property" (1961a, 183). Man is a material being. He lives in space. Rand's observation is echoed by Rothbard in his statement that humans "are not floating wraiths" (1974, 108), and by Den Uyl and Rasmussen who stated that men are not "disembodied ghosts" (1991, 116).

The right to property, Rand said, "is a right to action" (1964h, 94). Rights, as such, pertain solely to action. Rand's emphasis is on the product of man's actions—man has property rights because he has a right to the product of his mental and physical effort. This is Rand's basis for property rights. More fundamentally, one could argue that man exists in space. But she did not make this case. Rothbard stated that a man must have standing room (Hoppe 1998, xv; Rothbard 1974, 112). Men must "*stand* on land areas" (Rothbard 1974, 108). Although this might seem to be Rothbard's justification for property rights, it is not.

Sugden's approach to property rights was to examine biological roots of possession and territoriality (1986, 101–103), noting possible parallels with other species. Richard Pipes pointed out that even free-ranging animals are not free to move at random. They are limited in space to one or a few areas known as their "range" (Pipes 1999, 66). He found that for many species a female will not mate with an unpropertied male (1999, 68). Although Rand's ethics are biocentric, she did not look at biological roots for ties of territoriality to reproduction. To Rand, man ultimately stands or moves or acts for a purpose, to sustain his own life. The source of property rights is that property is created by man, which follows from the law of causality. Property is the result of man's thought and effort. The effect, wealth, is not possible without its source, intelligence (Rand 1961a, 183).

Rothbard noted that nothing can be produced with labor alone (1974, 112). Yet Rand stated that all property is the product of man's intelligence (1961a, 182). If taken literally, this would imply that matter is the creation of man's mind, a position with which Rand adamantly disagreed. Rand's first axiom is that existence exists independently of man's consciousness. "The function of consciousness is not to create reality, but to apprehend it" (Peikoff 1982, 303). Thus, man does not produce material values by using his mind alone. How, then, in the first instance does man acquire material values? Machan interpreted Rand's position on property rights to mean that "each person ought to be free to acquire things in nature"

(1975, 121). Rand said that man's survival is not dependent on a single limited resource. Man is not stuck on a lifeboat with a single jug of water. The planet provides unlimited resources, but he must acquire them (Berliner 1995, 354).

In the short run (and, perhaps, the long run), resources are limited. Locke's proviso was that a man had a right to that taken from the state of nature on which he had labored, "at least when there is enough, and as good left in common for others" (Locke 1984, 30). To this, Rothbard responded:

> If latecomers are worse off, well then that is their proper assumption of risk in this free and uncertain world. There is no longer a vast frontier in the United States, and there is no point in crying over the fact. In fact, we can generally achieve as much "access" as we want to these resources by paying a market price for them; but even if the owners refused to sell or rent, that should be their right in a free society. (1998, 244–45)

(Rand expressed a similar sentiment [1967g, 124].) In other words, new generations, some of whom may be propertyless, were not clever enough to be born earlier. Facetiousness aside, the issue is not whether one is or is not emotional about the fact that there are no longer vast unclaimed resources to settle. The question is: If there are no longer unowned resources, does this have any implications for the propertyless and for justice? Leopold Kohr suggested that a person needs property—not just property rights—to be free (1974, 52). He said:

> [I]t does not mean property is freedom. It is the source of freedom, and it is its only source by the strength of its very definition. For a person can be free only within the limits of a right that excludes the rights of all others. If he cannot exclude all others when it comes to making a decision, he cannot be free. (1974, 50)

Both Spencer and Mavrodes (1972, 261) said or implied that the propertyless live only by the sufferance of landowners—by permission, not right. Spencer ([1892] 1954, 104) said that the propertyless "are trespassers." What if the landowners do not suffer the propertyless? It is the right of the landowners to deny access. Johnson and Rasmussen stated that it would be murder if a landowner killed an unarmed trespasser (2001, 479). Trespassing is not a capital offense, they claimed. It is true that when trespassers come on one's property in the United States, it is customary to call the police (or the border patrol, if one lives on the border). But the reason trespassers usually go willingly with the police is that police carry guns. Force is implicit in the protection of property rights. Where do the propertyless go who are not suffered by landowners? They may travel public roads and sleep in public parks. But if all land were privately owned—roads included, as has been suggested by Rand (Sciabarra 1995, 277) and many libertarians—the vagrant would not have these outlets either. There would be prisons.

A person could be a criminal and face incarceration simply because he is propertyless. It is likely that in a free market, the number of individuals in this situation would be few. One can search history for examples of those who have not always fared well at the sufferance of "property owners." Jews were historically denied the ownership of property in land. (Pipes noted, for instance, that in eleventh-century England and thirteenth-century Germany, Jews did not own property, they *were* property [1999, 112].) Jews were denied property ownership by the state, not by individual property owners, who might have been willing to sell if permitted. In free enterprise economies, there are strong incentives to sell to buyers. There is a tendency, at least, for the market to be impersonal. Still, if there is widespread prejudice, there is no guarantee that the propertyless will find willing sellers. As Rand noted, the right to property does not guarantee that one will have property (1964h, 96).

Reality—Revised

OE claims that men do not need other men in a fundamental way (Peikoff 1991, 252–53). Primary virtues have to do with how man deals with reality, not how men deal with other men. Rand's cardinal values and virtues are consistent with those that (by a process of abstraction) can be derived by analyzing man alone on a desert island. However, on a desert island man has nature-given resources to transform. In society, once all resources are owned, what are a person's alternatives? He owns himself and whatever he may earn by selling his mental and physical effort to those who are willing to hire him. This is his avenue for acquiring property—space for the body he owns, a sphere of jurisdiction into which others may not intrude, a moral space in which he may be rational and virtuous. But to acquire that property he must depend upon others—property owners—to hire him. So how he deals and interacts with others becomes important. Not only does man dealing with other men become important, how he deals with others becomes vital to his existence. Others are the means by which he acquires property. So values and virtues that relate to other people (such as justice) become primary not secondary.

This does not mean that the propertyless man is "dependent" on those with property. Nor does it nullify Rand's tenet that each man is an end in himself. When I say that the propertied are the means by which the propertyless acquire property once all property is owned, this is analogous to saying that the grocer is the means by which one acquires his bread. My point is that once all property ("space") is owned by others, others must become part of reality. There is no choice if one is to acquire property other than to deal with others. Since one must deal with others for his survival (it is not an option), the values and virtues that concern others become cardinal. The trader principle would be an example of a cardinal principle.

The Problem of Equal Distribution

Spencer ([1892] 1954, 108), echoed by Hospers (1972, 270), pointed out the problems of trying to assign property rights to unowned resources on the basis of equal distribution. For one thing, all parcels of land would not be equal—not in terms of the natural resources with which they are endowed, or their productiveness, or their accessibility, or their climate, etc. This problem could be circumvented somewhat by dividing the land in parcels equal to the number of individuals and assigning each individual the same ownership in each parcel. So if there were 100 individuals, there would be 100 parcels of land and each individual would own a (1/100) share in each parcel. Individuals could sell their shares, so the exact distribution would be fluid. Land could still end up concentrated in a few hands.

If a society were to start from scratch, then unowned space might be distributed as described above. Still, this would not protect a person from himself. If someone decided to sell all of his space, then he would be alive at the sufferance of others—assuming that they would suffer him. One may be entitled, at a minimum, to an amount of space; say, equal to the dimensions of his body—standing room, Rothbard called it (Hoppe 1998, xvi; Rothbard 1974, 108). The problem with granting that a person is entitled to space is that if he is owed that, what else is he then entitled to? A response might be that space is different from other things. It is different in that no one produces it, as such. It is also different in that a person could be said to need to own some minimum space in order to be free.

Rothbard has said that one cannot sell himself into voluntary slavery (1998, 135). One cannot alienate his will. If one accepts that a person who owns himself cannot alienate his will, then how is it that a man can alienate himself from the space his body occupies? How can one be said to own his body if someone else owns the space it occupies? How can a person have free will—act in accordance with his own decisions—if the dimensions within which he acts are owned by another? It would follow that each individual could not sell this minimum required space so long as he lives. The space would not have to be the same throughout his life. If he owns no such space on earth, it would seem that he would forfeit his place on earth. He would become unfree.

This "solution" does not address those propertyless individuals who are born later, into a world in which all space is owned. An argument could be made that when a child is born he has a partial claim on his parent's property. A case has already been made for a child's entitlement to childcare from his parents. It would seem to follow that since one's body takes up space and one lives in space and space exists prior to man's existence—it is not created by him—that if a person brings into existence a being with these dimensions and requirements, then those responsible for that being should at a minimum yield some of their space to the new being. If this is the case, then perhaps each person should be prohibited from selling or giving away a space that exceeds his own dimensions by the amount of the space that would be required for his potential offspring.

As I noted earlier, people can get around the so-called inability to sell oneself into slavery. This would not only affect the individual but would also affect any innocent offspring he may bring into existence. Something similar to the idea that parents must have a minimum requirement of space before having children was tried in Bavaria. In that case, it was capital, not space, that was required; that is, "it was enacted in Bavaria that no marriage should be allowed between parties without capital, unless certain authorities could 'see a reasonable prospect of the parties being able to provide for their children'" (Spencer [1892] 1954, 9). The unforeseen consequence was that in Munich, 50 percent of the births were illegitimate.

Rothbard—Acquiring Property

Scarcity is a fact of life. It can lead to conflict among men unless property rights are defined. Property rights are in that sense useful. Machan criticized economists for focusing on the utilitarian aspect of property rights (1975, 136–37). But the focus of economics is scarcity. If resources were infinitely abundant there would be no economic problem, nor would property rights be necessary. In this sense, property rights can permit the coordination of cooperative activity among individuals. Rothbard acknowledged this aspect of ownership, but he did not justify property rights on the basis of utility. He said: "Justice, not the weak reed of mere utility, must be the motivating force if liberty is to be attained" (1998, 258).

Rothbard subscribed to the first-use or homestead principle for acquiring original resources. He used the state-of-nature abstraction to demonstrate how original property is thus acquired, beginning with Crusoe alone on an island, then adding a second person, Friday (Rothbard 1998, 47). The idea of property in land would only be relevant to Crusoe and Friday if scarcity in the land set in right away. But this has not been the case in many instances when land was first brought into use. Initially, land is oftentimes relatively abundant.

Pipes noted that: "'For some fifteen million years members of the family of man foraged as animals among animals'" (Pfeiffer 1977, 28; quoted in Pipes 1999, 86). Three Ice Ages transformed man's diet from one dependent primarily on plants to one dependent upon meat. When man supported himself primarily by hunting, he could not limit himself to a single piece of land. In the savannah, the limit was two persons to a square mile. The choice was to starve or move. And man did move over vast distances (Bronowski 1973, 45). About 20,000 years ago, hunting single animals eventually gave way to following the migration of a herd. This was not herding as such, since the animals followed were not domesticated. The humans moved with the herd, following the natural migratory pattern. But, as in herding, the animals were tended and were regarded as an inventory for food. The Lapps of northern Scandinavia, who follow the reindeer, are the last people that still do this (1973, 45–46, 48, 59).

At the close of the last Ice Age, about 10,000 B.C., a flourishing of ground vegetation encouraged the settlement of land. One noted settlement was the oasis of Jericho. At first, settlers harvested wild wheat. A couple of genetic accidents produced a larger grain that would not spread. It required being scattered by man. Similar cultivation commenced in other parts of the world (1973, 64–69). Cultivation of the land promotes a sense of ownership. Those who cultivate the land are more attached to it than hunters and gatherers, according to Pipes, because the process itself extends for months, even years, depending upon what is planted. It also requires vigilance. The effect of tenure on the psyche is one of growing propriety (Pipes 1999, 93).

The first domestication of animals began about ten thousand years ago. Unlike wild herds, sheep and goats do not have a natural migratory pattern. The nomadic herdsman leads his flock, rather than follows it as was and is done by the followers of wild herds. Nomadic peoples use land but they do not use the same land all the time. Property used by nomadic people may be scarce but it may not be scarce all year round. Eventually, it may become scarce all year round. In that case, it may be desirable for those who have been nomadic to settle on a particular piece of property rather than use it part of the year. But those who first settle a particular piece may not have been the first users of that land. Hunters and gatherers are often more interested in what is on the land than they are in the land per se. As land is used more, customs may arise to use it (what is on it) more efficiently. Examples include rights to acacia pods, beaver dams, trees, and rights to trap (Ridley 1996, 234–35, 241–42; Pipes 1999, 87). Hunting and gathering tend to be highly wasteful with respect to land usage. Prior to land cultivation, about ten square kilometers were required per capita. Once land came under cultivation, the need declined to between one and five square kilometers. Domestication of animals reduced the requirement even more, to less than one half square kilometer or less per individual (Pipes 1999, 92–93). According to Pipes, land ownership in the modern sense did not begin until cultivation (1999, 87).

Property in land cannot potentially come into existence until land becomes scarce. Scarcity exists for a resource when it would command a positive price if owned. (If the resource is used as an input into the production of some other good, once owned, it will fetch a positive price and will be utilized to some point at which the marginal product is positive. If the resource is a consumer good, when it becomes owned, consumers will have to pay for its use, and it will therefore be conserved. Its marginal utility will be positive, under the assumptions of that theory.) Unfortunately, simply because some form of ownership may become justified, this does not mean that the resource will become property. It may take some time for individuals to realize the resource is scarce. Typically, it will be apparent that a resource used on a particular plot of land becomes scarce before land itself is considered scarce. Rand said that it took several hundred years before nomadic tribes understood the concept of private ownership, particularly as it applies to land. This coincided with the birth of civilization, according to Rand (1967g, 129). As Bronowski noted, "civilisation (*sic*) can never grow up on the move" (1973, 60).

Once a piece of land was settled, the possessors may have felt territorial about it and may have fought off encroachers. If a piece of land was totally unpossessed or unused, then individuals or groups of related individuals may feel equally justified in claiming it for their exclusive use. If a fight ensued, neither side would be regarded as initiating force against the other (in a "rights" sense), since neither had possession of it prior to the dispute. Each would be equally "entitled." These possibilities are a far cry from the first-use criterion advocated by Rothbard. They are not as clear-cut because the exact point at which a piece of land becomes scarce may not be obvious to anyone. The point at which a piece of land becomes scarce is an economic, not an ethical, consideration. Scarcity justifies (in an economic sense) ownership. If land is so abundant as not to qualify as property, then it does not reflect the user's rationality, or lack of it, if he fails to recognize the resource as property. Similarly, simply because land is not scarce and the individual does not recognize the land as property, this does not confer upon him a nobility of character. Scarcity or the lack of it with respect to any resource in and of itself is simply an economic reality.

Justice may still apply, but there may not be a single overriding criterion. It is possible that some sort of custom will arise based on possession. Using a game theoretic approach to the establishment of property rights, Sudgen suggested that possession may be a salient feature in establishing a convention for property ownership. But possession was the sole criterion mentioned in that model. There may be others, since possession is not always unambiguous.

Rand—What's the Use

Acquisition of original property, according to Rothbard, is based on first use or the homestead principle (1998, 47). Rand and Den Uyl and Rasmussen (1991, 120) claimed that ownership is derived from the application of physical and mental effort—a process of transformation. "Use" could either mean use in the production process or use in consumption. Presumably, what is meant by "use" is production. What then constitutes effort? When it comes to unowned land, Rand gave a clue in her discussion of its proper method of distribution. She pointed to the Homestead Act of 1862, which awarded a legal title to a homesteader who worked a 160-acre farm for five years (1967g, 123). Is farming the only justification for ownership of virgin land? Generally speaking, when Rand referred to the application of physical and mental effort, this included a much broader range of productivity than farming, but the Homestead Act did not. A reading of Hospers might lead one to conclude that many, Locke included, would consider first use to mean the cultivation of land (Hospers 1972, 266). At one point, Den Uyl and Rasmussen seemed to have suggested a broader interpretation to what is meant by the transformation of virgin land, suggesting that picking an apple from a tree qualifies (1991, 120). If this broader interpretation applies, then hunting and gathering would be regarded as transforming virgin property.

If hunting and gathering are regarded as use, then this broadens considerably the standard for ownership. Pipes related that, since the beginning of time, out of the eighty billion human inhabitants of the earth, the majority, 90 percent or more, sustained their lives as did most untamed animals—through hunting and gathering. Of the balance, 6 percent and 4 percent were engaged in agriculture and industry, respectively (Pipes 1999, 86). Yet those who were hunters and gatherers oftentimes did not regard themselves as owning the land they used, nor should they have in many cases, since the land itself was not scarce (only things that were on it).

Transformation and Wealth

Rand believed that the application of man's mental and physical effort is what gives a thing value (1967i, 130). Den Uyl and Rasmussen stated that there is no such thing as untransformed wealth (1991, 118). A good can be transformed yet have no value. It may have no value because there is no demand for it. In this case, technically, it would not be called a good. A good may become obsolete, or it may become so abundant as to become a nuisance. When this happens, its utility would be zero or negative. (There may be disutility—if it is a nuisance or harmful).

Conversely, a good may have value even though it is untransformed. That is, there can be untransformed wealth. There are goods that are consumed directly without being transformed by humans. Most goods require some effort on the part of humans, even if that effort is no more than picking an apple from a tree. However, oxygen is consumed directly. No one produces it per se. It takes no mental or physical effort on our part to acquire it. Clean air has often been relatively abundant. When it is relatively abundant, it can be said to have no value in the marginal utility sense. However, it would still be said to have value in the total utility sense. (Assuming that marginal utility theory is valid, if a good is not scarce, it will be free and will be used until its marginal utility is zero. It would have no "value" in that sense. However, when a good's marginal utility is zero, its total utility is maximum. It would have maximum value in that sense.)

There is another sense in which transformation is linked to value, which is related to ethics but unrelated to rights. Objectivists believe that values cannot be divorced from one's own action. If unearned, a windfall of money would not be a value. With this Den Uyl and Rasmussen agreed, stating that those things that are valued "do not exist independently and apart from human actions to attain them" (1991, 63). This does not mean that if one inherits wealth or if one wins a lottery, it is not one's property. One would not have a right to it (N. Branden 1963, 22), but to be worthy of it, one must expend his own effort.

Common Property

Spadaro wrote that in the nineteenth century, the prevalent idea among historians was that communal ownership was pervasive in primitive cultures (1974, 146). Their error is identifying property with ownership of land. There is no evidence that any society did not recognize ownership of some goods (Pipes 1999, 76). As evidence of that, Pipes noted that in all societies theft is punishable (1999, 77). Pipes stated that in primitive cultures, property is either individual or tribal in nature. Tribal ownership typically covers land that is used exclusively by kin for hunting and fishing, primarily. Individual ownership includes personal items, such as clothes and tools, along with intangibles, such as spells, songs, and stories (1999, 79).

In primitive cultures, communal ownership is believed to be rare, even in societies characterized by hunting and gathering. H. Scott Gordon wrote: "Significantly, land tenure is found to be 'common' only in those cases where the hunting resource is migratory over such large areas that it cannot be regarded as husbandable by the society" (Gordon 1972, 98). In general, he continued, primitive societies characterized by stability seem to have recognized the perils of common property and taken measures to manage their resources (ibid.). Communal ownership is not the same thing as common property, although the effects at times may be the same. If there are rules or customs regarding use, then the so-called "tragedy of the commons" may be avoided (Ridley 1996, 235).

Agriculture, as Pipes noted, does tend to promote a feeling of propriety; but not in all instances. With nomadic cultivation, called slash-and-burn, the ownership is the in the crops, not the land. It is practiced when land is plentiful relative to the population. In Russia, the early Slavs would fell the trees in a forest, set fire to them, then spread seed on the earth, enriched by the ash. Once the soil became depleted, they migrated on to repeat the pattern in another expanse of woodland (Pipes 1999, 161).

Stationary civilizations were not immune from the tragedy of the commons. In New Mexico at Chaco Canyon, a site on which stood the largest constructed structure prior to the skyscraper, the surrounding woodlands were stripped of timber. The civilization became extinct. The Polynesians of Easter Island transformed a lush forest into a wasteland and turned to warfare and cannibalism (Ridley 1996, 219–21). There are no guarantees that the concept of property will be recognized; that rights will be assigned; that rights will be respected, enforced, or even enforceable. With a common property resource, the question is: How is mutual restraint—which results in mutual benefits—achieved when the attempted restraint of one person will only result in an increase in the unrestrained activities of the rest (1996, 225). If everyone reasons this way, there is no incentive for anyone to hold back. The incentive with common property is to weight the present more heavily in deciding to what extent to use the resource. As a result it will tend to be overutilized. If a two-person Prisoner's Dilemma is played repeatedly and defectors are punished by not being included in future games, then mutual cooperation tends to follow. With many players, defectors are not as easily identified. Assignment and enforcement of property rights "solves" the Prisoner's Dilemma for a two-person game. Assignment of property rights may also solve overuse of a common property resource with multiple users. However, ownership may not be easily discerned.

First Use and Resources That Move

There is a theory that man turned from hunting and gathering and toward land cultivation as a result of Paleolithic overhunting. At the end of that era, about 10,000 B.C.E. (beginning of the common era), Asians who had migrated to America had killed mammoths and certain bison species to the point of extinction. They had then hunted smaller creatures and, more and more, became dependent upon cultivation to sustain them, relying on small game to supplement their diets (Pipes 1999, 93).

Ridley noted that: "In the absence of government interference, people are remarkably good at developing ways of solving the collective-action problem for environmental restraint among themselves. . . . So how is it that they so signally failed to stop themselves [from] exterminating the megafauna of North and South America, Australia, New Guinea, Madagascar, New Zealand and Hawaii?" (1996, 240–41) He said that it is likely that the simplest response is the correct one and that is: "Animals move; irrigation systems do not . . . . Did nobody among the early Maoris sit down after a moa feast and say, 'You know, if we go on like this, we're going to run out of moas to eat; maybe we should let a few alone to breed'?

Evidently, if anybody did, nobody listened" (1996, 241). As with other unowned resources, the incentive with mobile resources is to place insufficient weight on the future. As a result they will be used up more quickly. Since with biological resources, future viability is dependent upon living resources being brought forward, overkill today may result in extinction tomorrow.

When the Ice Age ended, approximately 11,500 years ago, humans arrived in North America. Subsequent to man's arrival was the extinction of 73 percent of the large mammals in North America. After man's arrival, about 8,000 years ago, 80 percent of the large mammals became extinct in South America. Some have attributed the decline in species, known as Pleistocene overkill, to climatic change. But there is a good deal of evidence to the contrary. Supporting the notion that climate was not at fault is that regardless of climate, man's arrival coincided with subsequent elimination of species, usually within a few hundred years or less. Extinction of elephant birds and several species of primates occurred in Madagascar following man's arrival around 500 A.D. As recently as 600 years ago, the arrival of man in New Zealand led to the destruction of twelve species of giant moas. Similarly in Hawaii, half of its 100 bird species became extinct once man arrived. The pattern was repeated in Australia with large mammals (1996, 217–19).

So even though communal property per se may not have been a feature of primitive societies, exploitation of common property abounded. There is nothing instinctive in human nature that results in automatic restraint once a common property resource becomes dangerously depleted. As illustrated earlier, nonownership of a resource can transform a transaction that could yield mutual benefits into a zero-sum game. The problem is the incentive structure underlying unowned resources. The incentive structure is compounded for resources that move. As Ridley recognized, there was no restraint on the part of a hunter not to kill one of the last two mammoths on earth because if he did not, another hunter would (1996, 231).

The criterion of applying labor to an unowned resource to establish ownership does not eliminate the possibility of unintended overkill. For instance, if mastodons are scarce, then one would acquire them by hunting (by applying one's labor). But if everyone does this, it can lead to extinction. So the solution may seem to be to assign rights to the land on which they live. But mastodons move. So they still may be overhunted, since one property owner may not take into account how hunting mastodons on his land affects the mastodon population overall.

Assigning Rights to Fish

Economists have made significant inroads in the theory of renewable resources, particularly fisheries. Much of this theory could apply to any species that is reproducible and mobile. The interest in fisheries has been due to the practical need of solutions to the problem of overfishing of various species. From an economic perspective, the problem is one of assigning rights so that overfishing does not deplete the biomass to the point of unintended extinction. The concern is one of efficiency, not rights per se—although the solution may involve the establishment of ownership.

If the resource is not owned, fishers enter the industry without having to pay for the use of the resource. Since they do not have to pay, too many may enter the industry to the point that the biomass may be unintentionally harvested to extinction. The solution may be seen as one of limiting entry into the industry. One way of approaching this is to sell licenses or fishing rights in the biomass. To be consistent with other forms of ownership, the rights would have to be permanent. This may not sufficiently limit catch, however, as pointed out in appendix 2.3.

To correct this problem the government may sell licenses to fish to firms (fishers). The government would have to determine the number of licenses based on the optimal expected catch and estimate that on a per firm basis. Because of the dynamics of the industry, the number of licenses may have to be refigured each year or season. So each year or season, the number of firms might vary. This would introduce a great deal of uncertainty on the part of the firms in the industry since they would not know from one season to the next whether they would be granted a license.

This would not be full ownership by fishers in any sense of the word. It would be as if the government, in the case of gasoline, determined how many gallons it could sell per time period—say, per day—and filled up tanks at the pump on a first-come first-served basis. Even if the gasoline were given away (as was done in the case of land in the Homestead Act, which Rand [1967g, 123] endorsed and which formed the basis for her recommendation for airways ownership) this would be a case of government rationing gasoline. True, those who got their tanks filled would be the owners of the gasoline, but the government would be in control of the resource; that is, it would be in a position of managing the resource.

If the concern is not for optimality but for ownership, then the solution may be different. If the objective is to establish ownership, then perhaps it should make no difference whether fishers unintentionally deplete the stock to extinction or not—so long as they own the resource. In order to have both full ownership and also the likelihood that the resource will not be unintentionally depleted to the point of extinction, exclusive rights could be granted to a single owner—at least in theory. If the right to the resource is limited to one firm, the problem of unintended extinction of the resource may be avoided (Howe 1979, 272).

Limiting the property rights to a single firm is not an unheard-of recommendation in economic theory. The economic argument for government granting monopoly franchises to natural monopolies, such as utilities, is a notable example.

This would not be embraced by Objectivists or most classical liberals, not because of the establishment of monopoly, but because it is also recommended that natural monopolies should be regulated by the government. So the assignment of an entire resource to a single firm is not without theoretical foundation in economics. Nor is there any basis for objection to monopolies in Rand's philosophy.

As I have mentioned, full ownership has been generally advocated by philosophers who support liberal society. For instance, Den Uyl and Rasmussen and Rothbard have advocated 100 percent ownership. Rothbard's objection to assignment of ownership by government to a single firm would be the government involvement, since he objected to government (Hoppe 1998, xviii). Spencer was opposed to private ownership of land, because it violated the law of equal freedom ([1892] 1954, 111). It is likely that he would see the assignment of an entire resource to a single individual as unjust.

Now Rand's recommendation was unlike any of these. She recommended the Homestead Act in the case of land and argued that the same approach should have been used for the airways. Instead of government selling rights to use the airways, full ownership of the airways should have been given on a first-come first-served basis so long as those who received the rights subsequently applied their labor to the airways. The fact that frequencies were "limited" to ownership by a few individuals would not be a problem. According to Rand, latecomers who want a radio station would have to purchase one from an original owner, which is the situation for any kind of property (1967g, 124).

A fish biomass, like land and air frequencies, is scarce. The problem may be expressed as one of units. What is a unit of land? To homesteaders it was 160 acres. This was based on practical considerations, not theory. A biomass applies to a specific type of fish, not all fish. So if a monopolist were given a right to a biomass, he would be given the right to catch fish of a given kind. But this type of assignment of ownership—although theoretically feasible and potentially efficient from an economic perspective—is inconsistent with Rand's recommendation insofar as rights to land were concerned or rights to airways. If rights to resources on land had been assigned in the same manner as has been discussed with respect to rights to a biomass, the parallel recommendation would be that a firm or an individual would be assigned property rights in certain animals on land—not to the land itself.

To be consistent with Rand, a body of water would be divided into plots and the rights to those plots assigned on a first-come first-served basis. With the Homestead Act, ownership was based on farming. But, we do not—the Homestead Act notwithstanding—limit land ownership to the cultivation of farm products. If a body of water were to be parceled out, the rights need not be limited to fishing. Other rights would have to be acknowledged. Bodies of water are used as passageways, for recreation, for off-shore drilling, for scientific exploration. It may be preferable to keep some plots in pristine condition. So how should rights be assigned? A body of water could be divided into plots equal to the number of individuals in the population. To avoid the problem of some individuals getting better plots than others, each individual may have an equal share of each plot.

Because water moves, there may be the problem of some owners polluting the water and it affecting the water of other owners. This has been an argument against assigning property rights in bodies of water. J. H. Dales said: "Air and water . . . , however, seem to be owned in common because there is no alternative. There is no feasible way of separating a cubic yard, or an acre, of water from other cubic yards or acres, there is therefore no way of ensuring exclusive uses; fences simply don't work" (1972b, 311). Pollution is an issue in water ownership, but it is also an issue in land ownership. Land may be contaminated by chemicals, the air above it contaminated by car emissions. Another objection to the assignment of ownership in water is that some water uses may conflict with others that may be collocated. This can happen with land ownership as well (1972a, 175).

If a parcel were assigned to someone who did not want to use it in any way, he could sell it to a willing buyer. An enterprising person might be able to acquire enough acreage to use for offshore drilling or for recreational fishing or boating or for scientific exploration, etc. The question is, would this solve the potential problem of unintentionally overfishing a particular species? The answer is no, not necessarily. The problem is that ownership as assigned would be ownership of a parcel of the body of water, not the fish themselves, and fish move. This was the same problem faced by primitive people who depended on hunting for survival (Ridley 1996, 241).

Simply assigning ownership rights to plots of a body of water is not enough to solve the problem of overfishing, since a single fisherman still will not take into account how his efforts affect other fishers. In other words, some of the costs that result from his efforts will be borne by others (which violates Rand's trader principle). This would be true of land animals if we still relied upon wild game. Simply assigning property rights in land would not have solved the problem of overhunting.

If a person has exclusive rights to a resource (a monopoly), he will try to maximize its present value by considering the time stream of benefits as well as the discounted value of expected future costs. Since a single owner owns the resource, he will, by excluding nonowners, be able to capture all the benefits as well as bear all the costs (Gordon 1972, 91). The ownership to be assigned in the case of living resources—such as wild game or fish—is not of the land or of the ocean, but of the species itself. In particular, monopoly ownership of a species of fish, for instance, would more likely result in its efficient utilization. Unintentional overkill or extinction would be less probable.

But imagine that "solution" with land animals. Imagine landowners who own the land but others who own the species on it. The mastodon monopolist might take into account all present and future benefits and costs and thus not overutilize the resource. But mastodons live in space and unless the monopolist also owns the space on which the mastodons roam, there would be a conflict of interest between the mastodon monopolists and the landowners. If there were a monopolist for every species of animal, this could make it virtually impossible for the so-called landowner to do anything with his property. Consider the snail monopolist. He might be able to constrain a landowner's ability to build because it would kill the snails on the owner's property. In the extreme case, this could make one's land worthless, and it could as a result be snatched up by the enterprising snail monopolist. This is the position some property owners face when their property is declared a wetland by a government agency, except in the latter case it is the government that is the monopolist, not a private individual. (There is also the likelihood that the monopolist could sell his rights to several owners. So the original problem of overutilization is visited anew.)

Domestication of animals and land cultivation both had their geneses around ten thousand years ago. Small game still supplemented the diet, but reliance on large mammals as a primary food source was no more—largely because large fauna were becoming extinct. But had there been total reliance on wild game instead of agriculture and domesticated animals, private ownership of land would not have solved the problem of extinction of large animals, as land ownership under the sea would not solve the problem of overfishing. One might say that the domestication of animals may be a precondition for property rights. If man had been heavily dependent on wild game in his diet, it would have been much more difficult to establish private property for agricultural cultivation. One could have rights to use the land for growing crops, but unless there were wild game preserves set aside for hunting, it would have been difficult to subsist by hunting what was on one's own land, and it would have been difficult to police others from coming on one's land to hunt. Somehow property rights in animals would have to be assigned in order not to overkill them, but animals do not respect property boundaries.

Rand—On Distribution

Rand offered as her version of the proper distribution of unowned resources the Homestead Act of 1862. Here the government acted as the custodian of the unowned land and devised objective rules for its dispensation (Rand 1967g, 123). From Rand's standpoint (as well as Machan's [1998a, 67] and Rothbard's [1998, 36]), efficiency is not the overriding criterion insofar as ethics is concerned.

Efficiency may apply to Randian ethics in a couple of ways, however. If overutilization results in a threat to human life, then it threatens the foundation of Rand's ethics, since life is the ultimate value.

Property rights should be assigned to that which is scarce. If mastodons are scarce, then the property rights should be assigned to mastodons. If the basis is first-come-first-served, a people could end up as did the Easter Islanders. Each man will reason, based on the first-use criterion, if I am the first to kill the mastodon, I own it. If each reasons this way, then all will try to kill mastodons and this will eventually result in the extermination of mastodons. Therefore, an inefficient standard of assigning property rights can threaten a people's existence.

The second way in which efficiency, or lack of it, is relevant to ethics is that it can violate the trader principle. For instance, in the case of fisheries, even if rights are assigned to individual fishers, there is the problem that each fisher will not take into account the effect of his efforts on the other fishers (see appendix 2.3). Other fishers will bear the costs of his actions. In Rand's ethics, each person should bear the costs of his own actions.

For resources that do not move, such as land, once it becomes scarce, ownership will tend to result in more efficient utilization. If it remains unowned, since individuals do not have to pay for its use, it will tend to be overutilized. Lack of ownership may also lead to disputes over use. Rand has said that there are no conflicts of interest among rational men. However, if property rights are not assigned, there can be. One way of interpreting Rand is that property rights resolve potential conflicts among rational men. Another is that if men are rational, they recognize the need for property rights and assign them, so that no conflicts arise. A third is that there can be no conflicts if property rights are not assigned because a person cannot have an interest in that which he does not own, rights being synonymous with interests.

Taking the last position first, then the argument would be that one cannot lose what one does not own. If one accepts this position, then even if two individuals vie over a piece of unowned space and one of them does not win it, this is not a loss, because he did not own the resource in the first place. One cannot lose what he does not own. Still, there can be losses of other kinds—of time, of opportunities forgone (assuming that there were other opportunities), of being harmed or killed during the dispute. These, too, may not be interpreted as a loss in Rand's sense of the term. As Tara Smith stated: "We do not know in advance which of our efforts will succeed. The fact that a person's goals are not always realized is not a loss, however. It is the natural condition of all human activity" (2000, 180). But if these are not losses, it is hard to imagine what would be a loss. A loss is the sacrifice of a greater value for a lesser value. One way of interpreting Rand (and Smith) is that no one makes a (rational) decision to choose an alternative if one expects to lose. The actual outcome may be a loss, but the expectation is that one will not lose. This is similar to the way in which economists view decisions. However, it is possible that one may only face alternatives that involve losses. The decision-maker would then choose (for a given level of risk) the lowest expected loss. (How loss is defined is pertinent to the decision; that is, whether it is measured in dollars or utility or some other standard.)

The first position is probably more reasonable; that is, if property rights are not assigned, then the potential for conflict is present. Rand envisioned a Hobbesian existence in the absence of property rights. She said where property rights do not exist, there are clashes of opposing interests with no hope of resolution (1967f, 259). The situation takes on the characteristics of a zero-sum game. When a material thing is not scarce there is no potential for conflict, since it is abundant enough to satisfy all demands for it. It would be sufficiently abundant so as not to qualify as an economic good. A problem can arise when a fixed resource, such as land, is overtaken by a sudden influx of population. What is the solution? According to Rand, this would seem to be the time at which government should go about assigning property rights. That is, rational men would recognize the need for property rights and assign them. This is not entirely hypothetical. When the Europeans settled the Americas, the influx created resource scarcity where, in some cases, it had not existed. The problem was compounded by the fact that there were people already occupying the geographic region.

Johnson and Rasmussen claimed that Rand's position with regard to primitive people was that they have no concept of property and therefore they have no rights to respect (2000, 259–60n6). (This would follow from position three above.) One way of viewing native people is that they were living in a "Hobbesian" state of nature. Paul Beaird argued that American Indians did have government. He based this on conclusions drawn by Albert Jay Nock. From Nock, Beaird quoted: "Mr. Jefferson . . . remarked that the hunting tribes of Indians, with which he had a good deal to do in his early days, had a highly organized and admirable social order, but were 'without government'" (Nock 1973; quoted in Beaird 1976b, 23). Schoolcraft and Herbert Spencer echoed this observation. Nock countered that the natural rights position on rightful government is based on two principles found in Paine's *Common Sense* and Jefferson's Declaration of Independence: "'to secure these rights, governments are instituted among men,' and it 'derives its just powers from the consent of the governed'" (ibid.). Applying these, Nock claimed "'it is abundantly clear that the Virginia Indians had government'" (ibid.). Rand defined government as an institution that has the exclusive power of enforcement over a certain geographic jurisdiction of particular codes of social behavior (Rand 1964g, 107). The failure to recognize the governments of Native Americans is the identification of government with state (Beaird 1976b, 24).

Not only did Native Americans have governments but they also recognized property rights. According to Pipes, a study by Frank G. Speck noted that the Indians of northern America and Canada recognized exclusive rights to tracts owned by families and passed down from one generation to another (1999, 86). Where land was not scarce, it was not owned, per se. Pipes noted that North American Indians did not claim territorial rights when the animals they hunted grazed over too great of an expanse to make the protection of such claims practicable (1999, 87).

When the Europeans arrived, land that formerly may have been plentiful became scarce. Since it does appear that at least some tracks were owned or may have been owned on the basis of migratory patterns, then the Natives would have had first claim, so it would only have been proper to negotiate with the Natives. This appears to have been what was done in some cases. However, the natives had no concept of property in the way that the settlers did. They had a different relationship with the land in terms of use and in terms of their psychological attachment. As Pipes mentioned in a footnote, the familiar story of the Dutch "purchasing" Manhattan for sixty guilders is based on a misunderstanding. Manhattan Island was a hunting and fishing ground. The Natives envisioned yielding some of it now and then to meet the needs of the Dutch. They never imagined that they would be driven off the island entirely (Pipes 1999, 83n; from Ellis 1966, 25–26).

In many instances, land was taken by force, not by purchase. From the settlers' perspective, land was approached as if it were an unowned resource. Based on Sugden's game theory models, which were used to analyze property conventions in a state of nature, possessors should have had an advantage. The implicit assumption underlying Sugden's analysis did not apply here. The two sides were not evenly matched. Europeans had the advantage of numbers and firepower.

Rather than envisioning native people as not having government, the implication could be that they had governments, but that they were not proper. If a government is in place, but it is not proper, then other men may have the right to establish a proper government and, with that, property rights. Rand said that a proper government, such as that of the United States, has the moral right to defend the victims of one that is not. It does not have the moral obligation, however. If it is not in the interest of the United States, it has a moral obligation not to intervene (Rand 1974a, 363). Now, protecting people who are under the thumb of a despotic government is not the same thing as conquering a people or peoples who have government that an invading people do not regard as proper—which is what the settlers may be said to have done.

Even if it is argued that the Natives did not have government, nor an understanding of rights, it does not follow that they had no rights. Evers contended that

Rand's social contract theory was more Hobbesian than Lockean: "Ordinarily in political theory, natural law is right for man whether or not men consent" (1977, 191). There appears to be some contradiction in Rand. On one hand, Rand claimed that the source of rights is the law of identity; they are necessary by virtue of his nature for man's survival. They are not based on positive law or divine ordinance (1961a, 182). So government—the consent of the governed—is not the basis for rights. Not understanding rights does not mean that one has no rights to respect. Taking by force would appear to be ruled out—whether individuals recognized the land they occupied as their property or not; whether they had established rules for its dispensation or not.

The transition from man alone to man under a proper government may not be easy to trace theoretically and may be even more difficult to attain in reality. Not unrelated to this is the difficulty of recognizing at what point a resource becomes scarce and that ownership is necessary, and the further challenge of assigning and enforcing ownership rights.

CHAPTER NINE

Intellectual Property: Unilateral Transfers

Rand said that the basis for property rights is "man's right to the product of his mind" (1967i, 130). Consistent with this statement is Rand's advocacy of property rights in ideas—specifically, patents and copyrights. However, she argued that these should be limited in duration. She opposed altogether the ownership of ideas by discoverers of pure knowledge. Since property rights in ideas are limited or nonexistent, those individuals who discover, create, or invent can be said to provide benefits to others for which they are not fully compensated—that is, unilateral transfers. This chapter examines Rand's (1967i) positions on intellectual property.

Intellectual Property

The notion of intellectual property has been around for some time. In his book *Property and Freedom*, Pipes stated that patents are thought to have originated during the fifteenth century in Venice (1999, 142). Robert Lowie credited primitive peoples with customs reminiscent of today's rights that protect intellectual property. Covered were "intangibles" such as magical spells, songs, stories, and designs (1999, 80). The effect of a patent or copyright is to confer upon the holder exclusive control—a monopoly of sorts. Douglass North credited English patent laws with spurring the Industrial Revolution by encouraging inventors to make their inventions public (1999, 63).

Although patents and copyrights protect intellectual property, they must be given physical form. The property right, however, protects not the object, but the idea that gave it form. The law prohibits reproduction of the product without the creator's consent. This reflects the fact that it is not the physical labor of replicating an object that is of value but the idea behind its creation. Rand noted that the basis for intellectual property, such as copyrights and patents, follows from that for all other property—the right to the product of one's mind (Rand 1967i, 130).

Rand on Intellectual Property—Examined

Although Rothbard implied that rights to inventions should be held in perpetuity (1998, 123), Spencer and Rand both thought that there should be limits on the duration of intellectual property. The legal system in the United States (as well as in other countries) limits the duration of patents and copyrights. Spencer's reason for limiting the terms of patents and copyrights was because of the inclination on the part of inventors to come up with a new idea at approximately the same time. The term limits on patents and copyrights cannot be determined with exactness, but the right itself is still valid ([1892] 1954, 127–28).

Spencer's argument appears to have contradicted his claim that "nature's rules . . . have no exceptions" ([1892] 1954, 37). If a law appears to need a statement of exception to the contrary, it is the law that is imperfectly stated. "The so-called exceptions are in ourselves, not in nature" ([1892] 1954, 38). For example, in his argument against the legitimacy of existing titles to land, Spencer said that the commonly accepted notion is that land "held from age to age" is private property. He countered with the question: "How long does it take for what was originally a *wrong* to grow into a *right*?" ([1892] 1954, 105) Assuming the question is valid, one could equally ask with respect to setting time limits on patents and copyrights: "How long does it take for what was originally a *right* to grow into a *wrong*?"

Rand also supported the idea of time limits on patents and copyrights, although she offered different reasons from that given by Spencer. Rand stated that because it is not possible for intellectual property to be consumed, it cannot be owned in perpetuity. If ownership were of unlimited duration, this would have the opposite effect from that intended. Rewarding descendants would serve as a permanent mortgage on future generations that would stultify creativity. The price of a car would have to cover royalties to inheritors of all the patents used to produce one, from the wheel up. Rand said: "[C]onsider the accidental status of such descendants and the unreality of their unearned claims" (1967i, 132).

Although Rand's point sounds reasonable, she did not make the same case with regard to land ownership. She noted that intellectual property is not consumed. Her argument for limiting property rights in ideas was that "no debt can be extended into infinity" (1967i, 131). Yet land is not consumed either. She did not argue that land's ownership should be limited in time, nor was she opposed to its inheritance (N. Branden 1963, 22–23). Future generations pay landowners (who may have inherited it) for its use, over and over again. The latter observation originated with Mavrodes in his article "Property" (1972, 260). A response could be that patents and copyrights do create artificial scarcity; land is truly limited, but patents and copyrights limit the use of ideas that could otherwise be used by others (ibid.). Is this an argument for term limits (or, perhaps, an argument against intellectual property rights altogether)? Not necessarily. Ownership by its nature limits use. Intellectual property has "public goods" characteristics. The problem with public goods is that use by nonpayers cannot be restricted; therefore they tend to be underproduced. The challenge with public goods is finding a way to restrict nonpayers so that the goods will not be underproduced (or not produced at all).

Rand's case for limiting the duration of patents and copyrights was that personal virtues in general, and intelligence and ability in particular, are embodied and therefore cannot be transferred. Since intellectual property rights are based on one's right to the product of one's mind, then ownership should not extend beyond the creator's life (Rand 1967i, 132). Rand is correct that one's intelligence is embodied in oneself. One cannot hire out one's labor service after one is dead. But the products of one's efforts can exist beyond one's lifetime. Ideas that are or can be embodied in products live in those products. According to Rand, all wealth is a product of man's mind (1961a, 89). All productive effort is both mental and physical. This effort is embodied in material products. Patents and copyrights protect mental effort.

Ownership in natural resources is justified on the grounds that wealth cannot exist without its source, which is intelligence (1961a, 183). Land is owned indefinitely and is inheritable. Inventions, on the other hand, which require the greatest degree of mental effort, are limited to one's own lifetime. Based on the emphasis on mental effort in the creation of wealth in Rand's theory of property rights, it seems curious that rights that are designed to protect property that requires the greatest degree of intelligence should be limited in duration.

The argument that ability is embodied and therefore is limited to the creator's lifetime does not hold up if one compares patents with other forms of ownership. If the heirs choose to sell their land (or any inherited wealth), what they receive in return is the discounted value of the expected future income stream—a lump sum payment for all the rent to be received over the lifetime—*not of the owner*—but of the property being sold, the land. The same could exist for intellectual property. For instance, a patent could be sold by the holder of the patent to permit manufacture of the patented good, giving the manufacturer the exclusive right to produce and sell it. What the original owner would sell is the discounted value of the future income stream to be expected from the production of that product. If the patent were not limited in duration, that income stream would be calculated over the lifetime of the idea on which the patent is based, not the lifetime of the holder of the patent, unless these two lifetimes were the same. If the patent were limited in duration, the value would be discounted over the life of the patent. Inventions can have value beyond the lives of the inventor, just as land can continue to have value beyond the life of the original homesteader. One could say the lifetime for land is limitless. But that does not guarantee value. A barren desert may have no value, even though it may exist forever (or for the conceivable future). (Now if the lifetime is forever, the discounted value may not be much greater than if the patent was limited to, say, thirty years. The discounted value of $1,000 per year forever at a 10 percent discount rate is $10,000 whereas the present value of $1,000 per year for thirty years at 10 percent is $9,426.90.)

(Since anyone may use the idea behind an invention or formerly copyrighted material once the time limit expires, they will be used until they have a marginal value of zero. They will be attainable at a zero price. This may work against, say, new playwrights or authors of books. They must be paid, whereas those in public domain do not have to be. Users of newly patented inventions must pay for their use—but only the incremental value added. New inventors do not have to pay for the ideas they build upon.)

Although Rand suggested that intellectual property rights should be limited to the lifetime of the creator, she indicated that if so limited, investors would be discouraged from making long-term investments because of the risk involved if they thought there was a likelihood the creator would die soon (1967i, 132). Risk does not confer ownership or rights to someone else's property, however. If the patent should be limited to the person's life, then risk of others should not be an argument to extend a property right beyond a person's life. Even though Rand implied that limiting property rights in this case is to protect the right of (potential) investors, there is no right to protect. This is an argument based on expediency or efficiency, not rights. I am unaware of any other situation in which Rand expressed a concern for the risks of investors. Yet such risks abound. Any time investors put their money in a venture in which one or a few individuals have particular expertise, there is considerable risk involved. There are ways of hedging against some risks—for example, specific contracts and insurance policies. Similar instruments might be extended to reduce the risk of investment in new techniques. There are a variety of risky investments in a free market. One of the riskier investments is in another's education—particularly general education. Investing in employee training or lending money to students for their education is risky because of the difficulty of attaching a lien against human capital.

To protect and encourage investors in new ideas, Rand recommended extending copyrights beyond the life of the creator. She looked to the United Kingdom as offering the most logical solution to the question of duration, whose Copyright

Act of 1911 established the length of ownership as the author's life plus fifty additional years (1967i, 132). This would seem to put at a disadvantage those publishers who invest in the creative endeavors of the very old. A fixed number of years regardless of the lifespan of the creator would seem to make more sense. This is, in fact, what Rand recommended for patents. She noted that patents have the tendency to limit research in given areas. They can serve as "an unjustifiable barrier" to the advancement of knowledge. The legal challenge is to establish a time limit that provides the inventor with the greatest benefit "without infringing the rights of others to pursue independent research" (1967i, 132–33).

Here she claims that the rights of the inventor must be weighed against the rights of other researchers. If the argument favoring release of patented information (after a certain number of years) is that others are waiting in the wings to discover new techniques but are hobbled in their efforts because of patents, why should they be constrained at all? Why should a brilliant chemist or engineer have to wait twenty years for a patent to become public domain? What if the potential creator dies and his invention never materializes? Why favor a would-be inventor twenty years from now over a would-be inventor today? This could be an argument against patents altogether. Then again, if a budding inventor should have to pay for the use of a patent in order to build on the idea behind it—then why limit the right to twenty years? Why not make patent ownership permanent as is other property? Why should the budding inventor not pay for ideas that he did not originate?

In no other case did Rand, to my knowledge, argue in favor of any individual or group over that of the creator. In general, she said if there are those who by right are entitled to the production of others, this condemns the latter to "slave labor" (1964h, 96). If one person produces, while another distributes it, the former is a slave (1964d, 94). From the perspective of the would-be inventor, one could take a cue from the following Spanish proverb quoted by Rand: "God said: 'Take what you want and pay for it'" (1982a, 101). Rand said that the creator does not exist for other men, nor does he sacrifice for others (1961c, 79). Why should he be forced after twenty years, more or less, to release his claim on the product of his effort?

Since man must rely on his own mind, and since he must pay for knowledge acquired, it would seem to follow that part of the price of inventing something new would be to pay for the use of previous inventions. If one needs the ideas behind the invention of another to further his own creative purpose, he should acquire whatever knowledge is necessary. If that means paying for an engineering degree from MIT or paying for the use of a patent from the holder of it, then so be it. Rand made a similar point in "The Property Status of Airways," stating that latecomers who wanted a radio station would have to purchase one from the original owners, the same as all other property (1967g, 124).

Limiting patents to a few years has the effect of favoring those inventions for which patents can be avoided altogether. Rand mentioned that current patent laws encourage entrepreneurs to depend upon secrecy to safeguard inventions rather than risk patenting them (1967i, 133). Why should inventions that can be kept secret have an advantage over innovations that by their nature need to be patented because the ideas behind them can be easily duplicated by others? The argument that producers and consumers would still be paying patent holders of the wheel hardly holds up when it is acknowledged that we are still paying for land that has existed since the beginning of time. Milton Friedman stated that "there is a strong prima facie case for establishing property rights" (1962, 127) for patents and copyrights. However, conditions that apply to these rights, such as the period for which they are granted, "are matters of expediency to be determined by practical considerations" (1962, 128). Perhaps it is to expediency that one should look to make such an argument; however, according to Objectivism and classical liberalism, laws should be solely based on rights.

There are numerous "inventions" that cannot be patented because exclusion is impossible. Friedman mentioned the supermarket, a concept from which many benefited but for which the idea-man received no compensation from others who appropriated his idea (1962, 127). The same could be said of basic research. Rand made a distinction between a discovery and an invention. A discovery cannot be patented. By discovery, she meant uncovering basic knowledge. Patents relate to applied research and to the physical object that embodies it. They pertain to objects that may not have otherwise existed (Rand 1967i, 131). Basic research and those inventions that are not patentable by their nature are thus at a disadvantage relative to patentable inventions. They are public goods. Exclusion is not possible. Once known, others cannot be excluded from using them.

There may be the question of what basic research is and what applied research is in some cases. If someone discovered that a plant extract cured a disease because of some change that it produced at the body's molecular level, is that basic or applied research? Exclusion may be possible in a case such as this, so it would not be a public good, per se. It is patentable. If that were the criterion, then it would appear to be an invention, not a discovery. However, Rand's point was not that basic research *cannot* be patented. She asserted that discoveries *should not* be patented. They cannot belong exclusively to the discoverer since, first, unlike inventions, they are not created by the discoverer. And, second, once an idea is found by the discoverer to be true, he cannot insist that others rely on untruths unless they have his permission (1967i, 130). The discoverer may write up his discovery and have it copyrighted. He can insist on acknowledgment for the discovery, but he cannot claim ownership of the idea and require compensation for its use.

Rand's argument ultimately rests on the importance of the advancement of knowledge as such. This was one of the reasons she advocated limiting the duration of other intellectual property. It was Rand's position that others have a *right* to the product of discoverers of knowledge. Discoverers are deprived of the right to the product of or compensation for their efforts. This is an exception to her dictum concerning the right to own that on which a person labors. Patents and copyrights are the other exceptions (after a period of time). (Children are still another.)

Unilateral Transfers

Given Rand's argument for limiting patents and copyrights, it could be concluded that those who invent do not receive a return commensurate with their contribution. Limiting the duration of such rights entails a sacrifice on the part of the rights holder. Furthermore, according to Rand, a discovery is not patentable. Since a discovery of a scientific or philosophical principle or fact is not created by the discoverer, he cannot insist that others practice untruths unless they have his permission (Rand 1967i, 130). If it is assumed that the denial of such rights is justified, then it is true that the discoverer creates a benefit for which he cannot be compensated at all. This would qualify such work as a sacrifice. (The fact that a person may enjoy the creative process and not regard the endeavor as a sacrifice is not the issue. If a person expends labor, others benefit, and he is not compensated for it as a matter of rule not as a matter of choice, it is a sacrifice nonetheless. Unilateral giving qualifies as "service" [1963, 12]. The fact that a person may enjoy the process or get some partial compensation only reduces, but does not eliminate, the sacrifice.)

About those who discover new ideas, Rand said that they are permanent benefactors of mankind (1961a, 186). Yet, even though inventors and discoverers are not compensated fully, or at all, for their contributions to mankind, Rand did not condemn this as she did other sacrifices. Apparently, what is important to Rand is the *intent* of the inventor or discoverer. Although they are permanent benefactors of mankind, mankind or the benefits to mankind should in no way be their objective. Profit should be their (only) objective, according to Rand (1961a, 97). Here is an apparent contradiction as I see it. The fact that profit may be less than would exist if they were fully compensated (or in the case of unpatentable inventions or discoveries, there is no profit at all) makes it difficult to understand why anyone would undertake such endeavors. This introduces an aspect of irrationality into the decision to innovate or discover. Here productivity is not synonymous with profit (as defined above by Paterson [1968, 232] and referenced by Peikoff ([1991, 391]). If the creator works for nothing but his own profit, these creative endeavors are difficult to justify in OE.

Even though discoverers and inventors do not receive the full return on their contribution, Rand nevertheless praised them. She did not praise others who provide benefits without compensation or full compensation—those who do volunteer or charitable work, for instance (Berliner 1995, 83). One possible reason for the lack of praise in the latter cases is that such endeavors do not expand the bounds of knowledge and improve the productive capacity of the economy; at least that is not their objective. However, from the individual's perspective, the expansion of the productive base of the economy should be irrelevant if it involves a sacrifice on his part. Later, I will make a case for the rational (nonsacrificial) pursuit of innovation for which one may not be fully compensated as well as for other unilateral transfers (such as charity).

Personality Property

Although to my knowledge Rand never specifically developed a rigorous argument concerning the issue of personality property (even though it is clear she had ideas concerning biography (B. Branden 1986, xi–xiii)), it has been a subject of discussion in the Objectivist literature. Murray Franck included personality property in the definition of intellectual property (1995, 8). Personality property includes the right to one's own biography. Franck contended that the right to privacy protects the disclosure of the events of one's life without one's permission. Included also are publicity rights, which are property rights in one's name and likeness for commercial use. The property right in one's reputation is protected by defamation laws.

Franck's argument is based on his observation that personality property meets the same standards that are required for other property. It is the product of one's mental and physical effort—one is the author of one's own life. It also follows from the right to one's body and its actions. One's reputation is covered because it is derived from the facts of one's life as understood by others. It is one's reputation that determines the value of one's likeness and name for commercial use. Personality rights, according to Franck, are vital to one's survival. One's reputation can, through one's biography or the commercial use of one's likeness or name, provide the monetary return needed to survive. Defamation of one's character can result in the loss of one's livelihood and one's ability to survive. Franck noted: "Each person . . . requires tranquility against constant intrusion that can inhibit access to the subconscious and therefore to certain automated thought processes, and therefore to effective creative and productive thought" (1995, 8). Your rights to your personality can be violated by others disclosing the facts of your life (without your permission), "primarily through the media" (ibid.). He contended that no one else's rights are violated if one chooses not to disclose the facts of one's life or not to permit his likeness or name to be used commercially. Franck did allow exceptions. A public figure, particularly one in the political arena, will have narrower protection (1995, 9).

Spencer, writing long before Franck, agreed that a person has a right to property in one's character, or reputation. He also pointed out that, like other property, one's reputation is a product of one's labor ([1892] 1954, 128–29). Unlike Franck, Spencer did not address the right to one's biography or the rights to use one's name or likeness for commercial endorsement. He did address slander, but unlike Franck, Spencer hedged against regarding slander as a violation of the law of equal freedom—that law which prohibits trespass on another's own sphere of activity. Slander is more likely, said Spencer, an infringement upon the moral principle that prohibits infliction of pain on another, what he called negative beneficence. (Negative beneficence refers to psychological pain [{1892} 1954, 70–73].) Spencer claimed that there is no way of determining with certainty whether slander violated another's rights or is a moral breach ([1892] 1954, 130).

Of course, if it is a moral breach, it would not be subject to legal action. Only rights are protected by law, according to Objectivists and libertarians. So it makes a difference in terms of legal recourse on the part of the victim whether slander is regarded as a violation of one's rights or is a moral breach. Rothbard did not believe that libel and slander were rights violations. On the contrary, he argued that one had a right to one's own opinions and could publish for public consumption anything one wished, regardless of the truth of it. One's reputation is not a material existent. It is a product of the beliefs contained in the minds of others. One does not have a right to that which is in the minds of others. For example, if an investment newsletter erroneously predicted the future of a particular stock, and as a result of that prediction, the stock fell in price, the injured party could not sue for damages. Rothbard claimed that even if a person knows another is not a thief, he has the right to accuse the other of being one, to print the lie and to disseminate it (1998, 126).

Since one has the right to lie about another in Rothbard's opinion, it would follow that one would have the right to tell the truth about someone. Thus, one has a right to blackmail another. This follows from the right to one's own knowledge and the right to make that knowledge public (1998, 124). Although Rothbard didn't make this claim, it would seem to follow from the statements he made that since one has the right to lie about another, one could blackmail another by threatening to reveal information regardless of whether that information is true or not.

An exception to the right to disseminate what is in one's mind or to speak freely would be if one masterminded a crime. Even if one did not engage in the crime or otherwise benefit from it, he would be guilty of a crime. This would be particularly true, said Rothbard, if the mastermind told others to commit the crime. On the other hand, one could exercise his right to free expression if he, as a result of speaking publicly, were to incite a riot (1998, 81). As for the right to reveal knowledge that one is privy to, Rothbard did make an exception. That is, one would not have the right to use or make public information that was received from another on a conditional basis. For example, if, on the promise of secrecy, an inventor revealed to another the details of a patent he planned to file, the receiver of the information would not be at liberty to use it or to communicate it to others (1998, 123).

Discussion

If a person has an exclusive right to his biography as Franck (1995, 8) claimed, then if someone else published another's biography that would be theft—a forced unilateral transfer. If one owns his biography, what does this mean? If he has worked with others, then can he include his experiences on the job with his coworkers in his biography, or does that violate their rights to their own biographies? If he has been married, does his spouse's right to his spouse's biography prohibit him from mentioning his spouse? How does one write a biography without mentioning those who have influenced him, inspired him, taught him, or even betrayed him? The nature of a person's life is (unless he has lived on a desert island) that it is entwined with the lives of others, and it is difficult to reflect upon one's life without mentioning others.

There may be rights to privacy if there is a contractual agreement with another person that requires his permission before personal information can be disseminated. But by and large, most of the interactions one has with others are the subject of one's life and take place without privacy contracts. There may be a moral obligation to be discreet about experiences one has had with others, but in many cases when one experiences one's life it is in the company of others, and if one owns one's life, he owns those experiences. Experiences with others may be regarded as jointly owned. If so, it might be said that one must get the permission of the other party if one wants to disseminate information that concerns that party, but if one must have the permission of the other, then he does not own his history. In rebuttal, it could be said that one could discuss the events of his own life and keep the others parties' names anonymous unless he has permission to reveal them. This may sound logical, but it does not solve the problem of anonymity in many cases. One may refer to his ex-wife or his business partner, but not naming them will not protect their identities.

If one can relate experiences one has had with others because they are part of the history of one's own life, then a biographer could gather testimony from various acquaintances of the subject of the biography and base the book on those testimonies. There is little doubt that a biography based on the interviews with one's friends, family, etc. could be unsettling to the subject of the biography. But one does not have a right to tranquility, as Franck (1995, 8) suggested. And, except in those instances in which one had a contract of confidentiality with another, it would seem to me to be a violation of others' rights to free expression to limit what they can say if what they say is based on their own life experiences with the subject of the biography. There may be personal records that would be legally off limits. Medical, tax, and school records would fall into that category. One may own one's biography in that he can tell his own story and that story may be more truthful and more complete since only he is in command of all the facts of his life, but he cannot deny others the right to express their own experiences they had with him since they are jointly "owned."

Of course, if the biographer lies about his subject, that is a different matter. I do not agree with Rothbard's position on slander and libel. I think there is a difference between someone going to a restaurant, eating a meal, and giving his opinion on that meal (the service, etc.), and a person falsely accusing a restaurateur of selling liquor to minors. One is in the nature of opinion based on matters of taste. The other concerns a fact of reality. Either the restaurant owner did or did not sell liquor to minors. It is not a matter of opinion or based on a prediction about what the owner will do in the future. It is based on a statement that is or is not at variance with the facts of reality. There seems to be a contradiction in Rothbard's claim that one does not own what is in the minds of others when it comes to lying about a competitor's product or when one falsely accuses another of theft or murder, but when one lies about one's own product, somehow one gains ownership of another's mind. The latter lie is punishable, according to Rothbard, because it is fraud. If falsely accusing another person of, say, murder, leading to possible incarceration or death, does not violate another's rights, and if lying about another's product does not, how then is lying about one's own product a violation?

As for telling the truth about someone else, I would think it would be difficult to prohibit others from doing this if they have a right to free speech. Unfortunately, blackmail would be covered under the right to free speech, so long as the information was acquired legally, and it is true. I think that a case could be made that individuals do not have exclusive rights beyond their own domains. I think that the right to speech, for instance, does depend on the reasons one is on another's property. Rothbard did not regard an incitement to riot as a violation of anyone's rights; he regarded it as an exercise of free speech. Yet he did regard falsely shouting "fire" in a crowded theater a violation, whether by a patron or the owner. If the owner yelled, he would be culpable because, by interfering with the event upon which he based his sale, he has violated his patrons' rights. It would be a variety of fraud, presumably.

A patron who yelled would be violating the rights of the other patrons (as well as the owner) by robbing the patrons of the event they had paid to see. Rothbard quoted Hugo Black's argument that purchasing a ticket does not buy the right to make a speech (1998, 115). It was, said Black, not so much what the person yelled in the theater, but that he shouted. (It is not that the shouter somehow "owns the mind of others" by affecting what they think, but that he has been loud and disruptive.) According to Rothbard, if a patron shouts "fire" he is "violating the terms of his being there" (1998, 114). How is this different from someone inciting a riot? If one is on another's property when he incites a riot, it is very likely that he is violating the terms on which he has entered that property. Unless he bought the right to riot, he would be violating the rights of others by inciting a riot. This line of reasoning would extend to rights one does have outside his domain. If a person is on another's property, then he has certain privacy rights unless there is a presumption that he has forfeited them by the nature of the reason he is on another's property. For example, he would have the right not to be photographed or taped without his knowledge.

I find the exceptions to the right to disseminate knowledge curious from a number of standpoints. Rothbard claimed forcing people to be truthful or to keep promises is not under the purview of the law (1998, 79); i.e., keeping one's promises may be the moral thing to do, but it is not the function of the law to enforce them (1998, 133). If it is true that promises cannot be enforced, why would a person be guilty of violating an inventor's rights if he merely promised not to tell anyone and then broke his promise? If one follows Rothbard's logic, then, contrary to his assertions, it would also seem one could legally mastermind a crime so long as he did not otherwise participate in it. It follows from the right to free expression. (I do not agree with this line of reasoning. Exempt from prosecution might be, for example, those who mastermind war crimes as well as Charles Manson.) Telling others to pull it off should carry no extra weight at all since those who did so could not surrender their will (1998, 135). Nor would the mastermind own the ideas in the minds of others. It would follow that even if the mastermind threatened the others with bodily harm, he would be exempt from prosecution. Rothbard believed that the receipt of overt threats is a violation of one's rights (1998, 80). But a threat to another would seem to be an exercise of free speech, if one relied upon Rothbard's reasoning in other contexts. Having said that, I would conclude that whether threats are protected by the right to free speech would depend upon what is being threatened. A threat to do bodily harm to another (or his property or to someone he cares about) would not be covered under the freedom of expression provision. Rothbard (1998, 78) emphasized the immediacy and specificity of the threat, which makes sense.

CHAPTER TEN

The Social Contract

Although views of the social contract differ, the one I put forth in this chapter is that it is a bilateral exchange in which the individual's right to retaliate is relinquished in exchange for government protection of other rights—value is traded for value. Rand's view was that government is established by "the consent of the governed" (1967d, 332). Machan qualified that consent is not required from those who would violate the rights of others (1975, 176). Some do not see government as coercive if it is based on consent—whether explicit or implied. What is meant by implied consent is challenging to pin down. One argument is that if there are alternatives to the government, then it is not coercive, choice being seen as synonymous with freedom. I view government as coercive, since the individual is no longer permitted to exercise one of his rights—the right to (delayed) retaliation.

I offer two justifications for the existence of government. One relates to a point I made in chapter 7 that, under anarchy, those children (and others with diminished capacity) who are abused or neglected by their caregivers would be systematically excluded from rights protection. This violates the equal freedom principle. A second argument relates to the conflict of rights that exists when a person is accused of a crime. The decision is modeled as one of minimizing the risks one would face if he were accused of a crime under anarchy. A person may rationally think himself capable of just retaliation if he were a victim, but not believe that the odds favor his being treated justly if accused of a crime. He may rationally turn the function over to an impartial third party, but only under the condition that all others do so as well. If everyone reasons in this way and does so, then that would establish government.

I also address funding of government. I agree with Objectivists and libertarians who think that taxation is coercive. I examine two "voluntary" alternatives to taxation discussed by Rand (1964i) and find them to have coercive elements as well. My argument is that the exchange of the right to retaliation for protection (the social contract) requires that government produce protection. Production requires the use of scarce resources. Production and income are inseparable. Funding is not separate from, but integral to, that which is exchanged. The coercive aspect of the exchange is that one relinquishes his right to protection. Funding is not a separate coercive aspect, but part and parcel of the exchange. Without funding, the exchange is incomplete and empty.

Government and the Social Contract

A proper government derives its power "from the consent of the governed" (Rand 1967d, 332). And a proper government's sole function is the "forcible restraint of men" (1967d, 335). To Rand, government is an institution that has the exclusive power of enforcement of particular codes of behavior over a certain geographic jurisdiction (1967d, 329). The origin of the state, according to Robert Lowrie, was when authority became territorialized (Pipes 1999, 95); as Sir Henry Maine (1864) is credited with noting—"when bonds based on consanguinity yielded to those resting on territorial contiguity" (ibid.). Prior to this transition, the notion that individuals should be bound politically based on geographic proximity was thought "strange" and "monstrous" (1999, 96).

In contrast, Wolff defined the state as "a group of persons who have supreme authority within a given territory *or over a certain population*. A nomadic tribe may exhibit the authority structure of a state, so long as its subjects do not fall under the superior authority of a territorial state" (Wolff 1998, 3). Although a nomadic tribe may be said to have government, Beaird (1976b, 24) noted that it is an epistemological error to equate government with the state.

Pipes said: "Private property in the legal sense of the word comes into existence with the emergence of the state, that is, public authority. Until then, it is possession protected by physical force and/or customary law and legitimized by inheritance and/or prolonged usage" (1999, 97–98). Private ownership in land emerged in Greece in the eighth and seventh centuries B.C.E. when Athens's population was broken down into territorial political units, which replaced those based on blood ties. The idea was to cripple the clans' power (1999, 100). The transition from blood revenge to the rule of law was dramatized in *The Oresteia Trilogy*.

With the emergence of the state comes assumption by the state for retaliation. Private vendettas are forbidden (1999, 96). This exchange of obligations—protection for peace—is metaphorically referred to as the "social contract." In Hobbes's depiction, in the state of nature, there are only warring individuals. Every man has a right to everything including every other man, according to Hobbes. Men are compelled by self-preservation to surrender their natural rights to the state, the sovereign. It is the sovereign who establishes property and therefore has the right to it. He may tax it or take it at will, without the governed's consent (1999, 31–32).

Those who subscribe to natural rights regard natural law as existing prior to positive law.

> An essential element of the Law of Nature is the equality of man, specifically, equality before the law, and the principle of human rights, including the rights to property, which antedate the state, and thus are independent of it. (1999, 12)

Natural Law was a Stoic principle that dates to the fourth century B.C.E. (1999, 8). Laws were not thought to be made, per se, but "'there,' in the background, to be deduced from custom and the Law of Nature" (Atiyah 1979, 29; quoted in Pipes 1999, 127).

Rand claimed that prior to the existence of capitalism and the legal institution of private property, "private property existed *de facto*, but not *de jure*, i.e., by custom and sufferance, not by right or by law" (1967a, 13). This seems to contradict Rand's statement that inalienable rights "means that the same rights are held, individually, by every man, by all men, at all times" (n.d., 6).

Hobbes believed that property ownership was founded on consent, not on nature (Pipes 1999, 31). Similarly, Bentham (Pipes 1999, 104n*) and Hayek (Rothbard 1998, 229) saw rights as stemming from positive law, not being ratified by it. Holmes and Sunstein stated: "William the Conqueror created property rights, as they eventually came to exist under the common law, when he distributed plots of seized lands to the Norman noblemen who had helped him overrun England" (1999, 194–95). Those who subscribe to natural rights would argue that William the Conqueror did not create property rights. He encoded property laws that were inconsistent with individual rights.

Sunstein and Holmes called the social contract an exchange of "equal rights for social cooperation" (1999, 151). This sounds Hobbesian, but they clarified that to enjoy equal rights, each person "must renounce his 'natural right' to punish unilaterally all those who, in his subjective opinion, have injured him" (1999, 152). To the latter statement, Rand would have agreed (1964g, 110), even though she never mentioned the social contract per se. Machan dismissed the social contract, although he acknowledged that as an analytical tool it can provide important insights (1975, 173–74). If the "social contract" is interpreted as a metaphor for the establishment of government, then, unlike Hobbes, Objectivists would not regard it as an agreement to give up one's rights for state protection. They view government as the protector and enforcer of rights.

Consent and Anarchy

Although both Rand and Machan believed that a proper government is established by the consent of the governed (Machan 1975, 173; Rand 1967d, 332; Sechrest 2000, 170), Machan qualified this, stating: "The establishment of a proper government does not require the full consent of all those who might be subject to the laws of a free society. The protection and preservation of one's moral (self) interest does not require the sanction and consent of those who violate or threaten to violate them" (1975, 176).

Voluntary interaction is usually regarded as typifying individual freedom. If individuals have free will, and if they have a right to act on their decisions, it would seem to follow that the social contract would result from the independent exercise of each person's free will. It would also seem that to bar people from entering such agreements would be an infringement of their rights. Rothbard claimed, however, that such an agreement would be a barrier to freedom. In his view, individuals cannot enter contracts in which they agree to alienate their will. Thus a social contract, or any contract in which one agrees to alienate one's will, would be invalid. And if one cannot surrender one's will, he cannot surrender those of future generations (Rothbard 1998, 226, 232).

Wolff, in this respect, agreed with Rothbard, arguing that autonomy and state authority are incompatible and therefore concluded that anarchy is the sole moral doctrine (Wolff 1998, 18). Like Wolff, Rothbard was an anarchist. However, Rothbard was an anarcho-capitalist, whose case against government was founded on the theory of individual rights. He saw the state as coercive in at least two ways. One is that the state has a (compulsory) monopoly on the use of force. The second is that the state obtains revenue by compulsory means—through taxation (1998, 162). In Rothbard's vision of the anarcho-capitalist society, there would exist a system of privately competitive defense agencies. Individuals would also have the right to "take the law into their own hands" (so long as justice was proportional) (1998, 90–91). Rothbard believed the law and the state are independent of each other. Competitive private agencies would be shaped by market forces as would any firm in a free market. Although Rothbard did not believe that individuals could agree upon a social contract, he claimed that judicial agencies would all have to agree on "the basic Law Code" (Rothbard 1998, 236). Rothbard offered ancient Ireland as an example.

One of Beaird's arguments against Rothbard's vision of anarcho-capitalism is that the "primitive" communities (e.g., ancient Ireland) that Rothbard used to illustrate anarchistic societies were in fact governments (Beaird 1976b, 24); he claimed that Rothbard erroneously equated government with the state. A rightful government (based on Paine's *Common Sense* and in the Declaration of Independence) is founded on two principles. "[T]o secure these rights, governments are instituted among men," and it "derives its just powers from the consent of the governed" (1976b, 23). Based on these criteria, Ireland had government.

Responses to Anarchy

In response to Wolff, Machan said that if government is seen as a hired agent, providing protective services as would, say, a doctor providing medical services, then the citizen is not necessarily deprived of his autonomy. Machan interpreted Rothbard's objection to government as being due to a lack of choice regarding how a victim may respond to violence. Machan argued that a service is not compulsory if there is an alternative. Freedom, then, is the freedom to choose. He listed secession and the existence of competing (free) governments as alternatives. If these options exist, choice is not eliminated by the existence of government, according to Machan (1975, 143–55).

In my view, what is given up is not the freedom to choose among protection agencies but the right to retaliate. The government is not simply providing a service called protection. When democratic governments provide, say, medical services, they do not prohibit the private sector from also providing those services. Government provision of protection does not permit competition—at least in the area of delayed retaliation. The analogy with medicine suffers in the sense that healthcare is not a right, retaliation is. There are very few rights. There are the right to life, the right to property, and the right to retaliate. Others are derived from these.

It could be claimed that, in establishing government, what a person is agreeing to is not to initiate force against another. If that were all it entailed, then the person would not be relinquishing a right, since one does not have the right to initiate force. But to relinquish a right is to give up one component of freedom. To respond that government provides it for the person, and therefore he still has protection, does not address that point. By analogy, if man were to give up the right to property, the government would be charged with providing shelter, etc. However, classical liberals would not regard a government as proper if, as a condition of its establishment, individuals were required to surrender their property rights.

Kelley argued that market exchange assumes that property rights are in place and enforced. Having a market in enforcement would result in Mafia-like agencies (Kelley 1974, 247). Rand dismissed the idea of "competing governments," illustrating its inner contradiction with an example of two individuals, Mr. Smith and Mr. Jones, who are both customers of competing governments, A and B. If Smith suspected Jones of stealing from him and calls Police A to Jones's residence, and Jones, denying his guilt as well as the authority of Government A, responds by calling Police B, you can "take it from there" (Rand 1967d, 335).

Because of this, Machan asserted that there would have to be a "court of last resort—a court bound . . . by the law of the land—to be defined and enforced by a legal system's administrators in accordance with a system based on human rights" (1975, 151). If there were such a court, then a government would exist. It would seem to follow that private retaliation would be ruled out; otherwise it is questionable how effective that government would be.

Machan claimed that the protective agency would have to be a geographic monopoly, but the government would be a monopoly, per se, only if it were the only free society in existence. (This assumes that a person would be free to relocate to the alternative country.) Secession would be a second alternative to living under a government (1975, 150). Another option would be to "fire" (by not reelecting) those responsible for justice if they do a poor job. "In some cases, where the administrators try to prevent this—and thus subvert their essential function to serve the people—revolution is warranted" (1975, 151–52).

Like Machan, Beaird saw consent as justifying the establishing of government. The option of secession should be considered for its viability since both Machan and Beaird mentioned it. Rand did not speak of secession as an alternative to living under a government. Secession is unlike leaving one country for another or living alone on an island. When one secedes from a country, he stays within its geographic boundaries. The secession principle gives the person "the right to withdraw one's land from the government's jurisdiction" (Beaird 1976a, 12). Is secession a realistic alternative? First, one would have to analyze the circumstances under which one would secede. If one wants to secede so that he may violate the rights of others whom he might in some fashion coerce into seceding with him, then the government would be justified in prohibiting the secession in order to protect the rights of the coerced victim or victims. A person who values liberty and lives in a free country would have no reason to secede. A person who values liberty would only secede if his liberty were seriously threatened. If a country is seriously threatening its citizens' freedom, one would have to ask what the chances would be of the country allowing that person to secede. In practice, secession would seem to be unlikely.

Even if secession were considered in theory, problems remain. Suppose one secedes and lives peacefully on his own property; however, his neighbor, who is still a citizen of the country he has seceded from, kills his daughter. Can he exact punishment on his neighbor? His neighbor still falls under the legal jurisdiction of the government. Since the social contract specifically entails the relinquishing of the right to retaliate in exchange for government provision of retaliation, by seceding from the government, the victim (father) has given up the right to receive redress from the government. Even though he has seceded from the government, he should still have rights, since rights exist in a state of nature. By seceding, his right to retaliate on his own behalf would be restored. Would the government permit private retaliation under its jurisdiction? If a government has a monopoly on the use of force, as Rand contended, then by definition it would not permit private retaliation by its citizenry, or the father who has seceded.

A person who cannot protect his rights, has no rights. Yet, this appears to be the situation the father (and his daughter) would be in if he seceded. It would be wrong to conclude that this is simply the price one pays for going it alone. One retains the right to life, to property, and to retaliation, even in a state of nature. But as has been shown, it would be impossible to exercise the latter in such a circumstance. I would conclude that secession would not appear to be a viable alternative.

Why Government?

In an anarcho-capitalist society, Rothbard envisioned each person meting out justice on his own, or, more likely, leaving it to private agencies. The difficulty is, if one is incapacitated due to injuries suffered in an assault, he may find it difficult to do either. It is even more difficult to get justice if one is dead—for example, if one has been murdered. One might look to family members to see that justice is done, but as Rothbard noted, family members or heirs are under no obligation to seek retribution on one's behalf. As a possible solution, Rothbard suggested that individuals specify in their wills what the form of punishment should be if they are murdered (1998, 86). The victim could specify that an insurance company prosecute the alleged murderer.

In Rand's view, lack of "organized protection" would degenerate into gang rule (1967d, 330). Beaird (1976b, 23) pointed out that the tribe can be thought of as a governmental unit. So even though Rand categorized such social organizations as chaotic, and Rothbard (1998, 178) did not regard them as governmental units, they can have codes enforced to protect rights within the tribe. However, like other governments, the codes may not in fact protect individual rights, per se. Even if within the tribe rights are protected, between tribes there still may be warfare. Each tribe is like a country, and if one person within a tribe is injured by a rival tribe, then the tendency is to take action against the rival tribe, not the individual within the tribe who is responsible. Disputes between tribes are such that it is the tribe that bears the burden of guilt for an injustice and the tribe that bears the burden of seeking retribution if an individual of the tribe becomes a victim of a crime perpetrated by an individual in another tribe. So even if individual rights are protected within the tribe, between tribes the principle of equal rights for the individual would not be upheld. Guilt is communal; retribution is communal.

I should point out that the problem of a lack of respect for individual rights between governing bodies in disputes with one another may not be eliminated by governments becoming territorialized or by extending their range over larger geographic areas. Although England and other European countries were not based on full individual rights during the time of the settling of the Americas, they did have notions of property rights for their citizens. Respect for life and property, such as it was, did not extend to the natives of the Americas. Similarly, warring countries, like tribes in dispute, have been known to not have the same respect for the rights of individuals in the enemy camp as they do their own citizens. In practice, respect for rights, to the extent that it exists, is often confined to the tribe, whether the tribe is small or is geographically large, particularly in times of war. (This does not mean that some governments are not less warlike. There is a sound argument that countries that are relatively free tend to be more bound by trade with other countries and that trade makes aggression less likely.)

Children: A Case for Government

The question of children's rights and their protection in an anarcho-capitalist society was found to be problematic in Rothbard's theory. Rothbard claimed that children have negative rights. If one accepts this assertion, the question is, who protects a child's rights in an anarcho-capitalist society? Rothbard (1998, 100) held that parents are under no obligation to care for their children. This would mean that they are under no obligation to provide retaliation in the event the child was a victim of a crime. I have argued that parents are responsible for their children, and therefore would be responsible for providing protection for their child if he were a victim of a crime. This would seem to solve the problem of equal rights under the law for children. However, a problem arises if it is the parents who infringe upon the child's rights.

If a parent, or parents, kills his child, who will seek justice on the child's behalf in an anarcho-capitalist society? No one is obligated to do so. Since, according to Rothbard, the parents own the child, there is some question whether someone other than the parents could do so. In effect, it is the family unit, not the individual, that is imbued with rights in Rothbard's conception (Hoppe 1998, xli). In any case, if another person did seek justice for a child who was murdered by his parent or parents, it would be an act of charity. Since no one is obligated to do so, children cannot be said to have equal protection under the law.

It could be said that, should an adult be murdered, no one is obligated to seek justice on his behalf either. The adult must, in an anarcho-capitalist society, make arrangements to do that for himself. This is because each person is responsible for his own life. He has a right to life but he must support himself. Part of supporting oneself is protecting oneself. No one can guarantee another's life. It is his own responsibility.

So how is the situation of an adult different from that of a child? One difference is that an adult has reason and volition and the capability for planning and being productive. A child, particularly a young child, does not have these capabilities. He is dependent by nature. One could make the same argument about anyone with diminished reasoning capacity or who is severely disabled physically to the point that he is incapable of taking care of himself. He would not have equal rights under the law. So, if equal rights under the law are important, as Rothbard contended, and if equal rights do not exist for those who are not fully rational or who are otherwise severely disabled, then this could be a valid point of argument in favor of government protection of rights. Government is needed to protect the rights of those who are defenseless (on the basis of their diminished capacity). This would not mean that there would be government protection for children and private retribution for adults. If government were to exist, private retribution would be prohibited. This is the right relinquished when government is established.

The *DeShaney* Decision: The Default of the Furies

According to some interpretations of the function of government, a child may not be protected even if a government is established. Concerning the Constitution, Rand wrote that it limits government, not private citizens. "[I]t does not prescribe the conduct of private individuals, only the conduct of the government" (1967d, 336). This view was affirmed by the Supreme Count in the *DeShaney* decision (Holmes and Sunstein 1999, 89). The decision concerned a four-year-old boy, Joshua DeShaney, who had suffered severe brain damage as a result of beatings by his father, who had legal custody. The boy's mother filed suit against the Department of Social Services, since it had repeatedly returned the child to the custody of his father. The Supreme Court concluded that the child's "constitutional rights were not violated because such rights safeguard private individuals exclusively from public officials; they do not entitle people to state protection against their fellow citizens" (1999, 88). Holmes and Sunstein argued that (at a minimum) the ruling is at odds with the Thirteenth Amendment, which prohibits slavery (1999, 91).

If the state prohibits personal retaliation, it must take on that responsibility. If it does not, one could argue that it has been complicit in the crime. (Literally and metaphorically, it would be equivalent to someone—the State—restraining you while a thug beats you up.) Holmes and Sunstein implied this. They used the example of trespass. If the government failed to protect someone from trespass by a private citizen, then the state may be said to have "taken" one's property (Holmes and Sunstein 1999, 90)—a unilateral transfer. Since the property owner is prohibited from taking action (except if there is an immediate threat to his life), if the government fails to respond, the individual is rendered defenseless.

Costs and Cowardice

There are purely practical reasons for turning the function of justice over to a government rather than keeping it in private hands. One is cost. This does not mean that government protection of rights would necessarily be less expensive (in dollar terms) than private provision. Rothbard noted that protection provided by the government may be anything from a policeman for the country as a whole to a policeman and a tank per person (1998, 181). This is because protection is usually funded through taxation (which the government may increase to cover increased costs, whether those costs are warranted or not), and because there is no interplay of market forces to keep costs down. This makes it difficult to determine "how much" is "enough."

However, to the individual, the personal costs that he may anticipate if he takes on justice himself may seem large indeed. For one, he may have to risk his life. Similarly there is the cost of forgone opportunities that one would incur while seeking justice. There is also the possibility that one may not be able to take on the responsibility of justice oneself because one has been incapacitated as a result of the crime. One may be injured or dead. One could rely on family or, as Rothbard suggested, turn to a private agency. When reliance is on personal retaliation, particularly when it falls on family members, the burden on males can be particularly acute. They may have to forgo other endeavors at which they have superior skills. Their destinies may be simply stillborn because of the responsibility of protecting themselves and their families. Women may also be marginalized in such societies.

There is also the possibility that one may be a coward. It takes considerable courage to pursue personal justice. One may be inclined to hide behind the supposed virtue of forgiveness rather than to do the right thing. But unwarranted forgiveness has a high price if the victimizer remains a threat to oneself and to others. For this reason, it may be preferable to turn the protective function over to others—an agency. There is also the possibility that one may be legitimately fearful of accusing and punishing the wrong person. Since most crimes involve considerable uncertainty as to who the perpetrator is, one may prefer to hand the job over to experts, since they would be more experienced and may be less likely to charge the wrong person with the crime. Cost cannot stand alone as an argument for government, since, because of specialization, a private agency may also be less costly than an individual seeking retaliation on his own behalf.

Rights of the Accused and the Convicted: A Second Case for Government

R. A. Childs once criticized Rand for not trusting the individual in matters of justice. In the area of justice, the individual's judgment is "subjective and arbitrary" (although in all other decisions Rand regarded individuals as being objective—or capable of it). Childs contended that if this is the case, the problem cannot be eliminated by transforming the decision into a "collective" one (Beaird 1976a, 14). But the issue is not so much that a decision is being made collectively by turning it over to the third party. The purpose of turning protection over to a third party is to make the process as objective as possible by encoding rules that are impartial, systematic, and rational. A person may have perfect confidence in his own impartiality, objectivity, and rationality, but still may be fearful that if he is falsely accused of a crime, his pursuers will not be as fair as he. For this reason, a person may quite rationally prefer a system in place that is bound by certain principles, such as the presumption of innocence, rules of evidence, prohibition of unwarranted search and seizure, trial by a jury of one's peers. He may feel that it is less likely that his accuser will follow these rules if reliance is upon personal retaliation even if conducted by private agencies.

Not only would the accused prefer to be treated fairly but he has certain legal rights. In the United States and some other countries, there is the presumption of innocence. This may or may not be an absolute right of the accused. Still, it is a principle of justice that many recognize. There are other principles, such as trial by a jury of one's peers. These may or may not be derivative rights, but they are designed to protect the rights of the accused. Laws prohibiting search and seizure except under strict stipulations are derived from the protection of property rights, for instance. Beaird implied that a proper government is needed to protect the rights of the accused (1976a, 13). Evers criticized Beaird for not deriving these procedural rights from man's nature. Evers claimed that some who are natural rights liberals might advocate procedural standards for prudential reasons. But "[n]o consent doctrine is needed to favor prudent law enforcement" (1977, 192). Still, Evers offered no support for his assertion that prudential law enforcement would be forthcoming in an anarcho-capitalist society, other than to stipulate that it would.

I would agree with Beaird that the government is protecting the rights of the accused and the criminal, but theirs are not the only rights that should be protected. I would say that the need for government is that both the victim and the accused have rights and when a crime is committed these rights are in conflict, and it is for this reason that a third party (that is bound by certain objective and impartial rules) is needed. Rand pointed out that it is not simply the possibility of human immorality that makes anarchy objectionable. She said even if a society's citizens were perfectly rational and ethical, anarchy would not be workable because of the need for the arbitration of honest disputes based on objective laws (1967d, 334).

When a crime is committed, there is often considerable uncertainty about who is guilty, and if the guilty party is known, the nature of the guilt. (Even if an alleged perpetrator is known to have killed someone, it may have been self-defense, an unavoidable accident, or he may be insane.) Because of the uncertainty, there arises a conflict between the rights of the victim to justice and the rights of the accused. It is because of this clash of rights that a third party is needed to settle the dispute and mete out justice, protecting both parties' rights in the process.

Although Rothbard claimed that the accused "are innocent until proven guilty" (1998, 82), he did have a qualification. He stated that the police could use force against suspects of crimes so long as the suspect is eventually found guilty and the same methods of treatment are used against the police if the suspect is found nonguilty (ibid.). So the victim or his agents (police) may torture or beat up or confine the suspect so long as the police (or victim) are willing to face charges if the suspect is subsequently found not guilty. The qualification Rothbard offered could nullify the presumption of innocence principle.

On the other hand, it could be argued that the presumption of innocence is redundant. Exactly when would a person lose his rights if accused of a crime? Why should he lose any, so long as he has not been found guilty? This would render the presumption of innocence an absolute. However, if the accused retains all rights until found guilty, then the victim's right to justice may be compromised. For instance, if the accused retained all property rights, then even if a neighbor saw young boys enter his house and never leave, there would be no grounds to search the house. There must be instances in which there would be grounds for an orderly search of a person's premises for a specific purpose.

Rand has said that there are no conflicts of interests among rational men, but in the case in which a crime has been committed, there is a conflict—a conflict of rights. And since each party to the conflict has an interest in protecting his rights, it would be prudent for a person who might face either eventuality (i.e., of being a victim or being accused of a crime) to recognize the advantages to having a third party that is bound by certain principles of justice to settle such disputes. A person then may rationally forgo one right for the protection of another. He may willingly forgo his right to retaliation in exchange for the protection of his rights, particularly in the event that he is ever accused of a crime.

The reason he is willing to do this is that if accused of a crime the protection of those rights *is not under his control*. Without government the protection of those rights would be under the control of his accuser. Second, he cannot know who his accuser might be and how objective his accuser might be; he would prefer to put his trust in encoded principles of justice that a third party is bound by law to follow. The decision could be cast as one under conditions of uncertainty in which one person faces many potential opponents. The decision is one of minimizing injustice if one is accused of a crime. There is the possibility that one may be wrongly accused by another. One does not know who that person will be, and in a large community, the number could be significant. If personal retaliation is allowed, then each potential accuser may have his own ideas about justice (rules of evidence, the form justice will take, and so on). There is the possibility that the accuser may or may not be fair. If within a culture there is a tendency toward "tribal" justice (whatever the basis for the "group" might be), then guilt and retribution may not be individualized. "Tribal" justice may involve risk not only to oneself but to loved ones. Since the risk of injustice might be quite high, then another alternative may appear more attractive, particularly if its standards are known (with a relatively high degree of certainty) and are impartial.

If the alternative is to establish a government, this is not without a "price." Part of the price would be to give up private retaliation. Of course, unilaterally giving up retaliation would be useless. Assuming one would be willing to relinquish retaliation, it would only be with the stipulation that others would also agree to do so. It is that agreement (that others will not retaliate) which is the value one would gain. This is a public goods dilemma in the sense that one would only be willing to pay (by giving up his right to retaliate) if others agreed to do so. The reason everyone might do so is that everyone faces the same uncertainties. The (relative) certainty of a single (impartial) standard would be "worth the cost" so long as everyone paid it.

A criticism here is that I have cast this as "minimaxing" injustice (choosing the best of the worst alternatives). I have pitted personal (or tribal) retaliation against that of an impartial government; however, I have not included all of the alternatives—specifically private agencies under anarchy. Rothbard believed that private agencies would be impartial. He added, however, that all judicial agencies would have to agree to respect individual rights (1998, 236). If judicial authorities did reach this agreement, one could argue that the result would be a governing body. (Rather than citizens agreeing under a "social contract," the judiciary would agree.) Rothbard still allowed for private (personal) retaliation, however. The question is, if private retaliation were still permitted, would this agreement among judicial authorities be a governing body? One could argue that it would be. There have been governments in which private retaliation existed side by side with governmental retaliation. In some cases it may or may not have been legal, but it existed. Duels are an example of private retaliation that existed long past the establishment of government. In some Arab societies, private retaliation exists and is still culturally, if not legally, accepted. In other countries, such as the United States, private retaliation may exist (e.g., organized crime), but it is neither legally nor culturally sanctioned. In most cases, government takes a dim view of private competition in this area.

It is a legitimate question whether the existence of private retaliation undermines the authority of government. Certainly, if a citizen wanted some assurance of impartial treatment if accused, he would have to agree to forgo personal retaliation if he were a victim of a crime—so long as others did so—since this would be the only way he would be likely to have his rights protected if he were suspected of a crime. So, if respect for the rights of the accused is valued by a society, then the existence of private retaliation side by side with government could undermine confidence in the government to provide protection in the event one is suspected of having committed a crime.

A group of private agencies that agree on laws could be analyzed along the lines of a cartel agreement. Eventually, a cartel tends to break down internally because of incentives to cheat. Would there be incentives to "cheat" on the part of the private agencies comprising the cartel? Sechrest has compared the "common laws" on which the agencies would agree with "the voluntary adoption of a common set of time zones by the American railroads in the nineteenth century" (2000, 169). However, the time-zone problem would be a *coordination* problem, not one of *conflict*. Would there be a conflict of interests among private agencies that could lead to an internal breakdown of agreement? There might be if individuals bribed judges and other agents to act impartially, and there were no effective method of policing the cheaters. Even if there were no internal conflicts of interest, however, there would be external threats (competition) in the form of private individual retaliators who might not conform to the law. Although they, too, might be prosecuted, if there were enough competition of this kind, the "cartel" might collapse.

Buchanan and Tullock and the Social Contract

Buchanan and Tullock in *The Calculus of Consent* focused on the decision process for a representative individual facing collective choice. When Buchanan and Tullock referred to choice in the collective sphere, what they meant was voting. A vote reflects an either/or decision, but does not gauge intensity. In the market, individuals "vote" with dollars, and dollars express magnitude as well as direction. In the market sector, uncertainty is reduced by agreement and exchange. Buchanan and Tullock suggested that in the collective sphere, agreement and exchange can also take place to reduce uncertainty related to one's decision. Since votes occur over time, not once or in isolation, individuals can trade votes (log roll) (Buchanan and Tullock 1965, 122–23). Side payments are another possibility. The advantage of side payments is that they allow for the expression of intensity of preference.

Another difference between public and private choice is the degree of responsibility for decisions. In the private sector, there is a one-to-one correspondence between the decision a person makes and responsibility. In the private sphere, a given action by an individual is associated with an expected outcome. In the public arena, a decision can be made whether the individual participates in the decision (votes) or not. One may reap benefits or incur costs of a collective decision whether or not he participates. For these reasons, a person may not acquire the level of information needed to make a "good" choice. He may be "rationally ignorant" (Buchanan and Tullock 1965, 36–39; Gwartney 1976, 64).

Buchanan and Tullock offered an efficiency argument for the social contract. They argued that a rule of unanimity should apply at the constitutional level, but that a less-than-unanimous rule may be more efficient (less costly) at the operational level of government. The reason the cost is lower for government is that in the private sector unanimity is required for a decision to be implemented. The government can operate at less than unanimity. Why is this more efficient? The costs involved are two—decision costs and externality costs. Decision costs increase with the number of people needed for agreement out of the total number of people. Externality costs decrease with the number of people needed for agreement out of the total number of people. When these costs are summed, the resulting cost curve is U-shaped. It has a minimum at a point that is less than unanimity (1965, 63–72).

This explains why less than unanimity would be desirable from an efficiency standpoint, but it does not explain why individuals would be willing to go along with a less-than-unanimity decision rule. That is, why would individuals unanimously agree at the constitutional level (that is, as part of the social contract) to permit less-than-unanimity decision rules at the operational level? At the time when the constitutional decision is agreed upon, any given individual will be uncertain about the collective decisions that he will face in the future and what his positions on those issues will be. It is because of this uncertainty that the individual "*will not expect positive external costs to be imposed on him by purely redistributive transfers of real income*" (1965, 191). He will expect that on balance the external benefits he will gain at the expense of external costs that will be imposed on others will offset the external costs he will incur on other occasions (1965, 191). The expected net payoff is not negative over time.

Welfare economists use Pareto optimality as an efficiency criterion. A Pareto optimal position (and there may be an infinite number of them) is one in which any change would make (at least) one person worse off (in a utility sense). A position is non-Pareto optimal if (at least) one person can be made better off without making others worse off. A move is Pareto optimal if at least one person can be made better off without making anyone worse off (1965, 172). However, Pareto optimality is useless in analyzing purely distributional effects (1965, 202). Pareto optimality is concerned with efficiency only. Redistribution need not be inefficient (according to Pareto theory) but it can result in "externalities" (which can be negative or positive effects on third parties to a transaction).

If full side payments are permitted, then any decision-rule that is used for collective action, whether the rule is a unanimity, a majority, or a minority rule, will result in a Pareto-optimal outcome, even though the move itself may not be

Pareto optimal (1965, 189). When side payments are allowed, all collective action results in purely redistributional effects (1965, 190). Redistribution among individuals or groups cannot be prevented by the existence of side payments (1965, 191). Buchanan and Tullock concluded that attaining a Pareto-optimal outcome is insufficient to insure that no external costs will be imposed as a result of collective action. Even if other externalities are eliminated by collective choice, external costs associated with income redistribution will remain (1965, 195). Even though Buchanan and Tullock made a case for less than unanimity at the operational level, they pointed out that individuals would not agree to collectivize the distribution of income as part of the social contract (i.e., at the constitutional level) (1965, 192).

It should be noted that for some services, Buchanan and Tullock would be correct that an individual could expect benefits of collective decisions to offset costs over time. An example might be a service such as road repair. However, when government decisions involve restrictions on rights (for example, on the right to free speech or the right to bear arms), then those who see these restrictions as a threat to freedom would not regard themselves as winning if such legislation is not passed at one point in time and losing if it is passed at another. They would simply see themselves as not losing in the first instance and losing in the second.

Holmes and Sunstein

Holmes and Sunstein attempted to make the case for welfare rights as part of the social bargain (1999, 193). Their case is not based on an eleemosynary argument but a tactical one. They regarded welfare as a "side payment to the poor," an addendum to the original social contract (1999, 194). Their view of the poor is reminiscent of Marx's reserve army of the unemployed. They regard the poor as a class apart, as the propertyless. How can the propertyless "be deterred from looting and burning?" they asked. "[H]ow can wealth be made legitimate in the eyes of poverty?" (1999, 189) Their answer is welfare. They envisioned "welfare rights in part as bargains, as concessions granted to groups whose cooperation is necessary or desirable. In wartime, especially, property owners are confronted with their radical dependency on cooperation from the citizenry at large, especially the poor" (1999, 197). Those who own property "need to mobilize the poor, not merely sedate or placate them" (ibid.). Welfare makes the alienated feel included in the polity.

Holmes and Sunstein saw the poor as propertyless and as inclined to remain propertyless. They recognized two classes, the propertied and the propertyless—the wealthy and the poor. But that is not the way society is structured. In fact it is not structured. It is highly fluid and dynamic. Many of the "poor" own property.

And those who do not, may do so in the future, and, importantly, they own themselves. (At least this is true in a free society.) There is a great deal of mobility in a free economy—both up and down.

Holmes and Sunstein claimed that "wealthy people derive far more than fair value from their supposedly equal rights" (1999, 201). But one must ask, compared to whom? Compared to the wealthy in other countries? The poor in free countries derive far more benefits from equal rights protection by living in a free country than do the rich by living in a free country relative to how both groups would fare in a nonfree country. The rich can usually take care of themselves wherever they are. But compared with the poor in nonfree countries, the poor in free countries are immeasurably better off. Due process, rules of evidence, trial by jury, etc. are absent in other countries for rich and poor, but who suffers more by their absence? Being able to bargain with employers, retain one's wages, acquire a home, purchase a business are more important to those who have to work and do not have property than to those who live off of inheritance and on inherited estates.

As far as a bargain with the poor as an addendum to the social contract—the problems of determining who the poor are at any point in time and what poverty is and how these may or may not change over time would be a mind-boggling achievement to put into a document such as a social contract. And if the criterion of Pareto Optimality is accepted in analyzing collective choice, then, as Buchanan and Tullock concluded, "the individual would *never* choose to collectivize the redistribution of real income among members of the group. . . . If the distribution of real income among members of the society really does not matter, as would be implied by the argument, the most efficient way of organizing 'redistribution' is to do nothing about it" (1999, 192).

Buchanan and Tullock did not leave the analysis here since empirical behavior of individuals contradicts this conclusion. They offer an alternative explanation. They describe an income insurance scheme in which individuals insure against periods of low income (1999, 192–98). I see a number of problems with their proposal, however. One problem is that income is not some fixed amount that already exists out there in the future that can be "shape-shifted" to accommodate present needs. There may be those who would be satisfied with receiving a relatively low level of income throughout their lives if it were being supplied by someone else. If enough people chose this, then the larger income later on, which Buchanan and Tullock assume will exist, would not be forthcoming. In any case, such payments by the government would not be regarded as a right. Protection of one's rights is a right because one has given up a right (to retaliate). If government supplied income or any other good, one would not give up the right to provide it for oneself.

Taxes and Coercion: Alternatives to Taxation

If financing of government services were voluntary, then a less-than-unanimity rule would be a nonissue. At least it would not be considered a violation of rights since no coercion would be involved (although this is not entirely true for laws that are enacted in which the provision of goods is not a factor, e.g., censorship). Rothbard's second fatal principle in his case against government was that it obtains its revenues by compulsory means—through taxation (1998, 162). This is an objection to which Rand (1964i) would agree, not as an argument against the state, but as a case against taxation.

This is why Rand addressed voluntary alternatives to financing government. Rand suggested that government charge a fee—an insurance premium—equal to a small percentage of the dollar value of the transaction (set by objective standards to safeguard abuse) for any contract that the party to the transaction wanted to have legally enforced by the government. Those who wanted to rely on verbal promises could do so, but these agreements would not be legally enforceable. In the latter case, if either party defaulted, the other could not turn to a court of law for redress (Rand 1964i, 116–17; Machan 1975, 270–71). Rand mentioned that credit transactions are based on contract. Although Rand did not say so, since most transactions are paid for by debt (except for coin and barter transactions), they are based on some form of contract. Most payments that are not credit transactions are made by check or by fiat money, both of which are contractually based. Even if the government did not control the money supply, bank or promissory notes would very likely serve as a medium of exchange. If demand deposits and government or private debt are regarded as contractual obligations every time they are used in a transaction, then these premiums could generate a great deal of revenue.

Rand believed contract premiums would yield enough revenue "to finance all the other functions of a proper government" (1964i, 117). Another method of obtaining revenue for the government by voluntary means that Rand mentioned was a lottery (1964i, 116). Machan added that voluntary contributions could be requested as a temporary source of funds to finance national emergencies (1975, 271). Rand made it clear that these were not definitive solutions, that they were merely suggestive, and that she did not necessarily advocate them (1964i, 117).

Rand's suggestion of a fee for contracts for those willing to be insured by government is a voluntary means of financing government, but I think this suffers from a flaw in that it still allows for an element of coercion on the part of the government. It also violates one of the tenets of government, and that is equal protection for all. Those who do not pay the fee do not receive protection in case of default on a contract. It could be countered that that is true for all services, whether supplied by the government or privately. No one would force a person to pay the government the contract fee. However, if one does not, say, have health insurance, he retains the right to pay for a medical procedure out of his own pocket. He can use his savings or borrow or rely on charity, etc. He is not prohibited from taking other action on his own behalf. But this is, in effect, what would be the consequence of a voluntary fee for contract protection. Those who do not pay would not have legal recourse in a court of law, but they could not seek private redress on their own behalf.

The element of coercion that is involved here is that the individual is prohibited by government from carrying out a right—the right of retaliation. This is a right the individual relinquishes in exchange for government protection, but failing to get the protection robs him of the right altogether. Government is not providing protection, yet the individual is kept from providing it for himself. This seemingly has the earmark of a protection racket. First the individual gives up the right to protect himself in exchange for government protection, then the government agrees to protect him for a fee that he can "voluntarily" pay; but if he does not pay, the right that he originally gave up in order to get protection is not restored to him.

There are a number of goods and services provided by the government that are based on user fees—toll roads, for instance. But this is not what is being proposed here. Rand believed that this contract fee would finance all other functions of a proper government, not just those that are covered by the contract fee. All other victims of crime could use the courts, but pay no fee. However, a producer whose clientele paid on credit, but on the condition that no contract fee was involved, would have no recourse if a client defaulted on payment. This would violate the equal freedom principle on which a free society is based.

Thus a contract fee would violate the equal freedom provision and would be coercive. What of a lottery? It is true that a lottery would be a voluntary method of financing government. But so would the profits earned for any government-run enterprise. If the government can enter the lottery business in order to earn revenue, why couldn't it enter other businesses? If it is thought that governments should not own and run businesses, then a government should not run any enterprise, including lotteries.

This leaves voluntary donations. Since those goods that government funds, such as national defense and the justice system, are public goods, there is a logical argument that individual decision-makers will be disinclined to give voluntary contributions for government services for which everyone benefits and no one can be excluded. This is called the free-rider problem (Gwartney 1976, 519). There are numerous accounts of private organizations that have public goods characteristics that provide empirical evidence to the contrary. Thus, even though sufficient private funding would be theoretically unlikely, the verdict is out as to whether inpractice private donations could be solely relied upon to finance the government.

National Defense and the Public Good

Rand said that legitimate governmental functions fall into three general categories, all of which deal with the use of force and protection of rights. These include the police force, the armed forces, and courts of law. These protect citizens from criminals and foreign threats, and resolve disagreements in accordance with objective law (1967d, 334).

I have presented a number of reasons an individual might prefer a third party to carry out retaliation. Would those arguments apply to national defense? Why would one voluntarily give up the right to retaliate against an invader from another country? One practical reason is safety in numbers. Fidel Castro is unlikely to invade Key Largo if he were so inclined because Key Largo has the full force of the U.S. armed forces at its disposal. The counterthreat is much more formidable than if the citizens of Key Largo had to rely solely on their own resources. But then there is the question that, even though the citizens of Key Largo might like the full force of the rest of the country behind them if invaded, why would someone who lived elsewhere in the country, say Montana, care to defend the citizens of Key Largo? Such an invasion is unlikely to affect the Montanan's property. If one were simply concerned about protecting his property and he were motivated to combine with others because he saw the advantage of safety in numbers, he might be more inclined to join or otherwise contribute to a regional militia rather than military for the country as a whole. Insurance companies rely on spreading the risk, but there is not just one insurance company in existence; there are many. Some regions may be so remote or so unattractive to any potential invader that the people living in those regions would see no threat and feel no compunction to provide for defense for themselves or for the country.

If it were simply one's property that needed protecting from invasion, an individual might rely on a local militia. However, there may be things about one's country that might compel one to protect it as an entity, which would mean any region would warrant protection, regardless of whether one's own region seemed in danger. If the government is charged with protecting rights, then even if every person's property were not threatened by an invasion, each person's principles would be threatened. In this case, it would be the principles that would be worth protecting as embodied in the country as an entity.

If everyone sees the benefit of having national defense to protect everyone, there is no conflict of interests. Unlike disputes between citizens in which there exists a conflict between one citizen and another (of a victim's right to justice against an accused's right to property as embodied in the presumption of innocence), here all citizens benefit. The conflict of rights with the associated risks does not hold as an argument for turning over the provision of national defense to the government as it does for the police and the courts. If there are mutual benefits to all parties, then this would seem to make national defense a candidate for private provision.

There may be no conflict of rights involved here, but there is a conflict in the underlying incentive structure of the parties involved. In private transactions between two parties, there are mutual gains but there is also an incentive on the part of each party to agree to the transaction and then to default. This was illustrated in the Prisoner's Dilemma. The problem can be particularly acute if there is no mechanism to enforce agreements. Then each party must rely upon himself for enforcement. The existence of a government that protects rights frees each party from the burden of carrying out his own retaliation in case of default (as well as protects one's rights if he is falsely accused of reneging on a contract). In the case of a good like national defense, the incentive to default is multiplied. There is an incentive not only not to pay, but not to agree to pay—to conceal one's preferences. National defense falls in the category of being a public good. The word "public" does not mean the good must be supplied by the public sector; it describes the nature of the good. A public good has characteristics that tend to make it less likely to be supplied if reliance is on the private sector.

One characteristic of public goods is joint consumption. If one person is supplied with the good, all others also equally receive it. The other characteristic is the inability to exclude others if it is supplied to one person. The theoretical argument was first put forth by Paul Samuelson (Gwartney 1976, 519). By definition, national defense is for all the citizenry; if it is supplied to one individual, it is available to all. Also, by definition, since it is supplied to the nation as a whole, no one can be excluded from receiving if it is provided.

Recognizing that national defense is a public good, and as such is unlikely to be supplied if left to the private sector, citizens may agree to turn this function over to the government. In so doing, they will have to relinquish the right to private retaliation against invasion of their property by a foreign power. As in the case of private retaliation against a fellow citizen, one would not have to relinquish the right to defend oneself if one were in immediate danger—if someone invaded one's home, for instance, and the military was not available to assist him. What one would be barred from doing is carrying out delayed retaliation against a foreign power. By turning over the function to the government, one gives up the right to act independently because one's actions are no longer independent of effects on others within the country.

This is the public goods case for national defense. Other goods may be public goods or have public goods characteristics—dams, for instance. One could ask, if government is financed entirely through voluntary donations, as Objectivists and many libertarians contend, why should it be limited to the provision of police protection, the court system, and national defense? If the public goods argument applies to the protection of rights, why shouldn't government supply other public goods as well? In fact, why should government be limited to the provision of public goods? If the funds are obtained voluntarily, why limit government to the protection of rights only?

I think one reason is that the public goods argument cannot stand alone as a reason to turn a function over to government. The case for national defense is not simply that it is a public good, but that it protects the principle on which the nation is founded—liberty. In fact, ultimately, it is because liberty is indivisible that protection is a public good. Once private protection is relinquished, government must protect rights since that right is delegated to government, and, except for immediate threats, individuals are prohibited from protecting themselves. Herbert Spencer noted that government tends to be inefficient, and if the government assumed other functions in addition to rights protection, protection would be marginalized and since protection of rights is one function that can only be performed by the government and it is a right of individuals to have their rights protected, then to marginalize this function would be to marginalize this right (Spencer [1892] 1954, 247). Since all other functions are not prohibited in the private sector, and since the private sector tends to be more efficient, those functions should be provided by the private sector. Even public goods that may be undersupplied by the private sector because of their underlying incentive structure are not prohibited in the private sector. Retaliation is.

The other objection is that government-run or -financed enterprises would be nationalized enterprises. Even if financed through voluntary means, and even if private competition were permitted, they would be nationalized companies. Nationalized firms are, generally speaking, not consistent with the Objectivist or libertarian vision of freedom.

The Issue of Consent and Relinquishing Rights

Sechrest claimed that Objectivists reject consent (2000, 169). Although Rand did say that a proper government was based on consent, Sechrest's interpretation of Rand is that a person does not have the right to withhold his consent from the establishment of a proper government (2000, 170). Evers pointed to the position that "natural law is right for man whether or not men consent" (1977, 191). Rothbard's objection to the social contract, based on Evers's contract theory, was that an individual cannot consent to it because in so doing he alienates that which is inalienable—his will.

Lysander Spooner likened the institution of government to a corporation. The corporation argument was dismissed by Sechrest because corporations do not speak of themselves in the same terms as in the Constitution—as "we" or "people" (2000, 172). How an entity refers to itself can be merely semantics and not substantive, however. Some of the similarities between corporations and constitutional democracies are that the corporation, like a constitutional democracy, is a single entity that has laws (bylaws), its shareholders vote in which a less-than-unanimity decision rule prevails, and its shareholders relinquish rights. In the latter case, shareholders are not relinquishing the same rights as those within a constitutional democracy. What shareholders are relinquishing is some property rights with respect to ownership.

Even though Rothbard rejected the social contract, he did not object to corporations. In addition, he argued that property rights should be 100 percent; yet, that is not true for corporations. Nor did he have an objection to majority rule in corporations. He stated:

> Majority rule in the joint-stock companies, with respect to total shares owned, does not mean that the minority rights of owners are overridden. In the first place, the entire pooling of resources and the basis on which it is worked out are voluntary for all parties concerned. Secondly, all the stockholders, or owners, have one single interest in common—an increase in their monetary return and assets, although they may, of course, differ concerning the means to achieve this goal. Thirdly, the members of the minority may sell their stock and withdraw from the company if they so desire. (1993, 370–71)

The first reason in the above quote could be said to apply to the social contract as well. The social contract is supposedly based on consent—that is, it is voluntary. Whether this is true or not—either for the corporation or for the social contract—would seem to depend on whether alternatives exist, which is Rothbard's third point in the quote above. Presumably, Rothbard would not regard the existence of other alternatives, such as other free countries, as being sufficient to justify the establishment of government. Yet, the presence of other corporations (firms) would seem to be sufficient to justify the establishment of a corporation. But what if a single corporation dominated the economy?

Although Rothbard did not address this question specifically, he did discuss the possibility of an economy being dominated by a single firm or being exclusively comprised of cooperatives. (He likened a corporation to a cooperative [1993, 371].) He stated: "*[T]here must be in existence an external market to which the entrepreneur can refer*" (1993, 543). If there are no opportunity costs, resources cannot be allocated efficiently to maximize profits. Thus, a market consisting solely of cooperatives would not be possible. The same reasoning would seem to apply to a single firm (monopoly) dominating an economy. Of course, this assumes that the objective is to maximize profits. If the single firm (or cooperative) owned everything except the workers, then there would be a floor to worker salaries based on subsistence, which would ultimately affect the supply of workers. (This is consistent with the Malthusian or classical model: that is, that wages are limited by subsistence. If wages fall below subsistence, workers die and the supply curve shifts to the left; then wages return to subsistence.) There have been company towns that closely approximated this.

Like the social contract, many property arrangements result in individuals relinquishing some of their rights as a condition of purchase. Rights are rights to action. If, as a condition of ownership, a person agrees not to fully exercise all of his rights to action, he has in effect surrendered these rights as a condition of purchase. When individuals buy into, say, a gated community, they may be seen as willingly giving up certain rights (rights to act in certain ways with respect to their property) in order to buy something else (a quieter and/or safer neighborhood, etc.). It could be said that this is within a person's rights. But if every square inch of a country were covered by gated communities, then could individuals be regarded as free?

Since the problem of agreeing to restrict one's rights is that one will not be able to change one's mind later on and exercise those rights, the question seems to reduce to whether alternatives exist, since exercising one's will involves being able to have alternatives to choose from. For gated communities, so long as there are alternatives, one could make the case that there is freedom to exercise all rights—at least somewhere. Likewise, with corporate ownership, one does not have the option of exercising full ownership rights with respect to the firm one owns; however, alternatives exist as far as types of ownership arrangement for firms is concerned. One may choose to form a partnership with others or be a proprietor of his own firm.

If the existence of alternative property arrangements is a valid standard for corporations and other ownership agreements, then, as Machan (1975, 150) noted, if alternative free governments exist, government (provision of protection) is not compulsory, and a person retains his autonomy under a proper government.

Government and Inefficiency

It seems to me that even if there were no regional governmental bodies such as cities, counties, and states, so long as individuals can combine and agree on certain things, they will. If they are permitted to restrict ownership rights—as in the case of corporations or of some gated communities—they will. Even in a marriage contract, one attempts to alienate one's will. However, these forms of ownership or agreement may not ultimately restrict one's rights, so long as alternatives exist.

Buchanan and Tullock noted that: "An essential difference between market and political 'exchange' is absence of alternatives in the latter case" (1965, 104).

In the political sphere, decisions made at the ballot box tend to be all or nothing—either/or. This is not simply a rights issue; it is also an efficiency issue. Buchanan stated the following:

> [C]entral to an economic approach to choice problems is the possibility of variation *at the margin.* If such variation is possible, choices become "either/or" only for small incremental changes; and, considering a total complex, *some* of *all* alternatives may be chosen. Interest in or a desire for, a particular alternative becomes a function of its cost or price relative to the other alternatives available for choice. (1965, 322)

If, for example, road construction and maintenance is under the purview of the government or a private collective body, then the governing body chooses when to repair roads. For a particular time period, the decision to repair a particular road (or a portion of it) may be either/or. Over time, all roads may be repaired (Buchanan 1965, 148–58). On the other hand, if one owns the road associated with his own property, he can choose to repair his road whenever he likes based on how that fits in his overall budget. The decision becomes either/or but for relatively small (incremental) changes. Buchanan and Tullock's point is that services like this may be turned over to government, if it is less costly than a private alternative. Individuals would be willing to turn it over if, on balance, the expectation is they will not lose more than they gain over time.

Although in theory government may potentially be less expensive than the private sector, it suffers because there is no market mechanism to reward efficiency. In Rothbard's quote in the previous section, he noted that one difference between corporations and government is that corporations have a single objective. That could apply to a proper government as well. Instead of making profits, government would have the single objective of "protection." However, profits—and the market mechanism, in general—have the effect of rewarding efficiency. Government tends to be less efficient than the private sector. Although efficiency arguments have nothing to do with rights, per se, they can be relevant if government becomes involved in providing goods that could be more efficiently supplied by the private sector.

Decision-making that is collective tends to be bundled. This is a weakness of the political provision of goods. Gwartney stated: "The collective process is likely to be imprecise in reflecting the wishes of 'consumers' because they (voters) are usually forced to act through a broker (legislator) who represents a 'bundle' of political goods" (1976, 558). Bundling goods and services does not permit decisions at the margin. It allows for fewer alternatives. Feedback is cumbersome or nonexistent. Changes are not easily made.

There are goods that are bundled in the private sector as well. For instance, for lighthouses, bundling their payment in with another that is not a public good may be the only way in which to privately finance them (Barnett 1998, 163). Even in the private sector, when goods and services are bundled, the usual mechanisms that exist that reflect scarcity, demand, etc. cannot exert themselves as easily. Insurance coverage tends to be bundled. By their nature, premiums are not tied to usage. A customer pays a homeowner's premium with the hope that his house does not catch fire. But since usage is not tied to premiums paid, there can be abuses. One distinction between the private sector and government is that, in the former case, even when bundling of services exists, there is a market mechanism that tends to reward efficiency.

Police Protection: A Public Good

Sechrest recognized that police protection does not have the cost structure typically found for public goods. Public goods have a cost structure such that the marginal usage cost is zero. Police protection, unlike, say a dam, is not monolithic. It has an incremental usage cost that is positive. If police protection were supplied exclusively by the private sector in response to individual demand, then the customer could be charged based on usage. Those who did not pay for protection would not receive it. There would be no free riders. Payment would not be divorced from benefits. Sechrest, an advocate of anarchy, favored this funding approach.

Sechrest claimed that his arguments for anarchy are superior to the Objectivist case for minimal government (2000, 164). He distinguished between governance and government. With governance: "Decisions are primarily achieved by micro-level negotiation. Injustices can occur, but they tend to be small and localized" (2000, 179). What anarchists are opposed to and what they would like to see abolished is centralized governmental power (2000, 174). With centralized government, injustices, when they occur, are more likely to be systemic.

However, if, as Sechrest recommended, the law protects negative rights (the right to noninterference), but certain persons are systematically excluded from having any recourse to rights violations, then the law is not valid for those who are excluded, because it is not enforceable. If enforcement is tied to payment, one must be independent (have a fully functional rational capacity) in order to have the wherewithal to pay. If one is not independent in that sense, one must rely on a guardian who is legally responsible for one's care. But if the legal caregiver is the rights violator, the dependent has no recourse, particularly if the dependent has never qualified as having been independent. Since these individuals would be systematically incapable of receiving justice, there would not be equal freedom under the law.

If the equal freedom principle is accepted, not only in theory but in practice, then no one should be *systematically* excluded from protection. Those who are incapable (and have always been incapable) of taking care of themselves and whose rights are violated (which is especially problematic when they are violated by those legally responsible for their care) should not be excluded from the equal freedom principle. Yet, if reliance is a pay-as-you-go basis, those who do not have a fully functional rational capacity and are abused by their guardians will be incapable of receiving justice. *It is the nature of the principle* (that equal rights applies to all and yet cannot, in practice, be achieved by all under anarchy) *that makes protection of rights a public good, not the cost structure of the service provided.*

For public goods, exclusion is not possible, and therefore they are not likely to be provided in the private sector even though there would be benefits to their provision. The challenge in the private sector is to discover innovative methods of financing. For radio broadcasts, for example, producers turn to advertising. For near-public goods, methods may be devised to exclude nonpayers. Roads have public goods characteristics, but there are ways to deny access to nonpayers. There is an important difference between communities that combine to provide the neighborhood with roads and a government that provides protection. Since no one has a "right" to a road (unless he has paid for its use), it poses no moral problem to exclude nonpayers. For protection of rights, there can be a problem with exclusion (systematic exclusion as described above). Exclusion would invalidate the equal freedom principle.

Negative Rights and Costs

Den Uyl and Rasmussen pointed out that negative rights, which are natural rights, are basic—that is, "not derivable from other rights" (1991, 82). By turning over the right to retaliate to the government, individuals have a positive right to that function being provided by the government. Holmes and Sunstein stressed that rights protection has costs. They stated: "Since 'ought implies can,' and lack of resources implies cannot," (1999, 18) the issue of resources is morally relevant. They further stated: "To ascertain that a right has costs is to confess that we have to give something up in order to acquire or secure it. To ignore costs is to leave painful tradeoffs conveniently out of the picture" (1999, 24).

I have said that in the first instance the reason one has the positive right to protection is because the government, by taking it over, denies citizens the right to execute it. But that requirement in and of itself is empty. Someone must pay. So not only does one give up the right to retaliate in order to receive government protection, one must also pay for the protection. Objectivists and most libertarians would argue that the payment, once government has taken over the function, should be voluntary.

Sechrest stated that Objectivists are inclined to presume "a one-to-one correspondence between the moral and the practical" (1999, 92). He stated that Rand assumed that because rational men do not seek the unearned, and because most men are rational, most will voluntarily contribute to the government for the protective services they receive. However, he noted that if a service must be provided to everyone, but payment is voluntary, enough payment may not be forthcoming. Murray Franck argued "that Rand (incorrectly) advocated voluntary government financing because she was so devoted to the proposition that rational men will not experience conflicts of interest" (Sechrest 2000, 174). Of course, Rand recognized that not all men were rational. If all men were rational there would be no violation of rights. She also acknowledged that there could be honest disputes among rational men (1967d, 334).

Franck (1998, 15; cited in Franck 2000, 153) stated that a free market cannot exist without property rights, since trade is predicated upon ownership; but the enforcement of contracts is not just a private good; it is also a public good. It is the public good nature of defining and enforcing property rights that validates taxation. To Franck, because property rights cannot exist without government, "[c]onsent of the governed is irrelevant" (Sechrest 1999, 99). Additionally, because everyone benefits from enforcement of contracts and other rights protections, consent is not required for taxation (ibid.). In his view, coercion is not necessarily synonymous with the initiation of force. If force is in response to aggression, it is defensive in nature, whether a person does this on his own behalf or an agent (the government) does it for him (Franck 2000, 152).

Franck is correct that use of retaliatory force is nonaggressive. However, what he does not acknowledge is that it is not the use of retaliatory force that is the coercive aspect of government. The coercive aspect of government is that it prohibits retaliation (unless there is an immediate threat) on the part of citizens, which is a natural right. My argument is that the moral obligation to pay for protection follows from the moral obligation that a person has to seek retaliation if his rights have been violated (in a state of nature). The coercive aspect of payment is part and parcel of the same "exchange" that forms the basis for the "social contract." One cannot relinquish the right to retaliate in exchange for government provision of retaliation without providing for its payment. Turning over the right to retaliate to government involves relinquishing a right (which is coercive). Delegating that right means that it must be produced by government, and production requires resources which must be acquired. This is a fundamental economic reality. *Payment is not an additional layer of coercion; it is integral and inseparable from that which is exchanged in the "social contract."* Production necessarily implies payment. If payment were not part of the transfer, the exchange would be incomplete and empty.

Of course, the individual is forced to receive the benefit whether he can afford it or not. And government has no market mechanism to encourage efficiency. Sechrest (1999, 100) noted that efficiency is of no particular concern to Franck. To stem the expansive tendency of government, Franck stated that taxes should be limited by law (Sechrest 1999, 94). The idea of limiting taxes is consistent with Rand in the narrow sense that she recognized that some limits could be set by law. She recommended that the contract fee that she suggested as a method of government finance be legally fixed. She advocated a copyright law that was limited to the author's life plus fifty years (1967i, 132) and that a time limit should be set on patents. The Homestead Act, of which she approved, limited the homestead to a certain acreage and the homesteading tenure to a given number of years (1967g, 123). So a legal limit to the size of a tax would not be what Rand would find objectionable. It is the coercive nature of the tax to which Rand would object. My argument is that it is the transfer of the right to retaliate that is coercive and taxation is an inseparable part of that coercion.

Government and its provision of protection (with the requirement to pay for it) would not be coercive in the broad sense, if, as Machan implied, there are alternative free countries to which one may freely relocate. (However, it should be noted that Machan [1975, 150] was suggesting the "alternative free countries" argument for the governmental provision of protection, not for taxation by government. He did not approve of taxation.) It would be noncoercive on the national level in the same way a condo fee is "voluntary" at the residential level, if a person buys a condo unit. The condo fee covers the "public good" aspects of the condo. The condo fee may not be seen as voluntary, however, if a person had only one residence from which to choose.

Government and Governance

Sechrest asked the question that was raised by Spooner. Even if a social contract was forged by the consent of the governed, how can it be binding on future generations? (Sechrest 2000, 171) One approach to answering this is to consider what is bound over from one generation to another. One thing that is being carried forth is the principles set forth in the social contract. The principle of equal freedom can be binding and must be if property rights (including the right to life) and property titles are to be respected from one generation to the next. If the legal code that would result from such an agreement were not binding on future generations, the law could simply be renegotiated, wiping out former property titles and arrangements (e.g., contracts such as marriage) at some later date. The idea that legitimate property rights and titles and other contracts should be binding on future generations, with which anarcho-capitalists agree, is not inconsistent with what is metaphorically regarded as a social contract—at least one component of it. One difference is that under government, it is the citizens, not simply the lawmakers (as in Rothbard's vision of anarchy), who reach agreement.

According to Sechrest, it is not governance that anarchists oppose; it is central government (2000, 174, 179). The difference between government and anarcho-capitalist governance is that in the former there is an agreement to give up the right to retaliate in exchange for protection for everyone. It is this aspect of the social contract—the relinquishing of a right that is binding on future generations—to which anarcho-capitalists object.

The idea of a central government, in my view, elicits the question—central to what? If there is a territory that is bound by certain laws that protect the rights of the people within its boundaries, then as a territory it may need protecting because an attack against any part of it is a threat to the principles that bind the whole territory. So, because it is an entity, it requires protection as an entity. And as an entity it would need some central decision-making process and enforcement potential. The argument against central government may really be a case against governance over a large geographic area. A government in which all agree to protect the equal freedom principle need not be large. Although not an example of this specifically, the Mayflower Compact was a social contract of sorts and it covered very few people. Size becomes an issue insofar as practicability and efficiency are concerned. But if the principle of equal freedom for all within a geographic area is valued and the protection of that freedom is deemed necessary, some central decision-making will be called for. Smaller units may be preferred. Size may matter. But size is relative. Hong Kong and the United States are both relatively free. Cuba and China are not. Nor is a company town.

Ethics and Rights

Rand arrived at the noninterference principle (on which negative rights are based) from the nonsacrificial principle. Mozes stated that in order to generalize the noninterference principle as a principle of rights for everyone, Machan invoked the substitution principle. Although Mozes claimed that Rand never referred to the substitution principle (Mozes 1992, 88), she did say that a person respects another's rights if he wants others to respect his (Rand 1967h, 227). Mozes said of Objectivism "rights come later than ethics and are based on it" (1998, 11). He said that rights and ethics are distinct. He stated further that rights do not guide individual interpersonal action, as illustrated in the following example:

> Suppose A and B are two persons living alone on a desert island. A beats up B and takes the food that B has gathered. In evaluating A's actions, if you say "A initiated force, and what he did was immoral," you have, in effect, exhausted everything there is to say about it. If you then add "and on top of that,

> he violated B's rights!" what would that addition mean? It is, again, only in the context of an organized social system that bringing up B's rights has any meaning (since it would then imply that A should not only be morally condemned for his action, but also legally punished). (1992, 92)

According to Mozes, this was an example used by Peikoff in his course entitled *The Philosophy of Objectivism* and was endorsed by Rand as reflecting Objectivist theory (1992, 93n7). I do not believe that this is all that can be said. I have argued that B would be justified in retaliating against A and would be obligated to do so since no one else would be charged with doing it for him in a state of nature. If one violates another's rights, one has committed an ethical breach. If government did not exist, the wronged party would be under an obligation to seek redress in a situation such as this. If government takes over this function, one is generally not allowed to compete with the government in seeking redress. The government is charged with taking over one virtue—justice—as it relates to retaliation only. When the government takes over this function, the individual no longer has to, nor is permitted to, uphold justice in this particular way. However, there may be lesser slights that are not handled by the government, but fall on the (ethical) shoulders of private individuals.

The trader principle states that one should not give or receive the undeserved. Protection of rights stems from that principle. But that social principle is more inclusive than what is covered by rights and the protections of rights by government. It could include slights that would not be enforceable in a court of law (and should not be because of their nature). One's life is one's ultimate value and life is measured in units of time. One values one's time. There may be instances in which if another deliberately does not respect one's time, he has in a sense squandered some of one's life.

For example, if you have made a luncheon engagement with another and that person for no valid reason fails to show, that person has taken a little bit of your life. The trader principle would inform us that value has not been exchanged for value. What recourse does the "injured" party have? There are social conventions that many times cover this variety of breach. The no-show may apologize and that may be sufficient. But if he offers no explanation or apology, what recourse does one have? One alternative may simply be to sever ties with the person. The point is that the injured party may be under some obligation to do or say something. Simply not acknowledging the slight and continuing to interact with the individual as if the slight had not occurred (assuming no apology, explanation, or amends has been offered) would not be the right course of action, because it would signal to the other party that one did not value one's own time, and this might lead the other person to believe that one did not sufficiently value one's own life.

When government takes over the function of retaliation, it is sometimes seen as enforcing an aspect of morality. That is, government is seen as forcing individuals to respect the rights of others. However, whether in a state of nature or under government, the individual is free to act ethically or unethically. If he refuses to work, he is not being productive. He is not acting on that virtue. If he steals from another to support himself, he is being unethical. He is hurting himself, because he is endangering his long-run ability to survive. He is also violating the rights of another. The victim has the right to retaliate. He would also have the responsibility to do so in a state of nature. If he did not, he would have permitted the violator to take the unearned. If he did not retaliate, he would also risk eroding the principle involved, justice. When a person retaliates, he is acting virtuously (with qualifications previously discussed).

When government takes over the function of retaliation, the individual can no longer exercise this virtue. This does not mean that he cannot exercise the principle of justice at all, but he is prohibited from exercising it when his rights have been violated. The violator faces retaliation in either case, whether meted out by the victim (or his agents) in a state of nature or by the government if it takes over this function. In either case the individual is "forced" to respect the rights of others. The value that is affected (upheld) when the government assumes the retaliatory function is the retaliatory aspect of justice. The individual is prohibited from exercising or acting to uphold this aspect of justice, but is free to exercise all other virtues and all vices. Both virtues and vices will have consequences, however—whether in a state of nature or under a proper government.

Tara Smith has said that rights always trump ethics (1995, 111). Den Uyl and Rasmussen have said that rights are absolute—although like all principles, they may have limited applicability (1991, 85, 150), such as in emergencies. When rights come into conflict with ethics, the question is, which should predominate. If, for instance, a person (A) noticed that his neighbor (B) was drowning in (B's) backyard swimming pool, A would have to trespass onto B's property in order to save B's life. Although this might technically be a violation of B's property rights, it would in most cases be justified under the circumstances. However, if A were to enter B's property in order to save B's soul or to save B from the evils of alcohol, A's visits could be regarded as intrusions, even though A has B's best interests at heart—at least in A's estimation. The authorities, to the extent that they would be involved in such cases, would have to examine the reasons for trespass. When another's property becomes a factor in one's actions, rights can become an issue. Since it is the government's job to protect property rights, its agents may investigate a person's actions if he enters another's property (if he does so without invitation) even when the person's interest was to benefit the owner of the property. Ideally, adjudication should be just that—judging situations that would include determining whether some violations of property rights were warranted or not.

Independent Equals

Contracts fall under the purview of government. The question that has arisen in the United States in years past is, how involved should the government be in contracts between individuals? Much of the intervention by the government has come in response to redressing what has been regarded by some as an imbalance of power between contracting parties. This goes to that aspect of the trader principle that states that trade should be between independent equals and it should be noncoercive. The issue is, if the parties are unequal, does it follow that exchange may be coercive?

This was a question raised concerning children and their parents (even though this is not an issue of contracts, per se). And it was concluded that there is an element of coercion from parent to child and that this is not necessarily something that should be corrected by a third party (government). It is assumed that parents, by and large, have the best interests of their children at heart, and when they, say, restrict where their children may go outside the home, it is to protect the children. But children may be abused or killed by their parents. So there is a need for a third-party (government) response. This kind of response is after the fact, that is, after the abuse has been detected or reported.

Contractual interactions between adults are regarded as noncoercive since adults are independent equals. Noncontractual interaction is regarded as noncoercive unless there is some evidence of physical harm (or, if falsehoods are reported, possible harm to one's reputation). But there are unequal relationships that have the potential for coercive behavior on the part of the person in "power." Even among adults, the teacher/student relationship could have that potential. On merchant and other private ships, where individuals are confined and there is a hierarchy of authority, there is the potential for the abuse of power. (In the military, which is not in the private sector, the potential exists.) In many cases, the private sector has responded by establishing grievance procedures to deal with abuses of authority when they occur.

But the government has increasingly stepped in with legislation designed to redress perceived imbalances of power in the private sector before the fact. The government has established minimum wages and health and safety standards, for example. The assumption is that the worker is at a disadvantage in bargaining relative to the employer. Pipes has presented arguments to the effect that these laws have increasingly infringed on the rights of both property owners (employers) and workers (1999, 260–66).

CHAPTER ELEVEN

Value

This chapter compares Rand's value theory with that found in consumer theory. Ethics involves choice among alternatives as does the theory of consumer decision-making. However, economics is said to be "value free," even though there is a standard for judgment—efficiency. There are several points of similarity between Rand's view of value and that of economists. Both regard value as a relationship between man and an object (Rand 1967a, 22). Both reject the idea of intrinsic value (Rand 1967a, 24). Both acknowledge that value is contextual and that where no alternatives exist, values are impossible (1964a, 15). According to Rand, there is a hierarchy to one's values based on a comparative scale (1979, 40). Utility theory is now seen as a preference ranking of options a consumer faces.

There are several points of dissimilarity. Although Rand distinguished between the market value and the philosophical value of a good (1967a, 24), Objectivists are uncomfortable with the idea that the consumer determines the value of a product. They believe the producer's purpose should not be his beneficiaries, but his work (Rand 1961c, 79). This is consistent with the idea that others are not a fundamental part of reality. Rand's value theory has been labeled a labor theory of value in which the producer creates value (Sciabarra 1995, 248).

Utility Theory and Objectivism

Rand bridged the is/ought gap by proposing that what a man *is* determines what he *ought* to do. The consequence of this, according to Merrill, is that all choice is moral choice (Merrill 1997, 69–70). The economist Wickstead did not believe the laws underlying economics are any different from those underpinning the logic of choice (Spiegel 1971, 528). Yet, unlike Randian ethics, economic value theory is supposed to be "value free"—by which economists mean free of moral judgment. Machan noted that the difference between a theory of morality and a theory of value is that, unlike the latter, the former "focuses on value that is produced from right motives or intentions" (1998b, 99–100n16). Economic theory does have standards for judgment, however, efficiency being a primary one.

There are elements of both the labor theory of value and the utility theory of value that are consistent with Rand. The labor theory of value states that the value of a good is derived from the labor necessary to produce it. A more general version is that the costs of production determine the value of a good. Marx subscribed to a labor theory of value that was largely based on Ricardo's theory. The labor theory of value states that inputs used in production (specifically, labor) determine the value of a good. This view is often expressed when a person casually says something to the effect that doctors' fees are high because doctors have to spend so much time in medical school. The labor theory of value is associated with the classical economists as well as with Marx. Marx drew heavily on Ricardo in developing his theory (or theories) of surplus value, although Marx made the following distinction:

> [T]he mere *possibility* of this surplus-labour . . . does not in itself make it a *reality*. For this to occur, the labourer must first be *compelled* to work in excess of the [necessary] time, and this compulsion is exerted by capital. This is missing in Ricardo's work, and therefore also the whole struggle over the regulation of the normal working-day. (1968, 406)

A labor theory of value has been attributed to Rand by both O'Neill (1972, 212–13) and Sciabarra (1995, 248). However, Rand, unlike Marx, regarded the capitalist rather than the worker as being paid less than his contribution to the production process.

Values Must Be Discovered

Rand believed that values must be discovered as well as produced by man. She said that if one is forced to accept a value at the cost of surrendering his mind, it does not qualify as a value. "[T]he forcibly mindless can neither judge nor choose nor value" (Rand 1967a, 23). Gregory Johnson countered that something can have value to a person whether he has discovered that it has or not (1999, 141). For instance, based on one interpretation of Rand's quote, if an unconscious person received life-saving treatment, this would not be a value to the person if he had not given consent. In fact, it would constitute coercion (1999, 146). What Rand thought was of no value is for one to "surrender one's mind" to another, which is not the same thing as being unconscious and receiving aid or not being conscious of something out of ignorance. Consciousness is the natural condition of man. Rand was aware that a person could benefit "by accident." But this does not form the basis of a value system. Being unconscious is not the natural state of man. What is not natural is for man to surrender his mind to another. Anything that is gained when one *refuses* to think is not a value. Rand illustrated this in *The Fountainhead* with the character of Peter Keating. Peter Keating achieved recognition as an architect by passing off Roark's work as his own. Unmerited recognition is not a value. This kind of benefit can never be a value because it is the result of fraud.

A second example Johnson gave was oxygen. He asked, wasn't it "an objective human value before it was discovered and evaluated as such?" (1999, 147) I believe that Johnson misinterpreted what Rand meant by discovering something by one's own mind. Rand did not have a narrow concept of discovery or a narrow concept of reason. She was aware that man is not omniscient. More important to the current discussion is that value depends on context. Oxygen is a value in most cases, but it would be unwelcome if used to fan the flames of a fire that a person was trying to extinguish.

Economic Theory of Value and Rand

Context can manifest itself in many ways when applied to the concept of value (Peikoff 1991, 123). There are many points of comparison between Rand's view of value and the way in which economists now view value. She saw value as a relationship between man and an object (Rand 1967a, 22). Classical economists initially saw utility as a characteristic of a good or service; as its "usefulness." Adam Smith posed the diamond-water paradox to illustrate the difference between value in use and value in exchange. Water is more useful (value in use) than diamonds, yet diamonds are expensive (value in exchange). The "paradox of value" was later resolved by distinguishing between total value and the marginal increment. Gossen conceived value as a relationship between an object and an individual, in particular a marginal unit of a commodity and a consumer (Rima 1978, 207–208). There is more than one implication from this insight. One is that objects do not have intrinsic value (by intrinsic I mean value inherent in the object separate from a valuer), which is the Objectivist position. Another is that how much an additional unit of a good is valued depends upon how much of it has already been consumed. And that will depend, as Jevons recognized, upon its scarcity (Spiegel 1971, 513).

What is meant by relative scarcity in the latter context is how much the consumer values another unit of a commodity relative to how much he has already consumed. From the perspective of market demand rather than an individual consumer, an additional unit of a good (such as water) is valued relative to its supply. Edgeworth extended Jevons's utility function by including not only the amount of a product the consumer already has purchased or consumed but also the amounts of other products purchased or consumed. "[T]he value that a person attaches to another unit of food reflects not only how well he is fed but also how well he is housed, clothed, and so forth" (1971, 526). An updated approach to value, as described by Alchian and Allen, expresses one good's value in terms of the amount(s) of another good(s). An individual will willingly sacrifice some amount of one commodity in order to have more of other commodities (Alchian and Allen 1977, 25). Rand said that when there are no alternatives, values are not possible (1964a, 15). In economic theory, the value of a good is based on the highest valued alternative forgone.

Utility theory originally assumed that consumer utility was cardinal in measurement. Modern consumer theory assumes that consumers are rational but in a very limited way. All the postulate of rationality requires is that the individual be capable of ranking goods in order of preference (Henderson and Quandt 1971, 8). Given this ranking, it is assumed that (given prices and budget) the individual will choose that combination of commodities that ranks highest on this scale (Samuelson 1974, 97–98). Are such rankings feasible? Rand affirmed that they are. This provides philosophical support to an assumption that economists make concerning consumer behavior. Rand stated that, although measurement of the intensity of psychological processes is inexact, "conceptualization does not require the knowledge of exact measurements. Degrees of intensity can be and are measured approximately, on a comparative scale" (1979, 40). This is precisely the type of measurement economists assume underlies consumer choice. Rand stated:

> For instance, the intensity of the emotion of joy in response to certain facts varies according to the importance of these facts in one's *hierarchy* of values; it varies in such cases as buying a new suit, or getting a raise in pay, or marrying the person one loves. (Ibid.)

She emphasized that "*measurement requires an appropriate standard*. . . . [O]ne does not measure length in pounds or weight in inches" (1979, 50). If something does not appear to be measurable, it is because we have not yet devised a standard or, more likely, a precise standard has not been discovered. Rand said:

> If anything were actually "immeasurable," it would bear no relationship of any kind to the rest of the universe, it would not affect nor be affected by anything else in any manner whatever, it would enact no causes and bear no consequences—in short, it would not exist. (1979, 51)

Although economists have veered away from the notion of utility as sensation (Samuelson 1974, 91) and have merely assumed that consumers rank order commodities on the basis of preferences without delving into the bases for those preferences (as first developed by Wicksteed [Spiegel 1971, 527]), Rand acknowledged that emotions do underlie consumer decisions (and other decisions as well). The measurement Rand referred to in the quote above is of *psychological processes*. She is not referring to the measurement of cognitive skills in the quote, but emotions such as joy in response to buying, say, a new suit (1979, 40). The ranking of goods is based on preferences that are associated with emotions that correspond to one's hierarchy of values. The measurement of intensity of emotion as it relates to commodities may be done only comparatively, based on the hierarchy of one's values. The ranking of one's preferences is revealed by actions—in the market, on the basis of what consumers purchase.

Although there are parallels with some aspects of Objectivist philosophy and consumer theory, there have been notable criticisms, such as the following leveled by Machan:

> When we consider the details of economic theory itself, we find that it is not self-interested behavior but so-called utility-maximizing behavior that we are all driven to engage in, and the content of the utility is entirely subjective—thus the thesis ultimately comes to be tautological, since, of course, we all do what we do because we do it. By this "explanation" of human behavior, no wonder everything is fully explained, from suicide and marriage to bank robbery and multibillion-dollar corporate mergers. In all these cases, people do what they do because they want to do it, and the way we can test the truth of this claim is by noticing that they are indeed doing it. (1998a, 203n3)

Paul Samuelson recognized the apparent circularity of consumer behavior theory:

> Thus, the consumer's market behavior is explained in terms of preferences, which are in turn defined only by behavior. The result can very easily be circular, and in many formulations undoubtedly is. Often nothing more is stated than the conclusion that people behave as they behave, a theorem which has no empirical implications, since it contains no hypothesis and is consistent with all conceivable behavior, while refutable by none. (1974, 91–92)

However, the theory can produce meaningful hypotheses that are empirically testable concerning consumer demand using price, quantity, income, and other relevant measurable data. One such hypothesis is that, other things equal, a change in the price of a commodity will result in a change in quantity demanded in direction opposite that of the price change (1974, 109–111). This is the familiar law of demand. (The same axioms that are relevant to consumer preference can be derived using the concept of a utility function. The reason for the shift from preferences to the utility function is that the latter has more explanatory power. For instance, additional consequences can be derived from the axioms, and other hypotheses with behavioral implications can be posited [Green 1978, 79].)

Utility now stands for a preference ranking of options facing a consumer. Alchian and Allen echoed that now that utility is no longer regarded as measurable in a cardinal sense, the notion of utility maximization may simply appear to camouflage our ignorance of consumer behavior—i.e., regardless of what action a person takes, he could be regarded as "maximizing his utility." This perspective assumes that we cannot determine what can be regarded as commodities or goals and they cannot be classified by cost. Since we can make such determinations, refutable hypotheses can be tested other than those related to consumer demand. As an example, they stated that saving a child from drowning could be a goal, but whether one attempts to do so would depend on such things as whether the child is in a pond or in a "raging torrent with a 99 percent probability of drowning yourself" (Alchian and Allen 1977, 40). This idea of context is central to Rand's concept of value as well (1964d, 45).

The Consumer in Value Theory

Adam Smith said: "[T]he interest of the producer ought to be attended to, only so far as it may be necessary for promoting that of the consumer" (A. Smith [1776] 1937, 625). This is consistent with modern value theory, which sees the consumer as determining the value of a product. But it is not consistent with OE—at least it could be interpreted that way (Donway 1999b, 18). Rand (1961c, 78) thought the producer should be primarily concerned with the work itself, not the consumer. This is in keeping with Objectivism in that ethics should not be fundamentally concerned with other people. Producers should not regard their consumers as fundamental to the purpose of their work. Of course, if a producer cannot sell his product, he will not be able to stay in business. This is the essence of consumer theory.

Rand acknowledged that. She also realized that goods must be produced before consumption can take place. Only producers comprise a market, according to Rand. Rand said: "[C]onsumers *qua consumers* . . . are *irrelevant* to economics" (1982f, 130). No one can consume something that has not first been produced. And no one will have income unless he (or someone) has first produced something. However, from an analytical perspective, consumption must be isolated from production in order to identify its determinants.

The importance of the consumer (utility) in value theory (price determination) began in the mid-nineteenth century with Gossen (Rima 1978, 208) and was more fully developed in the 1870s with the publication of three independent works by Jevons, Menger, and Walras (Spiegel 1971, 513). From a macroeconomic perspective, John Maynard Keynes ([1936] 1964) theoretically elevated demand relative to supply with his publication of *The General Theory*. Keynesian theory has been interpreted as "demand creates its own supply." In its application, Keynesian theory has translated into the expansion of one component of demand—government spending, specifically, deficit spending. The idea has been that, through "the multiplier," output will be forthcoming if deficit spending increases.

Classical economists have been identified with the opposing phrase: "Supply creates its own demand," known as Say's Law (Spiegel 1971, 260). Since production results in income, and income is, in turn, purchasing power, it was thought that there could be no "over-supply" of goods in the aggregate. Neoclassical economists have revised classical theory, with special attention to the role of money on business cycles. Rand was more closely aligned in many respects with the classical view of macroeconomics.

Although Rand's theory has macro implications, she was primarily interested in the individual. To the extent that she addressed consumption, it was largely from an individual point of view. In OE, virtues are those actions that sustain a person's life, but consumption, although necessary for survival, is not a virtue. Consumption is valued, but it is not a virtue. Production is the virtue, the central virtue in OE. The distinction between value and virtue is an important one. Virtues are actions that result in the creation of values (Peikoff 1991, 239). Money is a value (1991, 232), but it would not be considered a virtue. Virtues are not ends in themselves. They are, according to Rand, entirely instrumental. "Virtue is not its own reward. . . . *Life* is the reward of virtue—and happiness is the goal and reward of life" (Rand 1957, 1021). Happiness is a value, not a virtue. It follows from or accompanies the exercise of virtue.

Rand recognized deferred consumption—saving—as productive (1974b, 345). Since production is a central value and productive work a central virtue, then since saving is productive, it follows that deferred consumption is a virtue. This, from a moral perspective, puts saving—a virtue—at odds with consumption—a value, perhaps, but no virtue. Rand was not an ascetic. She believed that happiness was the purpose of one's life. As Shelton pointed out, she also regarded productive work as the purpose of one's life. Therefore, on some level these two—happiness and productive work—are one. And in fact Rand did state this. She saw happiness and life's maintenance as different aspects of the same achievement. "Existentially, the activity of pursuing rational goals is the activity of maintaining one's life; psychologically, its result, reward and concomitant is an emotional state of happiness" (1964a, 29).

Rand also said that implicit in the law of supply and demand is that underlying both forces are the same individuals (1982f, 130). According to Sciabarra, Rand had an integrated or holistic philosophical approach (1995, 17). It might seem to follow that consumption could be regarded as a "reward" for productive work—pursuing one's values. Although one might draw this conclusion, Rand saw love as the "greatest reward" a person could receive for his virtues (1961a, 147), romantic love being its highest expression. To Rand, when it comes to love of another person, affirmation is inseparable from action. As for romantic love, the action takes the form of sex (Shelton 1995, 29–30). It seems to me that insofar as material goods are concerned, the action that most directly affirms one's appreciation is purchase. Purchase is affirmation in a very real sense, because it not only provides the producer with information (it provides a positive signal to the producer), it also provides the producer with his means of survival. Rand acknowledged that "the spending of money is a grave responsibility" (1982h, 6).

Purchase and Affirmation

In Rand's novel *The Fountainhead*, the architect, Roark, said to Wynand about the house he had designed for him:

> What you feel in the presence of a thing you admire is just one word—"Yes." The affirmation, the acceptance, the sign of admittance. . . . [T]he ability to say "Yes" or "No" is the essence of all ownership. It's your ownership of your own ego. Your soul, if you wish. Your soul has a single basic function—the act of valuing. . . . In this sense, everything to which you grant your love is yours. (1981, 564)

Rand was writing about art in this passage, but the same kind of sentiment could be applied to other kinds of purchase. One may not feel a strong affection for the more mundane purchases one undertakes—pencils, soap powder, and the like; nevertheless, Rand made an important observation about purchases. By acquiring something through purchase, one is in effect saying "yes." By choosing to purchase, one is revealing one's preferences for a product.

Rand said in the quote above that, in a sense, "everything to which you grant your love is yours" (ibid.). This is reminiscent of Adam in *Genesis*, who, as Elie Wiesel pointed out, by naming creatures, came to own them (1976, 10).) There is truth here, but affirmation cannot be divorced from action. When it comes to values, tacit approval is insufficient. Action is required, and purchase is that action when it comes to material goods. Purchase is affirmation in a very real way in that it literally keeps alive that which one values (the object of one's values). By purchasing a commodity, one is signaling the producer that this item or service is valued. Even more importantly for the viability of the value, the purchaser is providing income to its producer. One supports the product produced by supporting the producer of the product.

Purchase provides information, telling the producer, as well as others, that this product is valued. Moreover, it provides the incentive for him as well as other producers and potential producers to produce this product. Purchase provides a livelihood to the producer and the expectation of an income for potential producers. Purchase is an affirmation of the value itself as well as of the producer of the value. This is what economic theory tells us, but it does not make any value judgment about what is valued—whether it is good or bad. To a large extent, what is valued and whether it is good or bad depends on who is valuing the good and in what context he is evaluating it. Even goods that may generally be regarded as "bad"—addictive drugs, for instance—may have medicinal uses. In discussing objectivity, Peikoff noted the following: "The epistemological responsibility imposed on man by the fact that knowledge is contextual is the need of integration. The responsibility imposed by the fact that knowledge is hierarchical is: the need of *reduction*" (1991, 132). One could make a similar statement with regard to purchase. Whether a good is good or bad depends on context. It depends on how much of it one has already consumed, the basis for the use or purchase of it, the expectation of its future purchase, etc. These are based in consumer theory.

Hierarchy relates not only to where this good ranks with other goods one has purchased or plans to purchase, but to how this good fits in with one's overall hierarchy of values. One should ask not only how this purchase fits in with my other purchases at this moment, but how it fits in with my fundamental values. One should ask if the good is connected to one's own reality—the reality that is one's life. Just as, as Peikoff said: "Knowledge is *not* a juxtaposition of independent items; it is a unity" (1991, 122), so should one think of one's life and the products one consumes in one's life.

One's life is not a juxtaposition of independent events nor should purchase be a collection of independent items with no apparent relationship. Yet purchase can be viewed this way. There are individuals who purchase luxury cars without being able to pay for their child's orthodontia. The consumer's preference map should, through a process of reduction, be tied to one's hierarchy of values, and one's hierarchy of values should be tied to reality—one's own life. Although Rand did not discuss this directly as it relates to consumer choice, it is clear in her discussion of sacrifice that she believed one's purchases should be tied to one's values and one's values tied to reality. She said with respect to sacrifice that if a mother forgoes purchasing a hat for herself in order to feed her hungry child, this would not be a sacrifice, since she values her child more than a hat (1961a, 141). It is clear that when one takes ownership, one should be aware of what one may be sacrificing by making the purchase. This is consumer choice from a normative perspective.

Philosophical versus Market Value

Rand distinguished between market value and philosophical value. The market value of a product reflects its socially objective value. By philosophical value, she meant from the perspective of the "best possible to man," based on the standard of the person who is most rational and knowledgeable within a given context, category, and time period (1967a, 24). A microscope may be demonstrably more scientifically valuable than lipstick, Rand said. Yet the producer of the latter may make more income than the former. The question concerning value is—of value to whom? Rand noted that for a struggling young stenographer, a microscope may be of little value. Lipstick to her could transform self-doubt into self-confidence (1967a, 25). If the stenographer spent all of her income on cosmetics, and as a result could not afford to sustain her existence, then she would be budgeting her income improperly. But the fact that she purchases a lipstick does not mean that her preference ordering is irrational, or that it is not in line with her hierarchy of values, or that her values are not tied to the reality of her own life.

If purchases are made consciously and tied to values that are in turn tied to reality, and if in making a purchase the person is mindful that he is signaling to others that he values this product as well as supporting the producer of the product, then the consumer may place more value on that which he purchases. Even the mundane may take on more significance since a person will better see its importance in his life. One may come to have a greater appreciation for the process by which a product is acquired. In *Free to Choose*, the Friedmans related the impersonal forces of the market by illustrating the making of a pencil (from the story "I, Pencil: My Family Tree as Told to Leonard E. Read") (1980, 11–13). If one were more mindful of what it takes to bring such a seemingly simple product to market, one might appreciate not only the product more, but also the producers, as well as the system that allows for the product's creation. Although the work of Andy Warhol has been called mechanical by Objectivists and by the artist himself (Torres and Kamhi 2000, 269–70), in a sense, he and other pop artists of his time heightened the appreciation of everyday consumer goods by making them objects of art. This is instructive in the way in which consumers can choose to view the goods that they purchase. Goods can be appreciated on more than one level. A consumer who is making conscious choices can value the products he purchases from many perspectives, including the aesthetic, even for goods that are not objects of art per se.

Chapter Twelve

Productivity and Destiny

This chapter leads with a comparison between David Norton's and Rand's views on productive purpose—or one's destiny (Norton 1976; Rand 1964a). The reason for this is that Den Uyl and Rasmussen (1986a, 75) placed Rand's ethics in the perfectionist camp but regarded Norton's ethics as more complete than Rand's.

To Rand, in one sense, all work is productive if it employs the full range of a person's mental ability and it is pursued as a career (so long as no coercion is involved). An exception is the full-time humanitarian—that is, someone supported by almsgiving rather than trade (Berliner 1995, 83, 544). Objectivists see humanitarians as merely distributing income produced by others ("A Slogan" 1998, 4). Productivity is the central virtue in OE and productive purpose a cardinal value. This chapter discusses the Objectivist view of productivity and compares it with the way it is regarded in economic theory. The main reason productivity is valued in OE is that it sustains one's life. Peikoff (1991, 391) equated productivity with profit. From an economic perspective, if an economic unit does not cover its costs, it is being wasteful of resources. In Rand's view, it is parasitical on the production of others. However, according to OE, even if one were independently wealthy, he would still have to work, since it satisfies a psychological need—that of anchoring and prioritizing all other values. Productivity ranks above relationships with others and all other endeavors. It is a single purpose that is long-term in nature, requires the full range of one's abilities, and results in the production of a physical product (even though services qualify). Excluded are recreation, a variety of interests, knowledge for its own sake, and careers that rely upon charitable donations (Peikoff 1991, 292–303). I note that some of these descriptors are contradictory; nor do they all correspond to the way economists view productivity.

Destiny

Den Uyl and Rasmussen put Rand's egoistic ethics in the eudaimonistic camp; however, they regarded David Norton's perfectionist ethics as capturing "in more detail the substance of the doctrine that Rand struggled to express" (1986a, 75). There are a number of points of similarity between Rand's ethics and Norton's, although each has its own terminology. The central purpose in Rand's ethics is productivity (1964a, 25); in Norton's, it is one's daimon, or destiny (1976, 5). Both closed the is/ought gap by claiming that what man is determines what he ought to do. For Rand, this is related to man's nature. Norton was more specific. For him, it has to do with a man pursuing his own destiny. To Rand, joy is the reward and concomitant of work (1964a, 28); Norton used the Greek term eudaimonia (1976, ix).

One point of dissimilarity is that Norton regarded one's destiny as innate (1976, xi). Rand believed individuals were born tabulae rasae (1964a, 28). Both believed that each person was born with all potentialities. However, Norton believed that one's destiny was a perfection that could never be realized. Rand regarded man as efficacious. She would not have subscribed to an ideal that was unachievable by man. Both embraced free will, but Norton interpreted this more narrowly as the freedom to choose or not to choose one's destiny (1976, 16).

Merrill challenged Rand's acceptance of the "blank slate" assumption (1991, 121). He suggested that, based on recent argument, "basic moral principles are inborn, genetic, instinctive" (1997, 84), a position with which Rand would not have agreed. Merrill, however, qualified his statement by saying that moral sentiments—sympathy, for instance—are genetically based, but what one feels sympathy for or about is not (1997, 84–85). I do not think Rand (1964a, 28) would have disagreed with this qualified statement. She recognized that man had the capacity for emotions but thought he could not rely upon them to guide his survival (and therefore could not depend upon them as tools in making moral choices). Man is not born with a standard of value, only the capacity to reason. Recent research on the brain and cognition indicates that the brain has a great deal of plasticity in early development (Springer and Deutsch 1989, 235). However, individuals are not born with the same potentialities (Touchstone 1996, 161). It appears, based on what is known about brain development and its relationship to cognition and ability, that neither Rand nor Norton is completely accurate about innatism and its link to ability and, therefore, to one's "destiny." Some individuals do have tendencies for some skills relative to others. Innatism is probably a factor here, but exposure plays a role as well. Interest and motivation are also significant factors, and a great deal remains unknown about what their determinants are.

Both Rand and Norton had similar ideas on personal integrity. They viewed work as the integrating principle of a person's life. To Rand, a career is a discipline that is essentially long-range. To Norton, one's daimon is a single act that spans one's life (Peikoff 1991, 299–300; Norton 1976, 238–39). Worth or value is tied to one's work or destiny. To Norton, self-worth is manifested solely by living in concert with one's destiny (1976, 16). To Rand, self-esteem is the value, and pride is the virtue, which follow from productive work (1964a, 27). The concept of loyalty to one's career is akin to fidelity in marriage, according to Norton (1976, 195). Thus, having a "calling" is singular in nature. One should not have more than one profession at a time or more than one in a lifetime (1976, 196). Affirmation of one's career necessarily means saying no to "glittering and loud things" (1976, 220) on one hand, and entreaties for pity (1976, 88) on the other. Either would be at the cost of one's destiny. Yet one should not put oneself in the position of having to say no all the time (1976, 233). Every choice is drawn from its relationship to one's destiny. Rand also believed sacrifice to be a vice (1961a, 140); by this she meant the sacrifice of one's purpose to something one valued less or not at all. She did not believe in an ethic of denial. Therefore, one should only choose values that do not impede one's purpose (1961a, 130).

Norton regarded love—love of excellence—as the motivating force for adherence to one's destiny. The joy that accompanies it is eudaimonia (1976, 10). Similarly, Rand referred to noncontradictory joy as the psychological counterpart to the existential pursuit of one's purpose (1964a, 29). Norton referred to this love as eros, which he distinguished from egoism—the latter being Rand's basis for ethics. However, Norton's reference to "ideal selfishness" indicates that there is essentially no difference between his and Rand's conceptions of love in this context. Norton eschewed hero worship (1976, 12), an expression to which Rand adhered. But Norton's concept of emulation (1976, 13) was not dissimilar to Rand's hero worship. Both characterized envy as destructive to the spirit (Norton 1976, 10; Rand 1971c, 154).

Like Rand (1964d, 44), Norton did not regard love of others as essentially self-sacrificial in nature. He saw love as desiring the realization of the excellence of the other. The love of another does not embrace "lapses, defects, and infirmities," however. To these, one must serve as a "perpetual critic, calling for their rectification" (1976, 294). To do otherwise is not to be charitable but to be complicit in their defects. (I personally do not regard wanting another to realize his excellence as synonymous with being his perpetual critic. I address this obliquely below in a brief discussion of the difficulties involved in defining "perfection.") In a more general vein, Rand regarded moral evaluation as the coin paid to men for their character. If a person withholds reproach for vices it is "an act of moral counterfeiting" and if he withholds approval for virtues it "is an act of moral embezzlement" (1961a, 129).

Rand's perspective on love is similar to Norton's in that love is seen as a response to the virtues of another. She said that love was a reflection of a person's values. It is the greatest reward you can receive for your virtues. It is "the emotional price paid by one man for the joy he receives from the virtues of another" (1961a, 147). Her view of romantic love was unlike Norton's, however. Whereas Rand regarded romantic love as one's response to one's own highest values in another person—"an integrated response of mind and body, of love and sexual desire" (1968, 2), Norton saw romantic love the way Montaigne expressed it, as "'more precipitant, fickle, moving and inconstant; a fever subject to intermissions and paroxysms, that has seized upon one part of us'" (1976, 295). Friendship, on the other hand, is "'a constant established heat, all gentle and smooth'" (ibid.).

To Norton, a person best serves the interests of others by staying on his own path. Like Adam Smith, Norton pointed out that even though the good of others is not a person's objective, by fulfilling his potential, he benefits society (1976, 143). Thus, by following one's destiny and refusing to surrender to the persistent appeals from others—what Norton called "ideal selfishness"—one is not withholding from others. On the contrary, by actualizing one's true self, one manifests worth, and as a consequence contributes to others (1976, 89). This is because of the "complementarity of excellences" (1976, 10). Because each person has a different destiny, by fulfilling one's own potential, each person benefits society. Because each person can only fulfill his singular potential, he must rely on others to produce those excellences he does not. This is the source of interdependence among individuals (1976, 25). Interdependence manifests itself in "love, the division of labor, and justice" (1976, 275). (Or what Rand would call trade, trade, and trade. Rand regarded trade among independent equals as the basis for all relationships, whether in the economic or spiritual sphere [1964a, 31].)

Although reminiscent of Adam Smith ([1776] 1937, 424), Norton's departure from Smith's view of "specialization" is dramatic in that Norton did not subscribe to trade. In Norton's proposed economy, if each person followed his destiny, all the right goods would be produced in the right amounts. Norton claimed that: "[F]or every kind of work that must be done, there are persons for whom that work holds intrinsic rewards, and by whom that work shall be skillfully and lovingly done" (1976, 346). Although honorable work, it is difficult to imagine the intrinsic rewards of refuse handling or sewage work. My guess is, however, that if a sufficient dollar value were assigned to either one of these occupations, they would gain in appeal.

Norton mentioned nothing about remuneration, however. That is because each person has a right to pursue his unique destiny, and he is entitled to whatever support he requires in that endeavor. Performance is the only criterion and that is to be judged by experts in the field (1976, 342–44). But what is performance? Is it the best relative to others who perform the same task or the best that he can do based on his own skill level? Since we are all born with the same potentials, according to Norton (1976, xi), skill levels relative to others would seemingly be the criterion. Performance for some tasks—running, for example—is relatively easy to measure since speed is the primary criterion.

What of innovative ideas and novel artistic creations? Thomas Kuhn made the point that, in some ways, we are all prisoners of the existing paradigms (1970, 58–61), and, as a result, new theories, technology, art, etc. may go unappreciated by experts in a given field. This could be a real danger in Norton's economic scheme, but this can be a limitation of a market system as well. Obviously, there are those who cannot get their novels published or sell their works of art. Nevertheless, in a free market, it is the individual's choice whether he pursues an idea or not in the face of challenges. He is free to make the sacrifice in time and other resources if he chooses, even if his work goes unrecognized at first or is never acknowledged. Norton's "alternative" economy does not allow for this possibility.

My guess is that if each person could pursue what he wanted to do, people might be hard-pressed to find someone to pick up their trash. Dangerous and dirty occupations for which there is little excitement or glory may find few takers. Norton seemed to think that if we all simply rid ourselves of our prejudices and regarded refuse handling as equivalent to race-car driving, there would be no shortage in the former (or surpluses in the latter). Perhaps. But one must look at the world and ask, are there occupations that are also pursued for recreation or are undertaken voluntarily without pay? If so, perhaps the nature of the work of race-car driving is different from that of refuse handling.

Dislocations in the workplace may happen in a market economy. There may be coal miners who are out of work and, because of lack of mobility, remain so for some time. But most such surpluses are eliminated. If there are shortages—nurses are needed, for instance—these too are eliminated over time. The mechanism that eliminates surpluses and shortages is the price system. Prices signal and provide the incentive to reallocate resources. Adjustments do not happen automatically. It takes time for workers to find out where jobs are, for employers to discover where job candidates are, and for workers to be trained or retrained and to relocate. But the price system works far better than the scheme Norton seems to have in mind. No one may choose to be a garbage collector as a life's work, even though it's an honorable profession. It is dirty, hazardous, and physically demanding. If one wanted to develop and use these skills and inclinations, he might prefer to be a mountain climber. But, generally speaking, the price mechanism rewards garbage collecting more than mountain climbing, so there are a sufficient number of garbage collectors even though it is less attractive than some other more attractive occupations with similar skill requirements.

Free market exchange is the most efficient method of dealing with the problem of scarcity, according to free market economists. According to Rand, it is the most just way of interacting with other men. Norton, on the other hand, proposed to overcome the problem of scarcity by each person limiting his wants and by claiming only the goods he can maximally utilize in the pursuit of his destiny. Justice to Norton is based on love (1976, 317)—the love of excellence in oneself as well as others. One would not "claim" goods that could be better utilized by others in the pursuit of their destinies. Goods, like people, have potentials. Those potentials should be maximally utilized. Goods will be matched to individuals who have the requisite skill levels to maximally utilize them. Justice is distributive.

How is an individual to be trusted not to "claim" a Ferrari when it is not commensurate with his destiny? Norton said that those closest to the individual must be relied upon for corroboration. The complementarity of excellences will guarantee that the right goods in sufficient numbers are produced. Scarcity is eliminated by individuals limiting their wants to what is produced, and what is produced will be sufficient to meet the requirements for one's survival as well as for one's destiny. Justice is contributive.

From an economic perspective, Norton's proposal would quickly become bureaucratic and invasive and result in gluts of goods most people would not particularly want and shortages of vital ones. The free market system has an inherent mechanism that tends to eliminate shortages and gluts—the price system. The price mechanism provides the signals and incentives to punish those (with losses) who produce too much of a good and reward those (with profits) who produce those goods that people want and can afford. Norton relied upon specialization ("complementarity of excellences") to produce the right goods in sufficient quantities. But what causes specialization? Without trade, each person would be self-sufficient. The only alternative is a very bureaucratic command economy, which theoretically and practically has proven to be inefficient and unjust. In any case, it would not be consistent with Norton's eudaimonistic objectives.

Norton implicitly envisioned the economy as a fixed pie. "Claiming" one good would necessarily be at someone else's expense. For the very short-term, this may be true. It may be true for certain "goods"; for instance, if there is only one kidney and more than one potential recipient. However, generally speaking, the economy is not static, but dynamic in nature. If a person buys a good now, that person provides the incentive for more to be produced later. If a person likes the opera, a particular restaurant, or a brand of shoe, he, generally speaking, wants others to purchase it so that the producer will stay in business. Purchase encourages production. It also stimulates improvements in technology in the form of new competing products or cost-saving techniques.

Norton was critical of the maximizing principle as a principle of justice (1976, 315). His criticism was leveled against Rawls. (Although, at least in his solution, Rawls followed a maximin principle, not a maximization principle [Mack 2001, 7].) Rand's ethics are, like Norton's, a perfectionist ethics. If one does his best, he is a "maximizer," in effect. The emphasis in both Rand's and Norton's ethics is on the production side, not the consumption side. In the long run, maximization of production and consumption are not incompatible objectives, however.

Norton criticized the maximization principle as a principle of justice—i.e., maximization without limit (in consumption). But individuals do not maximize without limit. They cannot since they are constrained by their incomes. Even their incomes are a result of a decision between income (other goods) and the "good" leisure. Leisure itself is an ambiguous term since it encompasses all "goods" that do not go through the market yet are consumed by the individual. So even if one appears to have "enough" goods in the sense that a person chooses to work less and therefore make less income and as a result have fewer material goods, he is consuming more leisure. And leisure is also finite. Leisure is something of which there is only so much, regardless of how much income one has.

Consumers do not purchase irrespective of price, nor, if they are rational, should they. Since, by and large, individuals work for their incomes—which takes time and effort—they should not squander their incomes. To do so is to squander their lives—their time. They should not squander their incomes on those things they do not value or on those things that they value less than what they pay for them, because to do either is to give that which is undeserved. It would be validating something (the product) and someone (the producer), which and whom one does not value (or does not rate highly in one's value system). Although Rand did not explicitly make these statements with respect to consumption, they are consistent with her overall system of ethics. This is a maximization principle that demands of the consumer that he consider his choices as they relate to his value system. In a sense, it is a stricter maximizing principle than that assumed by economists because it requires (in a normative sense) that the consumer use principled reasoning about whether he is in fact maximizing. Economists are interested in modeling how consumers make decisions, not how they should make decisions.

Norton stated that one who maximizes without limit is an "ignorant, undisciplined, and uncommitted man, who wants everything, believes himself entitled to everything, and begrudges others their smallest gain" (1976, 315). One should probably separate wanting things—even if they are not founded on principled reasoning—from begrudging others. Utility theory assumes (generally speaking) that there are no interpersonal utility comparisons. One can have insatiable wants and still not begrudge another that which he has. Envy plays no part in basic consumer theory and is unnecessary to the assumption of maximization (although envy does play an implicit role in Rawl's theory [Rand 1982g, 111]).

Productivity

Keynes has been quoted often as having said: "In the long run we are all dead" (Spiegel 1971, 613). Rand's philosophy is not based on the near term or the short run as much as the long run. This does not mean that she was unconcerned with this moment or the next, but she thought that one should look at the long run to determine what actions should be taken in this moment or the next. Economists have specific definitions for the short run and long run that relate to the limitedness of resources. (In this context, I mean all inputs used in production, not simply natural resources.) From a microeconomic perspective, the short run is a period of time for which an input (i.e., resource) is fixed (capital, it is usually assumed). In the long run, it is assumed that all inputs are variable. Firms are assumed to operate in the short run and plan in the long run. Finiteness of resources, natural resources in this case, is also relevant to some growth theories. A general limit to natural resources is posited by some theories to result in a limit to growth.

Decision-makers are more apt to take into account the long-term opportunity costs of a resource—that is, to utilize it more efficiently—if they own the resource or have to pay resource owners for its use. It is the lack of ownership of fish, air, and bodies of water that tends to result in their overutilization. (Overutilization means to use or harvest a resource past the point that would be optimal if all opportunity costs were taken into account. These include discounted future costs.) Ownership is primarily an issue (in an economic sense) if the resource under consideration is scarce. Ownership also encourages the production of more and better goods over time. Property rights encourage growth by providing, through the price mechanism, the incentive and the wherewithal to innovate, to invest in capital formation, to explore, to train, and to educate.

Production is the means by which we overcome scarcity. It has been claimed by some that the establishment of property rights has "solved scarcity" (Wilkinson 2000, 17). This could be misinterpreted to mean that scarcity has been eliminated as such. But of course scarcity can never be eliminated. Some regard the existence of scarcity as a reason conflicts among men exist. Because of scarcity, one man can gain only at another man's expense. One person's gain is another's loss. The implicit assumption is that scarcity is the same as a fixed pie.

Rand asserted that no conflicts exist among rational men. Will Wilkinson claimed that this principle holds true "only under special circumstances, namely, when problems of scarcity have been solved by the emergence of property rights and market mechanisms" (ibid.). If a resource is scarce and unowned, one man may benefit in the short run at the long-run expense of everyone including himself (say, because a renewable resource is used to the point of extinction or exhaustion and this is undesirable from an optimal use perspective). If two persons or more vie over an unowned resource, then the "loser" may not be said to lose the resource since he did not own it in the first place, but he may lose other resources in trying to acquire the resource. So loss is still possible in both of these cases. In the first case, lack of ownership results in users failing to take into account the full opportunity costs (present costs and the present value of future costs) in their decisions and in their actions. There is a conflict of interests among users, and there is a conflict between a user's interests today and his interests in the future. In the second case, the nature of the conflict arises because ownership has not been established for a particular resource and, perhaps, both parties regard their own claims to the resource as having some merit. These kinds of conflicts among men may be resolved with the establishment of property rights.

However, those who regard scarcity as meaning a "fixed pie" see conflict as existing among men even if property rights are assigned. From their perspective, someone can get more of a thing only if someone else has less of it. Thus an egoist—one who pursues his own interests—is seen as one who strives to get more, and he can do this only if another or others have less. So in trying to sustain one's own life, others must sacrifice theirs. Life is by necessity zero-sum. Echoing Rand, Tara Smith (2000, 176) said that this is not the case, because by pursuing one's values, a rational egoist *creates* value. One creates value by producing.

Production is the means by which scarcity is overcome. However, even if there were a "fixed pie," as there is in the very near term, trade results in "more." This is because, by each person trading that of which he has relatively more, each trader gains in utility. Trade yields "more" in a utility sense, even if there are no more goods in total. In the longer term, more (in a physical sense) can be produced. Trade does at times result in some people being worse off than they were before. It is difficult not to regard these as losses. That does not mean that others gain at the "expense" of those who are worse off. When the electric bulb was invented, many candle makers were very likely worse off, some perhaps permanently. This does not mean that Edison and others benefited at the "expense" of the candle makers. They simply produced a product that was found to be extremely useful. As a result, consumers found less need for candles. Neither the bulb producers nor buyers were responsible (in any moral sense of the word) for the misfortune of those candle makers who had to close their doors.

There are situations that have the appearance of a zero-sum outcome, but the way in which Rand interprets "interests" makes them not zero-sum as such. An example of this would be the situation in which two individuals needed a kidney transplant but there was only one donor. Only one person could benefit from such a circumstance, but the other person would not be considered a "loser" in the sense that he could not lose that which he did not own. It could be true that the long run might be irrelevant to the person who did not receive the transplant. His situation would be unfortunate; still it could not be said that the transplant recipient had benefited at someone else's expense. A true zero-sum outcome would exist if one person stole someone else's kidney (or anything for that matter) against another person's will. In that case, the thief would benefit at the expense of the victim since the victim would have been the rightful owner.

Scarcity is a fact of reality. One does not overcome it in the sense that all goods will eventually be available at a zero price. However, scarcity can be mitigated by producing "more"—i.e., through growth. "More" can be defined as increased productivity. Productivity may be expressed as an increase in the number of units produced or as an increase in the number of units per worker (which translates into a decrease in per unit costs). Reduced scarcity has been defined as a reduction in per unit costs over time (Barnett and Morse 1963).

An entrepreneur, if he is successful, produces a good or a service that has a value that exceeds the sum of its "parts"—the values of the inputs used to produce it. This is, in fact, the definition of production given by Isabel Paterson (1968, 232; Peikoff 1991, 391). The entrepreneur's return for this, i.e., profit, is the difference between the market value of the products sold and the cost of the inputs used to produce them. The "parts" include material inputs as well as the services of plant and equipment and labor. Material inputs would include raw material as well as raw materials that have been fashioned into producer goods—"frozen intelligence," to paraphrase Rand (1957, 1064). Raw materials such as ore and fossil fuels may come from nature, but it takes human effort and ingenuity to extract them from the earth. Except for living space (untransformed land and air), the uses of most natural resources must be discovered. (Oil in the nineteenth century was considered a nuisance for those who discovered it on their land. It was not until many of the inventions of the late nineteenth and early twentieth century were developed—particularly the internal combustion engine—that oil came into its own as a resource.) Labor is the service provided by employees (included as well is the opportunity cost of the entrepreneur).

Rand assigned to innovation the role of the engine of economic growth. There are a number of reasons productivity may be increased. Economies of scale due to the division of labor or to technical factors (such as the reduction of relative risk in insurance as the number of insureds increases) are examples. Economies of scope associated with producing more than one product (e.g., combined distribution) and learning by doing are others. Using more (not better) equipment may increase worker productivity. Investment in human capital can also improve the productivity of labor. All of this can be achieved with existing knowledge and technology (Salvatore 1996, 274–93). However, as seen with growth (scarcity) models, with finite and/or depletable resources, eventually these improvements would be overcome and result in a decline in output per worker (diminishing returns). Rand is right in that, ultimately, innovation and discovery would be needed to improve the worker's productive standing. Ultimately, innovation and discovery would be necessary for growth to continue. Rand's concern is for long-term growth, and innovation is the engine that drives the growth of the economy in the long run. This is a dynamic perspective, not a long-run equilibrium perspective. If the limits to all resources that are finite and depletable were reached, innovation would be necessary simply to maintain a given level of income.

In the Malthusian model, diminishing returns are due to an overall limit to resources (a finite planet). Ultimately, a decline in output per capita will occur. Malthus assumed that land area, on which food production is based, is fixed. Food, which is necessary for survival, can increase arithmetically. Passion between men and women is necessary, and population if unchecked will grow at a geometric rate. Diminishing returns, which Malthus did not state explicitly, is implicit in his assumptions (Malthus [1803] 1963, 1–12). In his model, workers will receive no better than subsistence. If for some reason wages should increase (because of a larger "wages fund," in classical parlance), this would increase the number of workers. This is because a higher wage would allow for a lower mortality rate (and a higher birth rate), and since population is assumed to be the same as (or directly proportional to) the labor force, there would be more workers. The increase in population (labor supply) would put downward pressure on the wage. The population would increase (and therefore the supply of labor) so long as the wage rate was above subsistence. Once subsistence was reached, the wage rate would stabilize. If the wage rate should fall below subsistence, the mortality rate would rise, population would decline (as would the labor supply) and the wage would return to subsistence (Rima 1978, 108–109).

Conclusions like this one supposedly led Carlyle to call classical economists "the dreary professors of a dismal science" (Spiegel 1971, 369). More recent analyses by Meadows et al. (1975) and Mesarovic and Pestel (1976), using massive amounts of data and high-speed computation, have made dire predictions, not unlike those that can result from Malthus's assumptions. But Barnett and Morse, using an increase in unit costs as a measure of increasing resource scarcity, found that, on aggregate, the hypothesis of increasing natural resource scarcity was, in general, rejected (Barnett and Morse 1963, 235). As it turns out, growth itself induces antidotes to increasing resource scarcity by encouraging technological advances (Barnett and Morse 1963, 240; Johnson and Bennett 1980).

For resources that are finite and/or exhaustible, higher prices (that reflect rent due to scarcity) can conserve their use if they are owned. With those exhaustible resources that are not owned, such as whales, extinction may occur since there is no price mechanism to signal the resource's scarcity. The rents do not reflect an increase in productivity if a resource is finite and exhaustible (such as ores), but higher prices provide a signaling function. They, in effect, tell others that this is an increasingly scarce resource and encourage the resource's conservation. Probably more important is that higher prices encourage innovation. Higher prices do not necessarily spur invention—although they can—but they can encourage producers to bring into production inventions that were formerly considered too expensive to compete with resources or products currently available on the market.

Economists in general have tended to regard innovations as exogenous to the economic system and to be stochastic in nature (Barnett and Morse 1963, 235; cf. Chiang 2000, 267–274). Even Schumpeter, who made innovation the key contributor in the creation of business cycles, viewed it as random in pattern (Valentine and Ellis 1991, 355). Barnett and Morse regarded technological change as being causally related to the market mechanism (1963, 240–41). Innovation is scarcity-induced. Increased scarcity, by definition, is reflected in higher costs (of other inputs), and to avoid a cost squeeze, resource-saving technology is induced.

I have expressed the forgoing in passive tense to be consistent with Barnett and Morse. They stated that "resource-saving technology is induced," in the same way that one would say "prices increase." Prices can increase for any number of reasons, many of which are not under the direct control of the producer. Saying "technology is induced" makes it sound as if it were a variable that passively responds to market forces. It is not, of course. Barnett and Morse used the passive tense in their discussion, but the implication is clear. To avoid higher costs, producers look for new and innovative methods. The innovations themselves are the result of men's minds. Rand depicted this in *Atlas Shrugged* and also illustrated the process in reverse—i.e., what can happen when innovators and entrepreneurs go on strike. Higher costs do not automatically "induce" cost-saving innovations. In regulated industries, costs tend to increase and the increase in costs is passed on to the consumer by the regulatory agencies. There is little, if any, inducement to innovate in industries that are subsidized or that are government-owned, particularly if they do not suffer losses as a result of inefficiencies.

Barnett and Morse mentioned government involvement in exploration and research and development to overcome increasing resource scarcity (1963, 241). Research and development in these areas have value, but as Rand noted, one must ask, of value to whom? Even though Rand recognized the value of research and development in these areas (for instance, in the space program), she did not think that individuals should be forced to subsidize them (1969e, 8).

Barnett and Morse also hypothesized that people will tend to limit their numbers once they acknowledge that unlimited population growth will threaten their material well-being. Barnett and Morse regarded the problem as socio-cultural, however, and pointed out that little research had been done on the socio-cultural aspects of population growth (1963, 245–46). My point in chapter 2 was that, as alternative opportunities that are remunerative increase for females, nonpaid work—childrearing in particular—becomes less attractive. Becker (1995a, 267) argued that children are normal goods. There is evidence that does not support this. Unless there is a recognition by economists that children are something other than consumer goods, and virtues concerning childrearing are regarded as primary and significant rather than secondary and marginal by philosophers, the current trend may continue.

Even though Norton claimed that there is no hierarchy among different jobs, he listed a series of occupations that were arranged in descending order of value. In his list, childrearing and housekeeping rated only slightly above refuse handling (1976, 347). This is a single example, but telling nonetheless. So long as the value assigned to childrearing is considered only marginally better than refuse handling, the incentive to have children will fall. This can be a problem with "vocations" that by their nature are nonremunerative.

The Labor Theory of Value and the Value Theory of Labor

Rand attributed improvements in technology to the entrepreneur. She said that a factory employee is paid, not just for his own labor, "but for all the productive genius which has made that factory possible" (1961a, 185). That includes the investor who put his savings at risk, the engineer, the inventor of the product, the scientist who uncovered the laws, and the philosopher who has instructed man in how to think. Rand said that the standard of living of an employee working for her fictional steel producer Hank Rearden would be no more than what he could earn with his physical labor. "[T]he rest is a gift from Hank Rearden" (1961a, 186).

It is because Rand attributed innovation and its effect on productivity and growth to the entrepreneur that her value theory has been labeled a labor theory of value (Sciabarra 1995, 291). She envisioned the entrepreneur as being the source of innovation for which he can never be adequately compensated. The compensation the entrepreneur receives for his contribution is profit. There are various sources of profit, not all of which stem from innovation or discovery. A person may profit from the capital gain received from the sale of an asset—securities, for instance. Stock prices may increase because of a change in expected future earnings, but they can also rise due to a speculative frenzy. The latter would be unrelated to productivity improvements from any source.

Innovation is the application of an invention. It need not be invention, per se. It takes talent and risk to apply an invention, nevertheless, and there is a return to that (which may be positive or negative). Inventions may exist yet not be used in production because of cost considerations. If a particular resource or good increases in relative scarcity, its price will rise. The higher price may render new products produced with existing inventions more economically feasible. And if a particular (potential) producer thinks that demand for a new product will be sufficient so that he may be able to take advantage of lower unit costs as a result of, say, economies of scale, this would increase the economic attractiveness of the use of the invention in the production of the new product. Productivity can be improved by the introduction of technology in the production of new goods, or by producing existing goods with better techniques. Entrepreneurs create or produce products; they do not necessarily discover a new idea or create an invention. It is not just the worker who benefits from the invention and discovery of others; the entrepreneur does so as well. All of the improvements in the standard of living of the worker cannot be attributed to entrepreneurs, as Rand implied.

Rand had a labor theory of value in that she put the entrepreneur in a capitalist economic system at the apex of the ability pyramid. By innovating and creating, he contributes more than any other input in the production process and receives less in return for his contribution. A machine is seen as a "frozen form of a living intelligence" (1957, 1064). This is consistent with the rationale behind patent and copyright laws, which are designed to assign property rights to those whose new ideas can be expressed in physical form. Yet, Rand did not believe that patent or copyright holders should be compensated forever for their contributions. Unlike other property, which can be passed on to others (one's heirs) indefinitely, patents and copyrights should be limited in duration. Thus, inventors are not fully compensated for the contributions they make to others in the economy. At least this is the way I interpret the idea that innovators are undercompensated for their contributions.

As for the labor theory of value, modern value theory does not regard the value of a good as being determined by the value of labor (and/or other inputs) used to produce it. Modern value theory sees the value of labor (inputs) as being derived from the value of the product. And the value of the product is determined by the consumer. Worker productivity can be measured in units produced, but at the firm level, the value of a worker's contribution to the production process is the revenue attributable to employing the marginal worker (the marginal revenue product), which will equal (under competitive conditions) the wage or salary paid the worker. Of course, perfectly competitive conditions exist in neither the product nor the labor market.

Modern short-run theory of the firm defines the difference between total revenue (the sum of the marginal revenue products generated by employment of the variable input) and total variable cost as the quasi-rent payable to the fixed factor. Since the fixed factor (which is usually assumed to be capital, i.e., plant and equipment) cannot be altered in the short term, its marginal product cannot be directly calculated (Ferguson 1972, 410). The range of output that is considered "economic" begins once output per unit of labor input starts to decline (average variable cost begins to rise). This is the point at which the marginal product of capital (the fixed input) is zero. Additional units of labor will be employed so long as what labor adds to revenue is greater than what it adds to costs (the wage rate in a perfectly competitive environment). Since all workers will be paid the same wage for a given skill level (which will equal the change in revenue associated with the last unit of labor hired), the sum of the marginal revenue products of each worker (the total revenue) will exceed the sum of the costs (total variable costs). Or, the sum of the "contribution" of labor (the total revenue) exceeds the marginal revenue product of labor (of the last worker) multiplied by the number of workers. This assumes that all of the total product is due to labor.

Approached another way, the marginal product of capital can be implicitly computed. If returns to scale are assumed to be constant, in the "economic range" (that is, the range in which it would pay for the firm to operate), the (implicit) marginal product to plant and equipment is positive (and increasing), and the marginal product to labor is positive (and decreasing—that is, there are diminishing returns to labor). Both inputs contribute, and (with constant returns) adding the marginal contribution of both factors will equal the total product. Up to the point at which the "economic" range is reached, the (implicit) marginal product of capital is negative. Capital in this latter range of output would be so large relative to labor that it would be uneconomic to operate in that range. If demand for the product were this low, then a smaller plant would be preferred (1972, 150–51). (There would be excess capacity, an underutilization of capital.) From this perspective, the sum of the marginal products of labor would be the total product, but this would be less than the marginal revenue product multiplied by the number of workers.

This is an example in which A does not appear to be equal to A. But, in fact, the plant and equipment in all stages of production contribute to output in the sense that without the plant there could be no production. What this approach describes is the point in the production process at which there would be "too much" capital relative to labor for a given plant size (and vice versa, once labor expands to the point at which the plant is overutilized). In that range, plant and equipment contribute to output, but if workers were paid the marginal product of labor (of the last worker), there would be insufficient total product to "pay" workers.

From the perspective of the firm, marginal productivity theory is a theory of employment, not of factor prices. From the (perfectly competitive) firm's point of view, the supply curve for the (variable) factor is flat at the market price of the factor. The market price of the factor is determined by the supply curve and the market demand (which falls faster than the sum of the marginal revenue product curves for all firms). In a static state, the productivity theory would be an input price theory for a homogeneous input (given its market supply) (Rima 1978, 251). But any factor, not just plant and equipment, can earn a quasi-rent in the short run (that is, a surplus above its cost of production), since all inputs are relatively fixed in the short run (1978, 298). In the long run, wages (and other input prices) will more closely approximate their costs of production (for labor, the costs of rearing and training) (1978, 299). The theoretical exception is land (finite resources), which can (theoretically) receive rent in the long run. Land rent would, from the firm's perspective, reflect its opportunity cost, i.e., the price that would have to be paid to bid it away from the highest valued alternative forgone (1978, 297).

In the long run, all inputs are assumed to be variable from the perspective of the firm. Insofar as whether the marginal productivity theory is a theory of distribution, it suffers in a number of ways. One is that an input's marginal product is separable and calculable only if proportions are variable among inputs (i.e., the inputs are not used in fixed proportions) and substitutable for each other (1978, 237). Another problem is associated with returns to scale. If there are increasing returns to scale, paying factors the value of their marginal products will result in a shortfall, and with decreasing returns there will be a surplus if factors are paid on this basis (1978, 253).

Worker exploitation is described by economists as workers being paid less than the marginal revenue product of the last person employed. Rand's trader principle is a principle of justice. It assumes trade takes place between independent equals. "Exploitation" of workers would seem unlikely in a free market since all trade is voluntary, which means that neither the worker nor the employer is forced into the transaction. Rand did recognize that in some instances wages could be "too low," however. Nathaniel Branden mentioned that this could be true "particularly in small, isolated communities" (1967, 85). This condition can be met in a monopsony setting—i.e., where there exists a single employer for a given labor market. Although unusual in a modern industrial economy, company towns were once not that uncommon.

Even though it is true that the wage would be what the workers were "willing to accept," because they faced no alternatives (their opportunity cost would be, in effect, zero), they would receive a low wage relative to the market clearing wage that would exist under more competitive conditions. (Even though their opportunity cost may be zero in terms of alternative paid employment, workers can still consume "leisure." So rather than expend energy at a job for free, they would not offer their services if the wage were zero. In the long run, wages usually approximate the cost of rearing and training. But for unskilled workers this may barely cover "subsistence." Although a subsistence wage is a fuzzy concept, it is not entirely without content. If the wage becomes so low that the mortality rate rises, then the supply of labor will be affected.)

Workers' low (or nontransferable) skills and lack of mobility would be the main reasons for the lack of alternative employment. The lack of mobility in cases such as this may have been largely due to the inability to save. The inability to save may not have been simply due to the fact that wages were low ("subsistence"), but because frugality was rendered impossible because of the form in which their wages were paid. Workers could be paid in company scrip (shinplaster), which would only be redeemable at the company store. When a worker is paid in a unit of account that does not serve as a medium of exchange except in a store owned by the worker's employer, saving by the worker is not possible. This is regarded by economists as exploitation. If workers combine so as to act as one, countervailing power can improve wages (and possibly employment) (Ferguson 1972, 444–46).

There are disincentives for a firm's workers to unionize, however. The incentive structure has features in common with a public good, partly because of the number of workers involved. As I see it, there is more than one way to view the incentive structure facing the workers considering unionization. One way of viewing the payoff structure is similar to a cartel situation in which there is an incentive to cheat among participants. Although workers may initially agree to bargain collectively, each may separately have an incentive to accept a better salary from the employer (who would have an incentive to make the offer to one or some employees without making the same offer to all or most other workers). The monopsonist could offer better salaries to a few (say, the organizers) and break up the collective as a bargaining unit. I think a more realistic payoff structure is one in which, rather than an incentive to cheat on the part of some workers because of being paid off by the employer, each person has a disincentive to form a union because of negative repercussions. Each may reason that the small increase in pay he may possibly receive if he tries to form a union will be far less than he would lose if he were fired for unionizing, particularly under a monopsonist setting where there is, by definition, no alternative employment.

This is where an outside union would be needed to unionize the workers. The problem is that organizing workers is an enterprise in itself. If workers are paid in company scrip that is redeemable only for goods purchased at a company store, a union would have no incentive to unionize workers, since their dues would be paid in a medium of exchange that was not generally accepted. If a union did so, it would have to be with the certainty (or a very high probability) that one of its bargaining points would be that wages would henceforth be paid in a general medium, and the union would have to be certain to win. If not, unionizing workers under these conditions would be an act of charity on the part of the union.

Pinning Down Worth and Work

From an economic perspective, the "value" of the worker is not determined by physical productivity alone (the number units of output produced). It is related to the revenue generated. Although marginal (revenue) productivity theory is a theory of employment for the firm, not a theory of compensation, what a worker receives is not unrelated to consumer demand. Unless consumers purchase a product, the worker will not be compensated. Therefore, in that sense, demand for workers is a derived demand and affects worker compensation. The value to the consumer (the satisfaction or "utility" derived), will in turn affect the value of the work done to produce it. From the firm's perspective, the "value" may be determined by the value of the output produced by the last worker hired. Or it may be the addition to revenue generated by the last worker used in the production process. It could be the wage rate or it could be the change in costs associated with the last worker hired. This could equal the cost of rearing and training. All of these will not necessarily be equal. From the worker's perspective, there is the value of his human capital—the discounted value of his expected future income stream.

To Rand, the producer himself is the primary judge of value. His work also gives his life value (purpose). The result of productive work is self-esteem (self-worth) (1964a, 27). In a moral sense, all individuals have equal capacity for self-worth (Den Uyl and Rasmussen 1986a, 74). Although there may be a hierarchy of work in terms of what individuals receive in pay or in terms of how many units of a thing they produce, so long as a person regards his work as a discipline and uses the full range of his mental capabilities, his work has the same moral worth as any other individual's (Rand 1964a, 26–27). Rand recognized that the market value of a consumer good was determined by the consumer. She distinguished that from the philosophical value of a product (1967a, 24). Presumably, a philosophical value could apply to an input as well as a consumer good.

Even though the consumer is an important factor in determining the market value of a product as well as the inputs used to produce it, Rand did not believe that a producer's beneficiaries should be a (primary) consideration in one's work (Berliner 1995, 424). A man's relationship to other men, according to Rand, is secondary (1961c, 79). One might think by this she meant that one should not be emotionally dependent on others for one's self-esteem. For example, the phrase "social metaphysician" is used for one who relies on the opinions of others to determine his self-worth (B. Branden 1986, 269). But her relegation of men to second place is not limited to emotional dependence. What Rand meant was that man's "primary relationship . . . is to reality and not to other people" (Register 2000, 23).

In one's work, one's motive or intent should not be to create for others. Rand's character Howard Roark said that the creative person is not motivated by other people. Inventors, discoverers, producers, and artists are interested in that which they produce, not the people that use it. It is the thing itself that is the objective of one's work, not the beneficiaries or what they derive from it (Rand 1961c, 78). Because consumers determine, to a large extent, what is produced and in what number, and who gets compensated and by how much, economists have said that the "consumer is king" (Donway 1999b, 18). Advocates of Objectivism, such as Roger Donway, find the possible ethical implications of this unsettling. Productive work may be living in accordance with one's destiny, but it is also the means of acquiring income with which to sustain one's existence. If it is necessary to sell to consumers in order to acquire the income to live, wouldn't a person not only take the beneficiaries of his work into consideration, but also regard them as important? Of course, considering one's beneficiaries important to one's survival does not mean that a person puts his customers' wishes above his own values, that he sacrifices his integrity, that he "sells out."

Central to the question of value is, of value to whom? The Objectivist answer would seem to be: primarily to the producer. It is because Rand believed that a producer should not regard the beneficiaries as primary that she believed it unethical for a person to depend primarily on charitable contributions as his source of income (Berliner 1995, 544). Yet there would seem to be a subtle contradiction where charity is concerned, since in this case it is not the value the producer places on his work that is primary, but *who pays* for the product that determines whether it has value.

In OE, work is one's central purpose and serves to anchor one's values and to rank them. As such, it is a psychological need even when it is not an existential one. So, one must work even if he receives no pay for it (Peikoff 1991, 302). If a person receives no pay, yet works, economists assume that the person receives psychic income. The value that is produced could be pure consumption on the part of the worker (utility), it could be maintenance of human capital (e.g., training), or it could benefit others (e.g., charity). In the latter case, the utility of others would be part of the worker's own utility function, which would not necessarily be unethical from Rand's perspective so long as it was not the primary reason for work.

Psychic income can be "received" for work even if a person works for pay. In fact, both Norton (1976, 231) and Rand (1964a, 29) regarded workers as deriving pleasure from their work, which would be psychic income. If, for two identical jobs, a person takes the one that pays less because of some nonmonetary benefit he expects to receive (say, a quiet work environment), the difference in pay is assumed to be psychic income. The only reward to some jobs by their nature is psychic income. Parenting cannot be remunerative. Discoverers of laws of nature cannot charge for their use.

If no pay is involved, the question is, what is productive work? The purpose of work is to sustain a person's life. Yet, also according to OE, a person should work even if he is wealthy enough not to have to work for a living. Work satisfies a psychological need. To qualify as productive, a career should be singular and long-range. A hodgepodge of interests would not suffice, nor would recreation. A professional athlete would be considered productive, however. Yet work must take physical form. Still, services are recognized as productive even though no product is produced (Peikoff 1991, 293–302). There are some apparent inconsistencies among these descriptors.

In contrast to OE, economist Gary Becker categorized almost every activity as productive. Activities that would be categorized as consumption by most economists, Becker regarded as simultaneous production and consumption. If one is sleeping, he is simultaneously producing and consuming a sleep experience (Febrero and Schwartz 1995b, xxii). Becker's definition of productivity may be useful for some purposes, but it has the effect of diluting productivity to any activity that a person undertakes. Excluding from productivity those actions that one can *only* do for oneself—such as sleeping—would leave all those activities that could possibly be done in the market—housecleaning, and so on. Most economists might categorize the latter as productive activities, but they would not be regarded as productive in OE unless they were approached as careers.

Peikoff limited productive work to a discipline that is sustained long-range. He recognized athletics as a legitimate profession (1991, 301), but sports undertaken as recreation does not qualify as productive work. Nor would learning for learning's sake. Yet there have been those discoveries that have been the product of "esthetic curiosity" (Jacobs 1984, 222–23) by amateurs and hobbyists, such as Hedy Lamarr's contribution to radar technology. This would not qualify as productive work, yet a person who was committed to producing a product (say, two-legged stools) would be considered productive whether he sold any or not, so long as he had another source of income to sustain himself (inheritance, for example). At least that would be the case based on one interpretation of the Objectivist perspective on productivity. However, Peikoff (1991, 391) cited Isabel Paterson (1968, 232) as defining production as profit. Thus to be productive, the (market) value of the output produced would have to exceed the value of the inputs (costs). By that definition, the two-legged-stool maker would not be productive, but neither would some other efforts that Peikoff and Rand might consider productive (parenting and discovery, for example).

Productivity is the central virtue in OE because it is the means by which a person sustains his life—his ultimate value. Donway ("Roundtable" 1996, 6) noted that it is primarily the income-earning aspect of work that ties it to one's survival. From an overall economic perspective, if one sustains oneself by his own efforts, then he does not consume more than he produces (whether the return to that production is in the form of a salary, royalties, rent, interest, or dividends). If one consumes less than he produces, i.e., saves, then this would be productive, since saving (which must equal investment) increases productive activity.

Of course, if one consumes more than he produces, he has accepted the unearned. But what does it mean to receive the unearned? Bargain hunters keep prices down for those who are not conscientious shoppers. Those who buy new products create the volume to take advantage of economies of scale that reduce costs and prices. Obviously those who benefit from bargain hunters cannot locate and reimburse them. These benefits, it could be argued, are by-products of a market economy. But is an ethic needed that the consumer should be a conscientious shopper? Of course, if one is sacrificing time spent doing something more productive (brain surgery) to save a few cents on soap powder, this is a waste of resources. It can be shown that if one tries to minimize all costs, one may fail to minimize costs overall. So recognizing this is also an aspect of conscientious consumption.

One could also argue that those who "do-it-yourself" are also not being cost-effective. When someone undertakes activities at which he is relatively less well suited (even if he is better in an absolute sense), this reduces his income as well as shuffles someone who could have done the work relatively better into a job at which he is less suited. Does this mean that a person should hire others to, say, wallpaper his kitchen, simply because others may be relatively more suited? One might make an economic argument to that effect. One could possibly make an ethical case if one looked only at the earned and unearned, or if the emphasis is strictly on being productive, or on having a single purpose in life. But much can be learned by doing things oneself. This can be a source of education, recreation, amusement, fulfillment. It can result in an appreciation of the work done by others, and even lead to new discoveries by those who participate in such avocations.

What then of perfection? Rand's and Norton's ethics are both in the perfectionist camp. Must a person then be perfect at one thing or at everything one does? If a person cannot do something well, should he not do it at all? Norton seems to have suggested this. He criticized the dilettante (1976, 222), stating that there is no wholeheartedness in any of his acts. But much can be learned by "dabbling." Just as trying to minimize each cost can result in failing to minimize overall costs, trying to maximize productivity in all areas may not result in the greatest overall productive use of one's time. One cannot be perfect at all things all the time, nor can all values be affirmed all the time. The answer seems to be that if one limits one's values to a single purpose, then one can be (or can strive to be) perfect at that.

Norton (1976, 196) believed that one should have one purpose and it should be the same purpose throughout one's life. Rand also spoke of a single purpose. But a single purpose may not be realistic for many individuals. Rand and Peikoff acknowledged that reproduction could be productive if approached seriously (Rand 1964b, 7; Peikoff 1991, 302). However, reproduction is nonremunerative, so it could not serve as one's single purpose. One would have to have two purposes if one were a parent—one's work for pay as well as the care of one's child.

If one has a single purpose, one's purpose may be extremely hard, as Norton said, but decisions need not be that difficult. The answer to everything else is no. Choice necessarily involves saying no. By saying yes—by making a choice, one is always saying no to something. With one and only one purpose, a person must say no to virtually everything else (Norton 1976, 200, 220, 232–33). However, if one cannot find a job commensurate with one's purpose, one must work for pay as well as pursue one's destiny (Berliner 1995, 353). If one also has children, purpose is no longer singular. If one must care for a house, has other interests (even if commensurate with one's purpose), deciding what to say no to and when becomes much more challenging. Life may be no more difficult for this person than one with a single overriding purpose, but decision-making is multiplied. Multiple choice implies that one can make the wrong choice in that one may choose to affirm a nonvalue or, more likely, a value that is lower on one's hierarchy of values. Deciding what is the right (ethical) thing in a given context can become more difficult when a person has more than one purpose.

Market Limitations

Rand saw production as a good thing. To economists, production is not a good thing or a bad thing; it simply is. Of course, a reading of any Principles text will give one the impression that goods are good and growth is better. However, economists make no value judgments about the mix of goods and services produced. If consumers demand (buy) heroin, the market will determine its value just as it would any other good, be it insulin or a painted egg. Some things economists would regard as productive, Rand would not regard as such; however, she would not approve of the government prohibiting production of such "goods." Individuals should be responsible for their own value judgments and censor their own consumption.

Because the market will reward the seller of heroin and the seller of insulin alike, Rand realized that the market could not be relied upon to shape a person's ethics. Although she regarded capitalism as a moral economic system in that it is based on rights to life and property, individual ethics do not stop with simply recognizing and respecting the rights of others (Donway 1999b, 18). Rand stressed and, particularly in her fiction, showed the importance of not "selling out" either to the consumer or the employer, of not shirking work, of giving value for value, of doing any job well, of being conscious—not simply mimicking the actions of others, of not stealing the ideas of others, of bringing one's own identity and talent to the production process, of having a conscience—of not checking one's mind at the office door along with one's hat, of having integrity.

More than any other system, Rand recognized that a free market system rewards merit. However, she also knew it was no panacea. One cannot rely on the market mechanism to do one's thinking for one. Rand's cardinal values and virtues are reason/rationality, purpose/productivity, and self-esteem/pride. All relate to work. Productivity is the central purpose in life; happiness is the result. One might think that because the dollar value of what is produced is equal to the dollar value of what is spent, there may be some link in Rand's philosophy between production and consumption. But Rand did not regard consumption as a virtue, nor when she referred to happiness being the purpose of life did she mean the utility derived from consuming goods. She seems to have been referring to the happiness that accompanies one's work, much the way in which Norton used the word "eudaimonia." Economists realize that work might in fact have utility—bring some satisfaction beyond the receipt of a paycheck. It is this satisfaction—not consumption—that Rand meant when she referred to the happiness that results from productive work. It is pride in workmanship—which anyone can feel regardless of the work one does. Rand saw the creative process as not limited to artists and poets, and the productive process as not limited to industrialists and shopkeepers. Educators, novelists, and philosophers are productive. Bankers, barbers, and miners can be creative.

It should be noted, however, that the price mechanism does not work for productive effort that does not go through the market because of the nature of the work. For instance, parents don't receive pay for the care of their children. So these destinies are not compensated. There may be individuals who relieve the suffering of others—of children who have been abandoned, for instance—and consequently cannot be paid by their beneficiaries. Individuals who regard this kind of work as their "destiny" cannot rely on the price mechanism to compensate them for their efforts. (As a full-time endeavor, Rand would argue that such work is morally indefensible [Berliner 1995, 544–45].) Earlier I mentioned that unions would have no incentive to unionize workers paid in company scrip. There would be no market mechanism at operation here. The market may also underinvest in human capital development since a person cannot use his human capital as collateral. There may also be underinvestment in basic research since it is not possible to assign property rights in such knowledge. The market may not operate as efficiently for other goods that have public good characteristics, such as public health (infectious disease inoculation, for instance). There may be no price mechanism for those whose interest deals in caring for abandoned or abused animals. If a person's destiny involves professions related to these activities, then they will not be able to rely on the price mechanism to compensate them adequately and/or to provide for occupations in sufficient number.

CHAPTER THIRTEEN

Replacement Capital

The trader principle, the principle of justice in OE, is that value should be exchanged for value between independent equals. A person should not give or receive the unearned (Rand 1964c, 52). Productivity, the central virtue, requires of a person that he support his own life through his own effort. An honest person realizes that he cannot consume more than he produces (1961a, 89). To do otherwise is parasitic on the productivity of others. Unilateral transfers are difficult to justify in OE. Children, although a source of joy to their parents, are not independent equals and require (by right, at least some minimal) unilateral investment in human capital from parent to child for which the parent receives no return. (At least, parents should not be the primary beneficiaries [N. Branden 1962, 55].)

Inheritance is another unilateral transfer that is difficult to justify in OE. A person has a right to leave an inheritance. However, many inheritors are adults. In OE, a person is loved for his virtues (1961a, 147). An important virtue is independence. Therefore, why a person would give and why another would accept inheritance is challenging to explain within OE. According to Objectivist Nathaniel Branden, a person is worthy of his inheritance if he "brings more wealth into existence" (1963, 23). I take this to mean that, at a minimum, the inheritor would not trench on the value of his inherited wealth. It is a basic principle of economics with regard to a business that the value of its capital investment should be maintained (Simpson, Pirenian, and Crenshaw 1951, 263). Economist Gary Becker (1995f, 358–59) has implied that, for a parent, there is some trade-off between endowing his child with physical capital and investing in his human capital. In this chapter, I argue that human capital investment is an endowment that in significant ways is no different from an endowment of physical capital. And, like the inheritance of physical capital, its value should be kept intact. This could involve, as with physical capital, setting aside a sinking fund. However, human capital is embodied. Therefore, the investment should ultimately be embodied in another human being—typically one's children. This chapter presents my (stronger) case for "reproductivity" as a cardinal value in OE.

Unilateral Transfers and Sacrifice

Saving, according to Rand, is productive to the extent that it "applies *only* to financing the needs of production, *not* of consumption—and that its success rests on the investor's judgment of men's productive ability, *not* on his compassion for their feelings, hopes or dreams" (1982f, 132). In the latter case, she is referring to lending to others for their consumption, not for one's own consumption. Nevertheless, that which is saved is to be eventually consumed by the individual himself. Rand noted that those goods that are not consumed today by an individual "are available to him when he needs them tomorrow—and, in the meantime, these goods serve as fuel for the country's productive process" (1974b, 345). After all, if a person were to save indefinitely, this would be a sacrifice.

According to Peikoff, even a "tinge of self-denial" is a sacrifice (1991, 232). Rand said that a person should live for his own sake. He should not sacrifice himself to other people or others to himself (Rand 1964a, 27). If a person were to leave savings behind in the form of an estate, would this not qualify as a sacrifice of his life (his productive effort) for others? There are qualifications, of course. A person is responsible for his outstanding debts as well as for his children while the latter are (justifiably) dependent (N. Branden 1962, 55). However, leaving an estate to independent adults would be difficult to justify. One man loves another for his virtues (1961a, 147). Presumably this would include the other person's independence. Since a rational man "never seeks or desires the *unearned*" (Rand 1964c, 52), then it would seem unlikely that an independent person would accept an inheritance; therefore, there would be no point in leaving an estate to him. Since a bequest is unilateral in nature (it is not a trade of value for value), it would seem to fall into the same category as charity. Kelley said that to Rand: "A commitment to one's own life . . . is a full-time job. Any action not serving that end is at least a mild form of self-sacrifice" (1996, 7). Charity should be marginal (1996, 10). In addition to savings that are not consumed within one's lifetime, there are other forms of productivity that are difficult to justify within the confines of OE.

Parenting can be regarded as a productive endeavor, but the return is not monetary from the parent's perspective, nor, to the extent that the return is (eventually) monetary, does it accrue to the parent. At least, it *should not* according to

OE (N. Branden 1962, 55). Parenting has the apparent feature of being unilateral in nature. Although parents benefit from having children, the primary beneficiaries (in an investment sense) are the children. In that sense, parenting has a common element with charity. Neither Rand nor Peikoff categorized childrearing as charity, but if one tries to pigeonhole it into a category, it fits better in the category of charity than in productive work, since there is no profit in it. Yet, since parenting requires a long-term commitment and expenditures of one's time, effort, and money, it is not consistent with Rand's view of what charity should be (i.e., limited in duration and scope) (Peikoff 1991, 386; Rand 1964d, 47–49).

Kelley acknowledged that "the reasons why parents care for their children are more specific—and more powerful—than benevolence" ("Roundtable" 1996, 9). Rand said one should not have children simply to indulge her feelings (1964b, 7). Jennifer Roback Morse offered love as a reason for having children. She criticized the utilitarian perspective that one sees another person in terms of how he contributes to one's happiness (utility). She argued that we love another "not for what he can do for us," but for who he is (2001, 201). In this respect, the way Morse viewed love is not unlike Rand's view. To Rand, one loves another for his virtues (1961a, 147). But this does not fit well in the decision to have children, since potential children do not exist yet. They, therefore, have no virtues. Love is a response to another's worth, according to Rand. It is a reward to another for his virtues. It is not a response to *need* (1961a, 147). Yet children are needy by nature. They are not independent equals.

Rand believed childrearing was a serious, though optional, undertaking. Enright noted: "Rand once said that, if she were to have had children, she would have had to put her writing career aside in order to raise them" (1998, 232). Enright added: "Why would that be the case, if she did not think children were of great value?" (ibid.) But the point is Rand did not give up her writing career. Had she, she would have been sacrificing a greater value for something of lesser value. Children may have had a great value to her, but writing had more value; otherwise she would have had children. To have had children would have been altruistic. This does not mean that others who do so are altruistic. They obviously believe children to be of value. Yet, children do not fit in that well as values in the Objectivist system of values. Although Rand and Peikoff stated that childrearing could be productive, it is not in the same sense other careers are.

Gary Becker has argued that children are "consumer durables," and that the decision to have children is a consumer decision, much the same as other decisions (1995a, 243). It is true that all decisions require the decision-maker to consider alternative uses for his time and resources. In that sense, all decisions are economic decisions. To that extent, the decision to have children involves considering other trade-offs, which may be the purchase of consumer durables. But if children are "consumer durables," that would relegate them to the fringes of OE, since consumption is not a virtue. Having children then would not carry the ethical weight that productive work or saving does.

Even if it is agreed that from the parent's perspective the decision to have children is a consumer decision, the reality is that parents in effect invest in their children, and "human capital" is produced. This may not be the only or the most important result of childrearing, but it is a consequence. Childrearing is an investment, but like savings that is never spent within one's lifetime, it does not contribute directly to a person's (i.e., a parent's) self-preservation.

Justification for Receiving Inheritance

Although leaving an estate to another (or other) independent equal(s) does not seem to fit comfortably in OE, a person has a right to do so. That is not in dispute. And the inheritor has a right to receive it. That right follows from the right of ownership of the person leaving the estate. OE also supplies a rationale that justifies the receipt of an inheritance from an ethical standpoint. Branden said: "If an heir is worthy of his money, that is, if he uses it productively, he brings more wealth into existence, he raises the general standard of living" (1963, 23). "Using wealth productively" can be interpreted in more than one way. A reading of Peikoff (1991, 391) would lead one to conclude that to be productive, the value of an endowment should be increased. Quoting Isabel Paterson, a man has wasted his labor if he "plants one potato and gets only one potato as a crop" (1968, 232). Adam Smith's view of productivity is expressed in the following:

> We should not call a marriage barren or unproductive, though it produced only a son and a daughter, to replace the father and mother, and though it did not increase the number of the human species, but only continued it as it was before. ([1776] 1937, 639)

If Smith's view applies, at a minimum, an inheritor would leave the value of his inherited capital intact; i.e., he would not trench on the value of the capital he inherited. This idea is consistent with the Objectivist principle that one should not accept the unearned. It also has a basis in Rand's view on productivity. Rand said that a person whose consumption equals his earning carries his weight in an economic sense, but does not contribute to future production. A person who saves, regardless of his income, finances the future. The person whose consumption exceeds his earnings is a parasite, whether he earns a fortune or lives on the dole (1982f, 132). If a person were to draw down his inherited capital, this would be parasitic. Even if he earned income by other means, if on balance he consumed all of that income and drew down his inheritance as well, he would have been a parasite. Rand said that an honest man realizes that he cannot consume more than he produces (1961a, 89). If a person does trench on his inherited capital, he is not "honest." If he draws down his physical capital, his consumption exceeds the interest generated from his physical capital inheritance. If he trenches on his physical capital, he does so at the expense of the capital base of the economy as well. By his existence, the world is diminished (in an economic context).

A person may be entitled by right to receive an inheritance, but if he has not earned it, he is not morally worthy of it. If he consumes only what he produces (from his human capital plus the interest from his physical capital), then the initial endowment (its value) would have to be intact at his death. He will have carried his own weight, or "broken even," economically. He will have consumed all of his earnings (from his human capital) and only enough of the return (interest) from his endowment to leave capital intact (in a value sense).

Using it productively entitles an heir to inherit wealth in a moral sense, but for what purpose? If a person leaves the value of his inherited wealth intact (or increases its value), to whom should it be left after he dies? The obvious answer is to one's family. This is not a forgone conclusion in OE, however. Sciabarra stated that to Rand "the Family was a cultural institution that frequently undercut the individual's independence and autonomy, breaking 'a man's or a woman's spirit by means of unchosen obligations and unearned guilt'" (1995, 349–50; quote from Rand [June 1981], "The Age of Mediocrity," in Binswanger 2.3.5). Rand gave a clue as to who might be worthy of an inheritance in her discussion of the rightful heirs of patents and copyrights once they are in the "public domain." The rightful heirs would be the producers that keep the ideas viable (1967i, 132). Of course, in that context, she did not mean that producers should literally be the inheritors of the property rights in those ideas, but they were the inheritors in the sense that they could make them productive. Given what Branden said about those who inherit wealth—that they become worthy of it by making it productive—one might surmise that if one has an estate to bequeath, then one should leave it to those who could make it productive.

Human Capital Replacement

But who produces the producers? Rand proposed that man "is a being of self-made soul" (1961a, 131), just as he is of self-made wealth. Certainly this is true of an adult with a fully developed rational faculty. But humans do not, like Athena, emerge full-grown. They are born (at least insofar as the content of their minds) *tabulae rasae* (1964a, 28). Rand was aware of the importance of proper education in early childhood development (1971b, 190–212). It may be true that regardless of how one is reared and educated and otherwise cared for as a child, when one becomes an adult he is responsible for his actions; however, if a child has been exposed to the right values, educated, and otherwise properly nurtured, he has a better foundation for learning and choosing. As has been witnessed, a child kept in isolation during her formative years had difficulty even learning language (Springer and Deutsch 1989, 242–43).

Rand focused on adults, which is a natural starting point for a discussion of ethics, since adults have a fully formed rational faculty and all the rights accorded a human being. An adult is responsible for his actions. Kelley stated that the adult stage is the beginning point for a biocentric ethics ("Roundtable" 1996, 9). However, by concentrating almost exclusively on adults, one may exclude important aspects of the nature of human beings and what it means to be a (an ethical) human being.

Objectivists have made the point that parents have certain responsibilities toward their children. Those responsibilities end when a child becomes an adult (N. Branden 1962, 55). It has been argued not only that these are moral obligations, but that children have a right to some minimal care. What this care involves includes the imparting of values and knowledge to the child, which viewed narrowly in an economic context results in the development of "human capital." Implicit in a comment by Becker is that from the parent's perspective there is a trade-off between investing in a child's human capital and providing the child with physical assets (endowments). In some cultures in which reliance is on children providing parents with old-age care, the return to investing in the education of one's children has a higher payoff than investing in physical assets (1995f, 358–59). For the most part in our culture, parents rely on retirement, savings, and government-provided Social Security to provide for their latter years, not on their children.

The Objectivist position is that a child has a right to care, but is under no moral obligation to repay parents for the basic care he has received from his parents once he reaches adulthood. A person may choose to assist his parents so long as the assistance is reasonable and non-self-sacrificial (N. Branden 1962, 55). To claim that just because a parent has given a person life, the parent in turn somehow has some claim over the child's life, would be unjust and illogical. How can a person simultaneously be given life and not given it?

My view is that one's parents give a person life and are responsible for sustaining it in some (at least basic) way until a person is self-supporting. If a parent is in need, he is entitled to his (adult) child's help so long as he has not forfeited it by being a physically abusive parent. Beyond that, a child may rightly believe that it is his obligation to pay off any debts accumulated by his parents on his behalf for his education (specifically if the debts were incurred once the child was an adult and could have been self-supporting). The child can, of course, choose to provide gifts or necessities for his parents whenever he likes or deems it necessary so long as it is not at the expense of his own life (no rational parent would want his child to sacrifice his life for his parents).

As a child matures, it is reasonable to assume that he would be able to delineate basic necessities from other values that his parents have bestowed. From this he should be able to determine what the minimal amount is he owes his parents even if he feels no particular affection for them. It is too stringent a test to require that he "owes" them only if he has affection for them or shares the same values. Parents would be entitled (morally, not on the basis of rights) to assistance from their children if they were truly in need even if this required some sacrifices on the part of the child (although, not sacrifices of principle). These "sacrifices" would be no different from those one would make for outstanding debts (which are different from those to one's parents, since debts to creditors are owed by right).

I agree that one does not owe one's parents for the investment in his (basic) human capital. (This would be particularly true if it was incurred during the time in which a child could not have been self-supporting.) I would also argue that if a parent received the full return on his investment in his child's human capital, it would put the parent in the position of doubly benefiting. To the extent that a parent's parents had invested in his human capital, he would have benefited, and then he would also benefit from investing in his child's human capital. If a parent is not "entitled" to be taken care of in his old age by his children, then what would be the motivation on the part of a parent to invest in his child's human capital? To the extent a person "owes" anyone, it would be, in some way, to replace the investment in himself (by his parents). If a person does not invest or replace the human capital investment in himself, he has in effect consumed more than he has produced over the course of his life, which violates the trader principle. He has defaulted in an intergenerational Prisoner's Dilemma exchange.

To the extent that parents invest in their child's human capital, it results in an "income-earning asset," and in that sense is similar to an investment in physical capital. To the extent that the investment can be regarded as an endowment, it is analogous to the inheritance of physical capital. That is, that which a child inherits from parents in terms of human capital would be limited to the money, time, and effort that parents expended in developing and improving the child's character (values) and earning ability. This is as much in the way of inheritance as physical capital, since the parents could have spent their time, money, and effort in developing physical capital and giving that to their child instead. Both expenditures (on human and on physical capital) increase the earning potential of the child. How much parents devote to physical or human capital development will depend on any number of factors. The point is that parents have a choice as to what form the endowment they provide for their child takes.

To the degree that a person who inherits physical capital is a net beneficiary and becomes worthy of it by making it productive, it could be argued that the way in which a person earns his human capital investment is by making it productive. One could interpret this to simply mean that the person, once he becomes an adult, earns his own income. But if the person in turn consumes all of his income from human capital, he could be said to "trench" on his human capital by the amount of "depreciation" (specifically, the depreciation on that human capital in which noncompensated others have invested).

If a person were alone on a desert island and endowed with a quantity of hardtack, there is no reason to believe that he would want to leave any hardtack beyond his own life. If a person has just enough hardtack to keep himself alive, then his sole objective would be to ration it so as to keep alive. Hardtack is barren. Saving it will not create more of it in the future. The only reason to save it is so that one may keep more of oneself around in the future. There is no reason to leave any behind at the end of one's life, since there is no one to leave it to. If the castaway consumes just the amount needed to survive, there is no replacement value—for the hardtack or himself. He will have used up a quantity of hardtack without replacement. He will have left the world depleted by that amount. What it would have produced is his life, but he would not have replaced his life with a comparable value. In order to break even (that is carry his weight in an economic sense [Rand 1982f, 132]), he would have to produce the equivalent of that which he consumed. I have argued that if he were given an endowment, then, to be consistent with Rand, he would have to make it productive as well as support himself by his own efforts. In effect, he would produce to (at a minimum) sustain himself as well as keep the (value of) "hardtack" intact. In this way he would carry his weight from an economic perspective. In other words, based on the example presented in chapter 4, when he died the same quantity of hardtack (10,000 units) or an equivalent value of it (which would have a "value" of 6144.44) would have to be left behind.

But for whom? What the individual would have failed to do is replace himself. The question I have raised is, is he obligated to replace himself? For society he is not so obliged, nor for the economy as a whole. But if he is to "break even economically," then purely from an economic perspective, he has not broken even if he does not replace himself (or the equivalent). This is a simplistic approach on which I plan to elaborate.

A person is not born an adult. He is dependent for a period of time. If he is responsible, he recognizes that he has benefited because others have provided him not only with physical survival but also with knowledge and a set of values. Rand would say that he is self-made in that no knowledge or principles to which one is exposed are given to a person; they are earned by his own thought, his own effort. A person does not passively accept knowledge. However, during the child's development, there is equivalent effort on the other side of the learning process, and the child is the primary beneficiary of that effort. What the parent provides to the child is unilateral (in an investment sense). A child or adolescent does not give back anything. Value is not traded for value.

One may inherit a number of intangible values that may be classified as human capital. This would include education and skills, but also other values as well. Although intangible, these values require the expenditure of a number of resources. If a child has been provided access to education and other values, and has not expended his own resources (entirely) for their provision, he has received a net benefit. These values are intangible but they are embodied in the individual. If he is to keep these values intact, he must replace them. That is, individuals should keep intact that capital with which they are endowed by others. (I do not mean inherited traits. I mean that which has been learned by the child through the expenditure of time, effort, and materials of uncompensated others. And by knowledge I do not mean the identical knowledge of the parent.) This is consistent with Rand and Branden with respect to physical capital (N. Branden 1963, 23). However, the capital I am referring to here is human capital.

With standard income, as defined by Fisher ([1906] 1965, 111), depreciation is deducted from income. This is not how income is usually defined. If that portion of income that would qualify as depreciation is consumed (by the person himself), then under the definition of standard income, one is trenching on one's human capital by that amount. If it is saved, then that portion of saving is not an accumulation of capital, but is replacement investment (a sinking fund). Depreciation results because of the finite life of an asset. If the life of the asset were infinite and its value were based on a constant income stream, there would be no depreciation (see appendix 1.3).

For physical assets, a sinking fund may be set aside to keep its value intact. Since humans are not bought and sold, there is no "sinking fund," nor is one reckoned. A person owns himself. Until he is an adult, his parents provide considerable "informal" education and (oftentimes through taxes) pay for improvements in human capital through formal education. The Objectivist position is that the individual is entitled to all the return on his investment. His income is his with which to dispose. He owes no one for his life.

Human capital investment from uncompensated others (parents) can be viewed in the same way as endowed physical wealth. To keep (the value of) one's human capital intact in the way in which physical capital is kept intact, a sinking fund could be set aside to accumulate at compound interest. If one has been a net beneficiary in this sense, then if he consumed all that he produced (his actual income, not simply his "standard income"), he would not have carried his own weight economically. Would a sinking fund be needed to maintain the value of his human capital investment? That is one possibility. Most people do not deduct a sinking fund, however, because their children *are* their replacement capital. To both set aside a sinking fund and have children would be to replace one's human capital twice. For a person's consumption to (at a minimum) balance his production (so that he is not a net drain in an economic sense), he must earn enough to support himself plus earn an amount equivalent to replace the investment in his human capital (on the part of uncompensated others).

The theoretical argument for the purchase of life insurance is to protect the value of one's human capital in the event of an untimely death. The beneficiaries of life insurance are often one's dependent children. As has been shown by economists who have pioneered in this area (see Yaari 1965), it is during those years when one's children are young that the "bequest" motive that underlies the purchase of insurance is greatest. So if one had children, the children would be the beneficiaries of the value of this "human" capital in the event of the insured's death. However, insurance is purchased to cover untimely death. It is not purchased (primarily) because life is finite. Depreciation exists because life is finite. Thus depreciation would exist whether death's timing were uncertain or not.

Insurance may be necessary to replace one's human capital in the event of untimely death. But insofar as the "sinking fund" is concerned—that is, that fund set aside to replace the value of one's human capital due to a finite life, not an uncertain life—it *is* one's children. The idea that children are "replacements" of human capital is implicit in steady state growth models in which population (the labor force) is constant. In one of F. P. Ramsey's models he made this explicit, stating: "[E]ach man is charged with a share of that maintenance of such children as are necessary to maintain the population, but starts his working life without any capital and ends it without any, having spent his savings on an annuity" (1928, 557). In other words, Ramsey's model assumed that the both human and physical capital remained constant. Of course, what I mean here by human capital is more encompassing than the discounted earnings of labor income. It includes other kinds of knowledge that is instilled in or imparted to children—values and principles, for example.

From a parent's perspective, a reason to invest in their children's human capital is that their parents invested in them. The idea of parents investing in the human capital of their children is not new. However, the rationale or motivation for doing so has been attributed to such things as to maintain the species or for the benefit of the economy. To the extent that economists have addressed the issue, it has been from the perspective of the economy. Alfred Marshall said: "'The most valuable of all capital is that invested in human beings; and of that capital, the most precious part is the results of the care and influence of the mother'" (Marshall, 1930, 564; quoted in Pujol 1992, 126).

Marshall recognized that if the housewife stayed home to rear her children, she would forgo employment. Any improvements in her own human capital (through education) would go unrewarded (monetarily). For mothers, virtue must be "'for the greater part its *own* reward'" (Marshall 1930, 564; quoted in Pujol 1992, 128). In Rand's ethics, "virtue is not its own reward" (1961a, 131). Marshall's statement has the ring of self-sacrifice. This injustice loses much of its punch when children are regarded as the replacement of one's own human capital. The seeming paradox that caring for children is a productive activity that doesn't pay is recast. If one inherited a family business, then, based on my interpretation of the Objectivist view, the heir should regard it as incumbent upon himself not to squander it but to make it productive. If the heir chose to accomplish this objective by maintaining the business so as to leave it at least as well off as it was when he inherited it, he would not regard this as unproductive.

From an economic perspective, if one's parents invest in a child's human capital, that investment reaps returns throughout the child's life in the form of income above and beyond what the child could have earned if he were to grow up literally on his own. The childrearing part of the productive process is "maintenance." It would be equivalent to all the things one would have to do to maintain a business one inherited (or maintain its equivalent value). Replacement investment is a necessary part of maintaining a business. When one invests, he does so to reap future rewards. What seems curious about parents investing in their children, from an egoist's perspective, is that it is the children who will receive the return. That appears irrational if one looks at it prospectively. But one must also take the retrospective perspective. A person reaps rewards from his own human capital from investments that have been made (by others, for which they receive no material return) in himself before reaching maturity.

If one starts at the adult stage of analysis, then if one is to consume, he must produce. But the point is, how did he arrive at that stage? An adult may be self-sufficient on a desert island, but it is reasonable to inquire, how did he get to be an adult? If one is honest, he realizes (unless he has been horribly abused) that someone provided for his sustenance and invested (time, effort, money) in his human capital. Production does come before distribution, as Rand noted (1961c, 80), but not when it comes to a person's life. Consumption precedes production for many years. Production does precede consumption, of course. Someone else is producing in the early years of one's life. One's parents are.

David Ross said that "virtues aim at future values ("What Is Justice" 2000, 23). Virtues are prospective, as Ross implied, but, I would add, not exclusively. If one has purchased something and he has not paid for it, he owes the bill even if what he purchased has already been consumed in the past. One must look not only prospectively but also retrospectively in order to see the arc of one's life.

Sherlock Holmes said, in *A Study in Scarlet*: "Most people, if you describe a train of events to them, will tell you what the result would be. They can put those events together in their minds, and argue from them that something will come to pass. There are few people, however, who, if you told them a result, would be able to evolve from their own inner consciousness what the steps were which led up to that result. This power is what I mean when I talk of reasoning backward, or analytically" (Doyle n.d., 154).

One reason some people may reproduce is they think it is a way of achieving immortality. Rand rejected this idea (Berliner 1995, 397). Humans are mortal. From an economic perspective, children are replacement capital. That does not mean that is what they are exclusively. And that does not mean that is a justification for having children. It is not an ethic unless it is tied to the trader principle. Then it becomes an ethic.

This "reason" for having children fits into Rand's philosophy because it is consistent with the trader principle when seen from the perspective of the total of one's life. By focusing exclusively on the adult stage, it would seem as if a person would break even economically (which is the minimum required to be "honest" in Rand's view) by consuming no more than he earns. But economically, this would result in a net "loss," unless earnings are defined as "standard income"; i.e., actual income less depreciation.

Assuming that one has been the recipient of the efforts of others in the development of his human capital, then if one makes no effort to replace it, he is trenching on his human capital by consuming everything he produces and has "inherited." (At the end of his life, the individual not only would have consumed the interest from the capital but also would have drawn down all of the principal.) By leaving this life without imparting to others, one has consumed more resources than he has produced. When one dies, he leaves less than he started his (working) life with. To the extent that one inherits assets—whether tangible or intangible—from others (so long as resources were used in their acquisition and those providing those resources were not fully compensated for them by the recipient), one cannot simply consume everything one produces and break even, or carry his own weight, economically. To be "honest" in the Randian sense (Rand 1961a, 89), one must create a surplus in the sense that one must more than pay one's own way. One cannot produce and simply consume all he produces and provide nothing more.

In particular, if one values the values and principles he has acquired (particularly if they are, in part, the result of the efforts of uncompensated others), then one should not only affirm those values by living in accordance with them, but in some way provide for their maintenance in the future. Simply producing is not enough. One (generally speaking) is paid for the value of that which he produces (whether in wages or profit). (An inventor or discoverer may not get paid the full value because of limited or no property rights, however.) If he consumes all of his income, he has nothing left with which to sustain his values (those instilled in him or imparted to him by uncompensated others) after his life is over. He is a net beneficiary. On balance he has received a surplus. If he is honest, he will make an effort to maintain his values.

Thus, to replace one's human capital, one could, as with physical capital, set aside a sinking fund to accumulate interest so as to equal the value of one's human capital (the investment by uncompensated others in one's human capital) by the end of one's life. However, to keep human capital intact, one needs humans. Only humans can embody knowledge and produce, and so long as someone is producing humans (i.e., reproducing), this fund can be invested in humans who are, in turn, productive. But to keep one's *own* human capital intact, one would have to reproduce oneself. Of course, this is literally impossible. Even a clone would not be a reproduction of oneself. The equivalent in economic terms of keeping one's human capital intact is to reproduce and expend resources on the development of the human capital of one's offspring. So one may have a sinking fund set aside or one may have children and invest in their human capital.

Obviously there are differences between physical values and nontangible values. For instance, one cannot simply patent an idea of an invention; one must patent the object itself. By definition, Peikoff regarded production as "the creation of *material* values" (1991, 293). Peikoff noted that knowledge is not productive until it is embodied. By this he meant that it must take "some form of existence in physical reality not merely [in a person's] consciousness" (ibid.). By embodiment, Peikoff meant that knowledge in the consciousness of a producer must take physical (inanimate) form in order for production to take place.

In *Atlas Shrugged*, Rand called the machine a "frozen form of a living intelligence" (1957, 1064). But what of the human form of living intelligence? Is that not a value? The task and the purpose of the parent are to create that value—the living value that embodies living intelligence. The values that individuals create and hold dearest—such as Rand's trilogy: reason, productivity, and self-esteem—are embodied in their persons. We are tangible as well. We can create goods—such as machines—which embody human intelligence. These may have value, but inanimate objects cannot value. Life and value are inseparable. Only living organisms value. Only humans (living beings) can have values. The material objects to which Peikoff and Rand refer are not alive. Inanimate objects have no volition. They cannot act. They do not have values or virtues. Only human (living organisms) can embody values, and only humans can have virtues. Virtues and values cannot *be*, unless they are embodied. Once a person no longer exists, his embodied values and virtues die with him.

The individual not only has an obligation (in the same ethical sense as he would be obligated to produce) to replace those values or otherwise keep them intact, he has an interest in doing so. The individual values values as well as the principles on which they are based. Values and principles, like living beings, are mortal. But unlike individuals, the death of values and principles is not inevitable. Principles can be "immortal." But they cannot exist separate from human "being." Values and principles, ultimately, must be embodied in physical form, and the physical form in which moral values and principles are embodied is living beings—humans. These values can only be transferred to another person, not to a physical object. You may invest in the replacement value of oneself (a sinking fund), but if it is not embodied in a person or persons, it cannot be viable—i.e., alive.

A principle can exist separately from a person. It can exist as words on a page. But to have consequences it must be acted upon. Principles, like humans, can die. They too are mortal. To be sustained, principles must be affirmed. They must be acted upon. They must be embodied. The difference in mortality as it relates to a person and to his values is that a person's death is inevitable. The death of a principle, of a moral value, is *possible*, but it is not *inevitable*. If one values the best within himself—his embodied principles, his values and his virtues, that which he lives for and that which sustains him—he will acknowledge that he must die eventually, but that which he values most need not die.

The argument here is not that a person should be compelled to keep his human capital "intact" any more than individuals should be compelled to keep their physical inheritance intact or to be productive in order to keep themselves intact. The question is, should one do so in order to be moral or to do the ethical (as Rand said, "honest") thing? My point is, yes, one should, if one looks at the totality of one's life, not simply the adult stage.

Maintaining values beyond one's own existence is a sacrifice only if one regards it as a unilateral transfer from oneself to the future. It is not a sacrifice, or even a gift, if one has benefited by the contribution of others without having "paid" for it. Reciprocity demands that one keep intact what one has been given (if he values it) for which one has not paid. As such, it is not a gift one is giving; it is a value one is maintaining.

If a person values his values and principles, the way to keep them alive beyond his life is to instruct, instill, and impart them in others. What others? The obvious choice is one's own children. One may rely on other human beings to maintain the human race, but if one values principles and values, he will make an effort to create opportunities for the development of these in others. In this sense, reproduction is essential to one's life—not one's own personal survival per se, but the survival of those things that make one's survival possible—the survival of one's values and principles. Of course, reproduction cannot guarantee these things; but for principles to survive, they must be embodied in human beings. It is a precondition. There are risks in all ventures, especially those involving others. But all ventures ultimately involve other human beings.

One can see that if reproduction is essential to one's existence—and the argument is that it is essential to one's existence because it allows aspects of oneself to survive, specifically, those virtues embodied in oneself that have the potential for immortality—then all cardinal values cannot potentially be achieved alone on a desert island (as discussed in chapter 2). Man needs interaction—not just for his psychological well-being, or for the mental and material improvement it would allow, which are all extremely important—but because of his need to reproduce. And if one accepts that this is an essential part of man's existence, then more than the cardinal virtues of rationality, productivity, and pride are needed. These will still be vital to his existence, but other virtues will also be required—some virtue related to nurturance, perhaps. This would be required for the job of taking care of a child.

In Rand's ethics, a man is loved for his virtues (1961a, 147), such as productiveness, rationality, integrity, and justice. Many might regard these as sufficient for a person to be regarded as warranting love if one is only concerned with the necessity of each man sustaining himself, or if one is only concerned about men relating to other equals (i.e., as independent equals). But if reproduction is a value, one would need to exhibit virtues that make one appear to be deserving of love in a way different from that shown by these cardinal virtues.

Reason is needed for the expression of any virtue, but even Rand did not make rationality man's only virtue. She realized the importance of productivity and pride to man's survival. But one would not only need other virtues or another virtue if reproduction is important to his existence, he would have to exhibit it in order to be attractive to someone else, since it is because of one's virtues that one is loved. The reason it would be important to exhibit this virtue is that, without actually having children, a potential mate would not know if another would have the potential to be a good parent, and if that is essential to one's existence, then one would want to see evidence of that trait before mating. One would want to see evidence of an aptitude for the job of being a parent (of being capable of dealing with someone who is in a dependent position relative to oneself). So, just as one would want to exhibit traits of productivity so that someone would want to hire him for a job, one would want to exhibit traits of some aspect of possessing a nurturing nature if he wanted to be found attractive to a mate. This might take the form of showing some signs of being capable of caring for or about someone in a dependency position.

Rand focused exclusively on traders—people who are independent and rational, who are capable of making decisions and acting on those decisions; that is, people who are capable of being productive, of sustaining their own lives, and of reaping the rewards or bearing the consequences of their decisions, capable of owning property, of being responsible for that property. These people are adults. These would be adults who are sufficiently unimpaired mentally or physically so that they can perform or fulfill all of these functions. But reproducing involves traits that make one capable of dealing with people in a dependency condition. This is not the world of traders. One does not trade value for value with offspring. Many of the values that are transferred are unilateral in nature. Not that parents don't get anything in return; but to have a legitimate trade, the other party must be capable of agreeing to the exchange, and that is not what's happening with one's child or children. There may be many ways of exhibiting these traits, but the point is that since one cannot be a parent until one is a parent, one must exhibit some traits that make one seem to be attractive in that regard.

Now does every person have to have a child? Obviously not. Many don't. Many can't. Many who have, shouldn't have. A better question is, should every person think that he should have a child? After all, it is not necessary that each person support himself by his own efforts. Many don't. The question there is, should man support himself by his own efforts? And to this question Rand answered an unqualified yes. What about reproduction? It's essential if man cares not only what the future will be but that there will be a future. I've tried to make an argument in the affirmative (admittedly it need not be the only argument or even the most important, but it is an argument). So if a person does not reproduce, is he shirking a responsibility? One could counter that a person should not have a child unless he can afford to have one and has the traits to take care of a child properly. But insofar as productive work is concerned in Randian ethics, the imperative is not that a man have a job, but that the job be sufficient to support himself. The universe is benevolent, in the sense that man is efficacious—that is, capable of successfully dealing with reality. Similarly, it is not that man should have integrity. He must have it. So by analogy, the argument here could equally be that if reproduction is essential to man, he must be not only self-supporting but also capable of supporting a child, and he must have the traits necessary to be a good parent as well. These would not be optional. If they are essential to man, they should be necessary for all men. (This will be revisited and modified in chapter 16.)

CHAPTER FOURTEEN

The Consumption-Saving Decision

Production is the central value in OE and productivity its central virtue (Rand 1964a, 25). Consumption is a value, but no virtue (1982f, 130). In the short run, there is a trade-off between consumption and production. However, in the long run, maximization of consumption and production are not incompatible goals. This chapter examines some of the economic theory related to consumption and saving, both in the short run and over time. In the hardtack example of chapter 4, the castaway's decision was dependent in part on "time preference," which was a function of survival rates between two periods. The only return was his continued survival, since hardtack was fixed. Generally speaking, consumption is not fixed, and if an individual sacrifices consumption currently, he can expect a return (interest) in the future. For the decision-maker, the competing incentive with interest is time preference—since "tomorrow he may die." The rate of current consumption out of wealth (the marginal propensity to consume, MPC) is a function of the interest rate (r), the rate of time preference (i), and the elasticity of substitution. Under certain conditions, the inverse of the latter is defined as the degree of risk tolerance (ρ). The more risk averse a consumer is the more he will consume in the present out of an additional dollar of wealth. Also, the higher r is, the lower the MPC is; the higher i is, the higher the MPC is (Green 1978, 203).

The introduction of a bequest motive has a moderating effect on the MPC. With no bequest motive, a decrease in the probability of survival tends to increase the MPC. The effect of an increase in the probability of dying is ambiguous when a bequest motive is accounted for. If the bequest motive is weak, an increase in the risk of dying (πd_t) increases the MPC. However, if there is a strong bequest motive, then an increase in πd_t will lead to a fall in the MPC. A strong bequest motive is also positively related to life insurance purchase (Fischer 1973, 136–37). There are other risks besides death—risky assets for instance. If a person is risk averse, an increase in this risk will tend to lead to a higher MPC. If a person is a risk taker, an increase in risk will lead to a lower MPC (Levhari and Srinivasan 1969, 160–61).

The growth of consumption (therefore, production) over time will tend to increase with increases in r, decrease with increases in i, and decrease with increased risk aversion. If r exceeds i, consumption growth (g) is positive (Green 1978, 201–202). Under certain assumptions, if i (persistently) exceeds r, then over time g will decline, capital may be drawn down to exhaustion, and the person may be reduced to subsistence (Ramsey 1928, 555). An increase in πd_t decreases consumption growth (Yaari 1965, 143). However, the purchase of life insurance eliminates uncertainty in the consumption plan caused by death's timing (1965, 147). When a bequest motive is introduced, the bequest decision becomes separable (locally) from the consumption decision. Generally speaking, a strong bequest motive increases consumption growth and, therefore, production over time (1965, 149). Since productive purpose is central to OE, a conclusion that can be drawn is that if individuals care not only about their own lives, but beyond their lives as well, production will be greater.

In this chapter, I also derive and analyze several "permanent" probabilities using a net level insurance premium equation as a starting point. Long-run probabilities are relevant to OE. The long-run probability of survival is arguably the basis for ethical principles in OE (Merrill 1991, 115–17). The BUP is based on the long-run expectation of success—life being the standard (Peikoff 1976). The fundamental alternative is life or death (Rand 1964a, 15). Life's uncertainty is relevant to the calculation of expected lifetime earnings as well as replacement of human capital. Probabilities are also basic to decision-making under risk. In chapter 16, I make a case that probabilities of dying and surviving are relevant to decisions concerning charitable giving. What I refer to as "permanent" probability is unlike a long-run probability in that it is an "average" over time. The notion of a "permanent" probability of dying is inherent, I believe, in the derivation of net level premiums for life insurance.

For the reader unfamiliar with the economic theory discussed in this chapter, chapter 14 may be omitted without loss of continuity.

The Margin

To Objectivists, ethical principles are either/or. One cannot "trade off" a virtue for something else one may value. Peikoff said that one cannot trade off a "little" integrity for a "little bit more" money, yet still retain integrity. To Objectivists:

"Justice cannot countenance a single act of injustice" (Peikoff 1991, 264). This is in contrast to the way in which economists regard the "margin" in decision-making. To economists, decisions are rarely either/or in the sense that a person must choose to have all of one good or all of another. Generally speaking, there are trade-offs, but they are incremental in nature. Alchian and Allen said: "All desired things—standards of morality as well as trinkets in the marketplace—are marginally substitutable for each other. This is a fact of human behavior, which here we neither praise nor condemn" (1977, 26).

Consumption, Production, and Breaking Even Economically

The previous quote by Alchian and Allen is in direct contrast to the Objectivist position as expressed by Peikoff. Yet, there are trade-offs that must be made at the margin. Productive purpose is a primary value in OE and productive work a primary virtue. Yet, a person cannot work all the time. There is some trade-off between work and leisure. Saving, because it is productive, is also a virtue. Consumption, even though it is necessary for the continuance of a person's life, is not a virtue. However, one cannot save everything he earns. Rand's ethics are neither hedonistic (consumption is primary), nor ascetic (denial is a virtue). But where is the balance? Economists have grappled with this in growth theory. Michael Intriligator described the competing objectives in their extreme forms as, on the one hand: "Live today, for tomorrow we die" (1971, 398); and on the other, consume virtually nothing in order to expand the capital base and thereby increase future production. However, if humans consume everything today, there is none for tomorrow. If humans consume nothing, they die and there is no "tomorrow."

Maximizing consumption would seem to be a hedonistic approach to life. If a person tries to maximize consumption in the present, he may do so at the expense of the future. But if one takes a long-term view, the two objectives described by Intriligator are not necessarily incompatible. The long-term view is consistent with Rand's ethics. Consuming to the point of satiation as an objective in the short run can be "counterproductive," but maximizing consumption over time (or more accurately, utility) need not be, since in order to consume more, more must be produced.

The Consumption-Saving Decision—the MPC

The consumption-saving decision is relevant to Objectivism because of the centrality of productive purpose and productive work in its system of values. According to Rand, man must plan long term, and the consumption-saving decision is long-term in nature. It also involves trade-offs. Why would an individual choose not to consume to the point of satiation? There is a cost to consumption.

It may not be explicit, or out-of-pocket. There are opportunity costs. If a person consumes one good, he must forgo others. For an individual on a desert island with a fixed amount of hardtack and no other resources of any kind, the opportunity cost to current consumption of an additional unit is that he is sacrificing the wherewithal to sustain himself in the future. He is forgoing future consumption and, ultimately, the "return" that is his own life.

One of the factors considered by the castaway in his consumption decision was the probability of survival. The probability of survival was the only factor assumed to affect time preference in this simple model. Because consumption was equal for the two periods considered, the rate of time preference was approximated by the probability of being alive in the first period (period zero) divided by the probability of being alive in the second period (period one) minus one. (Since $(1/(1 + i) = \pi_{a1}/\pi_{a0}$, then $i= (\pi_{a0}/\pi_{a1} - 1)$.) There is no growth of hardtack and no return in that sense. However, there is a return in the sense that hardtack is used to extend human life. (See appendix 1.1.)

In the example considered in chapter 4 of an expected value of hardtack of 6,144 (based on 1,000 per year for 10 years and a force of mortality of 10 percent per year), the first year, the value of hardtack "grows" by 10 percent to equal 6,759 by the end of the year. The difference between 6,759 and 6,144 of 614 (or 10 percent of the expected value in the first year of 6,144) is the amount by which capital grows in value because the individual survives. The value return includes the interest of 10 percent plus the percentage of present value due to depreciation. In the first year the fall in value ("depreciation") between year one and year two is 385 (i.e., 6,144–5,759), which is the difference between 1,000 and 614 (approximately). Therefore the "value return" for the first year would be 16.27; i.e., the 10 percent "interest" plus "depreciation" for year one expressed as a percentage of value in year one (385/6,144=.0627, or 6.27 percent). (See appendix 1.2.)

In the hardtack example, if the castaway forgoes consumption now, he will maintain the same quantity of hardtack (assuming no physical deterioration). The "return" he receives on hardtack is that it can be used in the future to sustain his life. It cannot be enlarged in any other way to yield a return. But "off the island," if a person forgoes consuming his wealth today, he may have more wealth in the future. His wealth will increase as a result of forgone consumption by the amount of interest he will receive if he chooses to put it in an asset that will yield a return.

Generally speaking, consumption is not fixed, as is assumed in the hardtack example. If less is consumed in period zero, then that which is saved will accumulate interest and more will be available in period one. Under the assumptions that consumption, the interest rate, and the rate of time preference can vary, and given a utility function that exhibits constant elasticity of substitution (η), then a marginal propensity to consume (MPC) out of wealth for the first period (λ_0) can be calculated for a simple two-period model. The MPC (λ_0) is positively related to the rate of time preference, negatively related to the interest rate, positively related to ρ (where ρ is defined as the degree of risk tolerance in state preference theory and is equal to $1/\eta$) (Green 1978, 201, 321). (See appendix 1.4.)

When a bequest motive is taken into account in the consumption decision, it is found to have a *moderating effect* on current consumption. Other things equal, the larger the weight on bequests (b), the lower is the current MPC out of wealth (Fischer 1973, 134).

If there is no bequest motive and life's uncertainty is factored into the consumer's decision, then a decrease in the probability of survival increases the MPC out of wealth and therefore increases current consumption. If a bequest motive is now accounted for, then a change in the probability of dying can either increase or decrease the MPC, depending upon the significance of bequests to the decision-maker. If the weight on bequests is large, an increase in the probability of dying will decrease the current MPC, and if b is small, an increase in the probability of dying would increase the MPC. Stanley Fischer said that the more the "'eat, drink and be merry . . .' philosophy—in the form of a low [b]—prevail the more likely is it that an increase in the probability of death increases current consumption" (1973, 136). In some periods, the MPC could fall depending upon the importance "attached to 'posterity.'" The weight, b, will generally be greater when a person's children are young and dependent (ibid.).

When, in addition to the assumptions of uncertainty of survival and a bequest motive, insurance purchases are permitted, then in order for an insurance purchase to take place, the weight on bequests, b, must exceed the inverse of the rate of time preference plus one, $1/(1+ i)$ (Fischer 1973, 137). Fischer found that the greater b is, the greater the likelihood of buying insurance (1973, 143). (See appendix 1.5.)

There are other uncertainties besides the uncertainty of survival. One is the uncertainty related to investing in a risky asset—where risk is expressed as the variance in returns for a given average return. If the decision is confined to the effect of risk in return on the propensity to consume, then—as Levhari and Srinivasan noted—this will depend on the consumer's attitude toward risk as revealed by the value of ρ. If the value of ρ is one, then $\lambda = 1 - 1/(1 + i)$. (This λ is based on the assumptions of Levhari and Srinivasan's model and is constant over time.) Risk would have no bearing on the MPC because r would have no effect. The MPC depends solely on the discount rate. If the consumer is risk averse ($\rho < 1$), then increasing uncertainty would result in a higher λ. If the consumer is a risk taker ($\rho > 1$), more uncertainty would lead to a lower λ (Levhari and Srinivasan 1969, 160–161). (See appendix 1.6.)

Consumption over Time

A larger MPC results in more consumption in the current period, therefore less saving, and can (other things equal) lead to less production over time. The polar views from the perspective of the present are to "live today, for tomorrow we die" (Intriligator 1971, 398), or to invest all income to expand the capital base. Either extreme could be suicidal. Objectivism is consistent with the long view. If the longer view is taken, the maximization of (utility from) consumption and maximization of production are not incompatible objectives.

F. P. Ramsey (1928) was one of the first to examine optimal saving over time. Unlike some of the subsequent investigators of this subject, who employed optimal control theory, Ramsey used calculus of variations (Chiang 2000, 253). Ramsey devised the problem as one of determining the optimal consumption plan that maximizes utility for a community of a given size between the current period and "Bliss." Bliss is a time at which either the marginal product of capital (which equals the interest rate) is zero or marginal utility equals zero (satiation is reached) (Herfindahl and Kneese 1974, 103).

Because Ramsey's model is a growth model, it includes a production function. In his model, the marginal product of capital is implicitly assumed to be net of depreciation and equal to r. Since his model assumes that there is no growth in population, the total and individual models are indistinguishable. In consumer-saving decision models for an individual in which there is no accounting for the source of the growth in consumption—that is, there is no production function—r represents the interest rate. Once time preference (i) is taken into account, the relative rate of consumption growth over time for an individual can be expressed as:

(9) $g = dc^*/dt \; 1/c^* = \eta(r - i)$.

If the utility function is of the form shown in equation (3.1) appendix 1.4, then equation (9) would be consistent with the growth model of Ramsey (1928, 554), the optimal consumption plan given in Yaari's (1964, 309) model, and similar to that derived from the consumer model shown in Green (1978, 201).

The growth rate in consumption will increase with increases in the interest rate (r), increase with increases in the elasticity of substitution (η), and decrease with increases in the rate of time preference (i) (Green 1978, 201–202). When r exceeds i, consumption increases over time. When i exceeds r, the consumption plan decreases over time (Yaari 1964, 309). Ramsey found that under the assumption of a finite life, if the discount rate was greater than the interest rate, capital would be drawn down to the point of exhaustion, and borrowing would increase until a person could barely subsist once payments of interest were made (1928, 555). (It is not clear to me, however, that there would be anyone willing to lend if everyone faced the same prospect. The interest rate would have to rise to choke off this demand. So the interest rate would not reflect net return since no one would lend. It would only reflect scarcity. [See appendix 1.8.])

If equation (9) is viewed from the "community" perspective rather than the individual's perspective, then it would fail to allow for the possibility of population growth, n. Ramsey's model is a stationary state model; a steady state model permits growth in n. (A static system results in an equilibrium point. A dynamic model results in an equilibrium path. That path may be stationary, in which case the endogenous variables are constant over time, or steady, in which case the endogenous variable may increase at a constant rate over time [Gapinski 1982, 55].) Once population growth is permitted, then growth in consumption per capita would be:

$$dc/dt\ 1/c = \eta\ (f'(k) - \delta - n - i),$$

where depreciation, δ, is now explicitly recognized. The marginal product of capital per capita, $f'(k)$, must exceed $(n + \delta + i)$ in order for consumption growth to be positive (Intriligator 1971, 409–410).

For an *individual*, once uncertainty of survival is introduced, Menahem Yaari (1965, 143) derived the equivalent of the following if the assumption is that the utility function is that given in equation (3.1) appendix 1.4:

$$(10)\ dc/dt\ 1/c = \eta\ (r - i - \pi d_t(t)),$$

where $\pi d_t(t)$ is defined as the force of mortality for the relevant survival function (see appendix 1.9) and r is net of depreciation of physical capital. If the depreciation of *human capital*, ξ, is made explicit in one's consumption decision, then the growth in consumption becomes

$$dc/dt\ 1/c = \eta\ (f'(k) - i - \pi d_t(t) - \xi).$$

That is, depreciation of human capital would be separate from the effect of uncertainty of death in the decision-making process (if such a separation were possible). Depreciation of human capital is not accounted for in this way. If life's uncertainty is accounted for (by πd_t), it could be argued that its finiteness should also be represented. It is because of life's uncertainty that the need for insurance arises; similarly it is because of life's finiteness that depreciation arises. However, because replacement of human capital is one's children, depreciation is not accounted for, since those expenditures (on the human-capital development of one's children) are usually counted *as* consumption.

Yaari showed that the presence of life insurance eliminates uncertainty from the individual's consumption plan over time. Instead of equation (10), the growth in consumption would have the same appearance as equation (9). (Although the equation, call it (9'), would look like (9), the solutions would have different constants of integration.) Equation (9') would reflect the optimal consumption plan over time with uncertainty of survival "removed" (1965, 147–48). When a bequest motive is recognized along with insurance availability, then, in addition to equation (9'), there is a symmetrical equation (not shown) for savings (bequests). Insurance permits the two decisions (consumption and bequests) to be separable (locally, not globally). The optimality condition is that the marginal utility of consumption equals the marginal utility of bequests at each point in time (1965, 149).

A finding of the models considered here is that a strong bequest motive tends to increase consumption over time. Production will increase as well. Thus, if productive purpose is a value and productivity a virtue, one conclusion to be drawn from the analysis is that if individuals are concerned not only with their own lives, but after their lives as well, productivity will be greater.

Optimal Population?

In the approach in which utility per capita is maximized, the marginal product of capital per worker keeps pace with the increase in population so as to keep consumption per capita constant. An alternative model sums overall utility functions in the economy. So long as population is constant, the two approaches are the same with respect to the optimal consumption path (Herfindahl and Kneese 1974, 106–107). A problem with the per capita approach is that the product added by employing the marginal worker is less than average product (which is the same as average consumption if net investment equals zero), and a declining average product translates into falling consumption per capita. Thus, marginal product (the product added by hiring the last worker) is less than per capita consumption. If all workers were paid the marginal product attributable to employing the last worker, all wages would fall. Since marginal product is less than average product, wages would be insufficient to maintain average consumption.

In order to raise the marginal product to the average, Herfindahl and Kneese suggested managing the population (1974, 107). From the perspective of static analysis, it has been noted by Herfindahl and Kneese (based on a statement by James E. Meade [1955]) that the objective of per capita utility maximization carries with it the bizarre implication that those with low marginal products "should be eliminated in order to maximize per capita income" (1974, 106n⇑). (This assumes, apparently, that workers would be paid their marginal products rather than all workers paid the same wage based on the marginal product of the last worker employed.) In the case in which the objective is to maximize total utility, redistribution is assumed so that the consumption of those with lower marginal products is brought up to average (1974, 108). (Presumably, income would be taken from capital owners if all workers are paid the marginal product of the last worker hired.) Neither of these ideas (that is, redistribution or eliminating population) is ethically tenable, but they are the product of examining utility and abstracting from the reality of human nature as well as human rights.

At the golden growth path (analogous to Bliss in Ramsey's model), consumption and capital increase at the rate of population growth. All returns to capital are used for replacement investment and to provide capital for the increase in population. The per capita approach has the marginal product of capital per worker keeping pace with the increase in population. There is no growth in per capita income, nor is there a problem with income declining so long as investment keeps pace with population. Under the assumption of constant returns to scale (which has been assumed here), output increases by the same percentage as the increase in inputs. Declining marginal product would not have an effect over time unless there were some fixed resource, for instance a natural resource, as in the Malthusian model, or resources of declining quality, as in the Ricardian, that would result in declining returns. (See appendix 2.1.)

Herfindahl and Kneese (1974, 108) pointed out that the "optimal" population would be that which maximizes consumption per capita, which would be that which maximizes average product of labor. In static short-run analysis, that is the point at which the marginal product of labor equals the average product of labor, and with constant returns to scale, the point at which the marginal product of capital equals zero. (If population increased beyond that point, other things equal, the average product of labor would fall.) This assumes that those who hold capital would be satisfied with a zero return at the "optimal" population. In that case, no return would be necessary if the capital stock is fixed and does not grow and all returns are simply to replace depreciated capital. If population were optimal and did not grow, then there would be no need for (net) capital to be purchased as the population increases, since population would not increase.

This assumes that all of the product is attributable to labor and that there is no opportunity cost to capital (replacement investment). There is human capital. Human capital is different in character from physical capital in many respects. One is that the return to human capital cannot be for replacement only. Humans must consume. Physical capital per se does not have to "consume." However, the owners of physical capital do. They have an opportunity cost to their investment in physical capital. They can invest in their own human capital or another's human capital. Humans can invest in their own capital beyond that necessary to keep their productivity constant. Humans also have new ideas. This discussion assumes that technology is constant, but so long as individuals are free to pursue new ideas and to be rewarded for them, this assumption would be unrealistic.

Eventually there may be, because of the finiteness of the planet (and depending upon the prevailing political realities), a point at which declining returns set in and technology cannot keep pace with the increases in population. Of course, in the real world there are always, in the short run, limited supplies and bottlenecks, and over time there are lags in adjustment as well as improvements in technology. The world is much more dynamic than is accounted for in my brief discussion of these models. The discussion is still useful, so long as its limitations are kept in mind.

Standard Income and Depreciation

Like physical capital, labor commands a return. If there were no "interest," there would be no income. Permanent income, defined by Milton Friedman, is rW, if wealth (W) is all inclusive (1966, 247). In a stationary-state (no-growth) economy, labor, like physical capital, would have to be replaced as it "depreciated." The nature of human capital is different from physical capital. If there is no net investment, capital would be replaced as depreciated. Without interest, all that capital "earns" is equal to depreciation. In static-state discussions, the tendency is to ignore the opportunity cost of physical capital and to assume that all of the return is for replacement due to depreciation (e.g., see Valentine and Ellis [1991, 355–56]). On the other hand, because human capital is not bought and sold, there is a tendency to ignore its depreciation (particularly in models for the individual decision-maker).

For human capital, replacement investment means that a person would be replaced—by offspring. If one's income were to go solely for replacement, a person would have no income of his own to consume so as to sustain his life. If consumption were included in replacement investment so as to maintain individuals as well as replace them, this could be called "maintenance," but it would be different from maintenance of physical capital because of the nature of living beings. Humans must consume to survive. But if consumption were included in the definition as part of replacement, then other economic concepts would undergo revision or be superfluous (such as consumption).

Depreciation of human capital is part of (actual) income from human capital. Yet, as Fisher noted ([1906] 1965, 111), humans do not reckon human capital depreciation and deduct it from (actual) income. If human capital depreciation were set aside (in what Fisher called a sinking or depreciation fund), then the relevant income concept would be standard income. For the example of $1,000 per year at 10 percent interest for 10 years, PV=$6,144.44. Standard income would be r(PV) = Y_h = $614.44 (assuming that a sinking fund of $385.56 is put aside). The equation for standard income is: $Y_h = [1 - 1/(\$1.10)^{10}]\ \$1{,}000 = \$614$. Fisher pointed out that if actual income is $1,000 per year, then that is the relevant income concept in calculating present value—that is the amount that is discounted ([1906] 1965, 235).

Fisher ([1906] 1965, 111–12) mentioned that instead of a sinking fund for human capital, a life insurance premium could be purchased, suggesting that the two would be equivalent in amount (whether or not they can be equal is considered later). If a sinking fund were set aside, this would be commonly regarded as saving. A life insurance premium (if confined to a one-period term policy net of "loading") is a transfer payment (from those who survive to the beneficiaries of those who die). In this sense it is not unlike gambling. From the perspective of the individual, he may regard the policy as an asset (for which he will receive a loss if he lives, or a gain—to his beneficiaries—if he dies).

Friedman noted that an asset with a finite life, T, has a value given by the sum of the discounted yields per period, $W = \Sigma^{T}_{t=1} Y_t/(1+r)^t$, and that this finite stream of income "is equivalent to an income of rW per year indefinitely" (1966, 245). However, these are equivalent under certain conditions. One condition (for an individual's human capital) is that a sinking fund (or depreciation fund) be in fact set aside. Using the present value (PV) formulation for wealth, then income (Y) is: $Y = PV(r) + PV(r) / (e^{rT} - 1) = rPV / (1 - e^{-rT})$. For income to be defined as rW (or rPV, where W=PV), a sinking fund of $PV(r) / (e^{rT} - 1)$ must be put aside to accumulate at interest rate, r. If a sinking fund equal to the actual income less a perpetual annuity of the same present value is set aside, then the standard income definition would apply to the perpetual annuity value. There would be no trenching on capital. The capital value would remain intact.

(In the example, above I have used standard income for "permanent" income, because in the Friedman (1966, 245) reference he cast W in PV terms. Yaari (1964, 312) defined Y_h as Hick's income. According to my reading of Yaari, he stated that Friedman's preferred concept was given by the continuous and discrete formulas: $Y_p = r(W)/(e^{rT} - 1)$, or $Y_p = r(W)/[(1+r)^T - 1]$, where W is accumulated value. Yaari related that this was the same as Farrell's normal income concept. Based on my reading of Green (1978, 190), he attributed to Farrell normal income given by the equations: $Y_p = r(W)/(1 - e^{-rT})$, or $Y_p = r(W)/(1 - 1/(1+r)^T)$, where W is in present value terms. Either of the normal income definitions would result in Y_p = \$1,000 based on an actual income of \$1,000 per year, 10 percent interest, and T=10 years—where $Y_p = Y_h/(1 - e^{-rT})$.

If capital continued to depreciate, the idea that Y_h=rW would not be an accurate reflection of what would be taking place. Even though it would be possible to continually recalculate what an equivalent perpetual annuity would be, if there were continual depreciation, there would not be a perpetual annuity. For the economy as a whole, this is not generally an issue as such. There is a continual replacement and accumulation of both nonhuman and human capital. But from the individual's perspective, income from human capital is generally regarded as actual income (as Fisher noted [{1906} 1965, 235]). Fisher appears to be correct that a sinking fund is not put aside in reckoning income. If one spends all of his income, he is not typically regarded as trenching on his (human) capital. If he were, the concept of saving would be confined to "true" accumulation; that is, saving beyond replacement of human capital (beyond depreciation).

For the economy as a whole, there would be no net savings if there were no net investment, the age distribution of the population were constant, the labor force were unchanged, there were no technological advancement, and individuals attempted to leave estates of a given size (Herfindahl and Kneese 1974, 77). So an individual may appear to have positive savings at the end of his life (that is, there is positive net worth at T), but if it is for the purpose of keeping one's physical capital and human capital intact, there would be no net savings per se.

If it is assumed that an individual has a finite life and cares nothing about leaving an estate so that in the last period of life (T), $C_T=W_T$, that is, he consumes in period T all of his wealth in period T, then (at some point), the MPC out of wealth must increase. The idea of translating a finite income stream into a perpetual income stream of equivalent value would not be applicable to an individual in such a circumstance. (Nor would it be applicable to the individual on the desert island for much the same reasons. The individual would have a finite life and would not have any reason to leave anything behind when he dies.)

In order for standard income to be a viable concept to an individual, either T must be assumed infinite and/or he must care about bequests. Humans are mortal, so the idea of an infinite T is unrealistic. However, economic theory has circumvented this problem by assuming that utility is defined for the household, and the household may be thought of as having an indefinite future life (see Gapinski 1982, 144). Consumption decisions for an individual within a household ("head" of household) would include the future consumption of that person's heirs. (Permanent or standard) income could be defined as $Y=rW$. Inherent in this assumption is that there is no depreciation of human capital as such in the sense that the family can be regarded as producing its own replacement of human capital. A sinking fund would not necessarily be set aside, at least one equivalent to the full value of one's human capital, since one's children would be one's "replacement capital."

Replacement Capital and Life Insurance

Generally speaking, individuals have greater life insurance coverage during the time in which their children are young. Even then, the coverage is generally not the full amount of the present value of their lifetime earnings (Sachko 1975, 44–45). One reason that it is less is because they may have other assets and resources. Another is because insurance premiums are loaded, so they are less than fully insured. Another reason is that their children *are* their human capital replacement. To have both a sinking fund plus children would be to have twice the amount of human capital replacement value necessary. Similarly, to have children plus insurance would be to have more human capital replacement than may be necessary. One needs insurance to replace one's human capital in the event of one's untimely death, especially when one's children are young and not productive. (Other objectives are abstracted from.) In any event, one reason the coverage of insurance may be less than the value of one's human capital is that children are (in part) one's replacement capital, so there may be some overlap here in human capital replacement if one had full life insurance coverage *and* children.

"Permanent Probabilities"

Life insurance premiums are based on mortality rates. For a given year, an unloaded premium for a one-period term policy would approximately be equal to the expected mortality rate for that year; the rate being based on historical data. There are also various theoretical survival functions that can provide approximations for mortality rates. Although they do not perform as well empirically as historical data, they can be useful in theoretical discussions. In the following, I rely upon theoretical survival functions, not historical data, in discussing various alternative net level premium rates. Net level premiums are calculated for "whole-life" policies. The logic underlying them is that rather than pay a per-year premium that increases over time with increasing risks of mortality, a fixed amount is paid per year. This means that in the first few years the rate will have to be higher than the corresponding mortality rate. The surplus increases at interest (reserves) to offset the later years when the premium rate is lower than the mortality rate (although in the first few years, "asset share" is negative due to the relative significance of the front-end expenses [Huebner and Black 1976, 300–301]).

The reason that a net level premium (NLP) rate is relevant to this discussion is that it provides an "average" probability of dying over the corresponding period of the policy. In the following, I analyze and derive a number of net level rates. The rationale for this is similar to that underlying other "standard" or "permanent" concepts. Permanent or standard income is a long-run concept. The long run figures prominently in Rand's ethics. An ethical code facilitates deciding and acting long-range. The standard of OE is man's long-range survival (Peikoff 1991, 219). Probabilities also are central to Rand's ethics. Long-run probabilities of success are relevant to the derivation of moral principles, according to Merrill (1991, 114–17). The BUP is based on long-run success as a result of applying rational principles to one's life. The uncertainty of death figures into the fundamental alternative, which in Rand's ethics is life or death. This uncertainty also is relevant from the perspective of human capital replacement, particularly as it relates to the purchase of insurance. Probabilities are fundamental to decision-making under uncertainty. Probabilities of life and death enter in the decision for charitable giving that I present in chapter 16. There is a difference between a long-run probability and what I refer to as a "permanent" probability. A "permanent" probability results from an "averaging" of the long-term probabilities. I believe that the idea of a standard or permanent probability of dying is inherent in the derivation of a net level premium for life insurance.

Level Premiums—Comparisons

This section summarizes the results of a number of net level premium rates that are discussed more fully in appendix 1.11. It would appear that Irving Fisher ([1906] 1965, 111) saw the sinking fund per period and the premium to be paid for life insurance as interchangeable amounts. This is consistent with a level premium rate as shown in equation (13) in appendix 1.11. However, the sinking fund per period is insufficient to pay off insurance claims.

The NLP rate calculation used by insurance companies is that shown in equation (11) (or, similarly, equation (11^i)) in appendix 1.11. It is roughly equal to the sum of the discounted probabilities of dying divided by the sum of the discounted probabilities of surviving. Historical mortality rates are typically used for T years. To be consistent with the idea that what the insured person is protecting is the value of his human capital, I would think that, instead of actual mortality rates, depreciation rates (DR_t = depreciation divided by present value in year one) could be used, since they reflect a decline in value due to "aging." Still, a conceptual difficulty remains in that both the sinking fund and depreciation are relevant to the idea of replacement of the value of capital due to a finite and certain life, T, not because of the uncertainty of death's timing. If the objective was to examine depreciation and to arrive at an "average" rate of depreciation, then the focus should be on the replacement of capital of a given present value because life is finite, not on the replacement of the capital value due to life's uncertainty. Dividing by the sum of the (discounted) probabilities of surviving, as is done in equation (11), would not be relevant if the objective is to calculate the amount necessary to replace capital, since T would be known and certain. Dividing by T, rather than the sum of the (discounted) "survival rates," would be preferred if an average level of depreciation were the objective. Equation (P.1) in appendix 1.11, which gives the sum of the (undiscounted) depreciation rates divided by T, is an "average depreciation rate."

Of course, if it is the uncertainty of death that is of interest, (P.1) will not capture it. This leads to a third conceptual problem with using depreciation rates based on present value (PV) for mortality rates. In calculating present value, r is a return, not a force of mortality, ∂. One way of approaching this conceptually is, instead of using present value, to use the expected value of lifetime income (see appendix 1.2). Expected value (EV) assumes that yearly income is factored by the probability of receiving it, which I have simplified to be the probability of being alive. If the force of mortality ("mortality discount") is assumed constant and equal to ∂, then income per year would be weighted by $e^{-\partial t}$, the probability of survival (equation ($S3^i$) in appendix 1.11; although I used the discrete counterpart in the calculation of EV). From expected value of lifetime income can be calculated the equivalents of a sinking fund and depreciation. Expected value has as a "survival function," $S = (1 - \Sigma_{t=1}^{T} DR_{t-1})$ (see appendix 1.10).

A fourth problem is that if the objective is to isolate the effect of mortality alone (because of an uncertain life) in the calculation of a net level premium, it may be preferable not to discount (by the return discount, r, in the numerator and the denominator, as was done in (11^i). Thus, using depreciation (based on EV) as a percentage of expected value in year one as the "mortality rate," a net level premium rate can be calculated similar to that shown in equation (11^i) in appendix 1.11. However, if the numerator and denominator are not discounted (by r), then the premium rate would have a numerator equal to one (the sum of the "probabilities of dying" based on DR_t) and a denominator equal to the sum of the "probabilities of surviving" (based on one minus DR_t). The resulting NLP rate is shown in (P.2).

One problem with the approach in (P.2) is that an increase in the force of mortality, ∂, does not translate into a higher premium rate, which is contrary to intuition. Although the sum of the "probabilities of dying" is divided by the "sum of the probabilities of surviving," the latter sum does not decrease with an increase in ∂, as one would expect. The premium rate based on (P.2) is close to 1/T, regardless of the value of ∂, indicating that it is "driven" by T, the finiteness of life, rather than by its uncertainty. To correct for this, the premium rate shown in equation ($P.3^{ii}$) uses the sum of the "survival rates" given as $e^{-\partial t}$ (the discrete equivalents) in the denominator. It does result in a higher premium rate with a higher ∂. This aspect of the premium rate is more in line with expectations. However, as seen in ($P.3^{ii}$), the premium turns out to be the entire yearly income.

A variation on this premium is to retain the denominator of ($P.3^{ii}$), but in the numerator, instead of the value of one, use the sum of the "probabilities of dying" (where the probability of dying is = $\partial\ [1/(1+\partial)^{t}]$, based on the discrete version of ($S5^i$) in appendix 1.11). This results in equation (P.4). In this case the premium rate becomes ∂. The net premium would be ∂ multiplied by expected value of lifetime income, $\partial x EV_1$.

In appendix 1.12, I derive a "depreciation index" that shows the relationship between the force of mortality and "depreciation" based on the concept of expected value. If lifetime is infinite, then depreciation (the fall in expected value per year) equals the force of mortality, ∂.

Chapter Fifteen

Ethical Decision-Making

Rand was aware of the stochastic in life. The BUP states that success is the to-be-expected, if individuals act rationally (Peikoff 1976). Loss is possible; but, since principles are based on long-run success (survival *qua* man), it is the not-to-be-expected. In the application of principles to decision-making, therefore, the expected loss can be ignored. Ethical decisions can be approached as if they conform to a strict causal chain; only the expected gain of the ethical decision needs to be taken into account. (The expected loss for the unethical alternative would not be ignored.) This is particularly true if the choice is confined to ethical actions only, all of which have the same loss associated with them (given by the probability of loss—dying—multiplied by the associated "payoff"). Context matters, of course. In some cases, the risk of loss (death) may be high. Rather than choosing based on the greatest expected gain alone, the expected loss would also have to be taken into account. I note that even for an action in which the risk of death is high, one may choose it. Rand (1964d, 45–46) gave a standard on which to judge whether to risk one's life for another based on the degree of importance of a person in one's life.

In this chapter, I argue that identity—consistency in behavior—is a factor in this decision. Just as one may not abandon his principles if he is certain to die, he may choose to act on a principle, even if the risk of death is high (particularly if the alternative action is unethical). Many times, when one faces a decision in which there is a risk to one's life, it is in an unusual circumstance and the alternative (that is, the action associated with not risking one's life) is also ethical. The question is, would it be rational to risk one's life, given that life is one's ultimate value? To address this, one may look to the insurance decision as a point of comparison. With that decision, one may choose an action that has a lower expected monetary value (although it has a greater expected utility) than the alternative because of the starting point. One is born at risk. Death is inevitable. This aspect of the insurance decision may also apply to risking one's life. A person is born at risk. There may be circumstances where, to preserve a principle, one must risk his life in the process. Since principles are life affirming, this would not seem to be rationale. However, principles also have lives and can die if not affirmed. The difference is that one's own death is inevitable. The death of one's principles is merely possible. By acting to preserve one's principles, one may keep alive the best that is within (embodied in) oneself as virtue. In this chapter, I argue that both the rule-based (no deliberation) approach and the maximization principle are consistent with the application of OE. Which one is relevant depends on context.

Alternatives, Options, and Outcome

The following is a quote from a statistics textbook by Ya-lun Chou:

> [A] decision procedure involves the selection of a possible course of action which will lead to an outcome judged to be favorable or not, in accordance with its success or failure to fulfill some predesigned objective. (1969, 675)

Chou's quote served as an introduction to a discussion of statistical theory, but underlying it are a number of philosophical assumptions about man and reality that are consistent with OE. It assumes that the decision-maker is faced with more than one course of action. It assumes that the decision-maker can select among these alternatives—that one has free will. It assumes that the courses of action are possible—i.e., grounded in reality—and that one has the ability to discover what they are—i.e., one is conscious and has the capacity of rationality. It assumes that one can act on one's choice—i.e., has the freedom to do so. It assumes that an action will lead to an outcome. That is, there exist cause-effect relationships. It assumes that actions have consequences and that they are capable of being known beforehand. It assumes that outcomes can be judged favorable or unfavorable—that one can evaluate success or failure. The fact that outcomes can be favorable or unfavorable implies that it makes a difference to the decision-maker and that there is a basis for judgment. The standard on which the judgment is based is whether an action is successful or not at fulfilling an objective. That one can be successful or not assumes efficacy on the part of the one who acts. The assumption that the objective is predesigned implies that the decision-maker is goal-oriented and can plan. That one can plan implies that decision-making involves a time dimension.

Some decisions conform to a "strict causal chain" (Chou 1969, 675); i.e., they have an if-then structure that is certain. Thus, if a person were to choose a given alternative, there would be a consequence, and if he chooses correctly, the decision-maker will be successful (i.e., the result of his action will be that which he would deem favorable based on some criterion or standard). Decision theory deals with decisions for which there is more than one probable or possible outcome to a given alternative. When probabilities are estimable, then expected outcomes (based on monetary value, utility, or some other measure) can be calculated. This does not mean that there is no connection between decision and outcome. If there were no connection, there would be no reason to choose. Events would simply happen over which the individual would have no control. The individual's decisions or actions would be irrelevant to the outcome of events. Still, there is some probability that if one takes a given action, he will not be successful. In making decisions, decision theory assumes that the individual will weigh the expected gains and expected losses for a given action. For instance, a person may examine the expected values of the alternatives he faces in order to make a decision and choose the alternative associated with the greatest expected value (abstracting from variations in returns).

In determining an expected "value," the individual may, in effect, take an "average" of the possible "payoffs" associated with each possible outcome (state) by multiplying them by their respective probabilities and summing (although summation is not the only approach that could be used). For example, there may be two possible outcomes, a gain and a loss—say, life and death. Associated with each state would be a "payoff" as well as a probability of occurrence. By taking the expected value, it may seem as if the decision-maker is "averaging" life and death. In a sense, he is. Rand has said that there are two alternatives: one is right and the other is wrong, "but the middle is always evil" (1961a, 173). It may seem as if by taking an "average" of the expected "payoff" in the "life" state and the expected "payoff" in the "death" state that one is choosing a middle ground, a compromise. This is not the case. There is a difference in taking, or attempting to take, a middle ground between a right alternative and a wrong alternative, and, for a given decision, choosing between two alternatives: each of which has more than one outcome associated with it. For each alternative, one could calculate an expected value, which is not the same thing as "averaging" the alternatives themselves. The either-or decision is between the alternatives. One does not have a choice among the outcomes (states).

For a given decision, the number of outcomes may be many. For complex decisions, the alternatives may be presented in a decision tree. Construction of decision trees is dependent upon the knowledge of probabilities and "payoffs" associated with the various outcomes. The payoffs themselves may be dependent on other information, such as the assumed structure of the underlying probability distribution as well as the values of the parameters necessary to calculate a payoff for a given "state of nature" (see Winston and Albright 1997, 391–453).

Either/Or

A decision that conforms to a "strict causal chain" leads to a single "certain" outcome. For example, the switch to an electrical circuit results in a light turning either on or off (Chou 1969, 675). The only decision is whether to turn the switch off or on. The outcome of that decision is "certain." Although it is clear that Rand recognized the stochastic in decision-making (Merrill 1991, 115–17), in terms of moral choice, she might be viewed as regarding the outcome of making the right decision as conforming to a strict causal chain. That is, Rand's attempt was to uncover those principles that will lead to success—life being the Objectivist standard. Once discovered, if principles are applied to decisions, a person should have success. Success, according to the BUP, is "the metaphysically to-be-expected" (Peikoff 1976). Rand was aware that a given action could have more than one outcome. Still, she thought that failure was incidental, particularly if moral principles were applied consistently over the long run. Peikoff said: "[I]f you do, think, value, and act rationally, then you can (and barring accidents you will) achieve your values" (ibid.). That does not mean that failure is impossible. It is simply not the norm. One might interpret this statistically to mean that failure, speaking in terms of a "normal distribution," falls in a "tail" of the distribution. Rational principles will in the long run lead to a norm of success—success defined ultimately as survival (*qua* man).

"Choice—Two Mutually Exclusive Alternatives"

To Rand, the fundamental alternative forms the basis for all values (Peikoff 1991, 209). Rand described this choice psychologically, existentially, and metaphysically as one of life or death (1964a, 21). A person cannot choose some middle ground between right and wrong, between truth and nontruth, between life and death (1961a, 173). Rand saw the decision process (for questions of morality) as fundamentally dichotomous—a choice between two mutually exclusive alternatives. Rand said that for every issue, there are two sides—a right side and a wrong side (1961a, 173). Norton noted that there are usually many possibilities from which one might choose, but there is a tendency for choice to be cast as either/or (Norton 1976, 135). Peikoff clarified this point, arguing that on fundamental ethical questions, the decision is either/or; however, there are many options insofar as how one achieves what is right (1991, 323). For instance, a cardinal virtue is productive work. However, with some qualifications, the kind of career one chooses is largely optional. Thus "alternative" and "option" have different meanings (although they are typically used interchangeably when discussing decision-making).

Economists see choice between "goods" as marginal. Because of constraints (such as income), for a given time period, a person cannot choose an infinite amount of all goods (or consume all goods to the point of satiation). Nor, in most cases, does a person have to decide between only one good or the other. To obtain more of one good, less of another is required. Alchian and Allen regarded all "goods," including virtues, as "marginally substitutable for each other" (1977, 26). Peikoff rejected the notion of "trading off" ethical principles (1991, 264, 273). Virtues are either/or. They are mutually exclusive. There is no "quantity" of a moral principle that can be traded for a nonvirtue.

Mutually Exclusive Alternatives

A decision between two alternatives may be set up as follows:

		States of Nature	
		I	II
Alternatives	A		
	B		

A person must decide between A and B, yet both A and B are subject to states of nature "I" and "II" (Salvatore 1996, 568). The states of nature could be life and death or success and failure. Generally speaking it is assumed that the states of nature are not under the control of the decision-maker. They are given. They may have probabilities associated with them, which may or may not be known (or calculable). State of nature "I" will or will not occur. If it does not, "II" will occur, and vice versa. The probability that both will occur simultaneously is zero. They are mutually exclusive. The probabilities then are p for State "I" and (1-p) for State "II." However, there may be many states of nature, not just two. (It is often assumed that the probabilities for each state are the same for both alternatives.)

For this example, the choice is assumed to be between A and B. If the choice is between a virtuous act and one that is not, Rand would see these as mutually exclusive. One must choose between the two, and only one is ethical. Furthermore, if a person chooses the right action, he still may fail; i.e., State "II" may occur, but if it does, it is "accidental" (i.e., has a low level of probability—one outside the norm) and therefore would be irrelevant to the decision. (At least this is one way in which I interpret Rand. Later, I will present another.) In other words, if A is the right choice, then either of the two states of nature, "I" or "II," will occur; however, a person can ignore State "II" (failure) insofar as the decision process is concerned. That is, once a code of values has been adopted, then in applying that code to a decision, where one (A) is ethical and the other (B) is not, a person chooses which of two actions to follow based on that code of values. There may be more than one outcome (state of nature) to each decision, but insofar as the *right* decision is concerned—that is, A—state of nature "II" (failure in this example) is irrelevant to the decision. The decision process, as such, should treat the right decision as if it conformed to a strict causal chain. Ignoring failure for the unethical choice, B, would not be acceptable, however.

It might also be argued that Rand did not accept that probabilities are necessarily given. "Choice . . . is not chance" (Peikoff 1979, 149). And in many cases this is true. A person can take actions to change the probabilities themselves. This is well known in the insurance business. For example, a person may install a security system to decrease the likelihood that his home will be burglarized. Since principles are based on long-run success, that aspect would have been built into the probability of the ethical action. Therefore, the Alternatives A and B would very likely have different probabilities associated with each state of nature "I" and "II." Alternative A would be expected to have a higher long-run probability of success, and the probability of loss would be purely due to randomness.

What Alchian and Allen are saying in the above quote is that a person may have to choose between A and B, but the decision is made at the margin for most goods. A person may have some of both, but at the margin he may choose between more of one or of the other. In choosing between two assets, for instance, a person does not have to decide whether to hold his assets exclusively in money or exclusively in bonds, but may decide, for a portfolio of a given size, to hold more bonds. If he does so, he will have to sacrifice some money (Green 1978, 250–51).

What Peikoff is saying, in effect, is that in deciding between A and B, one cannot choose what is called a "mixed strategy." Chapter 5 discussed conventions of property, which are problems involving conflict over a resource leading to its permanent dispensation. Other problems, coordination problems, were mentioned—such as driving on the left or right side of the road. This convention involves the temporary use of a resource by more than one person. For these types of problems, under certain conditions (that is, when no particular strategy has been accepted as a convention) a mixed strategy may be "optimal." For instance, in deciding whether to drive on the right side or the left side of the street, a person may choose to follow both strategies a percentage of the time (where the percentages would add to one). Generally speaking, a convention results when a pure strategy (either A or B) prevails. In this case, it can be seen intuitively that because of the risks associated when both (or all) players follow mixed strategies, a pure strategy would yield greater "utility," assuming one of the pure strategies were to prevail (see Sugden [1986, 35–36]).

In some cases—driving on the right or left side of the road, for instance—either pure strategy would be acceptable (both would most likely yield the same "utility"). In that sense, the convention that emerges is "arbitrary." So long as one strategy, A or B, prevails, everyone would be better off than if each player were to follow a mixed strategy. A convention limits the choices facing the individual. His "freedom to choose" is curbed. But this is akin to limiting someone's freedom to trespass on someone else's property. I say "akin to" rather than "exactly like" because in this example the problem is how to use a resource that is "owned" or "used" by "everyone" (a road). Since two people cannot occupy the same space at the same time, some rule of behavior is needed to avoid the loss associated with probable accidents. If no rule is imposed (top-down), then one is likely to emerge "spontaneously." Those that emerge are conventions.

Once a convention is accepted, each person (as a general rule) does not face two alternatives—to drive on the right or the left. Nor are the two states of nature associated with each decision (with respective probabilities) relevant. Expected values (utilities) are not calculated for the purpose of making a choice, since they are irrelevant. Only one choice is acceptable. To Rand, principles should be based on long-range survival (*qua* man). I believe that there is essentially no difference between the way in which Rand viewed the application of a principle and the way in which, for example, Sugden described the application of a convention. The distinction is that a moral principle, unlike a convention, is not arbitrary. Driving on either the left or the right side of the street may be acceptable conventions. Honesty and dishonesty are not acceptable alternative principles. In applying principles, as with conventions, a person would consistently choose the principled alternative. He would not consider the unprincipled alternative in his decision set. As with a convention, in applying a principle, he does not calculate the odds and the payoffs for each state of nature each time he makes a decision. He does not calculate the expected gain every time because he expects the long-term gain to outweigh any short-run setbacks or losses. He ignores losses (in making the decision) because, even if they occur (or even if they are "expected" in the short run), they are not important, since in the long run he expects success. A person should not follow a "mixed" strategy where principles are concerned (i.e., when choosing between principled and nonprincipled courses of action).

For decisions involving ethical action, State "II," loss, can be ignored because it is incidental—not the norm. As will be seen later, this is why some decisions that are right yet "life-threatening" may be followed. (Also, as noted in chapter 3, there may exist exceptions in the application of principles, as there are with conventions—for instance, in the latter case, if one must temporarily swerve to the opposite side of the road to avoid an accident.)

Zero-Sum Games

Either/or decisions do not have to be zero-sum in the sense that there must be a winner and a loser to the outcome of a decision. There may be an occasion in which a person may have to choose between purchasing only one product exclusively or another product exclusively (not some quantity of each), but even so, no one necessarily loses. This is an example of choosing one alternative or another. In other words, a person may have to choose between spending all of his discretionary income on food or purchasing a lottery ticket. That is an either/or decision, but it is not zero-sum. However, for a given alternative (action), there may be more than one outcome. If the outcomes are that the person will either win or lose (a good), and as a consequence another party either loses or wins, then this would be a zero-sum game. If the person purchases the lottery ticket, it will follow that there will be one of two outcomes. He will either win or lose. If he wins, others lose. That is zero-sum.

Buchanan and Tullock asked, why would a person play a zero-sum game? (1965, 254) An obvious answer is that a person is willing to play a zero-sum game because he expects to win. But not everyone can win; so why would such games be played if the odds cannot be in every player's favor? It could be because individuals do not know what the odds are. However, in the case of gambling (lotteries, e.g.), it is well known that the odds favor the "house." Yet this does not discourage those who choose to play. The decision to play even when the odds are not favorable could reflect other motivations, such as the joy of playing the game. (Or it could reflect risk preference.)

Another reason why a person may choose a zero-sum game (that is redistributional or in which there is a winner and a loser) that has unfavorable odds is that the decision is the morally right one. As has been mentioned, where the application of a principle to a specific situation is concerned, one chooses the principled course of action because of the expectation of long-run success. There may be short-term setbacks, but those are regarded as incidental. A principle is adopted because it is life affirming in the long run. Application of that principle should lead to eventual success because of the nature of what moral principles are. The norm, the to-be-expected, is success. Failures are temporary anomalies. Since risk associated with failure is incidental, or marginal, it can be ignored insofar as the decision itself is concerned. For some specific decisions that are morally correct, the outcome may be zero-sum (and the odds may be unfavorable). However, Rand did not see ethical choice itself as zero-sum. (There may be more than one outcome to a decision, and one of those outcomes may result in loss, but that does not mean that another person wins. If a firm makes a loss, that does not mean that another firm made a profit as a result. The two are, for the most part, independent events. Zero-sum games that would not have an ethical dimension would be ball games or lotteries. It is questionable whether these can be regarded as entirely zero-sum, but they do have zero-sum elements.)

Another reason one may choose to play a zero-sum game for which the odds are not favorable is that the choices are between loss and a greater loss. It is the choice between the lesser of two "evils." If a person were risk averse, he would not, generally speaking, voluntarily enter a game if the odds were fair or unfavorable. If the odds are favorable, then he may do so. But with fair or unfavorable odds, a risk-averse person would enter a zero-sum game only under certain conditions. In an earlier discussion concerning a dispute over an unowned resource to which one believes he has a claim, if the choice is between fighting for control over the resource (thereby establishing it as property to which one has claim) or having no resource (no alternative and therefore dying—at least with some high probability), then a person may decide to fight even if there is a high probability of loss.

In some decisions one does not start from a certain (safe) place when he enters a decision in which risk (probable loss) is involved. For instance, in life there is always a positive probability of death regardless of the decision one makes; that is the nature of life. In the decision to purchase life insurance, for example, one begins at a position of risk (uncertainty about the outcome of a given action—in this case living or not). One may accept a "fair bet" (or, possibly, an unfavorable one) because it is preferable to one's original position (in an expected utility sense). In an article by Becker and Ehrlich (1972, 627), it is shown that the availability and purchase of insurance transform an "either/or" decision (or to be more accurate, a decision in which there is more than one outcome and only one will come to pass) into a marginal decision (one in which there is certainty insofar as the expected payoff in each state is concerned) if insurance is fair.

Certainty is neither a good nor a bad thing. One can be certain one will die if he takes an action to make it so. With fair insurance, the expected values for each alternative are the same; the expected value for the insured alternative is the same as for the uninsured. Because of diminishing marginal utility (if assumed), the expected utility with insurance exceeds the expected utility without insurance. (For instance, if a person expects to receive 1,000 if he lives and zero if he dies, the expected value without insurance is 500 [$=\pi_a \times 1{,}000 + \pi_d \times 0$], if the probability of dying is .5. If he could purchase a one-term (unloaded) policy for 500 [$= \pi_d \times 1{,}000$], the expected value with insurance is 500 [$=\pi_a \times 500 + \pi_d \times 500$]. That is, the expected value is the same whether the person is uninsured or insured, 500. However, if his utility function is $W^{1-\rho} / 1\text{-}\rho$, then if ρ=.5, the expected utility without insurance is 63.25, but with insurance is 89.44.)

Even if some risk remains (that is, there is "loading"), and one does not fully insure (so the expected value with insurance exceeds the expected value without insurance), one may be better off (in the sense of having a greater expected utility) with insurance than without it. Because of diminishing marginal utility, the expected utility associated with having insurance may be greater even if the odds are unfavorable. (This assumes that the utility functions are the same in both states, and that they are weighted the same—by that I mean that there is a bequest motive that gives the same weight to the death state as to the life state.)

Decision-Making—Probabilities Unknown

In some cases, there is more than one outcome to a decision and the probabilities are unknown or not calculable. (Technically, this is referred to as decision-making under uncertainty as opposed to risk. With risk, there is more than one possible outcome to a decision for which the probabilities are known or estimable.) There are criteria for handling these types of decisions. A typical decision matrix for two alternatives for which there are two states of nature, one for success and another for failure, could be presented as follows:

	State of Nature		
	Success	*Failure*	*Maximin*
Strategy			
Action A	100,000	-50,000	-50,000
Action B	0	0	0*

Action A results in an uncertain outcome. There are two states of nature and the probabilities of each state are unknown. Action B is a "do nothing" alternative for which there is a certain outcome under either state equal to zero. One decision criterion, the maximin, first selects the worst outcome for each strategy (shown in the Maximin column), and, of those worst-case scenarios, chooses the best (it chooses the best of the worst). In this example, the decision-maker would choose B and do nothing (shown above with an asterisk) (Salvatore 1996, 568).

The maximin criterion assumes that the opponent, in this case nature, is going to present the decision-maker with the most pessimistic state. It implicitly has a "malevolent universe" premise (see Rand 1964d, 48). In general "nature" is neither benevolent nor malevolent. To assume that "nature" would deliberately choose to present the decision-maker with the worst cases from which to select is equivalent to assuming extreme risk aversion on the part of the decision-maker (i.e., he is a coward). Rawls used the maximin criterion (difference principle) in his theory of justice. It assumes that those behind the veil of ignorance are extremely risk-averse. Each person "expects to be among the least advantaged" (see Mack 2001, 7). This is inconsistent with Rand's BUP, and, although it could describe some individuals, extreme risk aversion is not a defining characteristic of human nature. A case in which this criterion would be more realistically applied would be when the decision-maker is facing not nature but a conscious opponent (say, a competitor) and both are vying over a fixed objective (e.g., market share).

A strict "Randian" benevolent universe approach (my interpretation in this simplistic context) would be to ignore "failure" for the "right" action. Thus far, I have provided no information about Actions A and B. If A is an ethical alternative (and B is not), then it could be expected that the probability of failure for A would be low since that is true of principled action in the long run (although that may not be the case for this particular instance). Thus, failure would be unexpected and should be ignored. Action A would be chosen. Since probabilities are unknown, one would expect the best outcome for the ethical action. With no other information, the "expected payoff" would be 100,000. (Although Action A may be expected, the expected payoff of 100,000 would likely be a bit too optimistic.)

A second approach to decision-making when probabilities are unknown is to calculate a regret matrix. A regret matrix takes the largest value under each state of nature and subtracts each entry within the state from that value. In the matrix above, the larger number under success is 100,000. Subtracting the values for Action A (100,000) and Action B (0) from 100,000 gives 0 and 100,000, respectively. The larger value under failure is 0. Subtracting values for A (-50,000) and B (0) from 0 gives 50,000 and 0, respectively.

Regret Matrix
State of Nature

	Success	*Failure*	*Minimax*
Strategy			
Action A	0	50,000	50,000*
Action B	100,000	0	100,000

The Regret Matrix is an opportunity cost matrix. It gives the cost of the wrong decision. The decision criterion for a regret matrix selects the largest number for each action and then takes the lowest of those numbers (the least of the largest, or minimax). Action A would have the lower regret value. That is, if the decision-maker chose Action A and were wrong (that is, failure occurred) his loss would be 50,000, which would be less than if he had chosen Action B and were wrong (Salvatore 1996, 569–70).

The minimax regret criterion is a more optimistic approach to decision-making under uncertainty than the maximin criterion. It does not automatically assume a "malevolent" universe as does maximin. (Applying the BUP to this criterion, Action A would be chosen, since its loss would be ignored.)

Including Prior Probabilities

If probabilities are known or can be estimated, they can be used to calculate the expected value for each action. If no statistical probabilities exist (based on sample data), then probabilities based on chance may be used. These are called prior probabilities because they are based on something other than empirically estimated probabilities. (They could be based on experience, intuition, or chance.) From the payoff matrix, the expected values (EVs) for each alternative would be calculated as follows if chance is assumed:

EV for Action A = .5(100,000) + .5(-50,000) = 25,000

EV for Action B = .5(0) + .5(0) = 0.

The individual would choose action A since it has the higher expected payoff (Winston and Albright 1997, 398).

Again, if Action A is an ethical decision, then if one applies the BUP, the loss would be ignored. The payoff under the success state might reasonably be factored by the probability of occurrence to arrive at the "expected payoff" for Action A. Speaking of Objectivists' attitude toward defeat or failure, Peikoff (1976) said that "if there's a chance at all," they do not succumb to defeat—which I take to mean that the positive probability of success should be acknowledged. The decision, then, would be based on the expected gain of 50,000. The loss for the ethical action would be ignored. (Since Action B is assumed to be unethical, its expected loss would not be ignored. Of course, in this particular case, it is 0.)

Returning to the way in which decision-theory is typically approached, the prior probabilities may also be applied to the regret matrix to obtain the "expected opportunity loss" matrix.

Expected Loss
State of Nature

	Success	*Failure*
Strategy		
Action A	0	.5(50,000)
Action B	.5(100,000)	0

Expected Loss for A = .5(0) + .5(50,000) = 25,000*

Expected Loss for B = .5(100,000) + .5(0) = 50,000.

To minimize the expected loss, the decision-maker would select Action A. This is called the cost of uncertainty and is regarded as the unavoidable loss "due to chance" (Hirschey 2003, 591). Since under the BUP criterion loss would be ignored for ethical action, A would be chosen.

Note that the probability of success under Action A is only 50 percent. If Action A is the ethical choice, this probability may be too low. Ethical principles should be based on long-run success. If these were long-run probabilities, one would expect the probability of success to be higher, since success would be the "norm." This is one problem of choosing prior probabilities based on the assumption of chance (equal probabilities across states of nature). (And this is not the only problem with this approach, as will be discussed below under the section on the Bayes Theorem.) Generally speaking, an ethical person would not include an unethical alternative in his choice set. However, decisions are contextual and there may be times in which one may be forced to choose between an ethical and an unethical action.

To Ignore Is Not to Evade

Ignoring the expected loss in making a decision between an ethical and an unethical choice does not mean one should ignore the loss altogether. That would be evading reality. Neither should the cost be ignored. The cost of a decision is the highest valued alternative forgone, assuming the action with the greatest net benefit is chosen. However, the ethical choice may not be the one associated with the lowest cost. One must recognize the cost of a decision, even when cost is not the criterion on which one makes his decision. For example, suppose that a pharmaceutical company official discovers that an important ingredient has been mistakenly omitted from an over-the-counter medication. If the product is recalled, there will be a certain loss associated with this, which could be quite large. There is no probability associated with this figure. The company will be certain to incur it if it recalls the product. If it does not recall the product and the error is discovered, it could cost the company in lawsuits and reputation, but the probability of that, in the company's estimation, is relatively low, so the expected legal and reputation cost is lower than the certain recall cost.

Now, ethically, the company official should recall the product. The fact that the cost of recall exceeds the expected cost of lawsuits should not be the basis of the decision. But that does not mean the decision-maker ignores the cost of the decision (in this case, the explicit cost, which also in this particular case equals the expected loss). The cost of recall is real and must be incurred. It could result in losses in profits, possibly bankruptcy. Workers may lose their jobs, suppliers could go unpaid. One cannot ignore reality. But, insofar as the correct decision is concerned, one would not decide based on a cost comparison of the right decision and the wrong decision. (The health cost to the consumers if the product is not recalled would be included in the expected legal costs. It could be argued that these should not be factored by the probability of "being caught" since they would be incurred whether the company pays for them or not. They are an ethical cost to the decision to not recall the product.)

Choosing among Ethical Alternatives

If one were choosing among several courses of action, all of which were ethical, one could choose based on the expected value (or utility) of the ethical alternatives. This is consistent with decision-making under risk as typically presented using the Bayesian approach. However, if the probability of loss is the same across all of the alternatives, the expected loss could be ignored (particularly if the "payoff" for the loss state is the same under every alternative). The decision could be based on the largest expected gain. Jan Narveson has said of Rand's fundamental choice, life or death: "What you and I are nearly always choosing among are alternatives of much lesser moment, such as which brand of milk to buy, or where to go for vacation next year. Those are choices among options all of which, so far as we know, yield just about equal life expectancy—'life or death' just isn't where it's at" (Narveson 1998, 97). It is true that there is a probability of death associated with every action one takes, because there is always a chance one will die. Many of the choices we make have the same probability of death associated with them—such as whether to buy a brown suit or a blue one. (These might be thought of as "options" rather than "alternatives"; however, the same reasoning would apply to "alternatives.") For these decisions, the probability of dying is irrelevant.

Bayes Theorem

First in the calculation of expected value, it was assumed that the only probabilities that were available were prior probabilities, which were based on "chance." If there is some historical data, it may be used to revise the prior distribution. The revised distribution is called the posterior distribution, and it can be used to calculate updated expected values for each alternative (A or B).

Suppose that, using the historical data, for each distribution the probabilities $P(A_i|I)$ and $P(B_i|I)$ are estimated; that is, given A_i, what is the probability of I; likewise, for B_i. These probabilities, called likelihoods, can be used to revise the prior distribution (cf. Chou 1969, 684, 688).

Given the likelihoods $P(A_i|I) = p_1$ and $P(B_i|I) = p_2$, the probabilities for the posterior distribution would be:

$P(I|A_i) = .5P(A_i|I)/[.5P(A_i|I) + .5P(A_i|II)] = p_1'$, where .5 and .5 are the probabilities for the prior distribution.

$P(I|B_i) = .5P(B_i|I)/[.5P(A_i|I) + .5P(B_i|II)] = p_2'$.

(See Winston and Albright 1997, 432.) So, the revised probabilities in calculating the expected values for Alternative A would be p_1' and $(1 - p_1')$ and similarly for B.

Discussion

In his discussion of the scientific method and normative inference, Doug Fraedrich said: "To the Objectivist, the Bayesian model's major fault is its reliance on subjective prior probabilities" (2001, 37). However, basing prior probabilities on personal "degree of belief" is not necessarily subjectivist (2001,

45n8). I do not believe prior probabilities are subjectivist in the sense Rand meant. To Rand, subjectivism, from a metaphysical perspective, meant that there is no objective reality. If a person were a subjectivist, he would act without reference to reality or in opposition to it (Berliner 1995, 578).

Prior probabilities are often called arbitrary because they are based on chance (the assumed equal likelihood of all states of nature relevant to a decision). Chance in this context means that the outcome of an event will be the result of randomness alone. Given the states of nature, this means that there is an equal likelihood that each will occur. This assumes every possible outcome is known. One can see the problem with this assumption when referring to the probability of dying within a given timeframe. The number of possible outcomes are two. Yet it does not follow that the probability of dying for the given period is one-half. This is because there are factors other than chance (age, occupation, health, etc.) that affect mortality.

Peikoff stated that an arbitrary claim cannot be assessed by logic; it "has no relation to evidence" (1991, 165). This is not true of prior probabilities. They can be tested. If there are two possible states of nature, say being either male or female, and there is no clue what the probability of occurrence of each of these events is, one might begin by hypothesizing that the probability of being male is .5. Then one could test this against a randomly selected sample.

Since it may be costly or even impossible to get enough data (a census) to calculate the true parameter, one can use a sample to make inferences about the true parameter. Inferences are made based on assumptions concerning the sampling distribution. Because a sample is used, there will exist some error between the sample statistic and the true parameter. The error is the result of chance variation. If the sample statistic falls outside a range due to chance variation from the hypothesized parameter, then one could conclude that the true population parameter is not what would be expected based on chance alone. That is, for the hypothesis test on gender, it might be concluded based on a sample that the probability of being a male is not equal to .5. There is a probability that one is wrong when this conclusion is drawn (rejects the hypothesis that the percentage of males is one-half). Rejecting the null hypothesis (that the probability is equal to chance) when it is true is called a Type 1 error. The researcher usually selects the probability associated with this error (.05, for instance) prior to the test (see Beals 1972, 190).

Rand's objection to logical positivism was that logical positivists claim that certainty is not possible, and in its place claim "'percentages of probability,' not troubling . . . with such questions as how one calculates percentages of the unknowable" (1961d, 35). The percentage just discussed has to do with the probability that some observed characteristic or event might be due to chance even though there is significant evidence to the contrary (i.e., the probability of a Type 1 error, which in this case would be the probability of rejecting the hypothesis that the population parameter is due to chance and being wrong).

Thus the hypothesis that the probability of being male is .5 (chance) is testable. If one finds that this probability can be rejected, then one learns more about the underlying probability. The error in this test is a measure of chance variation based on the assumption of a normal distribution. This is not the same meaning of "error" that Peikoff used in the following quote: "'Error' signifies a departure from truth; the concept of 'error' logically presupposes that one has already grasped some truth" (Peikoff 1981, 9; quoted in Binswanger 1986, 479). The hypothesis here is not the "truth," per se. It is the "to be tested." The "error" is not a departure from the truth. Statistical tests such as these are not inconsistent with Rand's conception of knowledge as being contextual and open-ended. Certainty to Rand is contextual. Even though there may be much that remains unknown about the true parameter, what can be known with certainty in this example is the proportion of this sample that are males. That proportion is certain within the context specified. Knowledge is open-ended. Much may remain to be known about this question insofar as the population is concerned, but that is the nature of knowledge. Knowledge does not mean omniscience (Rand 1979, 104–105).

In using the Bayesian theorem, there is nothing particularly wrong with assigning prior probabilities based on chance or on the basis of casual observation if one has nothing else to base them upon. This is because "its very aim is to modify the prior probabilities . . . by experimentation" (Chou 1969, 141). Once the experiment is concluded, then the posterior probabilities replace the prior probabilities. In conducting further research, the new (posterior) probabilities are used as prior probabilities. Repeated estimation will eliminate the initial prior probabilities from consideration (1969, 141–42). The sole restriction is that the prior probabilities cannot be zero or one.

So long as the purpose of using prior probabilities based on chance is to establish posterior probabilities, I do not believe there are grounds for dismissing this approach. However, as mentioned earlier, it might be argued that in deciding between two (ethical) actions, one would expect, based on the BUP, that success is the "norm," the "to-be-expected." Therefore, if there were two states of nature, success and failure, for a given ethical action, the assignment of probabilities based on chance to the "success" state of nature would be inconsistent with this premise. One would expect the "success" state would not have the same probability of occurrence as the "failure" state but would have a greater probability. At least, this would be true of the long-run probability.

A second application of probabilities that has been mentioned is in deciding between two actions when one is ethical and the second is not. It was noted that a mixed strategy would be unacceptable since, even if a mixed strategy might seem to be suggested based on a cost minimization approach, unethical behavior would not be recommended. (It is likely that, if this strategy were (erroneously) recommended, it would be because the costs were not all inclusive.) This is not to say a mixed strategy would never be recommended. If the choice is between two or more ethical actions or "ethically neutral" alternatives, then a mixed strategy could be called for. If a country's military were trying to prevent an enemy from detecting its moves, it might choose a mixed strategy. A random approach might be appropriate here. Optimally, with a mixed strategy, each strategy would be utilized a given percentage of the time (where the percentages would add to one). The maximin principle is applied to the expected payoff to arrive at the optimal percentages (for one player). The opponent would apply the minimax to determine what percentage of the time he should play the strategies facing him (Chiang 1974, 754–59). The idea that one would apply a mixed strategy to ethical questions implies that choice itself is random. Even though a random strategy could be the best strategy to confuse an enemy, in general, ethical decision-making should not be based on chance. As Peikoff noted: "Choice . . . is not chance" (1979, 149).

The Fundamental Choice

In Rand's view, the fundamental alternative is between life and death. This alternative forms the basis for determining what a person values as well as what virtues are required to gain or keep one's values. Rand illustrated this with a thought experiment: an indestructible robot. Such a robot would have no values or virtues, according to Rand, because, regardless of what it did, it could not die. She said that: "Only a *living* entity can have goals or can originate them" (1964a, 16). Yet she called the robot "immortal," which means that it cannot die. This would imply that the robot is *alive*, but is incapable of dying.

Humans, and all living organisms, have sensations in order to cue them about their environment. It is likely that these would be unnecessary if an entity were indestructible. If the robot only had the capacity for programmed "thought"—like a computer—then this would not be a thought experiment, since such devices exist and it is obvious that they do not have values. A computer may "act" in the sense that it has been programmed to respond in certain ways to certain things. But to be "motivated" to act, in the sense described here, an entity would have to be endowed with the capacity not only to sense (in the "heat sensor" sense), but to have a negative or positive response to that sensation. There are heat sensors, but are they regarded as "sensing" heat? I think not. But if one did sense heat, one question would be, does it cause pleasure or pain?

Charles King considered the experiment under the assumption that the robot is capable of preferences or interests, and he concluded that it is the capacity for desire that is the basis for the existence of values and virtues (1986, 110). I addressed the same thought experiment with respect to art, asking whether art could exist without death (Touchstone 1993). One of the things I considered was whether anything would exist to force choice even if one were immortal.

Time preference is assumed to exist largely because humans are mortal. Even if time were unlimited in duration, it is still limited in that it is sequential or linear in nature. A being cannot do everything at one time. Space is also limited. A being cannot be all places at the same time. But these limitations may be insufficient to force choice, since eventually an immortal being could do all things. Would there be any standard(s) for preferring one alternative over another? Would preference exist for an immortal or would it simply act at random?

A more basic question is, would it act at all? Is there anything that would induce it to act? In humans, prolonged inactivity (stimulus deprivation) will result in boredom that will eventually be too painful to bear (Scitovsky 1976, 22). According to psychologists, this is a condition that will motivate action (1976, 31). Sensations are the "raw materials" required for living organisms to act. Lower organisms have "values" (those things necessary for their survival), but their actions are automatic (Rand 1964a, 19). If sensations could exist for an entity that was not threatened by the possibility of death, then it would seem to follow that the entity would value that which caused pleasurable sensations and avoid that which caused pain. If the responses to these stimuli were automatic, no choice would be involved. Given the capacity to choose, it would seem to follow that the hypothetical immortal would choose those things that caused pleasure. There would be values, but would the pleasure-pain alternative be fundamental enough to form the basis for a value system? A value system assumes a hierarchy.

If pleasure and pain were the fundamental alternatives, would it follow that the being would simply be a pleasure-seeking machine? Would all pleasures be equal? If so, then the choice would simply be limited to the avoidance of pain. This would not seem to be a satisfactory basis for a code of values. No one pleasurable alternative would be preferred to any other. However, too much of any activity, like inactivity, may induce change (Scitovsky 1976, 28). This is similar to the logic underlying diminishing returns ("utility") in economic theory. This could form the basis for not simply engaging in a single activity if that activity yields pleasure. After a point, another pleasurable activity would increase in value relative to the one in which one is engaged.

If the robot were capable of making errors and learning from his mistakes, and if he found errors unpleasant, then improvement might be important to him. There is also the possibility that even though the robot might want to avoid pain, he might enjoy inflicting it on others. Pain and its avoidance might be barometers of choice, but some higher level of abstraction might be needed in order to arrive at ethical choice. Rights might enter as well, since one robot might expect other robots to respect his person and territory. Enforcement of rights could be tricky since robots are immortal, but there might be some method of punishment if a robot could feel pain—perhaps the pain of ostracism would be sufficient.

It would appear that robots would, like humans, have to rely on reason to choose whether an action is right or not. If death is not a possible outcome, then it would seem that rationality would still be required for values to exist, but feeling would be required as well—in particular, there must be some negative feeling that can be avoided through right action. These would seem to be the minimal criteria necessary to make values determinant.

Since living entities, and humans specifically, are mortal, it may seem like a meaningless exercise to speculate on an immortal being and whether it would have values or not. It does support rather than detract from Rand's basic point, it seems to me; at least, insofar as the importance of rationality is concerned. That is, for humans, rationality is necessary for survival. Sensations are necessary for values to exist. Men may create heat sensors or develop computer programs that engage in "error-reduction," but unless these can be translated into positive or negative sensations, they cannot form the bases for values. Although feelings or sensations are basic to living things, they cannot be trusted as tools of decision-making. Virtues require choice and choice requires a higher level of cognition.

Rand argued that man must have an ultimate end, which is an end in itself. It is this ultimate end that makes a code of values possible (1964a, 17). King argued that a system of values needs a minimum of one end in itself, but there needn't be an ultimate end (1986, 107–108). Rand said that there could be no lesser values without an ultimate value (1964a, 17). In Objectivism, all goods can be traced back to life as the ultimate goal. For any decision, there can be an outcome that is negative. In business, one could make a profit or loss; in baseball, one could win or lose a game. Couldn't any loss serve as well as death in a system of values? The answer, it would seem to me, based on my reading of Rand, is in the question: Why would loss of any kind matter if death were not a possibility? If a negative outcome—such as pain—were a sufficient alternative, then it could be at least possible to have a system of values if one were immortal so long as there was the capability of a higher level of cognition—rationality.

Alternative versus Outcome

In Rand's ethics, principles are either/or. A person either practices a principle or violates it. Virtues are not mutually exclusive, however. Virtues, such as independence, honesty, integrity, and justice, are not practiced separate from, but along with, the primary virtues of productiveness, rationality, and pride. They are complementary. One does not have to choose between productiveness and honesty, for instance. To be productive, one needs to be honest. One cannot fake reality or ignore reality and be productive in the long run. There is no conflict between them. It is not necessary to sacrifice one of these principles for the other. One principle does not have to be violated for the sake of the other. Nor are they substitutable. A person would not trade off a little bit of honesty for a little bit more productiveness.

Most decisions do not require the violation of a principle, but many require that one value or principle be chosen or affirmed over another. Productive purpose is a value and productiveness is a virtue. Friendship is also a value and benevolence a virtue. Suppose a person had to choose between helping a friend (benevolence or generosity) and going to work (productivity). What would Objectivism recommend? (OE are contextual. The question at this point is, can anything be said in a general way about this decision?) In Rand's hierarchy of values, productive purpose is central. It is a cardinal value. Peikoff said that: "One cannot substitute people for work" (1991, 300). In response to an interviewer for *Playboy*, Rand said that if a man ranked family and friends above his career, that would be immoral (1964b, 7). Both Peikoff and Rand were referring to placing people primarily above work. According to Rand, a producer's work is his primary purpose in life, not other people (Berliner 1995, 82).

Rand had nothing against benevolence towards one's fellow man. She thought it was in one's self-interest (1995, 556). But she did not regard benevolence to be a response to need (Kelley 1996, 17). When applied to a moral code, she regarded need to be vicious (Berliner 1995, 576). Furthermore, one chooses one's friends in response to their virtues. Rand said that she did not have an expectation for help from others when in need, nor did she think it incumbent upon her to help another if in need, not on the basis of what she did or did not want, but because she thought it was the right code to live by (Berliner 1995, 558).

It would seem that if one were an Objectivist and his friend had the same set of values as he, and each followed the tenet mentioned above, a question of whether to go to work or help a friend would not arise. An Objectivist would not regard it as incumbent on himself to respond to such a request, and his friend would not make the request in the first place. This does not mean that one should never help a friend. First of all, love itself is exception making (Rand 1981, 515). Second, one should help another in an emergency whether the person is a friend or a stranger (so long as one does not risk his life in the process). (A person may choose to risk his life, and if he does, the degree to which he would do so would depend upon the value he placed on the other person.) Rand defined an emergency as an unanticipated occurrence that threatens normal conditions of survival and is limited in duration (Berliner 1995, 551). Thus, one consideration in making this decision (between work and a friend who needs help) would be the urgency of the generous act.

Both friendship and productive purpose are values. The latter is ranked higher than the former in an Objectivist hierarchy of values, but this does not mean that it always trumps all other values. If it did, what would be the point of having any other values? The question is, how does one move from one to two in a system of values? Although here a person would be choosing between two principles, a person cannot be said to violate the one not chosen. Still there is the threat of "sacrifice," i.e., of sacrificing a greater value for a lesser one. Sacrifice is regarded as evil (Berliner 1995, 295), and even an instance of it is regarded as wrong. The concept of sacrifice is clear when one surrenders something that is dear for something else that is worthless. But the difficult decisions are those in which one must choose between two values, both of which one values highly.

Of course, whether one is sacrificing productivity for friendship depends on the request of the friend and exactly what one is sacrificing in the way of productivity. If the friend wants you to help him move out of his house, yet if you do so you will fail to meet an important work deadline, then you may have to make some other arrangements for your friend. If, however, your friend has no one to take him for a chemotherapy treatment and your biggest fear about missing a day of work is confronting your boss with the request, then what you are giving up is not productive work. What is stopping you from helping your friend is moral cowardice, the fear of facing your boss with a legitimate request. As Rand noted, one must not fake reality. A person must examine the true reason for his choice.

If a person has a friend who needs chemotherapy and yet he is scheduled to perform brain surgery—the person has a tough choice. The person may make other arrangements to help his friend and make every effort to be there for him when he can and hope that in the future he is offered the opportunity to better plan his calendar. However, when a request is urgent and unanticipated, this doesn't permit a person to plan. These are the kinds of choices a person dreads. One may still be a productive person if he misses a day of work. He may still remain a friend if he makes other arrangements for his friend so long as the friend is not neglected (assuming, of course, he truly needs help).

Many decisions may differ in degree but not in kind from the one just described. Rand did not believe that there is necessarily a conflict between what one knows to be right and what one wants to do. I believe the conflict can arise when a person wants to do more than one right thing at a time. The person must consult his hierarchical code. Unfortunately, it only tells a person what is number one, two, and so on, not how to get from one to two in any particular circumstance. The example above is simply my interpretation of how one might apply such a code. Sometimes, with some creative thinking, a person may be able to reach a third solution. The solution is not necessarily a compromise, but it is not either/or in nature. There are other times, unfortunately, that a person must choose one value over the other. The one that is sacrificed (i.e., not affirmed) is, in economist's parlance, the opportunity cost of the value affirmed.

There is an element of the marginal about these decisions. One is not choosing, in the case described, between working and not working at all. One is deciding whether he can forgo a day of work. Sometimes this is not entirely under one's control—as in the case in which one must ask one's boss for the day off. In cases such as this, the cost of not working could be more than missing a day of work. One might have to decide, depending on the seriousness of one's friend's request, whether one can afford to lose one's job in order to honor the request. In most instances, decisions do not involve this level of sacrifice, or potential sacrifice, with respect to one's productivity.

Similarly, the issue is not whether, by choosing to not help a friend or making some other arrangement to help him, one is sacrificing friendship. Again, if it were a life/death situation, it could be cast in those terms. Short of a life/death situation, one is deciding whether one can help his friend without making a larger sacrifice with respect to some other value. Decisions such as these are not either/or in the sense that one will either have a job or have friendship. The decision is how one spends an increment of one's time. Which value does one choose to affirm and which is forgone?

If a person does not affirm a principle, he has not necessarily violated it. However, if one acts in opposition to a principle, that is a violation. The worst decisions for a person who wants to do the right thing are those that force a person to violate a principle. When there is force, the capacity for autonomy is limited or nonexistent. If the capacity for exercising volition is nonexistent, then a person cannot say he has made a decision. But there are times when an element of discretion remains. In his book *Generosity*, Machan presented a decision in which the alternatives are to lie to a Nazi storm trooper concerning the whereabouts of a Jewish neighbor that one is hiding or to tell the truth (1998b, 27). Clearly the right thing to do is to lie, but in so doing, one is forced to violate a principle. William Thomas stated: "The Objectivist principle of honesty . . . is the recognition that evading or misrepresenting the truth is not an effective means of gaining values from others, and that one benefits from grasping the truth and being open to facts" (Thomas 1999b, 19). In a similar example to Machan's, concerning secret police, Thomas said that they "are not offering any values. If one is *not* seeking to gain values from the interaction, then honesty offers no clear guidelines" (ibid.). This is not my reading of Rand. It seems to me that her argument for honesty hinges on the relationship between a person and reality, and that faking reality in any form (evasion, lies, fraud) is destructive to the person.

The person making this decision is forced to violate a principle (telling the truth) in order to preserve something more important—the safety of an innocent person, as well as the associated principle involved (justice, according to the context of Machan's example [1998b, 27]). What one risks by telling a lie is the death of a principle. (Although a single violation may only be "a little death," the cumulative effect can be serious if a person is forced to persistently lie.) Machan argued that when one is not free, one is not responsible for one's decision; i.e., one cannot be blamed or take credit for the "decisions" one makes and the actions one takes (1998b, 42). In the example above, there is a risk that the principle (honesty) will be damaged if one lies, but there are other risks as well. There is risk of death to oneself if he is found to be a liar. This is an example of an evil situation because of the presence of force in the decision process. Although there is an element of discretion and a morally preferred alternative, one's autonomy is limited. Some might argue, depending upon the degree of danger to oneself in such a situation, that one may not be responsible for his response.

If one does protect his neighbor, this does not mean that no harm has been done to the principle that has been violated. Principles, in a real sense, have lives of their own. The way they survive is by being affirmed. Affirmation is not simply agreeing with a principle. It requires acting upon a principle. Virtues are actions (to gain or maintain values). Many times, because of constraints (limited resources such as time, energy, money, etc.), one principle must be affirmed over another, as in the situation in which one must choose between benevolence towards a friend and productivity at one's job. The principle not chosen is not affirmed. In general (although not always), a principle is not affirmed when no action is taken to support it. It is violated when one actively goes against it. When one tells a lie, a principle has been violated. Even if the lie is justified, lying has the effect of eroding the principle. This is particularly true if an individual (or individuals) is forced again and again into the position of having to break a principle. The principle suffers regardless of the reason or reasons why one must break it.

Risking Death

In Rand's lexicon, the concept of sacrifice is when a person forgoes or gives up something of greater value in favor of something of less value. As a standard of morality, Rand called this altruism. It is demeaning to the decision-maker and to the object of his choice to refer to noble actions that may require effort or struggle as sacrifices (Rand 1961a, 141). To Rand, if one risks his life to save the person he loves, this is not a sacrifice. If a man works two jobs to put himself though college to acquire the knowledge and credentials necessary to have the career he wants, this is not a sacrifice. Out of respect for one's decisions and for that which one values, one should not refer to one's best efforts as sacrifices.

In her discussions, Rand cast alternatives as between one that has value and another that has less value or no value at all (1964a, 15). The fundamental alternative is between life and death. Life has value; it is the ultimate value. Death has no value. Life takes effort. It requires action. And, even though one can make an effort to die, inactivity will eventually (in relatively short order) lead to death. Generally speaking, this is true of other losses (besides death) as well. In business, one can make a profit or one can make a loss. Making a profit takes effort. But doing nothing (negligence) will result in a loss. Similarly, winning a ball game takes effort. One may lose for any number of reasons, but inertia will guarantee it.

Economists assume that the objective of entrepreneurs is to maximize profits. They would not choose to make a loss if another alternative were available. Economists use the term "sacrifice" differently than Rand does. In economic jargon a sacrifice is a cost; it is the highest valued alternative forgone. When resources are used in production, something is sacrificed. Rarely is that which is sacrificed of no value. Most resources have alternative uses and those uses are being forgone when resources are used in a given enterprise. This includes the alternative market value of the entrepreneur's time and effort (as well as any other resources that he may use in the production process). Even though the objective of the entrepreneur is to maximize profits, just because a business suffers a loss does not mean it will shut down. An entrepreneur may suffer losses on a short-term or temporary basis if he expects the long-term net worth to be positive. In business, one cannot look at losses in isolation; one must consider them in the context of what is expected over the long haul.

Generally speaking, one does not *choose* a loss. A loss is a probable outcome that exists for any course of action a person may choose. It is not an alternative in the sense that one would select it among a given set of alternative courses of action. Only in an extreme circumstance would someone choose death as an alternative. For most decisions, a person is choosing among two or more alternatives, and for each alternative, there exists a risk of death associated with it. Most decisions do not seem this dramatic; they do not seem as if they are life or death decisions. However, there is always a probability that one will die in the next instant regardless of the action one takes.

Does this mean one would choose only those alternatives for which there is a low probability of loss? In business, it is not unusual for a decision-maker to choose an alternative that has a high probability of loss if it can also result in a large expected gain. Large expected returns are often risky. Profit is often seen as a return to risk. A given action can have more than one outcome. There is risk involved because the outcome is not certain. For a given action, a person looks at the probabilities of gain and loss, but also must look at the payoffs expected under each of those "states of nature." The expected return would be the sum of the expected payoffs for each state of nature. The decision-maker would compare the expected returns for each alternative. He could select the alternative with the highest expected return for a given level of risk. How he would choose would also depend upon his attitude toward risk. (Risk may be reflected by the standard deviation of the returns.) For some decisions, instead of expected monetary return, he might decide on the basis of his expected utility.

In examining the life insurance purchasing decision, it is notable that individuals might be willing to purchase insurance even if it were not actuarially fair. In determining whether an individual would be interested in purchasing insurance, one must look at the starting position, which is one of disequilibrium. Individuals are "born at risk." A person knows he is certain to die, but faces an uncertainty concerning when he will die. Because of the starting point in the analysis, a person may be willing to move from a position of uncertainty to one of less uncertainty (or certainty if there is no loading). Therefore, even if the person is risk averse, the individual may accept a fair or even an unfavorable bet. That is, he may choose to purchase insurance even though the expected value of that decision is the same as or *even less* than his original position. The fact that a person is "born at risk" has implications not only for insurance purchases, but also for other decisions.

I think this is relevant in examining a decision in which a risk-averse person may risk his life. Even though the expected value of that decision (to risk his life) is less than his original position (the status quo) or the best alternative, he may choose to do it. Humans are born at risk. There is always a probability of dying; it is a risk associated with every decision. Also death is inevitable. This does not mean that a person would under normal circumstances risk his life. Context would be extremely important. However, a person may rationally risk his life under certain circumstances. There are important conceptual differences between purchasing insurance and a person risking his life to achieve some objective. One is that, in life insurance, it is assumed that the probabilities are the same under each decision alternative. It is the difference in the probabilities of the two states that makes the decision to risk one's life appear unattractive relative to the "safer" alternative. Another is that in deciding whether to purchase insurance or not, the expected loss in the uninsured "death" state is zero (if one is insuring his human capital). If one is deciding whether or not to risk his life, the loss if one dies would be, at a minimum, the expected value of human capital. There are other differences as well. The point is, however, that there is a logical rationale for accepting an alternative in which the expected value is less than the status quo, even when that person is risk averse.

In analyzing this question, I use decision theory. This does not mean that I believe people actually make these kinds of calculations when faced with a life/death situation in which a split-second decision is required. This is a framework for analysis that can explain the logic behind such decisions within the context of Randian ethics. I also use it to take into account aspects to decisions that are insufficiently incorporated into Rand's ethics (e.g., the inevitability of death).

I have noted that for many mundane decisions, it is probably unnecessary to take the probability of dying into consideration since the probabilities of dying are the same for all alternatives in any case and would not affect the outcome of the decision (e.g., whether to have chocolate ice cream or vanilla). (This would be particularly true if the expected losses were the same for each alternative.) I have interpreted the BUP to suggest that, in deciding between an ethical alternative and an unethical one, the expected loss could be ignored for the ethical action, since success would be the norm in the long run. Short-run setbacks and failures are so insignificant to that decision that they can be ignored.

It is questionable whether the expected loss should be ignored when choosing among alternatives that are all ethical. Decision-theory would suggest that, in applying the Bayesian criterion to ethically neutral alternatives, one should choose the alternative with the greatest expected value. I would think that, generally, when the decision set is limited to ethical alternatives, it would be preferred to base the choice on the expected value (utility) rather than only on the expected gain, since, even though principles are based on long-run success, for particular decisions, the loss for some alternatives could be quite large. This is possible because, even though the probabilities themselves are based on long-term success, other probabilities can be relevant. They may be other conditions that, if they were to arise, could significantly affect the probabilities associated with a given ethical action. These conditions may not be relevant for most decisions that appear with some regularity in a person's life. However, for some decisions, the possibility of one's own death has more immediate relevance. An example would be if one had to risk his life for another person.

In an emergency ("*and only in an emergency*"), Rand (1964d, 47) said that one *should* help others—unless one's life is in peril (1964d, 48). I take this to mean that one would not help another if the risk of one's death were high. Therefore, one would not ignore the probability of dying if the risk were high. In an emergency situation, the expected value might be irrelevant. The primary gauge of whether to act or not would be the extent to which one would be put in harm's way. Since Rand stated that one *should* help others in an emergency (unless one's life is in danger), I take this to mean that he would not base his action on choosing the alternative with the greater expected return. There may be some other action one could take at that moment that would yield a greater return than helping out; however, during an emergency one would sacrifice a greater value for a lesser value, if necessary (with the caveat of not risking one's life).

Even though one's own life is one's ultimate value in Objectivism, risking one's life for another is not outside the realm of OE. Concerning actions taken on behalf of a loved one, Rand said that, within one's hierarchy of values and within a given context, if a person risks his life for a loved one, it is not a sacrifice, if, by doing so, he gains what is of greatest value to him (1964d, 45). Commenting on Rand's position, Den Uyl and Rasmussen said: "[O]ne *can* say that risking one's life for one's lover is a part of Rand's doctrine in that taking risks for one's highest value would be a normal part of what one would be willing to do to try and keep such a value" (1978, 200). According to Rand, the risk one takes on behalf of another should be based on the degree to which the person is valued relative to one's personal happiness (1964d, 45). Such risk-taking would be an exceptional circumstance and not typical in ordinary life. Therefore, I would conclude that when it comes to risking one's life for a loved one, one would ignore the expected loss (risk of death) for that decision.

Some individuals choose extremely high-risk careers—firefighters, for instance. These individuals risk their lives again and again. It is their job. However, there are times in which an individual will go beyond the bounds that duty requires. A soldier might land on a grenade to save the lives of his companions. Is this rational or not? One could say that the soldier is choosing between alternatives. He could choose to not take any action and risk the lives of the men and his life as well, or he could risk his own life alone. The risk to his own life increases the closer he is to the grenade. Unless the grenade is a dud (and there is some probability of this, even if infinitesimal), the soldier will certainly die if he throws himself on the grenade. This is a life or death situation, yet one could argue that he is not choosing death. If he chooses to take action, he is choosing to save the lives of the men (with, say, a very high probability) that will cost him his life (almost certainly) as a result. Death is not an alternative he chooses, but a highly probable outcome to an action he is taking to achieve an objective.

The military knows that a soldier may not risk his life simply because it is his job. One may very well risk his life to save himself, particularly if an enemy is trying to kill him, but that person may feel no sense of obligation toward those with whom he fights. The military attempts to build a sense of loyalty among its men. This may be done among small groups, and then among increasingly larger units of men. The smallest unit may be no larger than two—a buddy system (cf. Shay 1995, 39). The group may expand to include others. If successful, this can be effective when combined with the actual element of combat. It is not unusual, given conditioning, camaraderie, and environment, for one soldier to look upon another as he would a family member. It is not that rare for family members to risk their lives for each other. This hasn't answered the question. It has merely recast it.

As mentioned, there may be times in which the expected loss would not be considered when making an ethical choice. This may not, on the face of it, appear to be one of those times, since both choices would appear to be ethical. My point is that it would not necessarily be unethical for a soldier to risk (sacrifice) his life in this situation, and whether he did or not would be his judgment call. Either decision could be justified according to my interpretation of the application of the BUP. The context of the decision is important in determining what action to take. A soldier may risk his life in a situation that a civilian may not. The fact that one is compensated as a soldier and not as a civilian would be a secondary consideration but not entirely irrelevant. More important would be what one thinks the job requires, and that one has committed himself to fulfilling those requirements. In a particular situation, what those requirements entail may go beyond the basic job description. The loss if one dies is the whole value of one's life. The value of that cannot be minimized. Nevertheless, it may not be infinite to the individual. The reason it may not be infinite is that death is, eventually, inevitable. This may figure into why, under certain conditions, a person may be willing to risk his life.

There may be many motivations for a man to voluntarily enter combat. He may feel compelled to defend his country, he may be seduced by adventure, he may fear the sting of humiliation if thought not brave enough to enlist, and I am sure there are many more. These plus the possibility that one may be unable to calculate the risks (danger, horror, death) may be factors that influence a man's decision. But the principles for which a war is waged can be a strong motivation. To rephrase Rand, a man may choose to die for a principle if he would find life unbearable without it. He may rather die than live in a world without freedom, for example.

When fighting in a combat situation there may be, in addition to the camaraderie a man feels for those with whom he fights, a principle he is defending. A man may fight harder and undergo extreme hardship if he believes passionately in the principle for which he is fighting (or at least if he believes those for whom he is fighting believe in the principle). Why would a man choose to die (or choose actions that can with a high probability result in his death) for a principle? As mentioned previously, principles have lives. If they are violated, they will eventually no longer exist. If they are not affirmed, they will eventually no longer be upheld. To survive, principles must be sustained. They are sustained through action—through acting on principles and by defending them if threatened.

Moral principles are life-affirming. It seems like a contradiction to say that one would be willing to risk his life for a principle when they are the means by which a person gains or keeps those things necessary for his survival. Humans have a unique capacity to reflect on their past. History, in general, has value. Humans also have a unique capacity to think ahead. The future is important. Humans have a unique capacity to be aware of their own mortality. We care about the future because we care about our lives. We also care about what happens beyond our life spans. This is not inconsistent with OE. To say one's own life is his ultimate value does not mean what happens beyond his own life is unimportant to a person. In Rand's interview with Tom Snyder, she said that her idea about death was taken from a saying of an unknown (to her) Greek philosopher, to the effect that she would not die; it would be the world that would end (Paxton 1998, 184).

This is not true, of course. One's own world will end, but existence will not. One wants his life to have meaning while he lives it, but he also wants it to have meaning beyond his life. But is it rational for that to be important? I believe that at the heart of whether a person is willing to risk his life is the question of identity. Ethics are designed to be those actions that if consistently followed would be life-preserving. If that is the case, then why wouldn't a person abandon his code of values if he were certain to die? Why wouldn't he steal—for instance, rob a bank? I believe the answer to this question is the same as to one that asks why a person would risk his life in defense of a principle (say liberty) if he is certain to die in the process. The reason is that a person has an identity and that identity is based on his values and his virtues. His virtues are embodied in him. They *are* him in large measure. To abandon them would be to forsake the best within himself. Identity is consistency. A person may act on his principles even when he faces death, because by acting consistently he is preserving his identity.

Of course, if a person is dead, he has no identity, or so one might think. But that assumes that legacy has no importance to a man; that he cares nothing about those values and principles that have sustained his life once he dies. When a man dies, his virtues die with him. Why then would a man risk his life to preserve a principle? Man is mortal and his virtues are embodied in him and to that extent his virtues are mortal. One's virtues die with one, but the principles one has lived by need not die. Principles are mortal. They can die if not sustained. To keep them alive, more is required than tacit assent. If principles are not acted upon, they risk death. Humans are also mortal. However, for a human, death is an *inevitability*. For a moral principle, death is merely a *possibility*. If one's principles are at risk, and the only way to keep them alive is by acting upon them, then one may risk his life to preserve them if that is what is required in a particular context. Sometimes that is the action that is forced upon a person. It may not be one he would otherwise choose. By risking his life to preserve a principle, he acts to keep alive the best within himself. Furthermore, that which he values most has the potential for immortality, even though he does not.

Duty

Rand defined duty as: "the moral necessity to perform certain actions for no reason other than obedience to some higher authority, without regard to any personal goal, motive, desire or interest" (1982a, 96). She regarded causality, instead of duty, to be the guiding principle in ethics (1982a, 99). A duty-centered, or deontological, ethics does not regard personal desire as having moral importance (1982a, 97).

Den Uyl and Rasmussen stated that there are two approaches to ethics, generally speaking: one is teleological; the other, deontological. A teleological ethics is end-oriented. It evaluates the morality of an action based on whether the consequences are good or not. A deontological ethics evaluates the action, i.e., whether it is moral or not, independently of the consequences (Den Uyl and Rasmussen 1991, 58). Den Uyl and Rasmussen said: "Rand's grounding of teleology in the very nature of living things is a novel and important addition to the Aristotelian tradition" (1986a, 66). Rand closed the is-ought gap by examining what man is and in that way determined what he ought to do. Man is a living being who relies upon his rationality to sustain his existence. The ontological basis for a code of values is life (Den Uyl and Rasmussen 1986a, 66; 1991, 42). Life is the standard. Man's life thus serves as the "basis for teleological measurement" (Saint-André 1993, 146).

Rand's ethics is egoistic, because it is one's own life that is his ultimate good. It is consequential (teleological) because moral judgments are outcome-based. However, OE are abstract principles based on long-run success. They have the appearance of being rule-based (Merrill 1997, 70). Hospers pointed out that in Rand's ethics "teleology gives way to deontology" (1998, 94). He said that a traditional egoist would violate another's rights if it were in his self-interest. In Rand's theory, rights are nonnegotiable.

This is not only true of rights in Objectivism; it is also true of honesty, integrity, and all other virtues. One would not lie because it may appear to serve his short-term interests. A person does not calculate temporary losses or setbacks in the application of principles, because the person realizes that consistent application of a principle will yield long-term success. There may be unethical courses of action that in a particular case may have a higher short-run expected payoff. The unethical course would be the expedient or pragmatic course and would be recommended by "traditional" egoists. But in Randian ethics, an unethical course would never be among a person's alternative courses of action, except in a case where one's freedom to choose is forcibly curtailed. For instance, if one must choose to tell an immoral authority (Nazi storm trooper) the whereabouts of an innocent person, he is justified in lying. A higher value is served by taking an unethical course. But in this case, one's freedom is constrained by the circumstance. This is why Rand's ethics cannot be regarded strictly as "rule-driven." Context matters (see Thomas 1999b, 19; Kelley 1997, 7).

No Calculation Required

Pure economic man has been depicted as a calculating machine, deliberating over every decision by tallying up the expected costs and benefits and applying the maximizing principle to the alternatives (Freeman 2004, 561–62). Machan has said that a virtue does not require calculation. Virtue is not a matter of deliberation (1998b, 1). Virtues are ingrained character traits. They are cultivated habits that are second nature and require no discipline in their application. They are acquired, yet there is an element of choice in their cultivation (1998b, 4). As traits, they cannot be counted on as exclusive guides to moral conduct. Focus is required, but it, too, according to Machan, can be acquired (1998b, 24). Kelley also regarded a virtue as a trait (1996, 36), but recognized that "virtues cannot operate automatically all the time. There are situations in which the right course of action is not obvious; we must deliberate about how to apply our principles" (1996, 20).

There seems to be some difficulty when virtues are categorized as traits. Traits are automatic, and yet some virtues, such as rationality, are by definition not automatic. They require effort. And rationality, according to Rand, is a primary virtue because every virtue requires rationality. Principles are embodied as virtues. But principles are contextual. The context is important. Therefore, deliberation may be necessary in the application of any principle. Although Machan regarded virtues as traits, which would seem to indicate that little struggle is required in their application (1998b, 3), he called the struggle to overcome drug dependency a moral act (1998b, 80).

Fred Groh interpreted Machan as "challenging the rule-following conception of morality, which implies that one must always deliberate and calculate about what to do" (1998, 15). Actually "rule-following" and "calculating behavior" are two separate approaches to decision-making. Rule-following is the application of a rule without thought. Calculating behavior requires deliberation for every instance. Rule-following is nonthought. Calculating is the "pure economic man" approach, which is not dependent on principles or rules—except the rule that one should "maximize utility." When Machan (1998b) stated that a virtue is a trait, the way I have interpreted this, based on my reading of the BUP, is that the application of a principle does not require one to calculate the costs (or, more accurately, loss, since the cost is the highest valued alternative forgone) and benefits for every decision a person makes. One does not examine the loss on every occasion that one applies a principle, because the expectation of loss is low or minimal (in the long run). In that sense, the application of a principle would be treated as if the decision conformed to a "strict causal chain." It would tend to be "rule-based." However, for decisions in which one must choose among alternatives all of which are ethical or ethically neutral, the expected value (utility) criterion could apply (particularly if the losses significantly vary among alternatives). These decisions would be more akin to the "pure economic man" approach.

The problem with charity is that the giver is not the direct beneficiary of his actions. So, if a person does not look at the costs (loss) to himself, only the benefit to someone else, then this can be sacrificial, since the primary beneficiary is a party other than oneself. This can lead to the altruist's trap. The altruist's trap is that giving is a virtue; one cannot be too virtuous; therefore, one cannot give too much. In the limit, this could be suicidal. Principles should be life-preserving and, if applied consistently, should result in one's long-run success (survival). For instance, productivity is a virtue. A person cannot be too productive, according to Peikoff (1991, 292).

Still one cannot simply produce; one must also consume. Consumption is not a virtue, however. The (Objectivist) "rule" that is relevant in this regard is that one should not consume more than he produces. There must be balance. This also applies to charity. Charity may be considered one among many virtues, all of which must be balanced. One problem is that charity, unlike other "goods," is not subject to the typical self-regulating market mechanisms. In chapter 16, I suggest a guideline that may be useful. In this way, charitable giving does not compete directly with other expenditure decisions. It is separable in that sense. Recall that when insurance purchase was discussed (under certain assumptions), the bequest decision was separable from the consumption decision (see Yaari 1965, 249). The analogy applies to charity and other expenditures.

In general, OE is at odds, it seems to me, with at least two ways of dealing with moral choice. One is strictly an application of rules without regard to context (and one's own interest). The other considers one's interests but from a "value-free" perspective. The latter is often associated with the maximization principle; i.e., maximization of utility. The former requires no deliberation or judgment. The second does require deliberation—the calculation of benefits and costs, and choosing the alternative that maximizes net benefits. The rules approach disregards a person's happiness altogether. The maximization approach is concerned solely with maximizing happiness (utility) without regard to "principles." The maximization approach is concerned with what is expedient or pragmatic. (It could be concerned with long-run happiness or short-run happiness—however, it makes no distinction.)

The "rules approach" to moral choice is a matter of "having to" follow certain dictates, whether a person "wants to" or not. The have-to school of morality leads to a way of thinking in which what is deemed "right" is often regarded as a chore or a drudge (see Kelley 1997, 7). This sometimes gets twisted around into the notion that if some deed is not a struggle, it does not have moral content. This leads to the paradox that if virtue is a trait that is automatic, then virtues have no moral content. George Bernard Shaw said: "Virtue is insufficient temptation" (Peter 1977, 512). W. T. Eldridge is quoted as saying: "Virtue does not consist so much in abstaining from vice, as in not having an affection for it" (ibid.). The latter quote comes closer to the Objectivist view of virtue. Nevertheless, practicing virtue (applying principles) may not be automatic; it may require deliberation.

Chapter Sixteen

Charity

This chapter covers several aspects of charity. Productive work is the central virtue in OE. Rand did not believe that one's beneficiaries should be the purpose of one's work (Berliner 1995, 540). If one's beneficiaries are the stated purpose, a risk is that their wishes will subvert one's own values. This position is consistent with the Objectivist view that other people are not a fundamental part of reality. According to Peikoff, production is the creation of a material object (1991, 293). However, in some professions, the production that takes place is embodied in human beings. I point out that in these professions, if it is not acknowledged that one's work is embodied in others, a person risks undermining his principles within that context.

Rand did not believe that a person should have a career that is primarily supported through almsgiving (Berliner 1995, 544). Those in charitable professions simply redistribute income created by others and are not productive, according to OE ("A Slogan" 1998, 4). This is consistent with the BUP, which states that accidents and loss are incidental metaphysically (Peikoff 1976). Therefore, charity should be marginal (Rand 1964d, 49). Consequently, a person should not devote his life to charity. Furthermore, recipients of charity are nonproducers. If charity were a major ethic, then devoting all or most of one's time and productivity to it would be justified. But if one did this, it would be suicidal to the giver as well as the recipient. It therefore cannot be major. In response to this line of reasoning, I argue that those who work in charitable careers are productive. Even though their incomes are paid by third parties, charity is not alone in being supported by contributions. Public goods and near public goods rely partly or entirely on "contributions."

Charity has some public goods characteristics. It falls outside the market and, therefore, is not subject to the price mechanism.

From the Objectivist perspective, consumption should not exceed production (Rand 1961a, 89; Rand 1961c, 80). This would lead to a net drain on productive capacity. Since charitable contributions may be expended on consumption, it can be a "net drain." If a person gives to charity, he may not regard it as contributing directly to his self-preservation—which is his ultimate value. Even if marginal, it may be seen as a mild sacrifice (Kelley 1996, 7, 10). I would agree that this argument could have some validity if the person has not been a net beneficiary of the productivity of others. However, this generally is not the case. Individuals are beneficiaries of productive work of those who have not been adequately compensated. They have not been compensated because their work falls outside the market, completely or in part, either because their work has public goods characteristics or the product is not or cannot be owned. This includes those who have created inventions and discovered new ideas as well as those who have established and preserved liberty. Although intangible, these are values with which many people are endowed. Like the inheritance of physical capital, I argue, these values should be kept intact or increased by their beneficiaries. Since individuals are net beneficiaries of these endowments, it is not a sacrifice to give to worthy others.

I believe that charity should be elevated to a major virtue; however, because it falls outside of the market mechanism, it is not subject to its self-regulating tendency. The information and incentives of the price mechanism are absent. I offer a heuristic for giving, a fraction that is derived from the BUP, the fundamental alternative, and decision theory under uncertainty (risk). Prospectively, one's expected income for a period is the probability of surviving multiplied by income plus the probability of dying (based on untimely death) times zero (if limited to earnings from human capital). The expectation, according to the BUP, is that one will live if he is rational. Therefore, the expected loss can be ignored. Retrospectively, if one lives, the expected loss (the probability of dying multiplied by income), which was unexpected (marginal and insignificant), is a bonus. As such, that amount can be used for charity. In addition to rendering this decision manageable, it also becomes separable from other spending decisions.

Self-Sufficiency, Independence, and the Purpose of Capitalism

Rand was an advocate of capitalism because it is an economic system founded on noncoercive exchange. Free enterprise is a system that is based on rights—the right to life and the right to property. It is voluntary exchange. Since there is no coercion in a free market system, it follows that individuals would not trade with each other unless there were the expectation of mutual benefits to both or all parties involved in the transaction. In a free market, value is traded for value; at least that is the expectation when parties enter an exchange with one another. This is a defining feature of Rand's trader principle (1967a, 19–20).

Mutual gains from trade can occur even if the identical number of goods *in toto* exists before and after the transaction. If Man A has two bottles of wine but is hungry and Man B has four loaves of bread but nothing to drink, there is an incentive to trade on the part of both men. Even if the total number of goods is the same, the benefits ("utility") after the trade will exceed the benefits that existed before trade. Rand attributed all the gains to trade to those men who have made discoveries or improved technology. She indicated that a person who had been abandoned as an infant on a desert island would not be able to achieve materially what a person would living among others. The "extra" that a person gets when living among others is not the result of the efforts of countless ordinary people, but the inventiveness of the man of ability. She saw the advantages of trade that result from specialization and the division of labor to be attributable to these men (Berliner 1995, 347).

Rand's point was that, in general, value is traded for value in a market system; therefore a person only gets "something extra" from those who do not trade value for value—the "men of mind." Rand is both incorrect and correct. Specialization (for a given state of knowledge and technology) can result in "more" being produced by both parties to a transaction. These benefits are not immediate, due to the production lag. For example, suppose (assuming constant returns) Man A can, on his own, produce either ten loaves of bread or ten bottles of wine. He settles on making five of each. B can produce either forty loaves of bread or ten bottles of wine. He decides to make twenty loaves of bread and five bottles of wine. For A, the cost of a bottle of wine in terms of bread is one loaf. Wine in terms of bread costs four loaves per bottle for B. Man A has a comparative advantage in wine production; B in bread. In total, the two men have twenty-five loaves of bread and ten bottles of wine. If A put all his effort into wine production, and B specialized in bread baking, they could, for example, produce, all told, as much wine but increase their bread production by fifteen loaves. (Adam Smith is credited with discovering the concept of absolute advantage; David Ricardo with comparative advantage (Salvatore 1998, 25).) It is true that "value is traded for value," but more can be produced (something extra) without any improvement in technology, as this example illustrates.

Rand is correct about the benefits derived from men of intellect. I interpret this to mean that, because of limited property rights in ideas, innovators and discoverers do not receive a return commensurate with their contribution. (However, in her discussion, Rand used the word "genius" as equivalent to inventor or innovator

(Berliner 1995, 348). Of course, there are men of superior intelligence—high IQs—who never invent a thing. It is also true that the inventor may not be the innovator.) Rand also believed that the men of ability can and do survive alone. It is because of these men that the less competent survive (Berliner 1995, 332). It is true that innovation is an engine of growth. However, as seen above, for a given state of technology, an exchange economy can produce more via specialization and trade than could be produced if each man were self-sufficient.

At the center of Rand's egoistic ethics is the independent man. The alternative of life and death is the choice between independence and dependence. To Rand, everything that emanates from man's independence has value. Everything that results from man's dependence on others is evil (Rand 1961c, 81). Capitalism is a moral system because it relies upon trade between independent equals. This is a second defining feature of the trader principle. Because of the reliance on independence in ethics, Rand objected to the characterization of capitalism as being a system of interdependence, equating "interdependence" with dependence (Berliner 1995, 95). In economics (Green 1978, 89, 93) and in probability theory, independence has a specific meaning. Independence in the probability sense is when, given two events, the occurrence or nonoccurrence of one has no effect on the probability of the occurrence of the other event (Beals 1972, 78–81). Interdependence is typical with respect to the marginal productivities of inputs. The marginal productivity of one input depends in part on the quantity (and quality) of others in use.

A third aspect of the trader principle is that voluntary exchange results in a general increase in the standard of living. Although the material welfare of the ordinary person is improved immensely with the introduction of free markets, Rand noted that this is not the purpose of capitalism or of the capitalist. The benefits to others are secondary. The primary goal is profit (Rand 1961a, 97). Rand implied that there is no purpose for capitalism (Berliner 1995, 365). Certainly entrepreneurs do not run a business in order to provide jobs for workers; nor do workers take jobs in order to provide owners with profits. But both owners and workers are trying to make a living and the owner's living is what is left over (profits or losses) after all contractual and other obligations have been met. Although it is not the purpose of any economic actor in the economy to provide someone else with income, it is certainly an objective of every economic agent to acquire an income. If capitalism failed miserably at that, it would be difficult to recommend it, since each person's life is his ultimate value and he must sustain it by his own efforts, according to OE. What can be said is that a primary motivation for each economic unit in a free market is to make a living and that capitalism's cornerstone (private property) and incentive structure (the price mechanism) encourage that.

Altruism Redefined

Although a free market system tends to improve the economic condition of men, Rand believed that the producer should not regard the purpose of his work as other people—whether those others are his workers, his customers, or humanity in general. Rand's ethics is one of rational egoism. From Roark's speech in *The Fountainhead*, Rand said that the first duty of a person is to himself. His primary goal should never be placed in others (Berliner 1995, 424). She defined altruists as those who put the welfare of others above themselves. She was opposed to regarding one's beneficiaries as primary in his work. Her harshest criticism was for careers whose beneficiaries could be characterized as suffering. Rand condemned the pursuit of a career in which one's primary motive was to relieve suffering (1995, 539). Although Rand defined altruists as those who trade a greater value for a lesser one, in one letter (to John Hospers) she referred to altruists as those whose satisfaction is derived from serving others' interests. She viewed these people as acting in opposition to man's nature (1995, 537). Altruism is thus redefined from sacrificing oneself to others to being employed in a career in which one's beneficiaries are one's primary concern—particularly, one devoted to the relief of suffering.

Rand distinguished suffering from the struggle, discomfort, physical danger, and/or effort one may have to endure on behalf of one's career. She said her criterion for judging a man is his dedication to his work and the active use of his mind to that end. The extent of the physical threat or discomfort involved in carrying out work is irrelevant. Thus, Rand is only morally opposed to the struggle one may have to endure in an occupation the purpose of which is the relief of suffering. The reason for this opposition appears to be that she believed suffering to be a necessary component of a career that has as its primary purpose the relief of suffering (1995, 539), whereas struggle, pain, and danger were simply incidental to other occupations. However, as I see it, humans are not all endowed with the same emotional equipment. One person's suffering may be another's struggle.

Relief of Suffering

It seems that it is not the relief of suffering per se that is objectionable to Rand, but the relief of the suffering of those whose suffering is a result of their own flaws. She did not view suffering as a value. However, a man's effort to overcome suffering is a virtue. If one person helps another who is suffering, he should do so on the basis of the person's character and because he is suffering unfairly. Rand saw this as a trade of one person's assistance for another's virtue. One should not help another on the basis of suffering per se. Another's misfortune does not represent a claim on a person (Rand 1961a, 180).

Rand wrote that one *should* attempt to relieve suffering that is the result of emergencies, but she drew a distinction between those and other bases for suffering. She said that all human misfortune cannot be categorized as emergencies. Ignorance, sickness, and poverty are not emergencies (1964d, 48). Even though it is permissible to help someone who suffers unjustly (1961a, 180), one should not devote one's life to those who suffer.

Some professions by their nature are involved in the relief of human suffering. In the case of the priest who worked in the leper colony, his motivation, she said, was irrelevant (Berliner 1995, 295). It was the relief of suffering as an occupation that was evil. Yet in a discussion of the career of the social worker, Rand found the motivation to be immoral. If one opts for this occupation, he dedicates his life to those who are ethically and cognitively inferior, with their lack as his primary purpose (Berliner 1995, 546). It would seem that to Rand if person A is in the business of relieving suffering, then A is responding to "lack," and if that lack is a result of an action (or inaction) of a potential beneficiary, B, then A should not intervene between cause and effect. Person B should bear the consequences or reap the rewards of his actions. In a person's work, as in the rest of his life, he should uphold his values and not relinquish them because of another's needs or values. One of the values he should adhere to is the law of causation, a basic principle of justice. Rand said that a person should always avoid severing the tie between cause and effect. For better or worse, a person should have to face the consequences of his conduct (1995, 558).

To follow Rand's logic, if a physician regarded his beneficiaries as the purpose of his work, he would be placing their values above his own. A physician should not sacrifice his values to the patient's wishes. As mentioned above, one principle an Objectivist should value is the law of causality, a basic principle of justice. A physician should apply this principle in treatment of disease. By stating that the purpose of a doctor is the treatment of disease rather than his patient's lives, the doctor is not in danger of compromising his principles or placing his patient's values above his own, according to Rand (1995, 539–40).

If a doctor adheres to his principles—that is, if he, for good or ill, should not prevent a person from experiencing the consequences of his behavior—then it would seem to follow that he should never perform abortions (as a method of birth control). (Whether pregnancy was the intended outcome of the patient's actions or not is totally irrelevant. Pregnancy is a known outcome of those actions. An intoxicated driver knows that one of the consequences may be that he could hit a pedestrian. His intent may be to drive from point A to point B, but since the possibility of endangering the lives of others exists, he would be responsible for his actions. Responsibility is not dismissed because of intent.) Secondly, since the doctor's purpose is to conquer disease, what specific disease would he be conquering by performing an abortion? Since the physician is not concerned about saving the life of (or the welfare of) any particular patient, he should not be concerned with this particular patient's problem. Since he should not put the patient's wishes above his values, then he should be more concerned with his integrity than the person's unwanted pregnancy. Integrity means not suspending one's judgment, and judgment means one should not evade certain principles—such as the law of causality. The doctor should not intervene between cause and effect by terminating the person's pregnancy.

Rand believed it was a person's right to have an abortion. One may agree or disagree with that. There are physicians who do not perform abortions, but I would venture to guess that for those who do not, the reason is because they believe in the right to life and regard an unborn fetus as a human life. I doubt that many do not perform abortions because they are upholding the principle of justice as expressed in the law of causality. But if Rand is right, then justice is the reason physicians should not perform abortions. So a person, according to Rand, may have a right to an abortion, but I would argue, based on her statement concerning the law of causality, that no self-respecting doctor would perform one; not because he believed in the sanctity of life (although that may be one reason), but because it would be a sacrifice of the principle of justice for the wish of a patient.

Similarly a doctor should not treat a patient for lung cancer if the patient has been a smoker or an AIDS patient who contracted the disease as a result of unprotected consensual sexual behavior. To do so would be to sever the tie that links cause to effect and prevent a person from facing the consequences of his acts (1995, 558). One might argue that treating a patient for a disease (or health "issue" in the case of an unwanted pregnancy) that is the direct result of the patient's behavior (when the patient had the capacity and ability to know that this was a highly probable outcome) would be to respond to a flaw.

Contrary to Rand, I think that if the physician's purpose is the treatment of the patient's health, the doctor does not suspend his judgment or sacrifice his values for the sake of the patient. However, he may reprioritize his values within that context in such a way that the patient's health would rank above "justice" (where justice would be, in this case, that a person [patient] should always bear the consequences of his actions). I think a person in any occupation has an obligation to uphold his principles. I do not believe a physician, for instance, should suspend his judgment in the treatment of patients. In a profession that has as its purpose the care of people, there may be the possibility one may be confronted with whether or not to treat someone who has essentially "brought the condition upon himself." That is a judgment call the individual has to make. In many instances, the physician's job is to intervene between cause and effect, however.

I think it is possible to separate motivation from purpose and purpose from integrity (living up to one's principles). If a doctor envisions his job as the healthcare of his patients—rather than conquering disease (1995, 540) or scientific effort (1995, 565)—this does not mean he will yield to their wishes. He would not, for instance, prescribe antidepressants simply because his patient thought it would make the patient happier or relieve his anxiety. In fact, this would not be in the patient's interest. The interests of one's patients (or beneficiaries, in general) need not be a doctor's (or any producer's) only objective, but it should be an objective. If it is not, the doctor (producer) risks compromising his principles.

Embodiment

Peikoff defined productiveness "as the creation of *material* values" (Peikoff 1991, 293). Knowledge (and its discovery) is important, but not for its own sake, according to Peikoff (in the "productivity" sense). It should bring about an existential value—for instance, a new piece of equipment. Unembodied knowledge is not a productive achievement. Knowledge cannot stay in a person's consciousness, but must take some physical form (ibid.).

Humans are regarded by economists as goods used in the production process. (They are distinctly different from other goods, but, because they are substitutable for other goods, they are treated as goods for the purpose of analysis.) When a person takes a computer-training course that is designed to improve his job skills, those training services become embodied in the person as human capital. The good that the trainer "produces" (or improves upon) is the worker. Training does not take place until it is embodied in a person.

When education takes place, it is embodied in the student. In keeping with her contention that a person's beneficiaries should not be the purpose of his work, Rand said that she regarded the purpose of teaching not to be one's students but spreading knowledge and creating a culture (Berliner 1995, 539). If one is an educator and values the preservation of knowledge, i.e., he wants to spread it, then ultimately it must be embodied in someone. Disembodied knowledge is a contradiction in terms. Similarly, doctors do not conquer disembodied diseases. Medical researchers may do so (in test tubes, for instance), but physicians do not. Diseases are embodied in humans and doctors treat patients. The service a doctor performs is embodied in the patient. It may be nothing more than telling a patient to change his diet, i.e., giving the patient information. Still, that information is embodied in the patient. And until that takes place, there is no productivity. (In medicine, the beneficiary may, at times, be a passive recipient. At other times, the beneficiary's involvement is required in the production process. The latter is true of education.)

For those people who work in services whose clients are human beings, production does not take place until the service that is rendered is embodied in a person. So returning to Peikoff's statement that productiveness is "the creation of *material* values" (1991, 293), the material values in the examples just mentioned are people. When Rand said that the purpose of one's work should not be one's beneficiaries, a difficulty arises for those occupations that produce services that must be embodied in people in order for production to take place.

Almsgiving

Rand found it morally reprehensible for a person to choose as full-time work a career that was backed by almsgiving, rather than based on exchange (Berliner 1995, 544). Rand maintained that charity can have value if the recipient is worthy. Misfortune is not the norm, however; it is the marginal in life. Charitable work should not be one's occupation. Additionally, a person cannot make a living at charitable activity since those who receive charity cannot pay for the benefits they receive. And, finally, according to Rand, if one does make a living at it, it must be at the expense of those who donate to charities—the producers (1995, 544–45).

From an economic perspective, the work done on behalf of those who may suffer (from, say, ill health or ignorance) can be regarded as productive and this work can have value. From an ethical perspective, I have stated that I believe people in these occupations can regard their purpose as caring for or informing their beneficiaries. In fact, to do otherwise can, in some cases, so alter one's professional priorities that he may sacrifice a greater value for a lesser within the confines of his profession. Nor is there any reason to believe that the provider would place the beneficiary's values above his own. By stating that one's job is to, say, treat patients, one's patients' values need not be placed above one's own; however, one's own values may be reprioritized within that context. I also do not think that those who regard their purpose as providing a service to beneficiaries who may be suffering (from illness or ignorance) are necessarily being motivated by lack. Loss, lack, or pain may be the exception in life and metaphysically unimportant, as Rand contended (Peikoff 1976), but to ignore it when it is present is to fake reality.

Regardless of the motivation of a person involved in this kind of work, he may still be regarded as creating value in an economic sense. If a service is provided, then the work may be regarded as productive. One explicit measurement of the value of a product is the market value. The market value is not equal to the utility derived by the person receiving a service. Generally speaking, if a person purchases a product, the expectation on his part is that the benefits derived from it will at least equal what he has paid for the product. If the buyer had valued the money more than the product, he wouldn't have purchased it; he would have kept the money.

In some instances, from the perspective of the seller, the value he receives from performing a service actually exceeds the explicit income he receives. The provider of the service may have enjoyed performing the service and this enjoyment is an unpaid benefit. It is "psychic income." If the value of the inputs used in production exceeds the value of the service or good produced, then this is a net loss. Rand would call this a sacrifice. Generally speaking, a firm will not stay in business if it continues to run at a loss; i.e., if costs persistently outstrip receipts. Capitalism is regarded as an efficient economic system because firms that continue to operate at a loss go out of business. Thus, resources that are valued more are not destroyed or otherwise expended in order to produce products that are valued less. If resources were infinitely abundant, destroying them would not be an issue. But resources are scarce. It is their scarcity (relative to the fact that they are demanded) that gives them a market value.

In the case of charity, there is a cost, but there is no price, per se. If a person donates to a charity, it is expected that the value of that contribution exceeds the value of the money spent by the contributor. However, in some cases, those who work for charitable endeavors receive less than they could otherwise. Cost may not reflect value. The following discusses instances in which reliance on the market to determine value would be inadequate.

No Value—Because No Production Takes Place

There are many ways to view the value, or lack of it, placed on work that is paid for by those who are nonrecipients of the benefits. One is that the activity has no value because no production takes place. Rand believed that since the focus of humanitarians is on distributing that which others produce instead of producing themselves, they are parasites (Berliner 1995, 83). If a charitable organization simply collected donations from some people and wrote checks to others, this would qualify as a redistribution of income. The question then would be, is this productive (in a "value-added" sense)? Insurance companies are involved in an activity in which premiums are paid by (all) participants and then awarded to a few (beneficiaries). This may appear to be a redistribution of income, especially for annual term policyholders (and in a real sense it is), but the company performs a service. The same rationale applies to lotteries. Abstracting from the motivation of the payers (of insurance premiums and lottery tickets), and focusing only on the redistributional aspects of the business, one could say that just because there is a redistribution of income does not mean that no service has been rendered.

The motivation of the payer is important since that determines the benefit he expects to receive (which represents the value of the service from the payer's perspective). In the case of lotteries and life insurance, some people who pay will necessarily "lose." But in both cases the expectation of gain must be present at the outset, since this is what makes the purchase worthwhile. In the case of the lottery ticket, the odds do favor the "house"; however, the person may play anyway, either because he does not believe the odds are against him, or because he enjoys the game. In life insurance, one must consider the original position. The question is whether the expected utility with the purchase is greater than the original position. The insurance company and the lottery are providing a service, not just because there are a few people who "win," but because every buyer has an expectation that he is better off with the policy or the ticket than he would be without it.

The second point is that, although some charitable organizations do take donations from some and write checks to others, this is not all they do. Many do provide services—health services, rehabilitation services, child placement, and so on. However, just because a person is productive in the physical sense does not mean that what he produces has value. A person may be very productive in that he can turn out a large quantity of a thing (Edsels), but it may not be able to generate sufficient revenue to cover the cost of production. The market is fairly efficient at letting producers know whether their output has enough market value to make continued production worthwhile. Since the market price of charitable services is zero, how is value—it if exists—assessed?

Value Is Zero Because Recipients Cannot Pay

From the perspective of the producer, there is no difference in the service that he provides, irrespective of who pays for it. If a doctor sets the broken arm of a child who injured it while climbing a tree or sets the broken arm of a child who is a victim of child abuse, there is no difference in the service provided if the former is paid by the child's father and the latter is paid for by a charitable organization. From the doctor's point of view, he is performing the same service. Would the latter not be a productive service because it is paid for by a third party instead of the child's father? The abused child would receive the medical care free of charge, but can it be said that no production has taken place? From the perspective of economists, it has.

The lack of an explicit market price paid by the abused child (or his parent) does not negate the fact that the doctor provided and the child received a service. The value of the service would seem to be the same from the perspective of the two children. (One is not supposed to make interpersonal utility comparisons. There is no reason to believe that the service is different. However, one cannot know how one person evaluates a good or service relative to another person.) But what Rand is implying in the above reference to "almsgiving" is that, if the consumer (i.e., the person actually receiving the service—the abused child in this example) pays nothing, production has not taken place. Regardless of the service provided by the doctor, unless the consumer (recipient of the service) pays for that service, nothing has been produced.

To a large extent this is the way economists view value. The consumer determines (assigns) the value to the good. But, generally speaking, this is not the way in which Rand viewed productivity. To her, the producer gauges the value of his work. Of course, the producer does create the product, but without demand there is no value. Demand is not just desire or need; it is the ability to pay. A product could (potentially) bring utility or satisfaction to a consumer, but without the money to back it up, there is no demand. Rand regarded trade as taking place between producers, because it is the producer who has the income necessary to buy a product (1961c, 80). Of course, someone is paying for the service in this example. If no one paid, the abused child would not receive care, no matter how much he might require it. Those who pay are third parties to the transaction; i.e., they are not direct beneficiaries of the service provided. Presumably, they are willing to pay because they see some value in the doctor providing this service to patients who cannot pay. And presumably they receive some benefit or they would not part with their money. They would spend it on something they valued more. If they benefit from the transaction as much as the child, then the (total) utility would be greater than if the beneficiary simply paid for the service himself, assuming he could.

Economists argue that utilities cannot be added across individuals. If such summations were permitted, one could see that the conclusion that would be drawn would be a bit perplexing. If one person receives more benefit from giving to charity than he would if he kept the money (or spent it on something else), and the person who receives the charitable service obtains as much benefit as one who pays for the service himself, then one could conclude (if benefits were additive) that the charitable service resulted in greater benefits than a noncharity transaction. Since there is no way to measure utility or add utilities, one could not draw this conclusion. (However, adding across individual demand curves is permitted. This is the way in which market demand is determined. In the charity case, it might be thought that there could be a summation across two demand curves for the service, since both the contributor and the beneficiary receive utility. However, demand is based not only on utility but also the ability to pay, so only the contributor's demand would be relevant.)

No Value—Resources Used Exceed Value Created

Another reason that charitable contributions may be perceived as lacking value has already been alluded to, and that is that the value of the goods and services used in production exceed the value of the output produced. This is a loss—a sacrifice in Rand's terminology. A higher value is sacrificed for a lower value. Rand's concern seems to have been if charity is considered a major virtue rather than a minor virtue, then it will lead to altruism, which she defined as the sacrifice of a higher value for a lower one or for something that has no value.

Rand's main point about charity is that the recipient does not pay for the good or service received. Recall that principles result in long-term success. If one produces and does not consume more than he produces, then a person will be able to sustain his life. This is necessary for man's survival. It is necessary for *a* man's survival. If a man consumes more than he produces as a long-run strategy, this would not result in success. As a principle this would be suicidal. It would be parasitic if one person relied on someone else to make up the balance with that other person's own productive return. As a general strategy, it would not be life sustaining.

The problem with charity is that those who live on charitable contributions consume more than they produce. (This point was made by Isabel Paterson in her book *The God of the Machine*. Charity must come from the "surplus" created by others (1968, 251–63).) From the perspective of the giver, it could be argued that for charity to be a major virtue, it would have to be an activity that would be admirable to practice on a significant scale. If it were as important as productivity in one's hierarchy of values, then contributions to charity could justifiably consume all of a person's income. For charity to be a major principle governing behavior, every person would be justified in devoting as much time to charity as he would to production or more so, and as much of his income on charity as possible. If charity were on par with productivity or above it, then one would necessarily be in a position of sacrificing a greater value for a lesser value. On balance, charitable giving on this scale would result in a loss. That is why it must be marginal in one's life. If a little charity is good, but more is better, and all is best, then the limit of giving is all of one's income and all of one's life.

Of course, if suffering and pain are not the norm in life, then those who are in need of charity should be few and therefore charity should consume only a marginal part of one's time and/or income. I do not believe, as Rand did, that some people should not devote their lives to charitable works, however. I think specialization works in the nonprofit sector. Some people have better talents for that line of work. They may be better fundraisers; they may be more nurturing by nature or more community-spirited than others.

Goods That Are Undervalued by the Market

Goods that are not owned will have no market price. A consumer good that is not owned will tend to be consumed until its marginal utility (MU) is zero (if marginal utility theory applies). An input, if unowned, will be used until its marginal product (MP) is zero. In either case, it cannot be concluded that neither has value. When the MU of a good is zero, the total utility is maximized. When an input's MP is zero, output will be maximum (under the short-run theory of the firm). Generally speaking, because workers own themselves, they command a positive wage and therefore will not be employed in the production process until their MP is zero.

An exception to this is when the work is done by volunteers. Since they receive no salary, they may be employed until their MP is zero (or even negative)

(Gapinski 1980, 584). The value of the product will be positive. Volunteer work is quite common in charitable organizations. Many charities are not-for-profit. Even though they are not-for-profit, the "profit-maximizing" solution would recommend using free inputs until their MPs are zero. (If the marginal cost of an input is zero, then the profit maximizing and the revenue maximizing solutions would be the same. That is, to maximize profits, marginal revenue is equated to marginal cost, which in this case would be zero, and therefore, total revenue would be maximized.) The result is seemingly paradoxical. The work has value (revenue is maximum), but, because the worker receives no pay, the marginal "value" of his contribution is zero.

Some "goods" by their nature cannot be owned. Children cannot be owned by their parents. Discoverers of new knowledge cannot own those ideas. (In some cases, such as patents and copyrights, property rights are possible, but are limited in duration by law.) In these cases, value or full value cannot be assigned to the work, since it cannot command a market price. There are other goods that are not provided by the market or not supplied in sufficient number because they are public goods or have public goods characteristics. They may have no market value (price) because there is no market per se. Economists argue that national defense is a public good and would not be provided sufficiently if left to the private sector. The incentive structure is such that the inclination for each person is to conceal his preferences, so national defense would not be provided (in sufficient quantity) privately. There is no market mechanism at work to provide the incentives or rewards to encourage production.

The military and police force (as well as many who work in the criminal justice system) rely on "contributions" for their support (usually by way of taxes rather than voluntary donations, although Rand would argue that only the latter is morally proper). Why are they not singled out as morally reprehensible by Rand, since soldiers, policemen, etc. choose, as full-time occupations, activities that are paid for by contributions? (Berliner 1995, 544) The argument that government should provide protective services is that private citizens are prohibited from seeking retaliation on their own behalf. They are legitimate functions of government because they are delegated to government by citizens.

Other goods, including public goods, are not functions of government, since their provision is not prohibited and since they are not rights. Therefore, it is up to the private sector to provide public goods, even though the incentive structure works against their provision. If they are provided, public goods or near public goods typically rely, to some extent, on donations ("almsgiving"). Rand objected to activities that are supported by almsgiving rather than by exchange (ibid.). The discovery of new knowledge is not supported by trading. Neither is parenting. The latter is not supported at all, except of course by the parent. Rand said that social work had a special status since it was noncommercial and relied on charitable contributions. Parenthood is also noncommercial and has a very special social status because it relies on no monetary support whatsoever.

Parenting has many characteristics that are often associated with charity. Of course, a big difference is that the support given by parents to children is provided by right. It is an obligation of parents to children. What parents provide children is not charity. But the characteristics of being noncommercial, of being outside the market, of involving unilateral monetary support, of being productive but not involving exchange between independent traders, are all quite similar.

Charity—The Price Mechanism Failure

There are features that charities share with goods that either cannot be owned or are public goods, the main one being that the market mechanism does not work for charitable contributions. There are, of course, those who would use charitable services if available. There are those who would be willing to provide these services if someone were willing to pay, and there are those who may be willing to pay, but there is nothing equivalent to a price-signaling mechanism to inform those people who would be willing to pay: who the people are who require these services, where the people are who require these services, and how much of these services are required. Nor is there a mechanism to let people know when or where there is "too much" charity.

I offer as a recent notable example the aftermath of September 11. There was an outpouring of generosity from all over the United States. Many people gave and were willing to give. Charitable organizations were flooded with phone calls with offers to give blood, money, and time. One of the reasons that people were so responsive was because they were aware of the tragedy. It was widely covered by the media, and when people are made aware of tragedies of this and even lesser magnitude, they tend to be responsive. This is what the price mechanism does in the private sector: it provides people with information. It tells producers when a product is making a profit or a loss. It lets customers know when a product is getting scarcer or more abundant. A single data point sums up considerable information; information that can lead to very good (theoretically optimal) decisions. There is no comparable mechanism in charitable activities. People must rely on the media and word of mouth, and must seek out information on their own.

The other thing that happened after September 11 was what could be called a glut of giving. Not that the recipients were not entitled to receive the outpouring of gifts and money, but the givers had no way of knowing how much had been given, how much recipients would receive, or who would be receiving it. Some charitable organizations were overwhelmed and understaffed to handle the response. There were claims by the media, some well founded, that charities were "dragging their feet." This is another thing the market mechanism adjusts to; i.e., it responds to an overabundance. The price system not only provides information concisely, it does so automatically, and it provides the incentive to act on that information. The market tends to be self-regulating. There may be short-run gluts or shortages, but they tend to be eliminated relatively quickly in most cases. There is no comparable mechanism for charities. Again, during the aftermath of September 11, people relied on the media to let them know that there were bottlenecks and inefficiencies and where they were.

Unilateral Transfers—Net Beneficiaries

There are individuals who are under- or uncompensated for what they produce. It could be because of market/price mechanism failure due to lack of property rights and/or the public good nature of the work. In any event, they provide benefits to others without being fully compensated. Those who benefit are unilateral recipients. I argue that they are net beneficiaries of "inherited wealth." Wealth in this context may be of a material form or of an intangible nature. Included are the inheritance of (physical and human) capital, of discoveries and inventions, and of freedom.

Trader Principle and Inherited Physical Wealth

The trader principle, according to Rand, "is the principle of *justice*" (1964a, 31). A rational man does not want the unearned; a trader earns what he receives and neither gives nor receives the undeserved (ibid.). Rand said an honest man realizes that his consumption cannot exceed that which he has earned by producing (1961a, 89). If a person should only consume that which he earns by his own efforts, where does that leave inherited wealth? A person who inherits wealth has not earned it. Yet, he is entitled to it by the right of the original producer, who can dispose of his earnings as he so chooses. According to Nathaniel Branden, "an heir is worthy of his money, that is, if he uses it productively, he brings more wealth into existence" (1963, 23). To bring more wealth into existence means that one would keep the initial value of wealth intact plus add to it. So by the end of one's life, one would leave behind an amount of wealth equivalent to the initial value plus some added amount. If one were not worthy of it, he would squander it—that is, his consumption over his lifetime would exceed the earnings he produced by his own effort. He would draw down or trench on his (physical capital) inheritance.

Inheritance—Ideas

There may be many people who do not inherit physical wealth from others, but most people inherit human capital investment from others, usually from their parents or guardians. And all of us inherit the ideas of those who have come before us. Rand said that everyone inherits the products of the ideas of others. We have inherited the wheel, for instance, and from that is made a cart, and from that a car, and so on (1961c, 79). According to my interpretation, the reason that ideas and the products of ideas are endowments is because we do not pay the full value due to less than full property rights. Because copyrights and patents are limited in time, ownership in ideas that take physical form is limited. Once something is not owned, it is free; i.e., it commands a zero price. Yet, it has a value. Since copyrights and patents are limited in time, the owners (originators) cannot receive the full return on their creations.

Since discoveries of new ideas cannot be patented (1967i, 130), and some inventions are not practical to patent (Friedman 1962, 127), these are provided free of charge at the outset. These discoverers and inventors receive no monetary return (for the discovery or invention itself), and others benefit without paying for that value. In other words, people receive a benefit without paying for it. This violates the trader principle, since value is not traded for value. A debt is owed to the beneficiaries in the same way a debt is incurred when one buys a product for which one must pay. However, this debt is not payable. It is a nonspecific debt in the sense that we cannot pay the producers for the value they have bestowed. Rand said the single major debt that is owed others is for the accumulated knowledge of our predecessors and to those among us with greater intelligence. The benefit is intangible, but the result of it takes physical form (Berliner 1995, 347).

If this is an inheritance, one is in the same position as one who has consumed more than he produced, or one who inherits property and has not "earned" it. How does one "earn" the inherited ideas of all those from whom one has benefited? Rand did not say. She did address the benefit side of the equation, however. To profit from the accumulated knowledge that others have bestowed, a person can add to it if he is of superior ability. If one is of lesser ability, one gets an "extra" (ibid.), according to Rand; but the fact is that we all get a bonus from the discoverers and originators who preceded us. The question is, how do we "earn" it or "repay" it? Since it is a nonspecific debt, there is no one we are required to pay in the sense that anyone has the "right" to collect it from us. This is a matter of our own "honesty" in the sense that, if one is honest, he does not want to accept an unearned benefit. He recognizes that he should not consume more than he produces. One's response to the debt would be rooted in the trader principle, the principle of justice. If one is a trader, he trades value for value. What value can one trade (and to whom) to match this bonus one inherits?

If a person simply produces, this is not sufficient, since if he does, he receives the value of the benefit derived from his productivity through exchange. Value is traded for value. The exception is if one also discovers a new idea or invents some new good or process. If one does, then he may never be repaid the value of his contribution to others. (And this is a "justification" of why such endeavors may not be "irrational" from a productivity perspective.)

On balance, most people—regardless of their level of creativity—do not create anything to match the inheritance of ideas with which they are endowed. So, in a sense, no contribution—however original and important—could "repay" that debt. The issue here is that one has derived a benefit for which he has not paid. One has consumed without producing something of equal value. It would seem to follow that to "pay back," a beneficiary would produce more than he consumes, that is, save or, equivalently, invest. But the return to saving (investing) goes to the investor. He contributes to productive capacity and reaps the return in terms of interest or dividends. If he consumes all that he receives in income from all sources (over the course of his lifetime), he still has received an unearned benefit.

To create something "extra," this would mean having some unconsumed income. But for whose benefit? To simply blindly give the savings to someone else would not be justified. In another context entirely, Rand gave an idea of how one might contribute to others. (I must emphasize that this was not her recommendation of how to pay back this debt. Although she recognized it as a debt, she did not, and would not have, suggested that anyone is under an obligation of any sort to pay it back. This is my interpretation of her trader principle, not hers.) Rand said that if one's objective were the relief of suffering, he would not start with the disadvantaged and the mentally inferior, but those with superior intellectual ability who risk dying psychologically of confusion and isolation (1995, 546).

Rand was referring to charitable works (of social workers). I am applying the same concept to the debt one owes to those creators who have preceded us. One response to that debt might be to produce more than one consumes and use some of that to benefit those who have the potential to discover and to create. This could be through contributing to scholarship programs or to basic research. The rationale for funding basic research is that the success of the latter is uncertain and the benefits when they do occur often do not accrue to the originator or discoverer. (It is a public good.) Scholarships and endowments can preserve and expand knowledge and the arts. I do not think that they should be limited to the gifted, however.

Liberty

For those who live in free countries, each person is born with a great inheritance of freedom. Isabel Paterson said:

> Whoever is fortunate enough to be an American citizen came into the greatest inheritance man has ever enjoyed. He has had the benefit of every heroic and

> intellectual effort men have made for many thousands of years, realized at last. (1968, 306)

It is claimed that freedom is a person's birthright. To say one inherits freedom makes it sound as if freedom is a gift rather than a right. If freedom is a gift, it can be taken away. Rand said that individualism means inalienable rights cannot be denied (Berliner 1995, 366). One could counter that one has the right to property, but no one is entitled to have property unless he has purchased it. Yet how would a person "purchase" freedom? Whom would he pay, and who would withhold it if he refused to pay? If one had to pay, that would give one person power over another, which is the antithesis of freedom.

To say that one has inherited freedom does not mean anyone can take that away from a person, anymore than if one inherited property someone could take that property away from the heir. The right one has to his inheritance is grounded on the rights of the producer. So if one inherits freedom, he has a right to it, as he would any other inheritance, and it is derived from the producer of it. But there is no "producer" of freedom, per se. Still, there are those who discovered freedom, and those who invented (in the case of the United States) the Constitution—the Founding Fathers, specifically. They did not "produce" freedom any more than Newton or Leibnitz "produced" calculus. Nevertheless, we owe them a debt for discovering freedom and inventing the Constitution, since they "produced" something that subsequent generations benefited from, and those who were the discoverers and inventors did not receive the full measure of the value that they bestowed on others.

If the Founding Fathers are discoverers and inventors, why should liberty be singled out as a separate category from other discoveries and inventions that we have inherited? One reason is that without freedom, there may be a body of knowledge out there that we could inherit, but it would be useless since we could not act on that knowledge. Ideas, discoveries, and inventions have immense value when one is free, when one may use the ideas, act on them, add to them, etc. If one is not free, it is like being at a banquet and not being permitted to eat. It has no value.

The other reason liberty is singled out as a separate category of inheritance is because a person in a free country is endowed with freedom, not only because of the great minds that discovered freedom and invented (in the United States) the Constitution, but because we are also indebted to the men and women who fought for freedom, defended and preserved it. Not all of these people were of superior intelligence. They had to be intelligent enough to understand the principle for which they were fighting, but they did not have to have the same degree of intelligence that Jefferson or Madison had. The virtue that was required was courage, physical courage in particular. One could say it required courage plus rationality, but without rationality all that remains is foolhardiness. To be a virtue in every sense, courage must be combined with rationality; rationality is required for every virtue. That is why reason is a primary value. This does not mean that the Founding Fathers did not have physical courage as well. Even those who were not in combat faced the threat of being convicted of treason and death by hanging for their deeds. One could say that physical courage is nothing more than an outward manifestation of mental courage. This is true. But one cannot minimize or dismiss the fact that when it comes to the protection of freedom, it is the physical manifestation of courage that is required.

Rand regarded courage as a practical necessity. Both she and Peikoff identified it with integrity (Rand 1961a, 128–29; Peikoff 1991, 261–62). Courage is separate from integrity, however. Integrity requires courage, but so do all virtues. Maya Angelou said that courage is the most important virtue because without it one can practice none of the others. I agree that courage is as important as rationality. Both are needed to practice all other virtues. That is why I consider courage a primary virtue.

The people who were brave enough to face the risk of death, to sustain injuries, and to pay with their lives to establish, defend, and preserve freedom bestowed upon their contemporaries and subsequent generations far more than they received in pay. That they may have acted on a purely selfish motive, for their own behalf, because they believed in the principle for which they fought and/or died, does not take away from their contribution to others anymore than Thomas Edison's or Henry Ford's contributions should be dismissed because their primary goal was not their beneficiaries.

Rand said that the creative and inventive men are humanity's true benefactors; that there has never been a humanitarian who has provided the benefits to mankind that Edison or Ford did (Berliner 1995, 82). I would agree that these men are important benefactors. I do not agree that the creative or inventive men are the only benefactors. Without the freedom to discover and invent, to patent and copyright, to own, produce, and sell, it would be impossible for the creative, productive man to benefit anyone, least of all himself. Rand said that the benefit that men of mind have bestowed on others is not material but it takes material form (1995, 347). This describes the "gift" of liberty. It is a right, but it is not inevitable. Like every value, it must be "produced." Like other values, virtues are needed to acquire and maintain freedom. To establish freedom, courage is required. To maintain it, vigilance is needed. These are not the only virtues, but they are important ones.

Also like every value, liberty is subject to its own mortality. For a value to stay alive, it must be preserved. But one does not preserve a principle or sustain liberty by simply being. One does not uphold a principle by tacitly agreeing with it. A principle or value is sustained through action. Simply because liberty is a right, and one is free, this does not mean one is free to take it for granted. Freedom is not attained once and for all.

One aspect of sustaining freedom is recognizing those who have contributed to its establishment, protection, and preservation. But is that all that is required? Branden said of inheritance that one earned it by bringing "more wealth into existence" (1963, 23). I interpret this to mean (in light of the trader principle) that one should leave the value of the wealth intact (at a minimum; otherwise one is trenching on capital) and, to the extent one can, add to its value. How does an inheritance of freedom compare with the inheritance of physical wealth?

Rand said that rights do not impose obligations. She said, referring specifically to the military draft, that the government—whose obligation it is to protect rights—cannot claim a person's life in exchange for providing protection. One's only obligation is to respect the rights of other people (1967h, 227). Rand used "obligation" to mean that one is legally obligated to do something. If one is obligated that means that the government has a right to force you to do something. It is the sense of the word that one would use if one purchased a product and was obligated to pay for it. The government can enforce the obligation to pay for a product that is exchanged because its function is the protection of rights. Used in that sense, I agree with her statement that one's obligation is to respect others' rights. If one values liberty, however, I would say one has a moral obligation to protect and preserve it in the same way that if one values one's life one is morally obligated to sustain it by one's own efforts. I use obligation in the same way Rand used "must" (1982a, 99). It is not an enforceable obligation.

Many have risked their lives and many have lost their lives establishing, defending, and preserving one's freedom. In my view, these benefactors have offered a benefit for which they were not fully compensated. It is unearned, but not undeserved. Everyone deserves freedom. It is one's birthright, but it is not costless. No value is. All values by definition require actions to acquire and maintain them. Those actions are virtues. As Rand said: "[L]ife is a value to be bought" (1961a, 127–28).

Must a beneficiary undertake any actions to preserve freedom? Yes—if he values it. Who "imposes" that obligation? A person imposes it on himself. And to whom is the debt owed? Ultimately, to oneself. Like any other inheritance, one should (if one values it) keep it intact and even, if possible, improve upon or add to it. This does not simply mean not violating the principle. A principle may perish because it is violated (especially if its violation is wide-scale, but every violation is a little death if someone does not act to correct it). A principle can also die from neglect in that there is always someone, whether through ignorance or intent, who is trying to destroy it. Preserving a principle means active support. A person does not necessarily have to enlist in the military if one's country is at war. I do not think that one owes his life for freedom, whether that means risking his life for it or spending most of his time preserving it in other ways. One may choose to risk his life under certain circumstances, but as a general way of conducting one's life, I do not think it is necessary or desirable.

As to what one might do to preserve freedom, that is up to the individual; but I will mention a few possibilities that may not seem so obvious. First, when others have established, defended, and protected freedom, they did so for all people. And, of course, freedom is indivisible. Rand said: "Since man has inalienable individual rights, this means that the same rights are held, individually, by every man, by all men, at all times" (n.d., 6). If this is true, why do we have borders? There are good reasons why we have borders, which I will not go into here. What is true is that there are other people in other countries who are not free. This does not mean free people are under an obligation to free everyone in every nonfree country. That would be self-sacrificial. However, there are measures individuals may take on behalf of other nonfree people that are not self-sacrificial. Although there may be many actions one may undertake, at a minimum one should not support unfree governments in word or deed. (This does not mean that a free government would never be in position of dealing with a nonfree country, but if they must, it means that citizens and governments that are free should always acknowledge that the country is not free. They should not evade reality.)

In my earlier discussion of rights, I mentioned that there are some individuals who do not have full property rights in themselves within free countries. These include children. Generally speaking, this does not create a problem. Parents have certain rights and responsibilities with respect to their children, and since parents usually have their children's best interest in mind, the fact that children have limited rights is not an issue. An exception was the case of Joshua DeShaney, who was repeatedly beaten and eventually (at age four) abused to the point of suffering severe and irreparable brain damage by his father. His (divorced) father had legal custody, and, although both his second wife and a doctor arranged for the boy to be placed in the temporary safety of a hospital, the local social services returned the boy to the custody of his father. His mother sued social services but the Supreme Court claimed that the boy "had suffered no constitutional wrong" (Holmes and Sunstein 1999, 88).

The actions of the father, social services, and the Supreme Court are all disturbing. It is difficult to figure what an outsider (such as the doctor mentioned above) could have done to prevent this from happening to the child, given the ineptitude of social services. The Supreme Court decision was unfortunate. The reason for bringing up this incident is that since children do not fully own themselves, and since parents have certain rights and obligations on their behalf, when parents abuse or relinquish those rights, children become at risk.

The problem is that if a child does not have full property rights in himself and if his parents, who have certain rights and obligations, abuse those rights and the rights of the child, what should the government do in response? If it is the government's responsibility to protect the (negative) rights of individuals, then the child's right not to be physically assaulted should be upheld. But, of course, this should involve removing the child from the custody of the parent (because the parent should be in jail). That, however, leaves the child without guardianship. Does the child have any positive rights or are rights only negative? If the state is charged with the expense of incarcerating the parent, why should a child who has committed no crime not be afforded some positive protection by the government?

According to OE, no one should be forced to care for a child whose parents cannot or will not care for him. Contrary to the Objectivist position and that of most libertarians and classical liberals, I have argued that at a minimum the government should be responsible for placement of the child in a safe home where he could get adequate care, as well as provide subsequent oversight. A similar case was made for those with limited capacity who are in similar circumstances. The care itself would rely primarily on charitable contributions.

These are areas in which the rights of some have "fallen through the cracks," so to speak. The reason I bring these cases up is that those who have inherited freedom have a responsibility to preserve it. Those who defended freedom did so for all people. Freedom is indivisible. However, there will always be a few whose rights are limited because of their own limited rationality and ability to care for themselves. (Their rights are limited by nature, not by the nature of their actions, as would be true of criminals whose rights have been abridged.) I believe it is incumbent on those who have rights and are capable of exercising those rights to be cognizant of those whose rights are limited in these kinds of ways. This is an area where a person can pay back those who have contributed to his inheritance of freedom, by helping those whose rights are limited by the nature of their capacities—i.e., by helping to right injustices done to them.

A third area is one in which rights cannot be assigned, but protection may be required, and that is protection of animals when they are mistreated. Again, there are laws on the books in many states and localities concerning cruelty to animals. But if people are found to be cruel to animals, what happens to the animals? This may not be an area of rights, per se, although, if there are laws against cruelty to animals, and they are enforceable, then the animals have some limited legal rights. The problem is that (as when children are abused) someone must recognize that cruelty, abuse, or neglect is taking place and report it. After the fact, there needs to be some method of dealing with the abused animal. This is an area in which charity is legitimate, since animals themselves are innocent (by innocent I do not mean virtuous) and cannot "look after themselves."

The point is that most individuals have received benefits for which they have not paid—unilateral transfers—and based on this, they should make unilateral transfers to others. In the cases discussed here, issues of rights were involved, but the unilateral transfers need not be limited to rights-related issues. That is up to the individual to determine.

Sunk Benefits

David Ross's view is that "virtues aim at future values" ("What Is Justice" 2000, 23). In economics parlance, sunk costs are those that cannot be recouped. Insofar as future decisions are concerned, sunk costs should be ignored. It matters not how much money you have invested in a venture; if the value of it is now zero, what has been spent should have no bearing now on what one decides to do in the future—it's sunk. I have described several examples of unilateral benefits, i.e., benefits that have been received by individuals for which they have made no payment. In fact, payment cannot be rendered because the debt is nonspecific in nature, is intangible, and is owed to those who, in many if not most cases, are no longer alive. These could be described as "sunk benefits." If so, then it could be argued that, like sunk costs, they should be ignored insofar as making future (ethical) decisions is concerned.

However, there is a distinction between sunk costs and debts. For example, person Y may have purchased a piece of property from Mr. X to develop an upscale resort, and then Z purchases the property adjacent to Y for a toxic waste disposal dump. Person Y's property now, let's assume, has no value whatsoever. The expenditure is sunk. Person Y does not count how much he has spent on the property in making future decisions about that property. However, this does not free him from his obligation of paying Mr. X for the property. He still owes that debt. By analogy, if the so-called "sunk benefits" were regarded as a "debt," they would not necessarily be disregarded when making future decisions.

Life, liberty, and property may be birthrights, but we still must pay for defense and police protection. Those are ongoing requirements that we pay to protect our own lives and property in the present. But that does not reduce the magnitude of the benefit we derive from those who have established and preserved freedom in the past. It is important that human beings regard their lives as a whole, not as fragmented experiences without unity. If the future is important, the past must be as well. To always live forward is not life-affirming, because a life is a whole, not disassembled moments. The existentialist perspective on time was given by William Barrett as: "Yesterday, which is *no* longer, and tomorrow, which is *not* yet, belong to the negative realm of nonbeing" (1973, 87). Not even the present is real. "No matter how far we go in shortening the interval we find always a finite duration in which past-present-future are joined together" (ibid.).

Marcus Aurelius shared a somewhat similar sentiment: "[A] man cannot lose either the past or the future: for what a man has not, how can any one take this from him?" (*Marcus Aurelius* 1982, 258) In a different context, Tara Smith said (echoing Rand): "A person cannot lose what he never had in the first place" (2000, 180). If applied to time, and if Aurelius was correct when he said, "[I]t is true that this [moment] is the only thing which [a man] has" (ibid.), then the future does not exist. If the future does not exist, and it does not except in one's mind, then no one can take it away from you. The idea of taking away from a person something that does not now exist nor has ever existed would seem absurd if the future does not exist. However, if a person is robbed of his life, it is his future that is stolen. And if the future exists, which has never been, then surely the past does, which indeed has been.

Although Rand's philosophy is optimistic in the sense that the expectation (so long as one is rational) is for success, it is not an entirely forward-looking philosophy. The penal code, she believed, should be based on retribution (Berliner 1995, 559). This is consistent (as I have discussed earlier) with the trader principle. But retribution is very specific. It applies to the punishment of a specific individual in payment for his specific criminal actions. It is not to be sought against family members of the accused (his tribe, clan, etc.). In the first instance, I have argued that retribution is a debt that is owed to the victim of the crime. Secondarily, a principle has been violated by the accused, and if principles are not upheld, they risk dying. So punishment of the violator of the principle is also necessary if the principle is to remain viable.

There are also debts owed for benefits derived from others. Obligations are backward-looking, in that the benefits received (which were received in the past) must be paid for in the future. This is the nature of contractual obligations. Contracts are a means of tying past and future in business transactions. They form the basis for most of the market exchanges that take place in a capitalist economy (Rand 1967a, 19). But these debts, like retribution, are specific in nature. The debts to which I am referring above (based on my concept of inheritance) are general in nature and not a result of contract.

To Objectivists, one should accept no unchosen debt (Branden 1962, 55). Branden said this with regard to one's parents. A debt owed because of the discoveries, inventions, and bravery in defense of liberty is even more nonspecific than that to one's parents. Since it is wrong to impose general retaliation, why should it be right to say there are nonspecific debts? To say that we are endowed with this inheritance and that, in turn (based on reasoning from Rand's trader principle and what Branden said about earning one's inheritance), we owe a "debt to the dead" may sound as if that is a mortgage on one's soul. It hints of "original sin."

The nature of the values to which I am referring is general. Liberty is general. So is the accumulated knowledge of our predecessors (Berliner 1995, 347). Values can be stated in abstract terms. As abstractions they are "spiritual" in nature. But they are no less real than material values. Like material values, they require actions (virtues) to acquire and maintain them. If liberty is a value, a person will, in the way he sees fit, preserve that value and extend it if he can. If knowledge is a value, he will take actions that he finds appropriate to preserve and advance it. If his life is a value, he will be productive so as to sustain it. The specific form that productivity takes is up to the individual. The debt to which I refer, if one chooses to honor it, is nonspecific. How a person chooses to maintain it is optional. There are many ways. It is no different in this respect from productivity. If one chooses to sustain his life, he must be productive. How he chooses to do that may be in large measure optional. One might regard the debts I mention as burdens. If they are, then all values are burdens. Productivity is a burden. Love is a burden. Life is a burden.

Rand limits the debt we owe to previous great minds to be simply recognition (and, perhaps, living up to one's potential, if you choose to stretch her suggestion that a person may profit by adding to it) (1995, 347). I do not believe that recognition of a value is sufficient to sustain it. Tacit acknowledgment or agreement is not enough. Action is required.

Charity

Rand believed it was proper to help someone in an emergency situation. In fact, she said that a person *should* do so. The basis for the benevolence one feels toward others follows from the value he places on his own life. She said that it is on the basis of a general sense of goodwill and respect that a person would come to the assistance of a stranger during an emergency, but this help does not extend to nonemergencies (1964d, 47); it is solely in emergencies that a person should help strangers, if he is capable of doing so (1964b, 48).

She defined an emergency as an unexpected occurrence that is limited in duration and produces an environment in which human survival is not possible. Her list included, primarily, natural disasters, such as floods and earthquakes (1964d, 47). (This list is different from the one she included in a letter to John Hospers, which included illness [cf. Berliner 1995, 551]. The reason she may have excluded illness in the list above is because it is not a metaphysical emergency.) In contrast, she regarded nonemergency situations, such as poverty and sickness, to be the normal risks of living. If a neighbor is in need and it is a situation of limited duration, then a person may—out of a sense of benevolence, not duty—provide him with food, etc., or collect a donation on his behalf. But such assistance does not extend to supporting him for the rest of his life or seeking out helpless people to whom to give assistance as one's life's work, according to Rand (1964d, 48).

The verb is changed from "should" in Rand's discussion on emergencies to "may" in her discussion on helping the neighbor. The change is because sickness and poverty do not qualify as metaphysical emergencies (ibid.). During an emergency, one should help others (but not at the cost of one's life). I interpret this to mean that an emergency is an exceptional case (that is, "unchosen") in which a person does not calculate the benefits or costs of this action and compare it with other alternatives. There may be other alternatives at that moment that might yield greater value; however, one would forgo those in order to help during an emergency. (This is why the qualifier that emergencies must be limited in duration is necessary.) The only criterion would be whether the risk to oneself is dangerous or life threatening.

Nonemergencies are different. One may help someone (so long as the person is not evil), but only if one can afford it and the help is limited in duration. Calculation in nonemergencies is warranted. What Rand opposed is subordinating one's own life to the relief of suffering of others as one's primary concern in life. Help should be "marginal and incidental" because disasters are marginal and incidental (1964d, 49; cf. Paterson 1968, 250–254). The latter requisite follows from her BUP. In answer to a letter asking Rand whether a person who was incapable of improving his situation without assistance should be helped by another if it involved a significant expense of time and effort on the part of the helper, Rand replied that the person should not do it. One should not put himself in a position of perpetual moral bondage to another. Charity is morally acceptable if it is marginal in nature (Berliner 1995, 552).

David Kelley expanded the motivation for benevolence to include providing for future potential trading partners. He stated that his argument is "that benevolence in general is a kind of investment in this sense: One invests one's time, attention, and concern in people in order to create opportunities for trade, even though many of them won't pan out" (1996, 47). It is a "*nonspecific investment in their potential*" (1996, 50). The rationale is that "opportunities for trade do not simply present themselves. They must be created by our own initiative" (1996, 26). So benevolence functions to create trading opportunities "by treating other people as potential traders" (ibid.).

To Rand, charity ranked of secondary importance because it is a response to suffering. If the universe is benevolent, success is the to-be-expected. Suffering is the not-to-be-expected and should not "be taken seriously." The virtues related to suffering are therefore also of minor importance (Kelley 1996, 14). However, since Kelley did not regard benevolence as a response to suffering but as a "nonspecific investment" in potential, he elevated it to a major virtue (1996, 17, 33).

A person who invests does not provide funds for someone because that person *needs* it. One does so because the beneficiary "can better his life with it" (1996, 50). The investor is not responding to need or suffering, but to another's long-run potential. Kelley does not see this as a sacrifice on the part of the investor (even though the investor will receive no specific return) so long as he gives "in accordance with his own hierarchy of values" (ibid.).

Conventional appeals to charitable giving view a person as splitting his time between taking care of his own interest and caring for others. This pits one's own interests against those of others. One's own interests and those of others are in conflict. Rand saw one's own interests—providing for one's own life—as a full-time job. Kelley noted that "any action not serving that end is at least a mild form of self-sacrifice, a use of our time and effort for things that do not benefit us, or that provide a lesser benefit than we might obtain by other uses of our resources" (1996, 7). He regarded investment in nonspecific potential as self-interested and nonsacrificial. The decision of how much help to give others "is an economic decision like any other. It is no different in principle from the decision of how much to choose between more work and more leisure" (1996, 50).

Since the giver receives no return on his investment, this would appear to potentially be a sacrifice. Although Kelley did not make this case, it is true that if giving is for investment (for which no return is forthcoming) instead of consumption, it is productive from the "total" perspective. There is no overall loss (and from the production side such a summation is permitted in economics—although it would be irrelevant to an individualistic ethics). The implication here is that the nonspecific investment is not parasitic in nature. Those who are receiving the contributions will use them productively. The contributions are not going to be used from a "total" perspective for immediate consumption by the recipients. If they were, they could, like other consumption, be a potential drain. If one practiced "productive charity" (i.e., nonspecific investment) then, as a principle, there would be no drain over time when viewed from a "total productivity" perspective, even though the income of the benefactor would be drawn down by the amount of the charitable contribution.

This would not be simply a redistribution of income from a benefactor to a beneficiary; it would be an investment in the productive capacity of the economy. If the beneficiary does use the funds productively, the pie will be bigger than it would have been if the beneficiary or the benefactor had spent the funds on current consumption. Even so, for an individualistic ethic, it is not the "total" that counts. An individual could not engage in this kind of investment if it took a significant portion of his income because he would not be the recipient of the returns; i.e., it would not be in his self-interest. In some ways this has similarities with parenthood, except, of course, for the obvious lack of emotional ties, and that children are owed care from their parents (including at least minimal investment in their human capital) by right. (In fact, I would add that for those who don't have children this is a way of replacing their human capital. That investment need not be in one's own offspring.)

Extending Benevolence beyond Nonspecific Traders

If the person who gives to others receives a benefit (utility) and the recipient benefits as well, then the total benefit is greater than if the person who received the benefit had paid for the service himself. Charity would result in double the benefits for a single payment—twice the bang for the buck. From a "total" perspective there would be much to recommend it. It could be regarded as an absolute virtue. But an ethic based on individualism should examine whether something is worthwhile from the individual's viewpoint, not from the "total" perspective, even if the "total" was valid (which it is not, according to economic theory).

If charitable expenditures were large in a person's budget (and life), one can see why Rand would believe that, as a principle, charity could not be a major virtue, since the money and time spent on charity would eventually drain one's income and productive capacity, and if carried to the limit, one would perish, and, of course, so would the object of charity as well. This is why Rand called charity parasitical. As a general or guiding rule of behavior, it would be. Altruism, according to Rand, is when other's interests are always above one's own. If one follows the logic I have put forth in making an ethical decision, then an altruist would only consider the expected benefits in making a decision. The benefits to others would be the only payoffs considered in a decision matrix. Losses to oneself would be ignored for the purposes of making the decision. This would be a justified approach for a decision if consistent application of the principle results in the decision-maker's survival. But it is not difficult to see that altruism as an overriding principle of behavior would be suicidal.

But so would productivity if a person never consumed. Productivity is a life-affirming principle, but a person must also consume. The caveat (of Objectivism) is one cannot consume more than he produces (Rand 1961a, 89). Like any other consumer good, one could spend *part* of his income on charity. As one spends more on a thing, according to consumer theory, its marginal value in terms of other goods declines. So if charity is considered like other goods, one would expect that as more is spent, its marginal value in terms of other goods will decline. Given an income constraint, one would not spend all of one's income on charity or on any single "good."

On the other hand, as noted above, sustaining one's own life is a full-time job. If so, charitable contributions would seem to be a sacrifice. According to Rand, sacrifice is wrong, whether it is small or large. If a thing is wrong, then one cannot do some incremental amount of it. Ethics is either/or. According to Peikoff, when it comes to principles, there is no trade-off between good and evil. Peikoff said that OE does not subscribe to the notion of "trade-off" (1991, 273). It would seem to follow that even if a sacrifice is small, it is evil.

Kelley said:

> The kind of altruism which says we must apportion our time between what we do for ourselves and what we do for others . . . offers no principled guidance on how to draw the line. If the needs of others create claims on our time and resources, why do we honor some of these claims but not others? (1996, 50)

Kelley claimed that by making nonspecific investments in potential in accordance with one's hierarchy of values, one does not sacrifice. Still, one could still ask, why would a person honor some nonspecific investments and not others? How does one apportion his time and other resources between these competing objectives? Kelley's reply was that it is an economic decision like the trade-off between work and leisure. However, if that is the case, since leisure is a "consumer good," then not only would nonspecific investments qualify as legitimate unilateral transfers, but unilateral consumption expenditures would as well.

Objectivists reject the argument for charity based on need. My argument for charitable giving is not based on the need of the recipient. There are many who are rightfully in need of help of one kind or another, but their need is an incomplete argument. In some cases, there is an issue of rights, such as children whose parents have reneged on their obligations. For charity in which rights do not enter in any way, the case for charitable giving cannot be based solely on need. My argument for charitable giving, the other prong of my argument, rests on the trader principle.

According to Rand, one should not give or receive the "unearned." One should trade value for value. This is the principle of justice (1964a, 31). Yet individuals by and large do receive net benefits. That is, they receive benefits for which they do not pay. They are net beneficiaries and as such, they are in "debt." Insofar as a person's total benefits and costs are concerned (over the course of one's life), if a person has received in his lifetime net benefits for which he has not paid—which I have argued many people have—then a marginal contribution to charity would not necessarily be a sacrifice so long as the recipient was justified in receiving it. The potential donor has received benefits for which he has not paid; so if he donates to a (justifiable) charity for which he does not receive a direct or monetary return, on balance he has not sacrificed.

When one examines a specific unilateral contribution narrowly (i.e., ignoring the fact that he has been a net beneficiary), then it could be viewed as a sacrifice.

Whether it is viewed as a sacrifice or not may depend on how much the person knows about the charity he is giving to. Generally, a problem with charity is that there is no market mechanism to provide that information and so the person will have to incur search costs. Economic theory (generally speaking) assumes knowledge is perfect. However, knowledge is imperfect and costly. This is why it pays for companies to advertise. Still, for goods that go through the market, the price mechanism provides information to decision-makers and the incentive to act on that information. With charity, there is no price mechanism to provide a signal, to give individuals information, to let people know if there are "shortages" or "surpluses," and to provide incentives on which to act. For that reason, it may be necessary to expend some effort to inform oneself. This may seem like a sacrifice as well. But with knowledge may come appreciation. This often happens even with consumer goods. If one is interested in a product, one may appreciate it more if he learns more about it. If this happens with the charity or charities to which a person chooses to donate, then one's estimation of it (them) will increase (i.e., one's own perceived benefits) relative to costs.

For instance, if a person dedicated some marginal amount of his budget to charity and knew it was to be used for this purpose, then initially, before the fact, one might regard the costs as exceeding the benefits (for that specific expenditure), particularly if he ignores the fact that he has been a "net beneficiary" because of the "inheritance" mentioned above. As he searches, his estimation may increase. So in the final analysis, charity need not be a sacrifice. But it still can be a "drain" in the same way any consumption can be. So it should be limited. And that should present no real problem because suffering should be a marginal issue in a benevolent universe. A problem here is that supply (of potential recipients) does tend to respond to demand. So if there is more charity provided, more people will tend to need (i.e., demand) it. A reasonable guideline is needed to keep charitable giving in perspective.

Marginal?

One way to approach decision-making under uncertainty is to look at the alternatives (say, A and B) open to a person, as well as the "payoffs" under different states of nature. (The "payoffs" need not be monetary, but should be measurable, at least ordinally.) Because a given action may have more than one outcome (depending on the state of nature), the payoff under each state is relevant to the decision. If the probability of each state is estimable, the Bayesian approach (Chou 1969, 682) would recommend calculation of expected value for each alternative.

In OE, ethics is tied to being; what a human is determines what he ought to do (Rand 1964a, 22). "Value" presupposes the existence of alternatives. If there were no alternatives, there would be no need to make decisions. Living beings face the fundamental alternative of life and death. "Alternative" does not necessarily mean choice. Humans must choose because they have no automatic means of survival. They must choose rationally. Reason is their tool of survival. In order to survive in the long run, humans must choose those actions that will achieve the highest long-run probability of success. These form man's code of ethics (Rand 1964a, 13–26; Peikoff 1991, 207–229). Rand's position is that every moral code has implicit within it an underlying premise about the nature of the universe. To Rand the universe is benevolent. The implication of the BUP is that suffering, pain, and failure are the not-to-be-expected. They are incidental, marginal, and unimportant. Pain, suffering, failure, and loss are "not to be taken seriously" (Kelley 1996, 13).

In terms of decision theory, I have interpreted the BUP to mean that if one confines his decisions to principled actions only, so that all the alternatives within one's decision set are consistent with a person's moral code, then each alternative will (like any set of alternatives under uncertainty) result in different "payoffs" depending upon the prevailing state of nature. Since, insofar as ethics is concerned, (principled) actions are tied necessarily to life and death, the relevant states of nature would be the life and death states. That is, the "loss" state would be the death state. However, if the alternatives are based on principled action, then the expectation is for long-term success. That, plus the BUP, would suggest that a person ignore the expected loss (probability of loss—or probability of dying—multiplied by that which would be forgone under the loss state of nature) in making one's decision. Thus, instead of the expected value (or expected utility) based on the sum of the expected payoffs in both states of nature, one would make the decision based only on the expected gain.

That is at least one interpretation of the BUP and the application of ethical principles to decision-making. However, risks of death may be higher for some ethical alternatives, and one may believe that those risks should be factored into those alternatives. So based on this interpretation, one chooses, as one would in decision theory under uncertainty using the Bayesian approach, the (ethical) alternative with the highest expected "value" when the decision set is confined to ethical choices. Since all alternatives are principled, there is no conflict between a principled course of action and an unprincipled course. One is simply choosing the principled action that has the highest expected "value" based on some measure of value (utility or some monetary measure that is either implicit or explicit). Now once the decision is made using the expected value (or expected utility) approach, the expectation would be (based on application of the BUP) that the return to that decision would be the expected gain. That is, the expected loss would be ignored after the decision is made, but not before. The to-be-expected from one's decision would be the expected gain (the probability of gain, i.e., of living, multiplied by the payoff under the "success" state of nature).

When confined to ethical alternatives (or those that are ethically neutral), whether the decision is based on the alternative with the highest expected value or with the highest expected gain, once the decision is made, the expected loss is ignored insofar as the to-be-expected is concerned. (If the decision is between an ethical and an unethical alternative, the expected loss associated with the *ethical* alternative would also be ignored.) If the gain results (success), then the expected loss (the probability multiplied by the loss) will be a bonus. Since loss is stochastic in nature, if success results, then the value of the expected loss will have been received as the result of good fortune, or luck. Since the expected loss is the "not-to-be-expected," is "not to be taken seriously," is metaphysically unimportant, it can be used for charity. This would be after the fact, that is, after one has in fact been successful. For example, for a given year, there is an expected income for the next year. The expected income (if confined to earnings from human capital) would be the probability of dying multiplied by income plus the probability of dying multiplied by zero (since if one dies he receives nothing). The expected gain for the next year is the probability of living multiplied by the income for the next year. (The expected income would be the same as the expected gain.) However, the expected loss of income for the year if one dies is the probability of dying multiplied by income. If one survives he receives the entire income. However, that portion that was an expected loss would be a bonus and can be used for charity.

For instance, if the probability of dying is 10 percent and yearly income is $30,000, a person's expected income is $27,000. If he person survives, his actual income will be $30,000, and the expected loss of $3,000 will be a bonus. It can be donated to charity. But this would be after the fact, that is, after the income has in fact been received—the person has survived. The amounts of gain and loss should be based on income rather than, as in the case of life insurance, the present value of lifetime income, since one is gauging from year to year what the expected gain and loss are for that year and looking retrospectively as to whether one has succeeded for that year or not. (If a person dies, his loss from earning would be his human capital. Because the decision here is made annually and after the fact, the focus is on the flow of income, not the stock of human capital.)

One might say that survival is not based on luck (primarily); it is based on one's own efforts—one's own rational efforts. That is what ethics is all about. But that part of survival—based on the rational approach to decision-making—has already been taken into account. One's principles are derived based on the long-run probability of success. One is only choosing among principled alternatives. That is why the to-be-expected, the norm, is a successful outcome to one's decision. The not-to-be-expected is metaphysically unimportant, but that does not mean there is a zero probability of its occurrence. What this means is the probability of failure can be ignored in applying principles. The BUP assumes bad luck is not the norm if one lives rationally. It does not assume it can never happen. Peikoff said, quoting Rand: "'It is not success but calamity that we regard as the abnormal exception in human life'" (Peikoff 1976). If loss transpires (in the application of rational decision-making), then it is "bad luck." If it does not transpire, that means that expected loss that did not occur can be regarded as "good fortune." Since it was considered unimportant and insignificant; since it was not expected and not relevant to one's decision; since it was ignored; since it is marginal and incidental, it can be used for charitable contributions. Since it was metaphysically unimportant—a result of luck—it is not a sacrifice to give it up.

Isn't this equivalent to the amount that would be put into a "sinking fund," if one were to replace the present value of his human capital? Isn't this the amount that a one-term life insurance premium would be (if life insurance were fair) for full coverage of one's human capital? If one is interested in one's replacement capital, one could have a sinking fund or children. Insurance would be a hedge against unforeseen contingencies (in this case death) that would result in the loss of one's human capital. Life insurance would remove uncertainty from the decision process. To use this amount for charity would be to renege on one's human capital replacement value. If that replacement takes the form of children, it would reduce the amount that one would spend on one's child for the purpose of human capital replacement. That does sound like sacrifice.

A distinction between the amount set aside for charity and that for insurance is that insurance is prospective in nature, whereas charitable giving would be retrospective. The former is a hedge against unforeseen contingencies, the latter a response to good fortune after the fact. A distinction between that portion given to charity and that portion that would be set aside in a sinking fund (or for children and/or would be used to pay for a life insurance premium) is that the latter is a decision concerning an asset (the replacement of one's entire human capital) and the former (charitable giving) tends to be a marginal decision, is income-based (a flow rather than a stock decision).

However, if a person does not have children and he wants to replace those values he finds important, i.e., if it is important for those values to continue beyond his life, he will want to sustain them in some way. Those values could include values related to earnings potential (human capital), knowledge, liberty, and moral principles. For those values and principles to be sustained, they must be embodied in human beings. For a person with no children, unilateral contributions (an endowment) to individuals or to organizations that support activities he regards as worthwhile may be one way of extending beyond his life that which he values. (That is, these would be "stock" decisions, not "flow" decisions, based on one's human capital replacement.) Even if a person has children, he may choose to do this if he can afford it. Although other individuals and organizations would not be as important as one's children, one's values may take many forms. Some values may be served outside one's immediate family.

A Rule

Although there may be cases in which a person would want to give a sizeable endowment to a charity, most charitable donations will be marginal amounts consistent in scope with other consumer expenditures. The individual would think in terms of the fraction of his annual income rather than the fraction of his lifetime wealth he would give. The probabilities of dying that are associated with the charity decision may be different from the probabilities used in the calculation of a life insurance premium. Several methods of calculating "average probabilities" were discussed in chapter 14 and examined in appendix 1. One of those might apply to the charity decision, since the probability of dying used for the charity decision should not be age-specific as it would be for life insurance (particularly term insurance). The probability of dying for charity should be some norm for the population as a whole and based on unforeseen reasons for death, not due to death's inevitability. Success is the to-be-expected if one is rational. Loss is stochastic. A guideline for the rate might be that given in appendix 1.12 for the so-called "depreciation index." There it is shown that as $T \rightarrow \infty$, the "asset" decays at a rate ∂ for every year it ages. ∂ could be used if it is to result solely from untimely death. Death's inevitability would not be a consideration since this percentage assumes that T tends to infinity.

Death, of course, is inevitable. For some decisions, not only life's uncertainty but death's inevitability may be included in the probabilities. It was found in appendix 1.11 that death's inevitability "drove" the premium rate as shown in equation (P.2) to be approximately equal to 1/T. If death's inevitability is relevant, then the appropriate "probability" might be given by (P.2). However, if the objective was to sustain the lives of one's values (so that they are "immortal"), then ∂ might be a better choice.

Life is a very crude measure of "success," and death of "failure." Life and death are inherent in Rand's fundamental alternative and form the basis for her code of values. However, within the context of charitable giving, I think it appropriate to view the probability of dying as having weight in one's decision because of the objective of (marginally) supporting other individuals in order to affirm values that exist within oneself as virtues, as well as to sustain values that exist independently of oneself as principles. To stay viable, those principles must be embodied in human beings. It is because one wants those values to survive independent of one's own life—which one knows to be limited—that one may contribute to others. (I mean this in a very broad sense. I do not mean to imply that a person would never contribute to those who are terminally ill.) In determining the probability that is relevant here, both life's uncertainty and its finality have meaning in the decision.

Thus, mortality enters into the decision because of the fundamental alternative a person faces—his life and death. This forms the basis for his values and virtues. The probability of (unexpected) death is relevant because of the role loss plays in the BUP. Mortality also enters into the decision because of the potential death of principles and because they must be embodied in humans in order to survive. The probability is relevant since it is a fraction and it is marginal. The probability of dying (mortality rate) (as a norm, not for any particular person) should be low in a free society under normal circumstances.

Therefore, the probability of dying one would use as a fraction of the previous year's income would be an average for the population under normal circumstances (assuming it is based on a rational society—i.e., one that is free). Theoretical probabilities may provide some guidance as well. This is, of course, simply a rule of thumb. If one's probability of death increased, this would not mean a person would contribute more to charity (unless he desired to do so). On the contrary, if the probability of dying were to increase for a person relative to the norm, then his decisions might differ from the norm. If a person faced more misfortune than the average person, he might very likely need more of his time and income to take care of his own situation.

The purpose of suggesting a guideline such as this is to keep charity marginal in nature. For those who accept the altruist creed of giving "until it hurts" (Vardey 1995, xxxii), such a guideline would limit his giving so that it would not be self-destructive. For those who might see any charitable giving as self-sacrificial, this would provide a rule of thumb. It is not merely heuristic, however, since it is based on the fundamental alternative (life and death along with their associated probabilities) and the BUP (which would, according to my interpretation, view as good fortune the probability of loss multiplied by the associated loss if the loss state does not transpire) as well as decision theory under uncertainty (risk).

The other reason a guideline for charitable giving is useful is that there is no price mechanism for charity. There may be those individuals who would want to give to those who may be justifiably deserving of charity. And there may those who are justifiably deserving of charity. However, unlike the market for other goods, there is no price mechanism in cases like this to provide information and the incentive to act on that information. The price mechanism performs this function automatically. Nor is there any mechanism with respect to charitable giving that signals when there has been "too much" given. The market system tends to be self-regulating. To the extent that charity is warranted, it needs to be acknowledged as a virtue. Since charity is by nature outside the market mechanism, it is incumbent upon those who give to seek out information about charitable giving. This serves at least two functions. Those who may not be inclined to give may be more inclined if they know more about the charitable causes that exist. Also, when a person is informed, there will be less of a tendency to give to unworthy charities—that is, those that are inefficient, or those that are glutted with contributions (to the point that there are bottlenecks).

Additionally, like the phenomenon of moral hazard in insurance (Becker and Ehrlich 1972, 641n44), there may be a tendency for supply to respond to demand. So there needs to be an ethic on the supply side to be prudent with one's giving and on the demand side to refrain from abusing the goodwill of others. If these ethics and guidelines are followed, then charity will tend to be marginal, which is consistent with the BUP (and a rational economic system under normal circumstances).

Rules and Objectivism

To say that one can use an equation as a guideline for determining the fraction of one's income to devote to charity sounds like a rule, e.g., a tithe. Rand was adamantly opposed to rules or duties. She regarded duties as unchosen obligations (1982a, 98). The idea of using a fraction of one's income (or, equivalently, one's time or other resources) is simply a guideline, not a rule. Since it is based on a probability, it may seem like an insurance premium, but it is not. Kelly, based on an insight by Donway, compared his conception of benevolence as a nonspecific investment in potential trading partners to a "kind of informal insurance" based on "custom rather than contract" ("Roundtable" 1996, 9). Maintaining the custom is in one's self-interest, since one may need similar aid in the future, according to Kelley.

I am not ruling out the motivation discussed by Kelley, but what I am referring to is not insurance, nor does one necessarily expect to be a beneficiary of this kind of giving later on. It may be in one's self-interest broadly defined and should be, but this is charity, not insurance. As Stephen Moses noted: "Insurance is a business, not a charity or a welfare program. Private charity and government welfare programs may be legitimate ways to help the uninsurable, but that's a different issue" (2002, 11). The fraction notion is simply a guide. However, it is not arbitrary. It follows from Rand's BUP (Peikoff 1976) as applied to decision-making, as well as the fundamental alternative (Rand 1964a, 15). It is far less arbitrary, I believe, than setting a certain number of years for a patent, yet limiting the duration of a patent to a given number of years is considered appropriate in Objectivist literature (Rand 1967i, 132).

The idea of a percentage may sound as if it is a "must." Rand's concern with charity being seen as a "must" is that it could very well become a legal requirement. In response to a letter from John Hospers, Rand said that if sacrificing for the benefit of other people were a moral imperative, then eventually a law would be enacted that would force people to do so, since a moral case against its passage would be invalid (Berliner 1955, 547). Rand argued that laws necessarily follow from what is ethically right. I don't believe that is necessarily the case, however. Laws should be about rights, primarily. Ethically, according to Objectivism, a person should work, regardless of whether he is independently wealthy or not. Yet in free markets, there is no law compelling people to work, nor should there be. Furthermore, as Machan pointed out, no one can take moral credit for actions that he is compelled to perform (1998b, 20–21). In fact, I believe that if charity or benevolence is elevated to a major virtue (which does not mean it would consume the major part of one's income or time), or at the very least is not considered a minor one, then there would be sufficient generosity in the private sector. (And the private sector has the added advantage of generally being somewhat more efficient, even in its nonprofit enterprises, than government agencies.)

In my discussion, I have included areas for charitable contribution that Rand and Kelley did not. Rand confined the verb "should" only to emergencies (1964d, 48). Kelley incorporated nonspecific investment into benevolence. I have added those whose rights have been violated and fall through the cracks because of limited rights due to diminished capacity. In these cases there is an issue not only of need but of rights. Charitable contributions would not be limited to these individuals, however. Ultimately, the choice would be up to the individual giver.

I would agree that in a rational economic system, success is the to-be-expected. It may not be the objective of capitalists to improve the lot of the ordinary person, any more than it is the purpose of the ordinary person to make profits for the capitalist (and these two groups of people are not necessarily mutually exclusive), but the outcome is that the vast majority are better off under capitalism. If one is concerned about the ordinary person, then it would be an act of generosity to encourage liberty and free markets in his own country and elsewhere.

However, there are those whose lives may still not be improved under any economic system—children who are abandoned and who have no support, for example. Capitalism may result in fewer abandoned children than would exist in a nonfree market, since the standard of living for the ordinary person is improved; so this may result in fewer parents abandoning their children. Also, capitalism offers more opportunities for women, and this tends to reduce the number of children women have. So, this may also have the effect of reducing the number (incidence) of abandoned children. Still, even though capitalism provides more and better paying jobs and more abundant and more affordable products, if a person cannot work and is not mentally capable of owning or caring for property, that person is not that much better off under capitalism in a material sense. However, others are. If they are generous, then someone who is abandoned or otherwise justifiably in need has the potential to be better off.

There are less likely to be abandoned and sick or dying children under a free market system, because the ordinary person is better off. It is difficult to separate tragedies such as these from the political and economic system, since if parents cannot afford to care for their children, they may be more inclined to abandon them. Rand regarded charity to be a social luxury (Berliner 1995, 545). I think charity is a social luxury in Calcutta. If, in a country that has a history of freedom, success is the to-be-expected, and loss the not-to-be-expected, then charity should be marginal, since there should be few who need it. That is, from the "supply" side, few people should be in the tragic situations I have described. From the demand side, it should be marginal because one's primary responsibility is to oneself, to support one's own life, so that one does not depend on others. By necessity, if one is taking care of himself and any dependents he may be responsible for, what one spends on charity should be marginal. Also, from the perspective of the potential to give to charities, in free economies, there is more likely to be a "surplus." Isabel Paterson noted that charity must come from the "surplus" created by producers (1968, 251). For a person who just subsists and consumes all of his income, such as the desert island "castaway," his expected income will be the probability of surviving multiplied by yearly income (hardtack). If he survives, the probability of dying times income will be a "bonus" because his life will have been extended beyond expectations. However, he will need the income to sustain his life. There will be no surplus to give to charity. This is not typical of an advanced economy.

Would it follow that charity, because it is marginal, is a minor virtue? A virtue need not be pursued in a significant way for it to be major. Consumption is not a virtue. Productivity is a virtue. Saving is a virtue because it is productive. Saving (investment) is an engine of economic growth, yet it generally comprises only a small part of one's income. If a little saving is good, why isn't more better? The trade-off between productivity and leisure or productivity and (other) consumption is in some ways more difficult than the trade-off of one consumer good for another, because only productivity is a virtue in OE and consumption is not. The only guide one has is that an honest man does not consume more than he produces. But clearly the saver is ethically elevated in OE. Where does one stop? Growth theory shows that there can be a balance.

If one follows the altruistic tenet that if a little sacrifice is good, more is better, then where does one stop? (Kelley 1996, 50) One could say that of any good, of course. If ice cream is good, why isn't more better? For other goods, the answer is (if there is diminishing marginal utility), the more you have, the less you value an additional unit of it. Or (even if the marginal utility does not decline), the more you have, the less you value it in terms of other goods. But other goods do not have the force of the altruistic creed behind them—for those who accept it.

Any expenditure on charity could be viewed as a potential sacrifice. As an either/or decision. As a life-or-death question. But this envisions wealth as a fixed pie that one redistributes. And for any point in time, that is true. Over time, given the proper incentive structure, the pie will grow. The proper incentive structure exists under capitalism. It is true that if too much is forcibly distributed, the pie will eventually shrink. If too much is voluntarily given to charity, the pie can suffer. But in a free market the number of charitable cases should be few, and if individuals keep the contributions in proper perspective, the productive capacity should not be affected. In fact, if charitable expenditures are worthwhile, the productive capacity could grow. Charity need not be a drain on the productive capacity. However, I do not think that the effect on productive capacity should be one's primary concern when making a charitable contribution. (That is, I do not think all [nonemergency] charity needs to be for nonspecific investment.)

Public Good

Public goods are goods that when provided to one consumer are simultaneously provided to everyone else, and for which it is not possible for nonpayers to be excluded. Since once a public good is provided to one, it is provided to all, there is an incentive for consumers to conceal their preferences and to be nonpayers, or free riders. Since everyone has an incentive to free ride, the public good will not be produced (Gwartney 1976, 519). National defense is one example. Even goods that are not pure public goods but have public good characteristics may be underproduced.

Economist James Andreoni regarded charitable contributions as public goods. No doubt some contributions that could be classified as charitable are expended on goods that have public good characteristics, e.g., museums, libraries, parks, and basic research. However, there are charities that benefit only some of the population, not everyone. Free clinics and charity hospitals benefit those who cannot otherwise pay for healthcare. Orchestras and other live arts have patronage, yet they still charge sizeable ticket prices and are only available to those who can afford the tickets. The same is true of endowed private institutions of higher learning whose students not only must pay tuition but are also screened for admittance. Even these, it could be argued, have public good characteristics. Those who do not directly consume these products may nevertheless indirectly benefit. For instance, those who have health insurance may derive benefits in knowing that the uninsured have access to medical care.

Andreoni's point was that even though charitable activities may be public goods, "each year they receive far more than token levels of support" (Frank

1988, 222). This is not what would be expected based on the supposed incentive structure that underlies public or near public goods. Robert Frank cited the following from Andreoni's research:

> More than 85 percent of all American households make private donations to charities, with an average gift of more than $200 in 1971 dollars. Religious organizations raised approximately $10 billion in 1981, health and hospitals over $7 billion, and civic orchestras more than $150 million. (1988, 222)

It is not possible to know all of the motivations for those who made these charitable contributions. My guess would be that the ethic that underlies much of this giving has its roots in Judaism and Christianity.

In Objectivism, producers have the moral high ground. Humanitarians are regarded by Rand as parasites, since their primary concern is distribution rather than production, and that which is distributed was produced by others (Berliner 1995, 83). Although Kelley (1996, 33) ostensibly elevated benevolence to a major virtue, rather than a minor virtue, and wrote of nonspecific investment in others as being in one's self-interest because they were potential trading partners, it is clear that he did not regard charitable activities per se as productive. He claimed in a television special *Greed* that Michael Milken had been a greater benefactor to humanity than Mother Teresa ("Sightings" 1998, 10). This view is consistent with Rand's ethics. Kelley said that one of his purposes for making the statement was to emphasize that it was not necessary for entrepreneurs to launder the money they earned by donating it to charity ("This God" 1998, 3).

Actually, there are (at least) two separate issues here. One is from the perspective of the giver to charity. The second is from the perspective of the person who does charitable works as a full-time occupation. Charitable giving could be regarded as a consumer expenditure or a nonspecific investment, depending upon how the donation is used. When a person purchases a consumer good, it is not regarded as productive. The person who provided the good is the producer. It's true that the consumer had to acquire the income to be a consumer, but purchasing a consumer good is consumption, not production. If the donation goes for production, then it can be seen as an investment and is productive. Of course, the giver does not receive a direct return from the production, but it is still productive. Objectivists' quarrel is with those who find charity to be superior to productivity insofar as an ethic is concerned. In OE, productivity is a central virtue. Consumption is not. Since charity is, or may be used, for consumption purchases, it is consistent to think of charity as not being a virtue, since one's own consumption is not a virtue. But there are other reasons that charity is a minor virtue at best, according to OE. One is that it tends to be, or can be, self-sacrificial on the part of the giver.

Unilateral transfers (charity) can be provided for any number of services, many of which may be viewed as productive, but certainly not all are. All could be considered productive in the broad sense of human capital maintenance and development. But what is called "maintenance" of human capital is oftentimes consumption. As has been seen in the discussion of parents' expenditures on children, it can be difficult to distinguish consumption from production. Becker regarded children (expenditures on children) as consumer durables. That may be the perspective of some parents, but expenditures on children are, in part, an investment in human capital ("replacement investment"). Children will eventually (it is hoped) become productive members of the economy. But human "capital" development is not limited to the productive capacity of the economy narrowly defined. It also includes the development of values and virtues that are not limited to those required on the job. So some part of the expenditure on charity may be regarded as productive in the narrow sense of improving abilities of the (potential or actual) workforce, and in the broader sense of developing values and virtues not limited to those related to work.

As for having a full-time occupation that is financed by charitable donations, Rand was clear. She regarded it as morally reprehensible to support oneself by almsgiving rather than by exchange (Berliner 1995, 544). I have argued that the same service is performed by an individual whether that individual is paid directly by the person receiving the service or by a third party. Value is traded for value, a service is being provided, but the person who receives the service is not the same person who pays. From the perspective of the provider of the service, it is irrelevant who pays, so far as the service rendered is concerned. A doctor who sets a child's broken arm is providing the same service whether the child's parent pays the bill or it is paid by a third party.

In Kelley's comparison of Michael Milken and Mother Teresa, it is clear that he did not regard her as productive. Like Rand, he regarded humanitarians as redistributors of income only. Milken was the greater contributor to mankind because he produced income rather than distributed income created by others—as Mother Teresa purportedly did ("A Slogan" 1998, 4). In an interview for the *Navigator*, Kelley indicated that he did not view going into slums and suffering, as did Mother Teresa, as a value. What is important is what individuals create ("And to Think" 1998, 4).

It is difficult to separate Mother Teresa from her faith and the virtues it espouses. Suffering is not in itself a value to Objectivists. It is a momentous case to argue that those things that cause suffering—cancer, evil, starvation—are values. Yet to Mother Teresa suffering and poverty are necessary "to know." Alice Walker has said: "Suffering is the school of the soul." Mother Teresa is quoted as saying: "Love until it hurts" (Vardey 1995, xxxii). According to Vardey: "It is the acceptance of suffering—not in a stoic, sacrificial way but with gladness of spirit—that brings joy into the work of these sisters and brothers" (1995, xxxiii). To say that suffering is joyful seems like a contradiction, unless what Vardey meant was "struggle" in the way that Rand (1961a, 80) used the term (which seems to have been what Norton meant by "noble" suffering [1976, 229]).

Although Mother Teresa's mandate was to relieve suffering (Vardey 1995, xxvii), and the relief of suffering can be viewed as a value in OE, she saw poverty itself as a value, since with it there were "fewer obstacles to God" (Vardey 1995, xxxi). Although I can appreciate the idea that those who depend on contributions for their livelihoods should keep expenses low, I do not agree that poverty is a value. On the contrary, I think that when one's focus is on physical survival there can be room for little else in one's existence. I think a higher standard of living can free a person from concentrating on bare survival and permit him to include less tangible values in his system of values. Secondly, it is only from the creation of a surplus by producers that suffering can be relieved.

Just as it is difficult to separate Mother Teresa's works from her faith, it is also difficult to separate the abandoned and dying that she cared for from the political and economic system under which they lived—and died. No doubt there would have been fewer poor people in general and certainly fewer abandoned children, had a free market system prevailed. But she became a citizen of India, and that country and some of the other countries in which her Missionaries of Charity were located were, in many cases, noncapitalistic. Her work must be evaluated within the context in which it took place.

I do not believe one measures productivity merely by the number of units of something a person turns out. Some teachers over the course of a career teach thousands of students. Plato may have had many. But had he only Aristotle, that would have been sufficient. A philosopher's productivity may be measured by how much he writes. Socrates wrote nothing. Jesus wrote nothing. Buddha wrote nothing. Marx wrote several volumes. Even how much income one makes is but a crude yardstick of value. Nor can a person's productivity be measured by his contribution to the "common good" (since, according to Rand, that is a meaningless concept [1967a, 20]). Does that mean productivity has no meaning? No. One can make comparisons for some purposes. One can compare two people who are doing exactly the same task, and determine which one is more productive. Comparisons can be made.

It is nevertheless difficult to determine the productivity for some jobs, because of the nature of the job itself. Retrospectively, a person's contribution may be easier to evaluate, but this may be after a person's lifetime. In occupations for which the payoff is long-term and/or uncertain, expected productivity is difficult to assess. Van Gogh barely sold one painting in his lifetime. Rand's books sold well during her lifetime; they still sell in the tens of thousands per year. Hero of Alexandria, inventor of the steam engine as a toy in the second century B.C., had no idea to what ends it would be put (Koestler 1989, 102).

The value of the work done by those who get paid nothing (because that is the nature of the job) is also difficult to assess. Parenthood (especially motherhood, since historically it has been a full-time or significant part-time occupation) is difficult to evaluate insofar as productivity is concerned. Was a parent who has three children more productive than a parent who has two? Was the parent who reared the James brothers (Henry and William) more productive than the parent who raised the James boys (Frank and Jesse)? Or can a parent take credit or blame for how an adult child turns out, since adults have free will? (Since the output of mothers is difficult to measure and is nonremunerative, it has also been at times underappreciated. This is not a recommendation for compensation by "society," since individuals by and large are replacing their own human capital—at least from an economic perspective—and individuals are, in that sense, the replacement capital for their own parents. No third party owes parents for their child's upkeep.)

Even though productivity may be difficult to assess, this does not mean that there are no yardsticks whatsoever, regardless of how crude. Some people have very impressive work histories. I believe this was true of Mother Teresa. (For a capsule discussion of Michael Milken's see Scott [1997].) Her motivation and philosophy aside, the sheer magnitude of her work is impressive. In the early part of her career, for nineteen years, she was a teacher, then principal of St. Mary's in Calcutta. Then, after recuperating from tuberculosis, she became regarded as "the quintessential, energetic entrepreneur" (Vardey 1995, xxiii).

In 1950, her Missionaries of Charity was founded in Calcutta. Her order founded homes and centers that are (or were) located in over twenty countries (Doig 1976, 174–75; Vardey 1995, 194). Examples of the homes include Prem Nivas. According to Lucinda Vardey, the land, built on a dump-yard, was donated, but the construction was done by the leper patients themselves. They built workshops and wards, clinics and schools, dorms and huts. Shishu Bhavan, a children's home in Calcutta, houses 300 children and provides employment for the children's mothers. The physicians there see 1,000 to 2,000 patients per week. They have adoption services. If a child is not placed by age ten, they may send him to boarding school, then to college, or provide work placement. Dowries are, at times, provided for marriage. The home provides meals for 1,000-plus people per day. Nirmal Hriday is a home for the dying. They have 105 beds and provide burial services by religion for Catholics, Muslims, and Hindus (Vardey 1995, 117–22).

According to Desmond Doig, in Prem Daan, Mother Teresa's small rehabilitation center provides work for the city's destitute, who collect green coconut shells discarded in the city streets. According to Desmond Doig, literally hundreds of tons of these shells litter the streets daily, since coconut milk is a popular drink. These shells are used to make rope, bags, and mats. Mother Teresa referred to this process as "changing garbage into gold" (Doig 1976, 121). In response to children suffering from malnutrition, Mother Teresa's nuns in Kidderpore began employing mothers to make paper bags. Paper is scarce and must be sought through donations and discards. They began with two mothers and expanded to seventy-five (1976, 121, 123).

Given the nature of the raw material Mother Teresa and her order had to work with, I believe they have been both constructive and creative. In order to evaluate a person's success, one must look at the context or environment within which he is working. There was a good deal of initiative, ingenuity, and effort as well as success on the part of Mother Teresa and the Order she established. I think this far exceeds the description of her as simply going into slums and suffering.

CHAPTER SEVENTEEN

Favors, Forgiveness, and Emotions

Rand did not believe one should accept an unearned obligation (1964a, 26). Gift-giving should, in the first instance, bring joy to the giver. She regarded need as "vicious" in ethics (Berliner 1995, 576). Yet, there is give-and-take among friends, which involves material gifts as well as favors. This chapter discusses these so-called unilateral transfers. Another gift one person may bestow upon another is forgiveness. I do not see forgiveness as an unqualified virtue. If it is unwarranted, forgiveness is an act of cowardice. I discuss forgiveness and the circumstances under which it may be or may not be warranted. Finally, Rand (Peikoff 1991, 228–29) believed one's emotions follow from one's thoughts. However, I argue that a person's emotions and thoughts are often out of sync, in part because of the dynamic nature of life and learning. Rand envisioned the trade-off between alternatives ("sacrifice") as being between two alternatives—one that is valued and the other that is valued less or not at all (1964d, 44). These are the relatively easy decisions. Those that are more challenging involve two (or more) alternatives, both (or all) of which one values. These conflicts are commonplace, particularly when productivity and childrearing vie for first place in one's hierarchy of values.

Favors and Gifts—Other "Unilateral Transfers"

Ridley believed the human brain to be an exchange organ: a reciprocity-calculating machine. It is a cheat-checker that seeks ways to screen for potential violators of exchange "contracts" (Ridley 1996, 130). Gifts, which are seemingly unilateral, are seen by many (consciously or subconsciously) as bilateral. Gifts can be used as bribes or to create obligation. But what creates that sense of obligation to arise in the first instance? (1996, 123) Although the brain may look for reciprocity, what is exchanged and under what circumstances it takes place may be the result of convention or tradition. Traditions often do imply reciprocity of some kind. When you graduate from high school I give you a gift; when I graduate you give me one. The idea is that you accept or perform certain traditions because there is an implied reciprocity. If you do not give a wedding gift, the idea is you have not pulled your weight, because when you are married the expectation is you will receive one.

Rand warned against the blind acceptance of tradition (Rand 1967j, 198). One might think that the words "trade" and "tradition" have the same etymology, but they don't. "Trade" comes from the Middle English and Middle Low German words for "track" or "path." Tradition comes from the Middle English, Old French, and Latin words meaning "a handing down" or to "hand over" (*American Heritage* 1969). A track or path suggests two-way or bilaterality. Handing over (or "surrender" in Middle English) is one way or unilateral. To "hand over" may imply tradition is a kind of trade; by accepting certain customs or performing certain behaviors, one gets something else—approval, membership in a group, or the "promise" of the same behavior in return on a similar occasion or circumstance. But it can be a handing down from one generation to another, and an acceptance by one generation of another's customs, rituals, behaviors, etc.

Potlatches were ritualized contests that included ostentatious displays of gift-giving as well as the destruction of valuables. Designed to embarrass rivals, they could include burning canoes and blankets, killing sea otters and even slaves (Ridley 1996, 121–22). Ridley described them as gifts used as weapons; they were examples of reciprocity run amok. But potlatches are not unique in applying the concept of reciprocity to situations where it does not belong. Ridley said social exchange is devised in the most inappropriate of settings. For instance, it is manifested when people deny the fact of good luck or bad luck, and instead believe these to be a reward or punishment for good or bad behavior (1996, 131).

The kind of reciprocity that underlies the Prisoner's Dilemma requires restraint and delayed gratification. Jennifer Morse claimed that self-restraint, delayed gratification, and trust—and thus reciprocity—are learned behaviors that parents teach children through interactions. It seems intuitively obvious that if parents are there for their infants and children when they are hungry, hurt, afraid, and so on, the children will learn to trust their parents. However, children also learn to be trustworthy. Morse said: "Restraining oneself is an integral part of being trustworthy. In fact, part of cooperating in the Prisoner's Dilemma is restraining oneself from taking advantage of opportunities for immediate gain" (2001, 41).

The link between the lack of restraint and the lack of respect for the law was noted by Frank: "The association between impulsiveness and criminal behavior has also been supported in numerous quantitative studies. One study of seventh graders even showed that tests of impulsivity in simple psychomotor tasks are predictive of future delinquency" (Frank 1988, 161). The cerebellum is known to be a significant coordinator for movement. The development of the cerebellum is a function of the degree and kind of body contact and movement experienced as a child. Restak described the following:

> When an infant is rocked or cuddled, impulses are directed to the cerebellum that stimulate its development, a process that goes on until age two. In fact, the cerebellum is unique, since it is the only part of the brain where brain-cell multiplication continues long after birth. (1979, 144)

There is also some evidence that an abnormally developed cerebellum is linked to dysfunctional behavior, perhaps violence (1979, 151).

Self-restraint largely follows from affection, not calculation, according to Morse:

> Politics, which appears to be about power and force, actually depends upon loving families at least as much as patriotism or civic-mindedness. The economic realm, which appears to be comprised of impersonal exchanges of material objects among strangers, is based on love. (2001, 49)

There is no doubt that dispositions toward trust and restraint are important between traders. However, there has to be in place a political and economic system that allows voluntary association and exchange to take place. Private property is necessary so that people own what they exchange. Self-restraint and trust are desirable under many circumstances, but within the political realm a legitimate question is, trust whom and for what? Is it a matter of Senator X trusting Senator Y to vote at a future date for a farm subsidy bill if Senator X will agree to vote for a gasoline tax hike now? Reciprocity can take many forms, not all of which have benign effects on third parties.

Love may be a factor in trust, but there must be opportunities to engage in reciprocal behavior that do not have the "zero-sum" aspects found in political exchange. The family can provide those kinds of opportunities. Free markets provide opportunities on a wider scale, but there have been relatively few free market economies. Where a free market is absent, the opportunity to practice reciprocity may not extend beyond the family or the tribe. The extension of trust beyond the tribe may be lacking.

Trade and cooperation are the forms of reciprocity on which Morse focuses. Reciprocity is not limited to trade and cooperation, however. It includes retaliation and retribution if another person defaults on trade or violates one's rights. To be just, retaliation should be confined to the individual who defaults or violates another's rights. It should not extend to his family, his tribe, or his friends. Tribal societies are based on reciprocity but it is tribal in nature. It includes cooperation among members of the tribe but distrust and retaliation, if crossed, against those outside one's tribe.

The value of a political system based on voluntary exchange is that reciprocity tends to lead to cooperation. There is less need for retaliation. The government's primary function is to protect life and property. Individuals are freed of the burden of private retaliation. They can devote their energies to productive enterprises and cooperative associations. Individuals are also freer to choose whom they marry, who their friends are, and with whom they work. Rand's trader principle applies not only to market exchange but also to what she calls spiritual areas. "Love, friendship, respect, admiration are the emotional response of one man to the virtues of another, the spiritual *payment* given in exchange for the personal, selfish pleasure which one man derives from the virtues of another man's character" (Rand 1964a, 31). According to Nathaniel Branden, friendship edges out family under capitalism, since unlike family, friends are consciously chosen.

> Under capitalism, men are free to choose their "social bonds"—meaning, to *choose* whom they will associate with. Men are not trapped within the prison of their family, tribe, caste, class, or neighborhood. They choose whom they will value, whom they will be-friend, whom they will deal with, what kind of relationships they will enter. This implies and entails man's responsibility to form independent judgments. It implies and entails also, that a man must *earn* the social relationships he desires. (Nathaniel Branden, "Alienation," in Machan 1967; quoted in Machan 1998a, 197)

Friendship is valued and friends are a value, but like values such as liberty, they cannot be exchanged or traded for something else (Machan 1998a, 69, 196). As Machan said, one does not sell out a friendship as one would trade in a car (1998b, 12). In friendship, trust is an issue. But trust to do or to be what? If friendship is a response to another's virtues, it would seem to follow that a person would trust a friend to be the person he is. In Rand's ethics, it would seem that the trade that takes place between friends is spiritual only. There is no other reciprocity expected or desired. In most societies there are cultural expectations of reciprocity in certain contexts. Each must be evaluated on its own merits. A person may dismiss those he finds self-sacrificial or otherwise irrational. This could be confusing to others, however. They may not realize that you have abandoned a particular convention in general, but think that you have neglected it in their specific case. You may risk sending crossed signals.

Sometimes even when a person follows a social convention, the effort can have more than one message, so there is a risk of being misunderstood. A gift may be a friendly gesture with no strings attached. Objectivists envisioned gifts in this way. It is selfish on the part of the gift giver. A gift is not given because it brings joy to the receiver, at least not as a primary motivation (Kelley 1996, 44–45). Yet if one is always the giver, buying gifts, picking up checks, doing another favors without receiving anything in return, there is more than magnanimity involved.

In most relationships in our culture, more is traded between friends than spirituality. Friendships usually have a degree of give-and-take of the material form—involving time, money, gifts. Some of the gift-giving may be ritualized—birthdays, religious holidays, graduations. Others may be regarded not so much as gifts, but favors. Even when a favor is done out of courtesy (not because one is asked), there may be, and often is, an implied sense of obligation for future reciprocity. The implicit understanding is that if a similar favor is requested in the future on the part of the giver, it will be honored. Sometimes if a person is on the receiving end of a favor, he may give a small gift in return as a token, a thank you. This gift is not generally thought of as strictly unilateral. It is or may be regarded as payment for the favor. The recipient may then see himself as free of the obligation of returning a favor in the future. The other party may not see it in the same way.

These kinds of exchanges (favors) are implied instead of explicit, generally speaking. There is usually a delay in time between favors, so there is an element of trust. There can also be some confusion as well. The trust is not only that a person will "pay back" the favor, but also that a friend will not take advantage. There is the trust that the friend will not request something you value (say, your time), unless it is very important. There is also the trust that a friend will not ask or expect one to compromise his principles. Principles are nonnegotiable.

Forgiveness

There are other gifts individuals give one another. Forgiveness is one. Kelley said that the dictionary definition of mercy includes the word "charity" (1996, 34). Peikoff called mercy "an unearned forgiveness" (1976, question period; quoted in Binswanger 1986, 290). Forgiveness, to the extent that it can be regarded as charity, is charity of a different kind from that which has been discussed thus far. So far, charity or benevolence has been assumed to be granted to innocents, or those assumed to be innocent. (Rand said: "A rational man regards strangers as innocent until proved guilty, and grants them that initial good will in the name of their human potential" [1964d, 47].) In the case of forgiveness, however, the person forgiven is not innocent. He has done some injustice to a person, and the person wronged is absolving him of that wrong.

In my view, forgiveness may be earned or unearned. If it is earned that means that the person who is forgiven has atoned in some way for his actions. If it is not earned, then forgiveness is unwarranted (assuming that the "injured" party was in fact wronged). In the first instance, the person who decides whether or not to forgive the offender is the injured party. The injured party is the person who is most affected by the offense. There may be secondary parties affected as well; they may also choose to forgive or not. Then there is the violation of the principle itself. As mentioned earlier, when a principle is violated, then it has been weakened. No one can "forgive" the violation to the principle itself. That damage is done. Secondary parties cannot forgive on behalf of the primary victim. That is why murder cannot be forgiven. The person most affected by the offender is dead, and only he can forgive the offender. Secondary parties (friends and relatives of the victim) can only forgive the harm that has been done to themselves.

For small offenses—slights, for instance—if the action of the offender was simply a mistake, then contrition may be sufficient "payment" to the wronged party. If the action was the result of thoughtlessness, then an expression of regret and that one will be more aware in the future may be adequate. The injured party is under no obligation to forgive. It depends on the extent of the injury suffered and whether the action was an isolated incident or not. If the action follows a pattern, then what one is forgiving is not a single slight but a character flaw. Forgiveness is for the exception, not for a character flaw. One may accept a person as a friend even though he has a flaw, but the decision then is to make an exception or exemption for the flaw itself.

As I see it, there is a risk to forgiving if there is no cost. The offender may have no disincentive to avoid future insults if he believes the slight was considered insignificant. He may not see the harm done. When a person is not forgiven or the forgiveness has not been earned, what he has incurred is an unpaid debt. Metaphysically and existentially, one has taken something and not paid for it. This is why some give flowers or other gifts to their friends if they have wronged them. It is a "peace offering." It does not undo a misdeed, but it is a way of unburdening a debt.

Even if one is forgiven, there is an unpaid debt to the principle that has been violated. It is one that cannot be paid in full, and in some cases it cannot be paid at all. Every transgression is a black mark against one's soul in the sense that one cannot correct the action itself or the violation to the principle. In the case of willful injury to a person that results in their death, one cannot be forgiven (by willful I also mean the refusal to think).

Forgiveness in and of itself is not a virtue. In my view, if one forgives another when it is not warranted, one has failed to uphold or support a principle. The principle has been doubly weakened. Rand said that the basic principle of justice is the law of causality and that a person should not try to sever the link between cause and effect. One person should not prevent another from experiencing the consequences of his behavior, for good or for ill (Berliner 1995, 558). Although, in an earlier discussion, I mentioned that there are instances in which intervention may be warranted, in cases in which a person has slighted another, the general principle applies. The offender should not escape the consequences of his actions. In this case, it is in large measure the wronged party (not nature or reality) who must determine what those consequences will be. (There may be cases in which the offender may find amends to be too onerous and unfair, in which case he may have to sever ties of friendship.) One consequence of a slight may be a refusal to forgive. If one forgives a transgression for which the offender is not sorry or is remorseful but will repeat anyway, or if one forgives an offense that significantly violates a core principle, then one is being unjust. By unjust, I mean one is not upholding a principle. Upholding a principle may mean not forgiving another when that person violates a principle. If one forgives another under such a circumstance, it is an act of cowardice.

Whether an aggrieved person forgives the offender or not, the offender may choose to forgive himself. If the action was the result of error of knowledge rather than the result of evasion of knowledge, then one may forgive oneself. But I agree with Rand that a true breach of morality "is an account of infamy growing in your soul" (1961a, 179), for which, in my opinion, one cannot forgive oneself. All one can do is to not repeat the breach and to bear the burden of the debt. It is a debt for which one keeps on paying (assuming one is alive—there are rights violations for which one should forfeit one's life. In this discussion, I am primarily referring to slights, not rights violations, although much of this could apply to rights violations). One does not necessarily keep "paying" the injured party. In some cases, that may not be possible or practical. One may take other actions. It might seem to follow that forgiving others may be a quid pro quo. It is not, since forgiveness in itself is not a virtue. One may, however, try to correct injustices done to others along the lines discussed with respect to charity.

Emotions

According to Rand, there should be no inherent clash between a person's reason and his feelings. Rand did not regard emotions as cognitive tools (1961b, 55). They are a consequence of one's value judgments. Rand said that in a fully integrated consciousness, a person's feelings should automatically follow from his convictions (Berliner 1995, 526). This would seem to follow from Rand's BUP, which states that: "Success and happiness are the metaphysical to-be-expected" (Peikoff 1976). So long as one is rational in his thoughts and deeds, he can expect to achieve his values. To Rand, life is the ultimate value, and she equated happiness to a life successfully lived (1961a, 123).

Rand stated that the lesson that her protagonist Dagny Taggart was supposed to learn in *Atlas Shrugged* was that it is happiness that is relevant, not suffering. Pain should not be regarded as important in a metaphysical sense—in the sense of being the essence of being. Joy, not the avoidance of suffering, is the purpose of life (Berliner 1995, 584). The pain to which Rand was referring is that which may have to be endured by external circumstance, not any pain that would come about by one's own actions (exercising one's free will through application of principles to decision-making). There should be no conflict there. Yet with any action, there may be loss, accidents, etc. These are not under one's control. Yet they must be put in perspective. Suffering is not the metaphysical norm.

Merrill claimed that Branden criticized *Atlas Shrugged* for advocating the repression of one's emotions (Merrill 1991, 80). Merrill regarded *Atlas* as "a powerful attack on repression" (1991, 81). This is evidenced by the emotional toll repression has on the character of Hank Rearden. Branden's point was that one should not dismiss a fact of reality. Branden used Rearden to make his point that if there is a clash between a person's values and his emotions, perhaps this is a sign that it is the values that are in error. Failing to acknowledge one's pain "is a form of failing to respect reality" (N. Branden 1997, 11).

I think that there are really two issues here. One is whether one should consider pain important in the whole scheme of things; i.e., whether one should take suffering seriously. It may be true that emotions are consequences of the values one holds consciously and/or subconsciously. But there are external injustices, accidents, losses, etc., that can justifiably cause one pain. (By external, I mean external to one's decisions, external to the rational application of principles. A person may live a principled life and still be involved in a car accident caused by a drunk driver, for instance.) This can be different from how one feels when he exercises a specific principle (which is "endogenous"; by that I mean pain should not as a rule follow from the exercise of principles). There may be no conflict between the person's values and one's emotions so far as exercising the virtue of productivity is concerned. Still, there may be a problem in the way a person envisions the world at the metaphysical level—that is, whether he sees it as being primarily a world that delivers suffering (external to oneself and one's decisions), or one that results in happiness if the person continues to think and act rationally. In the former case, the person may believe accidents to be the norm; in the latter, he would see these as metaphysical anomalies.

Rand believed that in exercising virtues one should feel joy, but she recognized pain could be caused by external events. External misfortunes should rightly cause one pain. The question is, whether the universe as such brings on too many of these exogenous accidents so that all one can expect is pain. Rand's view is that these exogenous occurrences are limited (to the stochastic or random) in nature. So pain should be as well—although it is felt when experienced. It is the day-to-day struggle to achieve one's values that should be ignored. Effort is part of being human. But that effort should to some extent be pleasurable.

Mental Conflict

To Rand, a sense of life is an emotional response to premises held subconsciously. Psycho-epistemology is the examination of the interaction between the subconscious and the conscious in one's thought. The term "psycho-epistemology," originated by Barbara Branden but first used in print by Rand (Sciabarra 1995, 194), is the study of the interaction of man's conscious mind with the subconscious (Rand 1969a, 18). Rand believed the subconscious to be an automatic "integrating mechanism" (1971b, 192). Its "ultimate programmer" is philosophy (1982d, 6). A person's sense of life is his emotional response to the philosophical premises that he holds on a subconscious or unconscious level and "is formed from the earliest moments of childhood as an unintended consequence or by-product of the child's contact with reality" (Sciabarra 1995, 191).

Sciabarra, in discussing Rand (1969c, 31), said that as a person begins to rationally derive his convictions, he relies less on his sense of life to guide his ideas and feelings. Rand recognized that many people may experience a conflict between the value judgments consciously held and their "sense of life." Sciabarra said: "In a clash of this nature, an individual's sense of life cannot be changed volitionally. It can be altered only after a long, difficult period of 'psychological retraining'" (1995, 193).

Although a person's philosophy programs his subconscious, Sciabarra said: "The task of evaluating the subconscious is a psychological, rather than a philosophical, endeavor" (1995, 192). Sciabarra claimed that both Rand and Nathaniel Branden attempted to understand the subconscious-conscious relationship. They recognized that habits of awareness could distort one's cognitive functioning (psycho-epistemology) and that such habits were as difficult to alter as one's sense of life. "[T]he older a person is, the more likely it is that his or her psycho-epistemology will remain entrenched" (1995, 195). It is obvious that Rand recognized that one's emotions and one's reason may not be in sync. She acknowledged that when there was a profound conflict between one's values and one's sense of life, one's sense of life could not be transformed through an act of will but required psychological retraining. This indicates that clashes of lesser import may be quite common.

Frank had confidence in emotions to solve what he called the "commitment problem" as depicted in the Prisoner's Dilemma (1988, 29–35). Frank believed emotions can be solving devices; i.e., they can commit individuals to pursue strategies that would serve their best interests, even though those strategies may appear to be at odds with one's interests, narrowly defined (1988, 4). The Prisoner's Dilemma is a problem of conflict between incentives—one of competing emotions, not the lack of emotions.

I doubt that many people actually have to fight a strong incentive to default on paying their bills. I believe that many people probably are virtuous and do not have to struggle against an evil side. Some may have a little difficulty getting out of bed to go to work. They may be battling a desire to be productive against a desire for rest or leisure. But I don't think most people are battling the desire to work against a desire to rob a bank. However, I do not believe, as Rand contended, that one always wants to do the right thing. A physician may enjoy practicing medicine but not want to tell a patient that he has three months to live. A judge may not want to sentence a convicted felon to twenty years in prison. A teacher may not want to flunk a student. Yet these may well be the right things to do.

As for most conflicts, I think they do not come about (for the most part) by trying to overcome a desire to do the wrong thing. I think many conflicts come about because individuals want to do the right thing but they must choose between two or more alternatives that they know to be right. The choice between whether to attend a business conference or go to one's son's piano recital can be a difficult one. Sometimes a person can find a "third way," some way of meeting both objectives. But that requires creativity and sometimes luck.

Out of Equilibrium

The reality is that life is a dynamic process. We are always in a state of change. Values and virtues are not self-evident. It has taken philosophers centuries to arrive at the point we are today. It is a lot to expect that a given person will get it right in one lifetime. Life is a constant process of learning and relearning. If one has not learned certain skills by the time he is an adult, it is a monumental task to acquire them as traits. Nothing makes this clearer than comparing a person who has been exposed to more than one language as a child to an adult who attempts to learn a second language. A child picks up two languages as easily as one. An adult may spend a lifetime trying to learn a second language and still never speak it as well as a person who learned the second language as a child. Or if a person has not learned to speak proper grammar in his youth, he faces a difficult challenge as an adult. He may learn the rules, but applying them may require conscious effort. It can be the same for a person who has not internalized such virtues as thrift, industry, or generosity. If not automatized by the time one reaches adulthood, these virtues may never be acquired as traits. That does not mean the person who has not acquired these as traits cannot be thrifty, industrious, or generous. It simply means the person may always be in the process of struggling to apply these principles in daily life. The effort to do so is heroic.

Rand's ethics are long-run in nature. They are based on what in the long run will yield success. This makes sense when discovering and applying ethics to daily life. But the emotions that correspond to those actions may be out of sync. Our emotions do follow from our thoughts to a large extent, but one may consciously realize that a certain course of action should or should not be taken and yet have difficulty willing one's emotions to follow one's thoughts. They may be in sync over time, but at any point in time they may be at odds.

It is also true that at different times in one's life or in different contexts, one's priorities will be different. When one is young, investment in one's human capital is usually more important than earning an income, yet earning an income may still be required. Both may compete for first place in one's hierarchy. If one has children, two purposes will compete for first place—one's income earning productivity and one's childrearing productivity. These are just two examples of the dynamic adjustments that can take place in one's life.

There are always competing emotions for any given action. There may be for some decisions the push and pull of vice and virtue. But the more difficult decisions for an ethical person are not the fights against vice; they are which one of two virtues to act upon given that a person has limited resources. When a person chooses to do one thing, he is always forgoing something else. The second thing—that which he is forgoing—may have little or no value. Those are the easy decisions. The difficult ones are those for which two alternatives are very close in value. Rand pitted life against death as the fundamental alternative. She defined a sacrifice as the surrender of a value for an alternative that has less value or no value at all (1964d). That, coupled with her belief that a person's emotions follow from his thoughts, would seem to make it relatively easy to choose the right alternative. However, there must be something attractive about the alternative for it to be an alternative. Otherwise no choice would be necessary.

I think the forgoing analysis complicates the decision process because I have introduced another value that is number one in one's hierarchy, and that is one's children. If and when one is a parent, he, in essence, has two jobs, but they are very different in some respects. Both compete for one's time and other resources. One cannot choose one or the other for all time. One must balance one against the other. Both are important. One cannot sustain one's life and one's dependents' lives unless one works, but one's work is not confined to employment that is remunerative. This makes conflicts possible, although solving those conflicts is not, generally speaking, impossible.

As for the decision to give to charity, I have laid a foundation for charity based on the trader principle. Individuals, by and large, inherit from others, not only the usual material goods that are thought of as inheritance, but also discoveries, inventions, and liberty, for which they do not pay. Individuals are net beneficiaries. They owe a debt, but it is of a general nature, and it cannot be repaid to the benefactors. I also pointed out there are rightful beneficiaries—those who "fall through the cracks" as far as rights are concerned, e.g., abandoned children. I think charity can arguably be regarded as a major virtue, but one that cannot take the majority of one's time and/or money. Therefore, I have set forth a practical guideline for giving based on the fundamental alternative (life or death) and the probabilities associated with those alternatives—decision theory under uncertainty (risk), and Rand's BUP.

Summary

In OE, life is the ultimate value. Productivity is a cardinal virtue because it supports one's life. All cardinal values and virtues are achievable by man alone. Other people are not a fundamental part of reality (Peikoff 1991, 252–53). OE's main social virtue is justice—the trader principle—the bilateral exchange of value for value between independent equals (Rand 1964a, 31). In this book, I have examined unilateral transfers. In OE, anything that is not life sustaining is self-sacrificial. Even a hint of self-denial is immoral (Peikoff 1991, 232). Charity, although not life sustaining, is acceptable in OE as long as it is marginal in scope. Only in emergencies *should* one help others (Rand 1964d, 48); that is, emergency aid has the force of a moral imperative. However, other charitable giving is morally optional. Having children is also morally optional in OE (Rand 1968, 3). Although parenting can be regarded as productive in OE (Rand 1964b, 7; Peikoff 1991, 302), it is difficult to justify as a productive endeavor since it is apparently unilateral in nature. It is not remunerative, nor is it life sustaining. The trader principle does not apply in the cases of charity and children, since both can be regarded as primarily one-way transfers. Also, the relationship between parent and child is not that of independent equals.

The trader principle is violated when there is a forced unilateral transfer; that is when a person's person or property is involuntarily employed by another. The victim is owed restitution or retribution. Retribution is sometimes seen as one-way in those instances in which a person is killed or maimed or his property is destroyed—the idea being that that which has been taken cannot be restored. There is a failure in these cases to acknowledge the preceding forced exchange. When a transfer of property occurs, rights are involved. When the transfer is voluntary, the person relinquishing his property has a positive right to compensation.

When a person's negative rights to noninterference have been violated, this confers on the victim a positive right for redress. This has its basis in the principle of reciprocity, a broader principle than the trader principle.

Objectivists and classical liberals regard rights as negative (Rand 1964h, 94; Machan 1998a, 121). The right to noninterference is necessary so that adults can be free to exercise their rationality, the faculty on which their survival depends. Rationality is the basis for rights (Rand 1967a, 18). Reason is not automatic. It takes effort. In fact, a human's rational faculty takes years to develop. The negative right to noninterference is necessary for the adult stage of human "being." Humans are not born with a fully functioning rational capacity. It must be developed and cannot be developed in isolation. I argue that the positive right to care from parents is a basic right. It is primary in the sense of being the first right needed for a human being. However, the right to care is not based on need alone. Parents have a responsibility because of the laws of causality and identity. Bissell's (1981, 30) argument for parental care of children is a liability argument. I think this case is valid, but it puts childbirth in the category of being an infringement of the negative rights of the infant.

According to Rand, dependency as a basis for morality is vicious (Berliner 1995, 576). Children are dependent by nature. In the parent-child relationship, that which is transferred is primarily from parent to child from a "productivity" perspective. Parents invest in their child's human capital, but for the most part, it is the child who receives the return on that investment when he becomes self-supporting. This aspect of parenting appears to be "self-sacrificial" and is difficult to justify within the framework of OE. However, this and other unilateral transfers may not be strictly unilateral if viewed over the course of one's life within the context of a broadened application of the trader principle.

For instance, inheritance is unilateral in nature. If, as OE claims, a person should not give or receive the unearned, then an independent man should not accept inheritance. However, the receipt of inheritance is justified in OE if the recipient in turn makes it productive. I take this to mean that he should not trench on the value of the inherited capital. This is in keeping with Rand's statement (1961a, 89) that, if a man is honest, he will not spend more than he earns (over the course of his life). Therefore, a person would keep the value of his inherited capital intact in value terms. This is a principle of business as well. The value of capital is kept intact by setting aside a sinking fund to accumulate at interest over the course of the capital's expected life. The interest (standard income) from capital can be consumed without trenching on the capital's value.

Gary Becker (1995f, 358–59) implied that parents have a choice of endowing their children with physical capital or human capital. Thus, I argue that human capital investment can be viewed as inheritance. Like the inheritance of physical capital, the value of human capital can be kept intact by setting aside a sinking fund to accumulate at (compound) interest. If a person consumes all of the income from the investment in his human capital (by uncompensated others—typically one's parents), he will have trenched on his human capital. However, most individuals do not set up a sinking fund, since their children are their sinking fund. If an individual's life is viewed as a whole instead of from the sole perspective of the adult piece, then both the receipt of inheritance and the having of children can be seen as intergenerational transfers of physical and human capital. Their "unilaterality" is more apparent than real.

Other unilateral transfers may not be strictly one way either. Certain gift-giving traditions subsume an implied reciprocity. This can also be the case with favors done on another's behalf. Forgiveness is also a gift, but it is unlike other unilateral transfers in that the person forgiven is not "innocent." That is why, if forgiveness is unearned, it is not warranted. By that I mean that forgiveness is not an unqualified virtue. In cases in which "slights" (not "rights") are involved, there are a number of informal ways in which the slighted party may be "paid back." Only the victim can forgive a person for the slight done to himself (and he is under no obligation to do so if a core principle is involved). The point here is that forgiveness should not be one way; the person seeking forgiveness should make amends in some way.

Unlike other unilateral transfers that have the potential for being bilateral if approached from a broader context, charity would seem to be truly unilateral in nature. Since value is not exchanged for value, charitable giving could be regarded as a sacrifice on the part of the giver. This would be particularly true if an individual had never been a net beneficiary. However, many people have received benefits from others who have been undercompensated or not compensated at all. Those who invent and create do not have full ownership of their intellectual property and, therefore, may be net benefactors since they are not fully compensated for that which they produce. Discoverers of new ideas cannot own the product of their efforts and thus are not compensated at all. Also those who have discovered, established, defended, and preserved freedom are net benefactors. If a person has been a net beneficiary, it is not a sacrifice to give to others (who are worthy).

However, since charity is outside the market system, it is not subject to its self-regulating tendency to eliminate shortages and gluts when they occur. The cues provided by the price mechanism to inform and to provide incentives to act are absent. Since charity is not directly life sustaining for the giver, if it is approached as an absolute virtue (with no regard to constraints), then in the limit, it could be suicidal. For that reason, I have derived a percentage for giving based on the BUP, decision-making under uncertainty (risk), and the fundamental alternative. This renders this decision separable from other spending decisions. In applying the BUP to decision-making under uncertainty (risk), I argue that both the rule approach and the maximization approach to ethical decisions are consistent with OE, depending upon context.

There are some one-way transfers that I regard as positive rights, which Objectivists and classical liberals would not. Positive rights are regarded as being the result of voluntary exchange (Den Uyl and Rasmussen 1991, 107). They may also result from infringement of a person's negative rights—what I refer to as forced unilateral transfers. Whether voluntary or involuntary, these positive rights are "reciprocity" based. The additional positive rights that I considered are not "reciprocity" based. They are unilateral in character. I presented two arguments, both dealing with those individuals who have less than a fully functioning rational faculty. The first argument starts with the position that everyone does not have the same negative rights. If it can be proven that a person has less than a fully functioning rational capacity, and he is abused or abandoned by his caregivers, he may be deserving of a positive right to care. The second (weaker) argument assumes that every person has full negative rights. If a person (because he is a child or has diminished capacity as a condition of his existence) is then denied a right, this is an infringement of his rights. This results in a positive right to compensation.

I make two cases for the existence of government. One is based on the systematic exclusion under the equal freedom provision of those who have less than a full rational faculty and are abused by their caregiver under anarchy. The second examines the decision for a person facing the risks of being wrongfully accused of a crime under anarchy versus those under a government with impartial rules.

I conclude that other people are a fundamental part of reality. Since I elevate reproduction to be on par with production, this introduces the necessity of (specific) other people in one's life. Also, I noted that once all original resources (space) are owned, the only way for a propertyless person to have access to property (moral space) is to trade with others. Other people become a fundamental part of reality in that respect. Values and virtues dealing with others—such as nurturance and justice—become primary. All of the cardinal values and virtues cannot be achieved by a man alone.

Appendix 1

1. Modeling Hardtack Consumption

Even though the consumption of hardtack may be considered a production decision, since what is being produced is human capital in the service of one's life only, I think it is more appropriately modeled as a consumption decision. When only one good exists, prices are in terms of that good. If only hardtack exists, a person can trade one hardtack for another, one-to-one. Fisher's hardtack example assumes a zero rate of time preference. However, it may be true that a unit of hardtack today may not have the same value as a unit later. It may depend on the probabilities of being alive in the respective periods. This will be considered explicitly below by weighting the utility functions by these probabilities.

For a single consumer, maximizing lifetime utility will be limited by his "budget" constraint. The Lagrangian function would be:

$$U_L = U^*(C_1, \ldots, C_T) + \mu\,(W_0 - \Sigma_{t=0,n}\,\pi_{at}\,C_t)\ t = 0, \ldots, T$$

where C_t is the amount consumed at time t, W_0 is the total amount of wealth with which one is initially endowed (hardtack), π_{at} is the probability of being alive at time t, so $\pi_{at}C_t$ is expected consumption at time t. In effect, C_t is weighted by the probability that an individual will consume C at time t, which here is shown as the probability of being alive. It is assumed that there are no bequests, i.e., consumption is zero at (T + 1). This expression, $\Sigma_{t=0,n}\,\pi_{at}\,C_t$, then could be regarded as equivalent to expected lifetime consumption (or income in the Fisherian sense [Fisher {1906} 1965, 254–55]), since if one is not alive, then one consumes nothing ($\pi_{dt}C_t = 0$), where π_{dt} is the probability of dying at time t. Typically, expected lifetime income or consumption is weighted by a discount factor, but since Fisher assumed that the interest rate and rate of time preference are zero in the hardtack case, future consumption is not discounted in this example.

The utility function, U*, above is in a general form. If it is assumed that the force of mortality is constant so that the π_{at} declines over time, then given both the "budget constraint" (which is a function of W_0 and π_{at} only) and the utility function, the optimal amount of consumption for every time period t will be fully determined (Green 1978, 196–97). With $C_2 \ldots C_{(T+1)}$ determined, then one can examine two periods, t = 0 and t = 1 (two adjacent time periods).

That is, with C_2 through $C_{(T+1)}$ fully determined,

$M_0 = W_0 - \pi_{a2} C_2 - \ldots - \pi_{aT} C_T - \pi_{aT+1} C_{(T+1)}$.

Therefore the constraint is:

$M_0 = \pi_{a0} C_0 + \pi_{a1} C_1$, or

$C_1 = [M_0/\pi_{a1} - (\pi_{a0}/\pi_{a1})C_0]$.

That is, the slope of the budget constraint (dC_1/dC_0) is $-\pi_{a0}/\pi_{a1}$.

To take account of the probability of being alive in each period on the castaway's hardtack consumption decision, each period's utility function can be weighted by the probability of being alive in that time period. If the probability of being alive is used as weights and if it is assumed that the utility function is of the form $U(C_t) = (C_t^{1-\rho})/(1-\rho)$, then

$U^* = \pi_{a0} U[C_0] + \pi_{a1} U[C_1]$, would become

$U^* = \pi_{a0} (C_0^{1-\rho})/(1-\rho) + \pi_{a1} (C_1^{1-\rho})/(1-\rho)$.

An indifference curve gives the various quantities of C_1 and C_0 that will keep the consumer's utility unchanged. The absolute value of its slope is the marginal rate of substitution of C_1 for C_0, which in this case is given by $\pi_{a0}/\pi_{a1} (C_1/C_0)^\rho$. If $C_0 = C_1$, then a one unit increase in C_0 accompanied by a π_{a0}/π_{a1} fall in C_1 will keep the consumer's utility unchanged. The point of tangency of the budget constraint with the indifference curve yields the following optimization condition:

$dC_1/dC_0 = -\pi_{a0}/\pi_{a1} = -\pi_{a0} (C_0^{-\rho})/\pi_{a1} (C_1^{-\rho}) = -\pi_{a0}/\pi_{a1}(C_1/C_0)^\rho$.

In traditional models of optimization over time, when $C_1 = C_0$, the slope of the indifference curve, –(1+i) (where i is the rate of time preference), is equal to –(1+r), the slope of the budget constraint, where r is the rate of interest (Green 1978, 198). Here, the slope of the indifference curve when $C_1 = C_0$ is π_{a0}/π_{a1}, which is the same as the slope of the budget constraint (ignoring negative signs). This may seem tautological, but it is not. Utility is weighted by the probability of being alive because it is expected that in making decisions on consumption over time, one's utility would be affected by the probability that one will be alive to benefit from the consumption of a good. One of the bases for time preference is that there is uncertainty surrounding the timing of one's death. I have assumed that the probabilities of being alive that are used as weights above do not take into account all of the uncertainties related to one's death. The ratio π_{a0}/π_{a1} may capture part of what is captured by time preference (i.e., $i = (\pi_{a0}/\pi_{a1} - 1)$), but would not capture all of the uncertainty under normal circumstances.

Consumption in the budget constraint in each period is weighted by the probability of being alive. This is consistent with expected consumption. To calculate the value of a stream of income, or in this case consumption, over time, it is reasonable to adjust consumption per time period by probabilities of receiving it. In other words, both the slopes for the budget constraint and the indifference curve would equal π_{a0}/π_{a1} at $C_0 = C_1$, but the reasons for weighting the respective functions by the probabilities of survival would differ. (The "return" would be $\partial = (\pi_{a0}/\pi_{a1} - 1)$, where ∂ is the constant force of mortality. See appendix 1.2.)

(The marginal propensity to consume (MPC) is discussed in appendix 1.4. Given the Lagrangian: $U_L = \pi_{A0}[C_0^{1-\rho}/(1-\rho)] + \pi_{A1}[C_1^{1-\rho}/(1-\rho)] + \mu(M_0 - \pi_{A0}C_0 - \pi_{A1}C_1)$, the MPC for period zero would be given as $1/(\pi_{A0} + \pi_{A1})$. If, for example, $C_0 + C_1$ were fixed, say, at 1,000 units, and $\pi_{A0} = 1.00$, $\pi_{A1} = .909$ and $\rho = .5$, then $C_0 = C_1 = 524$ if $M_0 = 1{,}000$. However, $M_0 = 500 + 500/1.10 = 954$. Therefore $C_0 = C_1 = 500$.)

2. Expected Value of Lifetime Income

To account for income's uncertainty due to the probability one will die from one year to the next (prior to T), another concept separate from present value is required. That concept is expected value. Expected value is calculated as income per period multiplied by the survival rates per period (Sachko 1975, 27–28). (The survival rates, π_{at}, are assumed to be simply $1/(1+\partial)^t$, or in continuous terms $e^{-\partial t}$, where ∂ is the force of mortality. See appendix 1.9, equations ($S3^i$) and ($S7^i$).) Expected value and present value are similar in appearance. Since the cumulative of survival changes over time, time enters the expected value concept. Thus, since the value obtained is based on the expected receipt of lifetime income, it has a "present value" aspect to it, but it is not the same as the present value of an asset partly because the "return" in each differs in interpretation and value.

If it is assumed that there is some probability of dying due to chance alone (i.e., over which the individual has no control), and that probability is 10 percent per year (abstracting from all other probabilities associated with untimely death), then if the person lives, he "gains" 1,000; if he dies his "payoff" is 0. The probability of survival in the first year would be 1/(1.10), so that the expected income for that year would be 1,000(.9090) = 909.90. There is also a probability that he will die and earn nothing and that probability is $\partial(1/(1+\partial)) = .10(.9090) = .0909$, or 9.09 percent (which is equivalent to the mortality rate). (The expected loss if he died would be 1,000(.0909) = 9.09.) Thus the expected income in year one would be .909(1,000) + .0909(0) = 909.90. If he lives, he receives 1,000, not the 909.90 that was "expected." He would receive a "return" of 9.09 over that which was expected of 909.09, (or 10 percent). This is a bonus in that it exceeds the "average" or expected income of 909.09. Expected lifetime earnings would be (in discrete terms) $[\Sigma^{T}_{t=1} (1{,}000)/(1.10)^{t}]$, where t = 10 = 6144.44. This would be the total income the individual would "probably" receive over his expected earning life.

3. Replacement Value of Human Capital

Irving Fisher defined standard income as that constant stream equivalent to a perpetual annuity which would keep the value of a capital asset constant. A sinking fund would be that amount per year that if set aside would accumulate at (compound) interest to equal the value of capital at the end of time T, the capital's life (Fisher [1906] 1965, 242, 332). If a sinking fund were set aside, standard income would be equal to income less the sinking fund per period. If a sinking fund were not set aside, standard income would be equal to (actual) income less depreciation (or appreciation). If a person inherited an income-earning asset that yields $1,000 per year with an expected earning life of 10 years at 10 percent interest, it would have a present value of approximately $6,144.44. In order to keep the value of that asset intact, a sinking fund of $385.55 per year would have to be set aside for 10 years at 10 percent interest.

In order that the inheritor not trench on his inheritance, he would set aside a sinking fund. To be worthy of it, he would be making it productive to the extent that the fund would accumulate to equal $6,144.44 at the end of 10 years. He would still be receiving the "standard" income of $614.44 per year of interest on this inheritance. (Although interest is considered a return to physical capital and I refer to it in this way, it may be viewed as income from his human capital because of investment decisions he makes and/or because of his abstinence from consumption.) The point is, at a minimum, he would be charged with maintaining the value of the capital ($6,144.44) in order to be worthy of it. In order to be "honest" (see Rand 1961a, 89), an individual would not consume more than he produced. Since he did not produce the value of $6,144.44, then in order for his consumption to be (less than or) equal to his income (from both his inheritance and his human capital), he would only consume income generated from his inheritance (of $614.44) plus any other earnings from his own human capital (salary income, for instance).

Instead of physical capital, a similar example could apply to human capital. For simplification purposes, one could retain the previous numerical example and assume that the investment in human capital has been $6,144.44 (and there is no inheritance of physical capital). The notion that a person is "self-made" assumes that the individual has been solely responsible for investment in his human capital. But since individuals are born *tabulae rasae* and if, as Becker (1995f, 358–59) implied, parents face to some extent the alternative of investing in their child's human capital or in physical endowments, then at least some portion of a person's human capital is due to unilateral investment by one's parents (i.e., parents do not receive a return on that investment). If that is true, then a person has been endowed with human capital investment. In order to keep that intact, as he would an equivalent value of physical capital, he would have to set aside a sinking fund of (to use the example above for purposes of illustration) $385.55 a year for ten years at 10 percent interest. In other words, the relevant income concept insofar as his own consumption is concerned would be standard income of $614.44.

In the example of a castaway who has at his disposal a limited quantity of hardtack, it is not possible to set aside an amount for depreciation (sinking fund), since hardtack cannot grow. The 6,144.44 is the value of hardtack because it is the probable amount that will be consumed over the life of the castaway. As was shown in chapter 4, survival rates per period can be used to arrive at a rate of "time preference." Time preference exists in part because of death's uncertainty. The expected value problem is thus "transformed" into a present value problem. (See appendix 1.2.) However, because of the limitations of the hardtack problem, there are some differences between it and the typical present value problem. The analysis is useful, nevertheless, because of the limitations it uncovers. If hardtack has an expected value of 6,144.44 based on consumption of 1,000 per year for ten years and a 10 percent force of mortality rate, then 385.55 would be the amount that would go into a sinking fund per year in order to maintain the capital value of 6,144.44. If one set aside 385.55 per year into such a fund for hardtack, one would have only 3,855.55 in ten years.

The reason that no sinking fund can be set aside for hardtack to accumulate at interest is that there is no alternative investment for hardtack. (See appendix 1.1, 1.7, and 1.8.) Hardtack is "invested" in maintaining a human life that is assumed to "depreciate" at a rate of $[\partial/(1+\partial)^{T+1-t} - 1]$ per year. This rate is applied to hardtack because hardtack derives its value from that which it maintains. Hardtack has a "return" in value of 10 percent so long as the individual survives, but it derives its value from being used at a rate of 1,000 per year to maintain an individual. In fact, if a depreciation fund of 385.55 per year were set aside, that individual (his "value") could not be maintained under the assumptions of the problem.

Nevertheless, for the hardtack case, what is called interest or a return is consistent with theoretical definitions. Each year that the person survives, there is a return. For the first year, if the castaway survives, the "growth" in value would be: 6,144 x 1.10 = 6759. This, less 1,000 units consumed for the year, gives the second year value of 5,759. "Depreciation" is 385.55 (i.e., 6,144–5,759). The "interest" on 6,144 is 10 percent, or 614.44; the difference between 1,000 and "depreciation" for the year. The person (or hardtack) could be said to depreciate by 385.55 that year because of a finite life. The 385.55 is the decline in PV (or more accurately EV, expected value) for that year. The value of 6,144 does not fall by 1,000 but 385.55, due in part to the readjustment of the probabilities since one survived the year before. (For example, once the second year arrives, now the castaway would be alive with the same probability that existed for the first year. If, in the first year, a person would survive with 90.9 percent probability, then the second year's probability would have been 82.6 percent. Once the first year has passed, the second year becomes the first and now the probability of surviving that year is 90.9 percent instead of 82.6, and so on.)

4. The Marginal Propensity to Consume

In the hardtack case, hardtack has value because of the survival of the castaway. The value of the hardtack and the castaway are inseparable in that sense. However, there is no "human capital" in the sense that the person in turn produces anything. So ultimately there is no return. There still may be a positive interest rate that reflects scarcity. In this simple example, if the interest rate were positive, it would be equal to time preference rate. If the time preference rate and the interest rate were both positive and equal, then consumption in each period would be equal. (See appendix 1.1.)

In the more general case in which growth is possible and there is more than a single person, the discount rate, i, would reflect other uncertainties besides survival, and interest, r, could reflect an actual return. Green presented the following lifetime utility function, which assumes that utility is additive over time and T is the length of life:

(1) $U^* = U[C_0] + U[C_1] / (1+i) + \ldots + \Sigma_{t=0}^{T+1} U[C_t] / (1+i)^t$.

The utility associated with C in (T+1) is that for one's heirs (1978, 196, 198). (Green did not offer a reason for a positive rate of time preference. If T is known and the probability of survival until then is 100 percent, then i would depend on other uncertainties.)

The wealth constraint would take the form:

(2) $W_0 = C_0 + C_1 / (1+r) + \ldots + \Sigma_{t=0}^{T+1} C_t / (1+r)^t$.

Given (1) and (2) and a single interest rate, optimal consumption over time is determined. Since the utility function is additive, the rate at which the consumer is willing to exchange one unit of consumption for another between two periods, say 0 and 1 (the marginal rate of substitution), depends on C_0 and C_1 alone. The indifference curve reflects the trade-off between C_0 and C_1 (for a given level of satisfaction or utility). The marginal rate of substitution (MRS) of C_1 for C_0 is defined as the negative of the slope of the indifference curve.

With consumption in all other periods determined, the constraint for periods 0 and 1 is:

$$M_0 = W_0 - C_2 / (1+r)^2 - \ldots - C_{T+1} / (1+r)^{T+1}$$

(3) $C_1 = [M_0 - C_0](1+r)$.

The slope of the budget constraint shown in (3) is $dC_1 / dC_0 = -(1+r)$. If

(3.1) $U = C^{1-\rho} / 1-\rho$,

then between two periods, 0 and 1, the Lagrangian function would be:

(4) $U_L = C_0^{1-\rho} / 1-\rho + [C_1^{1-\rho} / 1-\rho] (1+i)^{-1} + \mu [M_0-C_0-(1+r)^{-1}C_1]$.

Therefore:

(4[i]) $\partial U_L/\partial C_0 = C_0^{-\rho} - \mu = 0$

(4[ii]) $\partial U_L/\partial C_1 = (1+i)^{-1} C_1^{-\rho} -(1+r)^{-1} \mu = 0$

(4[iii]) $\partial U_L/\partial \mu = M_0-C_0-(1+r)^{-1}C_1 = 0$.

From (4[i]) and (4[ii]):

(4.1) $-C_0^{-\rho} / C_1^{-\rho} = -(C_1 / C_0)^{\rho} = (1+r)/(1+i)$.

Isolating the equality of slope of the indifference curve and the slope of the budget constraint from (4.1) (in absolute value terms) gives the optimization condition:

(4.2) $(C_1 / C_0)^{\rho}(1+i) = (1+r)$,

if $0<\rho<1$, marginal utility declines as additional units of a good are consumed. With additive utility functions, this means that an indifference curve is convex to the origin. When $C_0 = C_1$, the slope of the budget constraint, $-(1+r)$, equals the (negative of) the MRS, $-(1+i)$, which means $r = i$ at that point (1978, 197–98). It can be shown that if r increases relative to i, then (graphically) the budget line becomes steeper than the slope of the indifference curve at the point where $C_0 = C_1$. This means that the rate at which the individual is willing to trade C_1 for C_0 is less than the rate at which the person can trade C_1 for C_0. In effect, since (1+r) reflects the ratio of prices (P_0/P_1), current prices have increased relative to future; i.e., it takes more future goods to buy one unit of present goods. The individual will then save more (other things equal) and consume less during the current period. As he does, the marginal utility of current goods rises relative to future goods; the slope of the indifference curve steepens (the MRS increases). What this means is that consumption in period zero decreases relative to consumption in period one until the MRS is equal to the ratio of prices (of period zero relative to one).

A positive rate of time preference implies that present consumption is preferred to future. One thing that encourages an individual to postpone present consumption for future is that if one delays consumption he will receive a return in the form of interest. One reason that interest may be payable in the future is because of growth (in the physical productivity sense). If there is no growth, then interest will fail to materialize. (However, the interest rate may be positive in order to discourage borrowing—that is, it may rise to the point that no borrowing takes place. Since borrowing becomes prohibitive, no interest has to be paid. This is Böhm Bawerk's case in which income does not grow, but a positive rate of time preference induces a positive rate of interest [Green 1978, 203–208]. In the hardtack case, there is no lending market; a positive "interest rate" would reflect the cast-away's valuations. See my numerical example in appendix 1.8.)

Given (4.2), C_1 can be solved in terms of C_0 and substituted into the budget constraint (4^{iii}), thus obtaining:

(5) $C_0 = (1+i)^{1/\rho} / [(1+i)^{1/\rho} + (1+r)^{(1-\rho)/\rho}] M_0$, or

(5.1) $C_0 = \lambda_0 M_0$.

Thus, the marginal propensity to consume (MPC) out of wealth for the first period (λ_0) is positively related to i, negatively related to r, and positively related to ρ (where $\rho = 1/\eta$ is the degree of risk tolerance in state preference theory (Green 1978, 321). η is the elasticity of substitution, which Green described as "the most complex of elasticities" (1971, 198). It measures the percentage change in C_0/C_1 relative to the percentage change in the MRS.

5. Life's Uncertainty, Bequests, and the Propensity to Consume

An alternative formulation that gives an identical λ_0 as that shown in (5) is:

$U_M = U(C_0) + U[(M_0 - C_0)(1+r)](1+i)^{-1}$,

and if (3.1) is assumed, then:

(4^i) $U_M = C_0^{1-\rho} / 1-\rho + \{[(M_0 - C_0)(1+r)]^{1-\rho} / 1-\rho\}(1+i)^{-1}$.

The assumption underlying (4) and (4^i) is that whatever is not consumed in period 0 is consumed in period 1. Consumption in t = 1, the second period, is assumed to equal wealth for that period.

It is not necessary to assume that all wealth in the second period is consumed. The decision could be one of how much to consume in period 0 and to save in period 1. However, if one is alive now and will be alive next period, it would make little sense to assume that $C_1 = 0$. If one is alive, one consumes. Still, if one knew he was not going to be alive next period, the decision might be recast into how much to consume this period (t = T, the last period of one's life) and how much to leave in bequests next period (t = T+1). If the utility functions for consumption and bequests were identical (a simplifying assumption), then the MPC out of wealth in period T would be similar to that shown above in (5). There are one or two differences to account for, however. Even if the utility functions themselves were identical, it may make little sense to *discount* the second period (t = T+1) by time preference. If one is to die next year, there is no uncertainty, at least insofar as dying is concerned. One would weight next period's utility, but how much it would be weighted would depend on how important bequests are to the individual. If they have no value at all, the weight would be zero. If bequests yield utility, one would not consume all of his wealth in the last period of his life (T). If utility of bequests had equal weight to that of consumption in period T, then

(4^{ii}) $U_L = U(C_T) + U(C_{T+1}) + \mu [M_T - C_T - C_{T+1}(1+r)^{-1}]$.

If (3.1) is assumed, then:

(5^{i}) $C_T = 1/[1 + (1+r)^{1-\rho/\rho}]\ M_T$.

Thus if, as assumed, discount is irrelevant for T+1, and r = .10 and ρ = .5, then $\lambda_T = 1/[1+(1.10)^{(1-.5)/.5}] = .4762$. One would plan to consume *less in period T,* if both utility of consumption this period and that of bequests next period had equal weight. He would consume less than he normally would in the first period (period T in this case), because discount would not apply to the second period, T+1. That is, more would be available for bequests due to the interest that would accrue on that which is saved in period T.

It may seem a contradiction to say that a person places the same weight on consumption this period as he does on bequests next period, yet he plans to consume less this period than will be available next period for bequests. If he adjusts his decision so as to end up with the same amounts in each period, then the factor on bequests (b) could be the same value as the discount factor [1/(1+i)]. (This is because for C to be constant i = r. The MPC would be .524 if r = i =.10. See appendix 1.8.) The MPC for period T (the last period of life) is shown in the following (which is the same as that of Stanley Fischer [1973, 134]):

(5^{ii}) $C_T = [b_{T+1}(1 + r_T)]^{-1/\rho}\ (1 + r_T)\ /\ \{1 + [b_{T+1}(1 + r_T)]^{-1/\rho}\ (1 + r_T)\}\ W_T$.

In this case, the weight on bequests would have the same effect as discount would have had. Generally speaking, b would not equal (1/(1+i)). The greater the weight of the bequest function (b), the lower the MPC out of wealth for the current period. The bequest motive has a *moderating effect* on current consumption.

The usual situation is that one is alive now (with 100 percent certainty) but is unsure about next period. Next period he may be alive or dead. If he knew the probabilities, he might make decisions concerning consumption based (in part) on his expected utility for next period:

$E(U) = \pi_a U(V_a) + \pi_d U(V_d)$,

where V_a is the "payoff" if one lives and V_d is the "payoff" if one dies.

Since E(U) would be for *next* period, the "expected payoff" in the life state would have to be discounted. The "expected payoff" in the death state would be multiplied by a bequest factor:

$E(U) = (1+i)^{-1}\ \pi_a U(V_a) + b\ \pi_d U(V_d)$.

Instead of the general variable designations of V_a and V_d, it would be more accurate to recast expected utility next period based on the probabilities of (the utility of) either consuming (C) or leaving bequests (B) for period T:

$E(U) = (1+i)^{-1}\ \pi_a\ C_T^{1-\rho}\ /\ 1-\rho + b\ \pi_d\ B_T^{1-\rho}\ /\ 1-\rho$.

But this does not account for a "constraint"; i.e., that whatever is not spent in t = T-1 accumulates and is available either to consume or for bequests next period. If the individual is expected to die at t = T, then there is some probability of dying by the end of t = T-1. For these two periods, then

(4[iv]) $U_M = C_{T-1}^{1-\rho} / 1-\rho + (1+i)^{-1} \pi_a [(M_{T-1} - C_{T-1})(1+r)]^{1-\rho} / 1-\rho + b\, \pi_d [(M_{T-1} - C_{T-1})(1+r)]^{1-\rho} / 1-\rho$,

where $[(M_{T-1} - C_{T-1})(1+r)]$ is wealth in the second period (T).

However, if the individual lives, he probably will not consume all of $[(M_{T-1} - C_{T-1})(1+r)]$, but only a fraction of it; the rest will be saved. Therefore, under the life state, wealth in the second period should be subject to some factor, an MPC out of wealth. Intuitively, it would seem that the second period utility function (in the life state) should be multiplied by the MPC out of wealth, λ_T; however, the correct factor is $\lambda_T^{-\rho}$ (if the analysis is confined to deriving optimal consumption in (T–1), where T is the last period of life). Multiplying second period wealth in the "life state" by $\lambda_T^{-\rho}$ gives the following equation for $J_2[M_{T-1}]$ (where $J_1[M_T]$ is shown in (6) below):

(4[v]) $J_2[M_{T-1}] = C_{T-1}^{1-\rho} /1-\rho + (1+i)^{-1} \pi_a \lambda_T^{-\rho} [(M_{T-1} - C_{T-1})(1+r)]^{1-\rho} /1-\rho + b_T \pi_d [(M_{T-1} - C_{T-1})(1+r)]^{1-\rho}/1-\rho$.

To derive $\lambda_T^{-\rho}$, begin with the following equation, similar in form to (5.1):

(5.1[i]) $C_T = \lambda_T M_T$.

The indirect utility function given by Fischer (1973, 134) is:

(6) $J_1[M_T] = \lambda_T^{-\rho} M_T^{1-\rho} / 1-\rho \quad \lambda_T^{-\rho} > 1$.

Equation on (5.1[i]) implies that $U = [C_T]^{1-\rho} / 1-\rho = [\lambda_T M_T]^{1-\rho} / 1-\rho$, therefore

(6.1) $U' = [\lambda_T M_T]^{-\rho} = \lambda_T^{-\rho} M_T^{-\rho}$.

The MPC for period T-1 that is derived from equation (4[v]) is obtained in the same way in which (5) is derived from (4). (That is, by taking the partial derivative of (4[v]) with respect to C_{T-1}, setting it equal to zero and solving for C_{T-1}.) Although the MPC for period T-1 is not shown here, its properties can be discussed. Once a bequest motive (b) is accounted for, the impact on the MPC out of wealth as a result of changes in π_d (the probability of death) is ambiguous. If the weight on bequests, b, is high, an increase in π_d results in a lower MPC for the given time period. If the weighting on bequests is low, a rise in π_d will raise the MPC for the given period. Fischer said that the more the "'eat, drink and be merry . . .' philosophy—in the form of a low [b]—prevail, the more likely is it that an increase in the probability of death increases current consumption" (1973, 136); the pressure to consume now at the expense of the future is greater.

In Fischer's model, the MPC could fall in some periods, reflecting the weight "attached to 'posterity'" (1973, 136). The MPC out of wealth declines in some periods in Fischer's model, because of the weight on bequests, b. This weight is typically higher during times when a person's children are young (1973, 136). (The weighting function on bequests may be hump-shaped, reflecting greater weights during times in which one's dependents are young [1973, 133].)

One of Fischer's primary interests was in examining the determinants of insurance demand. When insurance is added to the decision then, if the individual lives, his wealth will be reduced by the amount spent on his life insurance premium. If m is that fraction of his savings devoted to premiums, then if he lives, savings will have to be factored by $(1 - m)$. If he dies, his savings will also be factored by $(1 - m)$; however, he will also receive a return, Q, on his insurance coverage, which would be factored by the proportion spent on insurance, m:

$$(4^{vi})\ J_2[M_{T-1}] = C_{T-1}{}^{1-\rho} / 1-\rho + (1+i)^{-1} \pi_a \lambda_T{}^{-\rho}{}_1 [(M_{T-1} - C_{T-1})(1+r)(1 - m_{T-1})]^{1-\rho} / 1-\rho + b_T \pi_d [(M_{T-1} - C_0)(1+r)\{(1 - m_{T-1}) + m_{T-1}Q_{T-1}\}]^{1-\rho} / 1-\rho.$$

This is very similar to Fischer's function (1973, 134). Fischer noted that for insurance purchase to occur, the weight on bequests, b, must be greater than $1/(1+i)$ (1973, 137). (Fischer's discount rate excludes the uncertainty of death [1973, 133].) He found that the greater the weight on bequests, the greater the likelihood of buying insurance (1973, 143).

Fischer continued the analysis by adding labor income. Labor income is more relevant for insurance decisions since that is the income that tends to be more greatly impacted by the death of the insured in most cases. The other thing Fischer added to the decision was an asset that had an uncertain return.

6. Risk and the Propensity to Consume

There are a number of ways to include uncertainty in the saving decision. One is to take it into account with respect to death's timing—as in the previous section. Another is to take into account uncertain returns (where risk is defined as a higher rate of variance in returns for a given average return). If it is assumed that the consumer's objective is to maximize expected utility; that the consumer has a given quantity of wealth, W_0, at time zero ($W_t \geq C_t \geq 0$); that yields of the risky asset are random and their distributions independent and invariant over time, then the optimal proportions invested in a risky asset and a safe asset will be independent of wealth and will be stationary over time if the utility function exhibits constant elasticity of substitution (that is, relative risk aversion must be constant—which means ρ is constant) (Levhari and Srinivasan 1969, 153; Mossin 1968, 218).

Like Fischer (1973), economists such as Samuelson (1969) and Levhari and Srinivasan (1969) derived MPCs under various assumptions. Both Samuelson (1969) and Fischer (1973) assumed a finite life. A more general MPC out of wealth than (5.1^i) is Samuelson's equation:

$C_{T-j} = \lambda_j W_{T-j}$, where ($j$ = the number of periods prior to T), and where:

$\lambda_j = [A_1{}^j (A_1-1)] / A_1{}^{j+1}-1 \qquad A_1 \neq 1$

$\lambda_j = 1 / (1+j) \qquad A_1 = 1$

$(6.2)\ A_1 = [(1+r)^{1-\rho} / (1+i)]^{-1/\rho}$.

The MPC out of wealth, $[1 - (1/A_1)]$ (where A_1 is given in [6.2]), is similar to that obtained by Levhari and Srinivasan in their examination of optimal saving under uncertainty with an *infinite time horizon*, and under the assumption that consumption per period was a *constant* proportion of wealth. If $\rho = 1$, then the uncertainty associated with the return on the risky asset has no effect on the optimal propensity to consume because r has no effect. That is, if the MPC (λ) out of wealth is based on $[1 - (1/A_1)]$ (and r in (6.2) is now a return on a risky asset), and $\rho = 1$, then $\lambda = 1 - 1/(1 + i)$. The propensity to consume depends solely on the discount rate (Levhari and Srinivasan 1969, 160–161; Samuelson 1969, 244).

Uncertainty, expressed as variance in returns, can affect consumption. How it will affect consumption depends on the individual's attitude toward risk. For instance, if $\log(1 + r)$ is distributed normally, then increasing uncertainty coupled with risk aversion ($\rho < 1$) will lead to a high propensity to consume out of wealth, λ (and a lower propensity to save). For the risk taker ($\rho > 1$), greater uncertainty will result in a lower λ and a greater propensity to save (Levhari and Srinivasan 1969, 160–161).

7. Definition of Time Preference

According to some definitions, time preference is equal to the marginal rate of substitution minus one:

$(-)dC_1/dC_0 - 1 = \partial U/\partial C_0 / \partial U/\partial C_1 - 1 = i$ (Allen 1967, 344; Henderson and Quandt 1971, 304).

For the utility function considered thus far (i.e., $C^{1-\rho} / 1-\rho$), this would be:

$i = (1+i)\,(C_1/C_0)^{\rho} - 1.$

Since $dC_1/dC_0 = -(1+r)$ is also the slope of the budget constraint at tangency, then $i = r$. For the utility functions of this form, this makes sense only if $C_1 = C_0$, which seems unrealistic as a rule of behavior.

If the intertemporal utility function is of the form:

$U = C_1\, C_2$

(4') $U_L = C_1\, C_2 + \mu\,[M_0 - C_0 - C_1\,(1+i)^{-1}]$

$\partial U_L/\partial C_0 = C_1 - \mu = 0$

$\partial U_L/\partial C_1 = C_0 - \mu\,(1+i)^{-1} = 0$

$\partial U_L/\partial \mu = M_0 - C_0 - C_1\,(1+i)^{-1} = 0.$

Solving for C_0 and for C_1 gives:

$C_1 = M_0\,(1+i)/2$, thus $C_0 = M_0/2$.

Given the expressions for C_1 and C_0:

$i = MRS - 1 = (-)\,dC_1/dC_0 - 1 = C_1/C_0 - 1 = [M_0\,(1+i)/2] / [M_0/2] - 1 = i.$

Therefore if $M_0 = 1{,}000$:

$C_0 = 1{,}000/2 = 500$, $C_1 = (1+i)(1{,}000/2) = (1+i)500$

$i = C_1/C_0 - 1 = [(500/500)] - 1 = 0.$

Thus, for this functional form of utility over time, if $C_0 = C_1$, then both i and r equal 0.

The equality of i and r is brought about by the consumer buying or selling bonds. From the *individual consumer perspective,* his actions alone have no effect on r. His *rate of time preference adjusts to the interest rate*. For instance, in the case in which i exceeds r, the individual places a premium on present consumption; the rate of interest is low. In response, he would sell bonds, increase his current consumption relative to future, until in equilibrium, the rate of time preference equaled the rate of interest, according to this point of view (Henderson and Quandt 1971, 305). (Given, $(C_1 / C_0)^{\rho}(1+i) = (1+r)$, then C_1 would rise relative to C_0, which, at least initially, would increase the MRS, but not i.) From the *perspective of the market,* however, the *interest rate adjusts to changes in the rate of time preference*. In the case in which i exceeds r, conditions are favorable to trade bonds for present consumption (C_0), thereby sacrificing future consumption (C_1). If this were true for *everyone* in the market, then bond prices would fall (due to the increase in supply—i.e., attempts to sell bonds), which means the interest rate would rise (since the price of bonds and the interest rate are inversely related). This would continue until r equaled i. (Given, $(C_1 / C_0)^{\rho}(1+i) = (1+r)$, as bond prices fall, the right hand side, specifically r, would rise.)

8. Fixed Cs, a Positive Interest Rate, and the Change in Present Value (M_0)

If $(C_0 + C_1)$ is fixed and cannot grow, then it would seem that M_0 (the present value for the two periods) would have to change with a change in the interest rate. When the Cs are not fixed, the (real) return would result in greater consumption in t = 1 if C_0 is sacrificed. With no growth, the change in r would reflect a change in valuation only.

If i = r = 0 and if the individual only consumed 500 units per period, the present value would be 1,000 (and given the utility functions of the form $C^{1-\rho} / 1-\rho$, expected utility would be $(500^{.5}/.5 + 500^{.5}/.5) = 89.44$). That is, if $C_0 + C_1$ is fixed and equal to 1,000, then, from equations (5) and (3) in appendix 1.4:

$C_0 = C_1 = 1/2\ M_0 = 1/2\ (1{,}000) = 500.$

However, if time preference is based on the probabilities of survival—as assumed in the example discussed in appendix 1.1, then if there were only a 90.9 percent chance of survival next time period (that is, the individual can expect to live only 90.9 percent of the next time period) would he choose to consume the balance (9.1 percent or so) today (in period zero)? If the rate of time preference increased to 10 percent, the present value would remain at 1,000. But this results in a higher MPC out of wealth in period zero. That is, based on equation (5), if i = .10, r = 0, then $\lambda_0 = .54751$, and

$C_0 = 547.51$

$C_1 = M_0 - C_0 = 1{,}000 - 547.51 = 452.49$

$C_0 + C_1 = 1{,}000.$

(Expected utility would fall to $(547.51)^{.5}/.5 + (1/1.10)(452.59)^{.5}/.5 = 85.09$.)

Based on (4.2), r would equal zero:

(4.2) $(1+i)\,(C_1/C_0)^{\rho} = (1+r)$

$(1.10)\,(452.49 / 547.51)^{.5} = 1.$

If C_0 and C_1 were fixed respectively at 500 each, then C_1 could not fall relative to C_0; therefore, r would have to increase to 10 percent. Typically, the mechanism by which this would happen is by selling bonds in the bond market. However, if there were no bond market, this would be the result of a revaluation on the part of the consumer(s). (The valuation on present goods relative to future—typically expressed as $P_{C0}/P_{C1} = (1+r)$—would rise.) Mathematically,

$(1+r) = (1+i)(500/500)^{.5}.$

Since $C_0 = C_1 = 500$, then, if (1+i) is given, based on the assumptions on which it is based (the probabilities of survival), r would rise to .10. By attempting to purchase more goods at the expense of future goods, the valuation of present goods in terms of future goods will increase. That is, if the rate of time preference remains at 10 percent, then to restore equilibrium, r must rise to 10 percent. The interest rate will rise in order to make the individual "satisfied" with consuming at the rate of 500 per period (as shown below).

This seems like sleight of hand. It appears to turn value theory on its head. How can the premium of future consumption over present consumption (i.e., the return) be positive when there is no physical return? The increase in the interest rate reflects a greater valuation of present goods relative to future goods because of an attempt to increase consumption of present goods to future (due to positive time preference) coupled with an inability to do so because of the fixed supply. The interest rate reflects relative scarcity in response to the subjective premium placed on present goods due to the lower probability of survival in period one relative to period zero. Consumption is fixed in supply in each period (and equal to 500 in each period). Its relative trade-off value between two periods is derived from the relative expected scarcity of one's life (based on the probabilities of survival) between the two periods. (It has been previously assumed that consumption overall is equal to 1,000 for the two periods, not that consumption is fixed at 500 per period. However, if r = i, consumption per period will be constant. It is not clear that r will rise to equal i if consumption overall is fixed, but can vary between the two periods.)

If the sum of the amount for periods zero and one are constrained to equal 1,000, then the higher interest rate may be shown to result in period one's consumption being discounted at a higher rate of interest; therefore, the present value (PV) will become:

$M_0' = 500 + 500/(1.10) = 954.54.$

(Expected utility would rise somewhat to 85.37.) That is, 454.54 will "grow" (in value) to 500 once t = 1 arrives. But why will it "grow"? It will grow, presumably, because (and if) one survives to consume it. In t = 1, the value of 454.54 increases to 500 because now the probability of being alive is 100 percent (since the person is alive).

When r increases to 10 percent (and i remains at 10 percent), the MPC out of wealth also changes to .5238. Now with λ_0 = .5238 and M_0' = 954.54:

C_0" = 500, and from equation (3)

C_1" = (954.54 – 500)(1.10) = 500 from equation (5).

(Expected utility would remain the same at 85.37.)

With the assumptions of ρ = .5 and r = i = .10, but with consumption in each period equal to 500, then M_0' = 954.54, and equations (5) and (3) give C_0" = C_1" = 500, amounts equal to that which result in the initial example in which i = r = 0, M_0 = 1,000, and ρ = .5. The only difference is that the PV is 954.54 instead of 1,000. (Although I am using the expression PV, it is a present value based only on the probabilities of survival, i.e., expected value.)

This example would not literally apply to the hardtack case, since in that case the overall quantity is limited; it is not limited to a certain quantity per period. If C_0 and C_1 were *not fixed at all* and M_0 = 1,000, ρ = .5 and r = i = .10, the MPC would become .52381, and

$C_0' = M_0\ 1/\{1+[(1+r)^{1-\rho/\rho}/(1+i)]^{1/\rho}\} = 1{,}000\ 1/\{1+[(1.10)^{.5}/(1.10)]^{1/.5}\} = 523.81$ from (5).

C_1' = 523.81 from (3).

Thus, $C_0'+C_1'$ = 1047.62.

(Based on the intertemporal utility function $U^* = C_0^{1-\rho} / 1-\rho + (1+i)^{-1}\ C_1^{1-\rho} / 1-\rho$, if i = r, the consumer would plan to consume the same amount in each time period, and the growth rate in consumption, $g = \eta(r-i)/(1+i)$ (Green 1978, 201) would be zero since r – i = 0. Even though consumption per period is constant, it is not "fixed." There is growth, even though there is no growth in consumption over time.) If C_0 and C_1 were physically fixed to equal 1,000, then these values of 523.81 per period with a PV of 1,000 might apply; however, they would simply reflect an appreciation of value, not more in total. If the total is fixed, it would seem more realistic to assume that the present value changes to something less than 1,000 (954.54 in the example above), if the probability of dying is positive. The "present" value would be lower because of the expectation that one may not be around to consume all of the 1,000 units in both periods.

9. Theoretical Survival Functions

Life insurance premiums are based on historical mortality rates (Huebner and Black 1976, 255). However, there are theoretical survival functions that can be consulted as well (although none of these perform well empirically). For example, if the survival function is $e^{-\partial t}$, the mortality rate is $-\partial e^{-\partial t}$ (∂ is used here, when referring to mortality, rather than r, which reflects return). The variable ∂ is generally referred to as the rate of decay (Chiang 1974, 294). For this survival function, ∂ is the force of mortality [cf. Jordan 1967, 15]). For a survival function (1 –t/T), the "force of mortality" is 1/T-t, whereas the mortality rate is 1/T.

The following is true of the uniform probability distribution:

(S1) $\int_0^T 1/T\, dt = t/T]_0^T = T/T - 0/T = 1.$

A more general expression for the probability distribution for any mortality rate π is:

(S1.1) $\int_0^T \pi(t)\, dt = 1,$

where $\pi(t)$ is the probability of an individual dying at time t.

For the uniform distribution (S1), the "survival function" for a group of lives, G, would be:

(S2) $E=G(1-t/T)$

where t is age, T is lifespan, and G is a group of new lives. The value of E gives the expected number of survivors by age t. The associated probability function for survival would be:

(S3) $S = (1-t/T).$

(This particular equation is shown in Jordan [1967, 3–6].)

The derivative of E is

(S4) $dE/dt = -G/T,$

the expected number of deaths per period. The derivative of S is

(S5) $dS/dt = -1/T,$

the probability of dying per time period (the mortality rate). The percentage rate of decline for E would give the force of mortality:

(S6) $dE/dt\ 1/E = -1/(T-t).$

To obtain the mortality rate, multiply the force of mortality by E and divide by G to get –1/T:

(S6.1) $dE/dt\ (1/G) = -1/T = dS/dt.$

Dividing (S6.1) by S gives the force of mortality:

(S7) $dS/dt\ 1/S = -1/(T-t).$

An alternative functional form for E, a survival function for a group of lives (G), could be one for a constant rate of decay ∂:

($S2^i$) $E = Ge^{-\partial t},$

where

($S4^i$) $dE/dt = -\partial\, Ge^{-\partial t}$

($S6^i$) $dE/dt\ 1/E = -\partial.$

That is, the percentage decline in the function would be constant. The mortality rate would be:

($S6.1^i$) $dE/dt\ (1/G) = -\partial e^{-\partial t} = dS/dt.$

The survival function would be:

(S3[i]) $S = e^{-\partial t}$

with derivative and percentage rate of change as, respectively,

(S5[i]) $dS/dt = -\partial e^{-\partial t}$,

(S7[i]) $dS/dt\ (1/S) = -\partial$.

The expression dE/dt 1/E, or equivalently dS/dt 1/S, has been labeled the force of mortality. Benjamin Gompertz in 1825 posited the following force of mortality function:

(S6[ii]) $\mu_t = Bc^t$, or Be^{kt}

(Jordan 1967, 21; Kurtz 1930, 111). Both c and B are constants.

Equivalent to dE/dt would be (-) $\mu_t E_t$, or

(S4[ii]) $(-)Bc^t E_t$,

or equivalently $(-)Be^{kt} E_t$ (Jordan 1967, 14) where

$E = G\, e^{-\int_0^t \mu y\, dy}$ and $-\int_0^t \mu y\, dy = -\int_0^t Bc^y\, dy$.

From this it follows that E (the survival function for a group of lives, G) would be:

(S2[ii]) $E = (G/g)\, g^{c^t}$,

where ln g = -B/ln c (Jordan 1967, 22).

Therefore, the equivalent of dS/dt would be:

(S6.1[ii]) $dS/dt = dE/dt\ 1/G = (-)\ 1/G\ \mu_t E_t$

(S5[ii]) $dS/dt = (-)\ 1/G\ Bc^t\ G/g\ g^{c^t} = (-)\ 1/g\ Bc^t\ g^{c^t}$.

The following:

$\int_0^t 1/g\ Bc^t\ {}_g c^t\ dt = 1$,

would be the probability distribution equivalent to $\int_0^t \pi(t)\ dt = 1$, under the Gompertz mortality assumption.

10. Mortality of a Value Function

The continuous formula for present value, where PV is present value, Y is income, r is the interest rate, and T is the "length of life" (or the relevant time period), is: $PV = Y \int_0^T e^{-rt} dt = Y(1 - e^{-rT})/ r$,

and the discrete formula is:

$PV = Y\ \Sigma^T_{t=1}\ 1/(1+r)^t = Y/r\ [1 - (1- (1/(1+r)^T))]$.

The sinking fund amount per period would be:

$SF = dPV/dT = PV(r)/ (e^{rT} - 1) = Y/ e^{rT}$,

and in discrete terms:

$SF = PV(r) / [(1+r)^T - 1] = Y/(1+r)^T$.

The rate of change in PV in relative terms yields the equation for the sinking fund rate:

$dPV/dT\ 1/PV = Ye^{-rT} \div (Y/r)\ (1-e^{-rT}) = r / (e^{rT}-1)$.

Note that dPV/dT is the change with respect to T, the "length of life," not t.

Since it is with respect to T, this would be the same as the depreciation rate. The sinking fund rate is constant for a given present value. But for a given asset that depreciates, each year the present value changes if a sinking fund is not set aside. So every year, a new sinking fund rate would be calculated. That sinking fund rate would be constant for that (new) capital value. In the examples that I consider, t (not T) is the only variable under consideration; T is assumed fixed. Therefore, I write the depreciation rate in continuous terms as $D_t = r/ (e^{r(T+1-t)} - 1)$ to distinguish it from the sinking fund rate, $r/ (e^{rT} - 1)$. That is, the sinking fund is constant, but depreciation changes from year to year for a given PV (if a sinking fund is not put aside). PV_t is multiplied by D_t to obtain the depreciation in year t. Depreciation as a percentage of the present value in year one gives the depreciation rate as $DR_t = (D_t)(PV_t)/ PV_1$. The sum of the latter rates over T years equals one, $\Sigma_{t=1}^{T} DR_t = 1$.

Survival functions pertain to a population, G, of a given age, that changes over time due to death. In this section, I relate the concepts of "force of mortality" and the "mortality rate" that are applicable to survival functions for a population to a value function for an individual. The comparable concepts to the "force of mortality" and the "mortality rate" for the PV function are, respectively, D_t—the depreciation rate as a percentage of present value in year t—and DR_t—the depreciation rate expressed as a percentage of the present value in the first year.

For example, a population of a given age G that declines at a constant rate (force of mortality) ∂ would be given by the survival rate function shown in equation ($S3^i$) (see appendix 1.9), survival for a population of size G would be given by ($S2^i$), the mortality rate would be given by (S5i), and mortality for a given population of size G would be ($S4^i$). The force of mortality would be ($S7^i$), and the force of mortality for a given population of size G would be ($S6^i$). Thus, for survival function ($S3^i$) $S = e^{-\partial t}$, in year zero the population of size G would be $E_1 = Ge^{(0)t} = G$. In discrete terms, this would be equivalent to the equation $E_t = G (1 - \partial)^t$ (or $E_t = G (1 + \partial)^{-t}$, although this is unconventional). Given a "survival function," E, for a population, G, then to find dS/dt (the derivative of a probability of survival function, S), take the percentage rate of change of E = dE/dt 1/E (which is referred to as the force of mortality), multiply that by E and *divide by G.* (Jordan [1967, 22] illustrates this for Gompertz's mortality function shown in ($S6^{ii}$) [appendix 1.9].)

Now if the objective were to translate these mortality concepts based on a population of initial size G to the value of a person's earning life, then the *equivalent of G* in value (dollar) terms for an individual is the present value of his lifetime income, which would be the *first year amount of PV_1*. The objective then is to obtain an equivalent "survival function," S, to substitute in:

$$PV_t = PV_1 (S)$$

where PV_t is analogous to E_t, PV_1 is analogous to G, and *(S) is the survival function and analogous to* $(S3^{i})\ S = e^{-\partial t}$. The survival function for present value would be $S = (1 - \Sigma_{t=1}^{T} DR_{t-1})$, where $DR_t = [PV_t(r) / (e^{r(T+1-t)} - 1)]/PV_1)$. "Survival" would be given by:

(V.1) $SV = (1 - D_t)\ PV_t = PV_{t+1}$,

or alternatively,

(V.2) $SV = (1 - \Sigma_{t=1}^{T} DR_{t-1})\ PV_1 = PV_t$.

The values for D_t in (V.1) are simply the depreciation rates, calculated as r / $(e^{r(T+1-t)} - 1)$. D_t is analogous to $\pi d_t(t)$, the force of mortality, and DR_t is analogous to $\pi d(t)$, the mortality rate.

To illustrate, if PV_1 is \$6,144.44, income per year is \$1,000, r = .10, and T = 10, then using (V.1), PV_2 = (1 – .0627)(\$6,144.44) = \$5,759.18. Similarly, PV_3 = \$5,335.30. The present value for year 3 can also be obtained using (V.2). Using (V.2) gives a $PV_3 = PV_1$(1 – .1316) = \$6,144.44 (.8682) = \$5,334.60.

The survival (of value) function, $S = (1 - \Sigma_{t=1}^{T} DR_{t-1})$, would give as survival rates for the first four years: 1.0000, .9373, .8682, .7923. D_t, the "force of mortality," is the percentage change in the survival (of value) function. For the corresponding four years these rates would be: (1 – .9373)/ 1 = .0627, (.9373 – .8682)/.9373 = .0736, (.8682 – .7923)/.8682 = .0874. DR_t, the "mortality rates," would be given by the change in the survival rates from one year to the next, or: (1 – .9373) = .0627, (.9373 – .8682) = .0691, (.8682 – .7923) = .0759.

11. Alternative Net Premiums

In the following, I consider a number of alternative net level premium (NLP) rates, the primary purpose of which is to approximate an "average" probability of dying. I also examine the idea of an "average" depreciation rate. The former attempts to capture the uncertainty of survival, and the latter, the finiteness of life as they relate to the average decline in value over time due to mortality.

Sinking Fund as Premium

One measure of human capital is the discounted value of a person's lifetime income. When a person buys life insurance, he buys it to cover this loss in the event of death. The sinking fund is a constant amount per period, $PV(r) / (e^{rT} - 1)$, that if set aside to accumulate at (compound) interest will equal the present value of lifetime income at the end of one's life (T). The first possibility I consider is that of using the sinking fund rate as the NLP. The idea of using the sinking fund amount per period as the life insurance premium was implicit in a comment made by Irving Fisher ([1906] 1965, 111–12). According to this view, a person could set aside a sinking fund of \$385.55 a year for ten years to replace a capital value of \$6,144.44 (based on \$1,000 per year for ten years at 10 percent), or he could pay a life insurance premium for $385.55 for a life insurance policy for $6,144.44 coverage (if there is no loading).

The sinking fund rate per dollar of present value would be:

(13) $r/(e^{rT} - 1)$,

or $r[1/(1+r)^T - 1]$ in discrete terms. If r = 10% and T = 10, then $p = r(1/(1.10)^{10} - 1) = .0627$. So, for a policy that fully covered the PV of $6,144, the NLP would be 6.27 percent of PV. Like an NLP and an NLP rate per period, the sinking fund and sinking fund rate are constant per period.

A problem with using the sinking fund rate, given in (13), as the NLP rate is that the premiums collected by the insurance company would be insufficient to pay off claims. For instance, if the present value of lifetime earnings is $6,144 and that equals the face value of the policy, then even under liberal assumptions concerning reserves, $385 per year for ten years (at 10 percent interest) would be insufficient to pay off claims. (Of course, insurance cannot exist for a single person. I based this conclusion on calculations in which I used typical actuarial assumptions in which expected premium payments, expected costs [claims], and interest accumulation on reserves [which I assumed to be equal to cash value] were attributed to a single policyholder. Loading was assumed to be zero and the same rate of discount was applied to reserves as on that used to calculate the premium rate [cf. Huebner and Black 1976, 280–81].)

Net Level Rate Based on DR_t

In equation (10) in chapter 14, the value $(-)\pi_t(t)$ is the percentage change in the survival function and is known as the force of mortality. The change in the survival function is the mortality rate, $\pi(t)$, and is the rate used in the calculation of the life insurance premium. It would be the premium rate for a one-period term policy (assuming no loading). (It is assumed, for simplification, that there is no loading in the examples that follow.) A net level premium rate would be given by the following:

(11) $p = \Sigma^{T}_{t=1} \pi d(t) / (1+r)^t / \Sigma^{T-1}_{t=0} \pi a(t) / (1+r)^t$,

where $\pi a(t)$ is the probability of being alive equal to $(1 - \pi d(t))$. The probabilities would be based on historical data (Huebner and Black 1976, 270–72).

Irving Fisher defined cash value of a life insurance policy for any given period as the difference between the discounted expected value of the face value and the present value of expected premium payments ([1906] 1965, 411). Although Fisher did not state this, these two values can be set equal to each other and solved for p (the NLP rate). Even though Fisher did not express these concepts mathematically, their equality could be given as:

$FV\ [\Sigma^{T}_{t=1} \pi d(t)\ 1/(1+r)^t] = p\ (FV)\ \Sigma^{T}_{t=1} (1 - \pi d(t))/(1+r)^t$.

Therefore, solving for p would give:

(11^{1}) $p = [\Sigma^{T}_{t=1} \pi d(t)\ 1/(1+r)^t] / [\Sigma^{T}_{t=1} [(1 - \pi d(t))/(1+r)^t]$.

This is the same as equation (11) above except for the upper and lower limits for the summation index in the denominator. This is because in equation (11), it is assumed that claims are due immediately, whereas interest is assumed to be received at the end of the period.

In (11^i), it could be assumed that $\pi d(t)$ is constant and equal to the sinking fund rate shown in (13). However, in calculating insurance premiums, it is usually assumed that the mortality rate increases over time (i.e., with the age of the insured). It is also assumed that the sum of the probabilities equals one as shown in (S1.1) in appendix 1.9. The sinking fund rates do not sum to one. Instead of the sinking fund rate, the depreciation rate could be used for $\pi d(t)$. Depreciation rates based on the formula:

(13^{ii}) $DR_t = PV_t\ (r)/\ (e^{rT+1-t} - 1)/PV_1$

increase over time, and they also sum to one (satisfying (S1.1)).

There is a logic underlying the use of the DR_t to approximate mortality. When a person buys life insurance, he buys it to cover the loss of his human capital in the event of death. I have calculated a "survival function" for value, by applying the same approach as that used for a survival function for a population. (See appendix 1.10.) In short, given the present value of lifetime earnings in year one, the present value in any year t would be:

$PV_t = PV_1\ (S)$,

where the "survival function" (S) would be $1 - (\Sigma^T{}_{t=1}\pi d(t-1))$. The values for $\Sigma^T{}_{t=1}\pi d(t)$ would be "cumulative probabilities" calculated as the cumulative sum of the depreciation rates, where depreciation rates are defined in (13^{ii}) as DR_t. For this survival of value function, DR_t is analogous to $\pi d(t)$, the mortality rate. The force of mortality for the survival of value function would be the depreciation rates, calculated as $D_t = r / (e^{r(T+1-t)} - 1))$.

Using DR_t for $\pi d(t)$ in the numerator of equation (11^i), at 10 percent interest for T = 10 years, would give a value for the numerator of .627. The denominator for (11^i), given as $[\Sigma^T{}_{t=1}[(1-\pi d(t))/(1+r)^t]$, is interpreted as the sum of the discounted probabilities of being alive for each year, where $\pi a(t) = (1 - \pi d(t))$. The sum of the "probabilities of being alive," given as $(1 - DR_t)$, discounted (at 10 percent for 10 years) is 6.2352. (It is assumed that the first year survival rate is 100 percent and no discount is applied for that year. This is consistent with the usual calculation of net level premiums when mortality tables are used to estimate the probabilities [see Huebner and Black 1976, 271].) Using these assumptions and equation (11^i), the NLP rate would then be equal to: p = .627/6.2452 = .1004. Based on the same actuarial assumptions discussed above, I found that this premium rate would generate sufficient reserves to pay out claims. In fact, I found that an NLP rate of about .09 would be sufficient—which would result in a premium of about $553.00 for a person who was fully insured and had a present value of \$6,144.44. This would be a little over half of the person's income (if, as assumed, he earns \$1,000 per year).

Alternative Net Level Rate 1

Of course, the depreciation rate is not a mortality rate per se, and it could be argued that what is being calculated above is not a net level premium, but an "average depreciation rate." However, if the objective were to calculate an average depreciation rate, then the denominator should be T, rather than the sum of the (discounted) "survival rates." Depreciation exists because life is finite. It would exist whether death's timing were certain or not. (If an asset's lifespan was infinite, and yield was constant at Y per year, the value of capital would be Y/r, and depreciation would be zero. It is because of a finite T that depreciation results—when income is a constant amount per year. It is possible to calculate a rate of decay in value for an asset that has an infinite life, but in computing depreciation, a finite life of the asset is typically assumed [cf. Hotelling {1925, 343}].)

Depreciation rates, defined in (13^{ii}) as DR_t, increase over time. If these were used as premium rates, then the premiums would increase over time, equaling all or almost all of income in year T. To avoid the burdensomeness of increasing premiums over time, an averaging approach would take the sum of depreciation rates and divide by T:

(P.1) $\Sigma_{t=1}{}^{t} DR_t/T = 1/T$.

Since the sum of the depreciation rates, $\Sigma_{t=1}{}^{t} DR_t$, equals one, this would give a premium rate of 1/T, or .10. Rather than a premium to cover an uncertain life, the result, (P.1), would be an "average" depreciation rate.

Alternative Net Level Rate 2

It could be argued that the relevant concept when death's timing is uncertain is expected value instead of present value. (See appendix 1.2.) That is, instead of the present value of lifetime earnings, the loss that is being insured against is the expected value. Expected value in discrete terms would be given as $EV = \Sigma^T_{t=1} Y_t/(1+\partial)^t$. (This is consistent with Sachko's approach to EV in her investigation of the demand for insurance [1975, 26, 28], except she used $\Sigma^T_{t=1} Y_t(1-\partial)^t$.) That is, expected lifetime income is the sum over one's life of yearly income multiplied by the survival rate per year $(1/(1+\partial)^t)$, where the mortality rate would be $\partial(1/(1+\partial)^t)$ per year and ∂ would be the force of mortality. (These are the discrete counterparts for the hypothetical survival function ($S3^i$) and the corresponding mortality and force of mortality rates, ($S5^i$), and ($S7^i$), respectively, shown in appendix 1.9.) Mathematically, the comparable equations (in continuous and discrete terms, respectively) for the "sinking fund" and "depreciation as a percentage of expected value in year one" are indistinguishable from those for PV:

(13^{i}) SF = $\partial/(e^{\partial T} - 1)$ and $\partial\,[1/(1+\partial)^{T} - 1]$

(13^{iii}) $DR_t = EV_t\,[\partial/(e^{\partial\,T+1-t} - 1]/EV_1$ and $EV_t\{\partial/[(1+\partial)^{T+1-t} - 1]\}/EV_1$.

One difference between the PV concepts and the EV concepts is that it is unlikely that r would equal ∂. Even though a sinking fund could be put aside to replace EV, since ∂ would not equal r, the return on the sinking fund would not have to equal r in order to replace EV.

Although it would be unlikely for ∂ to equal r, for simplification, I am assuming that it does in the following examples. With that in mind, another approach to deriving an NLP rate could be to use the approach in equation (11^{i}), where $\pi d(t)$ would be equal to DR_t, but now DR_t would be equal to (13^{iii}) not (13^{ii}). Of course, because of the assumption that ∂ is equal in value to r, the resultant NLP rate would be identical to that shown above; that is, p = .627/6.2452 = .1004.

In this context, equation (11^{i}) would be interpreted as being the sum of the *return discounted* "mortality rates" (the latter based on DR_t as shown in (13^{iii})) divided by the *return discounted* "survival rates" (the latter based on $(1-DR_t)$). I am using the term *return* discount, r, to distinguish it from *mortality* "discount," ∂, on which EV is based. It could be argued that for some analytical purposes, it would be desirable to separate the effect of "discount" due to mortality from the effect of discount due to interest. If the objective were to isolate the effect of uncertain death, then neither the numerator nor the denominator of the premium rate calculation would be discounted by r. If the "mortality" rates, DR_t, were undiscounted (by return, r), then the NLP rate would simply equal the sum of the "probabilities of dying" divided by the sum of the "probabilities of surviving." The sum of the probabilities of dying (based on DR_t given in (13^{iii})) would simply equal one. This numerator would be divided by the sum of the probabilities of survival (where it is assumed that the probability of survival in year one is 100 percent). The logic of dividing by the sum of the survival rates rather than by T—as was done in (P.1)—is to take into account the uncertainty of survival, not just death's inevitability. The resulting NLP rate would be:

(P.2) $\Sigma_{t=1}{}^{T} DR_t \,/\, \Sigma_{t=1}{}^{T}(1 - DR_{t-1}) = 1/\,\Sigma_{t=1}{}^{T}(1 - DR_{t-1})$.

Using (P.2), the NLP rate based on a 10 percent probability of dying and T = 10 would be 1/9.1479 = .1093. If the "force of mortality" (mortality "discount" rate) per year was 20 percent, one's intuitions would suggest that the sum of the probabilities of survival (based on 1 – DR) used in the denominator of (P.2) would be lower than if the mortality "discount" rate were 10 percent, thus yielding a higher NLP rate. However, the NLP rate based on 20 percent using (P.2) would be 1/9.1988 = .1087. An even higher mortality "discount" rate of 32 percent gives an NLP rate based on (P.2) of 1/9.2588 = .108. (A 3 percent force of mortality of dying, or mortality "discount" rate, would give an NLP rate of .1204.) Contrary to intuitions, the higher the force of mortality (mortality discount rate), the lower the NLP rate. The NLP rate in equation (P.2) is "driven by" the length of life T, not by its uncertainty, and it is the uncertainty of life that one would want to capture in a premium for life insurance or in trying to estimate an "average" probability of dying based on untimely death.

Alternative Net Level Rate 3

Since it is the uncertainty of life that a policyholder is hedging against when he buys life insurance, then the use of probabilities of dying might be preferred to depreciation rates if the objective were to establish a premium rate for life insurance. These probabilities could be based on the same theoretical survival function on which the EV was based—that is, mortality rates based on equation ($S5^i$), shown in appendix 1.9. Thus, instead of the sum of the "probabilities of surviving" based on $(1 - DR_{t-1})$ in the denominator as was used in (P.2), this third NLP (shown below in (P.3)) uses the sum of probabilities of surviving based on $1/(1+\partial)^t$—which approximates the survival rate per period (in continuous terms $e^{\partial t}$), where ∂ is the "force of mortality." The sum of the survival rates would be $\Sigma_{t=1}{}^{10}\ 1/(1+\partial)^{t-1}$, if T = 10. Since a survival function assumes that the sum of the mortality rates equals one (equation (S1.1)), the numerator of this third alternative NLP rate could remain equal to one, as was done in equation (P.2). Consequently, the NLP rate would be:

(P.3) $1/\ \Sigma_{t=1}{}^{T}\ 1/(1+\partial)^{t-1}$.

For $\partial = .10$, $\Sigma_{t=1}{}^{T}\ 1/(1+\partial)^{t-1}$ would be 6.759 (under the assumption that the probability of survival in the first year is 100 percent). Thus (P.3) would give an NLP rate of 1/6.759 = .1479. The advantage of using this NLP rate equation is that, unlike (P.2), (P.3) increases with increases in the mortality discount rate (force of mortality). The NLP rates for mortality discount rates of 3, 10, 20, and 32 percent are: 1/8.7864 = .1138, 1/6.750 = .1479, 1/5.031 = .1988, and 1/3.8681 = .2585, respectively.

The problem with (P.3) is that it results in an NLP equal in value to depreciation in year T as shown in ($P.3^i$). For instance, for $\partial = .10$ and T = 10, the NLP would be .1479(6144) = $908.70.

($P.3^i$) $[1/\ \Sigma_{t=1}{}^{10}\ 1/(1+\partial)^{t-1}]\ [Y\ \Sigma_{t=1}{}^{10}\ 1/(1+\partial)^t]$.

If the probability of survival in the first year is assumed to be $1/(1+\partial)$ instead of 1.00, then the NLP becomes equal to yearly income, as shown in the following:

($P.3^{ii}$) $[1/\ \Sigma_{t=1}{}^{10}\ 1/(1+\partial)^t]\ [Y\ \Sigma_{t=1}{}^{10}\ 1/(1+\partial)^t] = Y$.

With Y = $1,000, the premium per year based on ($P.3^{ii}$) would equal $1,000.

Alternative Net Level Rate 4

An alternative NLP rate would use the denominator of (P.3), but in the numerator, instead of using "one," the sum of the mortality rates given as $\partial(1/(1+\partial)^t)$ would be used. The logic of this is that if a quantity "A" decays at the rate ∂ per year, i.e., $V = Ae^{-\partial t}$, then the instantaneous rate of decay of V is (-)∂, and the change per period dV/dt is $(-)\partial Ae^{-\partial t}$. If A = \$1, then the per period rate is $(-)\partial e^{-\partial t}$, or in discrete terms $(-)\partial(1/(1+\partial)^t)$. Summing over the life span would give $\partial\, \Sigma_{t=1}^{10}\, 1/(1+\partial)^t$ (ignoring the negative sign). This would be divided by the sum of the survival rates (as assumed in the denominator of (P.3), $\Sigma_{t=1}^{10}\, 1/(1+\partial)^{t-1}$; although, an approximation to this of $\Sigma_{t=1}^{10}\, 1/(1+\partial)^t$ is used in (P.4)). Therefore, the NLP rate would be (approximately):

(P.4) $\partial\Sigma_{t=1}^{10}\, 1/(1+\partial)^t \,/\, \Sigma_{t=1}^{10}\, 1/(1+\partial)^t = \partial$.

To arrive at the NLP per year, ∂ would be multiplied by EV_1. For an expected value of \$6,144.44, the per year NLP would be \$614.44. (In this premium the finality of death is not taken into account in the premium rate (P.4), although it is inherent in the EV amount.)

Discussion

For the survival function given by equation ($S3^i$), the mortality function is given by ($S5^i$), and the force of mortality by ($S7^i$). To be consistent with Sachko's definitions (and ignoring negative signs), the probability of dying would be given by ($S7^i$), and the cumulative probability of survival up to time t would be based on ($S3^i$) (1975, 27–28). In the net level rate shown in (P.4), the numerator uses the sum of the mortality rates based on the discrete equivalent of ($S5^i$). The denominator of (P.4) uses the cumulative probabilities of survival based on the discrete form of ($S3^i$). The sum of the mortality rates given by ($S5^i$) equals one as T tends to infinity—which is consistent with equation (S1.1). However, the cumulative probability of survival for a given period does not equal one minus the mortality rate for that period; this is inconsistent with equation (11), the net level premium equation for life insurance. The mortality rates given by ($S5^i$)—which mathematically equals the force of mortality multiplied by the survival function for a given period—decline over time. This is because the cumulative probabilities of survival, given by ($S3^i$), decline over time.

For the net level rate given by (P.2), the numerator is based on the sum of DR_t, since the values given by DR_t reflect the "mortality rates" for a value function. The rates increase over time. The sum of these rates equals one, which is consistent with (S1.1). To be consistent with equation (11), the sum of the "survival rates" based on $(1 - DR_t)$ is used in the denominator. The values given by $(1 - DR_t)$ are not *cumulative* probabilities of "survival" (for a value function). If, as in (P.4), cumulative probabilities of "survival" had been used in (P.2), the net level rates would have been higher than those obtained using $(1 - DR_t)$; however, it would still be the case that the net level rates for (P.2) would decline as the force of mortality increases. This is at odds with intuitions. The force of mortality, ∂, operates like a return in (P.2). For a present value function, for a given level of income, a rise in the interest rate will result in shift in the relative values for interest and depreciation; interest will rise and depreciation will fall. Thus, for an expected value function, for a given income level per period, a higher force of mortality results in a lower depreciation rate, and therefore a lower "mortality" rate and a higher "survival" rate. The sum of the survival rates—the denominator of (P.2)—rises as the force of mortality rises. This explains the counterintuitive finding for rates based on (P.2) as ∂ increases.

12. Depreciation Index

Assuming a discount rate of 10 percent, an asset that earned one dollar a year with an expected life of ten years would have depreciation in year one of $1/(1.10)^{10} = .3855$. (This is because $\int_0^T SF\, e^{-rt}\, dt = e^{-rT}$, or $1/(1+r)^T$ in discrete terms, where SF stands for the sinking fund rate. In discrete terms, the depreciation rate in year one is $SF = r / [(1+r)^T - 1] = .0627$. The present value, PV, of \$1 $= \Sigma^{10}_{t=1}\, 1/(1.10)^t = [1 - (1 - 1/(1+r)^T)]/r = 6.1445$. Therefore, depreciation in year one would be $= (.0627)\,(6.1447) = .3885$.)

In continuous terms, the present value of one dollar per year would be $\int_0^T e^{-rt}dt$. If $T = 10$, then the sum of depreciation over the ten years equals the present value of income over ten years. This is because the sum of depreciation in year T through the first year equals the sum of discounted income from the first year through year T. The sum of depreciation is a sum of "mortality of value" function (the amount by which value declines over time). However, the sum of depreciation would be $-\int_T^o e^{-rt}dt$. The sum of depreciation for T years divided by the present value of income over T years would be equal to one. Depreciation for any particular year under the same assumptions would be: $e^{-r(T-t)}$. This amount, divided by the PV in year t, would be the depreciation rate. (For example, in the first year, the analogous formula in discrete terms would give depreciation of .3855. Based on a PV of 6.144, the depreciation rate in year one would be $.3855/6.144 = .0627$.) The sum of depreciation over the period $t = 0$ to $t = 10$ is

$$\int_0^T e^{-r(T-t)}dt = \int_0^T e^{rt}e^{-rT}dt = e^{-rT}\int_0^T e^{rt}dt$$
$$= 1/r\, e^{-rT}\, \{[\, e^{rt}]_T - [\, e^{rt}]_0\} = 1/r\, [1 - e^{-rT}],$$

which is the same as the PV. Thus the conclusion here is that

$$\int_0^T e^{-r(T-t)}dt = \int_0^T e^{-rT}dt.$$

If one dollar of income per period were subject to a "survival function" $e^{-\partial t}$, where ∂ is the "mortality discount," then an expected value of lifetime income could be derived analogous to present value. If r is reinterpreted as the "mortality discount," ∂, and if the "mortality discount" rate is 10 percent, then (based on discrete equations) the "probability of surviving" the first year is 90.9 percent and the expected income for the year is .9091 for \$1 of income. Summing the expected income per year over T years gives the income that would "probably" be received over one's life. This value function represents a lifetime expected income (based on survival). Mathematically, it is the same as present value. Depreciation can be calculated for the expected value function in the same way that it is for a present value function.

If depreciation is regarded as analogous to mortality of value, then a depreciation index could be derived using the expected value concepts just discussed. That is, if at time t = 0, the asset were (T – t) years old (for example, an asset of age six, this would be (10 – 4), then an index of the cumulative depreciation over that time period as a percentage of present value would be:

$DX_t = \int_0^{T-t} e^{-\partial(T-t)}\,dt \,/\, \int_0^T e^{-\partial t}\,dt$

$= \int_0^{T-t} e^{-\partial T} e^{\partial t}\,dt \,/\, \int_0^T e^{-\partial t}\,dt$. Since $e^{-\partial T}$ is a constant

$= e^{-\partial T} \int_0^{T-t} e^{\partial t}\,dt \,/\, \int_0^T e^{-\partial t}\,dt$. Therefore

$DX_t = (\,/\partial)\, e^{-\partial T} \{[e^{\partial t}]_{t=T-t} - [e^{\partial t}]_{t=0}\} \,/\, \{-(1/\partial)(e^{-\partial T} - 1)\}$

$DX_t = \{e^{-\partial t} - e^{-\partial T}\} \,/\, [1 - e^{-\partial T}]$.

And Lim $T \to \infty$ $DX_t = e^{-\partial t}$. That is, as $T \to \infty$, the asset decays at a rate ∂ for every year it ages.

For a finite life, under the assumptions considered here ($\partial = .10$, T = 10), for an asset that is t = 6 years old (T – 4), then the formula for DX_t would in its discrete formulation give: $DX = [1/(1.10)^4 - 1/(1.10)^{10}] / [1/(1 - 1/(1.10)^{10}] = .4842$. DX of .4842 is the cumulative probability for year six (equal to one minus the "cumulative probability of being alive" in year six = $[1 - \Pi^6_{t=1}(1 - D_t)] = [1 - (1 - .0627)(1 - .0736)(1 - .0874)(1 - .1054)(1 - .1296)(1 - .1638)] = (1 - .5159) =$ .4841). It is also equal to the sum of depreciation divided by the present (expected) value in year one $= \Sigma^6_{t=1} D_t\, EV_t / EV_1$ = (.3855+.4241+.4665+.5132+.5645+.6209)/6.144, as well as the sum of the depreciation rates expressed as a percentage of present (expected) value in year one $= \Sigma^6_{t=1} DR_t$ = (.0627+.069+.0759+.0835+.0919+.1011).

Appendix 2

1. Defining Scarcity

There are several relatively simple models that can be used to define scarcity. One is the no-scarcity case, where "no-scarcity" in this context means no natural resource scarcity. The no-scarcity model assumes that no price is charged for the use of resources, and the real cost, in terms of labor and capital (L+C) to acquire the resource, is zero.

In the no-scarcity case, optimal resource use will occur when idle resources are brought into use with L+C to the point at which the marginal product of resources is zero. At the zero marginal product of resource point, output (for the economy as a whole) will be maximized, given the amount of L+C employed. At this point, the average product of L+C—that is, the output per unit of L+C input—will be maximized and will be equal to the marginal productivity of L+C (Barnett and Morse 1963, 103). (This model assumes resources are divisible, and, therefore, the L+C input is not subject to increasing marginal and average returns.) Since average and marginal costs are inversely related to average and marginal productivity, and since at this point the average product of L+C is maximum, then the per unit costs of L+C must be minimized. Given the assumption of constant returns to scale (output increases at the same percentage as inputs increase), resource use does not result in increasing costs (1963, 104).

The Malthusian Scarcity Model assumes that there is an upward limit on resources. Until that limit is reached, resources are not scarce and the model is the same as the no-scarcity model. Once the limit is reached, diminishing (marginal and average) returns of L+C set in. This corresponds to increasing marginal and per unit costs of L+C, the latter being the definition of increasing resource scarcity (1963, 105–107). Output is at a maximum when the marginal product of

L+C is zero. Beyond that, output declines as additional units of L+C are applied. Correspondingly, the marginal product of L+C becomes negative.

In the Ricardian Scarcity Model, the assumption of an upper limit to resources is not necessary for scarcity to exist. All that is required is that resources be of declining quality. It is also assumed that individuals have full knowledge of resources and use them in order of declining quality. Resources are still assumed to be available at a zero price (1963, 113). One way of approaching Ricardian scarcity is to assume that resources of declining quality are converted into resources of a given standard through a resource conversion production function. This function reflects the transformation of labor and capital (L_r+C_r) and substandard resources (R_u) into resources of standard quality (R). R_u will be used to produce R up to the point at which the amount of standard resources per unit of labor and capital used in conversion (L_r+C_r) is maximized. This corresponds to minimum per unit cost of L_r+C_r.

The aggregate production function is a function of inputs of L+C, which includes labor and capital used in the production of final goods (L_g+C_g) (indicated by the subscript "g"), as well as labor and capital used to convert substandard resources (L_r+C_r). Optimal production results in diminishing marginal and average returns to L+C (1963, 112). Unlike the Malthusian case, diminishing returns set in right away, not after some limit to resources is reached. As with the Malthusian model, the condition of declining marginal productivity of L+C (increasing marginal costs) corresponds to an increasing implicit marginal product of the resource.

2. Defining Rent

Although an upper limit to resources is not necessary for the existence of scarcity in the Ricardian Model, in most expositions of Ricardian rent theory, finite resources are assumed to exist. In Ricardo's rent theory, rent is received by a landowner because land is owned; because land is finite; and because land varies in quality attributes, such as fertility (Spiegel 1971, 324). Both the differential principle and the marginal principle are in operation in Ricardo's theory of land rent. The differential principle is reflected in differences in land quality. That is, plots of land of the same size will differ in the amounts of output produced on them for given quantities of labor and capital. The higher quality of land will produce the same amount of output with less L+C input, i.e., lower costs. Since the output will fetch the same price regardless of where it is produced (due to competition), the owner of the higher quality land will receive a surplus, or rent. The marginal principle also applies. That is, intra-marginal land will be cultivated intensively until the return is equal to that of the extensive margin (Rima 1978, 129).

In an unsettled country, where land is plentiful, unowned, and free, it is assumed that the highest quality land will be employed first. No rent will be received for this land. It is when the second-grade land is cultivated, that the first-grade land will earn rent, calculated as the difference in the L+C costs incurred on the two different grades of land (Spiegel 1971, 324–25). Although Ricardo specifically addressed land, any factor of production that is limited in supply can receive a rent (or quasi-rent) that is in excess of its opportunity cost (Rima 1978, 305). (For a firm, quasi-rent is defined as the difference between the variable costs and revenue [Alchian and Allen 1977, 270].)

A. C. Bunce noted that when the United States was first settled, land was plentiful, rents were low, and soil-depleting practices were used. Eventually, increasing rents encouraged more intensive use of the land. Now "after 350 years there is no problem of population pressure on land in North America" (Dales 1972a, 174). In contrast to land, lack of property rights in water with zero water rents has resulted in overutilization and a reduction in quality as population has grown. Increasing land rents encouraged improvements in technology in land use. The absence of rents for water use has been accompanied by few technological advances (1972a, 175).

3. Go Fish—A Model

This section will examine a model for a resource that moves—fish. The purpose is to illustrate the difficulties involved in assigning ownership. Related to this is the effect on efficiency involved with various ownership schemes. The model in the following is based on Frederick Bell's paper "Technological Externalities and Common-Property Resources: An Empirical Study of the U.S. Northern Lobster Fishery" (1972, 148–158).

A fish population, or biomass (N_t), is assumed to follow a logistic growth function over time ($N_t = N^*/[1+be^{-at}]$). (The logistic model is too simplistic to reflect the complexities of most bioeconomic systems [Herfindahl and Kneese 1974, 168].) The assumption underlying a logistic growth function is that initially there would be rapid growth of the biomass, then, because of space constraints and predators (other than man), a leveling off to some maximum would occur and be sustained. A steady-state solution with intervention by man (fishing effort) would exist if the rate of growth of the biomass were just balanced by the loss due to fishing effort. The instantaneous rate of growth of the biomass as a function of time (without intervention by man) is:

$dN/dt \; 1/N = a[1-N/N^*]$.

For the steady-state condition, fishing effort must be subtracted from the biomass growth rate function. A simple functional form, F(E), can be posited for total industry fishing effort, E (where E reflects labor and capital), factored by a constant, k, giving $F(E)= kE_t$. Thus, the steady state condition becomes

$dN_t/Ndt = a(1-[N_t/N^*]) - kE_t$,
which, when set equal to zero, balances the growth of the biomass against the loss due to man's intervention.

The interest of the fishermen is the catch from the stock, Q_t. The production function relates catch (Q_t) to the inputs, (kE_t) and (N_t). It is assumed that the production function is a multiplicative function of the inputs; therefore, $Q_t = kE_t N_t$, where Q_t is the take from the stock. Solving for the biomass gives $N_t = Q_t/kE_t$. This can be substituted into the steady-state condition to solve for catch, Q_t, in terms of effort, E_t. The result is a parabolic function,

$Q_t = AE_t - BE^2{}_t$, where $A = kN^*$ and $B = (k^2N^*/a)$.

The maximum point on this function is the maximum sustainable yield (MSY), the maximum catch rate per time period that is possible without decreasing the fish population (Howe 1979, 260). The MSY can be found by taking the derivative of the Q_t function and setting it equal to zero and solving for the level of effort that maximizes the Q_t function. The derivative of Q_t is the marginal product of effort ($\partial Qt/\partial E_t = A - 2BE_t$). It represents the change in catch when another unit of effort is employed. The marginal product of effort function is downward sloping, representing diminishing marginal returns. The average product of effort, i.e., output per unit of effort, is found by dividing catch by effort (i.e., $Q_t/[E_t A - BE_t{}^2]$).

The situation for a firm in the fishery industry is at variance with that typical in the theory of the firm. For instance, the average cost curve is total costs divided by output, but in fisheries total (explicit) costs would only include the cost of effort (L+C). Since the fish industry is based on a common property resource, the cost of that resource would not be included in the firm's costs. In the theory of the firm, the average cost curve is posited to rise if there are diminishing returns. This is considered a short-run phenomenon since in the long run firms are assumed to be able to acquire more of all of the inputs used in production. That is, they may adjust their scale of operations to accommodate changes in demand. The inability to acquire more of the fixed input in the short run does not constrain output in the long run. Barring diseconomies due to the effects of red tape as scale of operation increases, long-run per unit and marginal costs are not expected to rise. In fisheries, however, the presence of diminishing returns is a long-run phenomenon. In the fishery industry, per unit cost is total cost of effort ($TC=cE_t$) divided by output, Q_t. The Q function is parabolic, indicating that as more effort is employed, output (catch) increases, reaches a maximum, and then declines. The per unit cost curve ($TC/Q = cE_t/[AE_t - BE^2{}_t]$) is therefore backward bending once effort is extended past the point of MSY.

In the short run, in a competitive fisheries industry, the firm would attempt to maximize profits by equating the revenue earned by producing the last unit of catch (the price) with the addition to cost incurred in producing the last unit (the marginal cost). From the fishers' perspective, they see their per unit (and marginal) costs as constant, c. Their actions are based on the perception that there are no diminishing returns (Herfindahl and Kneese 1974, 161). They do not take the biomass and their effect on the biomass into account in costs.

In the short run, the price may temporarily be above average costs, resulting in apparent profits (actually rent, see appendix 2.2). This would be a return to the natural resource for which the firm pays nothing. The firm's only (explicit) costs are for effort (L+C). However, any so-called profits would be short lived because other potential entrants would be attracted to the industry by the presence of profits (actually, rent) being earned by existing firms. This and the relative ease of entry into the fishery industry (that exists because potential entrants only face L+C costs and do not have to pay for the use of the common property resource) would encourage firms to enter the industry.

Competition does not cause price to fall and dissipate profits as in the typical competitive industry. What happens in the case of fisheries is that firms (fishers) enter the industry until price equals average costs (and rent is zero). At that point, the (actual) marginal cost curve (which includes the effect on the biomass, not merely the marginal cost of effort perceived by the fishers) is above average cost. This means there is overinvestment in fisheries. If demand continues to increase, MSY may be reached and surpassed, in which case the marginal product would be negative. Continued production (fishing effort) could result in unintended extinction.

The optimal price per unit of catch would (in steady-state equilibrium) equal the marginal cost of effort (MC_{L+C}) plus the opportunity cost (or user cost) of a unit of stock. That is, the price per unit should cover all marginal costs, not just the marginal cost of effort. The opportunity cost of a unit of stock should reflect what is sacrificed when a unit is taken from the stock—which includes not only what is sacrificed in the current time period but also the present value of what is sacrificed in all subsequent time periods. This would be an implicit price for a unit of stock; call it λ (Herfindahl and Kneese 1974, 162). However, since fishers pay no explicit price (nor do they impute an implicit price), they will continue to fish, and other firms will continue to enter the industry, until all so-called profit (rent) is dissipated. But these so-called profits reflect the opportunity cost of the resource. So effort continues to be employed as if $\lambda = 0$. Thus the apparent profits are equal to the present value of intertemporal opportunity costs and, under competitive assumptions, will be wiped out by increased entry into the industry (Howe 1979, 265).

The question arises: Would increasing costs by the amount λ be sufficient to reach the optimal steady state (static) solution for catch? The answer is no. The individual fisher perceives the marginal product of effort to equal the average product. Adding λ to costs would result in fishers employing effort until price equaled λ plus per unit costs ($P = \lambda + AC_{L+C}$), not at price equal to λ plus marginal cost ($P = \lambda + MC_{L+C}$) as the optimality condition would require. Another way of expressing this condition is that fishers should employ effort until price of catch less the implicit price of stock ($P - \lambda$) equals the MC_{L+C}. Equivalently, ($P - \lambda$) = $w/(MP_{L+C})$, where w is the cost of a unit of effort, or $(P - \lambda)MP_{L+C} = w$. But the individual fisher will continue to apply effort until $(P - \lambda)AP_{L+C} = w$, since the fisher perceives the marginal product of effort to equal the average product.

Thus, simply attaching the opportunity cost of a unit of stock, λ, to the price of catch will not be sufficient to attain optimality. What is needed is a charge, say δ, on effort equal to the catch price per unit net of λ multiplied by the difference between the average product of effort and the marginal product of effort, that is $\delta = (P - \lambda)(AP_{L+C} - MP_{L+C})$ (Herfindahl and Kneese 1974, 165). Since in optimal static equilibrium $(P - \lambda) = w/(MP_{L+C})$, the charge δ would equal $[w/(MP_{L+C})](AP_{L+C} - MP_{L+C})$, or $w[(AP_{L+C}/MP_{L+C}) - 1]$. The term (AP_{L+C}/MP_{L+C}) is, in discrete terms, the inverse of the output elasticity of effort and is equal to the percentage change in effort divided by the percentage change in catch and will be greater than one in the range of diminishing returns (Salvatore 1996, 250–51). Thus, in the range of diminishing returns, the growth of fishing effort will be greater than the growth in catch. So the cost per unit of effort (w) should be increased by a fraction that reflects the difference between this ratio and one.

Dynamic optimization indicates that in considering the rate of increase in λ over time, stock effects must be acknowledged. In the optimal control problem given by Herfindahl and Kneese, λ is now given as y_2e^{-rt} in their presentation (where y_2 is in current value terms) to reflect that it is a costate variable—the dynamic counterpart to the Lagrangian multiplier, λ (1974, 173). If stock effects can be ignored, then the stock should be altered to the point that one unit brought forward will increase rent by the return that could be obtained outside fisheries—the latter equaling ry_2, where r is the interest rate. But in fisheries, stock effects cannot be ignored. If the size of the initial stock is large enough, extinction as part of the optimal solution will be unlikely. Important as well is the interest rate (or the discount rate used in determining present values) in relation to stock effects. If the interest rate is low in comparison to stock effects, the rate of increase in rent will fall as stocks expand. Extinction will not be economically optimal. If the interest rate is high in comparison to stock effects, then y_2 will increase as stocks shrink. Extinction becomes an economically optimal possibility (Howe 1979, 265–66).

Dynamic analysis has revealed that the competitive nature of the industry in combination with biological responses of the biomass can lead to an unintended outcome of extinction of the biomass. As demand for fish continues, more fishermen will enter the industry. Without ownership of the biomass, individual firms will pursue short-term gain at the expense of the long run. Intertemporal effects on opportunity costs of the biomass will not be capitalized and thus will not be reflected in present value calculations. Nor will firms take into account their current actions on the productivities of other firms or on the biomass overall (1979, 267). Dynamic analysis has shown that ease of entry into the industry encourages firms to enter when it is profitable to do so, but firms are slow to leave when the tide turns (1979, 270).

Thus the common-property nature of the fishing industry can lead to an unintended extinction of a population of fish. The answer would seem to be, to establish ownership. With ownership, the intertemporal opportunity resource costs will be taken into account by fishers in determining catch. But this is insufficient to avoid unintended extinction of the population. As discussed, interfirm effects will still be ignored. The problem is compounded if fishers are quick to enter the industry when profitable to do so but are slow to exit when it becomes unprofitable, particularly once the critical level of the stock is approached. These can combine to bring about unintended extinction, even when ownership is established in a competitive fish industry.

Is there a solution to the possible outcome of unintended extinction of a population of fish? There are many solutions that do not involve establishment of ownership, such as government setting fees through selling a limited number of licenses, or giving away a limited number of licenses on a first-come-first-served basis, or limiting the technology that can be used, or limiting the fishing season. But none of these establish full property rights, if that is the objective. Then the question is, is there a way to establish full property rights and at the same time not face the possibility of unintentionally depleting the resource to extinction? The answer is yes. This might be achieved by limiting entry to a single firm (1979, 272). H. Scott Gordon mentioned that, in the case of lobsters, limiting entry has been successfully achieved in some cases by the fishers themselves. "In a few places the fishermen have banded together into a local monopoly, preventing entry and controlling their own operations" (Gordon 1972, 97). Variations on this practice are in use today, enhanced by advancements in detection of specific species of fish.

By granting exclusive rights to a fish resource to a monopolist, incentives would arise to limit the catch so as not to unintentionally deplete the stock to the point of extinction. Intertemporal opportunity resource costs would be taken into account in decisions, since the firm would own the resource. Since a single firm would own the resource, the firm could keep track of the effect of its effort on the stock and of diminishing returns (increasing costs). Interfirm effects will not exist nor will the problem of firms entering the industry attracted by so-called profits.

Profit maximizing monopolists tend to sell additional units so long as the additional revenue from selling the last unit is greater than what selling that unit adds to costs. With a single owner, the marginal costs would reflect all relevant costs. However, because price exceeds marginal revenue in the case of the monopolist, price will exceed marginal costs at the profit maximizing level of catch. What this means is that, from the consumer's perspective, the monopolist might be viewed as an overly stringent conservationist. The problem here would not be overfishing but underfishing. To clarify, this underfishing would be from the perspective of the consumer (demand side), not from the perspective of the effect the underfishing would have on the growth of the biomass (production side).

References

Aeschylus. 1966a. *The Oresteia Trilogy and Prometheus Bound.* Translated by Michael Townsend. Scranton, Pennsylvania: Chandler Publishing Company.

———. 1966b. *The Eumenides.* In Aeschylus 1966a.

———. 1979. *Aeschylus: The Oresteia.* Translated by Robert Fagles. New York: Penguin Classics.

———. 1982. *Eumenides.* In Hutchins 1982a.

Alchian, Armen and William R. Allen. 1977. *Exchange and Production: Competition, Coordination, and Control.* 2d ed. Belmont, California: Wadsworth Publishing Company.

Alexander, Richard D. 1974. The Evolution of Social Behavior. *Annual Review of Ecology and Systemics.* 5: 325–83. Cited in Axelrod 1984, 97.

Allen, R. G. D. 1967. *Mathematical Analysis for Economists.* New York: St. Martin's Press.

The American Heritage Dictionary of the English Language. 1969. William Morris, editor. Boston: American Heritage Publishing Company.

And to Think That I Heard It on Network TV. 1998. *Navigator.* 1(6) (February): 4.

Anthropology Today. 1971. Del Mar, California: CRM Books.

Atiyah, P. S. 1979. *The Rise and Fall of Freedom of Contract.* New York: Oxford University Press. Quoted in Pipes 1999, 127.

Axelrod, Robert. 1984. *The Evolution of Cooperation.* New York: Basic Books.

The Ayn Rand Letter. 1979. Volumes 1–4: 1971–1976. Palo Alto, California: Palo Alto Book Service.

Barnett, Harold J. and Chandler Morse. 1963. *Scarcity and Growth.* Baltimore: The Johns Hopkins Press.

Barnett, Randy E. 1998. *The Structure of Liberty: Justice and the Rule of Law.* New York: Oxford University Press.

Barrett, William. 1962. *Irrational Man*. Garden City, New York: Doubleday Anchor Books.

———. 1973. *Time of Need*. New York: Harper Torchbooks.

Baumol, William J. 1977. *Economic Theory and Operations Analysis*. 4th ed. Englewood Cliffs, New Jersey: Prentice-Hall.

Beaird, Paul. 1976a. On "Proper Government" 2. *Option*. 4 (1) (March–April): 12–14, 26–27.

———. 1976b. On "Proper Government" 3. *Option*. 4 (2) (May–June): 22–27.

Beals, Ralph E. 1972. *Statistics for Economists*. Chicago: Rand McNally & Company.

Beauchamp, Tom L. and James F. Childress. 1994. *Principles of Biomedical Ethics*. 4th ed. New York: Oxford University Press. Quoted in W. Smith 2000, 212.

Becker, Gary S. 1971. *Economic Theory*. New York: Alfred A. Knopf.

———. 1995a. An Economic Analysis of Fertility. In Febrero and Schwartz 1995a.

———. 1995b. *De Gustibus Non Est Disputandum*. In Febrero and Schwartz 1995a.

———. 1995c. Nobel Lecture: The Economic Way of Looking at Behavior. In Febrero and Schwartz 1995a.

———. 1995d. Investment in Human Capital: A Theoretical Analysis. In Febrero and Schwartz 1995a.

———. 1995e. A Theory of the Allocation of Time. In Febrero and Schwartz 1995a.

———. 1995f. Human Capital and the Rise and Fall of Families. In Febrero and Schwartz 1995a.

Becker, Gary S. and Isaac Ehrlich. 1972. Market Insurance, Self-Insurance, and Self-Protection. *Journal of Political Economy*. 80 (4) (July–August): 623–48.

Begley, Sharon. 1996. Your Child's Brain. *Newsweek*. (February 19): 55–62.

Bell, Frederick. 1972. Technological Externalities and Common-Property Resources: An Empirical Study of the U.S. Northern Lobster Fishery. *Journal of Political Economy*. 80 (1) (January/February): 148–158.

Berliner, Michael S. 1995. *Letters of Ayn Rand*. New York: Dutton.

Bidinotto, Robert James. 2000. The Moral Argument for the Death Penalty. *Navigator*. 3 (2) (February): 7–10.

Binswanger, Harry, editor. 1986. *The Ayn Rand Lexicon*. New York: New American Library.

Bissell, Roger. 1981. A Calm Look at Abortion Arguments. *Reason*. 13 (5) (September): 27–31.

Blumenfeld, Samuel L., editor. 1974. *Property in a Humane Economy*. LaSalle, Illinois: Open Court.

Boydstun, Stephen. 1994. Volitional Synapses. Part 1. *Objectivity*. 2 (1): 109–38.

———. 1996. Volitional Synapses. Part 3. *Objectivity*. 2 (4): 183–204.

Branden, Barbara. 1986. *The Passion of Ayn Rand*. Garden City, New York: Doubleday & Company.

Branden, Nathaniel. 1962. What Are the Respective Obligations of Parents to Children, and Children to Parents? *The Objectivist Newsletter*. 1 (12) (December): 55.

———. 1963. Intellectual Ammunition Department: Does Inherited Wealth Give Some Individuals an Unfair Advantage in a Competitive Economy? *The Objectivist Newsletter.* 2 (6) (June): 22–23.

———. 1967. Common Fallacies about Capitalism. In Rand 1967c.

———. 1997. Objectivism and Self-Acceptance. *IOS Journal.* 6 (6) (February): 8–12.

Bronowski, J. 1973. *The Ascent of Man.* Boston/Toronto: Little, Brown and Company.

Brontë, Charlotte. 1981. *Jane Eyre.* In *The Works of Charlotte and Emily Brontë.* New York: Crown Publishers. Printed exclusively for Longmeadow Press by Avenel Books.

Buchanan, James M. 1965. Marginal Notes on Reading Political Philosophy. In Buchanan and Tullock 1965.

Buchanan, James M. and Gordon Tullock. 1965. *The Calculus of Consent.* Ann Arbor: The University of Michigan Press: Ann Arbor Paperbacks.

Casson, Lionel. 1966. Introduction. In Aeschylus 1966a.

Chiang, Alpha C. 1974. *Fundamental Methods of Mathematical Economics.* 2d ed. New York: McGraw-Hill Book Company.

———. 2000. *Elements of Dynamic Optimization.* Prospect Heights, Illinois: Waveland Press.

Chou, Ya-lun. 1969. *Statistical Analysis.* New York: Holt, Rinehart and Winston.

Coates, Philip. 1998. Coates on Merrill's Critique of the Objectivist Ethics. *Objectivity.* 2 (6): 218–24.

Dales, J. H. 1972a. Land, Water, and Ownership. In Dorfman and Dorfman 1972.

———. 1972b. The Property Interface. In Dorfman and Dorfman 1972.

Den Uyl, Douglas J. and Douglas B. Rasmussen. 1978. Nozick on the Randian Argument. *The Personalist.* 59 (April) 184–205.

———. 1986a. Life, Teleology, and Eudaimonia in the Ethics of Ayn Rand. In Den Uyl and Rasmussen 1986b.

———, editors. 1986b. *The Philosophic Thought of Ayn Rand.* Urbana and Chicago: University of Illinois Press.

———. 1991. *Liberty and Nature: An Aristotelian Defense of Liberal Order.* LaSalle, Illinois: Open Court.

———. 1997. *Liberalism Defended: The Challenge of Post-Modernity.* Cheltenham, UK: The Locke Institute.

Doig, Desmond. 1976. *Mother Teresa: Her People and Her Work.* New York: Harper & Row, Publishers.

Donway, Roger. 1999a. Property, Liberty, Property. *Navigator.* 2 (10) (June): 1, 11–17.

———. 1999b. Markets or Morals. *Navigator.* 2 (8) (April): 18–19.

Dorfman, Robert and Nancy S. Dorfman, editors. 1972. *Economics of the Environment.* New York: W. W. Norton & Company.

Doyle, Arthur Conan. n.d.a. *Sherlock Holmes: His Most Famous Mysteries.* New York: Grosset & Dunlap.

———. n.d.b. A Study in Scarlet. In Doyle n.d.a.

Ellis, Edward Robb. 1966. *The Epic of New York City*. New York. Cited in Pipes 1999, 83n.

Enright, Marsha Familaro. 1998. Enright on Merrill's Critique of the Objectivist Ethics. *Objectivity*. 2 (6): 229–232.

———. 2002. If "Emotions Are Not Tools of Cognition," What Are They? *The Journal of Ayn Rand Studies*. 4 (1) (fall): 25–67.

Epstein, Richard A. 1993. The Killing Grounds. A review of *Life's Dominion: An Argument about Abortion, Euthanasia, and Individual Freedom* by Ronald Dworkin. *Reason*. 25 (6) (November): 58–61.

Evers, Williamson M. 1977. Social Contract: A Critique. *Journal of Libertarian Studies*. 1 (3) (summer): 185–194.

———. 1978. The Law of Omissions and Neglect of Children. *Journal of Libertarian Studies*. 2 (1) (winter): 1–10.

Fagles, Robert and W. B. Stanford. 1979. "A Reading of 'The Oresteia.'" In *Aeschylus*. 1979.

Febrero, Ramón and Pedro S. Schwartz, editors. 1995a. *The Essence of Becker*. Stanford, California: Hoover Institution Press.

———. 1995b. Introduction. In Febrero and Schwartz 1995a.

Ferguson, C. E. 1972. *Microeconomic Theory*. 3d ed. Homewood, Illinois: Richard D. Irwin.

Fischer, Stanley. 1973. A Life Cycle Model of Life Insurance Purchases. *International Economic Review*. 14 (1) (February): 132–52.

Fisher, Irving N. 1930. *The Theory of Interest*. New York: Macmillan Co.

———. [1906] 1965. *The Nature of Capital and Income*. New York: Sentry Press.

Fletcher, Joseph. 1974. "New Definition of Death," *Prism*, American Medical Association. 36 (January): 13–14, republished in *Humanhood*: 159–65. Quoted in W. Smith 2000, 174.

———. 1979. *Humanhood: Essays in Biomedical Ethics*. Buffalo, New York: Prometheus Books. Quoted in W. Smith 2000, 171.

Fraedrich, Doug. 2001. Revival of Objectivity in Scientific Method. *The Journal of Ayn Rand Studies*. 3 (1) (fall): 29–46.

Franck, Murray I. 1995. Intellectual Property Rights: Are Intangibles True Property? *IOS Journal*. 5 (1) (April): 8–10.

———. 1998. The State, the Market, and the Morality of Taxation: Taxation Is Moral—4. *Full Context*. 11 (1) (September/October): 14–16. Cited in Sechrest 2000, 152.

———. 2000. Private Contract, Market Neutrality, and "The Morality of Taxation." *The Journal of Ayn Rand Studies*. 2 (1) (fall): 141–59.

Frank, Robert H. 1988. *Passions within Reason*. New York: W. W. Norton & Company.

Freeman, Katherine B. 2004. Motivational Needs and Interdependent Utilities. *International Journal of Social Economics*. 31 (5/6): 561–71.

Friedman, Milton. 1962. *Capitalism and Freedom*. Chicago & London: The University of Chicago Press.

———. 1966. *Price Theory: A Provisional Text*. Revised ed. Chicago: Aldine Publishing Company.

Friedman, Milton and Rose Friedman. 1980. *Free to Choose*. New York and London: Harcourt Brace Jovanovich.

Gallistel, C. R. 1990. *The Organization of Learning*. Cambridge, Massachusetts: MIT Press.

Gapinski, James H. 1982. *Macroeconomic Theory: Statics, Dynamics, & Policy*. New York: McGraw-Hill Book Company.

———. 1980. The Production of Culture. *The Review of Economics and Statistics*. 62 (4) (November): 578–86.

Gladstein, Mimi Reisel and Chris Matthew Sciabarra, editors. 1999. *Feminist Interpretations of Ayn Rand*. University Park, Pennsylvania: The Pennsylvania State University Press.

Goldberg, Todd H. 1998. A Doctor Looks at Assisted Suicide. *Navigator*. 1 (7) (March): 1, 7–10.

Goodrich, Norma Lorre. 1989. *Priestesses*. New York: Franklin Watts.

Gordon, H. Scott. 1972. The Economic Theory of a Common-Property Resource: The Fishery. In Dorfman and Dorfman 1972.

Gould, Stephen Jay. 1981. Evolutions as Fact and Theory. *Discover*. (May): 35.

Green, H. A. John. 1978. *Consumer Theory*. New York: Academic Press.

Groh, Fred. 1998. Helping Hands. *Navigator*. 2 (3) (November): 1, 13, 15–17.

Gwartney, James D. 1976. *Economics: Private and Public Choice*. New York: Academic Press.

Henderson, James M. and Richard E. Quandt. 1971. *Microeconomic Theory: A Mathematical Approach*. 2d ed. New York: McGraw-Hill Book Company.

Herfindahl, Orris C. and Allen V. Kneese. 1974. *Economic Theory of Natural Resources*. Columbus, Ohio: Charles E. Merrill Publishing Company.

Hillier, Frederick S. and Gerald J. Lieberman. 1967. *Introduction to Operations Research*. San Francisco: Holden-Day.

Hirschey, Mark. 2003. *Managerial Economics*. 10th ed. Australia: Thomson South-Western.

Holmes, Stephen and Cass R. Sunstein. 1999. *The Cost of Rights*. New York: W. W. Norton & Company.

Hoppe, Hans-Hermann. 1998. Introduction. In Rothbard 1998.

Hospers, John. 1972. Property (Comments on Professor Mavrodes' Address). *The Personalist*. 53 (summer): 263–73.

———. 1998. Ayn Rand's Philosophical Significance. *Reason Papers*. 23 (fall): 92–95.

Hotelling, Harold. 1925. A General Mathematical Theory of Depreciation. *Journal of the American Statistical Association*. 20 (151) (September): 350–53.

Howe, Charles W. 1979. *Natural Resource Economics*. New York: John Wiley & Sons.

Huebner, Solomon Stephen and Kenneth Black. 1976. *Life Insurance*. Englewood Cliffs, New Jersey: Prentice-Hall.

Hutchins, Robert Maynard, editor-in-chief. 1982a. *Great Books of the Western World*. Vol. 5. Chicago: Encyclopaedia Britannica.

———. 1982b. *Great Books of the Western World*. Vol. 12. Chicago: Encyclopaedia Britannica.

———. 1984. *Great Books of the Western World*. Vol. 35. Chicago: Encyclopaedia Britannica.

Intriligator, Michael D. 1971. *Mathematical Optimization and Economic Theory*. Englewood Cliffs, New Jersey: Prentice-Hall.

Jacobs, Jane. 1984. *Cities and the Wealth of Nations*. New York: Random House.

Johnson, Gregory. 1999. Liberty and Nature: The Missing Link. *The Journal of Ayn Rand Studies*. 1 (1); 134–66.

Johnson, Gregory R. and David Rasmussen. 2000. Rand on Abortion: A Critique. *The Journal of Ayn Rand Studies*. 1 (2) (spring): 245–61.

———. 2001. Rand on Abortion, Revisited. *The Journal of Ayn Rand Studies* 2 (2) (spring): 469–85.

Johnson, Manuel and James T. Bennett. 1980. Increasing Resource Scarcity: Further Evidence. *Quarterly Review of Economics and Business*. 20 (1) (spring): 42–48.

Jordan, Jr., Chester Wallace. 1967. *Society of Actuaries' Textbook on Life Contingencies*. 2d ed. Schaumburg, Illinois: The Society of Actuaries, Publisher.

Kelley, David. 1974. The Necessity of Government. *The Freeman*. (April): 243–48.

———. 1992. Post-Randian Aristotelianism. *Liberty*. 5 (6) (July): 54–59.

———. 1996. *Unrugged Individualism*. Poughkeepsie, New York: Institute for Objectivist Studies.

———. 1997. Ruled—Or Principled? *IOS Journal*. 6 (6) (February): 1, 5–7.

Keynes, John Maynard. [1936] 1964. *The General Theory of Employment, Interest, and Money*. New York: Harcourt, Brace & World.

Khawaja, Irfan. 1997. A Perfectionist-Egoist Theory of the Good. *Objectivity*. 2 (5); 95–147.

King, J. Charles. 1986. Life and the Theory of Value: The Randian Argument Reconsidered. In Den Uyl and Rasmussen 1986b.

Koestler, Arthur. 1989. *The Act of Creation*. London: Arkana.

Kohr, Leopold. 1974. Property and Freedom. In Blumenfeld 1974.

Kuhn, Thomas S. 1970. *The Structure of Scientific Revolutions*. Vol. 2. 2d ed. Chicago: The University of Chicago Press.

Kurtz, Edwin B. 1930. *Life Expectancy of Physical Property: Based on Mortality Laws*. New York: The Ronald Press Company.

Levhari, David and T. N. Srinivasan. 1969. Optimal Savings under Uncertainty. *Review of Economics and Statistics*. 46 (April): 153–64.

Lewis, David K. 1969. *Convention: A Philosophical Study*. Cambridge: Harvard University Press.

Locke, John. 1984. An Essay concerning Human Understanding. In Hutchins 1984.

Loiret-Prunet, Valérie. 1999. Ayn Rand and Feminist Synthesis: Rereading *We the Living*. In Gladstein and Sciabarra 1999.

Machan, Tibor R., editor. 1967. *The Main Debate, Communism versus Capitalism*. New York: New American Library: 24–25. Quoted in Machan 1998a, 197.

Machan, Tibor R. 1975. *Human Rights and Human Liberties*. Chicago: Nelson-Hall Company.

———. 1977. Nozick and Rand on Property Rights. *The Personalist*. 58 (spring): 192–95.

———. 1998a. *Classical Individualism*. London and New York: Routledge.

———. 1998b. *Generosity: Virtue in Civil Society*. Washington, D. C.: Cato Institute.

———. 2001. Another Look at Abortion. *The Journal of Ayn Rand Studies*. 2 (2) (spring): 449–456.

Mack, Eric. 1986. The Fundamental Moral Elements of Rand's Theory of Rights. In Den Uyl and Rasmussen 1986b.

———. 1998. On the Fit between Egoism and Rights. *Reason Papers*. 23 (Fall): 3–21.

———. 2001. Blind Injustice. *Navigator*. 4 (7) (July/August): 5–8, 13.

Maine, Sir Henry. 1864. *Ancient Law*. New York: Scribner. Cited in Pipes 1999, 95.

Malthus, Thomas. [1803] 1963. *Principle of Population*. Homewood, Illinois: Irwin.

Marcus Aurelius. 1982. In Hutchins 1982b.

Marshall, Alfred. 1930. Principles of Economics. Repr. of 8th ed. London: Macmillan; Guillebaud ed. London: Macmillan, 1961. Quoted in Pujol 1992, 128.

Marx, Karl. 1968. *Theories of Surplus-Value: Part* 2. Moscow: Progress Publishers.

Matera, Mariane. 1999. No More Kids. *Portfolio Weekly*. (January 12–18): 15.

Mavrodes, George I. 1972. Property. *The Personalist*. 53 (summer): 245–262.

Meade, James E. 1955. *Trade and Welfare*. London: Oxford University Press. Cited in Herfindahl and Kneese (1974, 106n⇑).

Meadows, Donella H., Dennis L. Meadows, Jorgen Randers, William W. Behrens III. 1975. *The Limits to Growth*. 2d ed. revised. New York: Signet.

Merrill, Ronald E. 1991. *The Ideas of Ayn Rand*. LaSalle, Illinois: Open Court.

———. 1997. Objectivist Ethics: A Biological Critique. *Objectivity*. 2 (5): 67–93.

———. 1998. Merrill on Some of the Points of Coates. *Objectivity*. 2 (6): 225–28.

Mesarovic, Mihajlo and Eduard Pestel. 1976. *Mankind at the Turning Point*. New York: Signet.

Mill, John Stuart. [1869] 1970. The Subjection of Women. In Rossi 1970.

Morse, Jennifer Roback. 2001. *Love & Economics*. Dallas, Texas: Spence Publishing Company.

Moses, Stephen A. 2002. The Inherent Individualism of Insurance. *Navigator*. 5 (10–11) (November/December): 10–16.

Mossin, Jan. 1968. Optimal Multiperiod Portfolio Policies. *Journal of Business*. 41 (April): 215–29.

Mozes, Eyal. 1992. Deriving Rights from Egoism: Machan vs. Rand. *Reason Papers.* 17 (fall): 87–93.

———. 1998. Must Politics Rest on Morality? *Navigator.* 2 (4) (December): 1, 11–16.

Narveson, Jan. 1998. Ayn Rand as Moral & Political Philosopher. *Reason Papers.* 23 (fall): 96–100.

The Neanderthals. 2000. Video. Discovery Channel, Channel 4 and ITEL. Wal to Wal Television.

Nock, Albert Jay. 1973. *Our Enemy the State.* New York: Free Life Editions. Quoted in Beaird 1976b, 23.

Norton, David L. 1976. *Personal Destinies: A Philosophy of Ethical Individualism.* Princeton, New Jersey: Princeton University Press.

Nozick, Robert. 1971. On the Randian Argument. *The Personalist.* 52 (spring): 282–304.

———. 1993. *The Nature of Rationality.* Princeton, New Jersey: Princeton University Press.

Ogden, Annegret S. 1986. *The Great American Housewife.* Westport, Connecticut: Greenwood Press.

O'Neill, William F. 1972. *With Charity toward None: An Analysis of Ayn Rand's Philosophy.* Totowa, New Jersey: Littlefield, Adams & Co.

Paglia, Camille. 1991. *Sexual Personae.* New York: Vintage Books.

Patai, Raphael. 1983. *The Arab Mind.* Revised ed. New York: Charles Scribner's Sons.

Paterson, Isabel. 1968. *The God of the Machine.* Caldwell, Idaho: The Caxton Printers.

Paxton, Michael. 1998. *Ayn Rand: A Sense of Life.* Layton, Utah: Gibbs Smith.

Peikoff, Leonard. 1976. The Philosophy of Objectivism. Lecture Series (1976), Lecture 8. Quoted in Binswanger 1986, 50–51.

———. 1979. Analytic-Synthetic Dichotomy. In Rand 1979.

———. 1981. Maybe You're Wrong. *The Objectivist Forum.* (April): 9. Quoted in Binswanger 1986, 479.

———. 1982. *The Ominous Parallels.* New York: New American Library.

———. 1991. *Objectivism: The Philosophy of Ayn Rand.* New York: Dutton.

Peter, Laurence J. 1977. *Peter's Quotations.* Toronto and New York: Bantam Books.

Pfeiffer, John E. 1977. *The Emergence of Society.* New York. Quoted in Pipes 1999, 86.

Pipes, Richard. 1999. *Property and Freedom.* New York: Alfred A. Knopf.

Postrel, Virginia I. 1989. Reconsidering Roe. *Reason.* 21 (1) (May): 10–12.

Pujol, Michéle A. 1992. *Feminism and Anti-Feminism in Early Economic Thought.* Hants, England: Edward Elgar Publishing.

Ramsey, F. P. 1928. A Mathematical Theory of Saving. *Economic Journal.* 38 (152): 543–59.

Rand, Ayn. n.d. *Textbook of Americanism.* (Pamphlet) Palo Alto, California: Palo Alto Book Service.

———. 1957. *Atlas Shrugged.* New York: Random House.

———. 1959. *We the Living*. New York: Signet.
———. 1961a. Atlas Shrugged. In Rand 1961b.
———. 1961b. *For the New Intellectual*. New York: Signet.
———. 1961c. The Fountainhead. In Rand 1961b.
———. 1961d. For the New Intellectual. In 1961b.
———. 1963. How *Not* to Fight against Socialized Medicine. *The Objectivist Newsletter.* 2a (3) (March): 11–12.
———. 1964a. The Objectivist Ethics. In Rand 1964f.
———. 1964b. Alvin Toffler's *Playboy* interview with Ayn Rand: A Candid Conversation with the Fountainhead of "Objectivism." New York: The Objectivist. Reprint.
———. 1964c. The "Conflicts" of Men's Interests. In Rand 1964f.
———. 1964d. The Ethics of Emergencies. In Rand 1964f.
———. 1964e. How Does One Lead a Rational Life in an Irrational Society? In Rand 1964f.
———. 1964f. *The Virtue of Selfishness*. New York: Signet.
———. 1964g. The Nature of Government. In Rand 1964f.
———. 1964h. Man's Rights. In Rand 1964f.
———. 1964i. Government Financing in a Free Society. In 1964f.
———. 1964j. The Monument Builders. In 1964f.
———. 1967a. What Is Capitalism? In Rand 1967c.
———. 1967b. The Anatomy of Compromise. In Rand 1967c.
———. 1967c. *Capitalism: The Unknown Ideal*. New York: Signet.
———. 1967d. The Nature of Government. In Rand 1967c.
———. 1967e. America's Persecuted Minority: Big Business. In Rand 1967c.
———. 1967f. The Chasing-in: The Student Rebellion. In Rand 1967c.
———. 1967g. The Property Status of Airwaves. In Rand 1967c.
———. 1967h. The Wreckage of the Consensus. In Rand 1967c.
———. 1967i. Patents and Copyrights. In Rand 1967c.
———. 1967j. Conservatism: An Obituary. In Rand 1967c.
———. 1968. Of Living Death (2). *The Objectivist.* 7 (10) (October): 1–6.
———. 1969a. The Psycho-Epistemology of Art. In Rand 1969b.
———. 1969b. *The Romantic Manifesto*. New York: Signet.
———. 1969c. Philosophy and a Sense of Life. In Rand 1969b.
———. 1969d. Introduction to *Ninety-Three*. In 1969b.
———. 1969e. Apollo 11. *The Objectivist.* 8 (9) (September): 1–15.
———. 1971a. *The New Left: The Anti-Industrial Revolution*. New York: Signet.
———. 1971b. The Comprachicos. In Rand 1971a.
———. 1971c. The Age of Envy. In 1971a.
———. 1971d. Brief Summary. *The Objectivist.* 10 (9): (September): 1—3.
———. 1974a. The Lessons of Vietnam. *The Ayn Rand Letter.* 3 (24) (August 26). In *The Ayn Rand Letter* 1979: 361–66.

———. 1974b. The Inverted Moral Priorities. *The Ayn Rand Letter.* 3 (21) (July 15). In *The Ayn Rand Letter* 1979: 345–48.

———. 1975. A Last Survey: Part I. *The Ayn Rand Letter.* 4 (2) (November/December): In *The Ayn Rand Letter* 1979: 381–84.

———. 1979. *Introduction to Objectivist Epistemology.* New York: Signet.

———. 1981. *The Fountainhead.* Indianapolis, Indiana: The Bobbs-Merrill Company.

———. 1982a. Causality versus Duty. In Rand 1982c.

———. 1982b. The Metaphysical versus the Man-Made. In Rand 1982c.

———. 1982c. *Philosophy: Who Needs It.* New York: Signet.

———. 1982d. Philosophy: Who Needs It. In Rand 1982c.

———. 1982e. Selfishness without a Self. In Rand 1982c.

———. 1982f. Egalitarianism and Inflation. In Rand 1982c.

———. 1982g. An Untitled Letter. In Rand 1982c.

———. 1982h. The Sanction of the Victims. *The Objectivist Forum.* (April): 6.

———. 1982i. Philosophical Detection. In Rand 1982c.

———. 1990. *Introduction to Objectivist Epistemology.* Expanded 2nd ed. New York: Meridian.

Reber, A. S. 1993. *Implicit Learning and Tacit Knowledge: An Essay on the Cognitive Unconscious.* New York: Oxford University Press.

Register, Bryan. 1997. Has Objectivism Been Refuted? *Navigator.* 1 (3) (November): 6–9.

———. 2000. Should Ayn Rand Have Been a Feminist? *Navigator.* 3 (3) (March): 18–23.

Restak, Richard M. 1979. *The Brain: The Last Frontier.* New York: Warner Books.

Ridley, Matt. 1996. *The Origins of Virtue.* New York: Penguin Books.

Rima, Ingrid Hahne. 1978. *Development of Economic Analysis.* 3d ed. Homewood, Illinois: Richard D. Irwin.

Rossi, Alice S. 1970. *Essays on Sex Equality.* Chicago and London: The University of Chicago Press.

Rothbard, Murray N. 1974. Justice and Property Rights. In Blumenfeld 1974.

———. 1993. *Man, Economy, and State.* Auburn University, Alabama: Ludwig von Mises Institute.

———. 1998. *The Ethics of Liberty.* New York and London: New York University Press.

The Roundtable. 1996. *IOS Journal.* 6 (4) (October): 6–10.

Sachko, Anna Maria. 1975. *An Analysis of the Demand for Life Insurance.* Unpublished Ph.D. diss., Department of Economics, Columbia University.

Sadowsky, James. 1974. Private Property and Collective Ownership. In Blumenfeld 1974.

Saint-André, Peter. 1993. A Philosophy for Living on Earth. *Objectivity.* 1 (6): 137–173.

Salvatore, Dominick. 1996. *Managerial Economics.* 3d ed. New York: McGraw-Hill.

———. 1998. *International Economics.* 6th ed. Upper Saddle River, New Jersey: Prentice Hall.

Samuelson, Paul Anthony. 1969. Lifetime Portfolio Selection by Dynamic Stochastic Programming. *Review of Economics and Statistics.* 51 (August): 239–46.

———. 1974. *Foundations of Economic Analysis*. New York: Atheneum.

Sciabarra, Chris Matthew. 1995. *Ayn Rand: The Russian Radical*. University Park, Pennsylvania: The Pennsylvania State University Press.

Scitovsky, Tibor. 1976. *The Joyless Economy*. London: Oxford University Press.

Scott, Jeff. 1997. The Financier. *Navigator.* 1 (1) (September): 7–10.

Sechrest, Larry J. 1999. Rand, Anarchy, and Taxes. *The Journal of Ayn Rand Studies*. 1 (1) (fall): 87–105.

———. 2000. Taxation and Government Are Still Problematic. *The Journal of Ayn Rand Studies*. 2 (1) (fall): 163–87.

Shay, Jonathan. 1995. *Achilles in Vietnam*. New York: Touchstone.

Shelton, Ray. 1995. Epicurus and Rand. *Objectivity.* 2 (3): 1–47.

Sightings. 1998. *Navigator.* 2 (4) (December): 10.

Simpson, Thomas Marshall, Zareh M. Pirenian, and Bolling H. Crenshaw. 1951. *Mathematics of Finance*. 3d ed. Englewood Cliffs, New Jersey: Prentice-Hall.

A Slogan Is Born! 1998. *Navigator.* 1 (9) (May): 3–4.

Smith, Adam. [1776] 1937. *The Wealth of Nations*. New York: The Modern Library.

Smith, Dayle M. 2000. *Women at Work*. Upper Saddle River, New Jersey: Princeton-Hall.

Smith, Tara. 1995. *Moral Rights and Political Freedom*. Lanham, Maryland: Rowman & Littlefield Publishers.

———. 2000. *Viable Values*. Lanham, Maryland: Rowman & Littlefield Publishers.

Smith, Wesley J. 2000. *Culture of Death*. San Francisco, California: Encounter Books.

Spadaro, James A. 1974. The Impact of Invasions of Property on Financial Crises. In Blumenfeld 1974.

Spencer, Herbert. [1850] 1946. *The Man versus the State*. Caldwell, Idaho: The Caxton Printers.

———. [1892] 1954. *Social Statics*. New York: Robert Schalkenbach Foundation.

Spiegel, Henry William. 1971. *The Growth of Economic Thought*. Englewood Cliffs, New Jersey: Prentice-Hall.

Springer, Sally P. and Georg Deutsch. 1989. *Left Brain, Right Brain*. 3d ed. New York: W. H. Freeman and Company.

SPSS® Base 10.0 *Application Guide*. 1999. Chicago: SPSS.

Stone, Merlin. 1976. *When God Was a Woman*. New York: Dorset Press.

Sugden, Robert. 1986. *The Economics of Rights, Co-operation and Welfare*. Oxford: Basil Blackwell.

Tabarrok, Alexander. 2001. Rand the Moderate. *The Journal of Ayn Rand Studies*. 2 (2) (spring): 457–67.

This God, This One Word: "I." 1998. *Navigator.* 1 (6) (February): 2–4.

Thomas, William. 1999a. Abortion. *Navigator.* 2 (7) (March): 18–19.

———. 1999b. Why Should One Act on Principle? *Navigator.* 2 (9) (May): 18-19.

Torres, Louis and Michelle Marder Kamhi. 2000. *What Art Is*. Chicago and La Salle, Illinois: Open Court.

Touchstone, Kathleen. 1993. Can Art Exist without Death? *Objectivity.* 1 (5): 1–28.

———. 1995. Interdependent Decisionmaking, Game Theory and Conformity. *Reason Papers.* 20 (fall): 68–108.

———. 1996. Mathematics and Intuition. *Objectivity.* 2 (4): 93–182.

Valentine, Lloyd M. and Dennis F. Ellis. 1991. *Business Cycles and Forecasting.* 8th ed. Cincinnati, Ohio: South-Western Publishing Company.

Vardey, Lucinda. 1995. *Mother Teresa: A Simple Path.* New York: Ballantine Books.

What Is Justice For? 2000. *Navigator.* 3 (5) (May): 23–24.

Wiesel, Elie. 1976. *Messengers of God.* New York: Random House.

Wilkinson, Will. 2000. What Is Morality Good For? *Navigator.* 3 (7) (July/August): 13–17.

Winston, Wayne L. and S. Christian Albright. 1997. *Practical Management Science.* Belmont, California: Duxbury Press.

Winterhalder, B. 1986. Diet Choice, Risk and Food-sharing in a Stochastic Environment. *Journal of Anthropological Archaeology.* 5: 369–92. Cited in Ridley 1996, 102.

Wise, Steven M. 2000. *Rattling the Cage.* Cambridge, Massachusetts: Perseus Books.

Wolff, Robert Paul. 1998. *In Defense of Anarchism.* Berkeley and Los Angeles: University of California Press.

Yaari, Menahem E. 1964. On the Consumer's Lifetime Allocation Process. *The International Economic Review.* 5 (3): 304–317.

———. 1965. Uncertain Lifetime, Life Insurance, and the Theory of the Consumer. *Review of Economic Studies.* 32 (April): 137–50.

About the Author

Kathleen Touchstone is an assistant professor of economics on the Graduate Faculty at Troy University. She has authored articles on such topics as demand estimation and decision theory. She holds a Ph.D. in economics from Florida State University.

www.ingramcontent.com/pod-product-compliance
Lightning Source LLC
LaVergne TN
LVHW090259210926
848480LV00001B/70